Feasting on the Word®

Editorial Board

Feasting on the Word®

Preaching the
Revised Common Lectionary

Year B, Volume 4

DAVID L. BARTLETT and BARBARA BROWN TAYLOR

General Editors

WESTMINSTER
JOHN KNOX PRESS
LOUISVILLE • KENTUCKY

Book design by Drew Stevens
Cover design by Lisa Buckley

First edition
Published by Westminster John Knox Press
Louisville, Kentucky

This book is printed on acid-free paper that meets the American National Standards Institute Z39.48 standard. ♾

PRINTED IN THE UNITED STATES OF AMERICA

11 12 13 14 15 16 17 18 — 10 9 8 7 6 5 4 3

Library of Congress Cataloging-in-Publication Data

Feasting on the Word : preaching the revised common lectionary / David L. Bartlett and Barbara Brown Taylor, general editors.
     p. cm.
  Includes index.
  ISBN 978-0-664-23099-9 (v. 4: alk. paper)
  ISBN 978-0-664-23098-2 (v. 3: alk. paper)
  ISBN 978-0-664-23097-5 (v. 2: alk. paper)
  ISBN 978-0-664-23096-8 (v. 1: alk. paper)
  1. Lectionary preaching.   2. Common lectionary (1992)   I. Bartlett, David Lyon, 1941–
II. Taylor, Barbara Brown.
  BV4235.L43F43 2008
  251'.6—dc22

                                   2007047534

Contents

Publisher's Note

Feasting on the Word: Preaching the Revised Common Lectionary is an ambitious project that is offered to the Christian church as a resource for preaching and teaching.

The uniqueness of this approach in providing four perspectives on each preaching occasion from the Revised Common Lectionary sets this work apart from other lectionary materials. The theological, pastoral, exegetical, and homiletical dimensions of each biblical passage are explored with the hope that preachers will find much to inform and stimulate their preparations for preaching from this rich "feast" of materials.

This work could not have been undertaken without the deep commitments of those who have devoted countless hours to working on these tasks. Westminster John Knox Press would like to acknowledge the magnificent work of our general editors, David L. Bartlett and Barbara Brown Taylor. They are both gifted preachers with passionate concerns for the quality of preaching. They are also wonderful colleagues who embraced this huge task with vigor, excellence, and unfailing good humor. Our debt of gratitude to Barbara and David is great.

The fine support staff, project manager Joan Murchison and compiler Mary Lynn Darden, enabled all the thousands of "pieces" of the project to come together and form this impressive series. Without their strong competence and abiding persistence, these volumes could not have emerged.

The volume editors for this series are to be thanked as well. They used their superb skills as pastors and professors and ministers to work with writers and help craft their valuable insights into the highly useful entries that comprise this work.

The hundreds of writers who shared their expertise and insights to make this series possible are ones who deserve deep thanks indeed. They come from wide varieties of ministries. But they have given their labors to provide a gift to benefit the whole church and to enrich preaching in our time.

Westminster John Knox would also like to express our appreciation to Columbia Theological Seminary for strong cooperation in enabling this work to begin and proceed. Dean of Faculty and Executive Vice President D. Cameron Murchison welcomed the project from the start and drew together everything we needed. His continuing efforts have been very valuable. Former President Laura S. Mendenhall provided splendid help as well. She made seminary resources and personnel available and encouraged us in this partnership with enthusiasm and all good grace. We thank her, and look forward to working with Columbia's new president, Stephen Hayner.

It is a joy for Westminster John Knox Press to present *Feasting on the Word: Preaching the Revised Common Lectionary* to the church, its preachers, and its teachers. We believe rich resources can assist the church's ministries as the Word is proclaimed. We believe the varieties of insights found in these pages will nourish preachers who will "feast on the Word" and who will share its blessings with those who hear.

Westminster John Knox Press

Series Introduction

A preacher's work is never done. Teaching, offering pastoral care, leading worship, and administering congregational life are only a few of the responsibilities that can turn preaching into just one more task of pastoral ministry. Yet the Sunday sermon is how the preacher ministers to most of the people most of the time. The majority of those who listen are not in crisis. They live such busy lives that few take part in the church's educational programs. They wish they had more time to reflect on their faith, but they do not. Whether the sermon is five minutes long or forty-five, it is the congregation's one opportunity to hear directly from their pastor about what life in Christ means and why it matters.

Feasting on the Word offers pastors focused resources for sermon preparation, written by companions on the way. With four different essays on each of the four biblical texts assigned by the Revised Common Lectionary, this series offers preachers sixteen different ways into the proclamation of God's Word on any given occasion. For each reading, preachers will find brief essays on the exegetical, theological, homiletical, and pastoral challenges of the text. The page layout is unusual. By setting the biblical passage at the top of the page and placing the essays beneath it, we mean to suggest the interdependence of the four approaches without granting priority to any one of them. Some readers may decide to focus on the Gospel passage, for instance, by reading all four essays provided for that text. Others may decide to look for connections between the Hebrew Bible, Psalm, Gospel, and Epistle texts by reading the theological essays on each one.

Wherever they begin, preachers will find what they need in a single volume produced by writers from a wide variety of disciplines and religious traditions. These authors teach in colleges and seminaries. They lead congregations. They write scholarly books as well as columns for the local newspaper. They oversee denominations. In all of these capacities and more, they serve God's Word, joining the preacher in the ongoing challenge of bringing that Word to life.

We offer this print resource for the mainline church in full recognition that we do so in the digital age of the emerging church. Like our page layout, this decision honors the authority of the biblical text, which thrives on the page as well as in the ear. While the twelve volumes of this series follow the pattern of the Revised Common Lectionary, each volume contains an index of biblical passages so that all preachers may make full use of its contents.

We also recognize that this new series appears in a post-9/11, post-Katrina world. For this reason, we provide no shortcuts for those committed to the proclamation of God's Word. Among preachers, there are books known as "Monday books" because they need to be read thoughtfully at least a week ahead of time. There are also "Saturday books," so called because they supply sermon ideas on short notice. The books in this series are not Saturday books. Our aim is to help preachers go deeper, not faster, in a world that is in need of saving words.

A series of this scope calls forth the gifts of a great many people. We are grateful first to the staff of Westminster John Knox Press: Don McKim and Jon Berquist, who conceived this project; David Dobson, who worked diligently to bring the project to completion, with publisher Marc Lewis's strong support; and Julie Tonini, who has painstakingly guided each volume through the production process. We thank former President Laura Mendenhall and former Dean Cameron Murchison of Columbia Theological Seminary, who made our participation in this work possible. We thank President Steve Hayner and Dean Deborah Mullen for their continuing encouragement and support. Our editorial board is a hardworking board, without whose patient labor and good humor this series would not exist. From the start, Joan Murchison has been the brains of the operation, managing details of epic proportions with great human kindness. Mary Lynn Darden, Dilu Nicholas, Megan Hackler, and John Shillingburg have supported both her and us with their administrative skills.

We have been honored to work with a multitude of gifted thinkers, writers, and editors. We present these essays as their offering—and ours—to the blessed ministry of preaching.

David L. Bartlett
Barbara Brown Taylor

A Note about the Lectionary

Feasting on the Word follows the Revised Common Lectionary (RCL) as developed by the Consultation on Common Texts, an ecumenical consultation of liturgical scholars and denominational representatives from the United States and Canada. The RCL provides a collection of readings from Scripture to be used during worship in a schedule that follows the seasons of the church year. In addition, it provides for a uniform set of readings to be used across denominations or other church bodies.

The RCL provides a reading from the Old Testament, a Psalm response to that reading, a Gospel, and an Epistle for each preaching occasion of the year. It is presented in a three-year cycle, with each year centered around one of the Synoptic Gospels. Year A is the year of Matthew, Year B is the year of Mark, and Year C is the year of Luke. John is read each year, especially during Advent, Lent, and Easter.

The RCL offers two tracks of Old Testament texts for the Season after Pentecost or Ordinary Time: a semicontinuous track, which moves through stories and characters in the Old Testament, and a complementary track, which ties the Old Testament texts to the theme of the Gospel texts for that day. Some denominational traditions favor one over the other. For instance, Presbyterians and Methodists generally follow the semicontinuous track, while Lutherans and Episcopalians generally follow the complementary track.

The print volumes of *Feasting on the Word* follow the complementary track for Year A, are split between the complementary and semicontinuous tracks for Year B, and cover the semicontinuous stream for Year C. Essays for Pentecost and the Season after Pentecost that are not covered in the print volumes available on the *Feasting on the Word* Web site, www.feastingontheword.net.

For more information about the Revised Common Lectionary, visit the official RCL Web site at http://lectionary.library.vanderbilt.edu/ or see *The Revised Common Lectionary: The Consultation on Common Texts* (Nashville: Abingdon Press, 1992).

Feasting on the Word®

PROPER 17 (SUNDAY BETWEEN AUGUST 28 AND SEPTEMBER 3 INCLUSIVE)

Song of Solomon 2:8-13

⁸The voice of my beloved!
  Look, he comes,
 leaping upon the mountains,
  bounding over the hills.
⁹My beloved is like a gazelle
  or a young stag.
 Look, there he stands
  behind our wall,
 gazing in at the windows,
  looking through the lattice.
¹⁰My beloved speaks and says to me:
  "Arise, my love, my fair one,
  and come away;

Theological Perspective

Many modern exegetes have rightly urged us to read the love poems in the Song of Solomon for what they are: the celebration of love for love's sake, equally of the woman's love for her beloved and the man's for her. For its full impact, the Revised Common Lectionary selection should be rounded out to include the full poem by adding verses 14–17. The woman urges the man she loves to share the night with her ("he pastures his flock among the lilies"). The words telling what her man says to her (10b–17) only heighten the initiative she takes for their rendezvous. Celebration of the desire of woman for man and man for woman is valid on its own terms in this poem. Its imagery of nature, springtime, the change from winter rain to sunshine, perfumed flowers and fruit, animals like the gazelle and the turtledove, forms the poetry of a metaphoric garden of delights enjoyed by a woman and a man who belong together. We may read this poem and relish its celebration of the love between a woman and a man.

Choosing this reading from the Song, the brave preacher will also easily see abundant implicit theological claims. The Song of Solomon celebrates the relation of woman and man in God's gracious creation, reflecting the two accounts of God's word and action, God's rich and effective purpose, in Genesis 1:1–2:4a and 2:4b–25.

Pastoral Perspective

Love and play are intricately interwoven. In this passage from the Song of Solomon, flirtation, invitation, and joy are palpable. This most sensual passage in Scripture stirs in its readers a desire to be involved. Whether it is a love story about two human beings or an allegory about God's love for God's people, the sense of delight in today's text is striking. The author of the Song of Solomon poetically alludes to the transformative power of love. The lovers are each (and all) transformed by love.

The Ninth Assembly of the World Council of Churches had as its theme "God, in Your Grace, Transform the World." Already theologically complex, this phrase had to be translated into six different languages so that all those who were in attendance could understand it with some consistency. Each language brought its own difficulties, nuances, and interpretations to the theme. Turning the phrase around, one brave group of Brazilian scholars wrote a compilation of articles that became a book entitled *The Grace of the World That Transforms God*. Discussing the fun, joy, and wit of love, these articles engaged in serious conversation about how God is transformed by love just as human beings are.

In one of the articles, "This Gracefully Witty World," Vitor Westhelles says: "This world is funny and

¹¹for now the winter is past,
　　the rain is over and gone.
¹²The flowers appear on the earth;
　　the time of singing has come,
　　and the voice of the turtledove
　　is heard in our land.
¹³The fig tree puts forth its figs,
　　and the vines are in blossom;
　　they give forth fragrance.
　　Arise, my love, my fair one,
　　and come away."

Exegetical Perspective

An Orientation to the Book as a Whole. Throughout the ages, interpreters have agreed that Song of Solomon (also known as Song of Songs and Canticles) is a series of love poems voiced by feminine and masculine characters to one another, with the occasional contributions of one or more choruses. But these same interpreters have disagreed greatly regarding larger and more important questions: who *are* these characters, and what does love poetry have to do with the life of faith?

Responses to these questions have taken two apparently contradictory paths:

1. *The allegorical:* Already by the second century CE, some Jewish interpreters claimed that the book was an allegory of God's love for Israel. Such an allegorical reading may explain the book's connection with Passover, the Jewish festival celebrating God's special favor for Israel. In early Christianity, the poems were understood as allegories of Christ's love for the church, the human soul, and/or Mary, often called the bride of Christ to underscore her unique role in God's plan of salvation.

2. *The historical:* Among those who interpret the poems as referring to a human couple, one common interpretation is that these are poems written to be exchanged between King Solomon

Homiletical Perspective

The Song as Poetry. Many have noted that the Song of Solomon contains some of the most beautiful and evocative poetry in the Bible. It should not escape the preacher's attention that the words of the Song of Solomon come to us in poetic form. Whether one believes that the Song of Solomon is a single epic poem or a collection of some two dozen poems, it is clear that the form of the text before us is poetry. For the word of God to speak its wisdom on this particular Sunday, the preacher does well to allow its poetic force free rein.

The rhetorical force of poetry is contained in its use of metaphor, allegory, and simile. Each of these conventions employs language in a way to press toward deeper reflection and meaning by engaging the imagination of the listener. For example, Paul Scott Wilson describes the power of metaphor to engage the imagination by "bringing together . . . two ideas that might not otherwise be connected and developing the creative energy they generate."[1] Like two poles of a generator, the spark of imagination occurs when two ideas that seem to have no apparent connection are brought in proximity to one another. In approaching the poetry of the Song of

1. Paul Scott Wilson, *Imagination of the Heart: New Understandings in Preaching* (Nashville: Abingdon Press, 1988), 32.

Song of Solomon 2:8-13

Theological Perspective

The imagery of the garden in the Song of Solomon recalls the creation of man and woman in Eden (Gen. 2:4b–25). In this second account of creation, the Lord God brings the whole creation to its climax by adding the female counterpart and partner to the human being (*ha-ʾadam*) whom God has created from the dust of the ground (*ha-ʾadamah*). She is different from him. The Lord God creates her out of him, while he is asleep, without his participation. Phyllis Trible has likened the creation of woman (*ʾishsha*) out of man (*ʾish*) to a surgery, performed on his body while he is unconscious and therefore entirely without agency.[1] He is different from who he was before the surgery. He becomes a male as his partner is created female. She is also like him. Together in mutuality and relationship they reflect the image of God. Without her, the man would have been alone. The Lord God did not choose to create her without him, nor did the man have identity apart from her. This mutuality is the relationship between man and woman in partnership and in love. Neither is alone, but rather both are free to live together in covenant love, without shame.

The two Genesis accounts of creation imply God's intention for covenant. Karl Barth's interpretation was that creation is "the external basis of the covenant" (Gen. 1:1–2:4a) and covenant is "the internal basis of the creation" (Gen. 2:4b–25). Barth comments that nearly everywhere else in the Old Testament, *except in the Song of Solomon*, love and marriage—the partnership of man and woman—is an answer to the question of posterity, in which human parenthood by father and mother results in a family, a child, a son. Yet the affirmation of eros, of the mutual attraction and fulfillment of man and woman in a relationship of sexuality and of love, occurs both in Genesis 2:23–25 and in the Song of Solomon, which shows that such mutual attraction between man and woman is not peripheral to the Old Testament.[2]

In the Song of Solomon, the Old Testament offers a transforming context for the Christian community to proclaim God's goodness in creation and reorientation of the loving relationship between woman and man. The preacher could make a connection with Jesus' reaffirmation of the goodness of God's creation of male and female (and of the mutuality in marriage of one flesh, over against a patriarchal

Pastoral Perspective

facetious by its own gracefulness. . . . In Portuguese the word for 'grace' and its derivatives are used to denote both the theological meaning of grace as a gift as well as wit and humor which the English 'gracefulness' only vaguely connotes. The original title (*Mundo em Graca [do]*) entails a double entendre; it can mean 'a world in grace' as well as a 'funny world.'"[1]

In the Song of Solomon, we hear the invitation to come into such "a world in grace": "Arise, my love, my fair one, and come away; for now the winter is past, the rain is over and gone. The flowers appear on the earth; the time of singing has come, and the voice of the turtledove is heard in our land." Come, dear ones, into a world in grace! This world has transformative power in relationships, in nature, and in creation. However grim things may have been in seasons past, winter will yield to spring. The rain will go, flowers will appear, and the season of glad songs will arrive at last.

Who does not know the joy of the end of winter? People shed their heavy coats and scarves, trading them in on shorts and flip-flops. Gratefully they gather on college campuses or in public parks to enjoy a picnic of fresh vegetables in the sun, listening to music from the park stage, pretending not to notice as lovers kiss, turning to catch a glimpse of a game of Frisbee from the corner of their eyes. In such a season, love delights and explodes in playfulness.

Indian theologian K. P. Aleaz deepens the dimension of grace mixed with wit and humor in the element of play when he says, "God starts the play, with God as the starting point and then proceeds to creation. Humans, on the other hand, start the play in creation and then proceed to God. Both meet in play. The connecting link is play."[2]

In today's passage from the Song of Solomon, love and playfulness are profoundly integrated with all of life's realities. Even when love is frozen, hurricanes devastate creation, and summer has given way to icy cold, God's love for creation and creation's interplay with God explodes and blossoms anew. God's grace transforms the world, even as the grace of the world transforms God. Playful grace causes all kinds of metamorphoses to take place.

Too often, this love affair with life is limited to the natural, domestic, and communal world. Yet those

---

1 Phyllis Trible, *God and the Rhetoric of Sexuality* (Philadelphia: Fortress Press, 1978), 95–96.
2. Karl Barth, *Church Dogmatics*, III/1 (Edinburgh: T. & T. Clark, 1958), 312–13.

1. *The Grace of the World That Transforms God: Latin American Dialogues with the 9th Assembly of the WCC*, ed. Nancy Cardoso, Edla Eggert, and André S. Musskopf (Porto Alegre: Editora Universitária Metodista, 2006), 80.
2. K. P. Aleaz, "Play and Religion: Indication of an Interconnection," *Journal of the Asian Research Center for Religion and Social Communication* 2, no. 1 (2004), under "Conclusion," http://www.stjohn.ac.th/arc/play%20and%20religion.pdf.

Exegetical Perspective

and a peasant bride. Identification with Solomon is based on the explicit mention of his name in the book's title and in 3:9 and 3:11, as well as on the references to "the king" in 1:4 and 1:12. The wedding context is inferred from references to the woman as "bride" in 4:8, 9, 10, 11, 12, and 5:1, as well as the wedding scene in 3:6–11.

Most contemporary scholars, however, consider these poems as anonymous secular love poetry, similar in style and function to Egyptian, Arabic, and Syrian love poems of the same period. Like Songs, this parallel literature offers extended descriptions of the lover's body, called *wasfs*, and use "bride" and "sister" as terms of endearment. Hence, the Song's references to Solomon may be allusions to the great lover of ancient Israel (1 Kgs. 11:1–3) rather than a key to the book's authorship. In addition, the sexuality it celebrates is not necessarily marital, despite the "bride" and "bridegroom" headings added by some English translations, and the wedding scene may have been added to render the book more "Solomonic." When read through this historical lens, Songs reflects a less restrictive attitude toward human sexuality than do the legal materials of the Hebrew Bible and thus makes a distinctive contribution to an understanding of ancient Israel's view of sexuality and the human body.

The allegorical and the historical approaches are often considered at odds with one another, the first either pure or puritanical, depending on one's point of view, and the second either liberating or libertarian. Many recent commentators, however, have suggested that the approaches may be complementary rather than contradictory. The life of the soul (allegorical) and the life of the body (historical) are not distinct. To be in love is to live beyond the boundaries of the self and to enter a realm of sheer delight, in which the human and the divine can merge. Human love both allows us to celebrate God through our bodies and educates us in loving and being loved.

The Details of This Pericope. The Song of Solomon is often credited with providing more of a woman's voice than other parts of the Old and New Testaments, and indeed the passage begins with the woman speaking. She describes her lover appearing at her home to call her outside into the awakening spring. Often in the book, their trysts are outside (see 1:16–17). While the woman still speaks in 2:10–13, she turns to quoting what the man has said to her, presenting the reader with a series of nested

Homiletical Perspective

Solomon, one must make a choice at which level to read the metaphor. One option is to read the metaphors within the poetry ("My lover is like a gazelle"). In this instance, the metaphor is clearly given within a line of the poetic refrain. Another option is to read the entire poem as an extended poetic metaphor. In this instance, the particular metaphors within the poem must be understood as a part of the overall function of the entire poem. Extended poetic metaphor is akin to what has been traditionally called allegory.

At this point, the preacher must make an interpretive choice. Among the options available, one may read the Song of Solomon as a long lyrical poem about erotic love and sexual desire[2] or as an extended metaphor applied to Jewish aspiration.[3] There is also the long history of Christian interpretation that reads the Song as an allegory of Christ and the church. In each instance, the preacher must decide at which level she or he will allow the metaphor to play, as this choice will determine the shape of the sermon.

Messianic Expectation in Romantic Refrain. I suggest that the text be received as an extended poetic metaphor of messianic expectation in which the lyricist evokes heightened anticipation for the coming of the reign of God and the fulfillment of God's purposes. The particular refrain of 2:8–13 envisions the fulfillment of the coming of the long-awaited one and presupposes a long season of absence. That "the winter is past" and "the rains are over and gone" implies that one knows full well the reality of winter's chill and the gray despair of ceaseless rain. The lyric is filled with reference to the passing of one season and the emergence of another that at a deep theological level is connected to an apocalyptic turn of the ages. Such expectation is figured throughout the biblical story in both temporal (old/new age) and spatial (old/new creation) terminology. In the apocalyptic frame, the turn of the ages is initiated by God's intervention through the arrival of his servant. Further, our text for preaching this week indicates that the arrival of God's long-anticipated one supplies both the announcement and realization of God's new day.

2. J. Cheryl Exum, *Song of Songs: A Commentary* (Louisville, KY: Westminster John Knox, 2005), among many modern critical commentators.
3. See, for example, Louis Stadelmann, *Love and Politics: A New Commentary on the Song of Songs* (New York: Paulist Press, 1989), or James H. Hamilton Jr., "The Messianic Music of the Song of Songs: A Non-Allegorical Interpretation," *Westminster Theological Journal* 68, no. 2 (2006): 331–45.

Song of Solomon 2:8-13

Theological Perspective

interpretation of the Deuteronomic provision for divorce) in Mark 10:6–8 and parallels. With a more political and social ethical emphasis, the sermon might follow the implications of the Song's revision of Solomon's subordination of the relationship of man and woman to economic, political, and religious ends, as Walter Brueggemann suggests.[3] In either choice, the text invites critical reflection and joyous reaffirmation in place of oppressive human relationships and responsibilities.

Faithful preaching on this text from the Song of Solomon will proclaim God's good intention for creation in the relationship of man and woman over against the conflicting words about human sexuality in today's global culture. While we have human sexuality freely accessible, our free access does not automatically include our responsible, much less joyful, honoring of the goodness of God's intention. Sexual practice is often exploitive, especially of women and children. The accessibility of human sexuality becomes yet another means of objectifying and manipulating human beings, created in God's image for the Lord's own purposes.

Moreover, global markets make human sexuality into a commodity for the promotion and sale of goods and services. Treating human sexuality as a commodity is parasitic on the goodness of God's intended mutuality. Commercialization devalues and subordinates human sexuality for the sake of economic gain, instead of honoring and respecting God's intended gift and joy.

The thoughtful preacher, in pastoral relationship with the people of God, will be able to interpret for revaluation God's intended covenantal relationship between woman and man. The occasion might be a wedding. Or the pastor may seek occasions when, in good taste and playful seriousness, she or he engages the youth and adults of the congregation in careful conversation about the covenantal intentions God has for human beings in loving relationships.

CHARLES E. RAYNAL

Pastoral Perspective

who know the deep sacredness of play also know how necessary it is to move into delightful civic engagement with the larger political world. Dorothee Soelle, the late German theologian, adds that in the Song of Solomon "nature, animals, men and women partake of the joy, the abundance, the fullness of life. . . . I believe that our reflection on human sexuality is incomplete without a vision of *polis*. I call this sociopolitical dimension of our sexuality 'solidarity.'"[3]

For Soelle, political solidarity involves playfulness, humor, and witty engagement with the world. The erotic love that opens the hearts and minds of the man and the woman in today's passage from the Song of Solomon does not stop with their openness to one another. It also opens them to the hearts and minds of other people. Discovering their solidarity with one another, they discover their solidarity with all other human beings as well.

Whether the Song is read as a love story between two people or as an allegory about God's love for all creation, its beauty is that it invites all humankind to play as if life and love depended upon it (as they do). The pastor tuned to the deep needs of his or her congregation will welcome the opportunity to explore the ways in which the romantic love between individuals can spread in ever-enlarging ripples to encompass other people, other communities, all creatures and nations, as it swells toward the gracious God who goes on inviting us to play a while, that we may take part in the transformation of the world.

SUSAN T. HENRY-CROWE

---

3. Walter Brueggemann, *Solomon: Israel's Ironic Icon of Human Achievement* (Columbia: University of South Carolina Press, 2005), 206–14.

3. Dorothee Soelle, *To Work and To Love: A Theology of Creation* (Philadelphia: Fortress Press, 1984), 150.

Exegetical Perspective

voices: the words of the male character are reported by the female character, who is turn is described through the words of writer (likely male).

While other passages such as 5:9–16 and 7:1–5 will inventory in detail the lovers' bodies, the imagery here is primarily one of nature (fruit, wine, animals, and flowers), with appeals to multiple senses. The voices of the beloved, of the turtledove, and of singing are heard; the woman envisions the man as a gazelle, and he in turn looks at her through the lattice; and the blossoms of the vine give forth fragrance.

The male is depicted almost as part of the nature to which he calls the woman: he is a gazelle bounding over mountains. The female, by contrast, is portrayed as inside; the man sees her from behind the wall of the courtyard and through the lattice of the window of the house. Similar barriers between the lovers appear elsewhere in the Song. Their trysts are often hidden, secret, and threats of violence come from the woman's brothers (8:8–9) and the town watchmen (5:7). In 8:1–2, the woman longs for the freedom to express her love openly.

The male's speech calls the woman out into the freedom and budding sensuality of the world. The rainy season ended, (green) figs are on the vine and blossoms have begun to appear. Their love, like the season, is not fully ripened but intoxicatingly new, enticing, teasing, full of potential. Nature invites not only their admiration but their participation in its sensuality. The male's speech begins and ends with the same words, giving him a pleading, gently insistent, tone. He desires her and she knows it, repeats it, celebrates it.

When this pericope is read with its allegorical and historical aspects in creative play, it celebrates and perhaps even creates the feelings of passionate desiring and knowing oneself to be passionately desired. While loving and being loved are not the only goals of human existence, they can be transformative experiences that not only lead us to praise the One who makes joy possible but also exercise our capacities for love. Glimpsing oneself not as perfect but perfect for someone, wanted, sought after, is a cause for singing both secular love songs and hymns.

JULIA M. O'BRIEN

Homiletical Perspective

If this text is received as extended poetic metaphor for the coming reign of God, the sermon should function both to announce and to realize the inbreaking of God's reign. In order to accomplish this, the preacher might consider naming the trouble that lies behind and beneath this text. While the lyric of the song announces with some exuberance the arrival of the long-anticipated one, the meaning of this cannot be fully realized, experienced, or imagined without first making present the experience of the absence of God, the experience of winter or the rains.

The opening move of the sermon might first construct the narrative framework that imagines the long, seemingly endless season of waiting, watching, anticipating through the experience of absence/winter/rain. There are countless ways in which the preacher might draw this theme forward, allowing the language contained within the text to name the experience of absence. The good news announced in the text can be realized more profoundly as the preacher takes the time to name honestly and accurately, within the congregation's experience of reality, the trouble beneath this text, using the language and imagery supplied by the text.

Having named the experience of absence, the sermon is then able to imagine what it might mean to receive the long-anticipated one, to "arise . . . and come with" this one. Here the preacher does well to note the way the song employs the words "listen," "look," and "arise." The sequence in which these words appear is significant. Before one is able to see what is coming, one hears. Before one rises up, one has seen something. Words evoke vision, and vision summons action. In the second move of this sermon, the preacher might playfully allow the rhetorical development of this text to unfold. "Listen," the preacher invites. By inviting the congregation to listen for something different, the preacher introduces the possibility of presence into the experience of absence and the possibility that such listening might deliver new vision that summons us forth to participate in God's new creation.

STEPHEN C. JOHNSON

Psalm 45:1-2, 6-9

[1]My heart overflows with a goodly theme;
    I address my verses to the king;
    my tongue is like the pen of a ready scribe.

[2]You are the most handsome of men;
    grace is poured upon your lips;
    therefore God has blessed you forever.
. . . .
[6]Your throne, O God, endures forever and ever.
    Your royal scepter is a scepter of equity;
[7] you love righteousness and hate wickedness.
 Therefore God, your God, has anointed you
    with the oil of gladness beyond your companions;
[8] your robes are all fragrant with myrrh and aloes and cassia.
 From ivory palaces stringed instruments make you glad;
[9] daughters of kings are among your ladies of honor;
    at your right hand stands the queen in gold of Ophir.

Theological Perspective

Psalm 45 is one of about a dozen "royal psalms" in the Psalter. The royal psalms have several distinguishing features. One is the exalted terminology that refers to the king. In the case of Psalm 45, the king is worthy of honor (v. 1); the king is blessed by God (v. 2); the king holds the scepter of justice (v. 6); and the king is anointed with oil (v. 7). All these indications of royalty confer status and authority and power on the king. These honorifics do not, however, confer divine identity on the king. In this respect, the worship tradition of the Psalms is a contrast to surrounding cultures and traditions of the time. One commentator says, "It is beyond doubt that in Israel's worship the king was not the object of veneration."[1] The worshipers of YHWH made a clear distinction between God and anything in the created world.

The original context of many of the royal psalms may have been a coronation festival in Jerusalem. In the case of Psalm 45, a royal wedding is the context, made clear by the verses that follow this selected text. In accord with the messianic expectations of late Judaism, this psalm was understood as a messianic prophecy and included in the Psalter.[2]

Pastoral Perspective

At the ordination of a bishop in the Episcopal Church, the presiding bishop states that "a bishop in God's holy Church is called to be one with the apostles in proclaiming Christ's resurrection and interpreting the Gospel, and to testify to Christ's sovereignty as Lord of lords and King of kings."[1] A consecration takes place, during which the presiding bishop and other bishops pray, "Therefore, Father, make N. a bishop in your Church. Pour out upon *him* the power of your princely Spirit . . ."[2] Following the exchange of the peace, the new bishop may be escorted to the episcopal chair—the cathedra, or throne.

Even at the ordination of a female bishop, such language and ceremony suggest, if they do not still reinforce, a patriarchal system of power and privilege. The Episcopal Church at its best balances such hierarchy with its inclusivity as well as its electoral processes and representative forms of governance; nevertheless the monarchical model of leadership remains clear and prevalent.

The Episcopal Church is not alone among the churches in exercising the ministry of the episcopate and is by no means an exception among Christian denominations in appropriating the model of

1. Hans-Joachim Kraus, *Theology of the Psalms* (Minneapolis: Fortress Press, 1992), 111.
2. Artur Weiser, *The Psalms: A Commentary* (Philadelphia: Westminster Press, 1962), 365.

1. *The Book of Common Prayer* (New York: Seabury Press, 1979), 517.
2. Ibid.

Exegetical Perspective

Psalm 45 celebrates the marriage of a distinguished couple and most likely refers to a royal wedding ceremony, because the psalmist addresses a king and queen. It is possible, however, that the imagery expressed in this psalm may have been used in wedding services of the elite. The psalm can be divided as follows: (1) introductory remarks (v. 1), (2) an address to the bridegroom/king (vv. 2–9), (3) an address to the bride (vv. 10–12a), (4) a description of the ritual encounter of the bride and bridegroom in marriage (vv. 12b–15), and (5) a concluding blessing for the bridegroom (vv. 16–17).

When addressing the king, the psalmist praises his handsome appearance (v. 2), military prowess, and just leadership (vv. 3–7). The description of a ruler as physically attractive was common in the ancient world, and ancient Israel portrayed leaders in a similar way (e.g., 1 Sam. 9:2; 16:12). The political landscape of the ancient Near East also consisted of frequent military skirmishes between local parties of any given region, as well as more technologically advanced battles that were executed by larger forces. Ancient Israelite history consistently involved military conflicts over territorial control (e.g., Judg. 4, 6–8, 11–12; 1 Sam. 13–15; 2 Sam. 5, 8, 10; 1 Kgs. 15–16; 2 Kgs. 3–25). For this reason, the appeal of a leader was partly related to his success in

Homiletical Perspective

The language of Psalm 45 is alien to most twenty-first-century North American ears. It is language praising a king on the occasion of his wedding. It is poetic language that exudes a sense of being mesmerized by the king's outward appearance and military strength. It invokes all of the senses as it describes the setting of the wedding and the participants: robes are fragrant (v. 8), music delights the mood (v. 8), the queen and ladies of honor are described according to the opulence of status and dress (v. 9).

Not only are the images alien; they are also troublesome for many. Some readers experience discomfort with the sensual tone of the psalm—the praises of the psalmist sound like someone who is smitten by the show of power and voluptuous sights and sounds. Some readers and hearers may be troubled by the (seeming) pandering to the figure of a king and the glorification of a political ruler. Still others will read beyond the verses of today's lection and become troubled by the subservient role of women in the psalm. Though these questions remain, it is still helpful to see the images in their long-ago context.

Psalm 45 is an ancient psalm. It keeps company with other ancient cultures' myths depicting the marriages of gods that bring about life for the world. The male dominates, and the woman is the recipient.

Psalm 45:1-2, 6-9

Theological Perspective

Christian interpretation of the psalm quite quickly made the connection to Jesus Christ, as the king worthy of all authority and power, including divine status and identity. Verses 6 and 7 are quoted in christological context in Hebrews 1:8–9. They appear in the opening verses of the book of Hebrews as part of an extended argument to establish the full divinity of Jesus Christ. "In these last days," as the beginning of Hebrews asserts, God has spoken to us through a Son, one who is "the reflection of God's glory," "the exact imprint of God's very being" (Heb. 1:2, 3). To further establish this claim of divine identity, the author of Hebrews attributes to him indisputable divine attributes and kingly qualities. A throne, a scepter, a love of justice and hatred of evil, the anointing with oil—all these identified with the king in Psalm 45 are ascribed to Jesus Christ in the book of Hebrews.

From the perspective of Christian belief, then, this psalm can be understood as a prefiguring and identification of the Messiah.[3] The psalm can be treasured both as a royal psalm in its own original context and as a theological reflection on Jesus Christ as the king deserving of all honor (v. 1).

Some of the tensions and paradoxes that arise in a fully articulated Christology appear in this psalm as well. For example, the king who is filled with beauty and graciousness (v. 2) is also the warrior with a sword in his hand. The king who is committed to justice and truth also brings nations to submission (v. 4). The king who loves right and hates wrong is made glad by the sounds of stringed instruments (v. 8). These apparent tensions portray a complex picture of the king and, in christological terms, a complex picture of the Messiah.

The kinds of contrasts and paradoxes that Psalm 45 portrays can be seen in the particulars of the narrative of Jesus' life. It is perhaps not immediately clear that Jesus is "the most handsome of men," as the psalm says about the king in verse 2, yet the followers of Jesus perceive his beauty. The prophet remarked in a famous passage in Isaiah 53:2 that the Suffering Servant, understood to be the Messiah in Christian perspective, "had no form or majesty that we should look at him." Yet Jesus' relationships with women, children, and socially marginalized, as well as his healings and teachings, mark his life as radiant with beauty. His beauty is seen, most paradoxically of all, in the cross and resurrection, as Jesus absorbs and

3. James L. Mays, *Psalms,* Interpretation Series (Louisville, KY: John Knox Press, 1994), 182.

Pastoral Perspective

kingship for its leadership, governance, or practices at the congregational level. Any pastor of any church knows full well that royalty, some of whom generously tithe, reside in every community, and that volunteer leaders are as prone as ordained ministers to setting up functional monarchies among their members. In many ways and for many years the Christian community has shaped itself according to the biblical and historical precedent of kingship. However, whether it is a bishop or the congregation as a whole who identify themselves as the kingly figure, the Christian community always understands the image to function as a means of representing Christ to the world and embodying the kingdom of God.

Examining which attributes of royalty a church evidences and whether they are consistent with the character of the kingdom of God is a worthy pastoral exercise and a useful reflection for congregations discerning their mission and ministry. Pastors regularly see all manner of social, cultural, relational, and physical forces rob their congregants and communities of their agency, autonomy, and even basic human rights. The exercise of power in any realm—politics, a household, the workplace, or society—produces evidence of tyranny as well as benevolence and can be considered for its semblance to the power of the kingdom of God.

For centuries in Western Christendom, both church and state derived power through debate over the divine right of kings. Within the context of American democracy, the language and imagery of royalty employed by the church will resonate differently with worshipers, potentially creating some dissonance between the perceived values of the church and the principles of a free society. Current sensibilities around issues of gender, class, power, and equality make "prince" or "king" terms that inevitably provoke negative sentiments. Such challenges call upon the church to strengthen and clarify its vision of the kingdom characterized by the gospel of Christ.

The imagery and language of kingship found in such passages of Scripture as Psalm 45 invite the church to differentiate their heavenly ruler from temporal leaders. Interestingly, the psalm itself reflects the struggle to remain clear about the identity and nature of the divine king. Confused and confusing, the psalmist moves from addressing and describing the king (v. 6) to addressing God and describing the reign of God (v. 7) and back again (v. 8). What results is an attribution of divinity to the king. The psalmist conflates divinity with its representative.

Exegetical Perspective

warfare. Kings in the ancient world also advertised their rule as "just," and a sovereign's responsibility was sometimes perceived to include the stabilization of the social order, which included the protection of widows and orphans (e.g., The Code of Hammurabi, 18th c. BCE). When the psalmist declares that the king rides "for the cause of truth" (v. 4) and wields a "scepter of equity" (v. 6), the psalmist refers to this standard of just rule, which was not necessarily demonstrated by kings but was nonetheless ascribed to their leadership.[1]

Kings were often linked closely with the primary god of their region and/or culture. Many Neo-Assyrian kings (eighth to seventh century BCE) associated themselves with their chief deity, Ashur; Neo-Babylonian rulers (seventh century BCE) with their creation god, Marduk; and ancient Israelite kings with YHWH (or Elohim). The psalmist interprets the king's talents and Elohim's favor as interchangeable; because of the king's superior appearance, God has blessed him (v. 2), and because of his effectiveness as a just ruler, God has anointed him (v. 7). In verse 6a, the psalmist presents a confusing image: "Your throne, O God (ʾelohim), endures forever and ever." Because this phrase is placed within a section that addresses *the king* (vv. 2–9), it appears that the king is being addressed as "Elohim." In the context of foundational Israelite texts (e.g., Exod. 20:2–3; Deut. 5:6–7), however, this designation seems unfathomable, and for this reason, scholars have raised different solutions to explain the matter.

One suggestion is that the psalm we now have is missing a word in verse 6 that would complete the verbal action of Elohim. Since Elohim is the subject of two other verbal actions received by the king (vv. 2 and 7), verse 6a originally may have read something like "God *established* [*hekhin*] your throne forever and ever" (cf. the phrase "to establish a throne" [*kun kisseʾ*] in 2 Sam. 7:16; 1 Kgs. 2:45; 1 Chr. 22:10). Biblical scholarship is challenged by the sobering reality that much of our biblical evidence (e.g., the actual manuscripts that preserve this literature) was transcribed centuries after the texts were composed. In the process of transmission, sometimes words were omitted, and so it is always possible that we do not have the original version of any given biblical passage. Another suggestion is that "Elohim" in this verse is in apposition to "your throne" and should be

1. Verse 4a in the NRSV reads, "In your majesty ride on victoriously for the cause of truth and *to defend the right*." In place of the italicized phrase, both the Masoretic text and Septuagint provide, "and meekness and righteousness." The reason for the NRSV translation is unclear.

Homiletical Perspective

And though this psalm does not tell us about a divine marriage, and the king himself is not divinized, it still tells of a royal marriage that brings with it the divine promise for blessing. This king rules with God's "equity" (v. 6) and "righteousness" (v. 7). This king will bring about God's purposes for the whole land. While the king's power is only derivative, it derives from God.

This psalm is the responsorial psalm for the first reading, the Song of Solomon 2:8–13. This pairing is from the semicontinuous method used for designating the OT readings, one of two methods chosen for the Revised Common Lectionary. Because it is Year B in the RCL cycle, the OT readings are selected from the court stories as a way of complementing the Gospel according to Mark, which emphasizes Jesus as the Anointed One. The Song of Solomon reading for this day is a love poem, a profession of love from one beloved to another. It is an erotic poem that has been canonized. Even though later given allegorical interpretations in Jewish and Christian traditions, it celebrates sexuality and the human body. Set next to this reading, the psalm continues the sensual tone but directs it toward the praise of the king's prowess on his wedding day. It is intriguing to see these texts, then, alongside the Gospel reading with the Pharisees' question about uncleanliness and bodily defilement. Jesus' response speaks about disobedience that comes from within the heart rather than the body.

The images in the psalm are alien at a certain level. Yet the recognition of beauty, the use of the senses, and the value of the body are familiar to us. But familiarity with images and methods of description does not mean comfort with them. Because of our consumer-driven ethos we can celebrate and enjoy the human body well past the point of faithful stewardship, to reclusive and demeaning addictions instead. Or, despite the witness of Scripture, we can continue to cling to our discomfort with valuing the body. A gnostic distaste for the body permeates attitudes in the church. We are content to hear about the dangers of celebrating or enjoying the body. We are happy to define death as a time to escape the trapping of the earthly body. At the point of death, we think, the true self will live on.

In high contrast, the king in this psalm is anointed with the oil of gladness. It is a sign of his royalty. It is olfactory, visual, and apparent to the touch. It is done upon his body.

Psalm 45:1-2, 6-9

Theological Perspective

overcomes all brokenness, evil, and sin. The paradox of finding divine beauty, rooted in love, in the pain and death of a cross, has both comforted and challenged Christian belief throughout the history of the church. Especially in some contemporary contexts, the beauty of the cross is strongly challenged. In these contemporary contexts, faithful preaching must find ways to proclaim the love of God that was willing to take up and overcome even the violence and hatred of human systems. The cross, in striking tension, exhibits that divine love.

These verses of Psalm 45 give poetic narrative to other aspects of the life of Jesus as well. The language of a warrior king for the sake of justice and truth in verses 3 and 4 is enacted in many ways, often paradoxically. When Jesus overturned the tables of the money changers in the temple, he was a warrior for justice (Matt. 21:12–13; Mark 11:15–16; Luke 19:45, 46). But when he gathered the crowds together for the Sermon on the Mount (Matt. 5–7; Luke 6:20–49), he was no less a warrior king. His words, then and now, form his followers in the ways of peace and patience, of suffering in adversity, of repentance and faith, of mercy and humility. Kingship is portrayed as servanthood; power as self-giving.

The identity of Jesus Christ as the king in Psalm 45, whose beauty surpasses all others, whose sword serves justice, whose speech is gracious and wise, is made possible by the anointing of God. The psalm refers to the oil of anointing, an anointing that is commissioned by God. Only God can grant the kind of wisdom, grace, and power that the king needs. This language too has christological implications. The life, teachings, ministry, death, and resurrection of Jesus Christ have saving significance because God has anointed him to this office, to this servant kingship.

LEANNE VAN DYK

Pastoral Perspective

A king might be the first to make such a mistake. For example, contemporary secular leaders are subject to confusing their personal faith with their public roles, with perilous consequences at stake for people living in a pluralistic world amid global conflict. Leaders in any arena—political, ecclesial, industrial, intellectual, domestic—may not hold up to scrutiny according to the ideals of kingship identified in Psalm 45:1–2, 6–9. When we encounter duplicity and a poverty of language and meaning among public leaders, we might ask what it means for grace to flow from the lips of the king (v. 2). Is public speech merely an echo of popular opinion? Does it require truth?

The ministry of the churches as a manifestation of the kingdom of God is to bear witness to the reign of Christ in the world. If the scepter of God's kingdom is the scepter of righteousness, then the Christian community seeks to discover where, when, and how it might carry the righteousness of Christ into the temporal realms. The kingdoms of this world coexist alongside or within the kingdom of God. Therefore, individuals, local congregations, and the wider Christian community exercise citizenship in multiple realms at once. The fact that it is God's throne that endures for ever and ever (v. 6) may be both a source of fear and disappointment for those enjoying power and a source of hope and gratification for those enduring powerlessness.

As the prince of Psalm 45 prepares himself for his wedding, so Christ figures as both king and bridegroom. However the church might fashion itself for ceremony and governance, or even seat people around a table for potluck supper, it is Christ who was anointed (Mark 14:3); Christ who was adorned (Luke 23:11); Christ who bears the scepter (Matt. 27:29); Christ whom God blessed forever (Mark 9:3, 7); and Christ at whose feet we fall (Mark 15:19).

Above all, he emptied himself of all, and again was raised for all. Christ occupies the eternal throne of God, toppling the powers of sin and death, securing justice, bringing down the rulers of this world and raising up the righteous. To be wedded to Christ is to be wedded to freedom from iniquity, to receive and share God's blessing of righteousness, and to extend his reign in this world. Where leadership serves God and God's purposes, we bless and are blessed; where it confuses divinity with its representatives, we serve kings other than the one whom God blessed for ever.

ALLISON READ

Exegetical Perspective

understood as a superlative in the attributive position. Understood this way, verse 6a would read, "Your divine throne endures forever and ever." There are several examples where "Elohim" grammatically functions in this way (e.g., Gen. 23:6; 1 Sam. 14:15; and Jonah 3:3), and ancient Israelite kingship (especially in Jerusalem) was often described as divinely appointed (e.g., 2 Sam. 7; Ps. 89). Most notable is the reference in 1 Chronicles 29:23, "Then Solomon sat on the throne of the LORD, succeeding his father David as king."

In the context of ancient Israelite history, verse 6a likely conveyed the notion of divine approval of a king's rule, rather than declared the divinity of the king. Certainly ancient Israelite kings (along with other rulers in antiquity) were perceived to have an intimate relationship with the divine world (e.g., 2 Sam. 7:14; Ps. 2), but there is still much debate about how much any sovereign in the ancient world was believed to be equal to a supreme deity. Even Egyptologists debate how much pharaohs were perceived to be divine during their lifetime; there was a distinction between the divine office that the Egyptian king held and the king himself, and when and how these lines were blurred were not consistently expressed.

Because this song focuses on marital union, the psalmist also alludes to the consummation of the marriage. The sensate imagery of the king's perfumed garments (v. 8) is reminiscent of the romantic language in the Song of Solomon (cf. Song 1:1–17; 3:6–11; 4:1–16); and in conjunction with the procession of the bride to the king's palace (vv. 12b–15), this psalm hints at the sexual union that will solidify the couple's marriage and, hopefully, will produce male heirs for the kingdom (v. 16). Psalm 45 praises a traditional marriage in which the bride was expected to shift her loyalty from her home (and family traditions) to her spouse and his traditions (vv. 10–11). Although this psalm recounts a wedding celebration, it is told primarily from the perspective of a king and less so of the new queen; this is why the psalmist declares in the beginning: "I address my verses to the king" (v. 1).

PATRICIA D. AHEARNE-KROLL

Homiletical Perspective

And it is done to us. In baptism we are joined to the Anointed One of God, Jesus Christ. We are anointed with his dying and with his rising. And we, now sons and daughters of this king, are anointed for baptismal purpose. We too are to live with equity and righteousness. We too participate in the fecundity of the triune God in the world. The Epistle reading says that we are to be doers of the word (Jas. 1:22) and that this means: "to care for orphans and widows in their distress, and to keep oneself unstained by the world" (Jas. 1:27). Our power is derivative, but we are granted power that is to be used for the equity of all. As the king embodies the values of God, so do we bear these values in our bodily selves each day of our lives.

The preacher may choose to work with the interaction of the appointed texts of the day. Or the preacher may focus on proclamation from the psalm. Either way, the images are difficult because of the unfamiliarity with ancient royal wedding myths and, more so, because of the sensual language. The sermon is not to be a lecture on either of these subjects but a proclamation of the salvation of the world through the death and resurrection of Jesus Christ. The psalm gives us images for this proclamation: the king is anointed, yet even with all the accompanying ceremony and finery, this is for the purpose of faithfulness to God who wills equity and protection. Earthly kings are always judged according to the rule of Christ the Anointed One. Now we are anointed into this realm and this type of leadership for the purpose of serving all.

JENNIFER L. LORD

James 1:17-27

¹⁷Every generous act of giving, with every perfect gift, is from above, coming down from the Father of lights, with whom there is no variation or shadow due to change. ¹⁸In fulfillment of his own purpose he gave us birth by the word of truth, so that we would become a kind of first fruits of his creatures.

¹⁹You must understand this, my beloved: let everyone be quick to listen, slow to speak, slow to anger; ²⁰for your anger does not produce God's righteousness. ²¹Therefore rid yourselves of all sordidness and rank growth of wickedness, and welcome with meekness the implanted word that has the power to save your souls.

²²But be doers of the word, and not merely hearers who deceive themselves. ²³For if any are hearers of the word and not doers, they are like those who look at themselves in a mirror; ²⁴for they look at themselves and, on going away, immediately forget what they were like. ²⁵But those who look into the perfect law, the law of liberty, and persevere, being not hearers who forget but doers who act—they will be blessed in their doing.

²⁶If any think they are religious, and do not bridle their tongues but deceive their hearts, their religion is worthless. ²⁷Religion that is pure and undefiled before God, the Father, is this: to care for orphans and widows in their distress, and to keep oneself unstained by the world.

Theological Perspective

Early Christian converts interpreted the gospel using their former religious concepts. The writer of James, for example, used a Greek view of God and the universe and a Jewish view of the law. This mixing of concepts can be seen in the two divisions of this text: in 1:17–21 the writer discusses God's gift, adopting Platonic cosmology; in 1:22–27, the writer focuses on the call to be "doers of the word," relating to the ethical implications of the Jewish law.

In Greek philosophy, every being has its origin in the highest Being. This Being is also named the Source, Life, Light, Good, Truth, and Idea. Each being is placed in the hierarchy of beings, as on a ladder. Each receives energy from the Source above. If the being is closer to the top of the ladder, it receives and reflects brighter light; if the being ranks toward the bottom, it receives lesser light and stays shadowy. Calling the Christian God "Father of lights" (v. 17), the writer of James shows that every life-giving gift to Christians also comes from their Source. However, by stating "there is no variation or shadow due to change," the writer departs from Greek cosmology. In the Christian universe, every Christian receives this gift equally and not according to his or her rank in the hierarchy. The supreme gift that Christians receive is "birth by the word of truth" (v. 18).

Pastoral Perspective

"Every generous act of giving, with every perfect gift, is from above." This theological claim is the most important starting point for thinking about pastoral care, because it grounds human responsibility within the divine initiative. God cares for the whole world and creates it anew through the divine Word. God nurtures us, gives us gifts, and provides direction for our lives, often using human agency to do so. In God there is constancy of care and purpose, and no shadow of turning. God supplies the good things in people's lives (v. 17): from this basic affirmation, James instructs Christians about daily life. He names the things he is most concerned about. For example, James is keenly aware of the power of human speech both to build up and to destroy. In the vernacular, he says, "Be slow to use the tongue, or bad-mouth others, or go on the warpath, or raise Cain."

James was a keen observer of human nature, and he paid close attention to the details of everyday living. He noticed the generous acts, the small gifts, the gestures and the words we use. He knew that such small acts are the nuts and bolts of everyday life, holding together the scaffold on which we build community and the social order. Why was he especially concerned with the way we use words? Because they can make a big difference in the way we relate to one another. He knew that our words reveal

Exegetical Perspective

The Gift of the Father (vv. 17–18). The letter of James is addressed "to the twelve tribes in the Dispersion" (1:1). Designated as "the twelve tribes," the addressees are to turn to the Word to seek God's Torah, that is, God's rule of life. In daily life they are to be a Torah people, following "the perfect law," "the royal law, and "the law of liberty" (1:25; 2:8,12). As the Sinaitic Torah gave formation to the Israelites, so the Torah as taught by Jesus gives formation to the people now in Dispersion. It teaches them how to live as God's holy people in the tension between faith and culture (cf. Titus 3.3). The Israelites had to battle against religious syncretism as they lived in the promised land. James aims to put the new Torah as a fence around the believers in the Dispersion.

The imperative, "Do not be deceived" (1:16), looks backward and forward: "Do not be deceived" about what gives birth to death and what gives birth to new life (1:15, 18).

The gift of the Father from above underscores the otherworldly source of help for moral living. God's gift "perfects" or brings faith to maturity and produces actual deeds. James urges his readers to have a constancy that reflects the character of God with whom there is "no variation or shadow due to change" (v. 17). Those in the Dispersion are to

Homiletical Perspective

Renowned preacher Fred Craddock opines that if he had it to do over, he would preach more about God. It is common these days for sermons to avoid the subject of God. James 1:17–18, however, could make God quite a player, since every generous act of giving finds its origin in "the Father of lights." This claim summons preachers to center upon "the generosity of God," including the gift of new birth (v. 18a) as well as "every perfect gift" (v. 17a). The reference to new birth signals a critical intention of a purposive God. One may draw this out in terms of a theology and ethic of divine giving (John 3:16), giving being at the heart of the universe. Generosity grounded in the character of God and embodied in the mission of Jesus can unfold as an influential model of the Divine. To be generous is consonant with the nature of God. God comes through as reliable as well (v. 17c), even from a cosmic perspective.

On the way to the sermon, the preacher might also come at this text from the side of praise—which has indeed found surprising resonance in our contemporary world—focusing upon the grace of God in music and message. The doxology in particular affirms the God "from whom all blessings flow." We might cultivate a style of gratitude that bothers to count blessings, to "name them one by one." With particularly keen observation, Harry

James 1:17-27

Theological Perspective

The writer uses interplay between metaphors of the "word" to connect two points. First, the "word of truth" that gives birth to Christians is also a seed that grows. Second, this word is "implanted" and works for the salvation of one's soul (v. 21). In rabbinic Judaism, the word is the law. One looks at this perfect law and sees one's reflection of the Light, as in a mirror (v. 23). The word also symbolizes one's speech. Jewish law requires a response of doing, not just saying. One does not simply speak of God's word without bridling one's tongue (v. 26). One is to be "quick to listen, slow to speak" (v. 19). Moreover, God's law of liberty, which is the implanted word of truth, liberates one to ethical actions (v. 25). The seed produces fruits. Here the writer again departs from Greek cosmology, in which every good that proceeds from the Good eventually returns to the Source in an eternal cycle. But Christians who receive the gift of life from God become "a kind of first fruits of his creatures" (v. 18). Instead of returning their gift to the Source, they extend the gift of life to others. God's blessing for Christians comes full circle (vv. 18 and 25).

Finally the writer defines what doers of the word do: "Religion that is pure and undefiled before God, the Father, is this: to care for orphans and widows in their distress, and to keep oneself unstained by the world" (v. 27). Set apart from the pagan world, Christians become the source of life, light, goodness, and the word of truth to those who are placed at the lowest rank of Roman society.

Interestingly, in these sections the writer does not mention Jesus Christ. Some early Christians expanded the word/seed metaphor in their *logos* theology to equate the Word with Christ. Others understood the first fruit of God's creation to be Christ, developing a vision of the organic growth of Christ's body in the church. The fact that this letter was first accepted into the canon of Scripture in Alexandria in the third century—when Christianity was still an illegal religion in the Roman Empire—may indicate that the Alexandrian school of biblical theologians provided useful interpretation of this letter. Because of its large library, Alexandria attracted Hellenistic philosophers and gnostic teachers. There was also a large community of educated Hellenistic Diaspora Jews there, some of whom were noted rabbis. Alexandria was the legendary birthplace of the Septuagint, the standard Greek translation of the Hebrew Bible. Utilizing these resources, Christian thinkers such as Clement and Origen used both Greek and Jewish terms to teach Christian Scripture. They used allegory to explain

Pastoral Perspective

something about our motivation, intention, belief, and emotional life. Our emotional life grows from our earliest relationships with others and with the God who is Other. It also emerges from our relationship with our selves. Anger, for example, is an emotion that can be destructive. It can also be an emotion that alerts us to wrongdoing. Thus anger can be channeled in ways that lead to protest and improvement, so that we must make a decision about its meaning in our lives. James knows this and shows us his concern.

Words Create Worlds of Meaning. We use words to express ourselves; to convince and convict ourselves and others; to describe, name, blame, or label things; to win arguments; to sell an idea or object; to lecture; to expound a point, explain things into or out of existence, persuade, condole, console, counsel; to announce, denounce, deceive; to ask someone to marry; to declare war and make peace; to sentence someone, diagnose a condition, analyze a problem, deliberate or negotiate a deal. We cannot get along without words. Words can alarm, harm, uplift, inspire, degrade, or silence someone. They can reveal our inner thoughts. Where would we be without words?

According to James, we cannot bring about God's righteousness through revengeful or evil speech, which only spreads destruction. Get rid of that way of being in the world, James counsels. Destructive anger can poison our own lives and that of the community as well. It cannot give new meaning to life or inspire creativity. Words that serve such anger are worthless. Destructive acts can never be the means for illuminating God's presence or making room for divine goodness in our lives. They cannot produce God's righteousness.

Constructive and Destructive Expressions of Anger. James does not deny the importance or strength of anger. He does not tell us to "swallow" or "stuff" it. Rather, he encourages us to transform anger into a virtue. Be quick to listen, he says, and slow to speak and (therefore) slow to anger. This is hard work, especially for those of us who are quick to judge, impatient with ourselves and with others, especially when we are in disagreement or have already made up our minds. To resist such impatience requires discipline. "Rid yourself of all sordidness, and the growth of wickedness," James counsels (v. 21). Reverse your direction. Cultivate the virtues of a discerning and welcoming spirit. James counsels meekness, not weakness. James calls us to a standard that is higher than the one we already have.

persist in moral living, bearing fruit as intended by their Creator, in their challenging environment.

Quick to Listen/Slow to Speak (vv. 19–20). James implants wisdom in his "beloved children" by a series of imperatives. More than 100 imperatives punctuate the letter. Imperatives are vital because the "beloved" are being enticed by the dictates of the surrounding society.

For a covenant community, which is not immune to heated disputes, James urges his readers to be quick to listen, slow to speak. James undoubtedly sat through assemblies where contention fractured the community. He observed that human anger will not produce results that make things right. James is intense, using acid rhetoric: "rid yourselves of all sordidness and rank growth of wickedness," he admonishes (v. 21). On the other hand, he says, listening and being listened to open the door to the righteousness of God for the community.

Put Away/Receive (v. 21). "Receive [NRSV "welcome"] the *implanted word*" is set in contrast to "put away" [NRSV "rid yourselves of"]. A choice must be made. Either "put away" turpitude or "receive" the Word. Joshua challenged those assembled at Shechem to "choose this day whom you will serve" (Josh. 24:15). The double-minded get nowhere (Jas. 1:8; 4:8). Paul uses the same Greek word for "put away" in Ephesians, where he speaks of "putting away" all falsehood, speaking the truth in love, dealing with irritation, and not giving room for the devil (Eph. 4:22, 25–26). The implanted Word is an internal gyroscope, which guides the community.

Hearers/Doers (vv. 22–25). One not doing the Word is deceiving him/herself. This is like a person who looks into a mirror and then goes away unmindful of his or her faith. What is this deception about? On a practical level, someone might say, "I really believe in Jesus; I really believe in the resurrection," but then give no evidence of such faith in dealing with his or her neighbor (2:18–19).

The "implanted word" is able to "save your souls" (v. 21). Is James talking about eternal life? Probably so, but he does so in such a way that "being saved" is rooted in the present. It is connected with being "slow to speak and quick to hear" and with giving food to the hungry (2:14f). James cannot countenance a faith that does not love the neighbor actively. For James it is simple: "Every good tree bears good fruit, but the bad tree bears bad

Emerson Fosdick once observed that in his experience those who reflect upon their lives and conclude that they have received far less than they deserve tend to be among those from whom no great living comes. Others evaluate their lives, think they have broken about even, and conclude that they got about what they earned. Rarely do you see any exceptional living from them either. However, those who readily reckon they have received far more than they deserve are among those who do indulge in great living.[1]

James's remaining moral topics hang together rather well around the insistence on doing and not merely hearing (vv. 19–27) and bridling one's tongue (vv. 19 and 26b). Hearing without following up is as different from acting well after hearing as a lightning bug is from lightning. The larger passage contains two ornate passages that are downright aphoristic (vv. 22 and 27), bringing with them the power of the familiar. One tempting option would be to use one of these lapidary texts as a reiterative chorus. The tone of exhortation and imperative signals the urgency and importance of the issues at hand. To borrow a leaf from Tom Long, they might well influence the tone and even the structure of a sermon.

While the moral issues James raises may evoke general truths obviously applicable to home and work, they may also reflect congregational or denominational issues, providing models for handling conflict in the church. With a pastoral touch ("my beloved" at v. 19), the author confronts anger in the community with wise counsel indeed. He offers what amounts to a strategy for overcoming destructive anger: be quick to listen, slow to speak, and slow to anger. We often blow our tops and thrust people away. In marital relations we may have tin ears and caustic tongues that distance and wound.

James addresses the deception of passive faith (vv. 22–25) and offers a durable definition of pure religion (vv. 26–27), the word of God indeed. He develops the paradigm of looking into a mirror at oneself and then forgetting how one appeared as an analogy of hearing but not doing (v. 24). The peril of spiritual forgetfulness does not belong to the category of a moral misdemeanor. Gallery Christians represent a contradiction in terms (cf. Matt. 7:24–27). The Golden Rule contains the crucial provision "*do* to others" (Matt. 7:12; cf. Luke 10:37d). The Methodist minister Sangster turned the deep cellars of a church into shelters during World War II. He slept there five

---

1. Henry Emerson Fosdick, *Riverside Sermons* (New York: Harper, 1958), 174.

James 1:17-27

Theological Perspective

hard passages and difficult words in the Bible. The Christian community in Alexandria would have easily allegorized the metaphors of the word and law to read a Christian message into this letter that seldom mentions Jesus Christ.

Ever since Luther scorned the letter of James as "an epistle of straw," Protestants have tended to view it with suspicion. Uplifting Pauline salvation by faith alone, Luther saw only law and actions emphasized in it, erroneously equating it with "Popish" works righteousness. Yet even Luther understood the necessity of expressing the gospel of Jesus Christ to our neighbors in love. James speaks of the "law of liberty" (v. 25). In a similar way, Luther wrote, "A Christian is a free lord, subject to none. A Christian is a perfectly dutiful servant, subject to all."[1]

Historian Jeannine Olson noted Calvin's contribution to modern society through his creation of welfare institutions.[2] The city of Geneva during the Reformation period had many poor, widows, and orphans. Calvin himself came to Geneva as a French religious refugee. In his *Ecclesiastical Ordinances* (1541), Calvin established the General Hospital and designated the offices of deacon and deaconess to supervise citizens' works of mercy as the "doers of the pure religion" in care of the poor.

Throughout history, in all Christian traditions and world religions, women have proven to be doers of the word, daily serving the poor. The majority of the poor also continue to be women and children. How can the church be better doers, not merely hearers, of the word in today's world?

HARUKO NAWATA WARD

Pastoral Perspective

Actions Speak Louder Than Words. James counsels us to a practical morality that is quick to listen, slow to speak, and slow to anger. What we do matters, and what comes out of our mouths can make a difference, for good and for ill. But our actions speak louder than our words. Words may touch our emotional life and help us anticipate what is going to happen. But our actions establish the structures of meaning that build our worlds. Through faithful activity we create and re-create ourselves in trustworthy ways and help build worlds worthy of trust. Actions add value to our words and give them life. In this way, morality has the practical aim of creating relevance, meaning, and integrity in the world.

Worthless and Worthwhile Morality. James calls us to make a distinction between worthless and worthwhile religious morality. The discernment of the difference between these two kinds of religious morality is an ongoing process. It exists in a fluid relationship with the changing circumstances in which we find ourselves every day. Hence, James calls us to continual accountability and to a deeper appreciation of the vicissitudes of our emotional lives. By acknowledging and taking responsibility for our own anger, we may exercise self-control and become decision makers, architects of relationships, and builders of the beloved community. This is what James requires of us. He does not ask us to undergo psychoanalysis or psychotherapy, or to engage in fundamental character reconstruction. Rather, he calls us to be responsible, taking seriously our emotional lives, our religious faith, and our behavior. We can envision ourselves as early signs of God's new creation. We can begin by embracing the whole of ourselves and taking responsibility for our constructive and destructive potentials. Living this way can increase our critical discernment. It can foster the development of persons and communities. Such living, when joined by the faithfulness of many others, can become a strong current that helps to transform the world.

ARCHIE SMITH JR.

1. Martin Luther, *The Freedom of a Christian*, in *Martin Luther: Selections from His Writings*, ed. John Dillenberger (Garden City, NY: Doubleday Anchor Books, 1962), 53. See also, in same volume, Luther's *Preface to the Epistles of St. James and St. Jude*, 35–37.
2. See Jeannine E. Olson, "Calvin and Social-Ethical Issues," in *Cambridge Companion to John Calvin*, ed. Donald K. McKim (Cambridge: Cambridge University Press, 2004), 153–72.

fruit" (Matt. 7:17); faith without works is dead (Jas. 2:17).

The "law of liberty" engenders freedom. As the Israelites came out of slavery, they were a motley people who needed Torah, "household rules," to form them into the people of God. Rules allow rugby players to enjoy the game thoroughly. Without rules, there would be bloody mayhem. James does not want his hearers to forget that looking into the law of liberty provides rules for neighborly love. The "perfect law" matures faith in covenantal love in everyday interactions. The hearer/doer is called to look intently into the word and to persist in loving action. Looking intently into the law enhances memory.

It is not enough merely to hear the word. James promises that hearers will be blessed *in their doing* (cf. Luke 11:28; 12:43; John 13:17). The mere hearer is deceived; the doer is blessed. The doers can rejoice in knowing that their actions, born of the Word (1:18), demonstrate saving faith (Jas. 2:18, 22).

Good/Bad Religion (vv. 26–27). True religion watches out for the vulnerable and also for one's own vulnerability. Backbiting and slander, among other vices, characterize worthless religion. The tongue is capable of great damage. For James this cannot be overemphasized. James hammers against an abusive tongue and instructs his hearers to keep a tight rein on the tongue (3:3–10; 4:11; 5:9). The foundational imperatives of Israel enjoined the covenant people to refrain from slander and false witness (Exod. 20:16; Deut. 5:20; Lev. 19:16). The people of the Dispersion are people of a community Torah.

The commands to care for the orphans and widows reach back into Israel's experience as slaves in Egypt. Liberated by God, they were to treat the marginal with compassion. James says that those in the Dispersion, delivered by God, are likewise to care for the poor in their midst. This is foundational for Christian ethics.

James does not hold religion to be only social outreach. He emphasizes that the faithful must keep themselves under the influence of the Christian Torah. They are not to conform to or be stained by the world (1:27; 4:4; cf. Rom. 12:2). The integrity of faith embraces neighbor and self: "You shall love your neighbor as yourself" (Matt. 22:39).

AARON L. UITTI

years supervising the welfare of thousands, putting service ahead of services.

By way of illustration, there was a man who began cutting his grass on a scorching Saturday. He had a lot of lawn. Perspiring, he thought how good a tall glass of lemonade would taste. He went inside into the air-conditioning, poured an oversized glass, and settled into a big easy chair. He decided to look up the word "weed" in the dictionary and found "any plant growing where it was not wanted." He went back outside, surveyed the lawn, and decided that every blade stood exactly where he wanted it! He rationalized away doing.

The justly famous definition of genuine religion at James 1:27 is juxtaposed against a religion that is "worthless" (1:26), "barren" (2:20), or even "dead" (2:26), so the stakes run high. In a kind of dialectic of Christian existence, James understands pure religion as being inclusive of both social ministry and personal morality. One's relationship to God means showing mercy (2:13), striving for peace (3:18), helping the needy (2:15–16), loving the neighbor (2:8), and recognizing the social justice of a fair minimum wage (5:4). In terms of personal morality, it means keeping from the "stain" (Moffatt), and being "uncontaminated" (Jerusalem Bible).

Some Christians have discovered a social conscience but have dismissed personal morals, a great gain and a disastrous loss. Bunyan characterizes Mr. Looking Both Ways as having a sense of what is right but a love for what is wrong! The church would do well to find a renewed passion for troubled children, to stand behind Christian homes for children, and to salute parents who adopt children. Some churches can develop programs for "latchkey kids." The Baptist New Testament scholar Raymond Brown observed that those who scorn "do-gooders" in the name of biblical religion do so by scorning James 1:27. Given this wise dual insistence, we think of a Christian as a person for others and as pure in heart.

PETER RHEA JONES

Mark 7:1-8, 14-15, 21-23

¹Now when the Pharisees and some of the scribes who had come from Jerusalem gathered around him, ²they noticed that some of his disciples were eating with defiled hands, that is, without washing them. ³(For the Pharisees, and all the Jews, do not eat unless they thoroughly wash their hands, thus observing the tradition of the elders; ⁴and they do not eat anything from the market unless they wash it; and there are also many other traditions that they observe, the washing of cups, pots, and bronze kettles.) ⁵So the Pharisees and the scribes asked him, "Why do your disciples not live according to the tradition of the elders, but eat with defiled hands?" ⁶He said to them, "Isaiah prophesied rightly about you hypocrites, as it is written,

Theological Perspective

At first blush the warnings of Jesus in this text from Mark come across as straightforward and rather self-explanatory, not needing much in terms of theological commentary. It would appear that this passage is a critique of how we as religious creatures too often exalt our rituals above our ethics. Enamored with the religiously superior identity that we gain through the participation in our community's ritual symbolism, we get hung up on the religiosity of our set-apartness, overlooking the deeper truth that living out the heart of our religious tradition would instead call us to be an alternative to the larger "world" of our society by choosing and living out right relationships: kindness over cruelty, compassion over condemnation.

Instead, we get so wrapped up in the proper symbolic ways of representing our faith outwardly that we overlook the deeper demands of that faith to serve God by doing good, holding in check our own selfish desires so that we might better direct our energies toward the welfare of others and the larger community. Yet, as powerful and accurate a critique of human religiosity as this is, if we are content to stay at this level of meaning, we may miss the more subtle teaching about hypocrisy that Jesus provides for his listeners. Indeed, this may be part of the reason why some ancient manuscripts include an additional verse 16 in this passage (not included in

Pastoral Perspective

One Sunday morning I came into my office to find a note quickly scribbled and left on my desk. The author of the note wrote something like, "It seems that our youth don't know how to spell any better than they know the Bible." I walked to my doorway where I had a good view of the newly created bulletin board that welcomed kids and adults to the Sunday school wing of the church. In bright, happy colors it invited one and all to attend "Sunday Skool!" I chuckled as I realized that their intent was to get people's attention . . . and it had worked. I may have been mildly amused, but I was also angry. I knew the young people who had created the bulletin board had sacrificed part of their Saturday so we could feel welcomed to a new season of Sunday school. The person who had left the note on my desk was missing the deeper Christian message. In today's passage from Mark, I think Jesus is feeling something similar.

The Pharisees and the scribes, clothed in righteousness, come upon Jesus and his disciples in a moment of repose. The disciples are gathered together, sharing a meal without first having washed their hands. The Pharisees look to Jesus as the leader and ask, "Why do your disciples not live according to the tradition of the elders, but eat with defiled hands?" (v. 5). I cannot help but wonder if Jesus does not feel a little angry on behalf of his disciples. After

'This people honors me with their lips,
   but their hearts are far from me;
[7]in vain do they worship me,
   teaching human precepts as doctrines.'
[8]You abandon the commandment of God and hold to human tradition." . . .

[14]Then he called the crowd again and said to them, "Listen to me, all of you, and understand: [15]there is nothing outside a person that by going in can defile, but the things that come out are what defile. . . .
   [21]"For it is from within, from the human heart, that evil intentions come: fornication, theft, murder, [22]adultery, avarice, wickedness, deceit, licentiousness, envy, slander, pride, folly. [23]All these evil things come from within, and they defile a person."

Exegetical Perspective

It is difficult for Christians to comprehend the issue raised by the Pharisees in this passage, because the idea of physical holiness is alien to our understanding of religion.

Israel's religion included many laws concerning ritual purity or holiness, in conformity with Leviticus 19:2, "You shall be holy, for I the LORD your God am holy." There is no biblical law about washing hands before eating, but there is a requirement that priests wash hands and feet before ministering at the altar (Exod. 30:17–21). This was understood to include washing hands before eating holy meat from the sacrifices. The Pharisees took seriously the command of Exodus 19:6, "You shall be for me a priestly kingdom and a holy nation." They argued that this meant that all Israelites should be as holy as priests, and that consequently all Jews should wash their hands before eating.

Mark is exaggerating in verse 3 when he suggests that all Jews obey this tradition of the Pharisees. There must have been many others in addition to Jesus and his disciples who ignored the pharisaic rule.

Many of our modern translations have difficulty translating the adjective modifying "hands" in verse 2. The Greek word *koinos* does not in itself mean "defiled" (NRSV, REB) or "unclean" (NIV). It is the word for "common," that is, "ordinary." The Pharisees

Homiletical Perspective

Listening to these verses feels like walking in on a family argument: it is painful to hear and tempting to walk away. We may find it all too easy to dismiss the in-house disagreements between Jesus and the scribes and Pharisees as embarrassing or irrelevant, rather than probe beneath the surface to listen for the heart of the gospel's message. To further complicate matters, several verses have been omitted from the lectionary reading so that the sequence of Mark's narrative has been disrupted. The virulent tone of this passage and the verses omitted from it challenge us to look more carefully at the differing perspectives and arguments represented here and to appreciate Jesus' call to consider anew the inner workings of the human heart.

In our present context, when interreligious dialogue and understanding are essential to the well-being of individuals and nations, it is vital that preachers not only listen carefully to what Jesus says to those who challenge him, but that we recognize what he does *not* say. When he responds to the Pharisees and scribes, Jesus does not condemn their beliefs or denounce their important role in first-century Judaism. The Jewish leaders who confront Jesus about questions of ritual purity are not petty bureaucrats obsessed with matters of trivial pursuit. Rather, they are concerned that Jesus' disciples do

Mark 7:1-8, 14-15, 21-23

Theological Perspective

the NRSV) that echoes the spiritually hermeneutical refrain of Mark, introduced in 4:9, "Let anyone with ears to hear listen."

Hypocrisy refers to the disconnect between the moral values and standards that we espouse and those that we actually practice in our behavior. From its Greek roots (*hypokrisis* "acting out a theatrical role" and *hypokrinesthai* "pretending") we can see that hypocrisy is a negation of authentic life: it is life acted out to fool others, a role that we take on and pretend to be, that is not really us. It is a denial of our authentic self in favor of the fabricated persona that we wish to be. Religious hypocrisy, in particular, is a most destructive kind in that it uses sacred teachings about Truth itself to elevate self-deception. It makes our pretending both a distortion of Truth and a substitute for it. The hypocrisy of religious people not only damages the credibility of the message but creates idolaters who are convinced that their pretend piety is not idolatry at all. Hypocrisy is as common to our experience as love and hate. What Jesus is pointing to here is the quintessential human struggle to discover and maintain the integrity of the self.

How might we theologically analyze hypocrisy? One of the towering theologians of the twentieth century, Paul Tillich (1886–1965), described self-integration as one of the three basic functions of life (with self-creativity and self-transformation being the other two). What he meant was that, in order for life to be actualized from its potential being, it has to unfold in a process of finding our center, moving out from it in freedom and courage, and returning to it again enriched and deepened. This is how he described self-integration. The center is the core of the self; it cannot be divided, but it can be strengthened. To move out from our center is to exercise our free-dom, to risk disintegration, and this act is essentially a moral act, a function of the realm of the spirit. In Tillich's terms this also corresponds to a therapeutic model: spiritual health is the moral integrity, the self-integration of a person's center, whereas spiritual disease is the breakdown of moral integrity, the dis-integration of a person's center. Hypocrisy erodes our center by promoting disintegration rather than self-integration; moral inconsistency and disconnection from the dimension of the spirit rather than a deeper center in greater communication with the healing power of spirit.

More recently, theologian Robert Cummings Neville (b. 1939) builds on Tillich's theological assessment of the centered self and describes the human condition of sin as ontological self-

Pastoral Perspective

all, they have sacrificed a great deal to follow him. Some have given up family, others their careers, still others status—much more than a Saturday afternoon! In Jesus' response, we get a sense of what is important to God. Jesus quotes Isaiah, saying, "This people honors me with their lips, but their hearts are far from me; in vain do they worship me, teaching human precepts as doctrines" (vv. 6–7).

Human beings need a sense of order to feel secure. We need laws to organize our communities; we need doctrines to articulate our beliefs. Order and doctrines are not bad things. However, when we begin to worship what gives us a sense of order or bow down to a doctrine, we cease to be faithful to our Creator. Some of Jesus' contemporaries were very concerned with the details of ritual cleanness and uncleanness, purity and defilement. Some of the practices that came out of this concern were life saving. But the requirements of ritual purity in the first century could also become means of judgment and oppression.

Jesus takes this opportunity for a broad teaching moment. He gathers a crowd around him and says, "Listen to me, all of you, and understand: there is nothing outside a person that by going in can defile, but the things that come out are what defile" (vv. 14–15). The people are perplexed by this declaration. Jesus is challenging a basic religious belief of the day. The disciples are also confused. In private, they even ask Jesus exactly what he means. Jesus clarifies what is important to God. Jesus tells his disciples that the things we eat do not enter our hearts but enter our stomachs. In the stomach, the food is used as it is needed and then released to the sewer. It is those things that come out from our hearts that defile us, not the things that go into our mouths. Jesus says that evil intentions come from the heart and come out as "fornication, theft, murder, adultery, avarice, wickedness, deceit, licentiousness, envy, slander, pride, folly" (vv. 21–22). Today we may scoff at the first-century world's view of ritual purity and defilement, but we certainly are not above the evil intentions of which Jesus warns his disciples.

Our challenge today is to recognize how we, like the Pharisees, misinterpret what is important to God. Do we look at the dirty fingernails of our homeless brothers and sisters and think to ourselves, "They do not belong in our sanctuary"? Do we hear a crying baby during the worship service and think to ourselves, or even whisper to our neighbor, "Children should not be allowed in worship"? Do we watch a gay couple join the church and think, "They are not welcome here"? We seem to put our energy

believed that food should be eaten with sanctified hands, not ordinary hands.

A major transition occurs in verse 14. Now Jesus is criticizing not the Pharisees' tradition but their emphasis on ritual purity as that which makes Israel acceptable to God. Here he draws on the prophetic tradition, such as we find in Isaiah: "Is not this the fast that I choose: to loose the bonds of injustice? . . . Is it not to share your bread with the hungry, and bring the homeless poor into your house?" (Isa. 58:6–7). What makes Israel acceptable to God is not correct performance of ritual acts but ethical behavior. Similarly, Jesus declares that it is not scrupulous observance of the food laws that makes Israel holy, but morality.

The verb translated "defile" in the NRSV in verses 15, 18, 20, 23 is based on the adjective *koinos*; its meaning is "to make common," that is, ordinary. In a discussion of Jewish purity it means "render unsanctified, make unholy." Since the corresponding Hebrew verb is regularly translated "become unclean" or "be unclean" in the NRSV of Leviticus (5:2, etc.), NIV is justified in rendering verse 15, "Nothing outside a man can make him 'unclean' by going into him."

In Leviticus "unclean" refers to a status ritually unacceptable to God, a status that must be rectified through washing, sacrifice, or simply through the passing of the day into evening (e.g., Lev. 11:24). Even normal marital intercourse renders husband and wife "unclean"; they are required to remove the uncleanness through bathing (Lev. 15:18). It is certainly not sinful to incur "uncleanness" in this way, but ritual purity requires that the uncleanness be removed. The Contemporary English Version attempts to make this clear by its paraphrase of verse 15: "The food that you put into your mouth doesn't make you unclean *and unfit to worship God*" [the italicized words interpret "unclean"].

In verses 15, 18–19 Jesus seems to be rejecting the entire program of Leviticus concerning clean and unclean foods. Indeed, this is how Mark understands Jesus' words. He boldly announces, for the benefit of his Gentile readers, "Thus he declared all foods clean" (v. 19b). This is a paraphrase; the Greek literally means "cleansing all foods." It seems unlikely, however, that Jesus himself was such a radical. Is it reasonable to assume that Jesus ate pork? Probably he was employing the kind of argument that depreciates one matter, in order to give special emphasis to another.

In any case, Jesus' main point is perfectly clear: what really renders a person "unclean" in God's sight

not demonstrate reverence for the tradition of the elders, since the ritual of hand washing was considered an integral part of Jewish faith and identity. When Jesus turns the table on their concern, he does so as a deeply religious Jew who cites the prophetic tradition of Israel in denouncing the selfish interests of the scribes and Pharisees (Isa. 29:13). He asserts that their hearts are far from God, but he does not condemn all of Judaism and its leaders. We too must be careful not to preach and speak in ways that condemn whole groups of people or religious traditions that differ from our own. Otherwise, we will be guilty of the same hardness of heart that Jesus urges us to avoid.

In addition to understanding the complex relationship between Jesus and other Jewish leaders, at least two important questions arise when we explore this text today. First, what is at the heart of our own religious faith and traditions? Jesus uses the word "heart" three times in 7:1–23, and with each reference we sense the importance of the human heart for religious faith and practice. Since the heart was thought to be the center of one's will and decision-making abilities, to turn one's heart away from God (7:6b) or to have it filled with evil intentions (7:21) was a grievous sin. Passages such as 3:5; 6:52; and 8:17 also remind us that hardness of heart is among the most damning of spiritual conditions, revealing a lack of compassion toward others. In these and other verses, Christ urges us to examine our own defiled hearts rather than our neighbors' dirty hands.

In considering the heart of our faith it may be difficult to preach about the list of evil inclinations and activities cited in 7:21–22. We are all susceptible to sin and guilty of practicing one or more of the sins listed here. Each of the attitudes and actions Jesus names reflects a heart that has turned away from God. Each of these also impacts our relationships with others so that personal sin has social consequences. Evil intentions arise within the human heart and extend outward in their damaging effects. If we want to examine the heart of our religious faith, we must be willing to explore honestly whether our attitudes and actions reveal genuine love for God and compassion for others. In contrast to the list of evil deeds and intentions, it may be helpful for the preacher to offer an alternative list of attitudes and actions that reveal our more loving aspirations as followers of Jesus Christ. His words remind us that the growth in our capacity to love is directly related to an increased awareness of the hidden intentions of our hearts.

Mark 7:1-8, 14-15, 21-23

Theological Perspective

contradiction, or being divided against oneself in one's very being (Paul gives a profound firsthand experiential account of this in Romans 7). This contradiction is ontological in that human beings are created to be in a normative covenant with their Creator; therefore moral transgressions against the covenant are also transgressions against their own created being. To follow the covenant, for Neville, is to do right (practice righteousness) by striving to avoid harming one's neighbors, institutions, and nature, in other words, to avoid doing the "evil things" that Jesus mentions in verse 21.

How might such analyses of this text provide a vision of the faithful life? Living such a life means trying to avoid hypocrisy so that we might live more faithfully in relationship to God, with the centeredness of integrity maintained by moral consistency. One of the ideas for which Søren Kierkegaard (1813–55) is perhaps best remembered is that "purity of heart is to will one thing." For Kierkegaard this "one thing" is the Good. Only in the Good do we find truth and authenticity. Only by willing one thing can we achieve our true and authentic self.

But what does it mean to "will one thing"? "Will" is both a noun and a verb, our capacity and faculty for intentional choice, as well as the activity of our choosing and deciding. For Kierkegaard, to will the Good is also to will the eternal and the true at the same time. It is to will as God wills. Indeed it is to will God, to decide to make a choice for God. In Mark's text, this brings Jesus and his listeners squarely back to the real demand of the Jewish covenant traditions, especially the Mosaic covenant. To choose life is to choose self-integration and moral integrity. It is to be faithful to the covenant with our Creator, to choose right relations with God, each other, and our community over any pretended reenactments of that covenant.

LOYE BRADLEY ASHTON

Pastoral Perspective

into keeping people out of our sanctuaries, rather than into examining the sins that stain our own lives.

The human race has changed little in two thousand years. We cannot build prisons fast enough to hold our murderers, our thieves, our white-collar criminals. Marriages and families continue to be torn apart by acts of adultery and selfishness. We may not use words like avarice and licentiousness, but greed and lack of sexual restraint continue to be problems for us. We need to hear Jesus' teaching just as much as his followers and disciples needed to hear his words so long ago. We need to be reminded what is important and what is simply released into the sewer. The evil intentions that come from our hearts separate us from God. When we use religious rules inappropriately, we separate ourselves from one another.

The correct spelling of Sunday school is not important. Welcoming all into God's kingdom is important. We want to focus on the mundane because facing the sins that stain our own hands is so painful. However, when we face those sins, letting go of that which is unimportant, and turn to God, we are welcome in the sanctuary and at the table.

AMY C. HOWE

Exegetical Perspective

is what comes out of him or her. It is not what we eat but what we do that really counts with God.

The contrast between what goes into the mouth and what comes out leads the reader to expect that Jesus will emphasize sins of the mouth, such as lying, foul language, slander, and false promises. In the list of immoral acts in verses 21–22, only deceit and slander are sins of the mouth. Instead, attention shifts from the mouth to the heart, from which "evil intentions" (NRSV) or "evil thoughts" (NIV, REB, CEV) come. Jesus here stresses that the thought is father to the deed. We think a sin before we do it.

The list of sinful activities in verses 21–22 is fairly standard, echoing at least four of the ten commandments. It is interesting to compare this list with Paul's "works of the flesh" in Galatians 5:19–21. Missing from Mark's list are not merely such notable sins of the flesh as drunkenness and carousing but various sins of the spirit such as "enmities, strife, jealousy, anger, quarrels, dissensions, factions."

Two items in Mark's list, both missing from Paul's, are surprising: avarice and pride. These are striking because both refer primarily to attitudes rather than to behavior. The Greek word *pleonexia*, translated as "avarice" or "greed," literally means "a desire to have more." Why is it sinful to want more? Because it can make us stingy toward those who have little. In Luke 12:15 Jesus says, "Take care! Be on your guard against all kinds of *pleonexia*; for one's life does not consist in the abundance of possessions." Many of us who are innocent of most of the sins in Mark's list need this advice.

The word translated "pride" in the NRSV and CEV can also be rendered as "arrogance" (NIV, REB). Another English equivalent is "haughtiness." Arrogance is a disease of the spirit, reflecting resistance to God as well as contempt for other people. Christians rich and poor must heed the advice of 1 Peter 5:5: "And all of you must clothe yourselves with humility in your dealings with one another, for 'God opposes the proud, but gives grace to the humble.'"

DOUGLAS R. A. HARE

Homiletical Perspective

A second question worth exploring concerns our own holy habits and practices. What are the religious practices we pursue, and why do we pursue them? (Or, what are the religious practices we do not pursue?) Most of us do not think of religious practices in terms of what is clean or unclean, and we seldom use words like "holiness" or "defiled" when describing our faith. Yet there is renewed interest among many Christians in "practices," "values," and "spiritual disciplines" that encourage faithful living.[1] What kinds of ritual activities or practices may help us develop a meaningful relationship with God and our neighbors? How do practices of Sabbath keeping, charitable giving, public worship, private prayer, service work, hospitality, and forgiveness deepen our sense of God's presence and power among us?

This passage also invites us to consider anew the purposes behind our religious practices as well as their potential pitfalls. In terms of the purposes, we may look anew at the ways our daily habits (religious or otherwise) encourage our awareness of God and impact our relationships with loved ones and strangers. For example, does our Sabbath keeping remind us to trust in God for our well-being and to rest in ways that do not demand others to work on our behalf? In terms of the potential pitfalls, we may explore how we do or do not regularly evaluate the meaning or implications of what we do. It is entirely possible for our religious practices to become so entrenched that we have forgotten their meaning or value. Or we may not be aware of how our attitudes and actions impact others. Perhaps we have succumbed to moral rigidity, spiritual self-satisfaction, or, worse yet, a sense of superiority to others who are different from ourselves. However difficult or challenging Jesus' words may be, there is within them the hope of renewing our attitudes and actions so that we may reflect God's loving intentions for humanity.

DAWN OTTONI WILHELM

---

1. Miroslav Volf and Dorothy C. Bass, eds., *Practicing Theology: Beliefs and Practices in Christian Life* (Grand Rapids: Eerdmans, 2002).

Proverbs 22:1-2, 8-9, 22-23

[1]A good name is to be chosen rather than great riches,
    and favor is better than silver or gold.
[2]The rich and the poor have this in common:
    the Lord is the maker of them all.

. . . .

[8]Whoever sows injustice will reap calamity,
    and the rod of anger will fail.
[9]Those who are generous are blessed,
    for they share their bread with the poor.

. . . .

[22]Do not rob the poor because they are poor,
    or crush the afflicted at the gate;
[23]for the Lord pleads their cause
    and despoils of life those who despoil them.

Theological Perspective

The Revised Common Lectionary selects Proverbs 22:1–2, 8–9, 22–23, emphasizing the behavior of rich people. These verses aim at calling the rich to wise responsibility and stewardship of their wealth in their relationship to the poor, threatening them with poverty and loss by God's judgment if they foolishly disregard the wise counsel.

In contrast, the wisdom of proverbs addressed to the poor, not selected for the lection, appears nearby in both the collection of the Wise Sayings of Solomon (10:1–22:16) and in the Sayings of the Wise (22:17–24:34). These verses and others omitted from the lectionary aim at counseling the poor to accept their state with confidence that God will provide, warning them against laziness and foolish practices of debt.

Theological discernment of the lectionary selection for today therefore requires the preacher to be aware of the central message of the moral vision of Proverbs, obvious to anyone who studies the whole collection. The prime candidate for sin in Proverbs is foolishness, which is self-defeating in everybody, both rich and poor. The world not only is created by God, but also incorporates rewards for righteousness and punishments for folly. So in Proverbs the rich have higher standing. They live in a different world. The rich do live under the threat of punishment by loss.

Pastoral Perspective

Parents are fond of offering bits of wisdom and little lessons for life that usually fall upon disinterested ears, but are not soon forgotten. We remember from childhood: "Honesty is the best policy," "A penny saved is a penny earned," "Do unto others as you would have them do unto you." Today's reading is a collection of proverbs that fall into the category of sayings our parents taught us. Wise and true, these proverbs offer ideas and "best practices" of how to live a life of honesty and integrity where honor, justice, and good reputation are prized. Growing up in the southern region of the United States, where the Bible is one of the most often quoted (and misquoted) books, I learned that folk wisdom often comes from Proverbs and other scriptural sources. Only years later, in Sunday school, did I recognize how much of folk wisdom is scriptural wisdom.

My friend's mother had her children write the rules for summer, hoping that such rules might make life run more smoothly. She knew that if her three children made the rules, they might be more apt to follow them. They wrote dutifully, replicating both the tone and intent of the rules of their parents:

You shall not wear flip-flops in the pool.
You shall sweep the floor after supper.

Exegetical Perspective

The Passages on Their Own. In choosing noncontin-
uous verses from Proverbs 22, the lectionary follows a
long-standing tradition of treating this book as an
anthology of isolated sayings. The order in which
individual proverbs appear is understood to be
random, or at least not theologically significant.

The criteria for selection apparently are thematic:
all the verses challenge the assumption that wealth is
a good in itself. This theme fits well the concern of
the accompanying passage in James 2, which calls the
believer to love the neighbor as oneself and to
practice works of mercy. The Gospel reading, the
account of the Syrophoenician woman in Mark 7,
shows Jesus in the act of extending care and mercy.

The selected verses in Proverbs 22 include five
sayings: one each in verses 1, 2, 8, and 9, and an
extended saying that bridges verses 22 and 23. Each
saying makes a distinct claim about wealth, some
more directly than others.

Verse 1: This verse introduces the theme of wealth
indirectly, in the context of underscoring the
importance of a good reputation. Using the device of
comparison, which is widespread in Proverbs, this
verse gives a good name greater importance than
something already assumed to be a good: wealth.
The verse challenges the notion that wealth is of
ultimate value, but does not challenge its worth.

Homiletical Perspective

Preaching Wisdom Literature. Alyce McKenzie has
pointed out the challenge and necessity of preaching
the Wisdom literature of the Bible in our time,[1]
when there is a heightened awareness of the need
for character formation. Yet most expressions of
character formation are cast largely in terms of the
private self. In contrast, biblical wisdom partakes of
that form of prudence understood by Aristotle as
practical wisdom (*phronēsis*), the purpose of which
is to guide us into a virtuous life to benefit the
larger society. Biblical wisdom is concerned not
merely with the moral character of the individual,
but with the formation of a wise community
rooted in the peace and justice of God. Biblical
phronēsis offers itself for the benefit of the larger
social order, and preaching this *phronēsis* must draw
the listening community into engagement in the
public square.

This may present some difficulty when the church
has been relegated to the private sphere and matters
of faith are deemed personal opinion. Proverbs
resists this impulse, and the Old Testament lesson
before us on this particular Sunday requires us to

1. Alyce McKenzie, "Out of Character! Preaching Biblical Wisdom in a
Secular Age," *Journal for Preachers* 22, no. 4 (1999): 44–50; and more recently,
Hear and Be Wise: Becoming a Preacher and Teacher of Wisdom (Nashville:
Abingdon Press, 2004).

Proverbs 22:1-2, 8-9, 22-23

Theological Perspective

However, the poor, by their very poverty, are living examples of God's judgment. They have the assurance that their fear of the Lord is better than riches, but their poverty is due to God's disfavor. Perhaps those who selected today's reading from Proverbs 22 assumed that the hearers of the word for this Sunday would most likely be rich. Perhaps they wanted to emphasize to rich people and poor alike that the Lord takes the side of the poor in the court, threatening the rich who are unjust with loss. Whatever the basis of the selection, the *wise* preacher will consider not only the prudential ethic of the reward of riches and the punishment of poverty in Proverbs, but also the great encompassing message of the Old Testament vision of the covenant people of God, redeemed from slavery in Egypt and given a land of promise in Israel.

When we compare the fuller version of the relationship between wealth and poverty in Proverbs with the exodus tradition in the Old Testament and its refraction through the lenses of the Covenant Code (Exod. 21–23), Deuteronomy, and the prophets, we find a different kind of moral vision. In the Mosaic covenant at Sinai, the first four of the Ten Commandments require exclusive loyalty to the singular God of Israel. These make up the Great Commandment, to love the Lord as God alone (Deut. 6:4–6). The fourth commandment, "Observe the sabbath day and keep it holy, as the LORD your God commanded you" (Deut. 5:12), gives religious and institutional sanction to the worship of God alone and also to obeying the second table of the law, which requires the Lord's justice for the neighbor in the community.[1]

This Mosaic covenant and its later prophetic interpretation understood that the Lord redeemed all of Israel from slavery in Pharaoh's Egypt and that all lived by God's gracious provision for their need. Out of this covenantal tradition with its first obligation to the Lord and its second obligation to the neighbor, both embodied in Sabbath observance, came such requirements as the sabbatical from slavery, the welcome of the resident alien, the sabbatical seventh year for the poor and the wild animals, and the jubilee, when ancestral lands were restored. In the Mosaic covenantal tradition of Torah and its prophetic interpretation and later application, the poor become incorporated into the Lord's benefits of sufficiency in the body politic of Israel.

On this Sunday, preparation for preaching might compare the vision of retributive justice in Proverbs

1. Patrick D. Miller, *The God You Have: Politics, Religion and the First Commandment* (Minneapolis: Fortress Press, 2004).

Pastoral Perspective

You shall only buy Mister Softee (from the ice cream truck) once a week.

Somewhat more substantive than "You shall not wear flip-flops in the pool," today's appointed proverbs offer wisdom on matters of relationships, generosity, and justice. They remind the gathered community of the significance of seeing, understanding, and relating to the poor. The weight of theological grounding for this section is found in verse 2. "The rich and the poor have this in common: the LORD is the maker of them all." In God there are no distinctions.

In contemporary culture in the United States, much of our language reflects categories of identity that connote "otherness": "the poor," "immigrants," "gays and lesbians," "rednecks," "men," and "women." Proverbs 22 says, "The LORD is the maker of them all." In a theology of equality, pejorative labels of suspicion about otherness are morally and ethically wrong. Thinking and acting that result in unjust treatment of others leads to calamity. Justice and care result in blessing. Injustice will bring misfortune. Generosity issues blessing. The Lord will plead the cause of the poor and afflicted with consequences for the afflicters.

These proverbs are not only rules for ethical living but are also wise adages. "Do not rob the poor . . . , or crush the afflicted at the gate; for the LORD pleads their cause and despoils of life those who despoil them" (vv. 22–23). Overt or covert exercise of power over others brings harm not only to the oppressed but equally to the oppressor. Many people and communities understand this dynamic.

Abraham Johannes Muste graduated from Hope College and Union Theological Seminary. Inspired by the Christian mysticism of the Quakers, Muste became a pacifist and worked with many activist groups. After decades of work in civil rights, social justice, and disarmament, he sorrowfully saw the beginning of the Vietnam War. Because of his integrity, Muste was trusted by all groups and guided their efforts in ending the war. In 1966 he led a group of pacifists to Saigon. After trying to demonstrate for peace, they were arrested and deported. That same year, Muste flew with a small team of religious leaders to Hanoi, where he met with Ho Chi Minh, the Vietnamese Communist leader. They were two old men meeting in the midst of war, one of them committed to the path of violent change and the other to nonviolence.

During the Vietnam War, Muste stood many nights in Washington holding a candle in silent

Exegetical Perspective

Verse 2: Like many of the proverbial sayings, this verse makes an observation without spelling out its implication for belief or behavior. Does pointing to the common origin of the poor and the rich suggest that the poor are as valuable to God as the rich? Or, conversely, might it suggest that God allocates human wealth? As in the previous verse, wealth is not directly challenged; rather, its importance is relativized.

Verse 8: The cause-and-effect pattern of this verse suggests that human actions have (natural) consequences; it does not claim that God will punish the wrongdoer but that the unjust will reap the fruits of their actions ("you reap what you sow"). Paired in two synonymous phrases are "whoever sows injustice" and "the rod of anger." The word translated "rod" in the NRSV is the same one used elsewhere in the Hebrew Bible for a ruler's scepter, a weapon, and, as in 22:15, a tool for disciplining children. The Hebrew phrase might better be translated "the rod of *his* wrath," as in the NIV and the KJV, given the presence of the possessive pronoun. Another translation faithful to the Hebrew is "his rod of wrath," as in the *Tanakh* translation. Given the style of poetry here used (synonymous parallelism), the one who sows injustice is linked with the one who uses his or her position of authority to oppress others.

Verse 9: The word here translated "poor" can also mean "weak" or "helpless." Here, it seems to refer to those without sufficient food. As in the previous verse, consequences appear automatic, rather than the result of direct divine punishment. Together, verses 8 and 9 reflect an idea common in Wisdom literature: one must choose between two paths for life, the one of the righteous/wise that is secure, and the one of the wicked/fool that leads to ruin (Ps. 1). These verses contrast the paths in an interesting, even surprising way, juxtaposing the unjust and the generous rather than the generous and the stingy or even the just and the unjust.

Verses 22–23: These verses offer the only explicit admonitions in the pericope. Readers should not take advantage of the vulnerability of the poor, nor should they crush the afflicted at the gate, the site of justice in ancient Israel. The word translated "poor" is the same one used in 22:9; the word translated "afflicted" can also refer to the poor or the humble. Although both words are used elsewhere in the Old Testament to refer to a wide range of "lowly" life situations (the latter refers to barrenness in Gen. 41:52 and to the humility of Moses in Num. 12:3), the literary context of this verse does suggest that economic oppression is indicated.

Homiletical Perspective

consider the ways in which our lives as people of God belong to the larger social fabric of our world.

Further, biblical Wisdom literature takes up the task of searching and seeking out the fullness of life, received as gift of God, and manifested in the particularities of everyday lived experience. Though on the surface one may be tempted to view the counsels of this literature as broad, general moralisms for life, they grow out of and move toward concrete life experience. To preach biblical wisdom material will require the preacher to resist preaching these texts as simple moralisms and rather to work at the intersection of the theological claim they make and the world in which we live and move. Biblical wisdom, as McKenzie has put it, stands at all our daily crossroads and summons us to preach sermons that are God-centered, concrete, this-worldly, countercultural, and intergenerational.[2]

The Phronēsis *of Proverbs 22.* The instructions given to us in the selected couplets of Proverbs 22 rest upon a larger theological foundation than may be apparent when reading just these verses (1–2, 8–9, 22–23). These words proceed from YHWH sayings interspersed throughout Proverbs that declare God's creation and providence. God is the one who created all people regardless of their social or economic position. Therefore, all people are connected to one another. Those who mock the poor or disregard them insult YHWH, who is the creator of all. The preacher does well to allow the sermon to proceed first from these theological claims about God, God's favor for the poor, and God's relentless pursuit of justice for the downtrodden.

The instructions and sayings of Proverbs 22 are for the schooling of persons in regard to their participation in the larger society, especially those who will have considerable influence in public life.[3] While applicable to all who participate in the social order of their world, they are especially directed to those who will serve as government officials, judges, lawyers, and other legal officials. These sayings do not envision the kind of democracy in which we find ourselves, but certainly call all who have influence in determining the public well-being to exert that influence in the wisdom and life of God—especially in regard to matters of wealth and poverty.

---

2. McKenzie, "Out of Character!" 49.
3. For a good description, see Leo G. Perdue, *Proverbs*, Interpretation Series (Louisville, KY: John Knox Press, 2000), 200–205.

Proverbs 22:1-2, 8-9, 22-23

Theological Perspective

with the New Testament readings. In James 2:1–17, "the royal law according to the scripture, 'You shall love your neighbor as yourself'" (v. 8, quoting Lev. 19:18) becomes the foundation for prohibiting favoritism for the rich within the bounds of the Christian community. The letter of James, like Proverbs, incorporates a wisdom tradition for its ethical teaching; however, its proverbial character is based on the prophetic vision of a community in which rich and poor are united, where good works follow faith, and where rich oppressors of the community will be judged in the last days. Jesus gave birth to this vision of the community. Following the pattern of Elijah, ministering to the widow of Zarephath (1 Kgs. 17:8–24), Jesus gave the the Syrophoenician woman not just the dog's crumbs under the table, but the nourishing bread of life for her daughter (Mark 7:24–30). Jesus healed the deaf man, and the astounded followers found in the ministry of Jesus confirmation of Isaiah's announcement of the new community of God's people redeemed from exile in Babylon (Isa. 35). The readings from James and Mark envision a beloved community of compassion and sufficiency for the oppressed.

Our preaching on stewardship in the contemporary globalized economy can find purchase with the prudential ethic of Proverbs. We are fools if we do not address the widening gap between rich and poor. Terrorism will continue to exploit it, and military power alone will not quell it. The rich nations, as matters of wise policy, will come to address the injustice of the punishing gap between rich and poor. We could think of the immigrant communities in the United States who come for their own betterment. No fence will make our borders impermeable. Beyond mere prudence, the New Testament pushes the ethic of merit in Proverbs toward the prophetic tradition of a community in which the poor are already the blessed of God, in which all are members of the body of Christ.

CHARLES E. RAYNAL

Pastoral Perspective

protest outside of the White House. When asked by an incredulous reporter if he thought this would really change U.S. policy on Vietnam, Muste replied: "Oh, I don't do this to change the country. I do this so the country won't change me."

As the United States engaged in its only preemptive war at the beginning of the twenty-first century, great damage was done to the moral authority, the reputation, the credible voice, and the psyche of the United States. However rationalized or justified the intent of this war, it cost lives and damaged communities around the world. The once-prized reputation of the United States for its commitment to human and civil rights was compromised. The prophetic wisdom of Proverbs 22 cannot be overlooked: "For the LORD pleads their [the afflicted] cause and despoils of life those who despoil them" (v. 23).

The Michael Radford film *1984* opens with a scene in which workers stand in front of a screen for an indoctrination session called the Two Minutes Hate. The patriotic narrator informs the crowd that their land is one of peace, harmony, and hope. Winston Smith works in the Records Department of the Ministry of Truth, where he changes the newspaper reports of the past to reflect the present policies of the administration. Writing secretly in his journal, he says, "There is truth and there is untruth. Freedom is freedom to say two plus two is four. If that is allowed, all else follows." Meanwhile, at work he continues to rewrite the past to make it fit with the present. When a turn of events has to be rewritten, he writes in his journal, "Past is erased, the erasure is forgotten. The lie becomes truth, and then becomes a lie again." One day Winston says to his lover Julia, "It's not so much staying alive, but staying human that's important. We must not betray each other."[1]

This section of Proverbs is a call not to betray the family of God. Such wisdom includes the admonition to act generously, reputably, honestly, and justly, both as persons and as citizens of a nation.

SUSAN T. HENRY-CROWE

---

1. Anthony J. Clarke and Paul Fiddes, eds., *Flickering Images: Theology and Film in Dialogue* (Macon, GA: Regent's Park College with Smyth & Helwys Publishing, 2005), 279–81.

Exegetical Perspective

Here, for the first time in this reading, God's intervention in human affairs is made explicit. God directly advocates for the poor and ensures that those who sow evil will reap it.

Conclusions from These Passages. As a unit, these passages challenge the common wisdom that wealth is of ultimate value, but they do not suggest that poverty can or should be eliminated. Perhaps in keeping with the privileged circles in which the book likely was written, they suggest an attitude of charity, rather than one of challenge, to the disparities between poor and rich. Some contemporary readers may conclude that these proverbs do not go far enough in acknowledging the structural dimensions of poverty and that additional discussion of poverty and its causes is needed.

The Passages in Larger Context. Placing these sayings within the larger context of chapter 22 reveals that the attitude of Proverbs toward wealth is ambivalent. While passages selected by the lectionary are joined by 22:16 in challenging the inherent value of wealth, in 22:4 riches are seen as a reward for faithfulness, and 22:7 makes the (cynical) observation that the rich do indeed rule over the poor. Proverbs 22:27 protests the degrading nature of poverty.

This ambiguity also marks the book as a whole. While 28:6 claims that it is better to be poor and have integrity than to be rich and crooked, and 11:4 attests that those who trust in riches will fail, 14:20 and 19:4 observe that money makes friends, and 10:4 and 24:30–34 suggest that poverty is the result of laziness.

The wise interpreter, then, will find a way to honor this ambiguity as well as to honor the insistence of Proverbs on integrity, wisdom, and justice. One way to do so is to recognize how a given claim to truth resonates differently in different life contexts; another is to listen to the life stories and life truths of others.

JULIA M. O'BRIEN

Homiletical Perspective

The sermon should hold the theological claims of the text together with the experience of poverty in the public social arena, creating sufficient tension between the two so that a clearer vision of participation in the reign of God may be achieved. One fruitful image offered to us in these verses from Proverbs 22 is the legal one. The three couplets selected for our reading move from a theological declaration to the blessing of sharing food with the poor, and finally to a specific prohibition of exploitation that takes legal advantage of those in poverty. These verses are held within the theological claim that YHWH is the one who pleads the case of the poor in court, ensuring that justice will prevail. God is envisioned as the "redeemer" of those who can not secure their own defense. Because God is a "redeemer" of this sort, he calls his people to advocate on behalf of the poor and defenseless as well.

The sermon might be employed in various modes determined by a careful reading of the congregation. For some congregations, it may be most appropriate for this sermon to be proclaimed in prophetic mode. In this mode, the words of Proverbs 22 are offered as bold declaration of God's advocacy for the poor and critique of those ways in which the church has abdicated its role as partner with God in defense of the poor. The prophetic sermon might offer careful critique of those public officials who claim allegiance to God and yet shape and sustain public policy that disregards the poor.

For other congregations, it may be most appropriate for the sermon to be proclaimed in pastoral mode. In this mode, the words of Proverbs 22 are offered as assurance and certainty that God's favor does rest upon the poor and downtrodden. In the pastoral mode, the words "The Lord will take up their case" become "The Lord will take up your case." In either mode, the sermon begins and ends with declaration of God's nature, presence, and activity on behalf of the poor.

STEPHEN C. JOHNSON

Psalm 125

¹Those who trust in the LORD are like Mount Zion,
    which cannot be moved, but abides forever.
²As the mountains surround Jerusalem,
    so the LORD surrounds his people,
    from this time on and forevermore.
³For the scepter of wickedness shall not rest
    on the land allotted to the righteous,
    so that the righteous might not stretch out
    their hands to do wrong.
⁴Do good, O LORD, to those who are good,
    and to those who are upright in their hearts.
⁵But those who turn aside to their own crooked ways
    the LORD will lead away with evildoers.
    Peace be upon Israel!

Theological Perspective

Psalm 125 contributes to the theology of the Psalms of Ascent as it affirms confidence in God's providence and the longing of the people of faith for righteousness, which are typical of the Psalms of Ascent as a collection. It has several interesting theological affirmations of its own that are worth noting.

The psalm begins with an affirmation of the firmness and solidity of those who trust in God, just like the unshakable Mount Zion. An interesting possible variant in the translation of the first verse shifts the focus from the people who trust to a focus on God. The term "Mount Zion," *har siyyon*, may refer not to the physical location as an analogy of faith, but rather to God, the "Enthroned of Jerusalem." This would intensify the ascription to God of divine authority and faithfulness. "Those who trust in YHWH are like the Mountain of Zion; Never will be upset the Enthroned of Jerusalem."[1] Translations that render *har siyyon*, Mount Zion, as the Enthroned God or the mountain itself as an analogy of faith both convey the trustworthiness of God.

The psalm is divided into two sections: the first three verses and the concluding two verses. The first section is affirmation or instruction; its teaching is

1. Mitchell Dahood, *Psalms III*, Anchor Bible (New York: Doubleday, 1970), 214.

Pastoral Perspective

In a historic Colonial home in Old Wethersfield, Connecticut, a sick room is furnished with a full canopy bed for the invalid, the medical instruments of a visiting doctor, a wing chair for the family member or young woman from the community who sat vigil with the sick and dying, and a very large Bible from which the young woman would read aloud. A needlepoint genealogy on the wall in the kitchen across the hall reveals the sad fact that some half dozen children died in the home in one season. One floor above the sick room an exhibit of early American children's toys displays what may be a unique collection of antique dolls set up in a miniature schoolhouse. Among the miniature poster boards on the tiny schoolhouse wall is a placard that simply reads, "Do what is right and fear nothing."

On the one hand, this clear and simple rubric in the spirit of Psalm 125 might be useful and prove true in teaching children how to live and how to behave. Parents identify, and the community reinforces, what is "right" or "good" behavior. On the other hand, when painful mortality occupies an entire room in your small house on a continuous basis, and sudden illness consumes half of your many brothers and sisters in a single year, even a child may develop real and reasonable fears. Amid the more brutal realities of human existence, simply

Exegetical Perspective

Today's reading is part of a collection of psalms (Pss. 120–34) that most scholars believe was compiled as a literary unit. Each begins with the phrase "A Song of Ascents," which could refer to pilgrimages to Jerusalem (where people "ascended" to the city) or to other ritual settings (where sacrifices and prayers "ascended" to God). Many of these psalms also share other affinities, such as an emphasis on the importance of Zion (Pss. 122, 125, 126, 128, 129, 132, 133, and 134).

The notion of "Zion" in ancient Israelite literature signifies more than a particular location (i.e., Jerusalem). It always relates to the temple in Jerusalem, which was built at the highest point in the city and was sometimes referred to as the "mountain" or "mount" of YHWH (Exod. 15:17; Isa. 2:3; Ezek. 20:40; Zech. 8:3; cf. Ps. 125:1). In the ancient world, temples were not utilized like places of worship today; temples primarily housed the presence of particular deities. Rituals were performed in temple complexes, but they usually did not incorporate a congregation. Priests would administer these rituals to maintain the sacredness of the space so that the presence of the Divine would remain and the advantages associated with that deity would be sustained. One of these advantages was the perceived protection of the region by the god or goddess who was worshiped. The

Homiletical Perspective

"Do good, O Lord, to those who are good. . . . But those who turn aside to their own crooked ways the Lord will lead away with evildoers" (vv. 4–5). The psalmist's words have found a place in our mouths on Sundays. We make our corporate prayers to God and share the words of centuries ago when we plead with God to continue the work of good people and make the evil ones cease. Our repetition of these prayers is not a new thing. The words of this psalm would have been repeated again and again in their time because they were pilgrims' prayers. Psalm 125 is one of the Songs of Ascent, that series of psalms used by persons making the journey up to Jerusalem as pilgrims or as part of a festival procession. These psalms are short and easily memorized.

This particular psalm is about national concerns. It suggests that outsiders have control of the land (v. 3a) and that the righteous ones (the people Israel) are not to be led astray by imposing foreign empires (v. 3b). It is, therefore, a psalm about nation and nations. It is about the safety of one nation. The setting for this psalm is the postexilic time of regional unrest and of the continued threat of outside domination.

While twenty-first-century Christians are able to recognize these prayers on our lips—for the good and against the evil—we should not so easily align

Psalm 125

Theological Perspective

that the Lord protects those who trust in the Lord. The second section is a prayer to the Lord for blessing. The order is instruction, then prayer. First, God is extolled as the one who protects and guides. Then, the people pray for protection and goodness. Supplication, in other words, follows profession. We pray to one in whom we believe. This is a deep pattern of faithful worship and faithful living. Profession, then supplication is a pattern that protects our worship from vague generality, for it is *God* whom we worship and to whom our prayers are addressed. This pattern guides our Christian living, for the discipline of prayer in the context of God's faithfulness and care is a deep response of faith.

There are three fundamental theological affirmations in this psalm. First, Psalm 125 gives voice to the character of God. God is acknowledged as both good and great. Other divine attributes that are implied in the psalm include omnipotence, faithfulness, mercy, everlastingness, and righteousness. Many other psalms express these theological attributes of God as well. The Psalter is not only the "prayer book" of the Bible; it is also a deep and rich "theology text." The magnitude of God and the constancy of God's faithfulness to God's people is affirmed in confident terms. God's protective care is as obvious and as solid as the ring of mountains that surround Jerusalem.

The second theological affirmation concerns evil and its consequences. Verse 3 states that wicked rulers will not succeed in holding on to power and privilege. Patterns of oppression and injustice are not permanent. In its firm voice that evil rulers will not reign indefinitely, the psalm fully acknowledges the depth and variety of evil and shows an awareness that evil inevitably corrupts. The voice of the psalm in general makes clear that God opposes evil. Brokenness, sin, and evil are real in this world, in both individuals and institutions, but this is not the last word. God's relationship to evil is one of resistance, judgment, and, ultimately, victory.

This second theological affirmation is rooted in both a sturdy doctrine of creation and an expectant doctrine of redemption. In such brief scope, these doctrines are assumed rather than stated. It is assumed in this psalm that the mountains cannot be shaken, because they have been created by God. It is assumed that God's overall intent for goodness and righteousness will prevail, because the land is "allotted to the righteous" (v. 3), an expression of hope and assurance.

The third theological affirmation points out the connections between the good God, good people,

Pastoral Perspective

doing the right thing may not provide meaningful security or freedom from fear.

Today's culture of irrepressible greed and a climate of fear and anxiety generate a sense of heightened insecurity. A world of overwhelming violence and widespread corruption trivialize the notion that an individual's choice to do right bears much consequence. And contemporary American culture makes dramatic claims on its people. Pervasive entertainment industries and corporate media within a confessional culture readily produce and distribute distorted realities that leave few individuals, communities, belief systems, or relationships among the survivors. Even empirical science, politicized to coincide with our greed, fear, and anxiety, enters a cultural environment that leaves neither home nor land secure.

Psalm 125 insists that our most secure reality is God's solidarity with God's people. Our relationship with God provides a security as real and as certain as the strong, solid, physical landscape of Mount Zion and the hills of Jerusalem. Comparing God's solidarity with the people to mountains provides a convincing simile of protection even for today, when we still witness warriors—and terrorists—escape harm by seeking refuge in the impenetrable terrain of mountain ranges.

The relationship of solidarity between people and God is based on God's goodness, God's immovability, God's righteousness, and God's reign. It is our relationship with God that bears safety and security in the promise and power of God to do good and bring forth righteousness. Where the people figure into the landscape, the psalmist invites us to pay critical attention to who's carrying whose scepter of what. Quite possibly, we might mistake human reign with God's reign and claim that "God is on our side," rather than seek to stand where God resides. We might carry scepters of human power as though they bear God's righteousness and find we abandon our proper relationship to God, our communal covenant, as well as our accountability to those we lead. Indeed, the just may very well find themselves putting their hands to evil; consider how Americans painstakingly differentiate between support for U.S. troops and opposition to war. God's relationship with humanity abides forever, but human thinking does not stand fast forever. God is immovable, but a human course of action can be moved.

Who is carrying whose scepter is a question for which all people of God bear both responsibility and privilege. Assurances of security in relationship to

concept of Zion, therefore, conveys the inviolability of Jerusalem; because God's presence resided in the temple, Jerusalem would never fall. Many texts also associate Zion closely with the eternal rule of the Davidic dynasty (2 Sam. 6:6–10; 7:1–17; Ps. 89:1–37). Belief in Zion was a deeply rooted conviction for several leaders of ancient Israel: Isaiah exhorted Judah's kings to conduct their international relations according to this concept (Isa. 7:4–9; 37). When Judah fell to Babylon, writers struggled with the inconsistency between the assurances of Zion and the historical reality of Jerusalem's destruction. Those who had promoted the unconditional security of the city were condemned (e.g., Jer. 7; Ezek. 13:1–16), and YHWH was depicted as punishing the inhabitants of Jerusalem for their actions (Jer. 25:1–14; 27:12–22; 36:29–31; 52; Ezek. 8–10), engaging in battle against Jerusalem (Lam. 2), or even reneging on the initial agreement of protection (Ps. 89:38–52). When Cyrus II allowed the exiles to return to Judah and rebuild Jerusalem and the temple, several writers revived the hope in Zion (e.g., Isa. 44:21–28; 49:8–26; 51:9–16; 60; 62; Zech. 8:1–17).

In today's reading, the psalmist likens Zion—and all the connotations this word carries—to those who "trust in YHWH" (v. 1). In the OT, "trust" in the Israelite god is best understood as complete confidence in the protection of YHWH. In the ancient world, many believed that the divine cosmos could influence the challenges of daily life (e.g., childbirth, illness, and death) and the pressures of regional and international forces (e.g., exploitation and military invasion). Success and longevity were not simply associated with the god one worshiped, but often these results were seen to confirm the superiority of one's god. To trust in YHWH meant that one relied *only* on YHWH in times of need; the implied benefit was assured assistance for the petitioner. The psalmist reinforces this guarantee with the analogy of what Zion ensures; as Jerusalem is inviolable, so too will the believer always find security in a difficult world (vv. 1–2).

The psalmist describes those who trust in YHWH as "righteous" (*tsaddiq*) and explains how they will be shielded from opponents (vv. 3–5). In Wisdom literature, "the wicked" (*rashaʿ*) usually refers to *Israelites* who transgress from the Israelite-YHWH relationship, but in this psalm, the "scepter of wickedness" (*reshaʿ* [the nominal form of *rashaʿ*]) may refer to foreign rule (v. 3). Because this psalm most likely was composed after 600 BCE, the "scepter of wickedness" could allude to the Babylonian or Persian domination, but the psalm provides nothing to confirm these readings. "Those

ourselves as a nation against other nations. For unlike Israel in postexilic times, we are not a struggling small entity in the midst of powerful empires. America is still a (or the) powerful empire of the world. We might even think of another nation of our day that would pray these very words against us and have legitimate cause to do so.

Instead of caricaturing other nations, present-day interpreters of this text would do well to think about the divisions within our own nations. For while we may still hurt other nations and be hurt by them, we also injure one another within our own borders. This text is accompanied by the other texts of the day, which all speak of God's care for the poor, the marginalized, the afflicted, even the foreigner in our midst (see Prov. 22:1–2, 8–9, 22–33; James 2:1–10, 14–17; Mark 7:24–37). Given these foci, the concern of the psalmist translated for our time would not be that we are dissuaded from right action by foreign domination but that we might be dissuaded from right action when we ignore these divisions in our midst (v. 3). The concern is not that we might stretch out our hands to follow the dangerous values of encroaching empires but rather that we might not stretch out our hands to heal the divisions in our midst (v. 3). The danger that might undo us is not from outsiders; it is that which we have created and that which is a part of our nation.

This psalm is for the purpose of instilling trust in the pilgrims who make their way to the holy city Jerusalem. It is for the purpose of shaping them to trust, not only during that journey, but to trust God at all times, even in the face of foreign threats to nation and community. It is a call to trust God and not be persuaded by those who follow their own "crooked ways" (v. 5). Perhaps our act of trust as pilgrims on the journey of faith is to take account of how we have turned to our own crooked ways. This would be an act of trust—calling on God to set us right again as we honestly confess the ways that we are the foreign domination and the ways that we ignore the hurtful divisions in our own land.

The psalmist proclaims God's steadfastness even amid great threats of loss, death, and national annihilation. In this sense the text is eschatological—it speaks a word about how things will be, even when they are not completely that way yet. Though other nations (and internal divisions) may dominate, this is not the way that things will always be. There is future-tense language in this psalm. But present-tense language says this: those who trust in God are like Mount Zion. The church is the holy mountain.

Psalm 125

Theological Perspective

and good results. The connection is that God is the author and promoter of good and the resister and destroyer of anything that is not good. The psalmist longs for God's protection of the righteous so that evil will not overtake them. In fact, God can be trusted to cut down the wicked rulers so that the righteous will not be led into injustice (v. 3b).

The prayer of the psalm is that God will do "good to the good" (v. 4). We need carefully to avoid errors in theological and pastoral care that might come from this phrase. One error is to assume a necessary link between the goodness of God and material goodness. The petition for God to do good to the good does not imply that good fortune is a proof of God's blessing. Sometimes, as many psalms observe, the wicked prosper! Many other times, the righteous suffer. The relationship between divine favor and human fortune is not immediately transparent.

The prayer of the last two verses of this psalm does, however, affirm that the righteous long for God's goodness as surely as the hungry long for nourishment. God's goodness is the sustaining grace of all those who are "upright in their hearts" (v. 4). Similarly, the prayer affirms that the wicked have no claim to God's protection and goodness. God's rightful judgment is a dismissal into their own path of evil. There are instances when, in God's own divine purpose, the wicked are left to their own devices, allowed to reap the consequences of their actions. In this sense, the psalm's petition that "the LORD will lead away with evildoers" (v. 5) is fulfilled. The relationship that the psalm explores, between God, good actions, and good results is fundamentally the relationships that flow out from the shalom of Israel. One commentator says, "The *shalom* of the people of God is both well-doing and doing well, united in their interdependence."[2]

LEANNE VAN DYK

Pastoral Perspective

God can too easily reinforce the status quo, with the self-satisfied on one hand and the oppressed on the other. Those who do not experience oppression or even perceive it may see their good fortune as the way of God. For those experiencing oppression, the vision of Psalm 125 offers a promise and the truth of an alternative reality that will ultimately prevail.

Christ incarnates God's solidarity with the people and carries the scepter of God's righteousness into the world. The gospel calls us to follow Christ, bring in the kingdom of God, and incarnate God's solidarity with humanity over against whatever distorted realities erode and compromise God's people. Every local incarnation of this solidarity is unique, but the opportunity for such incarnation exists on every level of community life. The community assembled for worship replicates again and again Mount Zion and the hills standing about Jerusalem, figuring the safety and security of solidarity with God. A woman with terminal illness struggles with the isolation of her experience and dependence on others for her care as well as with immense physical, emotional, psychological, and spiritual discomfort. The psalm transforms her reality through the promise, if not the physical presence, of those who trust in the Lord standing fast for ever, encircled around by the presence of God, promised that the just shall not put their hands to evil. A diligent employee who observes privilege and wealth, acquisition and advancement in the hands of the unscrupulous may be encouraged to turn aside from crooked ways, trusting that God will show goodness to those who are true of heart.

Only within the narrative of God's solidarity with God's people does the rubric, "Do what is right and fear nothing," provide meaningful security. The solidarity of God mapped out in Psalm 125 assures us we have nothing ultimately to fear when the human condition confronts us with such powers as suffering and death. Psalm 125 also challenges us to be attentive to how human power creates conditions of fear and injustice. God's solidarity with the people is a relationship—clearly identified in the gospel of Christ and reinforced in Christian community—in which we participate, and in which we both rest assured and bear responsibility and power.

ALLISON READ

2. James L. Mays, *Psalms*, Interpretation Series (Louisville, KY: John Knox Press, 1994), 398.

Exegetical Perspective

who turn aside to their own crooked ways" (v. 5) could refer to Israelites, not necessarily to the "wicked" foreigners who ruled over them. Neglecting to conduct one's behavior along a straight course is used frequently in Wisdom literature to describe "wicked" Israelites (e.g., Prov. 2; 4:10–27). Those who act in defiance of the Israelite-YHWH relationship reap the consequences of their actions (e.g., Prov. 2:22, 3:33; 10:29; cf. Ps. 125:5b). Verse 5 may refer to Israelites *or* to foreign powers that supported a "wicked" foreign ruler, but the "wicked scepter" may signify *Israelites* who governed over the territory. There is precedent for critiquing Israelite leaders (e.g., 1 Kgs. 12–14; 16–22; 2 Kgs. 21). Even after the exile, not all who worshipped YHWH supported Zerubbabel's governorship (e.g., Ezra 4). Though the phrase "Peace be upon Israel!" (v. 5b) provides a nationalist sentiment, it is possible that the psalmist understood "Israel" to signify a specific group among YHWH devotees. If so, "the wicked" may refer to others who worshiped YHWH but in ways the psalmist viewed as flawed.

However one understands the opponents of the righteous, the psalm recounts the ways that YHWH will protect the righteous. YHWH will prevent political harassment of the righteous over the ownership of their land so that they will not be instigated to commit wrongdoing (*ʿavlah*) (v. 3d). Like the terms "righteous" and "wicked," the psalmist once again uses vague terminology, which implies that this psalm was composed for a community who understood what these terms signified and therefore had no need for further clarification. In other biblical texts, *ʿavlah* primarily refers to actions that conflict with what is considered to be just or right. In Job 24:20 and Psalm 119:3, *ʿavlah* refers more directly to actions that oppose the covenantal material (e.g., Exod. 20–23; Deut. 5–12; Lev. 19), but most of the time, this word and its masculine equivalent (*ʿavel*) only convey distortion of or disobedience from rules that are not clearly defined (e.g., for *ʾavlah*, see Job 5:16; 6:29–30; 11:14; 13:7; 22:23; 36:23; for *ʿavel*, see Lev. 19:15; Ezek. 3:20; 18:24–26; 33:13–18). In Psalm 125, God's protection prevents the righteous from doing *ʾavlah* (however understood), and the psalmist petitions YHWH to continue bestowing such benefits ("Do good, YHWH, to the good," v. 4).

PATRICIA D. AHEARNE-KROLL

Homiletical Perspective

We are the mountain of the Lord, the unshakable place of glory. And God is a mountain. God is, in fact, a mountain range surrounding Mount Zion. So the Lord surrounds the people, abiding now and forever. With this steadfastness of God we can risk acknowledging our crookedness and strive for true righteousness that is justice for all.

The preacher may look at all of the appointed texts for the day, working with the images and interactions in order to proclaim the word of God that inspires us for service in the world. God is a trustworthy mountain so that we are able to live in righteousness. Even our internal divisions are taken up in God who heals and sets things right. Or the preacher may focus on the psalm alone. If this is the choice, the preacher will do well to think carefully through connections between the ancient small nation of Israel and the current powerful nation of the United States. The parallels are tricky—we do not share the global dynamics of the postexilic period. We are the powerful with a great share of crookedness. But then theologically we would say this for every nation, for every people. Our prayer for peace (v. 5) accompanies our corporate confession of crookedness and our desire to be upright. It is God alone who makes the church as a mountain.

JENNIFER L. LORD

James 2:1-10 (11-13), 14-17

[1]My brothers and sisters, do you with your acts of favoritism really believe in our glorious Lord Jesus Christ? [2]For if a person with gold rings and in fine clothes comes into your assembly, and if a poor person in dirty clothes also comes in, [3]and if you take notice of the one wearing the fine clothes and say, "Have a seat here, please," while to the one who is poor you say, "Stand there," or, "Sit at my feet," [4]have you not made distinctions among yourselves, and become judges with evil thoughts? [5]Listen, my beloved brothers and sisters. Has not God chosen the poor in the world to be rich in faith and to be heirs of the kingdom that he has promised to those who love him? [6]But you have dishonored the poor. Is it not the rich who oppress you? Is it not they who drag you into court? [7]Is it not they who blaspheme the excellent name that was invoked over you?

[8]You do well if you really fulfill the royal law according to the scripture, "You shall love your neighbor as yourself." [9]But if you show partiality, you commit sin

Theological Perspective

James 2 builds upon the idea of "pure religion," manifested in care for widows and orphans (1:27). The first section of the chapter (2:1–13) deals with the topic of favoritism. The second section (vv. 14–26) deals with the topic of faith and works (continuing past the ending of today's text at v. 17).

Favoritism goes against godly living. The writer describes a scene in a certain "assembly" (a term better translated as "synagogue" or "community meeting"— v. 2), perhaps in a Diaspora Hellenistic Jewish synagogue in Alexandria. Wherever this assembly was, the writer saw disconcerting behavior showing favoritism toward certain wealthy individuals. These Christians treated a rich person with gold rings and in fine clothes with respect and flattery while they dishonored and humiliated a poor person in dirty clothes (vv. 2–3). The writer points to the naiveté of such action. Christianity was still illegal, and persecution was always a possibility. The rich man could be a local official checking to see if the Christians taught insubordination against Roman religion, acting as atheists (i.e., nonbelievers of pagan gods), as was rumored. Despite the special treatment, the official could take them to court; the judge could order them to prison, and finally to the arena for public execution. The officials would dishonor Christians' excellent name (of Christ) as criminals (vv. 6–7).

Pastoral Perspective

Why is being partial a sin? In the everyday world of sports, business, social affairs, and politics, we have to choose one value over another. During times of local or national elections, Americans are expected to show partiality. No one can stand everywhere and cast a vote for everyone. We are expected to stand somewhere and to cast a vote for someone in particular. Showing favoritism and partiality is inevitable in human affairs. So why is it a sin?

Perhaps James would agree that showing partiality in the ways described above is an expression of social order. But James has a more serious concern. He is concerned about the class distinctions that baptized Christians make among themselves in the faith community.

Showing Partiality between Wealthy and Poor Christians. In the new community called out in Christ's name, there is no place for distinctions between wealthy and poor Christians. James calls attention to the typical games that baptized Christians play. To paraphrase, "If a person comes into your assembly with a gold ring and dressed in fine clothes, and there also comes in a poor person, say a homeless and unemployed person, in dirty and tattered clothes, looking disheveled, and you pay special attention to the one who is wearing the fine clothes, and say, 'You

and are convicted by the law as transgressors. [10]For whoever keeps the whole law but fails in one point has become accountable for all of it. [11]For the one who said, "You shall not commit adultery," also said, "You shall not murder." Now if you do not commit adultery but if you murder, you have become a transgressor of the law. [12]So speak and so act as those who are to be judged by the law of liberty. [13]For judgment will be without mercy to anyone who has shown no mercy; mercy triumphs over judgment.

[14]What good is it, my brothers and sisters, if you say you have faith but do not have works? Can faith save you? [15]If a brother or sister is naked and lacks daily food, [16]and one of you says to them, "Go in peace; keep warm and eat your fill," and yet you do not supply their bodily needs, what is the good of that? [17]So faith by itself, if it has no works, is dead.

Exegetical Perspective

People of Faith or Judges of the Poor (vv. 1–4). James addresses his hearers as "My brothers and sisters" "in the Dispersion" (1:1–2). They walk in the wake of Israel and see the law as the biblical Torah. They are God's family, which, James insists, includes the poor! The issue at hand is partiality shown to the rich. This occurs within the thematic framework of the relationship of faith and works that permeates the letter.

James issues one of his many imperatives—there are over one hundred in the letter: "My brothers/sisters, *hold* the faith of our glorious Lord Jesus Christ without acts of favoritism" (2:1 NRSV variant reading). They are doing the opposite—claiming faith and showing partiality. "Our glorious Lord Jesus Christ" did not show partiality (Mark 12:14); he invited the poor and outcast to his table. The God of Scripture is impartial and just, compassionate and zealous for the poor and oppressed (Exod. 3:7–8; Lev. 19:2; Deut. 10:17f.; 15:11; 1 Sam. 2:7–8; Isa. 3:15; 10:1–2; 58:7; Luke 1:52; Rom. 2:11). God is the warrant for Christian faith, and this faith has no room for discriminating against the poor.

James gives an example of partiality (vv. 2–4). The rich are received with adulation in the synagogue, while the poor are being humiliated. The verb translated "make distinctions" in the passive form means "to face both ways" or "to be internally

Homiletical Perspective

Consider the parable of the prejudiced usher (2:1–4). This text from James juxtaposes sharp contrasts: one person is very wealthy and another is quite impoverished (cf. Luke 16:19–31). Should the preacher do something narrative with this text? One pictures the earliest Jewish believers in assembly. James's example/quasi-story is presented to them as hypothetical ("if"), although the problem of making distinctions between people seems to exist in the church already (v. 6).

Scene 1: The Entrance of a Rich Man and a Poor Person. Both a rich man and a poor person show up in the assembly, effecting a decidedly dramatic situation (v. 2) and raising immediate questions about how each will be received (cf. Luke 15:20–24, 28). We picture the rich man making a fine entrance, even if he is not an insider. After all, he wears two badges of belonging. Gold on his fingers sends a clear signal of his high social rank, perhaps a nobleman of equestrian or senatorial position. Perhaps he sports a little bling? The rich man's clothing is also rather splendid, literally bright, shining clothes. Bo Reicke theorizes that the visitor wore the *toga candide* as a Roman politician seeking supporters.[1] From a postcolonial perspective,

1. Bo Reicke, *The Epistles of James, Peter and Jude,* Anchor Bible 37 (Garden City, NY: Doubleday, 1964), 27.

James 2:1-10 (11-13), 14-17

Theological Perspective

It is not simply for the sake of self-preservation that Christians must not practice favoritism, but because favoritism is against God's intention (law). The writer explains the significance of the divine law in contrast to the Roman law. First, the writer reminds Christians of the "royal law" of Christ, which sums up the entire Hebraic law by saying, "You shall love your neighbor as yourself," alluding to Matthew 22:39, Mark 12:31, Luke 10:27 (v. 8). Second, Christians also affirm the Ten Commandments, especially the prohibition of harming others by adultery and murder (v. 11). To show partiality is equally sin and transgression against the whole law of God, who is the final judge (vv. 9–10, 13). By following God's perfect law of liberty (2:12, 1:25), Christians are free to act mercifully toward their more disadvantaged neighbors.

The writer notes the special favor God gives to the poor.[1] God, who gives to all generously (1:5), raises the lowly (1:9). If the poor are rich in faith and love God, God promises them the kingdom (2:5). Christians live out their faith in this God through works of mercy for the poor. Christian faith and good works are integrated and not separate (2:14). If faith is to produce fruit, it cannot remain dead in empty words. Faithful Christians supply "bodily needs" of the poor (2:15–17).

The temptation that led these early Christians to favoritism and unwillingness to give mercy was repeated in another time in history. During the Reformation period, the church distinguished worthy poor from unworthy poor. Late medieval Europe experienced rapid urbanization. Due to constant war, famine, and plague, uprooted people migrated into cities, seeking housing, food, medicine, and employment. Only the fortunate found such, and the streets were flooded with "beggars." During the Middle Ages, Christians had believed that beggars played an important role in the economy of salvation. Born at the bottom of the ranks of society, the poor in Christian nations depended totally on the mercy of God and Christians for their survival. While the more affluent escaped such a fate, the poor suffered vicariously in their stead. The poor symbolized Christ the poor. By assisting beggars, richer Christians honored Christ. However, the sudden increase of vagrants on the streets led to a change of attitude. Reformers

1. Reclaimed by Protestant and Catholic liberation theologians in Latin America during the 1950s, the term "God's preferential option for the poor" was adopted in 1968 at the Second General Conference of the Latin American Bishops in Medellín, Colombia. Since then it has become an important component of Catholic social justice.

Pastoral Perspective

sit here in a good place,' and you say to the poor person, 'You stand over there, or sit down by my footstool,' then you have made distinctions among yourselves, and become judges with evil motives." Many of us recognize ourselves or someone we know in that description. We are nervous if not irritated, when someone—a stranger with seemingly bad habits and odors—comes into our presence in the sanctuary. We may surmise, "You do not belong here." We may politely ask, "Are you lost?"

But let us reverse roles for a moment. If you were that poor person who happened to show up at a worship service, then you might feel shame and embarrassment along with physical hunger and other pains. These issues might be overridden by your deeper desire to hear a word of hope or to receive a modicum of respect from those who are known as "people of God."

James makes a theological point that may become, for us, the starting point for extending pastoral care. That starting point is *agapē* love, which enables us to bear one another's burdens under the most trying of circumstances. "Listen," James says, "has not God chosen the poor in the world to be rich in faith and to be heirs of the kingdom that he has promised to those who love him? But you have dishonored the poor" (2:5–6). Here pastoral care, Christian ethics, and moral responsibility are joined. James raises two paradoxical, yet linked, concerns: (1) God's image indwells the poor human being who moves against the odds, showing us the face of an uncommon and daring faith; and (2) in the congregation is more than one wealthy and socially acceptable person who is spiritually impoverished. The first shows us the face of humble courage with a rich faith. The second shows us the face of arrogant but shallow faith. It is tempting for us to call the first a failure and to see in him or her signs of divine disfavor. It is equally tempting for us to call the second hypocrites whose shallow faith is camouflaged by prosperity. James calls us to embrace both, without bad-mouthing or demonizing either one.

Here is James's radical challenge in a nutshell: "You shall love your neighbor as yourself." Isn't this impossible? It is surely problematic. Self-love can move us in many different directions. At one extreme, self-love may take the form of narcissism ("It's all about me"); at the other extreme, it may take the form of self-sacrifice ("It's all about you"). Partiality that contributes to either extreme cuts and sustains deep divisions in faith communities. It can also lead to seemingly irreparable harm between individuals.

Exegetical Perspective

divided." Those who show partiality divide the community according to wealth and poverty. Their favoritism for the wealthy aligns them with the world and places them at odds with God (4:4).

In essence, James queries, "In the synagogue you have made distinctions among yourselves between rich and poor, haven't you?" or "You are wavering, aren't you?" "Have you not become judges with evil thoughts, with discriminating purposes?" Each question expects a "Yes" in response. For those who show partiality, "gold weighs more than faith and love." It is not possible for them to have it both ways—to claim the faith of Jesus and to discriminate against the poor.

The Poor and the Rich (vv. 5–7). The first imperative is "Hold the faith of our Lord Jesus!" The second imperative is "Listen!" It is time to reason. James warmly engages his hearers as "brothers and sisters." The argument starts with God. "Has not God chosen the poor of the world to be rich in faith and to be heirs of the kingdom?" (v. 5). The response is affirmative. Faith is cognizant of God's election of the poor. Such faith exemplifies true wealth.

James reminds his brothers and sisters of their own painful experience at the hands of the wealthy. The rich oppress them and drag them into court. The rich blaspheme the name invoked over them that designates them property of God. In their own treatment of the poor, James's readers are endorsing the domination system of the powerful and rich. How can believers embrace that system and, as a result, put the poor at their feet? Their partiality for wealth sets them at odds with the essence of faith.

James does not want the oppression generated by secular social structures to impose itself upon the moral values of the church. He knows well how the syncretistic practices of the Israelites in Canaan led to the breaking of the covenant the people had with YHWH, resulting in the exile.

The Essence of Faith (vv. 8–13). Over against the practice of favoritism James sets the "royal law" of Scripture, "You shall love your neighbor as yourself" (Lev. 19:18). It is called the royal law because Jesus uses it to summarize the law in regard to others. Love of neighbor is the essence of Christian faith and obedience (Matt. 22:39; Gal. 5:14).

Showing partiality is sin. It is easy for people to look into the mirror and see themselves in step with the moral law of the faith (1:23f.), but James states that showing favoritism is glaringly at odds with the

Homiletical Perspective

Ingeborg Kvammen develops the thesis that any person wearing a gold ring did indeed belong to the equestrian order and was thereby representative of the empire. Furthermore, her research to date suggests that the bleached clothing fits.[2] We imagine a GQ gent, business casual with a flourish. He does not buy his personal jewelry online. He sends his people to Tiffany's.

The poor person, male or female, wears clothing quite the opposite of shining. The togs he or she wears are filthy, shabby. These clothes look as if they came from the clothes closet, their rumpled appearance out of style. The poor person's very gait implies a lack of confidence. He wears no Talbot tie. She could be a bag lady. Did he sleep under a bridge the night before? Is there a whiff of body odor?

Scene 2: The Reception of the Rich Man and the Poor Person. The doorkeeper scopes out both visitors. They are treated according to their attire. The rich man enjoys the red-carpet treatment with fawning courtesies, escorted to the best seat just behind mink row. Those of the equestrian order are routinely given privileged seats in assemblies. The usher relegates the poor person to standing or sitting on the floor by his footstool, figuring this "transient" will hit up a church member after services. He receives the cold shoulder of social snobbery. She is just not Junior League material.

Analysis. What is going on here? What values underlie the different receptions? Why does the usher disparage the poor and show a preference for the rich? Are the two receptions, different as salt is from sugar, doing a number on the church itself?

Why not do a brisk theological critique? With this hypothetical situation as a case study, what theological guidelines can be brought to bear? What about the incompatibility of favoritism and faith in Jesus (2:1)? Jesus actually went out of his way to honor the poor (v. 6). He celebrated the gift of two mites as though it were two mil (Luke 21:1–4). Even the enemies of Jesus observed that he did not evaluate people merely by position or appearance (Mark 12:14). And then there is the God who chose the poor to be rich in faith, thus heirs of the kingdom (v. 5). Actually the pious poor turn out to be rich both now and eschatologically.

James finds partiality and distinctions within Christian assemblies reprehensible. "Partiality" in

---

2. Ingebord Kvammen, conversation with author, December 1, 2006.

James 2:1-10 (11-13), 14-17

Theological Perspective

taught an ethic of hard work and self-reliance, but many beggars did not learn any new skills and kept on begging. Reformers considered these people too lazy and unworthy to receive charity. The churches aided only the upper-class "shame-faced," who suddenly lost their income in social upheaval and were reduced to poverty, but were too ashamed to beg. People no longer saw the image of Christ in these poor beggars but feared them as carriers of contagious diseases and moral decay. Cities banned begging, and cleaned up their streets by expelling them.

While Calvin distinguished worthy and unworthy poor, he also connected the "royal law" of Christ with the Ten Commandments (vv. 10–11). In his sermon on Deuteronomy 5:19, "You shall not steal," Calvin preached these strong words:

> Let us consider for a moment who the rich are: insatiable ones, who can never be satisfied and who are much more difficult to be content than the poor. [For example] if we were to make a comparison between the rich and the poor, we would find that just as there are some who are tormented and grieve, and who are led to steal, and engage in many adverse practices, so the majority are content to accept what God has given them and follow their course. But when we come to the rich, . . . we find that they are so inflamed and covetous for the goods of this world that we cannot satisfy them: indeed, they are almost grieved if the sun shines on the poor. . . . And although he draws their sweat and blood, it seems to [the rich] that when they eat at his expense they were wringing him of his very intestines and bowels. And unfortunately, this parsimony, or rather brutal cruelty on the part of the rich, is far too common.[2]

During the Reformation, while European Christians fought over correct doctrines of faith, they also exploited world markets for luxury goods such as sugar and spices, opened international banks, established unequal treaties with Asian nations, obtained massive American lands by force, and stole the free labor of millions of Africans. The majority of Christians were unaware that these activities produced great poverty, displacement, and oppression in someone else's backyard. As we strive to follow the royal law, we must ask how the churches in wealthier places might act justly and mercifully toward the churches in economically disadvantaged places today.

HARUKO NAWATA WARD

Pastoral Perspective

James calls Christians to a higher standard, the standard of *agapē* or divine love. This love excels all other forms of love and is the distinctive call to Christian communities and disciples. Such divine love constitutes a radical call to unconditional justice wherever the economic gap between poverty and wealth is great. How can wealthy Christians live lovingly and justly when brother and sister Christians live poor and destitute lives? In an ideal world of Christian faith, agape love trumps conditional love and partiality. But in the typical and limited world of everyday life, partiality appears to trump agape love. James's challenge is radical in that he calls all Christians, rich and poor, to show no partiality. He calls us to merge our differing self-understandings into a new, enlarged, and richer unity of identity as faithful followers of "our Lord Jesus Christ, the Lord of glory."

What Can Save Us Now? What can save us now is the distinction that James makes between a dead faith—faith without works—and a living faith that is always accompanied by works. We are not saved by faith alone. We are not saved by works alone. We are saved by faith and works conjoined. Spirit, body, and mind must be kept together. In this way we engage the struggle that releases the deep implications of agape love in community. In this way we discover a major resource for mental, spiritual, and physical health.

Where do we find signs of the kind of faith that can save us now? They are embodied in the small acts of impartial, divine love that we can build upon. Faith with works can lift us beyond the confusion and conflicts of our time and help us discern the working of God's hand, building the kingdom that is yet to be.

ARCHIE SMITH JR.

---

2. Benjamin W. Farley, ed. and trans., *John Calvin's Sermons on the Ten Commandments* (Grand Rapids: Baker Books, 1980), 193–94.

essence of the law. If one keeps the whole law, but fails in one point—showing favoritism—the whole weight of the law falls upon that person. Favoritism emulates, not the law, but the oppressive measures of the rich who do not show mercy. The polar opposite of favoritism is mercy.

Two imperatives charge the congregation to *speak* and *act* "as those who are to be judged by the law of liberty" (2:12; cf. 1:25). They will be judged by the standards they practice (Matt. 7:1–2). No mercy? No mercy! They are called to a higher standard, the law of Jesus. Such faith manifests itself in mercy toward others, especially the marginal.

They themselves hope to be on the receiving end of the law of liberty in the coming judgment that God will execute, after all. Have they clearly heard the law of liberty? The essence of the law is mercy. James has experienced mercy. He affirms this. He places a banner over the community, which reads "Mercy triumphs over judgment."

Practical Faith (vv. 14–17). Social discrimination (partiality) and halfhearted words of encouragement ("keep warm and eat your fill") do not arise from the royal law at the heart of Scripture. In the Scriptures, the poor and needy have pride of place (cf. 2:5). The commandments protecting the poor and alien are among the oldest in the OT. They are deep in the covenant. The people of Israel were delivered from bondage in Egypt and were, in turn, to show mercy to the stranger in their midst (Exod. 22:21–22). James expects no less of those in the Dispersion (1:1).

In this paragraph James twice asks, "What good is it?"—to have faith without works, or merely to tell someone to keep warm? Again, James asserts that faith without works cannot save, and faith without works is dead. This will lead to a discussion of two kinds of faith (2:18–26).

AARON L. UITTI

Greek literally means "to lift up the face on a person." James, who considers partiality a sin (v. 9), warns against the fallacy of favoritism. "God," insisted Paul, "shows no partiality" (Rom. 2:11; Gal. 2:6). The goal of Galatians 3:28 stands. We think of paid pews in Colonial Virginia or visitors having the audacity of sitting in our traditional places at church. James seems particularly concerned about the making of "distinctions among yourselves" (v. 4a), turning the church into a religious club. The integrity of the church is on the line. Some modern churches pop up designed for "winners." The suburban captivity of the churches removes many congregations from the environs of the poor. Some outstanding Christian leaders started life in trailer parks and institutional homes for children.

The text speaks not only to the profound issue of acceptance but potentially to the inclusion of the uncool. New people, whatever their social rank, need to be stitched into the social fabric of the church, not merely formally received as new members. Churches with fine, empty cushioned seats often do not invite the poor to sit in them. During the integration crisis some ministers took a stand for inclusion that cost their jobs. Incidentally, the text does not impugn all rich persons. Some are among the enlightened affluent, the compassionate rich, those who have overcome greed with grace (Jas. 4:1–10). The Buffetts and Gateses act on the stewardship of abundance that alleviates poverty conditions in Third-World countries. The text does criticize the church when it is not true to itself.

In his first year in seminary, Jim Wallis and friends did a thorough study to find every verse in the Bible that deals with the poor and social injustice. They came up with thousands, in the first three Gospels one out of ten verses, in Luke one out of seven! They could not recall a single sermon on the poor in their home churches. One of them found an old Bible and began to cut out every single biblical text about the poor. Much of the Psalms and prophets disappeared. That old Bible would hardly hold together. They had created a Bible full of holes.[3]

PETER RHEA JONES

3. Jim Wallis, *God's Politics* (New York: HarperCollins, 2005), 212–14.

Mark 7:24-37

²⁴From there he set out and went away to the region of Tyre. He entered a house and did not want anyone to know he was there. Yet he could not escape notice, ²⁵but a woman whose little daughter had an unclean spirit immediately heard about him, and she came and bowed down at his feet. ²⁶Now the woman was a Gentile, of Syrophoenician origin. She begged him to cast the demon out of her daughter. ²⁷He said to her, "Let the children be fed first, for it is not fair to take the children's food and throw it to the dogs." ²⁸But she answered him, "Sir, even the dogs under the table eat the children's crumbs." ²⁹Then he said to her, "For saying that, you may go—the demon has left your daughter." ³⁰So she went home, found the child lying on the bed, and the demon gone.

Theological Perspective

A traditional theological interpretation of these two stories from the second half of Mark 7 (the Syrophoenician woman and the curing of the deaf and mute man) is that these stories highlight both the universality of God's relationship with humanity and the tenacious faith of two Gentiles that allows them to witness to, demand, and participate in Jesus' saving power, even though they both remain outside of the recognized religious community. Three points are thus illustrated: (1) the power of faith knows no religiously demarcated boundaries; (2) as God's Anointed, Jesus is usually not understood and accepted in his true role by those closest to him (Mark's constant indictment of the disciples and his inclusion of the "messianic secret") but instead by those who truly have faith, even if they do not possess birthright membership in the covenant community; and (3) Jesus' messianic mission was always meant by God to go beyond the chosen people in order to fulfill God's universal plan for salvation and to attest to God's unlimited power of redemption. Mark's not-so-subtle political message is that the kingdom of God transcends and nullifies any claims of the Roman Empire to being truly universal.

If, however, you are looking for an alternative reading of this passage that is a little less safe, consider this instead. What if the placement of these

Pastoral Perspective

The Syrophoenician woman had everything going against her when she pushed her way into Jesus' presence. She was a woman and a Gentile from the wrong side of the tracks. She had no right to engage Jesus in conversation. Imagine a homeless person interrupting the dinner of the president of the United States to ask a favor.

Despite the dictates of custom, this woman does approach Jesus. She is driven by something more powerful than protocol; she is desperately afraid for her daughter's life. She bows before Jesus and begs him to cast the demon out of her daughter. We expect our kind, loving Jesus to say, "Of course I will save your daughter," but here Jesus is caught with his proverbial compassion down. He says to her, "Let the children be fed first, for it is not fair to take the children's food and throw it to the dogs" (vv. 26, 27). Jesus is telling this desperate woman that his mission is for the Jews and the Jews alone. He calls her a dog. Some commentaries have suggested that the word "dog" is not as harsh as it sounds, that Jesus is merely referring to her as a pet. No. The word is "dog," and dog is what he means.

Many who suffered those words might have crept away, feeling small and insignificant, but not the Syrophoenician woman. She boldly responds, "Sir, even the dogs under the table eat the children's

³¹Then he returned from the region of Tyre, and went by way of Sidon towards the Sea of Galilee, in the region of the Decapolis. ³²They brought to him a deaf man who had an impediment in his speech; and they begged him to lay his hand on him. ³³He took him aside in private, away from the crowd, and put his fingers into his ears, and he spat and touched his tongue. ³⁴Then looking up to heaven, he sighed and said to him, "Ephphatha," that is, "Be opened." ³⁵And immediately his ears were opened, his tongue was released, and he spoke plainly. ³⁶Then Jesus ordered them to tell no one; but the more he ordered them, the more zealously they proclaimed it. ³⁷They were astounded beyond measure, saying, "He has done everything well; he even makes the deaf to hear and the mute to speak."

Exegetical Perspective

We should assume that Jesus did not travel to the pagan city of Tyre. The "region of Tyre" extended eastward to an area not far from the Sea of Galilee. Although this was Gentile territory, many Jews lived there (see Mark 3:8). Because Jesus' meeting with a Gentile woman is treated as exceptional, we can take for granted that he did not enter this area to preach the good news to the Gentiles. Mark's simple statement in verse 24 provides no support for the hypothesis that Jesus was fleeing from Herod and other enemies. The sentence "He entered a house and did not want anyone to know he was there" suggests that Jesus was not there for public preaching. Perhaps Jesus sought temporary asylum from the multitudes that crowded around him in Galilee.

The travel note in verse 31 is curious. Why would Jesus travel from the region of Tyre through Sidon, which lay north of Tyre, if his intention was to return to the Sea of Galilee? And how could he be in the midst of the Decapolis and be near the lake? Perhaps Mark thinks of Jesus making a large arc north of Galilee that brought him from Tyre's territory to the region of Hippos, a Gentile city that belonged to the Decapolis. Hippos was situated near the east side of the Sea of Galilee. Although the population of this area was largely Gentile (as suggested by the herd of pigs in Mark 5:1–20), Jews

Homiletical Perspective

The two stories included in this week's Gospel reading double our opportunity to proclaim God's power at work among us. Both episodes recount marvelous healing events, but they also pose considerable challenges for the preacher. In Jesus' exchange with the Syrophoenician woman, we are disturbed by his insulting response to her plea for her help. After he heals the deaf mute, Jesus orders the man and his companions not to tell anyone about the man's healing. Each story includes intriguing details and challenging moments that provide more than enough material for their own sermon. Yet taken side by side, they present us with two particularly rich and provocative examples of God's power at work among us.

One approach to this text is to recognize that these two healing stories have much in common. First, both episodes take place in Gentile territory. The fact that Jesus gives attention and care to persons beyond his own ethnic enclave challenges us to reach beyond the ethnic homogeneity of our own congregations to worship and minister with persons who are different from ourselves.[1] Jesus' ministry

1. Recent studies have shown that growth in church attendance is more likely to occur among congregations that are multiracial and develop a clear sense of outreach and mission. See the study by the Hartford Institute for Religion Research as reported in the *Christian Century*, January 23, 2007, p. 14.

Mark 7:24-37

Theological Perspective

stories after the warnings about hypocrisy highlights not the shortcomings of Jesus' followers, but of Jesus himself? Given that Jesus has already performed a healing on a Gentile in Mark (the story of the demoniac of the tombs in chapter 5), the uncharacteristically rude response of Jesus to the woman seems out of place if Mark is interested only in using this story as way of emphasizing God's universality or testing her faith. Could the story of the Syrophoenician woman be a kind of "conversion" moment for Jesus, in which he realizes how (maybe in a very human moment of physical and mental exhaustion) he has lost sight of the point of his mission and has to be reconnected with it by someone assumed to be outside of it? Then for Mark the woman is more than simply rhetorically gifted: she is prophetic. She is an embodiment of Isaiah (e.g., Isa. 49:6), there to rebuke Jesus, straightening him out and opening him up. The story of the deaf mute that directly follows would then serve as an example of how being opened up empowers one to open up others.

It may be helpful to recall how over the last two decades feminist biblical scholars and theologians have challenged the traditional interpretation of the story of the Syrophoenician woman, told here and in Matthew's Gospel (15:21–28). Mary Ann Tolbert argues it is the woman's culturally unconventional and even shameful request (since it is not coming from a male member of her family) that draws the wrath and disdain of Jesus, not simply the fact that she is a foreigner. Further, since she bests him in the argument that ensues, it is the Gentile woman who teaches him, the Jewish man, the true meaning of what he has just reminded his own followers in the verse prior: that social conventions should not stand in the way of helping those in need.

Sharon Ringe disagrees with Tolbert's analysis and suggests that the harshness of Jesus is generated more by the political imbalance between the wealthy Gentiles of Tyre and the Jewish peasants of the region. Ringe suggests that the text serves to remind those with economic privilege not automatically to expect a place at the table in the coming reign of God. They will be lucky to get a space under the table, which is perhaps the price they must pay for their "costly discipleship." Analyzing the parallel passage of the Canaanite woman in Matthew, Gail O'Day points out that the mutability of Jesus and the remarkable boldness of the woman are both central to a larger theological analogy of the story. It is the courage of the woman to confront Jesus that changes him, just as it is the courage of Israel to

Pastoral Perspective

crumbs" (v. 28). Jesus' earlier prejudice was very human and his insight now perhaps divine. He instantly understands her challenge. His mission is not restricted to the Jews. God's love expands beyond all barriers. Rather than scolding her for her brashness, Jesus tells her, "For saying that, you may go—the demon has left your daughter" (v. 29).

The story that follows the tale of the Syrophoenician woman is also a story about healing. A deaf man with a speech impediment is brought before Jesus. The people beg Jesus to lay hands on the man and heal him. Being deaf in the first century was not merely about not hearing or speaking clearly. For many people, physical impairment was viewed as the consequence of sin. People who suffered from blindness, deafness, or withered limbs had little or no status. They were often barred from the social and religious institutions of the day. In those days, people were afraid of physical differences and did not understand the biology of birth defects as we do today. When Jesus healed people, he not only corrected their physical problems. He also restored them to community.

Jesus sees beyond this man's infirmity. He sees his value as a child of God. Jesus takes the man away from the crowd and puts his fingers in his ears, then spits and touches the man's tongue. Raising his eyes to heaven, Jesus says, "Be opened" (vv. 33, 34). Immediately, the deaf man can hear and speak clearly. Jesus has not only released him from the bondage of his affliction but has reunited him with his community as well. Whenever Jesus heals, whether it is a demon-possessed girl, a man with leprosy, a bleeding woman, or a deaf man, he heals not only the body but the fracture with community as well.

Human beings suffer from a deep insecurity that pushes us to create rules that give status and value to some while denigrating others. In the first-century, the poor, the infirm, the orphaned, the mentally ill, the alien, and many women lived with very low status. Years of lying on psychiatrists' couches and reading Freud have not seemed to dim our insecurities. In the twenty-first century, many of these people still live at the margins of society. We are no more inclined to forgiveness, preferring long prison terms and harsh religious judgment for those who stray from our secular laws or religious morals. There continues to be a sense that if people end up homeless or on drugs, they are weak and at fault. Our world teaches us to shun the dirty, smelly woman ranting on the bus next to us and not to embrace her. Countless children spend

were to be found there. Because there is no hint that the deaf man is a Gentile, we should assume that he, like the man in the pig story, is a Jew.

The first miracle differs from others in Mark in two significant ways. First, the exorcism is effected at a distance, as in the healing of the centurion's servant (Matt. 8:5–13; Luke 7:1–10). Secondly, Jesus has supernatural knowledge that the demon has been expelled.

The miracle itself receives little attention. The emphasis lies rather on Jesus' initial refusal to grant the woman's request: "Let the children be fed first, for it is not fair to take the children's food and throw it to the dogs." This harsh saying, which appears to insult Gentiles by comparing them to dogs, seems out of character for Jesus. There have been various attempts to soften its force. Some interpreters declare it inauthentic. They propose that it derives from conservative Jewish Christians such as those mentioned in Acts 11:2–3. Its effect was later modified by moderate Jewish Christians who added the words attributed to the Gentile woman. Other interpreters suggest that Jesus' saying would not have seemed so insulting in its original setting; it was simply a familiar proverb, roughly equivalent to our "Charity begins at home." To be preferred, however, is a third proposal. Jesus was convinced that he must not be distracted from his primary mission to his people, as expressed in Matthew's version of this story: "I was sent only to the lost sheep of the house of Israel" (Matt. 15:24; cf. Matt. 10:5–6). His sense of urgency is conveyed effectively by another harsh saying. To a would-be disciple who says, "Lord, first let me go and bury my father," Jesus declares, "Follow me, and let the dead bury their own dead" (Matt. 8:21–22).

Paul's mission to the Gentiles would have received less opposition had he been able to report that Jesus himself had ministered to many Gentiles. Instead Paul acknowledges Jesus' self-limitation: "For I tell you that Christ has become a servant of the circumcised . . . in order that the Gentiles might glorify God for his mercy" (Rom. 15:8–9). This conforms with Paul's understanding of the history of salvation: "To the Jew first and also to the Greek" (Rom. 1:16).

It is interesting to compare Mark's version of Jesus' saying with Matthew's. The latter reads bluntly, "It is not fair to take the children's food and throw it to the dogs" (Matt. 15:26). In Mark, by contrast, we find, "Let the children be fed *first*." By this one word Mark points forward to the time when Gentiles will also be fed.

affirms and anticipates the church's need to share God's gifts of grace, peace, and healing with all people. (See also Jesus' ministry among Gentiles in 8:1–26 and 5:1–20.)

The second feature common to both stories is that the persons who are healed do not approach Jesus alone but are aided by others. The young girl is freed of demon possession because her mother pleads on her behalf. The deaf man is brought to Jesus by friends who beg for his healing. In these stories it is not the faith of the disabled persons that brings about their healing but the active faith of their companions. Their stories remind us to approach Christ on behalf of others and actively seek the well-being of those who need help and care.

Finally, in both of these stories we witness something more than physical healing. Not only is the Syrophoenician girl healed of demon possession, but we recognize that a further transformation has taken place in Jesus, who experiences a change of heart and a shift in direction as he ministers among Gentiles (not only in 7:31–37 but through the feeding miracle of 8:1–8). When the man who is deaf and mute can hear and speak, we hear a gospel word of hope for all of us who have blocked our ears and/or refused to share the good news of Jesus Christ with others.

It is also important that preachers address what is most troublesome about these stories. In the first episode we are appalled that Jesus calls the Gentile woman and her daughter "dogs." It is not enough to excuse Jesus' retort because we suspect that he may have been weary from his earlier confrontation with the scribes and Pharisees (7:1–23). It is also less than satisfying to suggest that Jesus was simply focusing on his ministry to Jews rather than Gentiles. However, it is likely he was aware of the economic hardship that many Jews in the region of Tyre experienced due to the exploits of the Gentile landowners, and his rebuff of the Syrophoenician woman may well have reflected this.[2] But her faith in Jesus' healing power takes him by surprise. It is greater than that of his own people—including the members of his hometown, among whom he could not perform deeds of power because of their unbelief (6:4–6).

Thus, a sermon that addresses the shocking nature of Jesus' insult in 7:27 also needs to explore

---

2. According to Sharon H. Ringe, "[The Syrophoenician woman] is portrayed as part of the group in that region whose policies and lifestyle would have been a source of suffering for her mostly poorer, rural, Jewish neighbors." See "A Gentile Woman's Story, Revisited: Rereading Mark 7:24–31," in *A Feminist Companion to Mark*, ed. Amy-Jill Levine with Marianne Blickenstaff (Cleveland: Pilgrim Press, 2001), 85.

Mark 7:24-37

Theological Perspective

demand justice from God that moves God to respond, keeping with the prophetic tradition of the Hebrew Bible.

To read this text as a *metanoia* of Jesus raises serious theological questions. How can Jesus "change" if he is divine? Does this shortcoming of Jesus actually constitute an example of *sin*? Are we in the church so theologically constrained by our traditional readings of other New Testament documents (e.g., Romans, Philippians, Hebrews) and the Council of Nicaea and its doctrinal proclamation of "fully God, fully human" that we are unable truly to experience the profound theological tension that Mark provides for us? Is it possible to be "fully human" and without sin? In connecting this passage with the admonition about hypocrisy that precedes it, perhaps Jesus here faces his own hypocrisy and struggles to find his own center in God, moving through his own pain of self-integration. In other words, Mark is showing us that the incarnation is not a cakewalk.

To be the Son of God, the Messiah must suffer, not only at the hands of those of us who do not understand him, but also under of the conditions of existence, the challenge of the human condition itself. To be otherwise would not allow Jesus to be fully human. Furthermore, according to the tenets of process and liberation theologies, if he is also "fully God," Jesus cannot avoid this suffering either. Mark provides an interesting way of seeing how the divine and the human can be completely combined in the life of Jesus of Nazareth, a kind of "Ephphatha Christology." Jesus is fully God and fully human only if he can faithfully "be opened" to both at the same time.

LOYE BRADLEY ASHTON

Pastoral Perspective

empty, abused lives shuttled from one foster home to the next, forgotten and unloved by the world. Prisoners of other countries and religions can be blindfolded and humiliated because they are deemed undeserving of the same rights and privileges as those in power.

The Syrophoenician woman called Jesus to a mission of infinite compassion and mercy. New Testament scholar Mitzi Minor writes that Mark gives us God's initiatives in these stories. Jesus' actions illustrated that a "worthless, Gentile girl whose mind was devoured by a demon" and a "good for nothing deaf man who couldn't even speak clearly" were indeed children of God to be embraced and valued. Humanity's authentic response to God's initiative "calls forth recognition that there are no external barriers between God and any human being: not race, class, ethnicity, gender, age, or physical condition. Consequently, there should also be no such barriers between human beings."[1]

Perhaps it is too much to ask that a homeless person could interrupt the dinner of the president of the United States to ask a favor, but it is not too much to ask humanity to recognize that there are no walls made of withered hands, deaf ears, or troubled minds separating us from God or us from each other. Status is a product of our own imaginations, invisible to God. Once we acknowledge that there are no walls separating us, love and mercy flow unfettered, and all people are deemed equally valuable.

AMY C. HOWE

1. Mitzi Minor, *The Spirituality of Mark* (Louisville, KY: Westminster John Knox Press, 1996), 51.

Exegetical Perspective

The woman's quick-witted response wins Jesus' approval and healing. Mark is less interested than Matthew in the woman's faith. In the First Gospel Jesus makes no comment on the woman's response but says rather, "Woman, great is your faith! Let it be done for you as you wish" (Matt. 15:28).

How can Christians appropriate this story? First, it reminds us of our debt to Israel. As Krister Stendahl proposed, in Paul's view we Gentile Christians must consider ourselves "honorary Jews."[1] The Gentile woman humbly acknowledges the priority of the "children," even as she presses her request to be fed from the same table. Second, the woman's boldness inspires us to be bold in our prayers of intercession and petition. Even though our basic principle is "Your will be done," we must not prematurely abandon our prayers for healing, thinking they are futile.

The second miracle in the lectionary passage is omitted from Matthew and Luke, perhaps because it seemed to them reminiscent of the healings performed by magicians: the healing is done in private, using saliva, and a foreign word is employed. These similarities to the practice of magicians are superficial. The word *ephphatha*, whether Hebrew or Aramaic, was not a foreign word to Jesus' audience, and is translated for the benefit of Mark's Gentile audience. Since Jesus regularly heals in public, Mark cannot be accused of portraying Jesus as a magician in this and the private healing of a blind man in 8:22–26. The use of saliva is striking, but has a parallel in the Fourth Gospel, which by no means presents Jesus as a magician (John 9:6).

Like the other healing miracles, this one testifies to the fact that the proclamation of God's rule is accompanied by radical changes in the lives of individuals. When we respond to the gospel, our ears are opened and our tongues are released.

—DOUGLAS R. A. HARE

Homiletical Perspective

the shocking nature of the woman's response in 7:28. She accepts his priority of ministering first to the people of Israel, yet she is not satisfied with this. Her faith calls forth a larger vision of God's mission to the Gentiles. Jesus immediately recognizes the God-given wisdom of her words, changes his mind, and commends her outspokenness (cf. Matt. 15:28, where she is commended for her faith, not her outspokenness). In light of her words, Jesus does not simply have second thoughts: his vision and vocation are radically reoriented. We do not sense the diminishment of Jesus' power through this exchange but the expansion of it, as he blesses her heart's desire and heals her daughter. However unsettling this exchange may be, its resolution reveals that God is not unchanging or unresponsive but compassionate and merciful.

In the second episode, we are disturbed by Jesus' command that the healed man and his friends keep silent (7:36). Perhaps he ordered them not to speak because Jesus was concerned about their speaking prematurely, without knowing the fullness of his suffering, death, and resurrection to come. Or perhaps he understood that words are sometimes unnecessary.

Most of us are reluctant to share our faith with others and we find very good reasons to keep quiet: we may believe that our actions speak more loudly than our words, we may be afraid of the inadequacy of our speech, or we may fear that we will make a mistake and alienate those to whom we are speaking. Yet the healed man is every bit as insistent as the Syrophoenician woman. He and his companions give voice to God's presence and power among them. The characters in both stories embolden us to share whatever glimpse of God's mercy, love, and truth we have witnessed. Their stories and words remind us to focus our attention on God and to keep pointing others toward the reign of God proclaimed by Jesus Christ.

—DAWN OTTONI WILHELM

---

1. Krister Stendahl, *Paul among Jews and Christians* (Philadelphia: Fortress Press, 1976), 37.

Proverbs 1:20-33

20Wisdom cries out in the street;
  in the squares she raises her voice.
21At the busiest corner she cries out;
  at the entrance of the city gates she speaks:
22"How long, O simple ones, will you love being simple?
  How long will scoffers delight in their scoffing
    and fools hate knowledge?
23Give heed to my reproof;
  I will pour out my thoughts to you;
  I will make my words known to you.
24Because I have called and you refused,
  have stretched out my hand and no one heeded,
25and because you have ignored all my counsel
  and would have none of my reproof,
26I also will laugh at your calamity;
  I will mock when panic strikes you,

Theological Perspective

The foolish have already appeared in Proverbs as predators contending for a young one's life (Prov. 1:10–19). Now we meet Lady Wisdom as a sage turned prophetess, a street preacher turned apocalyptic by universal abandonment, and discover that the enemy already seems to have captured us all.

Wisdom's heart is a love for creatures that would share every mystery (Prov. 1:23; cf. 1 Cor. 13:2). This is gloriously confirmed when Christ, the wisdom of God (1 Cor. 1:24), shares the Spirit who searches, knows, and understands all (1 Cor. 2:11–12) with those whom God has made children and heirs. However, only briefly does the passage comment on those who heed her. It mainly reflects her schadenfreude at the suffering of fools who spurn her.

The retribution of wisdom unheeded is also the covenant's furious curse on unfaithfulness. It is the falling doom of apocalyptic prophecy. It is the psalms' and canticles' promises of swift reversal for the arrogant, and the biblical narrative's inexorable tide of justice. All these forms of judgment converge because wisdom participates in every embodiment of truth—Jewish and Gentile, divine and human, masculine and feminine.

The image of the Man of Sorrows laughing at calamity and mocking panic is disturbing. Yet Wisdom incarnate issues a similar warning in this

Pastoral Perspective

If the Proverbs have been marginalized in the Revised Common Lectionary, the church might at times confess that its wisdom has suffered a similar fate in the culture. Many eloquent voices make claims about how to live in the real world: talk-show hosts, cultural commentators, seminar leaders, life coaches. The church is but one voice among many, clamoring for the attention of the marketplace.

The writer of this proverb would have understood our challenge. "Wisdom cries out in the street; in the squares she raises her voice" (Prov. 1:20). How do the claims of God find a hearing in a culture that bombards its inhabitants with messages about the good life? Lady Wisdom raises her voice, just as a mother might with a resistant teenager. And so the culture, as sophisticated as it is, also resists wisdom: "I have called and you refused, have stretched out my hand and no one heeded" (Prov. 1:24).

Why does the culture (and the church) resist wisdom? The answer lies partly in the abundant wisdom that seems to surround us. We are overwhelmed with options, choices, and advice. At the same time, we often sense that guidance is offered to those who have little interest in amendment of life, not unlike an all-you-can-eat buffet prepared for those who have already eaten. In discouragement the church has often abandoned the tradition of practical

²⁷when panic strikes you like a storm,
  and your calamity comes like a whirlwind,
  when distress and anguish come upon you.
²⁸Then they will call upon me, but I will not answer;
  they will seek me diligently, but will not find me.
²⁹Because they hated knowledge
  and did not choose the fear of the Lord,
³⁰would have none of my counsel,
  and despised all my reproof,
³¹therefore they shall eat the fruit of their way
  and be sated with their own devices.
³²For waywardness kills the simple,
  and the complacency of fools destroys them;
³³but those who listen to me will be secure
  and will live at ease, without dread of disaster."

Exegetical Perspective

The first surprise of this passage is that its authoritative figure, its main speaker, and its primary focus is a woman. The second surprise is that she speaks like a prophet; she demands that her listeners decide now if they will hear her words and follow them. Wisdom Woman—whoever she is, and there is much debate about this—speaks here for the first time in Proverbs. Her tone is powerful and censorious because she knows that the consequence of deafness to her words is spiritual calamity. Wisdom calls everyone to a radical spirituality, to a way of being in the world and in right relationships. These right relationships get spelled out in abundant ambiguity in the collected sayings at the heart of the book (Prov. 10–31). After her dramatic invitation to listen (1:20–23), the bulk of today's text concerns the consequences of not listening (1:24–32) and concludes with one meager verse announcing the happy results of proper listening (1:33).

The Call to Listen (vv. 20–23). How, where, and to whom Wisdom delivers her demands are the subjects of the poem's opening verses. Like a preacher certain of the immense urgency of her words for her audience's well-being, she adamantly appeals for attention with a hammering sequence of verbs. She cries out, raises her voice, calls, and speaks (vv. 20–21). And

Homiletical Perspective

In this passage Wisdom, believed by many to represent the ever searching, ever calling, ever challenging Spirit of God, is personified. Wisdom shows up in the places where human beings live their lives. She shows up in busy streets. She shows up in the public square. She shows up in the bustling intersections. She shows up with a challenging question—"Is anyone out there listening to me?" She shows up with a stern warning —"To ignore wisdom is to choose destruction." She shows up with a compelling invitation: "Those who listen to me will be blessed."

This text gives the preacher many points of entry. The preacher may celebrate the ways in which Wisdom shows up in the lives of the congregation. Often she shows up in a moment of need, a moment of crisis, a moment of fear. In the fall of 2006 she showed up for the world in the form of a grieving and forgiving Amish community. On October 2, 2006, Charles Carl Roberts entered a one-room schoolhouse in the Amish community of Nickel Mines, Pennsylvania. He lined up ten young girls from the school and shot each at point-blank range, killing five of them. In the face of this unspeakable atrocity, the Amish of Nickel Mines insisted that if they were to be true to their faith, true to their heritage, true to the memory of the innocent victims, they must not be overcome by evil but

Proverbs 1:20-33

Theological Perspective

week's Gospel about those of whom he will be ashamed (Mark 8:38). This language is a strong rebuke to our cultural reflex to cast any suffering as victimhood that deserves sympathy. Wisdom's sympathy is always a free gift, and persistent scoffing and hatred for knowledge finally exhaust her patience (Prov. 1:22–23). When disaster comes, Wisdom's contemptuous response (Prov. 1:24–27) proves that these fools have no standing before God—not even the recourse of sympathy that a wayward child might use as leverage over loving parents.

Unconditional divine sensitivity toward sufferers is one conviction driving the theological trend toward universalism—the teaching, repeatedly condemned, that all will certainly be saved. But unconditional sensitivity would effectively hand the Lord over to sinners to be tortured by their folly. This is an idolatrous reversal of the outcome in Jesus' parable of the unforgiving servant (Matt. 18:23–35). The compassion of Proverbs' loving parents is palpable (Prov. 1:8–19). However, their loyalty to Wisdom surpasses even their loyalty to their own children—as Wisdom's loyalty to her divine Source (Mark 8:22–31) must surpass her loyalty to subjects (Mark 8:32–36)—because neglecting her is finally neglecting God himself.

In a world of foolishly and fatally misplaced sensitivities, Wisdom's insensitivity is thus essential to destroying the wisdom of the supposedly wise (Prov. 1:32–33, Isa. 29:13–14 in 1 Cor. 1:19) as well as moving the naive to maturity (Prov. 2:1–22; 1 Cor. 3:1–2). She seems deeply to desire both (Prov. 1:20–21). These desires are satisfied not through a prosperity gospel in which some are "saved" to become thriving sages, while others are "lost" to become condemned fools, but through good news of death and resurrection, in which the good sons and the prodigals alike leave the father's house in sheer foolishness and can return to life (Luke 15:11–32) through sheer grace.

First, the incorrigibly foolish will self-destruct, "killed by their turning away" (Prov 1:32b ESV). This is not an avoidable outcome. The very folly that beats paths to destruction sets up strongholds in our reason and will. Fools become self-righteous and reject as life-threatening the medicine that would heal them. And sure enough, Jesus' neighbors take offense at "this wisdom that has been given to him" and amaze him with their unbelief (Mark 6:1–5). Resistance spreads and intensifies until whole nations conspire to betray, arrest, condemn, and crucify the Messiah.

Pastoral Perspective

wisdom, and into the vacuum have come the therapist and the manager, each of whom speaks clearly and confidently, often with the use of spiritual language and even religious authorization.

Why do we resist wisdom? This predicament could be related to our human preference for knowledge. Ellen Davis speaks helpfully of knowledge as a "form of power," of knowledge "abstracted from goodness." In contrast, "Israel was not interested in any form of knowledge that is abstracted from the concrete problem of how we may live in kindness and fidelity with our neighbors, live humbly and faithfully in the presence of God."[1] And so the pastor gives thanks for those who compose the core of every congregation, wise men and women who listen for the still, small voice (1 Kgs. 19:12) that persists amid the background noise that is both distracting and discouraging.

The text does conclude with a glimmer of hope: "Those who listen to me will be secure and will live at ease, without dread of disaster" (Prov. 1:33). Listening in the Proverbs is always linked to obedience, and obedience is participation in the practices that lead to wisdom: hearing and reading Scripture, prayers of confession and intercession, humility before others and God. This wisdom has very little to do with knowledge in service of power, and more to do with insight that is in service of God and neighbor. In an insecure world, this wisdom is grounded in the voice of God, calling us into the way that leads to life. This wisdom is present among those who live in communion with God's people and, at times, in resistance to the persistent refrains of the culture. Wisdom is finally possible as we participate in the practices of the God who is wisdom. Craig Dykstra and Dorothy Bass describe these practices:

> Woven together, Christian practices form a way of life. This way is not shaped primarily by a certain cultural style, class, nationality or age; on the contrary, the way can embrace people in every circumstance, taking different shapes in different times and places. It becomes visible as ordinary people search together for specific ways of taking part in the practice of God, as they faithfully perceive it in the complicated places where they really live. It is like a tree [see Proverbs 3.18] whose branches reach out toward the future, even when the earth is shaking, because it is nourished by living water.[2]

1. Ellen F. Davis, *Getting Involved with God: Rediscovering the Old Testament* (Cambridge: Cowley, 2001), 94, 95, 96.
2. Dorothy Bass, ed., *Practicing Our Faith: A Way of Life for a Searching People* (San Francisco: Jossey-Bass, 1997), 203.

with equal emphasis, the text stresses the location of her efforts to accost the people. She demands attention in the streets, in the squares, at the busiest corner, at the entrance of the city gate. These are the sites of communal life, of the bustling relationships of daily life. This is where Wisdom demands to be heard, not in the privacy of homes, the sacredness of the temple, or even the quiet recesses of souls. She calls for allegiance smack in the thick of work and play, at busy intersections where people gather, and at the city gates, where legal and commercial deals take place. Ordinary life with its drama and busy social exchanges, with its joys and disappointments, is Wisdom's domain. In this passage and in the Wisdom literature in general, mundane human life is the hallowed place, the sacred ground where one may encounter Wisdom herself, if one is attentive.

Wisdom is not particular about who follows her. She does not call the chosen, the holy, or the privileged, but invites anyone who will hear her. She calls to the "simple," the "scoffers," and the ones who "hate knowledge" (v. 22). The "simple" refers to anyone who is not yet wise, and who is wise compared to Wisdom herself? She grows impatient because she has been calling to them for a long time. The scoffers and knowledge haters obstinately refuse to heed. "How long," she asks twice in her impatience, will they persist in their foolishness?

"Give heed to my reproof," she urges, and most of the passage is exactly that: reproof, criticism, and admonition. But before she warns, she makes a promise, and that promise is nothing less than to reveal herself to everyone who listens. "I will pour out my thoughts to you; I will make my words known to you" (v. 23). Her pledge is remarkable in the Old Testament, and it raises deeper questions about her identity. To her listeners, she promises to disclose her mind, her inner life, to form an intimate union with them. She longs to be with them in mutuality, to find communion with them, and to become one with them. Wisdom's promise uses language of self-revelation usually reserved for God's promises to prophets. But the text only suggests this connection in a mysterious glimpse of an identity never made completely clear.

Consequences of Not Listening (vv. 24–31). Wisdom is frustrated because she has tried so hard to win the people to no avail. She called, stretched out her hand, but they would have none of her warnings. Because they turn away from the life she offers, she will turn away from them when calamity strikes and

overcome evil with good. They said they would find a way to forgive. They embraced and cared for the families of the victims and the family of the shooter. To a country that speaks the language of revenge very well, to a people often addicted to the hope of getting even, the Amish said there is another way, a better way. Their story is eloquent testimony to the truth that Wisdom shows up in our lives, often in ways we do not expect.

The preacher may note that Wisdom does not mince words; she comes with a clear and stern warning. When she shows up she gets right to the point. "Because I have called and you refused, have stretched out my hand and no one heeded, and because you have ignored all my counsel and would have none of my reproof, I also will laugh at your calamity: I will mock you when panic strikes you" (vv. 24–26).

Many of us struggle with this side of Wisdom, this swaggering, self-assured, "I would listen to me if I were you" representative of God. Perhaps the poet who penned Proverbs overstates his/her case just a bit. Perhaps God does not actually laugh at the calamities we bring on ourselves. Still, it is difficult to argue with the truth of Wisdom's warning. When we forget about the ways of God, we often get ourselves into some terrible predicaments. When we think we are beyond the basic lessons of loving justice, doing kindness, and walking humbly with God, we often end up doing things and saying things we regret. When loving God and loving neighbor as we love ourselves are mere platitudes for us, it seems that disaster often finds us. It will always be true that bad things happen to good people and good things happen to bad people. It will also always be true that we have some responsibility for what happens to our families, our communities, our world, and ourselves. We need to pay attention to this brash messenger Wisdom and her insistence that "fear of the LORD is the beginning of knowledge" (v. 7a).

If the preacher chooses to lift up Wisdom's warning, he/she will also need to lift up her promise of peace. Preachers of conscience do not want to promise too much. They do not make assurances that will not materialize. They do not want to proclaim that all will be well when, in point of fact, all will not be well. Thus the preacher is right to be cautious in dealing with Wisdom's promise—"but those who listen to me will be secure and will live at ease, without dread of disaster" (v. 33).

Yet, to survey our congregations, to examine our own lives, is to see ways in which this promise is

Proverbs 1:20-33

Theological Perspective

Patristic ransom theories of atonement perceived the irony. Jesus of Nazareth is Wisdom made Proverbs' beloved son; and in seizing him, satanic humanity (Mark 8:33) seeks to capture none other than the loving God of Israel. Its fatal mistake exposes the world's folly and defuses its power. "Those who want to save their life will lose it" (Mark 8:35a); "the complacency of fools destroys them" (Prov. 1:32b). The world's rejection brings "suffering such as has not been from the beginning of the creation" (Mark 13:19), as the old order of folly collapses before the kingdom's advent.

However, the only wise God is *not* insensitive to the death of a righteous Son (Mark 15:39); and the Father lifts him up to perpetual security, free from the dread of evil (Prov. 1:33), as a new beginning for all things—including the foolish, dead in their folly but alive in God's gracious wisdom and power.

Second, the young will grow in favor as they grow in wisdom (cf. Luke 2:52). The wise and the foolish alike who begin anew in the kingdom of God can listen to Wisdom and find new rest (Prov. 1:33; Luke 24:25–27). Insensitivity has a place here too. It jars us into sobriety (2 Cor. 11:16–19) and calls us into new lives of urgent vigilance. "Beware that no one leads you astray," Jesus cautions (Mark 13:5–37), and in parallel passages he warns of the risks of being unready for the Son of Man's sudden coming (Matt. 24:36–25:46). Trial and error is an unaffordable learning strategy in such a perilous time. Wisdom will be unavailable when it is most urgently needed (Prov. 1:28), so it must be stockpiled while still available. Like the Torah and the prophets—and apostolic teaching (Jas. 3:1–12) with wisdom from above (Jas. 3:13–18)—Proverbs is a training ground for entering and dwelling in the apocalyptic future (Prov. 1:7, cf. 1:29).

Wisdom's callousness thus turns out to manifest divine love. The heavens cry out with affirmation of the God of Israel, but our depraved world hears nothing (Ps. 19:1–4). "No one heeded" (Prov. 1:24). We are truly a ship of fools. Yet "those who listen to [Wisdom] . . . will live at ease" (Prov. 1:33). Fools do not become wise through persuasion, let alone sympathy, but through the gift of a new mind. Only through conversion and new creation will our words and thoughts become acceptable to our rock and redeemer (Ps. 19:14).

TELFORD WORK

Pastoral Perspective

The living water might be the Proverbs themselves; the earth's shaking might be the difficulties we experience in life; to attempt to take part in the practice of God (wisdom) is to walk in integrity, even in the complicated places where we live. The writer speaks of an occasion when "panic strikes you like a storm, and your calamity comes like a whirlwind"(Prov. 1:27). The pastor is aware of occasions where people inhabit the complicated places: the parent of a teenager whose child is in the midst of substance abuse; a couple sorting out the possibilities of staying together; the aftermath of a natural disaster or a traumatic accident.

At times the pastoral ministry is smooth, constant, almost boring. But at other times the winds and waves crash upon us, and we are aware that the resources of wisdom are either present or absent. The "fear of the LORD," which is the beginning of wisdom (Prov. 1:7), is the experience of contact with a power greater than our own, before whom we give up control (in the Old Testament, the crossing of the sea, and in the New Testament, the relinquishment of the cross). A wise person knows that she or he is not all-knowing and therefore is in need of guidance; such a person possesses what John Calvin described as "a teachable spirit." This "fear of the LORD" is a form of humility or reverence, and, again, it is not obvious that such wisdom is valued in a culture that prefers power and control.

And so wisdom cries out, in the church and in the culture; some resist the claims of wisdom, others become attentive to wisdom, over time, with hearts inclined to understanding (see Prov. 2:2). Those who reject the wisdom of God are lost, reaping what they sow (see Gal. 6). But for those who have ears to hear, there is the promise of the gospel: they will abide in the shadow of God's wings (Ps. 17:8), safe and secure, in the words of the hymn, from all alarms.

KENNETH H. CARTER JR.

Exegetical Perspective

will laugh at their distress. They should have been pursuing her with the same intensity and absolute devotion with which she pursues them. This is the way to life.

The miserable fate of scoffers will not be her fault but theirs, the inevitable consequence of refusing her counsel to live in the "fear of the LORD." "Fear of the LORD" does not mean sniveling terror before God. The phrase is an ancient code for the proper behavior of the religious person in relation to God and creation. It involves awe, respect, and obedience; it summarizes righteous living. People who fear the Lord have their feet planted on the ground, see around them truthfully, and live in harmony with God and world. The foolish, by contrast, are to be abandoned to the "fruit of their way," to "be sated with their own devices" (v. 31).

Wisdom's call ends with a proverb, the first half of which concludes her reproof: "Waywardness kills the simple, and the complacency of fools destroys them" (v. 32). With the authority of the wisdom of the ancestors, the proverb summarizes her warning. Failure to follow Wisdom leads to death.

Consequences of Listening (v. 33). The proverb's second half arrives finally at the benefits of listening to Wisdom's advice. What she offers is true security, trust, and freedom from fear, because disaster will not come to her followers. The text does not say how this can be so, but it implies that true security comes from relationship with her. She will not merely lead them, but will live with them, reveal her thoughts to them, be in kinship with them. She will accompany them and keep them secure.

Whether or not Wisdom is God in this text, she reveals herself like God, makes demands like God, and promises freedom and life to her followers like God. Whoever she is, her appearance destabilizes complacency, closed-heartedness, and death-dealing behavior that comes from ignorance, hatred of knowledge, and refusal to commit to the way of Wisdom. Wisdom invites everyone to a life of harmonious balance in the midst of daily life.

KATHLEEN M. O'CONNOR

Homiletical Perspective

made known. When people take time to listen to those they disagree with, they often find ways to move beyond tension-laden conflict, conflict that consumes and destroys. When people find ways to honor God—simple, time-tested ways like saying a prayer or going to church—they find that life can have a rhythm and cadence that feels right. When people recognize their need to forgive and be forgiven, they find a peace that is good for body, mind, and spirit.

To walk in the ways of Wisdom is demanding. The promise Wisdom makes when she says that good things come to those who walk with her needs to be qualified by the words "often," "sometimes," and "it is not surprising when." We should not be distressed if it can be proven that the poet of Proverbs overstates both peril and promise.

Yet, in promising that Wisdom does show up, in warning that we ignore Wisdom at our own peril, in promising that there are benefits in paying attention to Wisdom, the preacher is in good company. Indeed, the preacher is walking the road that Wisdom walks—showing up, pleading, promising, predicting—and there is comfort in this. There is the comfort of walking a road that is valued by our tradition. There is the comfort that our work has meaning and purpose. There is the comfort that we are planting seeds that may produce a bountiful harvest. Wisdom's bold speech, brash approach, and lack of concern for diplomacy make us squirm, yet she is simply seeking the good of each and the good of all. The preacher does well to take her words both to heart and to the congregation.

H. JAMES HOPKINS

Psalm 19

¹The heavens are telling the glory of God;
    and the firmament proclaims his handiwork.
²Day to day pours forth speech,
    and night to night declares knowledge.
³There is no speech, nor are there words;
    their voice is not heard;
⁴yet their voice goes out through all the earth,
    and their words to the end of the world.

In the heavens he has set a tent for the sun,
⁵which comes out like a bridegroom from his wedding canopy,
    and like a strong man runs its course with joy.
⁶Its rising is from the end of the heavens,
    and its circuit to the end of them;
    and nothing is hid from its heat.

⁷The law of the LORD is perfect,
    reviving the soul;
the decrees of the LORD are sure,
    making wise the simple;
⁸the precepts of the LORD are right,
    rejoicing the heart;

Theological Perspective

Psalm 19 is the meditation of a close observer of the world. The psalmist's observations are threefold, linked to the world and its patterns, the pervasive energy of the sun, and the encompassing perfection of God's law. The psalm concludes with the impact of these observations on the observer, specifically the prayer to be found "acceptable," blameless, worthy. The greatest portion of the psalm is devoted to the articulation of the observations themselves. The last four verses, however, confess humility and awe before the architectural splendor of natural and moral order that is accessible to humankind and yet, in its grandeur and comprehensiveness, all but unattainable. Beyond value, it commands a harmonic obedience to which the observer and all creation are bound. Such magnitude, beauty, and perfection can only inspire the psalmist's critical self-examination and hopeful prayer.

The first two sections of the psalm focus on the natural world. In the first six verses there is only one reference to God, to the glory of God as it is revealed in the world. The emphasis is instead on the glory itself. The heavens tell of it, the firmament proclaims it, the day speaks of it, the night declares it. The natural world resonates with testimony to the glory of God. The psalmist, however, acknowledges that all

Pastoral Perspective

The pastoral implications of what C. S. Lewis took to be "the greatest poem in the Psalter and one of the greatest lyrics in the world"[1] make Psalm 19 a worthwhile focus for preaching. A hybrid between a nature psalm (vv. 1–6) and a Torah psalm (vv. 7–14), the text as a whole juxtaposes creation's witness to God's glory with Scripture's revelation of God's will, thereby inviting worshipers to consider their attitudes toward both.

Nature's Call to Worship (vv. 1–6). If the whole realm of nature constantly proclaims God's glory in a continuous, ecstatic pouring forth of spiritual knowledge (v. 1), then what might be the spiritual ramifications of living sequestered from nature in office cubicles, in shopping malls, or in front of our home entertainment centers? The Westminster Shorter Catechism (Q. 1) states that "the chief end of man is to glorify God and enjoy God forever." If we are deliberate about spending time in nature, and if we belong to faith communities that retreat regularly to wilderness places where God's majesty can be neither ignored nor domesticated, perhaps our "chief end" will come to us more naturally.

1. C. S. Lewis, *Reflections on the Psalms* (London: Collins, 1958), 56.

the commandment of the Lord is clear,
  enlightening the eyes;
⁹the fear of the Lord is pure,
  enduring forever;
the ordinances of the Lord are true
  and righteous altogether.
¹⁰More to be desired are they than gold,
  even much fine gold;
sweeter also than honey,
  and drippings of the honeycomb.

¹¹Moreover by them is your servant warned;
  in keeping them there is great reward.
¹²But who can detect their errors?
  Clear me from hidden faults.
¹³Keep back your servant also from the insolent;
  do not let them have dominion over me.
Then I shall be blameless,
  and innocent of great transgression.

¹⁴Let the words of my mouth and the meditation of my heart
  be acceptable to you,
  O Lord, my rock and my redeemer.

Exegetical Perspective

With a spirit of wonder, awe, and deep reverence, the psalmist celebrates God's glory revealed through creation (vv. 1–6) and God's goodness made manifest through Torah (vv. 7–10). Then, with candor and humility, the psalmist addresses God directly (vv. 11–14), and closes with an expression of profound confidence, "O Lord, my rock and my redeemer" (v. 14c). Although the poem appears to be two psalms (vv. 1–6 and vv. 7–14), tradition had melded the material together into one glorious hymn of praise and proclamation. This psalm may have had its origin in the cultic tradition, and the two diverse topics may have been joined together for the purpose of public worship.

The psalmist opens the hymn to creation (vv. 1–6) with a song of praise being sung by the heavens, which are "telling the glory of God" (v. 1a). Joining in the joy is the firmament, which proclaims God's handiwork (v. 1b). Here "handiwork" refers to the constellations (cf. Ps. 8:3). For the psalmist, the starting point for portraying creator God is the cosmos—the universe—not the earth. Hence, with these initial images, personified as having human qualities, the psalmist invites the community of listeners to enter the world of marvel and imagination.

Homiletical Perspective

Jews and Christians have turned to the Psalter to shape their prayers for thousands of years. As a pastor, I try to encourage the people among whom I serve to explore the psalms as a pathway into biblical faith and toward deeper prayer lives. Therefore, as a preacher I try to remember that the lectionary offers four (and not just three) texts on which to preach each week. That said, however, I confess that I do not personally find it easy to preach on the psalms, and I suspect I am not alone.

The challenge for me is akin to the difference between attending a poetry reading and trying to teach a great poem. When teaching is done well, the community of learners is invited into an expansive world. But too often the poetry itself can take a back seat to didactic and pedantic prose *about* the poetry. I think of that great scene in the film *Dead Poets Society*, when the teacher, played by Robin Williams, urges his students to rip out the pages of the pompous essay on how to read poetry and instead encourages them simply to read the poetry. We do well to follow that advice by daring to enter into the more expansive world of the poet rather than reducing the poem to didactic "lessons."

The psalms have the potential to evoke the wonder and awe that the church in our day so desperately

Psalm 19

Theological Perspective

this testimony—though pervasive and enveloping—is in some way also imperceptible. Even as the entire world cries out, the psalmist tells us, unless one has ears to hear, it goes unheard. Silently the whole world testifies aloud, and the observer must give his or her attention to the natural world. Then even what is inanimate testifies.

The second section of the psalm (vv. 4b–6) builds on the comprehended and uncomprehended majesty of God. Without explicit mention of God's glory, the psalmist moves into a description of the sun that conveys the brilliance of its light and the power of its radiant heat, its pervasiveness and the inescapable certainty of its course. The glory of God is not always comprehended, but to miss it is not to be missed by it. Like the sun's illumination and its inexorable heat, nothing is exempt, nothing can hide, nothing can escape. Nevertheless, the image of the sun is not a negative one; rather, its rising is likened to the confident pleasure of the bridegroom emerging from the wedding canopy, an athlete reveling in the race. The allusion to God is that God is not only glorious, but as imposing, as magnificent, potent, and grand.

In the third section (vv. 7–10) the psalmist abruptly shifts to a discourse on torah, or the law of the Lord. As with the one who hears silent testimony, the reader must be attuned to make the connection between this section and the first two. In contrast to the first half of the psalm, here there are seven references to the Lord. A parallel is implicitly drawn between the role of the sun in the natural world and the law of the Lord in the human community. And yet torah is superior to natural law. Though the ubiquitous testimony of all creation pours forth freely for all who have ears to hear, it nevertheless requires interpretation. Torah alone is an adequate and explicit moral code; torah alone encompasses natural law yet exceeds it. For those who attend to it, torah revives the soul, confers wisdom, and grants us joy.

The law of the Lord, the psalmist declares, is perfect, sure, right, clear, enduring, true, and righteous altogether. Suggested within this litany is the all-encompassing nature of the law that restores the soul, imparts wisdom to the mind, gladdens the heart, and reveals the way to live. Instructing heart, mind, soul, and strength, torah is holistic in its effect. More than this, however, torah is supreme. The psalmist compares it favorably with honey and gold. Torah is attractive, precious, satisfying; sweeter than the sweetest substance, more valuable than the most valuable wealth. By the same token, departure

Pastoral Perspective

This is especially relevant to children's spiritual development. Early and ongoing positive exposure to nature benefits children intellectually, physically, and spiritually, says journalist Richard Louv, but such exposure is becoming increasingly rare. His book *Last Child in the Woods: Saving Our Children from Nature-Deficit Disorder*,[2] demonstrates how the sharp decrease in nature play among today's children is harming them, body and soul.

Nature's ongoing witness to God's glory constitutes a sacred text, inaudible to the human ear (v. 3), but somehow not entirely beyond human perception (vv. 2, 4). Human-induced climate change with its disruption of weather patterns, ocean life, animal and plant habitats, and whole ecosystems, desecrates this sacred text. The cosmic chorus is confused. Creation groans where it once praised. The magnificent poetry in verses 1–6, having served first as a call to worship, may upon further reflection constitute a call to action on behalf of the heavens, the firmament, and all that dwells below the skies.

Many Christian leaders report having had formative religious experiences in church camps as children and youth. A liturgy might include a Minute for Mission about outdoor ministry with reports or testimonials from campers. The hymn "God of the Sparrow, God of the Whale" follows the thematic structure of Psalm 19 and invites worshipers to give imaginative or artful voice to the natural world through a series of questions: "How does the creature say 'Awe'? How does the creature say 'Praise'?" A children's sermon might take a similar tack: if a mountain could speak, what would it say to God? How about a firefly? A whale? A star?

Psalm 19 is also a perfect text for introducing basic Christian theology to seekers who may consider themselves spiritual but not committed to the church or any particular faith tradition. Nature's testimony to God's glory (general revelation) is something seekers and practitioners of New Age spirituality can affirm. As glorious as this testimony may be, God has provided something even better and more useful to guide and direct human life: the revelation of his gracious will in the Scriptures (special revelation) and ultimately in Jesus Christ, the Word made flesh.

Torah's Call to Faithfulness (vv. 7–14). If nature speaks generally of the Creator's glory, the Scriptures speak specifically of a God of history who loves and

---

2. Richard Louv, *Last Child in the Woods: Saving Our Children from Nature-Deficit Disorder* (Chapel Hill, NC: Algonquin Books, 2005).

Exegetical Perspective

Verses 2–4a are ironic. The heavens and the firmament tell of God's glory and handiwork continually—"day to day" and "night to night." Their voice goes out "through all the earth" and their words "to the end of the world" (v. 4a), and yet "no speech," no "words," and no "voice" are heard (v. 3). The theology embedded in these two verses is profound. God's first word was creation; creation, in turn, is a powerful witness to God's silence. By its sheer "being-ness," creation makes known God's glory. Hence the revelation of God's glory happens not only through action but also through "being." Finally, the verb "pours forth" (v. 2) evokes a sense of fullness and richness. Creation is lush with the glory—the presence—of God.

In verses 4b–6, the psalmist uses vivid figurative language to highlight these verses' central image—the sun—which has a tent in the heavens, placed there by God. This tent imagery draws on an ancient mythical idea of the sun-god building an abode for himself. The psalmist's emphasis on God having placed the tent in the heavens displaces the mythic nature of the reference and gives clarity to Israel's theology, namely, that Israel's God is the sovereign One. The comparison of the sun to a bridegroom coming out from his wedding canopy sheds light on the wonderful effects that love can have on a person, causing a person's face to glow and even to radiate like the sun. The reference to the sun running its course with joy "like a strong man" (v. 5b) hints at the ancient cosmology and belief that dominated the thoughts of poets and scientists alike for centuries, namely, that the sun revolved around the earth.

The second half of the psalm focuses on torah (vv. 7–14). Here, torah pertains to instruction and does not refer to a set of obligations, stipulations, or laws to be obeyed. In praising the Law, the psalmist praises God who is revealed through the Law. For the psalmist, the Law is "perfect" and reflects who God is—perfection (v. 7). For the Jewish people, torah was a way of life based on love that found its expression in right relationship with God, self, and one another (cf. Deut. 6:1–9; 10:12–22). The decrees (v. 7b), precepts (v. 8a), commandment (v. 8b), and ordinances of the Lord (v. 9b) are the ways that can help one live out torah. Through a series of participial phrases, the psalmist makes clear that living according to God's instruction is delightful. These sentiments are accented by the use of a double simile in verse 10. Verse 7a parallels verse 9a. Just as the law of the Lord is perfect and revives the soul, so too the fear of the Lord is pure and endures forever.

Homiletical Perspective

needs. In our polarized world, imagination may well be the key to finding our way through rigid orthodoxies on both the left and the right by helping us to see the world through new eyes. If the preacher is willing to trust the poetry to cultivate imagination (rather than trying to "explain" it or make it fit into previously defined theological "orthodoxies"), then real transformation may result. When that happens, the assembled hearers of the Word become doers of that Word, and spiritual gifts are unleashed and claimed and used by God's people.

Martin Luther suggested that the Psalter "might well be called a little Bible," for "in it is comprehended most beautifully and briefly everything that is in the entire Bible."[1] Similarly, one could make the case that the Nineteenth Psalm could be called "a little Pentateuch," for in it is comprehended most beautifully and briefly everything from the first chapters of Genesis ("the heavens are telling the glory of God") to the Sinai experience that unfolds from Exodus to Deuteronomy ("the law of the Lord is perfect"). This expansiveness, however, also poses a challenge: the temptation to try to summarize the entire Pentateuch. What makes for great poetry, however, is not sweeping generalizations, but particularity. I think of Mary Oliver's poem "The Summer Day," where the poet doesn't simply ask, "Who made the grasshopper?" but, "Who made *this* grasshopper . . . the one who is eating sugar out of my hand?"[2]

Moreover, we Christians have perhaps come to a point where we can move beyond law and grace polarities in order to (re)discover that torah really does revive our souls, and is sweeter than honey. Perhaps one path toward recapturing this wisdom is in the practice of Sabbath keeping, which is not primarily about the list of things we are prohibited from doing one day a week but about the discipline of making time in our busy lives to be still and know that God is God, a time for loving both God and neighbor.

While all ground is holy ground, and God's handiwork can be discerned in all the world, most of us have specific places where God's presence is more palpable and obvious than others. There is a Celtic saying that heaven and earth are only three feet apart, but in those thin places where we glimpse the glory of God, that distance is even smaller. The

---

1. *Luther's Works*, vol. 25, *Word and Sacrament I*, ed. E. Theodore Bachmann (Philadelphia: Fortress Press, 1960), 254.
2. Mary Oliver, "The Summer Day," in *New and Selected Poems* (Boston: Beacon Press, 1992), 94.

Psalm 19

Theological Perspective

from the law is considered "great transgression" while keeping the law promises "great reward." As with the sun, there is nothing insignificant or optional about the law of the Lord.

In its final two sections (vv. 11–14), Psalm 19 asserts the human dilemma before the law. The law is perfect, but human beings are not. The law revives and enlightens; however, human beings resist and hide. Having glimpsed the power and beauty of God reflected in the natural world, and having testified to the completeness and goodness of God's law, the psalmist registers uneasiness and concern. The glory of the Lord is everywhere and yet we miss it. The law of the Lord is clear and yet we become lost. The ultimate power of the law will not be denied, and yet not even mere appreciation of it is the same as its fulfillment. The law of the Lord serves as a warning; still the psalmist laments that we do not perceive our own faults.

The psalmist turns directly to God in prayer and asks to become observant and responsive to God's law. The prayer includes both confession of sin and petition for guidance and reform. In verse 12, the psalmist recognizes not only intentional sin, but those faults we cannot see in ourselves. In verse 13, the psalmist further acknowledges the contagious nature of insolence and prays not to be drawn away from God by the lure of the arrogance, laziness, and contempt of the crowd.

Still, Psalm 19 is positive and hopeful. The psalmist quietly asserts that blamelessness and innocence are possible, and prays to become both inwardly and outwardly acceptable. The psalm concludes with a return to the parallels with which it began, as it ascribes to God a word from the natural order and a word from the law—"O Lord, my rock and my redeemer"—thus proclaiming again both the silent music of nature and spiritual harmony with God.

SUSAN B.W. JOHNSON

Pastoral Perspective

calls us, one by one, into the beloved community of the faithful. God reveals himself personally in the "torah"—usually translated "law" but signifying, in a larger sense, God's gracious will for humanity, which delights, inspires, and instructs those who take it to heart.

Faithfulness to the law (torah) is not a matter of social conformity through adherence to a set of rules. It is, rather, a way of being in the world that holds God dear. This way of being means that we rest in the presence of God, converse with God through meditative engagement with the Scriptures, and ultimately translate our faith into action.

Some in the congregation will have had prior experiences in churches where the Bible was used to control, manipulate, or shame. Acknowledging that this might be the case can assist those who are still healing from such experiences to embrace the Scriptures differently. Stories and examples that illustrate the positive, life-giving benefits of torah-centered living (vv. 7–9) can help achieve this transformation of perspective.

Indeed, earnest study of the Scriptures (torah) can be more profitable than "gold, sweeter also than honey" (v. 10). In Patricia Polacco's *The Bee Tree*, a group of villagers drop their chores to dash through the countryside pursuing a honeybee to its tree, where all enjoy a taste of honey. Afterward, a grandfather spoons a dollop onto the cover of a book and gives it to his granddaughter. "Taste," he whispers. "There is such sweetness inside of [a] book, too . . . adventure, knowledge, and wisdom. But these things do not come easily. You have to pursue them . . . through the pages of a book!"[3] Like honey, like gold, the wisdom of torah is worth every effort to obtain it.

Getting Personal. Much has been made of Psalm 19's theological shift from general to special revelation, but of equal significance is its linguistic shift from the third person to the first person (vv. 11–14). It is not enough to talk about God and leave it at that. We do not praise God as unbiased observers but as creatures who, in pondering the magnificence of our Creator, come to terms with who we are in the cosmos. The goodness, glory, and wisdom of God lend us our dignity as human beings and define our identity as grateful but imperfect servants (v. 12) who long for a right relationship with our Maker (v. 14) through torah living.

RUTH L. BOLING

3. Patricia Polacco, *The Bee Tree* (New York: Putnam & Grosset Group, 1993).

Exegetical Perspective

"Fear of the Lord" is synonymous to "love of the Lord." At the heart of torah is love of the Lord, a love that is life-sustaining (v. 7) and enduring for all time (v. 9).

The last part of the psalm features the psalmist talking directly to God (vv. 11–14). Having outlined the benefits of torah and a life lived accordingly, the poet acknowledges that the decrees, precepts, commandment, and ordinances of the Lord serve as a personal warning, and that there is great reward in keeping them (v. 11). The "reward" would include living securely on a fruitful land (Lev. 25:18–19; Deut. 11:13–17), long life (Deut. 11:8–9), and peace (Deut. 11:22–25). The phrase "your servant" is the self-identification of the psalmist, who, like Job, appears to be blameless and upright, fearing God and turning away from evil (v. 11; cf. Job 1:8). Although upright, the psalmist petitions God to blot out all his hidden faults, and to keep him from the insolent (vv. 12–13a). The psalmist desires God to straighten him out completely so that he can live and act righteously and justly, especially toward and among the insolent (v. 13b).

For the psalmist, outward and inward attunement to God and God's ways is of utmost importance. Mere adherence to the Law is insufficient. One's whole life needs to embody and become a living example of torah. The psalmist closes his song with a "dedicatory formula" (cf. Ps. 104:34; 119:108) that was originally spoken during the presentation of a sacrifice but that is now spoken at the close of a hymn (v. 14). Here, the psalmist offers a prayer and in essence offers himself to God as a sacrifice. The psalmist has given over his whole life to God, who is his "rock" and his "redeemer." The personal pronoun "my" preceding both of these nouns suggests that the psalmist has experienced God's protection and deliverance in the past. For the psalmist, creation and torah are both revelatory.

CAROL J. DEMPSEY, OP

Homiletical Perspective

preacher might do well to ponder for a bit where his or her own thin places are, not in search of the perfect sermon illustration, but as a way of entering into the world of this poet.

Two of my own thin places, where Sabbath rest and joyful contemplation of God's good creation come together, are the Outer Banks of North Carolina and a family cabin in southern Vermont. When three generations of my extended family gather in Duck, North Carolina, each July, we eat and rest and play together. It is a place where even old unresolved sibling rivalries seem to melt away; a place where cousins fly kites and ride their bikes and play in the surf together. The warmth of the sun (even when we are lathered in SPF 30) declares the glory of God in that place as the sun's daily journey across the sky ("like a strong man running his course with joy," v. 5) evokes a sense of awe and wonder.

Similarly, for almost fifty years my wife's family has gathered at a family cabin in the hills of southern Vermont where we can take in the breathtaking foliage each October and go cross-country skiing in the winter. Lovers gazing at the stars see compelling evidence of the One "who made the Pleiades and Orion, and turns deep darkness into the morning" (Amos 5:8). Those stars declare the glory of God: "there is no speech, nor are there words; . . . yet their voice goes out through all the earth."

So this psalm invites those of us who are privileged to preach not simply to speak about God's good gifts but to help those among whom we serve to encounter (or more likely remember) God's holiness, a holiness that can never be confined to the church. The wisdom of this particular psalm can be discovered in the seamless connections the poet makes between creation and torah; together they lead us to doxology and then send us back into the world that God has created and loved and redeemed.

RICHARD M. SIMPSON

James 3:1-12

¹Not many of you should become teachers, my brothers and sisters, for you know that we who teach will be judged with greater strictness. ²For all of us make many mistakes. Anyone who makes no mistakes in speaking is perfect, able to keep the whole body in check with a bridle. ³If we put bits into the mouths of horses to make them obey us, we guide their whole bodies. ⁴Or look at ships: though they are so large that it takes strong winds to drive them, yet they are guided by a very small rudder wherever the will of the pilot directs. ⁵So also the tongue is a small member, yet it boasts of great exploits.

How great a forest is set ablaze by a small fire! ⁶And the tongue is a fire. The tongue is placed among our members as a world of iniquity; it stains the whole body, sets on fire the cycle of nature, and is itself set on fire by hell. ⁷For every species of beast and bird, of reptile and sea creature, can be tamed and has been tamed by the human species, ⁸but no one can tame the tongue—a restless evil, full of deadly poison. ⁹With it we bless the Lord and Father, and with it we curse those who are made in the likeness of God. ¹⁰From the same mouth come blessing and cursing. My brothers and sisters, this ought not to be so. ¹¹Does a spring pour forth from the same opening both fresh and brackish water? ¹²Can a fig tree, my brothers and sisters, yield olives, or a grapevine figs? No more can salt water yield fresh.

Theological Perspective

The book of James is as theologically fascinating as it is exegetically frustrating. Indeed, one of the perpetual dangers its readers face is that its lack of clarity about, for example, author, location, audience, and literary style tempts readers to treat it as addressed uniquely to them. This temptation is exacerbated by its peculiarity as the lone book of Wisdom literature in the New Testament.

The temptation manifests itself in at least two ways. The first is to react against James, either by childishly rejecting it for so regularly speaking in the imperative ("You can't tell me what to do!") or by focusing on one or two offending passages and devaluing the whole of the book on that basis, à la Martin Luther's claim that James is an "epistle of straw." The second manifestation of this temptation is the inverse of the first: to pull out specific passages as particularly appropriate to one's (or, more likely, someone else's) context: provocative verses become invitations for superficial, pedantic, and context-free appropriation.

The irony in this temptation is that Wisdom literature calls its readers to avoid doing the very thing the temptation invites. Becoming wise means learning how to think carefully and act virtuously in complex situations where one is tempted to think simplistically and act recklessly. Or, said differently, one becomes

Pastoral Perspective

"Not many of you should become teachers, my brothers and sisters, for you know that we who teach will be judged with greater strictness" (v. 1). So begins this exhortation on the dangers that our speaking can generate. As I am one who teaches and who teaches others to teach, this passage gives me pause. Why are teachers judged more severely? Does being a teacher imply a closer relationship to God or a greater mastery over sin? Is it because our speech is more public than others or that it is invested with more authority? In this perspective we explore the nature of teaching as it relates to this passage, assigned in September, when the church is likely to be celebrating and recognizing those who have agreed to take up this calling for the year.

Who Is the Teacher? One tends to picture a teacher standing at a lectern, delivering an oration to a rapt audience of students. With such a picture of teaching, it is easy to attribute the need to control the tongue to a select few with graduate degrees and important titles. However, when we think about growing in faith, rather than being tested on a body of knowledge, teaching is much less clearly defined. Are our parents, who modeled their faith by attending church or reading Scripture, teachers? Are mentors, who guided us through claiming our

Exegetical Perspective

Martin Luther called James "a right strawy epistle" and is said to have quipped about 3:1 ("Not many of you should become teachers, my brothers and sisters, for you know that we who teach will be judged with greater strictness"), "Indeed you should have observed that yourself!" Because Luther thought James contradicted Paul's doctrine of justification by grace through faith, he even questioned its status as canonical,[1] and here questions the author's status as teacher.

The passage that caused Luther the most trouble, however (2:14–26, part of which was last week's Epistle lection), seems addressed to a situation in which someone teaches a distorted view of "faith" in the service of a callous and uncaring attitude toward the poor. Some interpreters have wondered whether or not the discourse on the tongue is addressed to some particular teacher who is responsible for disseminating that disruptive doctrine opposing faith and works, although the contingent situation of the letter of James is notoriously difficult to see. The accusation is quite general and could apply to any who speak from positions of authority. Surely this discussion of the power of speech to accomplish both good and ill should give pause to all who teach or preach.

1. Luke Timothy Johnson, "The Letter of James," in *The New Interpreter's Bible* (Nashville: Abingdon, 1998), 12:177.

Homiletical Perspective

Preachers wise enough to know that they preach chiefly to themselves will spend some time praying this passage before attempting to interpret it to their congregations. "Not many of you should become teachers," James says to those who aspire to speak while others listen, "for you know that we who teach will be judged with greater strictness." Whether judgment is by God, our congregants, or the world, James does not say, although most of us would testify that the judgment is not future but already under way.

Thus begins James's tight essay on right speech, one of the three marks of true religion that he lays out in 1:26–27. The other marks (both verbs) are "to care for orphans and widows in their distress" and "to keep oneself unstained by the world." Those who fail to substantiate speech with action are not only possessed of worthless religion (1:26); they also disembody the word of God, by peeling Christian speech away from Christian practice.

The act of speech *is* a Christian practice for James, made all the more important by his conviction that "the tongue is a fire" (v. 6a), capable of setting the whole cycle of nature ablaze. Preachers hoping to use this text to address problems caused by parish gossip may need to think again. For James, an unbridled tongue is not a local problem but

James 3:1-12

Theological Perspective

wise by learning to integrate one's thoughts, will, and actions to one's context in faithful ways.

In James 1:26–27, its author gives us an overview of what true wisdom will look like: taking care in how we speak, giving care to those in distress, and being careful about what we let into our lives. Designed less like a rational argument than a homiletical mural—as we might expect of any book that aims at promoting wisdom rather than knowledge—much of the rest of the book elaborates what becoming wise looks like.

Sounding as much like a contemporary philosopher as an ancient theologian, James places questions of language use at the intersection of thought, action, and context. Treat James 3:1–12 as a meditation on the power and dangers of language. He begins the passage with a self-reflective warning: those who teach are especially obligated to carefulness, because they train others in wisdom—which is to say, they teach others to think and use words virtuously. Since the wise know that everyone makes mistakes, those whose mistakes are most likely to be mimetically repeated are the ones who must be most careful. Given James's concerns about the dangers of forgetting who we are (1:23–25) and thereby speaking in double-minded ways (1:8; 4:8), the reflexive character of the first two verses of chapter 3 is both appropriate—even necessary—for him to write and important for those of us who teach and preach to remember.

What makes language so powerful? Or, to use James's phraseology, what makes it possible for a member of the body as small as the tongue to boast of such great exploits? James lays out two reasons for its power. First, language acts as a kind of representational catalyst: it is a small and even ephemeral thing that makes big things possible. Second, language can be a wild thing (wilder, even, than any animal species): it does great good and great harm and therein reveals how much it is caught up in the evil of human sinfulness.

For James, evil is not defined by consistently foul action but by its capricious movement between the fair and the foul. (Such a definition, incidentally, is all but mandated by an anthropology that recognizes humans as both made in God's image and capable of cursing others.) The combination of catalytic power and volatility makes fire a particularly appropriate image for James to use—and the fires of Gehenna (judgment; NRSV "hell," v. 6) an intensely appropriate image for the way double-tonguedness both reveals and reinforces double-mindedness.

Pastoral Perspective

baptismal promises, teachers? Is the woman whose house we build on a mission trip our teacher? Are the children who sing their faith in worship our teachers? Is it our small-group leader on a spiritual retreat? Are we the teachers as we live out our lives through our vocation? What should be evident from this series of questions is that we are all teachers and that we are all taught when it comes to faith, just by virtue of living a life of discipleship.

It is in those moments in which someone else is investing us with authority, however, that we are most closely judged. This means that teaching is a communal activity. It is not something we do in isolation. In the life of community it is natural that we should use our voices. Language was one of the first gifts God gave to the human. We were asked to name those whom God created. Already the first teacher is being given authority, and much is expected of this one. Already there is the potential to hurt with language, as well as to heal.

The Tongue as Blessing. The teacher uses the gift of language for blessing when giving praise to God. We praise God when we remember each other in prayer, when we lift our voices in song, when we affirm those who are learning. We bless God when we read the words of Scripture. Calling our children by name, welcoming a stranger, and speaking the truth in love are other ways that our tongues bless God. As teachers we do all these things as well as retaining and using the vocabulary of faith that is handed down in the church community and sharing testimony of God's working in the world.

One example of teaching as blessing may be confirmation or new member preparation. As we help others profess and claim the promises made at their baptisms, we are loosening their tongues in some ways, teaching them the vocabulary of the faith community, asking them to testify to God's working in their lives, and naming them before the congregation as full participants in the life of the church. As teachers and mentors, we bless the journey that has led them to this place and call them to greater maturity as they continue to grow in relationship to God. When our tongues bless, we praise the living God, but it is not always so.

The Tongue as Curse. The teacher does not always use the tongue for blessing. Sometimes we gossip, slander others, or disrespect those whom we teach. Perhaps we arrogantly present pat answers, leaving little room for questions. Sometimes we are so busy

Exegetical Perspective

The central section of the letter consists of three discourses: 2:1–13, against partiality; 2:14–26, on faith and works; and today's lection, 3:1–12, on the tongue. This third discourse picks up a note sounded at the beginning of the letter ("let everyone be quick to listen, slow to speak," 1:19), and James reprises his discussion of the power of speech to do harm or to heal in 4:11, where he exhorts the entire community ("brothers and sisters") not to "speak evil against one another." Here in chapter 3 he reflects specifically on the responsibility of teachers, who will be judged more strictly than their students. He uses traditional Jewish theology about the two sides of human nature, our dual capacities for righteousness and for wickedness, to think about the power of language. Both the "evil impulse" and the "good impulse" mark human beings, according to Jewish anthropology, and the righteous life is marked by one's holding the evil impulse in check so that the good impulse leads one to do justice. In the world of early Christianity, where multiple understandings of the faith compete with each other, teachers are powerful people, and their speech carries weight.

James's thinking about the tongue, this power of speech, echoes similar observations in other Jewish Wisdom literature:

> Honor and dishonor come from speaking, and the tongue of mortals may be their downfall. Do not be called double-tongued and do not lay traps with your tongue; for shame comes to the thief, and severe condemnation to the double-tongued. In great and small matters cause no harm, and do not become an enemy instead of a friend; for a bad name incurs shame and reproach; so it is with the double-tongued sinner. (Sir. 5:13–6:1)

> To watch over mouth and tongue is to keep out of trouble. The proud, haughty person, named "Scoffer," acts with arrogant pride. (Prov. 21:23–24)

"For all of us make many mistakes," James continues—not only teachers, all of us. "Anyone who makes no mistakes in speaking is perfect, able to keep the whole body in check with a bridle. If we put bits into the mouths of horses to make them obey us, we guide their whole bodies" (vv. 2–3). The teacher who speaks wisely—and correctly—enables his or her listeners also to be wise; one who errs, though, leads a whole community into error. Here we see not only the influence of Jewish tradition but also Hellenistic ethics. James's comparisons of the tongue to a horse's bridle and the rudder of a ship are commonplace among pagan moralists. The

Homiletical Perspective

"almost a cosmic force set on evil"[1] with full apocalyptic potential.

James is a wisdom writer, which means that he looks to the natural world for demonstrations of divine truth. There is no theological speculation here, no doctrinal exposition. Instead, James counts on real life to help him make his point, coming up with illustrations that will allow his listeners to judge for themselves the truth of what he says. Today's text yields at least seven: how bits work in the mouths of horses, how rudders work on ships, how small fires cause big fires, how humans tame wild animals, how no single spring pours forth two kinds of water, how fig trees do not produce olives, nor grapevines figs.

James's facility with such examples frees preachers to follow suit, either by matching James's examples to recent stories in the news or by coming up with examples of their own. James knew nothing of germ theory or nuclear fission, for instance, yet both of these provide further evidence of the ways in which small things can produce very large and dangerous results.

As preachers head into the substance of the sermon, they may approach the text through any one of several doors. The most obvious door opens on the harm done to congregations and communities by practitioners of loose speech. Call it tongue toxin. Since teachers are of special concern to James, this harm includes conflict between the teachers in a community, who may subtly or not so subtly seek to increase their own followings by casting doubt on the authority of others. Insofar as preachers are the tongues of their congregations, it also includes clergy whose poisonous caricatures of other clergy, congregations, people, or nations make it easier for their parishioners to do the same thing.

Speaking of the harm small things can do, there is nothing quite so devastating as a carefully placed interrogative. Here is how it works: after someone has praised another person in your presence, telling you how much that person's example of faith has meant, you cock an eyebrow and say, "Oh?" That is all it takes to introduce doubt. That is all it takes to lay a match to the dried twigs at the base of a redwood tree.

Another door into the text opens on the harm done by faithful speech that remains unrelated to faithful action. This is of central concern for James, for good reason. Even today, the most frequent

1. Luke Timothy Johnson, "Letter of James," in *The New Interpreter's Bible* (Nashville: Abingdon Press, 1998), 12:204.

James 3:1-12

Theological Perspective

James's warnings about language are all the more pressing at the beginning of the twenty-first century. As we move ever further into the information age, we also move ever further into the disinformation age. Error, miscommunication, deception, slander, and libel have become so common that we expect them from reputable sources and all but insist on them from sources we think of as disreputable. Always powerful, language now reaches farther faster. James's warning ought to be ever before us.

It is easy to read this section of James with trepidation and a sense of dourness. The warnings of judgment, the imminence of mistakes, the power of sin, and the dangers of corruption/impurity pile on top of each other so quickly that it is surprising James doesn't press his readers toward vows of silence. But such a reading, while not inaccurate, is incomplete. James 3:1–12 is absolutely exuberant in its use of language. There is a kind of joyous playfulness in what the author can do with language, whether through his use of wide-ranging sources (including a rather disparate variety of philosophical traditions and Old Testament allusions), his fertile metaphors (horses' bridles, ships' rudders, tongues as fire), or his subtle language games, including the playful double alliteration of verse 5—*micron melos estin kai megala auchei*: "a small member boasting of great exploits."

So even as James warns us of language's dangers, he uses language in deliberately provocative ways. What are we to do with this apparent incongruity? One answer would be to point to a degree of obliviousness—of double-mindedness—on the part of the writer. And certainly this may be so: we are often most critical of the very faults in others that also most deeply reside in us. But it is hard to imagine this is the whole of the answer to the question.

Perhaps this incongruity also points to a kind of grace in language, which, like all good things, is a gift from God and a means by which we more clearly become creatures created in the image of the One who gives us birth by the word of truth (1:17–18). Perhaps becoming wise means, at least in part, learning how to use language in ways that are both increasingly playful and increasingly pure, both admitting our many mistakes and resisting the many temptations to make them.

MARK DOUGLAS

Pastoral Perspective

propounding our own viewpoints that we forget to listen to others. Often we converse only with those who speak as we do and do not search out those on the margins. This is also the way of a learning community.

Dietrich Bonhoeffer had one rule for the community of his underground seminary students in Finkenwalde. It was that no one should speak about another student in his absence or tell that student if he did.[1] His former students recalled the many times they broke this rule and how they learned from their mistakes. Gossip damages the body of Christ. It inflicts self-doubt and shame on the community. The church is an even more diverse community of teachers and learners than the community of white male theology students found at Bonhoeffer's seminary. It contains people with different backgrounds, of many ages and temperaments. One could infer that avoiding the pitfalls of language would be even more difficult with the varieties of faith expressed within the congregation.

Silence. Should the teacher simply not speak then, if there is potential for abuse and harm? Is James advocating for a commitment to silence the tongue? One could come to this conclusion by reading verses 4–5 or verse 8 in isolation. In the larger context of James, it does not appear that silence or isolation is the answer. We are admonished to strive for control of speech, even though our experience would tell us that this is difficult. Teachers can lead the way to more authentic community by creating spaces where differences can be voiced and listened to. The classroom, broadly defined, can be space for creative resolution of tensions and discernment of the Holy Spirit.

If we dedicate our tongues to the language of God, our actions will follow. Our tongues, which bless and curse, can also ask for forgiveness. Teachers are not perfect, but must choose words carefully, because God has given us authority to build up the body of Christ.

KATHY L. DAWSON

---

1. Described by Eberhard Bethge, former student of Bonhoeffer, in *Dietrich Bonhoeffer: A Biography* (Minneapolis: Fortress Press, 2000), 428.

metaphor compares the teacher's tongue to the ship's rudder, which goes "where the impulse of the pilot desires" (my trans.). This again evokes the Jewish doctrine of the two impulses. It is not only the teacher's own righteous life but also the life of the community that is at stake here. Whether the teacher speaks love and praise to God or speaks falsehood, hatred, and curses shapes the community's actions.

James then compares the size of the tongue to its power to boast of "great exploits" (v. 5a). He apparently sees this boasting as perilous, since verse 5a provides a transition to verse 5b and the image of a destructive forest fire. A small spark can ignite a huge blaze, as can human speech. It is not human speech in general, but particularly boastful or arrogant speech that worries James, for the second half of the discourse builds on and expands the image of the forest fire.

"The tongue is a fire," he says, "a world of injustice" (v. 6, my trans.). The one who shows partiality to wealthy guests and dishonors poor ones (2:1–7) or who offers pious blessings to the poor and refuses to alleviate their suffering (2:14–17) does a world of damage. Damaging speech, James says, does three things: it stains the body, sets on fire the cycle of nature, and is itself set on fire by hell. This is a global, even cosmic indictment of wrong teaching. In no way would James affirm the classically American childhood rhyme, "Sticks and stones can break my bones, but words can never hurt me."

The discourse ends (vv. 7–12) with a summary that repeats both the difficulty of controlling speech and the necessity to do so. Although other animals can be domesticated, human speech resists being tamed. Its dual nature—due, of course, to the dual character of human nature—means it can address God with blessing and God's creation with a curse. The logical impossibility of this all-too-possible human experience causes James to wonder, "Does a spring pour forth from the same opening both fresh and brackish water? Can a fig tree, my brothers and sisters, yield olives, or a grapevine figs? No more can salt water yield fresh" (vv. 11–12).

E. ELIZABETH JOHNSON

reason given by those who steer clear of churches is the duplicity of Christians. Many of these people can tell you the exact details of how many times they have showed up at springs marked "Fresh Water" with cups in hand, only to end up with mouths full of salt water. You can remind them that no one is perfect. You can tell them that churches are made up of human beings, after all, and that there is always room for one more hypocrite. They still have a point. James knows they have a point. If God's word does not show up in the flesh of a congregation—if those who hear the word do not also incarnate the word—then the tongue has worked a wicked spell on them. "Why do you call me 'Lord, Lord,' and do not do what I tell you?" (Luke 6:46)

In this same vein, tongue toxin is at work when people of faith indulge in glib speech, making what is difficult sound easy, or what is mysterious sound plain. Churches worried sick about waning membership can sometimes make the gospel sound like the South Beach diet: try it and see how good it makes you feel. This is the language of the world, not the church. When James speaks of keeping oneself "unstained by the world" (1:27b), this may be one aspect of what he means.

The third door into the text is the most difficult one, but it remains an important one for those committed to the Christian practice of right speech. At this level, preachers will focus on James's cautions about the essential untrustworthiness of the human tongue. "For all of us make many mistakes" (v. 2a). Whether we mean to or not, we construct worlds with speech. Describing the world we see, we mistake it for the whole world. Making meaning of what we see, we conflate this with God's meaning. Then we behave according to the world we have constructed with our speech, even when that causes us to dismiss or harm those who construe the world differently.

The cure for all of these tongue toxins, James suggests, is the steady practice of faith. Preachers can find the details in the verses that precede and follow today's text, but they all come down to this: to love the neighbor as the self is the way of wisdom, in this world and the next.

BARBARA BROWN TAYLOR

Mark 8:27-38

[27]Jesus went on with his disciples to the villages of Caesarea Philippi; and on the way he asked his disciples, "Who do people say that I am?" [28]And they answered him, "John the Baptist; and others, Elijah; and still others, one of the prophets." [29]He asked them, "But who do you say that I am?" Peter answered him, "You are the Messiah."[30] And he sternly ordered them not to tell anyone about him.

[31]Then he began to teach them that the Son of Man must undergo great suffering, and be rejected by the elders, the chief priests, and the scribes, and be killed, and after three days rise again. [32]He said all this quite openly. And Peter took him aside and began to rebuke him. [33]But turning and looking at his disciples, he rebuked Peter and said, "Get behind me, Satan! For you are setting your mind not on divine things but on human things."

[34]He called the crowd with his disciples, and said to them, "If any want to become my followers, let them deny themselves and take up their cross and follow me. [35]For those who want to save their life will lose it, and those who lose their life for my sake, and for the sake of the gospel, will save it. [36]For what will it profit them to gain the whole world and forfeit their life? [37]Indeed, what can they give in return for their life? [38]Those who are ashamed of me and of my words in this adulterous and sinful generation, of them the Son of Man will also be ashamed when he comes in the glory of his Father with the holy angels."

Theological Perspective

This whole passage is scandalous. First, there is Peter's confession that Jesus is the Messiah, a title which Jesus promptly upends in a way that Peter never intended. Then there is the startling prediction of Jesus' suffering and death, which has prompted theologians ever since to try to decipher what it means to say that he "*must* undergo great suffering . . . and be killed" (v. 31). Finally, Jesus offers the bleak and cryptic call to discipleship as "losing one's life." After reading these verses, it is a marvel that anyone at all is left being a follower of Christ.

"Scandal" is a term that has been associated with the Christian gospel since Paul's first letter to the Corinthians (1 Cor. 1:23), and it gained popularity among Western theologians in the twentieth century. The gospel is scandalous because it offers the startling and inexplicable claim that this person Jesus of Nazareth is both a real human being and God incarnate. This has been called the "scandal of particularity," because it insists that God has been encountered in a Palestinian Jew in the first century CE. This challenges classical assumptions about God as "a Spirit, infinite, eternal and unchangeable, in his being, wisdom, power, holiness, justice, goodness, and truth."[1] When

1. Westminster Shorter Catechism, question 4, in *The Book of Confessions* (Louisville, KY: Office of the General Assembly, 1999), 175.

Pastoral Perspective

When strangers meet, there is a fairly standard ritual followed as they seek to get acquainted. It begins with the names, of course. Then follow the questions: Where do you live? Are you married and do you have a family? Where did you grow up? What is your job? Where did you go to school? What are your hobbies? A stranger turns into an acquaintance and we get a sense of who the other person is when we gain a context.

But if the relationship develops, there are other insights to be gained: the values that shape behavior and decisions; the vision of success that provides the sense of direction; the awareness of whether the other is trustworthy, whether the other has integrity, whether the other treats people with dignity and compassion. Thus an acquaintance turns into a friend. And with further experience, a friend may turn into a life companion.

But there are limits to how much we can know about another person. In everyone there are secrets of the heart that will not be revealed or that cannot be discerned. Even two people who have lived together in a wonderfully shared marriage for half a century and more will find there are surprises in the other, and ever new insights to be gained. It is the wonder of life in human community that people are

Exegetical Perspective

Questions of Identity and Lifestyle. The shadow of the war between the Jews and Rome (66–70 CE) loomed over Mark's community. Clearly Jesus, whom they confessed as Messiah, had not freed them from Roman oppression and domination. Who was he, then? What did it mean to be his followers? Today's Gospel reading comes at the midpoint of the Gospel that was the community's answer to those questions. Throughout the first half of the book, two narrative threads intertwine: growing affirmation of Jesus' gifts as a teacher and healer, on the one hand, and building tension between him and the religious authorities, on the other. Following this passage, Jesus and the disciples head for Jerusalem, in a journey that seems to move at an ever faster pace—a downhill run to its inevitable conclusion on the cross, with only the enigmatic empty tomb for solace.

This hinge passage of Mark's Gospel consists of three moments. The first, verses 27–29, puts on the table various titles by which his contemporaries might understand who Jesus is. The second, verses 30–33, presents the hard lesson about what lies ahead that Jesus has to teach the disciples and that the community has to understand. The final, verses 34–38 (and 9:1), spins out the implications for faithful followers of such a messiah.

Homiletical Perspective

Although we should be, no one is really shocked by Peter's confession or Jesus' description of the true meaning of being the Messiah. The domestication of Jesus as the Christ makes it hard to renew the shock of Peter's declaration and Jesus' teaching about the nature of the Messiah and the meaning of discipleship. Therefore, the text needs to be retold by the preacher in such a way as to bring up this truly meaningful twist. Jesus' open rebuke of Peter seems harsh to the contemporary listener, and the call to discipleship is, regardless of age, era, or context, a perennially disturbing text. Imagine the disciples' shock on hearing that the restored anointed one should suffer in the same way that Israel has. If the Messiah suffers in this same way, how can the Messiah restore Israel? And to add insult to injury, to serve this restored king means to suffer the same humiliation and torture as well.

After we come to claim Jesus as the Messiah promised to the Jews, we are forced to accept the radical and strange meaning of Jesus as this Messiah. Regardless of the possibility that years of Sunday school have properly indoctrinated us into the "right" answers about who Jesus is and the meaning of his life, the radical new meaning of being the Messiah found in this text is not what we inherently wish for or expect at a fundamental level as human

Mark 8:27-38

Theological Perspective

we affirm that Jesus Christ is this God in human flesh, it challenges any straightforward philosophical assertions about the nature of divinity.

A particular scandal is the claim we encounter in this passage: that this one who came as the great liberator, the Messiah, must suffer humiliation, torture, and death at the hands of religious and civil authorities. When Jesus asks the disciples, "Who do you say that I am?" and Peter declares, "You are the Messiah," Peter likely has in mind a political liberator who would free the people of Israel from tyranny. Yet as soon as Peter identifies him as Messiah, Jesus forbids him to speak about it and begins to describe the suffering that is to come to the "Son of Man." This utterly changes what is meant by "Messiah" or "Christ"—no longer a title of triumphant power, but a name associated with suffering, rejection, and public execution.

What does Jesus mean when he says, "the Son of Man *must* undergo great suffering" (v. 31)? In what sense are his suffering and death *necessary*? Anselm in *Cur Deus Homo* (ca. 1100) interpreted the cross as a necessity in order to resolve the tension between God's judgment and God's mercy. Because God is both just and merciful, the fall of humanity poses a conundrum: divine justice requires that the debt be repaid, but divine mercy drives God to reach out to sinful humanity. Jesus Christ, God incarnate, shows God's mercy in paying the debt, and his payment simultaneously fulfills divine justice. Because God's justice and God's mercy both had to be satisfied, Christ's suffering and death are necessary.

Many recent theologians, however, have objected to this understanding of the "necessity" of the cross for a number of reasons. First, some interpretations of Anselm (if not Anselm himself) suggest too sharp a divide between Father and Son, making Jesus Christ the one who obeys the will and endures the judgment of the Father. Second, this view posits a problematic tension between divine love and judgment as two warring impulses within the heart of God. Finally, and most pointed, Anselm's schema suggests that God is subject to some kind of external logical necessity beyond God's own desire.

An alternate way of interpreting Jesus' insistence that the Son of Man "*must* undergo great suffering" is that he needs to endure the depth of human pain in order to reconcile humanity with God. For Jesus Christ to bring full humanity into communion with God, he must bear the fullness of human experience, including suffering and death. As Gregory of Nazianzus said, "that which he has not assumed he

Pastoral Perspective

endlessly fascinating as they express in attitude and word and deed who they are.

In today's Scripture lesson, Mark pictures a scene that takes place some considerable time after Jesus and his disciples have begun their relationship with each other. Jesus begins this moment in their life together by asking the disciples what they have heard people say about him. People obviously have been talking about him, because the disciples have something to report. Then Jesus moves to the critical question: "But who do you say that I am?" Peter answers. From what he has come to know of Jesus, from what he has seen Jesus do, from what he has heard Jesus say, he affirms, "You are the Messiah." Jesus seems to accept this title that Peter uses.

On the basis of our relationship with Jesus, on the basis of what we have come to know of him in the biblical witness and in the life of the Christian community, we make our own assessment and judgment about who he is. There are many titles or descriptions that we can use. We too can call him Christ or Messiah. We can call him Lord, Savior, Master, Friend, Teacher, Prophet, Son of God, Redeemer, Exemplar.

But then in this exchange with Peter and the other disciples, Jesus says a rather strange thing: "he sternly ordered them not to tell anyone about him" (v. 30). Why not? Why not tell others about him? There may be reasons we do not understand why Jesus admonishes his disciples so strongly to keep quiet about him, but the subsequent conversation with Peter suggests at least one reason. It comes clear that when Peter calls him the Messiah, he may have the right title but the wrong understanding of what the title means for Jesus. When Jesus declares "quite openly" that he is going to suffer and be rejected and be killed, Peter does not want to hear that. One wonders if Peter even hears the last part of Jesus' statement, the part about rising after three days. Peter does not want to hear about a suffering Messiah. He apparently is looking for a Messiah who will establish God's rule with power and authority, and who will bring his followers glory and reward.

The experience of Peter serves as an alert for us. We can indeed use our experience of relating to other people as an analogy for how we can relate to Jesus, and we can express our understanding of who he is for us in various ways. But when we speak of Jesus and who he is for us, we need to do so with the humility and the reserve that comes from awareness that we may have the title right but may not fully understand its meaning. What does it mean for us if

Exegetical Perspective

Who Is This? (vv. 27–29). The story is set in the villages of Caesarea Philippi, a locus of the Roman colonial presence on the northern fringes of Galilee. The scene looks to us like a stopover on a political campaign, where the candidate and his entourage are checking on the results of their focus groups along the way. What are folks saying? Are they getting the message?

In Mark's Gospel, though, Jesus is not portrayed as marching forward on a campaign that has been clear from the beginning. The time of sorting in the wilderness following his baptism by John the Baptist (1:12–13) appears as the first step in a process during which Jesus himself is portrayed as clarifying his mission and realizing bit by bit the depth and breadth of its implications. In a culture where one's identity and vocation were defined by the community's perception rather than by an individual's existential discernment, the question "Who do people say that I am?" would have been an appropriate vehicle by which to identify the next steps in his ministry. In this case, the response places him clearly in the line of prophetic spokespersons anointed to bring God's word to the people.

Not That *Kind of Messiah! (vv. 30–33).* People familiar with Matthew's version of this story (Matt. 16:13–23) expect Peter to be praised for his clear confession of Jesus as Messiah. Instead, in Mark that confession is met first by a command to tell no one (v. 30), then by a harsh prediction of the future awaiting Jesus, and finally by an exchange of mutual rebukes by Peter and Jesus (vv. 32–33), ending with Jesus linking Peter to Satan! Something has clearly gone wrong!

The sticking point is the summary of the coming events of the passion in verse 31. This is the first of three "passion predictions" in Mark (8:31; 9:31; 10:33–34), each of which incorporates details of the account that will unfold in chapters 14–15: events of Jesus' arrest, prosecution, and punishment, and various groups of his opponents. The shared memory of those days had to have been painful and terrifying to the community of Jesus' followers. It might at least begin to move into perspective if the community could understand that Jesus went into those days fully aware of what lay ahead, not as a victim of imperial power schemes and incarnate evil. The detailed nature of the prediction suggests that the specifics of these verses may have taken shape with the clarity of hindsight. Those details, though, would surely have found a framework in Jesus' and

Homiletical Perspective

beings, given our fallen condition. But only when we have heard the true meaning of what it means to be the Messiah are we in a place to hear his call to us: follow me. Discipleship, therefore, is the necessary outcome of confessing *this* Jesus to be the Messiah.

After imaginatively reopening the crucial twist in the story for the congregation, the preacher can then pursue the really difficult and uncompromising teaching found in Christ's call to discipleship. This is not any mere analogue. Rather, in the reading of the sacred text among the gathered people of God and in its proclamation by a minister of the gospel, Jesus calls us again to the paradoxical task of discipline under his yoke. We are tempted to make some kind of flat-footed analogy between the narrative or imagery in a biblical text and our own situation, and this is often good to avoid. In the case of this lection, however, the analogy between the disciples and our own congregations, between Peter and one of us as disciples of Jesus, or between the crowds and the unchurched, may well be analogues of which we would like to take advantage. Indeed, the text may even demand that we do so.

Moreover, we can ask certain questions that may help this text do something explicit in the life of our particular congregations or communities. Are there those who would deny that Jesus is the Messiah, or simply relativize the radical meaning of following this Jesus? Does our community want a "softer" gospel? Would some like to see Jesus as blending in nicely with current political, economic, and social norms?

Or, worse, do we find the radical political, social, and economic ramifications of this kind of Messiah easy to smooth over into a "Gentle Jesus, meek and mild" who is unconcerned with such earthly matters? Are there some who are unable to see that, as radically political, social, and economic the ramifications of Jesus as Messiah might be, these flow out of and are defined by the greater world of the kingdom of God that Jesus ushers in, and not the other way round? Are there some who find the cost of discipleship a little too "cheap"? Or who see the call to discipleship as nothing more than a call to radical social reform, rather than a participation in the pattern of the suffering Messiah? The questions easily flow.

A sermon on this text could take many shapes. One could do a straightforward expositional-style sermon that takes in the sweep of the entire narrative: the confession of Peter—the rebuking of Peter—the call to discipleship. On the other hand, one could focus in on a certain point or "principle" that one would like the text to convey to the

Mark 8:27-38

Theological Perspective

has not healed."[2] According to this interpretation, Jesus' suffering and death are not an extrinsic necessity imposed from outside, but an intrinsic necessity, the outworking of God's decision to enter into and reclaim the whole of human existence.

No matter how we interpret the place of suffering in the atonement, this passage makes it clear that the title "Messiah" is being reinterpreted. This helps illumine why Jesus rebukes Peter, saying, "You are setting your mind not on divine things but on human things" (v. 33). Although this might suggest a strong dualism of divine and human worlds, it is better understood as a clash of understandings of what it means to be Messiah. According to human conceptions of "Messiah," suffering should be conquered rather than embraced, but according to "divine things," suffering and death are necessary to being God's anointed.

The final scandal in this passage is Jesus' call, "If any want to become my followers, let them deny themselves and take up their cross and follow me. For those who want to save their life will lose it, and those who lose their life for my sake, and for the sake of the gospel, will save it" (vv. 34–35). This introduces the tricky theme of self-denial, raising the question: what is the self that needs to be denied? While Calvin embraced self-denial as the summary of the Christian life, many feminist and other liberation theologians have questioned the usefulness of this language. For those whose selves have already been denied by systems of oppression and violence, is "self-denial" really good news? Contemporary preachers need to wrestle with this: in what sense are Christians called to "lose their lives"? What is the life that needs to be lost in order to be saved?

This scandalous passage addresses the question of what it means to confess that Jesus is Messiah. It suggests that "Messiah" is not a straightforward human title, but a mysterious name that means suffering and death, bearing the cross and losing life—so that life may in the end be saved.

MARTHA L. MOORE-KEISH

Pastoral Perspective

we call Jesus Savior? What does it mean for us if we call Jesus Son of God? What does it mean for us if we too call Jesus Messiah?

Jesus tells Peter that he is getting it wrong because "you are setting your mind not on divine things but on human things." Of course Peter is looking at things from a human perspective; he is a man, after all. How else can he look at things? How else can he understand Jesus except from a human perspective? We bring our humanity to our relationship with Jesus as well. We see him as one who will support our human wants and desires. We see him as one who will sustain the values we want to enhance. We see him as one who will enable us to become what we want to become.

But Jesus' word to Peter suggests that he can and must gain another perspective, that he can set his mind on "divine things." In our relationship with Jesus, there is the promise and the hope that somehow the divine perspective on who we are and what we are about breaks through. In him God enables us to find a way that is different from the way of the world, enables us to discern how life is fulfilled as God intends, enables us to live by values that are not embodied in the normal course of human affairs.

Jesus puts God's perspective in stark terms for Peter and for us. We are to deny ourselves and take up our cross and follow him into a life of serving and giving and sacrificing. Then the promise: "those who lose their life for my sake, and for the sake of the gospel, will save it."

HARRY B. ADAMS

---

2. Gregory of Nazianzus, "Epistle 101," in *Christology of the Later Fathers*, ed. Edward R. Hardy (Philadelphia: Westminster Press, 1954), 218.

Exegetical Perspective

the disciples' recognition that if Jesus continued on his path, powerful people would rise against him and his followers.

A Life of Paradoxes (vv. 34–38). The exchange between Peter and Jesus portrays the Gospel writer's acknowledgment that this suffering Messiah is not the one the disciples planned to follow. If that is hard to accept, the situation only gets worse when Mark begins to speak directly about the life of discipleship. Only a series of paradoxes can set forth the logic that defines both identity and lifestyle according to the gospel. The first paradox—that discipleship entails "denying oneself" and taking up one's cross—is found in both Mark and the additional source shared by Matthew and Luke (Matt. 16:24//Mark 8:34//Luke 9:23; Matt 10:38 and Luke 14:27). The second—that those who want to save their life will lose it, and those who lose their life for Jesus' sake will find it—is found in three of the sources of traditions about Jesus (Matt. 16:25//Mark 8:35//Luke 9:24; Matt. 10:39 and Luke 17:33; John 12:25). From the beginning, the community clearly recognized these teachings as fundamental to their life.

It is tempting to dilute these teachings into advice for a more disciplined life or for putting up with burdens or responsibilities. The language and the literary and historical contexts of the sayings in Mark do not support that temptation, however. "Themselves" is the direct object, not the indirect object, of the verb "deny" (as in, "deny something *to* oneself"). To deny oneself is to remove oneself from consideration, just as Peter would later do to Jesus (Mark 14:30, 66, 72). "Picking up one's cross" is not accepting just any burden, but rather being prepared to put one's life on the line for the sake of Jesus and the gospel. The disciples are indeed called to be prepared to share in the fate of the one they follow, and to recognize that it is there that true life is found.

SHARON H. RINGE

Homiletical Perspective

congregation. One could focus on one of the three major structural parts of this passage. So, for example, the preacher could focus on the continuing importance of confessing Jesus as the Christ today and in every age. Or the preacher could focus on the stark difference between what we would like Jesus and his being the Messiah to mean and the actual radical truth.

Finally, the preacher could focus on the existential, practical, and soteriological significance of Christ's calling us to be his disciples. And, of course, the imagination allows for all sorts of other ways of proclaiming this text. The pastoral and contextual issues of the preacher's congregation, recent events in the world or in the congregation and its community, and the preacher's own inspiration must contribute to deciding the best approach.

This text does not call, ultimately, for a carefully outlined sermon that would allow for a few good sermon notes to take home after church. This is a text that moves us far beyond information to commitment. This text demands from faithful readers a decision: will we follow this man to the place that he is going? It therefore demands that the preacher convey the reality and urgency of this decision in the life of the individual congregant and in the life of the congregation as a whole. That may well be a cross for the preacher to bear.

NATHAN G. JENNINGS

Proverbs 31:10-31

¹⁰A capable wife who can find?
   She is far more precious than jewels.
¹¹The heart of her husband trusts in her,
   and he will have no lack of gain.
¹²She does him good, and not harm,
   all the days of her life.
¹³She seeks wool and flax,
   and works with willing hands.
¹⁴She is like the ships of the merchant,
   she brings her food from far away.
¹⁵She rises while it is still night
   and provides food for her household
   and tasks for her servant-girls.
¹⁶She considers a field and buys it;
   with the fruit of her hands she plants a vineyard.
¹⁷She girds herself with strength,
   and makes her arms strong.
¹⁸She perceives that her merchandise is profitable.
   Her lamp does not go out at night.

Theological Perspective

"A capable wife who can find?" (Prov. 31:10a) Because this passage draws from the patriarchal assumptions of its home cultures, preaching it in the midst of the pitched gender politics of our age is like stomping through a minefield. Many in today's ideologically diverse audiences will claim it for their side of our culture war, or designate it enemy territory. Few will really hear its challenge to all, let alone accept it.

Despite its patriarchalism (31:15, 23, 28, and esp. 31), this passage portrays a marriage that is neither egalitarian nor inegalitarian. This is because it is not interested in comparing husband and wife to one another. Comparison, whether of equals or of unequals, implies a kind of opposition; but what characterizes the relationship here is mutual support. Generous and empowering, it flows from each to the other and overflows into blessings on the family, the marketplace, and the whole city.

Such support will take different forms in cultures with different gender roles. These roles may appear more egalitarian in some and more patriarchal or matriarchal in others; but whatever the specific forms and expectations a society has for its marriages, wisdom can transform them (31:26) as thoroughly as foolishness can ruin them.

Pastoral Perspective

While Proverbs seem to be marginalized in the Revised Common Lectionary and subsequently in pastoral practice, this text is the exception. While Psalm 23 is the most frequently chosen Old Testament passage for memorial services, Proverbs 31 is often chosen as well, particularly when the deceased is a woman, a grandmother, a mother, or a wife. Yet, like Psalm 23, this is a text for the living, and it should not be confined to memorial services or eulogies.

The writer of Proverbs speaks of the qualities of a capable wife, literally a woman "of strength." In these verses wisdom is personified in a woman of integrity, energy, industry, creativity, and compassion. The proverb concludes with a crowning description: "Charm is deceitful, and beauty is vain, but a woman who fears the LORD is to be praised" (Prov. 31:30).

This passage of Scripture contains both bad news and good news. This is a word that cuts two different ways, and it can be heard as judgment or affirmation. For many women who read this proverb, it seems like an overwhelming ideal, an impossible job description, almost a portrayal of a spiritual Martha Stewart: make your own clothes; get up in the middle of the night to get everyone else going; take care of the family business; work into the

¹⁹She puts her hands to the distaff,
  and her hands hold the spindle.
²⁰She opens her hand to the poor,
  and reaches out her hands to the needy.
²¹She is not afraid for her household when it snows,
  for all her household are clothed in crimson.
²²She makes herself coverings;
  her clothing is fine linen and purple.
²³Her husband is known in the city gates,
  taking his seat among the elders of the land.
²⁴She makes linen garments and sells them;
  she supplies the merchant with sashes.
²⁵Strength and dignity are her clothing,
  and she laughs at the time to come.
²⁶She opens her mouth with wisdom,
  and the teaching of kindness is on her tongue.
²⁷She looks well to the ways of her household,
  and does not eat the bread of idleness.
²⁸Her children rise up and call her happy;
  her husband too, and he praises her:
²⁹"Many women have done excellently,
  but you surpass them all."
³⁰Charm is deceitful, and beauty is vain,
  but a woman who fears the Lord is to be praised.
³¹Give her a share in the fruit of her hands,
  and let her works praise her in the city gates.

Exegetical Perspective

The wife in this poem certainly is "capable," as the NRSV translates its opening phrase. But the Hebrew carries a far stronger meaning. The woman is more literally a "strong woman," a "woman of worth," a "warriorlike woman." She is a mysterious figure who greatly rewards anyone who settles down to live in her household. The poem about her comes at the conclusion of Proverbs, and her behavior summarizes the virtues of wise living promulgated by the book and enjoyed by anyone who follows her call.

Proverbs 31:10–31 is an acrostic poem, arranged in alphabetical order, each line beginning with a letter of the Hebrew alphabet. The presence of the acrostic, combined with language repeated from earlier poems about personified wisdom, suggests that this woman is more than the average mortal. In the book's introduction (Prov. 1–9), Wisdom Woman calls out to the "simple." The "simple" refers to anyone who is not yet wise, that is, to everyone. She urges her listeners to obey her commands, to eat at her feast, and to choose her instead of the Stranger Woman, also known as Dame Folly. The book sets forth the choice between these two women, as if its readers, presumably young men, were selecting a life partner. The way of wisdom requires that much commitment. To choose Wisdom

Homiletical Perspective

In the church of my youth, a church that did not follow the liturgical calendar and paid no attention to the lectionary, Proverbs 31:10–31 was the Scripture of choice on Mother's Day. "A mother's work is hard," we were told as our pastor interpreted the Scripture. "The work God has given to mothers needs to respected by all, as it is respected in the Scripture," we were informed. "Those of you who are godly mothers deserve our praise," ran the sermon. "Those of us who were raised, those of us who are being raised, by mothers who labor long and hard on our behalf need to thank God and thank those women," we were reminded.

This was all fine and good and true. The problem was that the same church was firmly against women in the pulpit, women in public places of power, women who rejected the traditional roles of wife, mother, and subservient member of the community, and any mention of equal rights for women.

The way the text was used in my church is an example of the way preachers limit its bite by sentimentalizing it. If this text is only about remembering to say thank-you to mothers on Mother's Day or to pay fitting tribute to a "godly wife and mother" on her death, then the preacher is doing the text a disservice. By using this text only

Proverbs 31:10-31

Theological Perspective

An embodiment of wisdom, this wife's example has inspired women and men for generations. She rises early (v. 15), not because of her subordination but because of her determination. She helps her husband, not because he holds power over her but because her character is trustworthy and her work fruitful (vv. 11–12). Her business flourishes because of her initiative and creativity (vv. 13–14, 16). Her generosity is not coerced but reflects her kind heart for needy strangers (v. 20) as well as her own children (v. 21). She is energetic and strong because of her self-discipline (vv. 17–19). She is not an appendage or bondservant of her spouse but a true partner. She embodies the prosperous one this week's psalm extols (Ps. 1:3). Indeed, in a world tempted to acknowledge only a woman's charm and beauty as her own (v. 30) and grant only her husband public recognition and control over the family name and resources, her goodness compels all to respect and reward her (vv. 28–31).

In all these ways and more, her virtue shines through the confining social structures of her world and impresses the fear of the Lord upon all who know her, regardless of their stations in life. Along with Joseph, Moses, Elijah, Esther, Daniel, and many others, she is a type for the suffering Son of Man, servant of all, whose wise love overthrows the foolish tyranny of sin (Mark 9:30–37).

She is also a type for the Lord's bride. And here the question that haunts this whole passage—"Who can find?"—gains special figural significance. This woman inspires generations, but no one compares to her (v. 29). What people so fears the Lord that it abounds with all these qualities? What people is so trustworthy that the Lord can delegate authority so freely and confidently? God has not found one. It is not because of Israel's righteousness that God has chosen it (Deut. 9:5–7). Try as we might, we will find that we always fall short, whoever we are.

However, the Torah is not for *finding* the wise. Nor are the prophets, the Psalms, the Proverbs of Solomon son of David and king of Israel (Prov. 1:1), or the gospel of Jesus Christ the Son of God (Mark 1:1). These *make* wise, and mature in wisdom (Prov. 1:2–7). Through their good news God woos the unlovely and crowns the irresponsible (cf. 31:30), not tolerating our flaws but promising to abolish them. The commonwealth of Israel (Eph. 2:12) is "holy and without blemish" (Eph. 5:27) because Christ the holy one gave himself up for her (Eph. 2:13; 5:25–26). This passage describes Christ's head by nature, and Christ's body by grace.

Pastoral Perspective

night; and, oh yes, have something to give to those in need; always be strong and dignified, and have something profound to say; but also laugh a little; and, finally, do not take yourself so seriously. Your children will affirm you, your husband will appreciate you. And do all of this with a reverence for God.

Many women hear all of this and react with nervous laughter, or their response may be one of resistance, as if to say, "*That is not me.*" This proverb can be read as a confirmation of our culture's pressure to overfunction.

Yet there is also good news here. How a story (or a biblical book) concludes is never accidental, and it is significant that the Proverbs find their consummation in these words about wisdom. Further, it is not accidental that wisdom is portrayed as a woman. Embedded in these words are the values that sustain our lives, our minds, our bodies, our souls: trust and integrity in personal relationships, sacrifice, going the extra mile, providing for our children, opening our hands to the poor, doing whatever needs to be done—and yet doing it with a sense of humor, because, really, what is the alternative? Many pastors would note from experience that these are patterns of life found in the women who sustain local congregations.

Wisdom may be defined as a life well lived, a life that matters. Wisdom in the Bible is not enlightenment. Rather, wisdom is a lifetime of obedience to God, discipline honed in daily decisions. Wisdom in the Bible is never mere knowledge. In our culture, knowledge is a form of control, exercised for the benefit of the one in possession of learning acquired through privilege and maintained through credentialing. In Scripture, wisdom is a way of life that includes justice, righteousness, humility, compassion, and fairness.

How do we discover this wisdom? We see wisdom in other people, and as we consider this text, we reflect on the women of faith across our spiritual journeys, sensing how they are often used by God to teach us about wisdom. One thinks simply of Paul's letter to Timothy, with its remembrance of how Timothy's grandmother and mother took part in his spiritual formation (2 Tim. 1:5).

Pastors often have the honor of sitting with families of adult children when stories are shared about wisdom, about mothers (and fathers) whose activities do resemble the portrayal in Proverbs 31: a mother who encourages her daughter to finish college; a mother and father who leave the comfort of their retirement community to help their daughter, a single mother and widow, in the raising

Exegetical Perspective

Woman is to choose life. The husband is a stand-in for all her followers.

Of course, this assessment of the woman as personified Wisdom is only one possible interpretation. She may depict a rich woman drawn from the lives of real women in the ancient world.[1] In this case, the poem gives us a window into the lives of a few elite women. But wherever the portrait comes from, the poem conveys the benefits of anyone who chooses to become wise. The particulars of that choice are expressed in the collected sayings in chapters 10–30, comprised of many actions, and attitudes in the midst of daily life in community. These decisions flow from a full-fledged commitment, akin to the decision to choose a partner for life.

One benefit of living in Wisdom's household finds expression in the acrostic form. The orderly pattern of the alphabetic structure suggests a life of comprehensive harmony and a completeness of good things, extending from A to Z—more precisely, from ʾaleph to taw.

The poem opens with a question: "A strong woman who can find?" (31:1, my trans.), as if it is unthinkable that one might find such a woman. But besides commenting on her warriorlike character, the question indicates that life with Wisdom commences only with a diligent search. Wisdom needs to be sought, is not easily acquired, but once attained, she is "far more precious than jewels" (v. 10). Life with her is a life of devotion, of trust, and it will bring "no lack of gain" (v. 11) to her household.

As a poetic figure, the woman moves between the symbolic worlds of human wife and suprahuman dynamo. A summary sentence opens the list of further benefits available to Wisdom's followers. "She does him good, and not harm, all the days of her life" (v. 12). Active verbs show her to be a woman of power and action (vv. 12–22). She seeks, she works, she brings. She rises at night, provides food, and supervises her servants. She considers and buys a field, plants a vineyard, sells merchandise, spins clothing. And in works of justice typical of the wise person, she opens her hands to the poor, even while she provides good things for her household. She herself is dressed in strength and wears attire of royalty, fine clothing of purple linen.

A comment on the benefit of her actions for her husband interrupts the list (v. 23). Because he lives

1. Christine Roy Yoder, *Wisdom as a Woman of Substance: A Socioeconomic Reading of Proverbs 1–9 and 31:10–31* (Berlin and New York: Walter de Gruyter, 2001).

Homiletical Perspective

when it has a ceremonial function, we keep it safely away from the power structures of our churches and communities. By using it only when it comes time to "say something nice about women," we limit its clear message that the place of women is not apart, above, beneath, or outside the life and leadership of the community, but at its very center, at its very heart.

This text is not just for Mother's Day, memorial services, and women's retreats. It is for communities that are struggling to come to grips with the roles for women that justice demands, Scripture portrays, and God expects. This text is for those times when the preacher needs to say, "The women in our community have been put on pedestals but not accepted as peers; the woman in our church have been revered but not respected; the women in our culture need equal rights, equal pay, equal opportunity, equal status, and equal accountability." This text is a gift from the past that speaks to some very current situations.

Another caution is needed. An unintended message of this text is that for a woman to feel good about herself, to live up to God's expectation of her, she has to be a never resting, always striving overachiever. Can any woman, or any man for that matter, truly be the "good at everything they touch" person suggested by this text? Is the only pathway to self-esteem for women that of being industrious, wise, and respected household managers? Is the only pathway to a sense of self-worth that of being wonderful mothers, supportive wives, accomplished artisans, skilled household managers, successful business persons, wise teachers, prudent planners, and tireless workers?

Perhaps what the preacher needs to do is suggest that it is not likely that all these admirable traits, characteristics, and accomplishments will be found in one person, to suggest that what looks like the portrayal of a single wonder woman is actually a composite of some of the ways that women make a difference. Perhaps it will be truly good news for someone who has been beating herself up because she cannot be "all things to all people" to hear that this passage of Scripture simply lifts up some of the ways human beings can work together for the common good. Suggesting that this text calls for men and women to consider together what the tasks of a family, church, or community are, and to consider the ways they can share in those tasks together, might be a way for the preacher to say something that really needs to be heard.

Nurturing families can be stressful, lonely work. It is work not limited to one gender. It is work for

Proverbs 31:10-31

Theological Perspective

So we fools can show "who is wise and understanding" among us (Jas. 3:13) after all: by displaying wisdom "from above" (Jas. 3:17a). This woman's marvelous conduct (Jas. 3:17b) is heaven's gift of eschatological sanctification. Her virtues resemble the virtues in this week's epistle (cf. Jas. 3:17b). That makes a paradigmatic figure for missional apostolic witness in the world, "for it is God's will that by doing right you should silence the ignorance of the foolish" (1 Pet. 2:15). Christian family life, commercial life, and political life yield the kingdom's peace in both the tumultuous and broken fellowships that call on Christ's royal name (Prov. 31:28) and the tumultuous and broken cities that host them (v. 31).

As the kingdom's ambassadors, Wisdom's sisters and brothers face the uncomfortable theological task of contrasting Proverbs' vision of freedom through subversive obedience with both our culture's contemporary ethics of liberation through rebellion against injustice (whether begotten in the American Revolution or the French Revolution) and our contemporary ethics of peace through passivity under domination (whether in a rule of law or a cult of power). Some will want to exchange or confuse this woman's strength for rebellion. Others will want to exchange or confuse her obedience for passivity. Both groups will miss the dynamic of radical mutual empowerment by which her holy family thrives. Christ does not micromanage the church, but delegates dominical authority to his people by bequeathing the very Spirit who anointed him. The church does not possess its royal character as its own, but always respects its source and goal. The result is an order of mutual deference and trust with features of both classical patriarchalism and modern feminism, but neither one's totalizing ideology, preoccupation with power, and spirit of envy.

So this pressing theological task is also a precious gift to males and females, singles and spouses, feminists and patriarchalists and egalitarians. All need to trust that her family's glory is meant for all of us. "Resist the devil, and he will flee from you. . . . Humble yourselves before the Lord, and he will exalt you" (Jas. 4:7, 10).

TELFORD WORK

Pastoral Perspective

of children; a mother who works the third shift in order to be present for her children as they rise in the morning and as they return from school. Of course there are many women of wisdom who do not have biological children, and yet shape and form the lives of others. In our first pastorate, situated in a rural community with strong multigenerational families, my wife and I were blessed to know two women who adopted our youngest daughter as their own.

These brief experiences are suggestive of others that come to the pastor in the midst of congregational life. In conversation, in teaching, and in preaching, the pastor leads God's people in reflection on the purposes of life and those who give us life, acknowledging their sacrifices and standing amazed in the presence of those who hold every-thing together, embodying the ties that bind us. Surely at the heart of all of this is wisdom. At the beginning of Proverbs we read, "The fear of the LORD is the beginning of knowledge" (1:7). And at the conclusion of the book we read these words: "Charm is deceitful, and beauty is vain, but a woman who fears the LORD is to be praised" (31:30).

The reverence in this proverb is not for women. Women do not need to be placed on pedestals. The expectations there are exhausting, and the fall from grace is destructive. The reverence, the fear of the Lord, is for God. This is the beginning, or the better part of wisdom.

Wisdom is a quality that has less to do with charm or beauty, or whatever the current social constructions of charm or beauty are, and more to do with what the writer calls "fear of the LORD," which is the place that we all stand before God and which is also, Ellen Davis reminds us, "the deeply sane recognition that we are not God."[1] This is surely good news for women and men who seek after wisdom.

KENNETH H. CARTER JR.

---

1. Ellen F. Davis, *Getting to Know God: Rediscovering the Old Testament* (Cambridge: Cowley, 2001), 103.

Exegetical Perspective

with Wisdom, he prospers at the city gates, the public place of legal decision and commerce. Her labors for him set him among "the elders" with influence and leadership in the city. But the poem shifts its focus back to her (vv. 24–31). She beautifully clothes the members of her household, but her clothing is "strength and dignity." And, in a lovely proclamation of her trust in life, God, the future, and her preparations for it, she "laughs at the time to come."

Because Wisdom has provided for the needs of all, no tragedy can disturb the equanimity of her family. She speaks wisely and persistently "looks well to the ways of her household" (v. 27). Rather than the woman praising her family, her family praises her, thus reversing gender expectations of the ancient world. She surpasses other women because she embodies the right attitude at the heart of religion. In the code of the Wisdom literature, she "fears the LORD" (v. 30). To "fear the LORD" does not mean to live in abject worry but in awe, wonder, gratitude, and reverent humility before the Creator. It is to follow every good feature of true faith. The poem concludes with a summary line that takes praise of her and her works on behalf of her household into the public arena, revealed to all at the city gates.

This poem moves back and forth between the life of a wife and mother and the personification of the virtues that display wisdom, particularly as seen in the collected sayings of chapters 10 to 30 of Proverbs. The poem concludes the book of Proverbs, having selected a woman as the chief embodiment of wisdom, adding strength to the interpretation that she is Wisdom herself. At the very least, the poem invites all readers to search for wisdom as if for a precious stone, to live committed to the path of wisdom with the utter loyalty and allegiance of a person setting out in life with a beloved partner. She may not be God in this poem—a much debated point—but she works for her followers as if she were.

KATHLEEN M. O'CONNOR

Homiletical Perspective

women and men to take on together. Envisioning the future can be stressful, lonely work. It is work not limited to one gender. It is work for women and men to take on together. Making wise use of the resources available to us can be stressful, lonely work. It is work not limited to one gender. It is work for women and men to take on together. Caring for the hurting and broken of the world can be stressful, lonely work. It is work not limited to one gender. It is work for women and men to take on together.

This text not only praises women, but it presses us to think about partnerships between men and women in the work of the community. It presses us to consider the value of these partnerships; it presses us to ponder their lack. Indeed, this text is helpfully interpreted not as an eloquent hymn to a solitary individual, but as a sermon on interdependence, partnership, and the contours of community.

A hymn that might be paired with this text is "Lord, Whose Love in Humble Service." This hymn concludes with these words: "Called by worship to your service, forth in your dear name we go to the child, the youth, the aged, love in living deeds to show; hope and health, goodwill and comfort, counsel, aid and peace we give, that your servants, Lord, in freedom may your mercy know, and live."[1] Like the text, the hymn points us not to solitary labor, not to women's work or men's work, but to needed work that is best accomplished together, work that expresses faith, hope, and love in ways that build people up and bring people together.

H. JAMES HOPKINS

---

1. Albert F. Bayly, "Lord, Whose Love in Humble Service," © 1961, 1988, Oxford University Press.

Psalm 1

¹Happy are those
  who do not follow the advice of the wicked,
 or take the path that sinners tread,
  or sit in the seat of scoffers;
²but their delight is in the law of the LORD,
  and on his law they meditate day and night.
³They are like trees
  planted by streams of water,
 which yield their fruit in its season,
  and their leaves do not wither.
 In all that they do, they prosper.

⁴The wicked are not so,
  but are like chaff that the wind drives away.
⁵Therefore the wicked will not stand in the judgment,
  nor sinners in the congregation of the righteous;
⁶for the LORD watches over the way of the righteous,
  but the way of the wicked will perish.

Theological Perspective

Psalm 1 is a gentle and confident wisdom psalm in its own right, with its own shape, imagery, and meaning. It is also, however, the first psalm, and therefore a kind of introduction or preface to the entire collection of the book of Psalms. Everything that can be said about Psalm 1 serves at another level as a kind of primer also instructing the reader in how the rest of the book should be read. Book 1, Psalm 1 opens the Psalter with a benevolent word to the wise; Book 5, Psalm 150 concludes the Psalter on a note of joyous praise. The psalms in between range across the spectrum of human emotion, communal life, theological reflection, and spiritual inquiry. What binds the psalms together is outlined in the opening psalm. Fittingly, the very first verse of the opening psalm is a beatitude.

A beatitude, as the description of what it means to be happy or blessed, is at once both promise and counsel. "Happy are those who" is a formulaic meditation that promises happiness to anyone who heeds its advice. In this way, Wisdom literature is inherently laissez faire; the reader is free to accept and act upon the counsel of the wise, but also equally free to reject it. Psalm 1 promises happiness to the person who devotes himself or herself to the law of the Lord. As the Psalter's introduction, Psalm 1 begins with an elaborated beatitude that

Pastoral Perspective

A pastor working with marginalized Korean immigrants in New York City attempted to encourage his congregation by emphasizing the message that God would bless those who followed God. After a year or two he discovered that his church members were becoming disillusioned. They were in fact following, but they had not experienced any improvement in their lot in life, the circumstances of their daily living, their financial security, or their status in the community. What were they to make of this?

The problem with preaching Psalm 1 is that it reads like a false promise. Its dualistic worldview and theology of retributive justice do not square with reality. A sermon on this text must acknowledge what listeners already know: faithfulness to God does not guarantee prosperity, and wickedness often prevails.

A sermon on Psalm 1 probably needs the book of Job as an additional point of reference. While the disparity between one's faithfulness and one's fortunes is rarely as great as it is for Job in his trials, many experience more than their "fair share" of senseless suffering. Job's friends did not help the situation by suggesting that his sufferings were a sure sign that he had done something terrifically wicked. Interpreting Psalm 1 to mean that "the good life" is a sign of faithfulness, while misfortune befalls the

Exegetical Perspective

With creativity and simplicity, the poet of Psalm 1 sets up a contrast between the righteous and the wicked, and describes the two possible ways that people can live out their lives. As a preface to the entire Psalter, this psalm serves as a guide, and becomes an instruction on how to choose life or choose death (Deut. 30:19). Those who do not follow the way of the wicked will be blessed with life and prosperity, unlike the wicked, whose way will lead to naught (cf. Deut. 30:15–20).

Psalm 1 is a didactic poem. The "two ways" theme can be found elsewhere in the Bible, for example, in Jeremiah 17:5–8 in the OT and in Matthew 7:24–27 in the NT. The psalm reflects a new situation in Israel: no longer are all Israelites part of the congregation of the righteous (v. 5). Some people have gone astray, with the root cause probably being either idolatry or apostasy, or both. Forgetfulness or abandonment of God leads to forgetfulness or abandonment of God's ways (cf. Deut. 31:16–21; Isa. 1:1–20). The psalm can be divided into three sections: a description of those who are blessed because they are righteous (vv. 1–3); a description of the wicked and what is to be their lot (vv. 4–5); and a summary statement that pulls together the contrast between the two ways (v. 6).

The first section of the psalm opens with a beatitude (v. 1), signaled by the word "happy." The

Homiletical Perspective

Charles Wesley wrote "O for a Thousand Tongues to Sing" in 1739 to commemorate his conversion. For more than two centuries it has been the opening hymn in Methodist hymnals around the world, setting the tone for all that follows. One might even say that the entire hymnal is about the invitation to sing "my great Redeemer's praise" and the "triumphs of [God's] grace." Psalm 1 serves a similar purpose as the gateway to Israel's hymnal, the Psalter. It too sets the tone for all that follows. Old Testament scholar Walter Brueggemann suggests that this psalm "announces that the primary agenda for Israel's worship life is obedience, to order and conduct all of life in accordance with God's purpose and ordering of the creation. . . . [It] affirms that the well-oriented life fixed on torah expectations is one of happiness and well-being."[1]

The psalm's prominent placement represents both a challenge and an opportunity for the preacher. The challenge is to resist the temptation to try to preach the entire Psalter in one sermon. The opportunity is to see the Psalter itself in miniature through this particular psalm, and in so doing get to the heart of the matter of why we sing to God in the first place.

1. Walter Brueggemann, *The Message of the Psalms: A Theological Commentary* (Minneapolis: Augsburg, 1984), 38–39.

Psalm 1

Theological Perspective

impresses upon the reader a grounding in torah, the law of the Lord.

The book of Psalms begins with the tacit instruction to find one's delight in meditation upon the law. Although the word "law" in English suggests legislated prohibitions, torah is not merely a set of rules restricting the behavior of the people of God. For the people of Israel, torah was a description of life with God through stories and laws, a constructive design for life with God as presented through the story of God's relationship to God's people. Both proscription and prescription have a place in that story, but the story is about one's whole life: identity, personal relationships, ethical precepts, and the health of the wider community. The way to happiness is revealed, through torah, as willing and obedient relationship with God. Psalm 1 presents a contrast between two attitudes toward life with God: righteousness or wickedness. It is not a legalistic decision, but, for the psalmist, it is a binary choice. "Happy are those," the Scripture says, who do not follow the ways of wickedness, but set their hearts on life with God.

In the first two verses of the psalm, the "way" of the wicked is delineated. One should not follow the advice of the wicked; one should not take the path that sinners take, and one should not sit in the seat of scoffers. Psalm 1 appears to be about the company we keep. Indeed, it might almost seem that Jesus himself violated the sensibility of this wisdom psalm, eating and drinking with sinners, prostitutes, and tax collectors. However, we need to take a more careful look at the intent of this psalm. It does not condemn the people who surround us, or even the company we may invite to sit with us; it is about the way we allow their company to affect us. The righteous do not follow the advice of those who should not be advisors; the righteous do not take the path they already understand leads to destruction. The righteous do not comfort themselves with the perspectives of those who only express contempt and tear down. The steps into wickedness are, in some ways, incremental. Gently but persuasively, Psalm 1 is exposing not only two attitudes, but two incremental and yet slippery paths. The ideas, the projects, and the rationalizations of the wicked are to be avoided.

The second half of the psalm is devoted to the contrast between the righteous and the wicked. The righteous are compared with trees planted by streams of water. Just as the righteous meditate upon the law, the trees are fed by living streams. They bear good fruit in due season, their leaves do not wither,

Pastoral Perspective

wicked, would essentially offer a biblical justification for one of human nature's worst habits—blaming the victim—and should be avoided.

Since we know from human experience that God does not dole out good fortune in proportion to our goodness, or misfortune as a consequence of our misdeeds, how do we interpret this text? What kind of prosperity is promised to those whose "delight is in the law [torah] of the LORD" (v. 2)? Throughout the Old Testament, YHWH shows consistent concern for the physical well-being of God's people, so it would be a mistake simply to spiritualize the prosperity envisioned in Psalm 1. Those who delight in and meditate on the law (torah) know that theirs is a God who acts in history to save the oppressed and to establish justice. The image of trees planted by streams of water does not refer to the afterlife. Nor does it represent some sort of internalized, metaphysical groundedness that makes the trials and vicissitudes of this present life bearable, as if to say that the poor and the hungry are really okay because they prosper spiritually.

God is genuinely concerned about the way real people spend their precious God-given years on this earth. God cares. God provides. We can choose to take to heart God's gracious will for humanity and allow God to use us in the grand unfolding of God's opus. Or we can choose to live as if God were not actively caring and providing for God's people— which is to say, we can opt out. God's blessing belongs to those who opt in, centering their lives on God's law (torah).

Even if the external circumstances of day-to-day living leave much to be desired, the faithful can take heart—for God is at work even now, setting things right, and God is recruiting each of us to help "make it happen." When the poor and the marginalized delight in this aspect of God's revelation, they are empowered to act in ways that reject systemic oppression and bring into present reality the blessings hitherto denied.

Psalm 1 is most useful in pastoral situations where there are relatively clear choices to be made. Recovering addicts, for example, face such choices "24/7" as they struggle to live alcohol- or drug-free, or to go another day without gambling. The only healthy, and consequently the only faithful, choice for a recovering addict is to resist the addictive substance or behavior 100 percent of the time. The choice is clear, and there is no margin for error. Taking just one drink will, for the alcoholic, unleash patterns of behavior with unhappy consequences.

Exegetical Perspective

beatitude follows a typical pattern that begins with a congratulatory formula, followed by a word or clause that describes either a particular kind of character or conduct worthy of praise. The opening beatitudinal word "happy" occurs frequently in the Psalms (see, e.g., Pss. 2:12; 32:1f.; 33:12; 34:8; 40:4; 41:2; 65:4). The phrase also occurs in other wisdom poems (see, e.g., Prov. 3:13; 8:34; 20:7; 28:14; Job 5:17; Sir. 14:1f.).

Those whom the psalmist deems "happy" refrain from three kinds of behavior. First, they do not follow the advice of the wicked (v. 1ab). Those who are wicked have committed some sort of injustice and have been proven guilty in court. The wicked reject Torah, follow their own ways, and are excluded from the sanctuary by an order of a priest. Second, the righteous do not take the path of the sinners (v. 1ba). "Sinners" are those who have violated a specific commandment or prohibition; their deeds label them. Third, the righteous do not sit in the seat of scoffers (v. 1bb). "Scoffers" are those who typically mock God (Ps. 74:22). Scoffers are popular figures in Wisdom literature (see, e.g., Prov. 9:7–8; 13:1; 14:6; 15:12; 19:25; 21:11, 24; 22:10; 24:9) and also appear in the writings of the prophets (Isa. 28:14; 29:20). The righteous do not engage in negative activity.

Verse 2 begins with a *waw* conversive in Hebrew or, in English, with a coordinating conjunction "but" that signals not only a continuation of thought but also a contrast to what has been stated previously. Thus, verse 2 stands in stark contrast to verse 1. Verse 2 describes why the righteous are "happy": they delight in the law of the Lord (v. 2a) and meditate on it continually (v. 2b). Here the law of the Lord is "instruction" and refers to the whole body of tradition that reveals the ways of God. The law's core and central focus is love (see Deut. 6:1–9; 10:12–22). Those who are righteous are also reflective: they ponder unceasingly God's law—the ways of love—in order to embrace, embody, and live out Torah.

The efforts and choices of the righteous are not done or made in vain. In verse 3, the psalmist uses an extended simile to capture the beauty of the righteous, whose lives flourish because of their positive choices. The righteous are like fruitful, forever foliaged trees planted near nourishing streams of waters. The comparison of persons to trees is not uncommon in the OT (see, e.g., Jer. 11:19; Ezek. 17:5ff.). Full of life, the righteous are prosperous (v. 3c).

In verses 4–5, the psalmist shifts the picture dramatically, by not only introducing a description of the wicked but also introducing sinners. Both sets

Homiletical Perspective

The NRSV uses the word "happy" to begin this psalm, which is potentially problematic. It brings to mind Bobby McFerrin's song "Don't Worry, Be Happy," which can be a bit disconcerting. In our social and cultural context, happiness tends to be self-centered and self-absorbed, something we find by listening to Dr. Phil or browsing the self-help section in our local bookstore. The preacher needs to be aware of how easily this text can be manipulated into a proof text for a prosperity gospel that asserts that you too can be rich, successful, and happy (like a tree "planted by streams of water") *if you are counted among the righteous.*

The alternative translation that begins "blessed are they" may especially help Christian hearers who may remember Jesus delivering the Beatitudes in the Sermon on the Mount. In both this psalm and those Beatitudes, we come to a touchstone for what discipleship is all about. Either way, the preacher stands among God's people to speak truthful words about God's many blessings, while at the same time seeking to avoid the trap of being heard to preach the "be-happy-attitudes" of popular religion and culture.

A further challenge the preacher faces, even before she opens her mouth (especially among Christians well schooled in Luther and Calvin), is that it is difficult for Christians to *delight* in the Torah (verse 2). We have simply been too well trained to follow Paul's juxtaposition of law and grace. (Or is it Luther's reading of Paul?) If we hear "law" as a list of rules and prohibitions that cannot save us (but, rather, exists solely to convict us of our sin), then we will be unable to grasp the joy and gift that the psalmist perceives Torah to be.

One way to move toward a deeper appreciation of the psalmist's love for God's Teachings is to back up to the exodus narrative and to explore the move from slavery toward freedom. That journey, both in Israel's memory and in our own experience, does not happen overnight. It is a journey that sometimes seems to take a step forward and a half step back. Pharaoh's economy is ordered around the welfare of the powerful. Alternatively, Torah is given as a gift in the wilderness to a people called to order their welfare around God's abundant gifts, gifts that make neighborhoods possible. It is given as *Instruction* in order to shape a people after God's own heart. With Sabbath keeping as its fulcrum, Torah is summarized succinctly in both testaments: love God and love neighbor.

The poet's insight is that those who are oriented toward this wisdom find purpose and meaning in

Psalm 1

Theological Perspective

and even in a time of drought they are fertile and serene. The image is one of groundedness; the righteous are utterly secure in the law of the Lord. The wicked, according to verse 4, are not so. They are whipped up and tossed away like chaff in the wind. The wind blows and the wicked are easily disturbed. They are insubstantial and are effortlessly carried away.

The contrast between the righteous as fruitful trees and the wicked as useless chaff becomes the primary image of the psalm. The wicked are plainly short-lived; they do not abide. And yet, contrary to the forceful judgment that might be pronounced on the wicked from a prophetic perspective, this wisdom psalm allows us to see that the wicked have, in a sense, judged themselves. God does not actively seek to punish the wayward; in their waywardness they will punish themselves. The way of the righteous, we are told, is under God's protective watch; the wicked are haplessly on their own. Consistent with Wisdom literature, the book of Psalms places the self-condemnation of the wicked at the beginning. The psalms are not intent upon judgment but wise counsel and true consolation. Through the law, God grants the righteous substance and durability, while the wicked vanish from the face of the earth.

Finally, the psalm creates one more contrast: that of the individual and the group. This is lost in inclusive language versions, which sometimes necessarily blur singular and plural. In Psalm 1, God's law is a *personal* preference. The individual is formed by what he or she loves and reflects on continually. The crowd goes off in a direction determined by a gust of wind. But the one who delights in God's law endures.

SUSAN B.W. JOHNSON

Pastoral Perspective

Wickedness will have room to play through self-destructive behaviors that ensnare others in webs of deceit and distress. Staying clean and sober is the only choice that will allow a recovering addict to be blessed in all the wonderful and ordinary ways that God desires for God's beloved creatures.

Psalm 1 is less easily applied in complex situations where good and evil commingle and the law of unintended consequences is apt to play itself out. Corporate America's enslavement to the bottom line all but ensures that individual employees—from assembly-line workers to corner-office-holding executives—routinely compromise their core values just to get the job done. Similarly, those who work in government or the social services often find that they serve bureaucracies more than people in need of services. As consumers, we participate in a global economy that exploits the world's poor and pumps CO_2 into the atmosphere at rates that threaten to collapse the earth's ecosystem. We all participate in structures that perpetuate evil all the time. Choosing right paths is no simple matter. A prayer of confession can help to articulate this unsavory truth, laying the groundwork for further elaboration during the sermon.

Psalm 1 does not tell us what to do in any given situation, but it offers us a process in which we take our cues for living from our understanding of who God is and what God intends for human life on this planet. Delighting in God's word and meditating on it are dynamic processes that continually inform our choices, turning us toward the good and rooting us in pleasant places where God's grace and God's blessings are accessible.

A liturgy centered in this text might feature a meditative style of music, such as songs from the Taizé community, or lively, rhythmic music that conveys a feeling of "delight" in the law of the Lord. Consider offering a variation on the standard pastoral prayer that is more meditative in nature. Follow up the sermon with an invitation to join an adult Bible study group, or offer a class on the *lectio divina* method of Scripture reading. Since Psalm 1 is an introduction to the Psalter, the entire liturgy could make use of psalms, serving to reintroduce the Psalter as a prayer book and devotional guide for God's people.

RUTH L. BOLING

Exegetical Perspective

of characters contrast with the righteous. Unlike beautiful trees, the wicked are like chaff that the wind drives away (v. 4). The psalmist uses an effective simile from the agrarian world. At threshing time, a farmer scoops up the grain, lets it fall to the ground, and lets the wind blow the scraps—the chaff—away (cf. Job 21:18; Ps. 35:5; Isa. 17:13; Hos. 13:3). Unlike the righteous, the wicked are not nurtured or nourished; they are rootless, and their fate is to be scattered about by forces greater than themselves. In verse 5, the psalmist reminds his audience that the wicked will not stand "in the judgment," nor sinners "in the congregation of the righteous." The phrase "in the judgment" implies that the wicked do not have access to the act of sacral judgment; they cannot gain entrance to the judgment court. Sinners, because they will not have access to the congregation of the righteous, will not be able to praise God in the holy place (Pss. 111:1; 118:19, 20). Thus, through the use of two similes, the psalmist has made a distinction between the righteous and the wicked, has set up a sharp contrast between them, and has linked the first section of the poem (vv. 1–3) with the second section (vv. 4–6). This unity is accented by the image of the wicked and sinners in verse 1 that reappears in vv. 4–5.

In verse 6, the psalmist draws the poem to a close. Divine attentiveness is toward the way of the righteous, but not so for the way of the wicked which will perish. Of note, the psalmist stresses that the "way" of the wicked will perish, not the wicked themselves. The text hints at the transformative work of God that will, in the end, change all into goodness and godliness.

CAROL J. DEMPSEY, OP

Homiletical Perspective

their lives, and ultimately true happiness and blessing. This is not to suggest that there are guarantees in life or to rule out any sense of life's precariousness. Bad things can and do happen to God's people, and there are other songs within the Psalter that will need to be sung on those days. Those whose central icon is the cross know full well about those songs of loss and grief and trouble. But this poem encapsulates the wisdom that parents and grandparents of every generation want to teach their children and their children's children. It is wisdom around which we can orient our lives—even when we know that there will also be seasons of disorientation through which we will struggle.[2] The way we live our lives does matter, and a life lived in relationship with a good and loving God is a life that bears fruit.

I think of my grandmother, who in spite of financial struggles chose gratitude, and who in spite of great loss in her life chose hope over despair. Her choices did not negate the fact that life is not always fair. But her choice to see blessing and offer thanksgiving, even in the face of life's hardships, reminded all who knew her that whatever life brings can be an occasion for responding with thanksgiving and fidelity. One prayer puts it this way: "We thank you for setting us at tasks which demand our best efforts, and for leading us to accomplishments which satisfy and delight us. We thank you also for those disappointments and failures that lead us to acknowledge our dependence on you alone."[3]

So the community that gathers around this psalm knows that it is not the *last* word. But it is the *first* word, a word that invites the baptized community to orient their lives to the One who has come that we might have life, and have it abundantly.

RICHARD M. SIMPSON

2. See Brueggemann, *The Message of the Psalms,* for his distinction between psalms of orientation, disorientation, and new orientation.
3. *The Book of Common Prayer* (New York: Seabury Press, 1979), 836.

James 3:13-4:3, 7-8a

3:13Who is wise and understanding among you? Show by your good life that your works are done with gentleness born of wisdom. 14But if you have bitter envy and selfish ambition in your hearts, do not be boastful and false to the truth. 15Such wisdom does not come down from above, but is earthly, unspiritual, devilish. 16For where there is envy and selfish ambition, there will also be disorder and wickedness of every kind. 17But the wisdom from above is first pure, then peaceable, gentle, willing to yield, full of mercy and good fruits, without a trace of partiality or hypocrisy. 18And a harvest of righteousness is sown in peace for those who make peace.

4:1Those conflicts and disputes among you, where do they come from? Do they not come from your cravings that are at war within you? 2You want something and do not have it; so you commit murder. And you covet something and cannot obtain it; so you engage in disputes and conflicts. You do not have, because you do not ask. 3You ask and do not receive, because you ask wrongly, in order to spend what you get on your pleasures. . . . 7Submit yourselves therefore to God. Resist the devil, and he will flee from you. 8aDraw near to God, and he will draw near to you.

Theological Perspective

The church has regularly understood the book of James as a counterweight to the Pauline theological emphasis on faith apart from works, treating it as a book emphasizing the importance of works for revealing faith. While the relation between faith and works may be worth an argument, those arguing for the "works" side of things should not be too quick to turn to James. In spite of this (rather forced) reading of the latter half of James 2, the book as a whole isn't about works so much as about wisdom. And true wisdom, as discussed in the theological analysis of last week's text, is not about actions so much as the integration of thought, will, action, and context. Not faith *or* works; faith *and* works made coherent in wisdom.

So why is wisdom not more obvious? And what does wise living look like? These are the questions of James 3:13ff. James's answer to both questions is that there are two kinds of wisdom: earthly wisdom and wisdom that comes down from above—and the two kinds of wisdom oppose each other. To be clear: James does not describe earthly wisdom as some simulacrum or imitation of heavenly wisdom. It is a kind of wisdom that is self-absorbed and destructive. It is false but in the way that a lie is false.

The idea that there are contrasting wisdom traditions is characteristic of apocalyptic literature, including such varied New Testament texts as

Pastoral Perspective

This portion of James offers three questions for the Christian community: Who is wise and understanding among you? (Jas. 3:13a) From what do conflicts and disputes arise? (This is a paraphrase of Jas. 4:1) What does God want? (An interpretive question arising from Jas. 4:5 and lived out in Jas. 4:7–8a)[1] We will look at each of these questions in turn and give examples of how the answers to them might be lived out in the church.

Who Is Wise and Understanding among You? One might think that the answer to this question would be the clergy and church officers of the congregation. Isn't this how they attained their important offices within the life of the church? We would certainly hope that wisdom and maturity of faith would be criteria for such decisions, but this is not what James says. In this passage, James lifts up a number of markers of the evidence of God-given wisdom in the life of individuals. These include: gentle or humble (Jas. 3:13b NRSV and NIV), pure (3:17), peaceable (3:17), willing to yield (3:17), full of mercy (3:17), without a trace of partiality or

---

1. My inspiration for this structure arises from the commentary on this passage of Luke Timothy Johnson, in *New Interpreter's Bible* (Nashville: Abingdon, 1998), 12:209.

Exegetical Perspective

Although James is structured as a letter with a stereotyped salutation (1:1) and addresses itself to Christian "brothers and sisters" (1:2, 16, 19, etc.), it ends abruptly without closing greetings, and scholars have found it difficult to discern what particular ecclesiastical context may have elicited the writing. We know nothing of its author, its intended recipients, or their situation. There are no references to external events, and the traditional quality of the exhortations makes them appropriate any time from the second century BCE well into the Christian era.

Although much is sometimes made of the meager references to Jesus in James (only at 1:1 and 2:1), it is clearly a Christian work and addressed to believers. The literary genre is paraenesis, or moral exhortation. In James's 108 verses there are 54 imperatives, which may go a long way toward explaining the letter's lack of popularity in a church that generally does not like to be told what to do. Many interpreters have therefore looked to the content of James and seen that it has more in common with traditional Wisdom literature like Proverbs, Ecclesiastes, Sirach, and the Wisdom of Solomon than with the New Testament letters of Paul or Peter. At the outset, James exhorts his listeners to seek wisdom from God (1:5), much as Solomon prayed for wisdom (1 Kgs. 3:9–12; cf. also Wis. 7:7: "Therefore I prayed, and understanding was

Homiletical Perspective

As differently as James and Paul approach the good news of God in Christ, both prize peace. For Paul, "God is a God not of disorder but of peace" (1 Cor. 14:33). For James, "a harvest of righteousness is sown in peace for those who make peace" (3:18). In their letters, both of these early teachers scold their congregations for infighting, just as both beg their hearers to let God turn their enmity to unity. When James lists the attributes of divine wisdom in 3:17, he could be singing a duet with Paul, who offers a similar list for love in 1 Corinthians 13. However they get there, both of these saints arrive at the same proclamation: those who truly love God cannot fail to live in peace with one another.

If the James who wrote this letter is the same James who led the church in Jerusalem after his brother Jesus' death, then Luke gives us evidence that he practiced what he preached. When Paul and Barnabas came before the apostles and elders in Jerusalem to defend their unorthodox mission to the Gentiles, it was James who invented a way for that mission to continue (Acts 15:12–21). When Paul's ministry continued to provoke some believers in Jerusalem, James was among those who came up with a way for Paul to demonstrate his regard for Torah (Acts 21:17–26).

If the preacher of today's passage faces warring church factions, James faces more. If the preacher of

James 3:13-4:3, 7-8a

Theological Perspective

1 Corinthians 1–4, parts of John's Gospel, and Revelation. In these books, apocalyptic wisdom, as Christopher Rowland highlights, "is not an avoidance of what is there, a diverting opiate, but another way of perceiving. . . . [It is] the product of insight into the nature of things, which recognizes the contradictions and sees 'through' them to a more complete understanding."[1] The apocalyptic wisdom tradition assumes that some type of special revelation is needed in order to see the world as it truly is, namely, a site in which cosmic forces are at work.

Yet James is fascinating in its regard—or lack thereof—for those forces. On the one hand, he assumes such forces, both of good and evil. The text is peppered with comments about demons and the devil, as well as God's supremacy. On the other hand, his treatment of the forces of evil emphasizes their weakness and even their cowardice. "Resist the devil, and he will flee from you. Draw near to God, and he will draw near to you," James writes in 4:7b–8a. The forces of darkness are no threat to those who see with heavenly wisdom, and so James's call is not to engage in heroic battle against the forces of darkness. That battle is settled, at least for those of faith.

Instead, the conflicts we face are those that come from within us—from disordered and conflicting desires that, when they come into contact with the disordered desires of others, lead to disputes and conflicts. The true battle is for self-awareness, self-control, and enough self-mastery to know that we ought not take on the task of trying to be masters of our own fates. The battle, in short, is for heavenly wisdom.

And the fruits of this wisdom manifest themselves in both publicly visible and surprisingly mundane ways, given James's apocalyptic scope. Be "peaceable, gentle, willing to yield, full of mercy and good fruits, without a trace of partiality or hypocrisy," he writes in 3:17. Such virtues would likely benefit a small and embattled community surrounded by a larger society that is largely hostile to it, so James might be perceived as offering a kind of appeasement morality by highlighting them. However, it is hard to square such a reading with James's strong emphasis on purity. For James, these virtues flow out of the community's set-apartness and its concurrent tendency to isolate itself from

1. Christopher Rowland, "'Sweet Science Reigns': Divine and Human Wisdom in the Apocalyptic Tradition," in *Where Shall Wisdom Be Found? Wisdom in the Bible, the Church, and the Contemporary World*, ed. Stephen C. Barton (Edinburgh: T.&T. Clark, 1999), 61–62.

Pastoral Perspective

hypocrisy (3:17). Does this describe anyone that you know?

These are difficult traits to live into. They speak of a life that is not ego-driven, not grasping or envious. In a society that is centered on self-gratification, often at the expense of others, these words sound alien and countercultural. As you continue reading this pastoral perspective, envision members of your congregation who embody these traits. How do they live this out in their daily lives? What practices or habits help them to live into God's wisdom? Are there ways that what they are doing can be applied to the life you share in the church community?

From What Do Conflicts and Disputes Arise? Within any relationship, family, or community, there will be times of disagreement. James looks at these conflicts and sees at their core the attitude or sin of envy (3:16; 4:1–3). He may call it different things—selfish ambition (3:16), cravings (4:1), coveting (4:2)—but it really comes down to desiring what another has. James sees this as a sin that feeds on itself, craving ever more, asking for the wrong things, escalating in violence until the taking ends in death (4:2).

When we look at our society, we see this "earthly, unspiritual, devilish" wisdom all around us. Children desire brand-name clothing, because they see others who wear that clothing as popular and happy. Youth crave the latest in tech toys so they can communicate and promote the self 24-7. Adults look for the greatest car, house, and job that will promote the lifestyle that they believe will bring them fulfillment. Sometimes family members are objectified in this way, looking for the "best provider," "show wife," or the "genius children" as a measure of self-worth and achievement.

Marketing capitalizes on these attitudes. We are told via commercials that we can be happy if we just use a particular toothpaste or weight-loss remedy. We envy others who appear to embody or have what we want, making over ourselves and our homes in their images.

One of the most frightening commercials of the past year promotes a family vehicle. The father arrives with excitement, having just completed a tree house for his children. He finds his young sons playing cards in the vehicle. When the father invites the boys to come play in his creation, the boys respond with a series of questions, asking if the tree house has leather seats, a DVD player, and amazing speakers, among other things. Is this what the family relationship has become, simply a weighing of the attributes of different products?

Exegetical Perspective

given me; I called on God, and the spirit of wisdom came to me"). James returns in this Sunday's text to reflect on what God's wisdom accomplishes among those who ask for it.

The lectionary's editing of the passage is curious. Two more-or-less complete thought units (3:13–18 and 4:1–10) are linked by the language of peace in 3:18 and warfare in 4:1. Together they can be seen to constitute a single reflection on the function of divine wisdom in human experience, making peace and restraining violence. The omitted sentences in the middle of the lection lend it a much more somber tone, however, with their warnings against complicity in the world's wickedness and the promise of judgment:

> Adulterers! Do you not know that friendship with the world is enmity with God? Therefore whoever wishes to be a friend of the world becomes an enemy of God. Or do you suppose that it is for nothing that the scripture says, "God yearns jealously for the spirit that he has made to dwell in us"? But he gives all the more grace; therefore it says,
>
>   "God opposes the proud,
>   but gives grace to the humble." . . .
>
> Cleanse your hands, you sinners, and purify your hearts, you double-minded. Lament and mourn and weep. Let your laughter be turned into mourning and your joy into dejection. Humble yourselves before the Lord, and he will exalt you. (4:4–6, 8b–10)[1]

Whether preachers read the entire text or only its edited version, they owe the author some attention to the full passage. The image of friendship with God, for instance, as contrasted with friendship with the world (4:4), speaks directly to the character of wisdom. The Wisdom of Solomon says that wisdom "passes into holy souls and makes them friends of God" (7:27). So also, the exhortation to "draw near to God, and he will draw near to you" in James 4:8a fails to do justice to James's argument without the moral exhortation that follows it.

The connection between divine wisdom and human peace is familiar from the earlier Sirach 1:18,

1. Perhaps the lectionary hopes to avoid speculation about Jas. 4:5. The verse is notoriously difficult to translate, since "the spirit" may be either the subject or the object of the verb. Compare "Or do you think Scripture says without reason that the spirit he caused to live in us envies intensely?" (NIV) with "Or do you suppose that it is for nothing that the scripture says, 'God yearns jealously for the spirit that he has made to dwell in us'?" (NRSV). The words cannot be found anywhere in the Old Testament, although they may allude to passages that remind people that God longs for them or that urge people to long for God.

Homiletical Perspective

today's passage has had it up to here with church conflicts and disputes, James feels your pain. He is sick and tired of hearing what people think about faith in God. He is unimpressed by wisdom and understanding, at least the kind that people use to pound one another. The only wisdom that interests James is the wisdom from above, which has nothing to do with having good ideas and everything to do with living good lives.

The first choice the preacher has is whether to try and preach the same sermon that James preaches, or to tweak James's sermon by practicing a little more of the peacemaking that he commends. Preachers who exercise the first option will not have to scold their congregations; they can let James do that for them. Following James's basic outline and using some of his same basic techniques (leading questions, appeal to lived experience, accurate description of the consequences of human behavior), the preacher may construct a similar sermon, focusing on divisions that the congregation cannot fail to recognize.

In this case, the point is not to shame one's hearers but to name the existential fallout of "bitter envy and selfish ambition" in such a way that one's hearers feel the real sting of it. Since North American culture depends on active envy and ambition as heavily as it depends on fossil fuels, plenty of people find ways to deny the pain of this sting. Church can be one more place where this denial takes place, as believers strive against one another for first prize in faith. Or church can be one of the few places where people hear their envy and ambition exposed for what it really is ("earthly, unspiritual, devilish," 3:15), as well as for what it really does ("disputes and conflicts" 4:1), causing war within people and between them). Wisdom from above focuses on the needs of others, not on its own self-establishment.

The peculiar omissions from today's text rob James of his prophetic edge. If the lectionary had allowed him to cry, "Adulterers!" (4:4) then we might have cause to remember Ezekiel, Jeremiah, or Hosea. If it had allowed him to say, "Cleanse your hands, you sinners" (4:8b), then we might remember the opening verses of Isaiah, where God refuses to listen to the prayers of those whose hands are bloody (1:15). Still, the lectionary leaves the verses that address the murderous cravings (4:1) and quarrel-producing covetousness (4:2) that thrive in congregations, making Christian denial of these toxins more difficult. A sermon that aims no higher than

James 3:13-4:3, 7-8a

Theological Perspective

that society. These aren't principally the civic virtues necessary for living in a pluralistic society; they are the ecclesial virtues beneficial to living in the community of faith.

So understood, James's moral vision contains both irony and frustration for those of us who do not live in small, embattled Christian communities. The irony of James is that although heavenly wisdom requires enough special revelation actually to see the cosmic scope of what is going on around the community of faith, James's advice on how to live into that wisdom ends up emphasizing the type of ethic that general revelation of the sort that natural law—or one's mother—would provide: Be careful whom you spend time with. Watch your tongue. Be kind to others. This is not exactly earthshaking stuff.

But perhaps that is part of James's wisdom: that a distinctly Christian vision of the world does not remove us from addressing the commonplace obligations that come with everyday life. For James, being "heavenly wise" doesn't mean disconnecting ourselves from the routines of life as if we could sunder ourselves from matters that are now beneath us. Instead, it is recognizing that Christian wisdom expresses itself in the routine and mundane matters of living in but not of the world.

The frustration of James is that the author spends so little time in theological description. That is, neither this particular text nor the book as a whole spends much time actually doing theology in order to shape the church's ethics. Missing from the book is, for example, a focused Christology, an evangelical or missiological impetus, an eschatological attentiveness, or any discussion of the most significant theologically driven moral question of the whole New Testament: how much do Gentiles have to behave like Jews in order to be Christians? While James is about wisdom rather than a faith vs. works debate, it would be helpful to see him spend a bit more ink on the way faith is integrated into wisdom. And at a time when many in the Western church find it easier to preach on "Christian morality" than "Christian theology," the frustration of James can be a temptation of which to be wary.

MARK DOUGLAS

Pastoral Perspective

What Does God Want? In this part of the assigned readings we come to a break in the lection. The assigned text moves from 4:3, with its alarming description of earthly wisdom, directly to 4:7, which exhorts us to submit ourselves to God. This implies that we are to repent, turning away from this grasping lifestyle that leads to violence. But in this jump we lose the blessing of the third question, embedded in 4:5. The question as it is found in the NRSV asks us who will be our authority. God is yearning and searching for the human spirit that mirrors God's own image. Therefore, in choosing to draw near to God, we are throwing off the power that earthly wisdom has over us.

What then does life look like in the church community that lives by God's wisdom? Here are some of the marks of a wise church that this passage provokes:

— Church officers are chosen on the criteria of godly wisdom, rather than how much money they give to the church.
— Worship leadership is not just handled by the paid staff, but is shared among the church membership of all ages and stations.
— Disputes are handled with mercy and love, seeking peace above selfish ambition.
— Stewardship becomes not just a season of pledge collection, but a yearlong spiritual discipline taught and lived by the community.
— Prayer is not selfish, asking for what will feed individual desires, but seeks the good fruits that will meet the needs of all.
— Peacemaking and social-justice ministries become ways of addressing the earthly wisdom that surrounds us.
— Our primary identity is measured by our closeness to God rather than the possessions we accumulate.

The way that this last expression of Christian identity is enacted at the church I attend comes in the words used at every baptism. As the minister performs the baptism, he or she tells the congregation that the world will give us many messages about who we are to be, but our primary calling is as children of God, and we are to remind each other of this wisdom.

KATHY L. DAWSON

Exegetical Perspective

"The fear of the Lord is the crown of wisdom, making peace and perfect health to flourish," which echoes King Solomon's prayer for insight that he might rule the nation wisely and "discern between good and evil" (1 Kgs. 3:9). James exhorts the wise person to exhibit behavior that shows the "gentleness born of wisdom" (Jas. 3:13), a trait he earlier relates to believers' reception of God's word (1:21). Gentleness—or humility or considerateness, as the word is sometimes translated—marks those who know that God is the source of their wisdom rather than presume to have made themselves wise. Such divine wisdom is emphatically relational rather than individual in character, since its opposite is "bitter envy and selfish ambition," boasting and falsehood (3:14). Human envy and ambition result in "disorder and wickedness of every kind" (3:16), because they cause people to covet one another's goods and do violence to acquire them (4:1–3).

James then turns to another result of one's failing to ask for God's wisdom—the failure to be a friend of God. This equation of friendship with the world and enmity toward God (4:4) calls not for asceticism or renunciation of the world's created goodness, but instead seeks primary loyalty to God, whose righteousness is made accessible in God's wisdom. Second Temple Jews and Jewish Christians like James frequently connect wisdom and righteousness this way, because they see God's wisdom as embodied in God's law, the revelation of God's righteousness. One must choose to serve God or the world; no middle ground is possible. Only God's righteousness can make people righteous and ensure their harmonious life together. This understanding of God's law as God's wisdom is important for Christian preachers to bear in mind, particularly as we have been encouraged to draw such a deep distinction between "law" and "grace." James does not understand God's law as some kind of joyless prescription of behaviors whereby we might earn God's favor, but rather God's own gracious granting of divine wisdom to human beings.

E. ELIZABETH JOHNSON

Homiletical Perspective

calling the faithful to be nicer to one another will fall seriously short of James's mark.

Preachers who note that James's harsh tone does not match his call to peacemaking may decide to tweak his sermon, coming up with something more pacific. In this case, the preacher might compose a sermon that compares "wisdom from below" with "wisdom from above," hunting for instances of each in the local and global news, as well as in the lived experience of the congregation.

Whether the preacher focuses on how both kinds of wisdom function in the life of the individual believer or how they bang against each other in the life of the congregation, it is important to remember that for James, wisdom is not in the head but in the behavior. It is a way of life, not a way of thinking or believing. While theological dualism is the name of the game in this letter, preachers committed to a more unitive vision of life with God may avoid deepening the divide between "above" and 'below" by pointing out the ways in which God can work from either end.

Preachers may find support for their arguments in Scripture, just as James supports his argument by citing Proverbs 3:34 and alluding to the prophets. Luke's Magnificat provides one stunning comparison of two kinds of wisdom (daring preachers might even contrast the wisdom of the capable wife in today's reading from Proverbs 31 with the wisdom of Mary in Luke 1). The Beatitudes provide another obvious choice, along with today's reading from the Gospel according to Mark, which flips on its ear conventional wisdom about greatness.

Whichever option preachers choose, those who want to remain faithful to James's own theology will prepare sermons that center on God instead of Christ. James's letter is theocentric, not christocentric. Good Jew that he was, James did not build his argument on the mystery of his brother's death and resurrection but on the elemental faith in God that allowed his brother to live and die the way he did. In Jesus, wisdom from above met wisdom from below, so that everyone could see which one was which. In him, God's Word became flesh indeed.

BARBARA BROWN TAYLOR

Mark 9:30-37

³⁰They went on from there and passed through Galilee. He did not want anyone to know it; ³¹for he was teaching his disciples, saying to them, "The Son of Man is to be betrayed into human hands, and they will kill him, and three days after being killed, he will rise again." ³²But they did not understand what he was saying and were afraid to ask him.

³³Then they came to Capernaum; and when he was in the house he asked them, "What were you arguing about on the way?" ³⁴But they were silent, for on the way they had argued with one another who was the greatest. ³⁵He sat down, called the twelve, and said to them, "Whoever wants to be first must be last of all and servant of all." ³⁶Then he took a little child and put it among them; and taking it in his arms, he said to them, ³⁷"Whoever welcomes one such child in my name welcomes me, and whoever welcomes me welcomes not me but the one who sent me."

Theological Perspective

There are two distinct parts of this passage, each with its own set of theological issues. Both, however, raise questions of inclusion and exclusion: verses 30–32 *exclude* the disciples from others in Galilee; verses 33–37 *include* a child in the midst of the disciples. In addition, the first verses present another prediction of Jesus' suffering, death, and resurrection, raising the question, why is the scandal of the cross so difficult to understand?

In verses 30–31, Jesus passes through Galilee, and the Gospel writer pointedly says, "He did not want anyone to know it; for he was teaching his disciples." Though the passage does not explain Jesus' secrecy, it does suggest that some teachings are offered only to those who have a relationship with the teacher. Is the news of Christ's death and resurrection so shocking that it can be heard only by those within the community? Though the disciples do not understand, does this verse suggest that relationship with Christ precedes full announcement of his mission? This suggestion of boundaries between the disciples and other Galileans poses puzzling questions for contemporary practices of evangelism and Christian formation.

Privately, Jesus tells the disciples, "The Son of Man is to be betrayed into human hands, and they will kill him, and three days after being killed, he will

Pastoral Perspective

As the author of Ecclesiastes notes, there is "a time to keep silence and a time to speak" (Eccl. 3:7). There are many occasions when it is appropriate to speak: when we want to express an opinion on an important issue; when we want to deepen a relationship with another person; when we want to take our part in a social conversation; when we want to offer sympathy or encouragement or understanding to another. But there are times to keep silence: when we really do not know what to say about an issue; when we can vent nothing but destructive hatred; when we confront a mystery that is beyond our capacity to explain; when there is such pain that any word is shallow and only a loving presence can be offered.

But it is not always easy to know whether it is a time for silence or a time for speaking. Sometimes we talk too much and try to dominate a situation in which we should be more open to the views and needs of others; sometimes we are silent when we should speak out in opposition to injustice or evil. Sometime we speak when we do not really know what we are talking about; sometimes we hesitate when we could offer a word of comfort or support or insight.

As Mark describes the interaction between Jesus and his disciples in Mark 9:30–37, he indicates that twice the disciples were silent when they heard what Jesus was saying. Their silence is ambiguous. Their

Exegetical Perspective

Hard Teachings—Again! Today's Gospel lesson, like the previous one, addresses the Markan community's struggle to understand who Jesus is and what that means for their own lives. It presents another private tutorial session in which Jesus attempts to instruct the disciples. Like the session depicted in 8:31–38, this one has two parts. The first again forecasts Jesus' fate (9:30–32), and the second spins out consequences for the disciples' lifestyle (9:33–37). Together these teachings grant the premise underlying the disciples' confusion: the disciples' lives will mirror the one to whom they are committed. Instead of leaping immediately to examples of Jesus' glory and power as their models, however, they need to recognize that Jesus is first and foremost anointed to suffer at the hands of the world's powers. In accepting such a life contrary to the world's wisdom, they will share in the resurrection that is God's final word on Jesus' life.

A Second Try at Understanding the Future (vv. 30–31). Once again Jesus uses the enigmatic term "the Son of Man" to speak of the future. The Gospel writer clearly understands it as a title of Jesus, linking him with both the eschatological judge forecast in Daniel 7:13 (NRSV "human being") and the prophet who is given a task by God in Ezekiel (NRSV "mortal"; e.g., see Ezek. 2:1, 2, 6, 8). As the

Homiletical Perspective

This text follows immediately upon the narrative of the transfiguration and the exorcism of the demoniac boy, which, in turn, immediately follows upon Peter's confession and the call to discipleship. The crux of Mark's story has already occurred, and we are now on our way to Jerusalem, the cross, and the empty tomb. The real surprise inherent to the narrative itself comes when Jesus takes a small child and tells the disciples that in receiving such a one they receive him—and through him they receive "the one who sent me" (presumably, following the rule of faith, the Father). Given our domestication of Jesus, however, this often comes across to our congregation as another "cute" story about Jesus and little children.

Our sheer familiarity with Jesus and the narrative of the Gospel sometimes softens how radical Jesus' teaching about the nature and meaning of being the Messiah is. Even more so, our familiarity with a "gentle Jesus, meek and mild," makes any pericope of Jesus with little children very quickly turn into treacle, domesticating its radical gospel content. The problem, then, is in making this text something fresh for a congregation to hear.

A sermon on this text could find several shapes. One could focus on a certain point or "principle" that one would like the text to convey to the congregation, such as Jesus' attention to the

Mark 9:30-37

Theological Perspective

rise again" (v. 31). Once more Mark presents the scandal of the cross: Jesus' prediction of his impending suffering, death, and resurrection, and the disciples' inability to understand his words (cf. Mark 8:31ff.; 10:32–34). Why is it so difficult to understand and accept this teaching?

One way to answer this question is to assert a deep divide between human knowledge and divine revelation. This passage, in part, highlights the human difficulty in understanding the ways of God, because we are not God. "For my thoughts are not your thoughts, nor are your ways my ways, says the LORD" (Isa. 55:8). Human limits of knowledge and wisdom in this case simply make it impossible for the disciples to comprehend what God is doing in Christ's passion.

Another angle suggests that the disciples' failure to understand the scandal of the cross points not simply to natural difference between human knowledge and God's revelation, but to the deeply corrupting power of sin. John Calvin suggests this, marveling that the disciples cannot comprehend such a clear pronouncement from their teacher. Calvin laments, "So great is the influence of preconceived opinion, that it brings darkness over the mind in the midst of the clearest light."[1] The "veil of foolish imagination" darkens their vision so that they are unable to see the truth of the one who stands before them.

Yet Calvin's comments also suggest another way of reading this passage, one that focuses neither on God's radical otherness nor on the depth of human sin, but on the discontinuity between Israel's expectation of a Messiah and Jesus' way of being Messiah. In part, the disciples fail to understand Jesus' teaching because they have inherited a particular understanding of who the Anointed One was going to be, an understanding that did not include suffering and death. Jesus Christ as Messiah is utterly other than what they had come to expect. This raises a question long debated among Christian theologians: to what extent is Jesus Christ a *continuation* of the triune God's relationship with the children of Israel, and to what extent is God doing something startlingly *new* in Christ? The early church ruled out absolute discontinuity between the God of Hebrew Scriptures and the God of Jesus Christ when in 144 CE it declared Marcion a heretic. Marcion had taught that the God of Jesus Christ is a

1. John Calvin, *Commentary on the Harmony of the Gospels*, vol. 2. Calvin Translation Society, Comm. Matt. 17:22.

Pastoral Perspective

first silence comes after Jesus again tells his disciples that he is going to be betrayed, and killed, and raised from the dead. "But they did not understand what he was saying and were afraid to ask him" (v. 32). Why did the disciples not ask him to explain further? We can understand their hesitation if we discern that they had heard enough to get some idea of what he was talking about, but did not want to believe that he really meant what they were hearing. There are times when we are silent because we do not want to hear what we fear we might hear. It is easier to keep quiet, to pretend that we do not understand, than to ask and run the risk of hearing something we might not like.

Their second silence comes after Jesus asks them what they have been arguing about. This time the disciples seem to have been silent because they are ashamed to answer. "But they were silent, for on the way they had argued with one another who was the greatest" (v. 34). It is hard to imagine that the disciples had so little understanding of what Jesus had been saying to them that they were arguing about which of them was the greatest. It is hard to imagine that, at least, until we realize how often we would be silent if Jesus were to confront us and ask us what we have been talking and fretting about. Some of us spend a lot of time worrying about our status, trying to get the symbols of prestige, and seeking to maneuver so that we get the acclaim. Many of us would fall silent if we were asked to explain how what we are doing and saying accords with the way of life that Jesus sets before us.

On one occasion I was responsible for making the seating arrangements at a head table. At one end of the table a person with experience was placed next to a newcomer in order to make him feel welcome. When the experienced person saw his place card, he promptly picked it up and moved it to the center of the table, next to the person who would be presiding. It takes a certain amount of chutzpah to do such a thing, and the action reveals a profound need to be in a perceived status position.

It must have been difficult for the disciples when they realized that even if they were silent, Jesus somehow knew what they were talking about, as it is difficult for us to come to awareness that our lives are open before God. Jesus proceeds to speak a word to them and to us. "Whoever wants to be first must be last of all and servant of all" (v. 35). He illustrates what he is talking about as he takes a child, puts his arms around the child, and declares that in welcoming the weak and the helpless they will be welcoming him.

translations indicate, the term need not be a specific title, but may be understood simply to refer to a person, a human being (just as a "son of Israel" can mean an Israelite). It might even stand in popular speech as a third-person reference to the speaker. In the Gospels, only Jesus is said to use the term; no other character uses it to refer to him. The Gospel writers seem to assume that it refers to Jesus himself, but a specific equation of the two ("I am the Son of Man") is never found.

The wording in the NRSV of verse 31, that the Son of Man is to be "betrayed" into human hands, seems to invoke Judas's act of betrayal of Jesus, for which he is well known in the tradition. In fact, though, the word is usually translated more generally as "handed over" (e.g., in Mark 15:1, 10, and 15) or even "handed on" (1 Cor. 11:23). The prediction is thus simple: Jesus will be placed in human hands, and human beings will kill him. God, however, will pronounce a different verdict, and "three days after being killed, he will rise again." The disciples' inability to understand this teaching is a problem not of complex grammar or obscure vocabulary, but rather of a fate they can not fathom or accept.

Upside-Down Hospitality (vv. 33–37). The second part of the reading once again connects Jesus' fate to parallel and difficult consequences for the disciples' life. Jesus has caught them in an argument over who is the greatest. Competition for power, wealth, and prestige infected all of the cultures included in the Roman Empire (as it does the cultures of the modern world), and apparently the disciples shared in those values. Just as, paradoxically, for Jesus the Messiah resurrection would follow on a gruesome death inflicted by human forces, so also for the disciples the highest prestige would be found in service. The words translated in the NRSV of verse 35 as "servant" is *diakonos*. While that word came to refer to a person in ministry, in the Greek of Jesus' and Mark's day it meant someone who served meals. The person who was "servant of all" was the lowest in rank of all the servants—the one who would be allowed to eat only what was left after everyone else had eaten their fill.

The concluding verses of this section (vv. 36–37) are puzzling to modern readers of the English text. First, they seem to represent an abrupt change of subject from a "servant" to a "child." Mark's Greek-speaking audience would make the connection more easily, though, especially if we understand that they were principally hearers and not readers of the

vulnerable. One could do a straightforward expositional sermon that takes the sweep of the entire narrative: the disciples' confusion regarding Jesus' messianic teaching to the acceptance of a child as an example of discipleship. One could focus on one of the two major structural parts of this passage. So, for example, the preacher could focus on the continuing difficulty in understanding or accepting what it means to say that Jesus is the Messiah. Finally, the preacher could focus on the existential and practical meaning of accepting the One who sent Jesus by accepting a little child in Jesus' name.

The preacher has the burden of conveying to the congregation the radical spiritual calling of Jesus as Messiah. The congregation and the preacher will come with certain notions of Jesus as Messiah—often far cries from the Messiah of sacred text. Jesus the Messiah surprises us, sometimes beyond, sometimes against our own wishes for what a savior ought to be. But it is only upon accepting Jesus' teaching about his role as Messiah that we come to a place where we, as disciples, can be servants of all and receive a little child in Jesus' name. Servant leadership, therefore, is the necessary outcome of confessing this Jesus to be the Messiah.

This text has some obvious implications for the lives of Christian disciples trying to live in community with one another. This is one of many Gospel texts that show that leadership and authority among the Christian community is based upon service and humility. The disciples have trouble understanding Christ's teaching about being Messiah, and directly following this, he shows them that leadership in the community is like receiving a child. One obvious literal ramification of the text would be to ask, how does our congregation minister to children? Next would follow questions based upon the analogy of children to other people who are vulnerable or low in social status: the marginalized, the poor, other races.

Although it is good to avoid simple analogies between the imagery or narrative of a biblical text and our congregation, situation, or cultural context, in the case of this lection the text may demand that we explore the analogy between the disciples and our own congregation, or the little child and the children (or anyone on the margin) of our congregation or society. The preacher needs to help the congregation imaginatively engage the crucial teachings concerning the radical nature of being the Messiah on the one hand, and the radical teaching that flows from it—that among Jesus' disciples the first will be last.

Mark 9:30-37

Theological Perspective

God of love, while the God of the Old Testament was a God of law. The church judged that this sharp distinction was unfaithful to the teachings of Christ himself, who said, "I have come not to abolish [the law] but to fulfill" (Matt. 5:17). Yet Mark 9:30–32 suggests that there is real disjunction between the disciples' messianic expectation and the "new thing" being done in the cross and resurrection of Christ. This passage presents an opportunity to notice both continuity and discontinuity between the two testaments.

In verses 33–34, the disciples quarrel about who is the greatest, prompting Jesus to remind them to be "last of all and servant of all" (v. 35). Then, bringing a child into their midst, he says, "Whoever welcomes one such child in my name welcomes me" (v. 37).

What is the role of the child here? Is Jesus emphasizing helplessness and dependence, or humility, or lowly social status, or relation of child to parent (implied by Jesus' own relationship to God the Father)? Any of these interpretations is plausible. Certainly, children in that time were regarded as nonpersons, or not-yet-persons, possessions of the father in the household. For Jesus to hold up a child as an emblem of living in God's household, and as a stand-in for Jesus himself, was to offer serious challenge to social norms of the day.

Joyce Ann Mercer suggests that Jesus' treatment of children shows his "struggle and resistance to the purposes of empire." Imperial politics favors relationships of power and privilege, while the politics embodied here lifts up the lowly, those with no power or privilege. Jesus first calls the disciples to emulate the child, thus renouncing social status; he then calls them to welcome the child, to make space for those with no social status, since to do so is to welcome Jesus himself—and the One who sent him. According to this story, a child enables God to be known as one who overturns social hierarchies, welcoming the lowly into God's embrace. The "gift of children" is thus not only about the delight and wonder that children embody, but also about the way that children draw Jesus' followers into resisting all imperial powers of our time, struggling against all that opposes the "kin-dom of God."[2]

MARTHA L. MOORE-KEISH

Pastoral Perspective

Again we can note how difficult it was for the disciples, as for us, to grasp what Jesus was saying to them. In this passage he tells them that if they want to live in the way of one who gives his life for others, they will identify with the children and welcome them, for they are in need of love and protection. In the very next chapter of Mark, people were bringing children to Jesus, and the disciples spoke sternly to them and tried to turn them away. And Jesus "was indignant" (10:14).

Finally it can be noted that the word of Jesus— that those who would be first must be last, that those who would find status before God will do so as they serve the needy—comes as a liberating word rather than an onerous demand. There was a pathos about the man who was so concerned about where he sat at the head table that he would take it upon himself to change the place cards. It is sad for a person to be so consumed with what others think about him, to be so insecure in who he is that he must seek public recognition of his importance. We are truly significant when we welcome Jesus in the child who finds comfort and aid and security in the arms in which we enfold her.

HARRY B. ADAMS

---

2. Joyce Ann Mercer, *Welcoming Children: A Practical Theology of Childhood* (St. Louis: Chalice Press, 2005), 50–52, 54.

Exegetical Perspective

Gospel. They would have made that connection in the first place on the basis of vocabulary, because the word used here for "little child" (*paidion*) is closely related to another word for "servant" (*pais,* whose inflected forms also contain a "d" sound).

In the second place, that connection would have been recognized as more than one of vocabulary, because Mark's audience would have heard the word "child" as referring to someone like the servant who served meals to everyone else in the household, in that both were seen as without "honor" or high social standing. A child did not contribute much if anything to the economic value of a household or community, and a child could not do anything to enhance one's position in the struggles for prestige or influence. One would obtain no benefit from according to a child the hospitality or rituals of honor or respect that one might offer to someone of higher status or someone whose favor one wanted to curry. Children and servants were of equally low social status.

Against this background, both the coherence of this section of the Gospel and the offensiveness of Jesus' teaching becomes clear. Not only is Jesus himself said to honor and welcome a mere child (v. 36), but the saying in verse 37 equates one's welcome of such a child with welcoming Jesus himself—and even more, with welcoming the God who sent him. This passage, then, is far from a saccharine scene in which Jesus cuddles sweet little children and welcomes them to Sunday school, as it is often misrepresented. Instead, it is a powerful and even shocking depiction of the paradoxical values of God's will and reign, which confront the dominant values of human societies and assign worth and importance to every person.

SHARON H. RINGE

Homiletical Perspective

One thing that may be difficult for a congregation today is the way in which the disciples are afraid to ask Jesus to explain what he means by his obscure messianic teaching (v. 32) and their being afraid to tell them what they were talking about (v. 34). Why does our Jesus "meek and mild" berate his disciples so much that they simply become afraid to be open with him anymore? Even without our contemporary domestication of Jesus, these texts are stern. In discussing this aspect of the text, we hit upon something that is not merely analogical: as disciples of Jesus, are we not also afraid to engage Jesus' radical messianic teaching? Are we not also afraid to admit to him the posturing and power struggles that we have among one another as his disciples?

This text does not call for a simple Sunday homily where people feel sentimental thoughts about the innocence of childhood—if there really is any such thing. How are the various leaders of the congregation getting along with one another and with the people whom they are leading? What is their mode of leadership and their approach to decision making? When we consider the transition in the text from Jesus' teaching about himself as Messiah to Jesus' teaching about the community of his disciples, these questions simply follow. And, if we follow the rule of faith in our interpretation, then reading the community of disciples as nothing less than the body of this radical Messiah deepens this important connection.

This text, therefore, demands decision: are we willing to accept the kind of authority that this Messiah is willing to give to us? The text demands that the preacher convey the reality and urgency of this decision in the life of the leaders of the congregation and in the life of the congregation as a whole as it serves in positions of leadership in the world. Radical servant leadership is not just for the church; it is also the witness of the church to the world.

NATHAN G. JENNINGS

Esther 7:1-6, 9-10; 9:20-22

⁷:¹So the king and Haman went in to feast with Queen Esther. ²On the second day, as they were drinking wine, the king again said to Esther, "What is your petition, Queen Esther? It shall be granted you. And what is your request? Even to the half of my kingdom, it shall be fulfilled." ³Then Queen Esther answered, "If I have won your favor, O king, and if it pleases the king, let my life be given me—that is my petition—and the lives of my people—that is my request. ⁴For we have been sold, I and my people, to be destroyed, to be killed, and to be annihilated. If we had been sold merely as slaves, men and women, I would have held my peace; but no enemy can compensate for this damage to the king." ⁵Then King Ahasuerus said to Queen Esther, "Who is he, and where is he, who has presumed to do this?" ⁶Esther said, "A foe and enemy, this wicked Haman!" Then Haman was terrified before the king and the queen. . . . ⁹Then Harbona, one of the eunuchs in attendance on the king, said, "Look, the very

Theological Perspective

The house of Xerxes (Ahasuerus) is not the righteous family of last week's reading (Prov. 31:10–31). The concupiscent king prizes only Queen Vashti's fleeting beauty and charm (Esth. 1:10–11, cf. Prov. 31:30), and her rebellion sets back not only her own cause but women's freedoms throughout Persia (Esth. 1:12–21, cf. Prov. 31:31). Royal intrigue and ethnic pride lead to murderous plots (2:21–23) and counterplots (3:2–6), with Israel's life finally hanging in the balance.

Can a good woman find a fruitful place in this depraved, conniving, and confining world?

Indeed she can. We first meet Esther as an orphaned cousin of an exiled people in a far-flung province of a shaken empire, when she is snatched away from her former life to be a pagan emperor's sexual plaything. A beautiful woman in a man's world, she rises in royal favor, becomes queen, and saves the king's life (Esth. 2:15–23). This week's passage relates the turning point in her reign. She maneuvers through treacherous court rules and fortuitous circumstances to eliminate a mortal threat to her own people (7:3–6). She shows extraordinary courage in identifying with her doomed people and fingering the king's edict and his viceroy Haman (7:3–6). By story's end she is "Queen Esther, daughter of Abihail" (9:29–32), as proudly Jewish as

Pastoral Perspective

The book of Esther is an enigma. For Christians it is little known among the biblical books, and yet Esther serves as the narrative source for Purim, the most joyous festival of the Jewish year. Its religious meaning is sometimes questioned: the name of God is not mentioned, and there are moral ambiguities even among the heroic characters. Yet Esther conveys a message that is consistent with the entire biblical witness: the survival and salvation of God's people, remembered and reenacted through celebrative ritual.

Esther is set in the most secular and least holy of locales, Susa, in the far eastern sector of the Persian Empire. In this context we discover the people of God, fully immersed in the surrounding culture and its values and assumptions. The book of Esther contains no mention of worship, torah, food laws, or distinctive dress, and this is indicative of how God's people had adapted to a new world. However, before we become too judgmental, North American Christians might consider our own bewildering ways of making sense of who and where we are: patriotic observances, sporting championships, musical festivals, celebrity obsessions, and economic forecasts. These events shape the rhythms of our lives, and the liturgical year is at best an alternative to the dominant ethos that surrounds us. Contemporary

gallows that Haman has prepared for Mordecai, whose word saved the king, stands at Haman's house, fifty cubits high." And the king said, "Hang him on that." ¹⁰So they hanged Haman on the gallows that he had prepared for Mordecai. Then the anger of the king abated. . . .

9:20Mordecai recorded these things, and sent letters to all the Jews who were in all the provinces of King Ahasuerus, both near and far, ²¹enjoining them that they should keep the fourteenth day of the month Adar and also the fifteenth day of the same month, year by year, ²²as the days on which the Jews gained relief from their enemies, and as the month that had been turned for them from sorrow into gladness and from mourning into a holiday; that they should make them days of feasting and gladness, days for sending gifts of food to one another and presents to the poor.

Exegetical Perspective

The book of Esther celebrates the escape of the Jewish community from genocide under the Persian Empire. The lectionary reading presents a chopped-up version of the story of Esther, including its climax in chapter 7 and its concluding account of the institution of the feast of Purim in chapter 9. One of the book's larger purposes is to provide a story of origins for this feast. In the process, the book offers a hilarious but biting critique of the oppressive Persian Empire. The book appears in the canon among the Megilloth, the five scrolls recited on various Jewish feasts. Contemporary celebrations of the feast of Purim include dramatic readings from Esther wherein the audience, often dressed in costumes, participates by boos, hisses, and cheering as the drama unfolds.

By chapter 7, Esther has stopped ignoring her Jewish identity in order to meet cultural expectations of the Persian court and to become the queen. She has taken a bold stand at the urging of her uncle Mordecai, going against the rulers to appear before her husband, the Persian King Ahasuerus. The book delights in making subtle fun of the Persian Empire, of the king—a monarchical buffoon—and of the empire's ridiculous, rigid, and unalterable law. The king is a weak ruler, blind to the moral character of others and ignorant of his people, and he has come

Homiletical Perspective

Commentaries are quick to point out that Esther is the one book in the Bible in which is God is not mentioned. This leaves the reader to puzzle over this omission. Are we to understand that the teller of the story simply assumes God's presence? Is there something else going on? Without getting caught in the web of too much speculation, we need to recognize that it is the preacher's craft to know when to speak God's name and when to leave the name unspoken. It is the preacher's craft to know when to use God's name and when we do God a disservice by saying "God" too quickly. Thus the preacher might begin by identifying with the teller of the story, a human struggling to know exactly where God fits in.

Still, we are drawn to Esther's story and to the hope that though God is not named, God can still be known. Because innocent lives are saved by Esther's courageous request that her life and the lives of her people be spared, the case can be made that God is present and active. Because the humble are lifted up and the haughty brought down, the case can be made that God is present and active. Because the experience of Esther's people was turned "from sorrow into gladness and from mourning into a holiday" (9:22), the case can be made that God is present and active.

God is present and active in the life of Esther. The preacher might consider the lives of other women in

Esther 7:1-6, 9-10; 9:20-22

Theological Perspective

she is proudly regal, feared by all under the king, immortalized in the canon of Scripture, and celebrated by Jews for millennia.

Yet Esther's harsh world seems to find a place in her too. A sheep among wolves (see Matt. 10:16a), she accommodatingly enters a royal life that almost certainly breaks the rules of Torah. If she saves her people through wisdom, it is the shrewd wisdom of a serpent (Matt 10:16b). And when (in passages the lectionary reading conveniently omits) she uses her favor to exact a second day of retribution upon the Jews' enemies (Esth. 9:11–17), she seems to have lost whatever dovelike innocence she might have had. We seem to be in a time like that of the judges, in which God raises up deliverers whose lives are puzzlingly and distressingly unfaithful to and even ignorant of the covenant.

Mordecai's suggestion that Esther's rise may be providential (4:14) is the only hint of divine action. Yet divine action is the indispensable theme of the plot (Ps. 124:1–5). It takes shape subtly and anonymously, in the "butterfly effects" of a predatory beauty contest (Esth. 2:1–4) and a sleepless royal night (6:1–3). These cascade into deliverance and holy war on Israel's "Agagite" (3:1, cf. 1 Sam 15:4–9) enemies. This is not the forceful interventionism of a suddenly existing universe, angelic plagues, fire from heaven, and other deeds of power (Mark 9:38–39). It is what the science-and-theology dialogue calls "noninterventionist objective special divine action." God heals his groaning creation through both styles. So disciples can pray for and celebrate both ordinary and extraordinary signs of God's redeeming and perfecting providence (cf. Jas. 5:13–18).

The queen's actions do save the day. Yet they lead to Persia fearing not the Lord (cf. Prov. 1:29; 31:30) but the Jews (Esth. 8:17). Esther's request that her people be spared (7:7) yields no lasting peace; countering an irrevocable royal death warrant (3:13) with another irrevocable royal right of Jewish self-defense (8:11) only kindles a civil war in which Israel survives by killing its enemies (9:1–10). Even in victory its life remains precarious, tied to its access to conventional power.

Purim (like Hanukkah) is a sign of God's kingdom that is worth celebrating. However, Israel is right to keep it a minor feast alongside its five covenantal ones. Queen Esther and viceroy Mordecai (Esth. 9:29–10:3) are as fleeting as King Solomon and Emperor Constantine. As long as a people's fate rests upon worldly power, it is insecure. Xerxes answers the queen's request with temporary relief;

Pastoral Perspective

Christians thus have the same capacity for adaptation in our present cultural climate. Some see this as a missiological strategy, while others lament our failure of nerve and lack of historical memory.

In the text we meet Esther, by heritage a Jew but now fully assimilated into a nonreligious culture, at the mercy of a male-dominated political system and yet, in the end, possessed by a cunning that allows her to overcome. We are a great distance from tent, temple, and synagogue; in fact, we find ourselves at a feast, a banquet prepared by Esther for the king. As pastors we are often present at these gatherings, not knowing quite what to do, sensing an ambiguity about the appropriateness of our presence; one thinks, for example, of wedding receptions, or sporting events, or civic club meetings! And yet we have been there. The king possesses human power, in the form of unilateral political decision, and so he grants a wish to Esther. She had been prepared for this moment in the warning of her uncle Mordecai: "Who knows? Perhaps you have come to royal dignity for just such a time as this" (4:14). And here she is, in the presence of the king, with the power to change the course of events.

Pastors understand the dilemma before Esther, the power that is given to us, but also the implications of a faithful response. A bishop of the church once urged a group of candidates for ordination to understand the human capital they would acquire through ordinary acts of ministry—visitation of the sick, burial of the dead, baptisms, weddings—and then she added, "You will come to the time when you will be called to spend that capital for some important purpose." While the economic metaphor of capital is imperfect, the truth of the admonition is clear. The pastor finds himself or herself in the presence of power, with an invitation to use that power for the common good.

Esther responds to the king: "If it pleases the king, let my life be given me—that is my petition— and the lives of my people—that is my request" (7:3). An opening has come to Esther; she has come into the kingdom for such a time as this. The wise pastor will reflect on his or her own place in the kingdom, his or her own use of power. At times, the congregation has access to political and economic resources, and the pastor is a participant in outcomes that affect persons and communities beyond those who gather for worship. At other times, the congregation is marginalized and must speak a word of truth against principalities and powers. Esther is bold: she asks for the survival and

under the sway of the "wicked Haman," one of his courtiers. Because Uncle Mordecai has refused to bow to him, Haman decides to murder all the Jews and to do it legally by persuading the king of an imagined threat to him personally.

When Esther learns of Haman's plan, she decides to appeal to the king, but she does it craftily, with artifice and charm, rather than blunt attack. In today's reading, she is about to expose Haman to the king. She chooses to do it at a festive meal, one of several in the book, and one of the most revelatory. Her brave visit to the king in the court wins his favor, so she invites him and the wicked Haman to dine with her. Haman is so happy to be included with the royals that he brags about it to his family. But at this feast, the king presses Esther to reveal her request and promises to give her anything, even half of his kingdom (7:2). Then Esther reveals Haman's plot to the king. With language depicting the excess of Haman's evil plan, she says to the king, "We have been sold, I and my people, to be destroyed, to be killed, and to be annihilated" (7:4). But clever Esther does not leave the matter as a threat to the Jews alone; she tells the self-centered king that she would not speak if it were only about her and her people, but this plot will cause "damage to the king." She teaches him that the safety and well-being of his subjects also concerns his own well-being.

Astonished by this revelation, the king demands to know who is behind the plot. Esther answers, "A foe and enemy, this wicked Haman!" (7:6). Today's reading omits the king's outrage and the funny scene that follows, where the king misconstrues Haman's appeal to Esther as an assault upon her. The reading resumes with a satisfying ironic reversal in the plot. The seventy-five-foot high (fifty cubits) gallows that Haman has prepared to execute Mordecai will become the gallows for Haman's own execution.

When the lectionary reading moves to chapter 9, it reenters the story at the equally ironic reversal of the legal orders to slaughter the Jews. Mordecai has replaced Haman as the king's chief courtier, prevents the genocide, and sends out urgent letters enjoining the Jews to keep the feast of Purim. The purposes of the feast, actually two feasts, are to celebrate the rescue of the Jews from their wicked enemies, their escape from death that turned their "sorrow into gladness and . . . mourning into a holiday" (9:22). This liturgical feast was to be made unique by its exuberant gladness, the sharing of gifts of food with one another, and the giving of presents to the poor.

The celebration of Purim is iconic, emblematic of the Jews' life as God's people, though God is nowhere

which God is present and active, women such as Hannah and Mary the mother of Jesus. In the prayers of Hannah in the Hebrew Scriptures and Mary in Christian Scriptures the belief is expressed that God is in the business of lifting up the oppressed and bringing down the oppressor. As she prepares to leave her young son in the care of Eli the priest, Hannah prays, "The LORD makes poor and makes rich; he brings low, he also exalts. He raises up the poor from the dust; he lifts up the needy from the ash heap" (1 Sam. 2:7–8a). As she anticipates the birth of Jesus, the Son of the Most High, Mary prays, "He has brought down the powerful from their thrones, and lifted up the lowly; he has filled the hungry with good things, and sent the rich away empty" (Luke 1:52–53). Certainly these prayers tell us that if we are looking for evidence of God's presence, we do well to consider those times and places when there are great reversals and dramatic changes of fortune.

Even if God's presence is irrefutable, not all people have the privilege of freely using God's name. Those of us who live in a time and place where we are free to use God's name both publicly and privately, both reverently and flippantly, quickly forget that such freedom is not a gift given to all. Throughout our world and throughout human history, there are entire populations who must trust that though God cannot be named, God is at work to put things right, to deal justly with both the oppressor and the oppressed. We wonder what we can do for those who are clinging desperately to this hope. In our attempts to identify and empathize with these unknown sisters and brothers, we do well to hold on to the story of Esther, noting both her courage and her initial reluctance to speak any word that might save her people. We do well to pray, "Loving God, there are those who are not free to name your name. Be known to them. Be known to them as you made yourself known in Esther's time— remembering the forgotten and saving those who were pawns in the games of the powerful. Amen."

This prayer leads to the second central question of Esther's story; Is there hope in history? Again we dare not answer this question with a hurried, "Of course"—for to do so would be to deny the pain and suffering that so defines the human experience. To do so would be to ignore the tears and travail so descriptive of so many.

When President Barack Obama was still a member of the United States Congress, he remembered being moved by a sermon preached by

Esther 7:1-6, 9-10; 9:20-22

Theological Perspective

but the Father answers her implicit prayer with a Son whose name stands forever above heaven and earth, who grants not just a reprieve from the latest generation of Agagites, but a Passover that delivers from sin and death.

So while this saga helps set the stage for the Messiah's coming, Israel's ultimate enemies must be defeated in a different way. It is not the way of vengeance that turns Haman's own weapons back on them (Esth. 7:9–10) but a salting with fire that spares no one (Mark 9:49–50). Jesus is targeted and does not escape; he is delivered and does not avenge. The wine at Purim flows until celebrants can no longer tell the difference between "cursed be Haman" and "blessed be Mordecai," but the wine at the Eucharist flows to cover victims and perpetrators together (Mark 14:24).

Where does this leave us readers? Esther's story can inspire us to pray confidently for wisdom (Jas. 1:5–7) so that we will face our own trials with joy and endurance (Jas. 1:2–4). It can encourage us to support agents of providence the way Mordecai does (Esth. 4:1–14), for Esther could not have won the Jews' freedom alone. It can remind us to distinguish carefully between the Lord, who alone is our help (Ps. 124:8), and the lesser powers through which our help may sometimes arrive. Above all, it can spur us to gratitude to the Father of lights who sometimes works wonders and sometimes works behind the scenes, and whose every perfect gift fulfills his ultimate purpose (Jas. 1:17–18), not of overwhelming personal adversaries but being "at peace with one another" (Mark 9:50).

TELFORD WORK

Pastoral Perspective

salvation of her people. The prophetic voices of the recent past have displayed this same boldness: Martin Luther King Jr., Nelson Mandela, Alexander Solzhenitsyn.

The courage of Esther shapes the destiny of the two other main characters in this text, Haman and Mordecai. Haman is motivated by evil and plans to have Mordecai hanged (5:9–14). Esther's word brings about a great reversal: Mordecai is saved, and Haman is killed (7:10). Thus the proud are humbled, and the humble are exalted. In the relationship between Haman and Mordecai we sense the providence of God, who works through historical events, and the faithfulness of God, who preserves the righteous.

The text concludes with a description of the feast of Purim and its historical origins. The occasion of the survival and salvation of God's people was one of feasting and celebration; God's people had gained "relief from their enemies," transforming "sorrow into gladness" and "mourning into a holiday." They were commanded to send food to one another and to gather presents for the poor (9:22).

The Christian community can learn something from this ancient Jewish practice. How do we celebrate the survival of a person in the military who returns home safely? How do we rejoice when a lost individual discovers grace? How do we give thanks when a community remembers the forgotten and marginalized and intervenes on their behalf? The distinction between the royal feasts in the story of Esther and the inauguration of Purim is clear. Eugene Peterson distinguishes between the "pursuit of happiness," which is commercialized in our culture, and the "irrepressible feast of the community" that is Purim. "Joy, separated from its roots in God and pursued apart from the community of faith, becomes mere sensation."[1] The pastor remembers the story of survival and salvation, even in the midst of a secular culture, and courageously calls the people of God to celebration.

KENNETH H. CARTER JR.

---

1. Eugene Peterson, *Five Smooth Stones for Pastoral Work* (Grand Rapids: Eerdmans, 1980), 201.

Exegetical Perspective

mentioned in this book. They feast at table, they give gifts of food to one another, and they bring in the poor among them. This celebration is a remembrance of attempted genocide, their escape from it, and their continued life together in community. The escape occurred because of Mordecai's resistance to the arrogance of Haman and because of Esther's recognition of her identity as a member of the persecuted Jewish community under the Persian Empire. Hence the story, with all its charm and its excesses and its deep pain, stands as a critique of the ways of empire, of governments that benefit only a few and harm others. The story lauds the fidelity of the less powerful as they seek to gain security and a life of dignity.

The text does not tell of the overthrow of the Persians but of the downfall of one member of its governing class, driven by shallow self-concern and by hatred for everyone who threatens his sense of privilege. His conniving wickedness fails him, but the empire continues, with the excluded now among the rulers. That God does not appear in the Hebrew version of this text has created challenges to interpretation, but God's presence may be deduced from the loyalty, goodness, and triumph of the weak. It may be surmised from the reversals of fortune where the good triumph over the wicked, despite all expectation to the contrary. And God's presence is suggested by the liturgical feast of Purim, where food is shared, community strengthened, and the poor invited to the table. For Christians, the feast of Purim calls to mind eucharistic feasts and, in the context of Esther, serves as strong warning against social systems that benefit the powerful and harm others.

KATHLEEN M. O'CONNOR

Homiletical Perspective

the Rev. Dr. Jeremiah Wright entitled "The Audacity of Hope." In the sermon Wright recalled a fellow pastor preaching a sermon in which he described going to an art museum and seeing a painting entitled *Hope*. The painting was of a harpist, "a woman who at first glance appears to be sitting atop a great mountain. Until you take a closer look and see that the woman is bruised and bloodied, dressed in tattered rags, the harp reduced to a single frayed string. Your eye is then drawn to the scene below, down to the valley below, where everywhere are the ravages of famine, the drumbeat of war, a world groaning under strife and depravation . . . And yet . . . the harpist is looking upwards, a few faint notes floating upwards to the heavens. She dares to hope . . . She has the audacity . . . to make music . . . and praise God . . . on the one string . . . she has left!"[1]

The hope that stirred President Obama is the hope expressed in Esther's story. A young woman in the court of a mighty king, a young woman valued more for her beauty than her brains, a young woman willing to risk her own safety and security for the well-being of her people calls attention to a desperate situation. She has only a few words at her disposal, words that must be very well chosen. She speaks. History is changed. Esther gives the preacher an opportunity to nurture the embers of hope.

H. JAMES HOPKINS

---

1. Barack Obama, *Dreams from My Father: A Story of Race and Inheritance* (New York: Three Rivers Press, 1995, 2004), 292–93.

Psalm 124

¹If it had not been the LORD who was on our side
  —let Israel now say—
²if it had not been the LORD who was on our side,
   when our enemies attacked us,
³then they would have swallowed us up alive,
   when their anger was kindled against us;
⁴then the flood would have swept us away,
   the torrent would have gone over us;
⁵then over us would have gone
   the raging waters.

Theological Perspective

Psalm 124 is a stunning fusion of communal theological reflection and personal emotional response. Liturgical in form, the psalm calls for collective affirmation of God's protection and care upon deliverance from grave crisis, even certain death; yet the psalm also conveys in very powerful terms the breathless terror one experiences in the face of calamity. A relatively brief psalm, composed of just eight verses, it is the collective voice of the people of God, who affirm the active presence of God in crisis. But it is also the voice of one who is only just on the other side of sheer panic and fear.

The psalm opens and closes in praise of God's powerful presence with us, even in the midst of the calamitous adversity. Its opening two verses proclaim not simply that the Lord is with us, but that the Lord is indeed "on our side," an active and steadfast presence who comes to our aid. Its closing verse expands upon this proclamation by further identification of the source of our protection. Our help comes from the creator of heaven and earth, our creator and the creator of all of life. God is the creator of both the earthly and the heavenly realms; the One who creates life will sustain it also.

Throughout the psalm the liturgical form is maintained. In verse 1, the proclamation of God's care is interrupted by an explicit direction that the

Pastoral Perspective

This is the psalm of a particular community that attributes victory in battle and deliverance from natural disaster to God's favor. It celebrates two exceptional experiences when life did not run its normal course but took an unexpected turn for the better. It is a corporate psalm, providing liturgical evidence of a community both wholly dependent on and publicly grateful for God's saving help. The opening line, "If it had not been the LORD who was on our side," repeated with the stage directions, "let Israel now say," indicates that the community members were in the habit of reciting together the disasters that would surely have befallen them had YHWH not taken up their cause. The recitation ends with an astonishing theological claim (v. 8): this community's special helper is none other than the Creator of the cosmos!

These experiences of unmerited favor give the ancient Israelites a glimpse into the nature of God. Not only is God all-powerful; God is also vigilant in showing grace to those whom God loves. Israel was to experience this saving grace at critical junctures throughout its history. The early Christians concluded that the life, death, and resurrection of Jesus was the perfect demonstration of this saving grace, consistent with Israel's earliest experiences, but extending to benefit all of humankind. Through

⁶Blessed be the LORD,
   who has not given us
   as prey to their teeth.
⁷We have escaped like a bird
   from the snare of the fowlers;
   the snare is broken,
   and we have escaped.

⁸Our help is in the name of the LORD,
   who made heaven and earth.

Exegetical Perspective

In a reflective posture, the psalmist recounts the sentiments of the community as it confesses to God's assistance in the face of its enemies that were about to become a devastating force against the Israelites. Psalm 124 is intended for liturgical use and is classified as a community thanksgiving psalm. In this poem, the psalmist joins images of danger with images of deliverance to create a picture of God's greatness and goodness.

Exactly what the national danger was remains obscure, but the community is certain of one thing: if God had not been on their side, they would have perished. Implied in this poem is a portrait of God as warrior God, the commander in chief of the hosts of armies, both heavenly and earthly. With peoples and nations at war with one another, the image of a warrior God fits the social and political scenario of ancient biblical times.

The poem can be divided into three sections: a reflective statement of affirmation (vv. 1–5); a hymn (vv. 6–7); and a statement of confidence (v. 8). In verses 1–5, the psalmist uses two sets of phrases that are cataloged. Through the first catalog, namely, the use of the phrase, "If it had not been the LORD who was on our side" (vv. 1 and 2), followed by the gripping statement, "when our enemies attacked us" (v. 2b), the psalmist creates a grave and consternating

Homiletical Perspective

The Book of Common Prayers includes daily offices of prayer for morning, noon, evening, and night. In the final prayers for the day, the last verse of Psalm 124 calls the community together for the service of compline:

> Officiant: Our help is in the Name of the Lord;
> People: The maker of heaven and earth.[1]

What would it be like for us if we allowed this one verse to shape our lives in community and in communion with the living God? What would it be like to lie down at night and go to sleep confident that we really can let go of what has been done (or not done) during that day? How might our lives be transformed if we could simply let go and rest in God?

In Psalm 121 the poet lifts his eyes to the hills and wonders: "From where is my help to come?" The response is a bold expression of personal trust and confidence: "*My* help comes from the LORD, the maker of heaven and earth" (my trans.). But that trust and confidence takes on even deeper meaning in the psalm appointed for today, as the pronoun shifts from *my* help to *our* help. This move from personal to corporate faith represents a challenge

---

1. *The Book of Common Prayer* (New York: Seabury Press, 1979), 127.

Psalm 124

Theological Perspective

people of Israel join in the psalmist's declaration that the Lord was with them through a terrible time. Following a description of the crisis averted, the psalmist pronounces the utter blessedness of God. Invoking a common liturgical formula, "Blessed be the Lord," in verse 6, the psalmist affirms that the God who saves us is holy in an awesome sense, as overwhelming in goodness as the source of our terror was in its destructive power. In the last verse, the psalmist calmly and confidently asserts not only that it is the Lord who comes to Israel's aid, but that the people of God are to call upon God in times of distress. In writing that their help is "in *the name* of the Lord" (emphasis added), the psalmist reminds the gathered community that God's help is sure and we can remember that it is not to be taken for granted. In gratitude and awe, the name of the Lord is to be praised.

What is remarkable about this psalm, however, is not its liturgical form alone, but its breathless expression of nearly overwhelming threat. Beginning in verse 2, the bulk of the psalm is given over to a rapid-fire sequence of graphic depictions of terror. In all there are six different descriptions of certain death, delivered in as many verses: the premeditated attack of angry enemies, being swallowed alive, the violent sweeping action of a flood, the act of drowning, the savagery of a predatory animal, and capture in a hunter's trap. The sense of powerlessness and dread is nearly palpable. Though these experiences are recounted in the past tense, the threat has only recently passed. One cannot but imagine the pounding of one's heart, the rush of adrenaline, the combined knowledge of one's own death and the incapacity to act. This psalm, though it conveys the ultimate power of God, conveys a close call in the battle between evil and good.

It is important to note, however, that these near-death experiences do not describe literal events, since no one could have survived all six experiences simultaneously or even in close succession. By creating such a list, the psalmist may be recalling a specific incident in Israel's collective experience; however, just as surely, the graphic descriptions themselves are inviting each individual to remember his or her most overwhelming personal experience of terror and peril. What is remarkable is that the psalmist is able to evoke the psychological state of fear and invoke trust in the Lord in very nearly the same moment.

The psalm stands as a lovely statement of the relationship God has chosen to have with the people

Pastoral Perspective

the power of the Holy Spirit, God's saving grace remains at work in the world, undergirding the fabric of human life, supporting the powerless in times of trouble, and surprising the faithful with unexpected blessings. Christians might rephrase the summary statement in verse 8 to declare, "Our help is in the name of the Lord, who made *and redeemed* heaven and earth."

Problems arise when we try to turn the particularity of the first seven verses of the psalm into general principles applicable to every person in every situation. Having the Lord "on our side" is no guarantee that things will go our way when troubles arise. Neither are suffering, defeat, and death signs that we have fallen out of God's favor. It would be absurd to conclude, for example, that those who died in the terrorist attacks on the World Trade Center or in the fury of Hurricane Katrina did so because God was against them. In fact, it is more in the character of God to side with history's victims. Through his death on the cross, Jesus went down with history's losers once and for all. Through his resurrection, he showed that God is on everyone's side, winners and losers, sinners and saints.

This is the wider context within which we read and interpret the psalm. Against this backdrop, we listen to the text and discover that through it we can overhear our ancient Israelite brothers and sisters as they worship YHWH. What do they say? What wisdom do their words hold for us today? Three sets of questions emerge from close reading:

Testimonials. On the basis of Psalm 124, Augustine invites us to "consider whose work thy salvation is."[1] How, when, where, in what settings and circumstances have we experienced God's saving grace? Are we encouraged, in our congregations, to tell and retell our faith stories? Are we invited to imagine—as the worshipers do in Psalm 124—how differently our lives might have turned out apart from God's grace? Do we express our gratitude to God publicly? Joyfully? Convincingly? What difference would it make if we put more of ourselves and our personal histories into the worship event?

Reliance on God. How much do we really believe that "our help is in the name of the Lord," and in what other forms of personal protection do we invest (i.e., health insurance, home security systems,

---

1. Philip Schaff, ed., *St. Augustine: Expositions on the Book of Psalms*, vol. 8, *A Select Library of the Nicene and Post-Nicene Fathers of the Christian Church* (Grand Rapids: Eerdmans, 1974), 124.10.

situation. This quickly shifts in the next three verses, which feature a second catalog of "then" clauses that describe what would have happened to the community if God had not been on its side when the enemy had attacked the people. A people against whom the enemies' anger was kindled would have experienced being swallowed up alive (v. 3), swept away by flood waters (v. 4), and then overpowered altogether by the raging waters (v. 5). The community's enemies would have been like sea monsters (cf. Jer. 51:34) who would have eaten the people alive and then left them in the sea to be washed away and washed "under" by sweeping, torrential, raging waters. Here the psalmist brings to light the community's feeling of powerlessness in the face of one who was able to wield greater strength and force.

In verses 1–6, the poet also brings to light a basic theological assertion that plays out time and again throughout the OT, namely, that God acts on behalf of the oppressed to thwart enemies and to rescue "the poor" from bondage (see, e.g., Jer. 20:7–13; cf. Ezek. 34:10, 12). Throughout the Psalter, one hears a member of the community crying out to God to be rescued from peril (see, e.g., Pss. 31:2; 35:17; 69:14; 71:2, 4; 82:4, 144:7; see also Prov. 24:11). Elsewhere in the Psalter, God is extolled for having remembered the community in its low estate and for having rescued it from its foes (Ps. 136:23). God's care is attributed to God's steadfast love (see Ps. 136:24).

In verses 6–7, the psalmist features the community blessing God for not delivering them into the hands of the enemies. The phrase "blessed be the LORD" is common in OT literature. God's people are forever blessing God, who is always saving them from the snares of death (see, e.g., Exod. 18:10; Pss. 28:6; 31:21). The psalmist captures the ferociousness of the enemies by portraying the enemies as predators and the community as prey. The simile sets up the enemies to be like lions (Ps. 7:2; 17:12; 22:21) or vultures (Lam. 4:19 NEB). The image of the community as "prey" is also a common one (see, e.g., Isa. 42:22)

The psalmist uses a second image in verse 7. Here he uses a simile to convey the community's experience of how God rescued the community from peril: "We have escaped like a bird from the snare of the fowlers" (v. 7a). The same language is heard in Proverbs 6:5, where a father advises a child to save himself/herself "like a bird from the hand of the fowler." In Psalm 11:1, the speaker quotes God, who has said "Flee like a bird to the mountains" in order to escape from the bow of the wicked. In 124:7, the

to the dominant piety of North American Christian culture.

So the poet dares to speak on behalf of the community: *our* help comes from God. It is one thing to discover (or rediscover) after hitting some bumps in the road that "Jesus loves *me*." But it is a richer and more mature faith that is able to claim God's love for *us*. This psalm articulates what it is like for a community to go through an ordeal and come out on the other side, not as a collection of isolated individuals, but as a community of faith.

The preacher might begin by reminding the congregation about the Babylonian exile. What would it have been like to have worshiped in the holy city of Jerusalem, praising God in the temple day after day, until one day the Babylonian army marched into town and destroyed the temple? What would it be like for that community as their leaders were carted off into exile? What would it be like to lay up one's harp and wonder if it would ever again be possible to sing the Lord's song? What would it be like to lose one's home and experience the social dislocation of a refugee? And yet afterwards (admittedly a long time afterwards) the community was able to recognize that it did not become "prey to their teeth" (v. 6). Indeed, like an escaped bird, the people must have experienced their homecoming as a second exodus. With one voice they are able to affirm: "If the LORD had not been on our side, . . . then they would have swallowed us up alive" (vv. 2–3, my trans.). But of course the Lord *was* on their side.

One of the real challenges in our polarized world is that it has become more difficult to imagine shared tragedies that function to bring us together as one people. We remain deeply divided on a range of issues that make it very difficult to speak about *us* and how *we* are experiencing the world. If the preacher is too quick to generalize, she risks alienating those members of the congregation who see the world from a very different perspective.

And yet the preacher can proclaim the good news of this sixth-century-BCE text by juxtaposing the psalm's message with the proclamation of the church that there is one Lord and one faith and one baptism. We proclaim that in Christ there are many members but one body. Surely we can acknowledge our differences and still celebrate the life we share in the risen Christ.

I think of the conflicts around human sexuality that my own congregation and denomination have been experiencing that have caused pain and hurt on all sides. Yet even when we are not of one *mind*, we

Psalm 124

Theological Perspective

of Israel, that the Lord is on their side. However, it also creates a kind of exoneration for those who suffer. The descriptions of distress are unvarnished and awful. Whether in relationship to mortal enemies or natural disaster, human life is depicted as fragile, vulnerable. The psalm tacitly expresses acknowledgment of risk as well as a realistic assessment of predation and evil. God is present in the midst of such suffering and threat, and yet the knowledge of God's saving presence is almost more than the human mind and heart can perceive in the whelm of assault.

A memory of rescue, Psalm 124 is a psalm of praise and a vow of reliance upon God. But it is also gratitude for survival, the recognition of the fragility of human life, and a documentation of wonder and sheer joy at the triumph over adversity and evil. Penultimate in the psalm (but prior only to the concluding affirmation of God's care) is the tender illustration of the escape of a bird from the fowler's snare. There is no panicking quite like the fluttering of a captured bird, nor is there any freedom quite like the soaring flight of that same bird. The psalmist has evoked for us the wonder and joy of one who barely escapes, and the freedom that life with God gives.

In the end, this little psalm manages to convey two major theological truths: the presence of hope even in the midst of impending disaster, and the obligation of thanksgiving to God in the celebration of escape. There is a realization that "if it had not been the LORD who was on our side," we would not be here to testify now, and implicit in this is the compulsion to testify and praise. In this time of heightened concern over terror and disaster in our world, this is a psalm of comfort that teaches us to hope and to praise while we yet live.

SUSAN B. W. JOHNSON

Pastoral Perspective

vaccinations, handguns)? Where do we draw the line between responsible stewardship and overreliance on commodities that promise to keep us safer? If we depend on God and God alone, can we justify the military budget of the U.S. government? Can we justify our own expenditures? If we trusted God more, would we be more generous with our money? When can we count on God to help us, and when does God expect us to use our own God-given talents and resources to help ourselves? Are we ever beyond help?

Priorities. Our help is in the name of the Lord, and so it is our mission to help others. How hard do we try to be helpful? If God is by nature grace-full, do we as the people of God act in ways that mirror God's grace? How well are we doing at aligning our priorities with God's priorities? How ready are we to take up the cause of those who are powerless in the face of evil? How willing are we to work to change systems that perpetuate imbalances of power?

A sermon on Psalm 124 would be particularly helpful for a congregation that has recently been through a trauma, perhaps a fire, or been under attack from a negative element within the community. Following the psalmist's example, the preacher can encourage the church to start telling its story differently, shifting the emphasis away from the bad things that have happened to focus instead on the remarkable ways God has helped it to cope, heal, and move forward. A sermon along these lines can plant the seeds for individuals with a history of trauma to begin to reframe their view of themselves in much the same way. Familiar hymns such as "Amazing Grace" and "Our God, Our Help in Ages Past" can reinforce the message of the sermon. The psalm, sermon, and liturgical setting thus combine to facilitate an encounter with God—in whose presence we find perfect safety, both now and forever.

We can count on this safety, but we can't manipulate it for our own purposes. Psalm 124 teaches us to trust in God who shows up on God's terms and acts on behalf of those whom God chooses to love. Psalm 124 teaches us that we are among those whom God has chosen. We are loved.

RUTH L. BOLING

Exegetical Perspective

community has indeed escaped from the trap of the fowlers who have attacked the people (v. 2b). "Fowlers" in verse 7 is synonymous with "enemies" in verse 2.

A "snare" is a trap. References to traps occur often in the OT. Snares can refer to physical or spiritual modes of entanglement. The snare imagery reflects the community's culture. The people were not only farmers but also hunters. In the ancient Near East, pits were often covered with camouflaged nets, which, in turn, became traps for animals being hunted. Elsewhere in the OT, the image of a snare is associated with a trap for human beings. In Job 18:8–10, Bildad waxes eloquent about the calamity that the wicked bring upon themselves. They entrap themselves. Unrighteous practices are also referred to as "snares" (see, e.g., Exod. 23:33; 34:12; Deut. 7:16; Josh. 23:13; and Ps. 106:36). Throughout the Psalter, one hears repeatedly that the wicked will fall into their own pit, net, or snare (Pss. 7:15; 9:15; 35:8; 57:6; 59:12). One also hears how the wicked repeatedly set traps to seize "the poor" (Pss. 10:9; 35:7; 119:85; 140:5). Finally, Jeremiah describes the wicked as fowlers who set traps to catch human beings (Jer. 5:26).

The psalm closes with a statement of confidence. For the community, their help—their deliverance—is in the "name" of the Lord who is the creator of heaven and earth, the creator of the cosmos. For the community and for the psalmist, God's name has redemptive power (Pss. 20:1; 54:1; cf. 1 Sam. 17:45). Thus this psalm celebrates a God who cares for those who are in need. It also provides a glimpse into the faith of the Jewish people, who now have reason to sing and proclaim, "If it had not been the LORD who was on our side. . . ."

CAROL J. DEMPSEY, OP

Homiletical Perspective

do occasionally glimpse that by the grace of God we are still (like it or not) one *body*. And slowly but surely we are beginning to learn in the midst of our varied thoughts and feelings around such issues to put more trust in God. It is not our management or technical skills that will "fix" what ails the church in our day. But by God's grace, we glimpse from time to time that we need each other, that we are called to love one another. God is becoming *our* help as we become more and more aware that the church doesn't belong to us.

The church in our day has experienced something of a Babylonian captivity as we have begun to come to terms with our own grief and loss at the death of Christendom. We do well to remember, however, that just as the God of Abraham, Isaac, and Jacob did not need the temple to be God; so the church of Jesus Christ does not need Christendom to proclaim the gospel.

For an exilic church like ours, this is an encouraging word of hope that points us to God and neighbor, especially the neighbor with whom we do not agree. This psalm calls us to a greater sense of intentionality to find experiences in our world and in our congregations that bind us together, so that we might pray with one voice as the community that exists solely by God's mercy. Difficult times can, and do, shape a congregation's common life together, and by God's grace it is out of those experiences that the people of God begins to form. The preacher has the opportunity to stand on this day among a people who need to know, now as much as they ever have needed to know, that the God who was our help in ages past will be our hope for years to come.

RICHARD M. SIMPSON

James 5:13-20

¹³Are any among you suffering? They should pray. Are any cheerful? They should sing songs of praise. ¹⁴Are any among you sick? They should call for the elders of the church and have them pray over them, anointing them with oil in the name of the Lord. ¹⁵The prayer of faith will save the sick, and the Lord will raise them up; and anyone who has committed sins will be forgiven. ¹⁶Therefore confess your sins to one another, and pray for one another, so that you may be healed. The prayer of the righteous is powerful and effective. ¹⁷Elijah was a human being like us, and he prayed fervently that it might not rain, and for three years and six months it did not rain on the earth. ¹⁸Then he prayed again, and the heaven gave rain and the earth yielded its harvest.

¹⁹My brothers and sisters, if anyone among you wanders from the truth and is brought back by another, ²⁰you should know that whoever brings back a sinner from wandering will save the sinner's soul from death and will cover a multitude of sins.

Theological Perspective

At the close of the theological reflection on the James text of last week (p. 90), I noted a frustration with the text, namely, that the book as a whole spends so little time doing theology proper in shaping wisdom. However, the absence of explicit theological development does not mean that James lacks theology. The opening verses of this week's lesson depend upon a profound theological claim, namely, that Christian wisdom—and therefore Christian life—turns on the twin convictions that God is compassionate and that God acts powerfully in the world. That both those who suffer and those who are cheerful are encouraged to pray (songs of praise being a form of prayer) makes sense only if prayer can effect change, and prayer can effect change only if God hears and responds to prayer. In theological terms, then, James's emphasis on prayer reveals the centrality of two classical attributes of God in his theology: sovereignty and compassion.

At the same time, James so emphasizes prayer's efficacy that he risks swamping his own theological boat. Prayer itself saves, and prayer (at least in James's estimation) becomes increasingly efficacious as the one praying is increasingly faithful. The first claim—that prayer saves—seems to undermine claims about Jesus' uniquely salvific work and, therein, God's sovereignty. The second—that the

Pastoral Perspective

The power of prayer seems to be one of the overarching pastoral themes of this passage. James picks up on some of the earlier themes, such as the importance of speech rightly used and the wisdom found in seeking relationship with God. These two themes are combined in the speech act directed to and with God, known as prayer. In this perspective we will look at two aspects of prayer found in this passage: when to pray and how the community is involved with prayer.

When to Pray. In these few brief verses James provides examples of many different occasions of prayer. We are to pray when we are suffering (5:13), happy (5:13), ill in body (5:15), and ill in spirit (5:16). We are to pray for ourselves (5:13) and we are to pray for others (5:14, 16, 19–20). The types of prayers mentioned roughly break down into the old educational formula: ACTS (Adoration, Confession, Thanksgiving, and Supplication) with adoration and thanksgiving being combined into praise (5:13). As we think about each of these modes of prayers, we see them in evidence both within our personal prayers and in the life of the church. For this section we concentrate first on the personal aspect, saving the community's practice of prayer till a little later.

When we praise God in our personal prayers, it is often linked with thanksgiving for what God has

Exegetical Perspective

It is interesting that the lectionary, after appointing all of James 3 and part of James 4, proceeds to omit James 4:11–5:12, a section that addresses the dangers of wealth and the tendency of the rich to oppress the poor, before it picks up again with the power of faithful prayer in 5:13–20. Perhaps James's railing against conspicuous consumption and crass materialism (5:1–12) cuts too close to the lives of many in North America and the image of the judge who stands at the doors (5:9) is a bit too uncomfortable. Nevertheless, the preacher owes James attention to the literary context, since his discussion of prayer and community solidarity in this Sunday's lesson follows directly on his indictment of those who wield power in the world and who therefore cause the powerless to rely as heavily on prayer as they do.

James advises prayer from "all sorts and conditions of [persons]," as the *Book of Common Prayer* puts it.[1] Whether one is suffering or cheerful, sick or sinful, prayer is the proper response of the people of God. This is not only a call to individuals to lay their lives and circumstances before God in prayer but an expressly communal obligation to intercede for one another. The "elders of the church" (v. 14), perhaps those who hold specific ecclesiastical

1. *The Book of Common Prayer* (New York: Seabury Press, 1979), 814.

Homiletical Perspective

These are the last eight verses of James's letter, in which he finishes calling his congregation back to the wisdom of God. The wisdom of the world has led them into all kinds of trouble, not least of which are the divisions that sin and sickness have caused among them. In characteristic fashion, James does not try to explain how this works, since their trouble is not in their minds. Their trouble is in the concrete acts of their life together, which is why James gives them concrete things to do: pray for one another, sing songs of praise, call for the elders, anoint with oil, confess to one another, bring the wanderers back home.

Before the preacher can explore the ways in which such acts open the way to divine healing even now, it will be necessary to help modern listeners over the hump of equating sickness with sin. While James does not connect the two as strenuously as Mark does in the story of the paralytic (Mark 2:1–12), he still connects them. Preachers may explain this as a prescientific understanding of why bad things happen to apparently good people, or they may decide to support James by exploring how what he says is still true.

One way to do that is to point out the ways in which illness and wrongdoing really do separate individuals from their communities—illness by isolating a person physically from others and

James 5:13-20

Theological Perspective

prayers of the faithful are more powerful—seems to make prayer's effect contingent on the one praying, rather than the One to whom the prayers are directed. It thereby downplays the centrality of God's compassion in order to advance a case for the power of human fidelity; there is, after all, a great deal of difference between a compassionate actor and a grace-dispensing machine. So what are we to do with this emphasis?

There are at least three things we can do with it. First, the texts ought to remind us that James is writing during a time of great theological fertility in which the early church is hardly settled on matters of Christian faith and life. The continuing fecundity of the Christian faith is due at least in part to the fact that Christianity is not the result of some settlement on the part of its early writers as to the meaning and significance of the Christ event. Instead, a tradition that begins with multiple voices is able to continue because those voices stay multiple. So the least we can do is to treat peculiar texts charitably while not venerating them. James's emphasis on prayer ought to be a sign for us that at least parts of the church have long understood prayer to be both significant and powerful and that prayer uniquely binds human and divine activity together such that it is difficult to see where one ends and the other begins.

Next, we can locate the texts in the context of James's writings. Given James's three central concerns—taking care in how we speak, giving care to those in distress, and being careful about what we let into our lives—his concluding focus on prayer invites us to note how prayer brings all three of these focal points together. Take the three in turn. First, after so much teaching on language and its potential dangers and in light of his own admission that everyone makes mistakes, James offers us a way out of the kind of muteness that is born of a potentially disabling preoccupation with endlessly erring in our speech: wise speech simply *is* prayer. What Luke does with language in the early chapters of Acts, and John does with the Word in the first chapter of his Gospel (i.e., line out a theological vision of how God relates to grammar), James does at the end of his text through his focus on prayer. The wise speak always as if before and to God.

Second, prayer for James is not a private matter. Instead, it helps to shape a particular kind of community in which people are committed to each other. The sick call for elders to pray over them. Sinners confess to one another. The cheerful sing. For James, the community that prays together stays

Pastoral Perspective

given us. This is true whenever we say grace before a meal, bless the beauty of God's creation, or appreciate the returned health of a loved one. It is a test of faith whether we can still adore or thank God in the midst of suffering and illness. There are many scriptural examples of those, strong in faith, who are able to praise God in difficult times. (See Job, Jonah, Hannah, Mary, and Jesus to name a few.) It is often in our brokenness that we can hear most clearly God's reply to our prayers. When we are too broken to speak our prayers, it is often through remembered hymns and spiritual songs of praise from our youth that we are able to continue the conversation with God.

When we are agents of our own distress or others', we are not passive participants in prayer, but also take responsibility for our actions in prayers of confession. The forgiveness we receive from God is balm to our wounds. In our times of personal confession we seek God's ear, but our public professions also help us be accountable to our neighbor. In confessing to at least one other, we make ourselves vulnerable and ready for healing.

But, it is not just for ourselves that we pray. We pray for others that we know personally who are in need and those whose needs are known to us in the wider world. This allows us to see the image of God embodied in others, to share in their suffering, and to add our voice in God's hearing for the good of the world. We can do this on our own, but the power of prayer is seen most clearly in the praying community of the church as these concerns are voiced aloud in worship and other gatherings of God's people.

The Praying Community. The church as praying community engages in all these types of prayers. We sing together, minister to the sick, and confess to one another. These times of prayerful engagement contrast with earlier portions of James (see Proper 19 and 20). Here the tongue is not used for slander or envy, it is rightly attuned to God-talk.

Language rightly used in God's service empowers the sick to call on the leaders of the church to pray for them. Those who are ill are not helpless, but charged with asking for the help they require. The elders in turn are expected to come to the sick, pray for them, and lay cooling hands on their bodies. In the spirit of James's example of the effectiveness of Elijah's prayer, I offer the following example of an ordinary and actual church community gathered around a sickbed. A beloved organist is suffering from a heart condition that is expected to be fatal. The clergy gather and so do other church leaders,

office, but more likely those who are "older" in the faith, should pray and anoint the sick and sinful with oil (v. 15). The practice of anointing with oil for healing is ubiquitous in antiquity. Isaiah 1:6 describes the suffering of Judah as untreated injuries: "From the sole of the foot even to the head, there is no soundness in it, but bruises and sores and bleeding wounds; they have not been drained, or bound up, or softened with oil." Ezekiel 16:9 uses the same metaphor to say God has ministered to the nation: "Then I bathed you with water and washed off the blood from you, and anointed you with oil." The church continues the practice, apparently after the example of Jesus himself. Mark 6:13 describes the ministry of the Twelve in response to Jesus' commission: "They cast out many demons, and anointed with oil many who were sick and cured them." And Jesus says of the man mugged on the road to Jericho that the Samaritan "went to him and bandaged his wounds, having poured oil and wine on them" (Luke 10:34).

Similarly, the practice of laying hands on the sick has precedents. In the New Testament we see Jesus laying hands on the sick to heal them (Mark 6:5; Luke 4:40; 13:13), and Luke tells of Paul's doing likewise (Acts 28:8). Luke's pairing of the laying on of hands with prayer particularly echoes James's advice. James writes, "The prayer of faith will save the sick, and the Lord will raise them up" (5:15a). This "prayer of faith" is faithful prayer, prayer that trusts God to answer the petition. Modern people sometimes look askance at such apparently naive confidence in so-called "faith healing." That stems from a distinctly modern understanding of illness, though, one that presumes scientific analysis alone is able to assess a person's state of health. James says that anointing, prayer, and the laying on of hands "will restore the weary" (my trans.), which is substantially more than merely prescribing antibiotics can do.

This restoration is the redemption that God alone accomplishes, which is why James draws a connection between sin and sickness: "anyone who has committed sins will be forgiven" (v. 15b). This too is common in antiquity. The disciples in John, for example, ask Jesus about the man born blind, "Who sinned, this man or his parents?" (John 9:2). This is not mere magical thinking or the absence of modern scientific medical knowledge, but a way of interpreting the experience of illness significantly different from Western medicine's. The relationship between human life and the divine realm seemed a

wrongdoing by isolating a person socially. While illness is no sin, plenty of sick people carry guilt about their sickness. Maybe they did not wash their hands enough. Maybe they did not get enough exercise. They probably ate too much, drank too much, smoked too much, thought too many of the wrong kind of thoughts. Anyone who thinks there is no shame to illness has not been paying attention. Just ask the sick how many of their friends disappeared when they took to their beds. If they can still speak, they can name the names, along with the names of those they never expected, who showed up bearing jars of flowers and pots of soup.

Another way to support James is to point out how sin and sickness both heighten the vulnerability of human beings. In both cases, for different reasons, people fail to meet the human ideal. They come down with acute cases of the human condition, exposing their vulnerability in vivid detail. While the typical human reaction to such exposure is to look politely away, James recommends a different course of action.

In the case of the sinful, he recommends confession—not to the ceiling but to another member of the community, whose own confession will follow in due course. In the case of the sick, he recommends an audible call for the elders of the church. Flowers and soup are good medicine, but they are not enough. The person whose weakness has caused her to be cut off from the community needs the representatives of that community to come to her where she lies, both to anoint her with oil and to cover her with their prayers. She, in fact, is the one responsible for calling them to come.

Like the sinner, she is to use her vulnerability to engage the vulnerability of others, in a community where people agree not to look politely away—where mutual confession is practiced, along with anointing of the sick and pervasive prayer, sin and sickness cannot isolate people for long. Through these communal acts of faith, attention is removed from the individual self and returned to the larger body, so that God has more room to work. In this way, the wisdom of God edges out the wisdom of the world, at least for today.

Preachers who remain true to the spirit of this letter will not spend much time explaining it. Instead, they will connect the health of their own congregations with concrete, communal acts of faith, beginning with things that are already taking place. Even if the list is short, listeners may not have thought of the ways in which something as routine

James 5:13-20

Theological Perspective

together—which is no small feat when there are so many things that can divide a community, many of which he has addressed throughout the book.

Third, James treats prayer as a kind of treatment for impurity—a therapy for the toxicities of the world. Modern readers may find it odd that James conflates illness and sinfulness the way he does in verses 14–16. Illnesses, after all, are physical conditions, and sin is a metaphysical one. But as our own environmental and health practices have shown us of late, the morally troubling things we do to our bodies and the world around us have the tendency to affect not only our individual health but the health of the beings around us. So perhaps we would do well to attend to James's suggestion that lives lived in the prayerful awareness of God's activity in the world may be as important to our physical well-being as advances in modern medicine and environmental science.

Finally, we can note that though James's emphasis on prayer ends the book, it does not really close the book. Indeed, the writer of James faces a conundrum: how to end a text about something that does not, itself, end. Heavenly wisdom, after all, is never exhausted. His solution is to use prayer to bring the book full circle without bringing it to a conclusion. Thus a book that begins in address to those who are dispersed (1:1) ends with blessings promised to "whoever brings back a sinner from wandering" (5:20). While James spends almost no time in describing eschatology, in an odd way, the book has the effect of exemplifying it. The abruptness of the closing verses can remind us that things are not yet ended, that the world is still full of sin, death, and those who wander, but that the wise Christian can, in and through prayer, continue to engage the world in hope for a time when what has splintered can be reunited.

MARK DOUGLAS

Pastoral Perspective

but many other church members come in twos or fours or fives. They pray, talk, and sing. One group of Indonesian members, who work in health care, bathes the woman's body and freshens her with sweet-smelling perfume. A group of church members led by clergy hold an impromptu healing service in the waiting room. The woman, unconscious through most of these visits, suddenly awakens, recovers, and is able to go home. While not all prayers of the community have such immediate and visible answers, those forty or more who came at one time or another to this bedside are reminded once again that prayer changes lives and has saving potential (5:15)

The prayers of the community shape the congregation and allow the people to become more nearly the body of Christ. In churches I have attended, it is not unusual for prayer times to last from twenty to thirty minutes, when individual members of the congregation voice their prayers of supplication in worship. While some find listening to the joys and concerns of members' lives tedious and too long, I am grateful and excited to hear how God is working and to know how to pray for others. In communal prayer we have the opportunity to listen for and be God's voice in the world. Through prayer the congregation is empowered to carry out Christ's mission. It is a practice in which all ages can participate. Prayer changes relationships and lives. It should be our first practice as a congregation, if we are truly to walk in James's concept of godly wisdom.

KATHY L. DAWSON

Exegetical Perspective

great deal more intimate and embodied to the ancients than it does to us, and their social construction of broken and ailing bodies is not of invading microbes but of their estrangement from or loss of the good life intended by God.[2]

The "prayer of faith" in verse 15 recurs in verse 17, where James says "the prayer of the righteous person works with great power" (my trans.). This is apparently why he invokes the example of Elijah (vv. 17–18). James draws from the story in 1 Kings 17–18 about the prophet's prediction to King Ahab of severe drought (17:1) and the report in 18:1, "After many days the word of the LORD came to Elijah, in the third year of the drought, saying, 'Go, present yourself to Ahab; I will send rain on the earth.'" Interestingly, 1 Kings does not mention Elijah's praying either to stop the rain or to renew it—he merely informs Ahab of the impending drought and then receives the "word of the LORD" that it will cease (17:1–2; 18:1). The story does, however, record between Elijah's two conversations with Ahab the prophet's fervent prayer on behalf of the Shunamite widow's son: "He cried out to the LORD, 'O LORD my God, have you brought calamity even upon the widow with whom I am staying, by killing her son?' Then he stretched himself upon the child three times, and cried out to the LORD, 'O LORD my God, let this child's life come into him again.' The LORD listened to the voice of Elijah; the life of the child came into him again, and he revived" (17:20–21).

Here indeed is the prayer of a righteous person that works powerfully. Elijah is the model for James's Christian community.

E. ELIZABETH JOHNSON

Homiletical Perspective

as a Wednesday night supper offers chances to pray with the suffering and sing songs of praise with the cheerful. Does someone routinely take plates from such suppers to those who are too sick to attend? Why not send an elder or two along for the ride? Whether or not they take oil, the point is for the community to go in search of those at risk of being lost to it. The point is to go to them when they cannot or will not come to you.

Few preachers will choose to be as directive as James, but those willing to imagine the congregational possibilities out loud may find that they stimulate the imaginations of their listeners as well. They will almost certainly find resistance, since it is no small thing to dislodge the self-serving wisdom of the world with the community-healing wisdom of God. To paraphrase James's opening questions, are any among you ready to be the first to confess your sins to the community? Are any ready to welcome church elders into your bedroom before you are well enough to change your nightgown? It would be a great mistake to assume that the faithful are eager to surrender their privacy to the church, much less their individualism. The preacher who can articulate their resistance with clarity and compassion will not only earn their ears; that preacher will also engage them in mutual confession whether they open their mouths or not.

There are also a couple of sermons in this text on the prophet Elijah. The preacher who wishes to follow James's lead may focus on the fervor and success of the prophet's prayer life (good luck convincing the congregation that Elijah was "a human being like us"), or borrow the verse directly proceeding today's lection (v. 11) to focus on the differences between Job and Elijah. In either case, the preacher will have ample opportunity to join James in praising those who manage concrete acts of faith in the face of great suffering.

BARBARA BROWN TAYLOR

---

2. Although he concentrates on healing narratives in the Gospels, John J. Pilch, in *Healing in the New Testament: Insights from Medical and Mediterranean Anthropology* (Minneapolis: Fortress, 2000), offers valuable insight into the social construction of health and illness in the ancient Mediterranean world.

Mark 9:38-50

38John said to him, "Teacher, we saw someone casting out demons in your name, and we tried to stop him, because he was not following us." 39But Jesus said, "Do not stop him; for no one who does a deed of power in my name will be able soon afterward to speak evil of me. 40Whoever is not against us is for us. 41For truly I tell you, whoever gives you a cup of water to drink because you bear the name of Christ will by no means lose the reward.

42"If any of you put a stumbling block before one of these little ones who believe in me, it would be better for you if a great millstone were hung around your neck and you were thrown into the sea. 43If your hand causes you to stumble, cut it off; it is better for you to enter life maimed than to have two hands and to go to hell, to the unquenchable fire. 45And if your foot causes you to stumble, cut it off; it is better for you to enter life lame than to have two feet and to be thrown into hell. 47And if your eye causes you to stumble, tear it out; it is better for you to enter the kingdom of God with one eye than to have two eyes and to be thrown into hell, 48where their worm never dies, and the fire is never quenched.

49"For everyone will be salted with fire. 50Salt is good; but if salt has lost its saltiness, how can you season it? Have salt in yourselves, and be at peace with one another."

Theological Perspective

Demons and Hell. The images of casting out demons and threats of hell present particular difficulties for post-Enlightenment Christians who want to make the gospel comprehensible to sophisticated audiences. A preacher confronted with this passage, therefore, does better to face these challenging themes head-on rather than evading them. There are certainly dangers in saying too much about such matters. New Testament scholar Markus Barth was once asked, "Do you believe in the devil?" His response: "No, and you shouldn't, either."

Christian theology since Augustine has rightly been wary of any stark dualism of light and darkness, since God created *all* things and pronounced them good. To focus too intently on the powers of evil is to grant them an ultimate power that they do not have. Furthermore, Christians rightly pause at detailed discussions of demons and hell, since accusations of demon possession have often been used to target and punish powerless groups, as in the witch hunts of the fourteenth to seventeenth centuries, and threats of hellfire have in many cases drowned out proclamations of God's abiding love.

Yet there are also dangers in moving too quickly to dismiss demons and hell as quaint but outdated concepts. Demons pose a real threat to people's health and well-being in the Gospels, and many

Pastoral Perspective

A strong community enhances the lives of its members. The community is a place of identity, where people have a sense of belonging because they are known and recognized. The community provides protection and support. The community shapes values and provides cultural norms.

But there are risks in a strong community. The expectations and demands of a social order may restrict the freedom and creativity of a person. The past ways may not be suitable for the challenges of the future. A strong community may be so focused on itself that it loses the capacity to relate to those outside.

There is a constant tension between being inclusive and being exclusive, with serious questions to be faced. How far should a community go in relating to other people who are different, and how far should it go in excluding those who have different standards and values and customs? How far must a community go in isolating itself from outsiders to keep its values? How does a community keep its identity if it recognizes the validity of differing ways and structures of other communities? How do people in a community fellowship with others without losing their defining distinctiveness?

The concern about inclusiveness and exclusiveness is particularly intense for the church.

Exegetical Perspective

No School for Scandal. Today's Gospel reading addresses two difficult subjects for Mark's fledgling community of believers. The first is the issue of boundary maintenance: how to identify who is in and who is out, and what to do when the membership status is unclear (vv. 38–41). The second is a list of rules, or rather of actions that are not acceptable for members of the community (vv. 42–50).

Boundary Maintenance (vv. 38–41). The issue is an outsider—someone "not following us"—who is doing ministry in Jesus' name. The question is posed by John, who, with Peter and James, constitutes the inner circle among the disciples (Mark 5:37; 9:2; 14:33). We are not told the motive for the concern, and any speculation about such is inappropriate. In fact, Jesus' response goes not to motive but to consequences, both for the community (v. 40) and for the person doing a good deed in Christ's name (v. 41).

The phrase "in my name" or "in Christ's name" merits a closer look. It is found in Mark only in 9:37, 38, 39; and 13:6, and in the supplementary ending at 16:17. On one level the phrase means simply "on behalf of," as perhaps is the case when one welcomes a child "in my name" in 9:37. The remaining instances are weightier, for they connect the "name" to the power and identity of Christ. The community that

Homiletical Perspective

It is always good to remember that understanding Scripture does not depend upon our ability to reconstruct a historical context or circumstance. So, before getting bogged down in the strangeness of the historical issues surrounding a text like this one, it is good for the preacher to ask, "What is the text evoking and demanding from the Christian reader?"

This text demands many decisions, at several levels: will we condone the exorcists who do not follow Jesus in *our* community? Are we prepared to lead one of Jesus' "little ones"? Are we going to cut off our hands and feet and gouge out our eyes in order to gain access to God's kingdom? Will we have salt in ourselves and be at peace with one another? And, if so, where and how do we get this salt that does not lose its saltiness? Every passage of this canonical text demands real and urgent decision. The job of the preacher is to convey this urgency and the life-giving abundance that a decision for the kingdom is sure to yield.

One problem that such a text presents for the preacher, however, is that it is basically a selection of Jesus' didactic teaching, with no real narrative context or interaction. Placing this text back in the narrative context of the call to discipleship, the turn toward Jerusalem, the transfiguration, and the exorcism of the demoniac boy will help the

Mark 9:38-50

Theological Perspective

Christians attest to their continuing power today. More importantly, however, they do not pose a real threat to Jesus. If we reduce demons to figments of primitive imagination, then we miss the point that casting out demons is a significant "deed of power," and that it is Jesus' name that accomplishes this deed.

In Jesus' Name. Key to the exorcism story (vv. 38–41) is the repetition of the phrase "in [Jesus'] name" [v. 38] and "the name of Christ" [v. 41]. This raises the question: what is the significance of the *name of Jesus Christ*? Some theologians have argued that to act in the name of Jesus Christ is simply to act in a manner consistent with his character. Others suggest that to act in Jesus' name means to act *on behalf of* Christ. Still others have insisted that the name "Jesus" itself is powerful, conveying the grace it signifies in a sacramental manner. "The name 'Jesus' contains all: God and man and the whole economy of creation and salvation. . . . His name is the only one that contains the presence it signifies." This latter approach has given rise to practices such as the Jesus prayer in the Eastern Orthodox tradition.[1] In this story, the "other exorcist" seems to be using Jesus' name explicitly as a powerful tool for casting out demons. This is not like Matthew 25:31–46, in which some people behave in a Christlike manner without realizing it. This is not an example of "anonymous Christianity." Rather, Jesus here suggests that an exorcism in his name works as a kind of "converting ordinance," a powerful act that cannot leave the performer unaffected: "No one who does a deed of power in my name will be able soon afterward to speak evil of me" (9:39). This passage, in the end, may be less about the power of demons and more about the power of language itself to change the speaker and to shape the identity of the community.

Back to Hell. Just as it is important not to dismiss demons, so also it is important not to ignore Jesus' words about Gehenna. The second part of this passage (vv. 43–48) repeats three times the fearful warning that if one places a stumbling block in front of a believer, or if one stumbles, it is better to drown or to cut off a part of the body rather than go to hell. Passages like this have given rise to one popular interpretation of the afterlife as a system of rewards and punishments for behavior here on earth. Those who behave well will be rewarded with eternal life in heaven, while those who behave badly will be cut

1. See *Catechism of the Catholic Church*, 2nd ed. (Washington, DC: United States Catholic Conference, 1994, 1997), nos. 2666–68.

Pastoral Perspective

For the church community is bound together not just by common interest or mutual enjoyment, but by convictions about the fundamental issues of human existence: what we believe most deeply, what gives value and meaning to our existence, under what obligations we live, how we define and achieve the good life, who we are.

When we deal with such fundamental and significant issues, it often becomes more difficult to be sensitive and accepting of those who have different convictions. To offer one example: Immediately after the 9/11 attacks, at an outdoor service at a baseball stadium in New York, prayers were offered by religious leaders from many different traditions. A group in the diocese of a bishop who participated in this service started a movement to depose him because by participating he had recognized the legitimacy of the prayers of others.

How do we keep the integrity of our own community without isolating ourselves from others? The first followers of Jesus confronted the issue when they came across someone who was casting out demons in Jesus' name. They tried to stop him "because he was not following us." He was not one of "us," one of their group, and they wanted to keep the integrity of the way of Jesus and the power of Jesus. What would happen if everybody started doing things in the name of Jesus? Jesus had certain powers, and through him the disciples had been given powers. The disciples were averse to allowing others outside their own group to exercise such power, even if it was in the good cause of casting out demons.

When they told Jesus about the person, he somehow did not seem as concerned about the situation. He said to them, "Do not stop him; for no one who does a deed of power in my name will be able soon afterward to speak evil of me." Preserving the power of his own group was not a priority for Jesus. If good were being done by others, their actions were to be affirmed. Jesus went on to say to the disciples that as they are ministered to by outsiders, it will come as blessing both to themselves and to those who aid them: "For truly I tell you, whoever gives you a cup of water to drink because you bear the name of Christ will by no means lose the reward."

How can a community keep its own identity and still be open to those outside? There is no simple answer to that question, but every community needs to be aware of where the line is drawn between insider and outsider, and of the impact that the decision of how to relate to others has on both those within and those without. The word of Jesus to his

acts in Christ's name in effect becomes his continuing presence in the world. Mark's community is wrestling with the implications of that responsibility as the gathering of disciples takes shape as the church.

"Do Not Scandalize!" (vv. 42–50). The countercultural but very gentle teachings about a reversal of status (becoming first by being servant of all) and about a community open to all who call on the name of Christ are followed by what sounds like an explosion of disproportionate and gruesome threats and prescribed punishments. There is no way to mitigate the forcefulness of the teachings, but a closer examination of the details may clarify their intent.

First, what the NRSV translates as "put a stumbling block" in front of people or "cause to stumble" is the verb *skandalizein*. It is much harsher than what we might hear in the word "stumble." The English cognate "scandalize" sounds quaint in a world where no action or behavior seems to shock anymore. The sense of the verb, however, is of being so horrified that one simply cannot remain in the place or go forward along the path where one had that experience. In this passage, the reference is to actions or words that would divert one from one's faith or discipleship or lead one to sin.

The first of the warnings focuses on things that would be harmful to "the little ones who believe." (The words "in me" are missing from some manuscripts, but they are implied.) That phrase is often seen as a term of endearment referring either literally to children or to people new to the community of faith. The context of the earlier issues of relative greatness of prestige or power, and the model of those who would be great becoming servants of all (9:33–37) suggest a social reference, namely, to those on the lower end of the social hierarchy, for whom the believers have a particular responsibility. The seriousness with which the offense is taken is seen in the "better" consequence of being thrown into the sea with a millstone around one's neck—a sure route to death.

Despite the parallel pattern in verses 42, 43, 45, and 47 of the verb *skandalizein*, followed by a drastic action that would be "better,"[1] there seems to be a change of subject in the last three examples. Instead of referring to one's responsibility for others in the community, verses 43, 45, and 47 speak of various body parts that would be better removed if they

1. Verses 44 and 46 are identical to v. 48, and are missing in the best ancient manuscripts.

preacher bring the more didactic nature of Jesus' teaching to life.

The text itself does have its own surprise. Why is the story of the dialogue between Jesus and John about an exorcist wedged between the flow of a discussion about receiving a child and being careful not to cause such a child to sin? Why does the text move from preserving a child from sin to preserving oneself from sin? It is also surprising that the text then moves from the fires of hell to the fire of sanctification. This text is a catena of many gospel demands, but central to them all is the continuing narrative demand to follow Jesus on his way to Jerusalem, the cross—and ultimately to vindication.

The work of the preacher is to reintegrate this text into the narrative that surrounds it. Could the disciples' pride be still smarting from Jesus' rebuke concerning the demoniac boy? Why should others successfully invoke Jesus' name when even his own disciples are unsuccessful in their ministry of exorcism? Jesus directs the disciples' attention to a child when they question their authority in the kingdom. He then warns them not to lead such a one astray. At issue is not just accepting a child, but "accepting," leading that child the "right way." With Jesus' face set toward Jerusalem, the demands of entry into the kingdom take their contextual meaning from the coming passion of the Messiah. Will the disciples be willing to take up their cross, deny themselves, and "cut off" eye and limb?

In terms of focusing in on the preacher's own community, this text can be preached with an emphasis on humbling "group pride": "whoever is not against us is for us" (v. 40). Further, the dangerous call of leading "little ones" in the life of the gospel can be a means of focusing on the life of the congregation. If this path is chosen, the preacher can pick up on the immediately previous lections and their focus on Jesus' teachings about himself as Messiah: in what way does Jesus' radical teaching about the nature of being the Messiah challenge the role of the teacher or preacher of the gospel? Are there those in the congregation who need to hear this kind of challenge?

Finally, the rigors of the Christian call to sanctification and Jesus' warnings about the end of a life that avoids that call are perennial themes for Christian sermons. Is your community within a tradition that has downplayed sanctification? Is the community one that has denied the hell that life becomes outside of Christian discipleship? Or has the community heard about the call to holiness so

Mark 9:38-50

Theological Perspective

off from God and dwell in "unquenchable fire." Dante's *Inferno* presents one classic version of this view of hell.

Yet it is important to note that this is not the only way of understanding hell, and it does not even make particularly good sense of the passage at hand. There is a strong countercurrent in Christian theology that resists speculation about eternal torture and focuses instead on hell as a strong symbol for separation from God. Many Christian theologians from the early twentieth century to the present reject a notion of a literal hell because it contradicts the basic christological affirmation that God loves the whole world and desires that all be saved. Instead, as Daniel Migliore puts it, "hell is simply wanting to be oneself apart from God's grace and in isolation from others. . . . Hell is self-destructive resistance to the eternal love of God."[2] Migliore's words offer an ironic twist on Sartre's grim declaration in *No Exit* that "hell is other people." We can resist God's love in Christ, and such resistance bears its own consequences, but separation from God is neither God's will nor the focus of Christian proclamation.

In this passage, Jesus does not describe hell in order to seal anyone's eternal destiny, but to motivate his audience to pay attention to the "little ones" and not to impede their path. The reference to "little ones" (v. 42) recalls 9:36–37, in which Jesus points out the little child as the one to be emulated and welcomed. Perhaps then the dire warnings about being thrown into hell are Jesus' stern caution about putting up roadblocks to those who would enter Jesus' community. Looking back from this standpoint, it appears that the whole trajectory of Jesus' teaching in this passage is to warn his disciples against obstructing the path for those who may turn out to be his followers— all "little ones," and even the "other exorcist" casting out demons in Jesus' name (v. 38).

MARTHA L. MOORE-KEISH

Pastoral Perspective

disciples reminds us to be sensitive to the issues involved, and his word pushes us to run some risk in relating to those who are not part of our community.

After dealing with the disciples' unwillingness to welcome the outsider, Jesus pointed to some other concerns his disciples would face as leaders, concerns that all of us who seek to minister in Christ's name will face. First, he warned against putting stumbling blocks in the way of others who are seeking to find their way toward faith in him. In vivid language he warned that "it would be better for you if a great millstone were hung around your neck and you were thrown into the sea." We need to ponder the risks for us if our failures of love, our distortions of the way of Christ, our too narrow understandings of the truth, our quickness to pronounce judgment cause others to stumble as they are trying to find the way of faithful living.

Second, Jesus warned his disciples and us about the risk that we may stumble ourselves. Again in vivid language, he declared that if our hand or foot or eye causes us to stumble, it is better to get rid of it than to miss the way of God and end up in the torments of hell. These words were spoken not to outsiders but to those who were seeking to follow him. His vivid words alerted them and us that the righteousness of God must be taken seriously.

Finally, Jesus talked about the salt of the disciples, the qualities that would preserve and enhance their community. From all that Jesus said as he journeyed the way to Jerusalem with his disciples, it becomes clear that their saltiness involves being humble in their relationships with each other, giving of themselves for others, reaching out and accepting all the people around them. They are to "be at peace with one another."

HARRY B. ADAMS

---

2. Daniel Migliore, *Faith Seeking Understanding*, 2nd ed. (Grand Rapids: Eerdmans, 2004), 347.

Exegetical Perspective

cause such an offense or threat. The very idea of such self-mutilation is grotesque, and the language of the text is offensive by any standard. Reading these verses in the context of the teachings about life and relationships in the community of believers, however, suggests that they may be drawing on the common ancient use of a body metaphor to refer to a social group. If that is the case here, the point may not be a counsel of self-mutilation, but rather that members with various roles in the community be removed if their actions threaten the integrity of the whole (see 1 Cor. 5:1–5).

Such betrayals are of inestimable importance, as can be seen in the eschatological language of the contrast of entering "life" (vv. 43 and 45) or "the kingdom of God" (v. 47) once the offending part has been removed. Those terms are equivalent here and are contrasted to being consigned to "Gehenna" (NRSV "hell") with the body intact. Human sacrifices were just some of the forbidden religious practices that took place during the Judean monarchy in the valley of Hinnom to which "Gehenna" referred. With Jeremiah's oracle of judgment against Gehenna (Jer. 7:31–34), that name came to mean "hell" as the place of eternal punishment and suffering—a picture amplified by the reference to the "unquenchable fire" that burns there and by the dire language of Isaiah 66:24, which is quoted in verse 48.

The images of punishment segue into an emphasis on purification in verse 49, where one is "salted with fire." That saying provides a catchword by which several sayings about salt are joined to the passage. Whether this is a deliberate reference to the disciples as "the salt of the earth" (Matt. 5:13) is unclear. In any case, in the ancient world salt was a precious commodity—to flavor and preserve food, for medicinal purposes, and as "salary"—for example, Roman soldiers were paid in salt rations. Here the reference is not to salt as part of the Roman imperial economy, but to their having that resource in themselves. The final verse, "Have salt in yourselves, and be at peace with one another," also emphasizes the gathered life of the community, and the use of salt to seal covenants with God and with one another (Lev. 2:13).

SHARON H. RINGE

Homiletical Perspective

much that it is now time for a fresh and challenging approach?

Outside of a straightforward expositional style, this particular lection lends itself to exhortation or teaching. In terms of exhortation, the theme of the first portion of the text could be taken up: acceptance of those who work in Jesus' name but not on our terms. Or, the second portion of the text could be addressed, by taking up the theme of sanctification, or of the dangers and responsibilities of leading Jesus' "little ones" in the life of the gospel. In terms of Christian teaching, the second portion of the reading lends itself to a discussion about hell, sanctification, or, even more interestingly, both. This text could be used as an opportunity to talk about the nature of damnation and sanctification and their odd and paradoxical relationship to one another in Christian teaching. How is it that both damnation and sanctification are described in terms of (an everlasting) fire? What—or who—is that fire? In the end, we get what we want. The question is, what—or whom—do we really want? And what are we willing to deny in order to get that one thing needful?

Accepting the breadth of those who call on Jesus' name—taking care in leading Jesus' "little ones"—responding to the call to sanctification and its paradoxical relationship to damnation—are all inescapable demands on the life and prayer of the disciple who follows the Jesus of this narrative, whose face is set toward Jerusalem.

NATHAN G. JENNINGS

Job 1:1; 2:1-10

[1:1]There was once a man in the land of Uz whose name was Job. That man was blameless and upright, one who feared God and turned away from evil. . . .

[2:1]One day the heavenly beings came to present themselves before the LORD, and Satan also came among them to present himself before the LORD. [2]The LORD said to Satan, "Where have you come from?" Satan answered the LORD, "From going to and fro on the earth, and from walking up and down on it." [3]The LORD said to Satan, "Have you considered my servant Job? There is no one like him on the earth, a blameless and upright man who fears God and turns away from evil. He still persists in his integrity, although you incited me against him, to destroy him for no reason." [4]Then Satan answered the LORD, "Skin for skin! All that people have they will give to save their lives. [5]But stretch out your hand now and touch his bone and his flesh, and he will curse you to your face." [6]The LORD said to Satan, "Very well, he is in your power; only spare his life."

[7]So Satan went out from the presence of the LORD, and inflicted loathsome sores on Job from the sole of his foot to the crown of his head. [8]Job took a potsherd with which to scrape himself, and sat among the ashes.

[9]Then his wife said to him, "Do you still persist in your integrity? Curse God, and die." [10]But he said to her, "You speak as any foolish woman would speak. Shall we receive the good at the hand of God, and not receive the bad?" In all this Job did not sin with his lips.

Theological Perspective

It is obvious to any reader of the book of Job that the most difficult of all theological questions is illustrated by the plot and raised explicitly within the dialogues. Theologians call this the theodicy question, namely, how the goodness of God can be vindicated in the face of the various evils in the world to which innocent persons are subjected. However, the tale is also about God's vindication of the innocent person who suffers. The book of Job actually scores three main points: first, while some suffering is brought upon ourselves through our own sin and foolishness, at least some, perhaps even most suffering is undeserved; second, to argue contrariwise misconstrues the character of the person who suffers unjustly as well as that of God; and third, how God can be affirmed as good and just in the light of such innocent suffering is a mystery beyond our finite human comprehension.[1]

Job is described as "a blameless and upright man who fears God and turns away from evil" (2:3; cf. 1:1). These words are spoken by God when conversing with "the Satan" (the "adversary" or "accuser") who serves in the heavenly council as a sort of prosecutor. Two things are noteworthy here. Satan is not yet the diabolical opponent of God's

1. Mayer Gruber, "Job: Introduction," in *The Jewish Study Bible*, ed. Adele Berlin and Marc Zvi Brettler, Jewish Publication Society *Tanakh* translation (Oxford and New York: Oxford University Press, 2004), 1499–1500.

Pastoral Perspective

No.

No, no. no.

Nobody is really like this: "blameless and upright, one who feared God and turned away from evil" (1:1). At least nobody in any congregation I ever served was like this, even Ed and Millie who were there every time we opened the doors. (Actually they had their own key.)

This is a setup. The text is another didactic setup. We all know the drill. "Ed and Millie or _____ (substitute the appropriate name here) are just saints. They are such a good Christian family with those ten wonderful children (1:2). Why, I can't imagine that either of them has ever had an evil thought. And they are just so faithful to the church."

But I knew Ed and Millie. Ed had been in the pastor's office now and then to set me straight in no uncertain terms about "how we do things around here." And Millie? She had some long-buried stuff in her life. You could see it in the lines of her face and the way her eyes were instinctively cast down in company. That was not humility. That was pain.

The whole story never came out, not even at Millie's hospital bed that time. The most anyone knew was the trouble with a couple of their kids, and some anger around town about how Ed had treated some of his employees.

Exegetical Perspective

This masterpiece of religious thought, in which the tragic suffering of a righteous individual occasions a probing theological investigation of the divine economy, was apparently written by someone (not necessarily Israelite) in Edom (or Egypt or Mesopotamia) sometime between the tenth and second centuries BCE as a historical account (or an imaginative parable) all wrapped up in a dramatic presentation replete with superb Hebrew poetry. Huh?

This lack of certainty regarding the diachronic data compels a more synchronic approach. *Sola Structura!* Perhaps the vagueness is intentional. By setting *Star Wars* "long ago, in a galaxy far, far away" George Lucas invites us to see that epic battle between good and evil as a timeless conflict applicable to all. Much the same could be said of Job. We are not reading historical accounts here; we are being asked to contemplate the weighty issues that arise in the course of the story.

And there *is* a story. Readers have long noticed that the (in)famous central core of poetic give-and-take between Job and his "friends" and then between Job and God (3:1–42:6) is enclosed by a compelling narrative of Job's suffering and restoration (1–2; 42:7–17). Though disputed, the literary architecture of the book is reasonably coherent and falls into a concentric structure:

Homiletical Perspective

Dare the preacher enter the pulpit with the book of Job in hand? After all, this book has confounded its interpreters for millennia, unraveling those who seek to unravel it. The book of Job is a complex work, exploring the intricate intersection of divine sovereignty, human faith, and innocent suffering. It is also a troubling work—troubling for the unsettling questions it poses to a neatly arranged, tidy faith. It is no wonder that its searing inquiry is given only a small parcel of acreage in the landscape of the lectionary! And yet the preacher would do well to grapple with its difficult questions for the sake of questioning the easy, feel-good faith that is too often proclaimed in place of gospel news.

Many Questions. Faced with the challenges that the book of Job offers, it may be useful for the preacher to begin with questions—questions with which the book itself wrestles. The prologue of Job (chaps. 1–2) yields many of them: What is the relationship between blessing and faith? Do persons believe in order to be blessed? Or is faith instead an expression of gratitude because we have been blessed? For many it is, but what constitutes that blessing? (And what happens to faith when those blessings are no longer perceived to be present?) Why is there suffering, and what effect might it have on faith? In our own time,

Job 1:1; 2:1-10

Theological Perspective

righteous purposes as he later appears in Jewish apocalyptic writings, including the New Testament. In this story, Satan works for God! This provides us with a clue about the mystery of God's relation to evil: Satan cannot act at all without God's permission. Furthermore, God is depicted in less than flattering terms as being vulnerable to Satan's persuasion: ". . . you incited me against him, to destroy him *for no reason*" (2:3, emphasis added). Perhaps God is *not* as good as we like to think.

Satan, who is depicted as having a rather astute mind for theological disputation, raises the critical question of the book as a whole: "Does Job fear God for nothing?" (1:9). According to Israel's wisdom tradition, "the fear of the LORD is the beginning of knowledge" (Prov. 1:7). But what is meant by "the fear of God"? John Calvin distinguished between two kinds of religious fear: servile fear and proper fear. Whereas most people fear God's punishment, true believers "fear offending God more than punishment."[2] Servile fear is fear for oneself. Proper fear, by contrast, is respect and reverence for God. James M. Gustafson has written of the contrast between a "utilitarian" religion that justifies religious faith by its benefits for human persons and a genuinely "theocentric" piety and fidelity focused on serving God and God's purposes without reference to the self.[3] Job himself articulates the question in slightly different terms when his wife suggests he curse God on account of his misfortune: "Shall we receive the good at the hand of God, and not receive the bad?" (2:10). Underlying these various formulations, the issue is the same: why be religious at all? Can we truly serve God for God's sake alone, apart from reference to the self?

Christianity has historically been a religion of redemption focused on the salvation of human beings. There is a proper concern with human well-being that motivates us to work toward the eradication of disease and oppression, as well as to ameliorate the devastating effects upon persons of hurricanes and other natural disasters. But, theologically considered, the issue is how we understand our place in the universe in relation to the rest of God's creation. Do we see ourselves as being in the center of things? Did God make the world for the sake of humanity? Has God designed

Pastoral Perspective

What always seemed odd, at least until understanding dawned, was that the congregation did not ever seem interested in the whole story. Ed and Millie were saints, everybody said. It was as if the congregation needed them to be saints. They were the designated holy ones, unblemished by evil, "blameless and upright." And thus they could stand in for everything the rest of the congregation would never be—or maybe even never want to be. Their iconic status would enable the rest of the congregation to avoid facing their own conflicts and failings or ever having to speak with each other plainly.

When the hyperbole starts piling up—in the case of Job, four straight adjectival descriptions of praiseworthy behavior—start sniffing for a rat. Something is going on. Nobody is really like this. So somebody is telling this tale for a reason.

Congregations, ancient and modern, are irresistibly drawn to melodramas of righteousness. How else can we account for the proliferation of children's "sermons," usually the most overt didacticism in a congregation's collective life? Here the adults give the children a moral object lesson in good behavior, almost always a lesson that no child can understand. But the adults respond regularly with warm laughter, because it would be so much more convenient if the life of faith were more like the instructions for assembling the new television stand: insert end A into slot B and tighten with screw C.

Of course, the appeal of didacticism to our congregations is a perfect mirror of our culture. We are always being to told what to think and how to feel. Each day brings a torrent of advertisements for products and services of every kind, mostly in the form of moral tales of salvation bottled for a mini-bar. I failed to watch my kid, but here's a towel that can wipe up any spill. I can't sleep for thinking about my falling out with my best friend, but here is a pill that will carry me off to the land of Nod. There's a ready answer for everything and a right solution to every situation.

Little wonder that so many sermons treat the Bible like an advice book, or reduce every text to a folk tale with a moral, or steadfastly cling to the happy talk of a consumer society. Is it Mother's Day? Salute the mothers, and pay no attention to the women who were unable to have kids. Is it Thanksgiving Sunday? Salute the plenty of the land and admonish everyone to use it well, and say nothing about the assumption that everything is here for human use—the assumption that underlies exploitation of God's good creation. It's the story of Job?

---

2. John Calvin, *Institutes of the Christian Religion*, trans. Ford Lewis Battles, ed. John T. McNeill, 2 vols., Library of Christian Classics (Philadelphia: Westminster Press, 1960), 3.2.27, cited in the customary manner according to book, chapter, and section.

3. James M. Gustafson, *Ethics from a Theocentric Perspective*, 2 vols. (Chicago: University of Chicago Press, 1981, 1984), 1:16.

Exegetical Perspective

A Introduction 1:1–5
B Job Loses All 1:6–2:10
C Three Friends Arrive 2:11–13
D Dialogue between Job and Friends 3–31
X Elihu Speeches 32–37
D′ Dialogue between Job and God 38:1–42:6
C′ Three Friends Depart 42:7–9
B′ Job Receives Double 42:10–13
A′ Conclusion 42:14–17

The lectionary's cropping of over half the verses in the first half of the narrative, however, obscures two further structural features helpful for interpretation. First, following a succinct portrayal of Job's exemplary piety (1:1–5) the author meticulously presents the heinous stripping of Job's possessions and health by means of two virtually identical panels:

Panel One 1:6–22
A Presentation of the Adversary v. 6
B YHWH's question v. 7
C YHWH praises Job v. 8
D The Adversary slanders Job vv. 9–11
E YHWH gives limited permission v. 12a
F Adversary departs v. 12b
G *Property and children* taken vv. 13–19
H Job's trust in YHWH vv. 20–21
I Job did not sin v. 22

Panel Two 2:1–10
A′ Presentation of the Adversary v. 1
B′ YHWH's question v. 2
C′ YHWH praises Job v. 3
D′ The Adversary slanders Job vv. 4–5
E′ YHWH gives limited permission v. 6
F′ Adversary departs v. 7a
G′ *Health* taken v. 7b
H′ Job's trust in YHWH vv. 8–10a
I′ Job did not sin v. 10b

In both panels the discussion between God and "the adversary" (*ha-satan*) concerning Job's piety, the provisions for the testing of such, and Job's profession of faith remain constant. The only palpable difference concerns the object of Job's loss. In G Job is systematically deprived of his property and children. In G′ his health is taken away. Despite the similarity, however, the repetition provided by the paneling should be seen as an intensification of Job's suffering, not merely duplication. By the way, "Satan" in the NRSV does not refer to the devil, a dualistic concept unknown in preexilic Israel; the presence of the article (*ha*) "the" indicates the *satan* is a member of the heavenly council functioning as an official "adversary" or "accuser." Readers are, therefore, understandably horrified by *God's* sanction of these calamities.

Homiletical Perspective

we wonder: Why do conscientiously healthy people suddenly grow terminally ill? How can those who worked and saved for a lifetime lose everything to corporate malfeasance? In a world of such abundance as ours, how can tens of thousands of people still starve to death every day?

In raising such questions, a sermon may probe those places where the congregation assumes a connection between faithfulness and blessing, or unfaithfulness and suffering. Or it may comfort a congregation where faithfulness has not yielded evident blessing, reminding them of the competing voices within Scripture that bear witness to the complexity of faith.[1] After all, the reality is that sometimes faithfulness does indeed yield blessing; but sometimes faithfulness yields only suffering. Such ambiguity surely tests faith! The inclusion of the book of Job in the canon stands as a reminder to the church that things are not always as simple as we may want to believe—but amid the complexity, God is present.

Why Suffering? One can hardly utter the name of Job without summoning to mind the realities of suffering—particularly the suffering of innocent persons. In his work *Amazing Grace: The Lives of Children and the Conscience of a Nation*, Jonathan Kozol stares unflinchingly into the deep pain and suffering of impoverished children living in the South Bronx of New York City. Drug abuse, violence, and hunger crowd the landscape in which young children grow up there. Kozol wrestles with his own despair as he reflects on these bitter realities, which have no easy solutions. Attending a worship service one evening in which a pastor spoke words of hope of God's future action to mothers whose sons were in prison, Kozol writes on the back of the bulletin, "Then where is He? What is He waiting for? Come on, Jehovah! Let's get moving."[2] The book of Job offers no easy answers to the suffering and injustice of this world (indeed, it was likely written to challenge any easy answers that had been offered). It does, however, articulate clearly that such struggles belong before God.

Why Believe? Among all of the questions raised in Job's prologue, the one most difficult to answer is

---

1. Walter Brueggemann, for example, considers the book of Job to be a part of Israel's "countertestimony" to the received testimony at the core of Israel's faith. See his *Theology of the Old Testament: Testimony, Dispute, Advocacy* (Minneapolis: Fortress, 1997), 317ff.
2. Jonathan Kozol, *Amazing Grace: The Lives of Children and the Conscience of a Nation* (San Francisco: HarperPerennial, 1996), 229.

Job 1:1; 2:1-10

Theological Perspective

the world in such a fashion that persons always get what they deserve? If not, then human happiness is not the end for which God created the world. Does this not suggest that our concern for salvation, however conceived, needs to be subordinated to that of discerning our appropriate place within the whole of creation?

Job is depicted as a model of theocentric piety and fidelity. In spite of everything he suffers, Job "persists in his integrity" (2:3). He serves God without expecting reward or complaining about misfortune. He does not put himself in the center of things. There comes a point, however, when even Job has to call into question the justice of God, in light of the enormous suffering inflicted upon him. Such lamentation is legitimate, even for a person of faith. To make matters worse, Job must defend himself against the suspicions of his "friends" that he must have done something sinful or else these bad things wouldn't be happening to him. But this theological thesis turns out to be false: God vindicates the righteousness of Job. We thus learn that, in the world as designed by God, suffering is not always the consequence of one's sin and virtue does not always entail happiness. I once heard someone who was in the middle of a deep personal crisis remark, "God doesn't owe me anything." Like Job, this person understood that true service of God is not motivated by hope of reward for oneself. That is the kind of fidelity exemplified by Job. Such is the wisdom born of a proper fear of God.

PAUL E. CAPETZ

Pastoral Perspective

Praise Job for his integrity, make a joke about the "foolish woman" (while assuming the superior moral wisdom of men), tell everyone that whatever befalls them it is God's will (even if you have now made it impossible to tell the difference between faith and fatalism) (2:10).

But somewhere in the congregation, some folks are sitting there scratching their sores. They do not understand. They know that neither their own aspirations for righteousness nor the ambiguities of everyday life are amenable to didactic instruction manuals. So be a pastor for them.

Be a pastor for Job, sitting in the ash heap scratching himself with a piece of broken pottery. He has not said a word. See if you can get across to him that you understand the setup, that you know something of how his life has really been with those ten kids, that you honor his silence now.

Find a way to let Job know that you realize the real dishonor here: that he has been reduced to a stand-in for everybody's illusions about their own righteous aspirations, that he is a stick figure in somebody else's melodrama, that he has not even been granted the dignity of the truth. Because what good is it, really, to be faithful to a God who jerks you around like a puppet on strings and does not have the good grace even to tell you what is really going on?

Tell Job that God is not like that. Hang in there. Wait. There is more about God than this tale reveals.

Somebody in the congregation will hear it too. Somebody will hear that we do not need Ed and Millie to be our saints, that we are all in this mess of joys and sorrows together. Ed and Millie might even hear it too and grow in their trust that life together is a continual discovery of God sitting in the ashes beside us.

That is not in this text. But maybe God is not either.

THOMAS EDWARD FRANK

Exegetical Perspective

Perhaps that is why the material is also divided into a series of five scenes that alternate between earth and heaven:

Scene 1 (1:1–5) *on earth*, Job's righteous character
Scene 2 (1:6–12) *in heaven*, God and the adversary discuss Job
Scene 3 (1:13–22) *on earth*, Job's first trial
Scene 4 (2:1–7a) *in heaven*, God and the adversary discuss Job
Scene 5 (2:7b–10) *on earth*, Job's second trial

Dividing the action into earthly and heavenly arenas provides readers with information unknown to Job. We know that Job's trials (scenes 3 and 5) are the result of conversations in the heavenly council (scenes 2 and 4) concerning the reasons for Job's exemplary piety, displayed in scene 1. Deprived of this knowledge, Job must continue to wonder, "Why?"

But to what does the "Why?" refer? Our passage introduces the burden of the book of Job. Job is usually assigned to the Bible's Wisdom literature, which also includes Proverbs and Ecclesiastes. These three books, however, are very different theologically. Proverbs, the Bible's parade example of retributive justice, maintains that righteousness is rewarded and sin is punished (e.g. Prov. 1:29–33). That Job is a frontal assault on this rather simplistic theological position is evident from the start. The description of Job as "blameless and upright" (1:1a), a description twice affirmed by God (1:8; 2:3), is defined as "one who feared God and turned away from evil" (1:1b), which comes right out of the exhortation in Proverbs to "fear the LORD, and turn away from evil" (Prov. 3:7b). In the following four verses we hear of the rewards this exceedingly pious individual enjoyed. So far, so good. But the remainder of our passage reveals (to the reader, not to Job!) that heaven is about to unleash a totally inexplicable assault on Job's theologically proper existence by afflicting him with undeserved pain and suffering. Despite his wife's intuitive understanding of the futility of maintaining one's faith in the retributive system (see her ambiguous statement "Do you still persist in your integrity? Curse ["bless" in Hebrew] God, and die" [2:9]), Job continues to live as he had before, without sin (1:22; 2:10b).

Our passage thus sets the stage for a vigorous theological debate. What does one do when one's theological doctrine, that the universe runs on the principle of reward and punishment, is manifestly at odds with one's experience? Subsequent Sundays will further explore this theme.

MARK A. THRONTVEIT

Homiletical Perspective

this: In a world of both blessing and suffering, *why is there faith at all?* What good is faith? If persons of faith suffer as much as any other, then what's the use? Why not follow the counsel of Job's wife, and curse God and die?

The book of Deuteronomy connects faithful obedience with blessing, and disobedience with curse (see Deut. 30:15–20). Job's friends will reinforce this connection when they join him at the ash heap, assuming that Job's suffering testifies to his disobedience. Like the Satan, they assume an unbroken connection in which faith and blessing reinforce one another. The questions of Job's prologue are particularly troubling to a faith in which one good (faithful obedience) is offered in exchange for another good (blessing). The Satan offers God the challenge of placing a proverbial stick in Job's spokes, wagering that removing the "hedge" of Job's blessings (his family, his fortune, and his health) will be enough to send Job over the handlebars, undoing Job's faith. Why *does* Job believe, after all?

That's not a bad question for the rest of us. Why *do* we believe? Is faith a commodity? There are some who believe because through faith they are convinced that good will come: material prosperity, eternal reward, internal peace, or whatever else. When those goods are somehow threatened, then faith is jeopardized.

In his *Screwtape Letters*, C. S. Lewis records the advice of a senior devil, Screwtape, to his nephew Wormwood, who is trying to undo the faith of a recently converted Christian. At one point, Screwtape says to Wormwood, "Our cause is never more in danger than when a human, no longer desiring, but still intending, to do our Enemy's [i.e., God's] will, looks round upon a universe from which every trace of [God] seems to have vanished, and asks why he has been forsaken, and still obeys."[3] Such a stance is testimony to a faith that is much more than a means to some selfish end.

J. S. RANDOLPH HARRIS

---

3. C. S. Lewis, *The Screwtape Letters* (New York: Collier Books, 1961), 39.

Psalm 26

¹Vindicate me, O LORD,
  for I have walked in my integrity,
  and I have trusted in the LORD without wavering.
²Prove me, O LORD, and try me;
  test my heart and mind.
³For your steadfast love is before my eyes,
  and I walk in faithfulness to you.

⁴I do not sit with the worthless,
  nor do I consort with hypocrites;
⁵I hate the company of evildoers,
  and will not sit with the wicked.

⁶I wash my hands in innocence,
  and go around your altar, O LORD,

Theological Perspective

Vindicate me? Are you serious? Are we really to pray asking God to turn the tables on our enemies on the basis of our "integrity" (v. 1)? Our trusting without wavering (v. 1)? Our eschewing of the worthless, the hypocrites, the evildoers and the wicked (vv. 4–5)? Christians of all stripes have loudly and consistently insisted that God justifies us *in spite of our sins*. God does not look down, decide that we are better than others, and grant us the reward we deserve. Psalm 26 is all backwards. Furthermore, in my own pastoral and spiritual experience, the folks who insisted most loudly on their own holiness, well, they were unwittingly hinting that something was wrong, spiritually speaking. And just when I am most sure of my own righteousness I am probably most blind to my own misdoing. It was G. K. Chesterton who famously called original sin "the only part of Christian theology which can really be proved."[1] If that is so, the psalmist did not get the memo.

Perhaps a historical vignette will help us see how the church has come to interpret this difficult psalm. The culture of Augustine of Hippo, in late fourth- and early fifth-century North Africa, was not so far removed from the days when Roman authorities

1. G. K. Chesterton, *Orthodoxy: The Romance of Faith* (New York: Image, 1990), 15.

Pastoral Perspective

The writer of this psalm sounds like a person who is too good to be true: "I have walked in my integrity, . . . I have trusted in the LORD without wavering. . . . I do not sit with the worthless. . . . I wash my hands in innocence. . . ." The psalmist is not shy about tooting his own horn. In fact, he wears his integrity like a badge of honor, polished to a point of near-blinding brightness.

But interspersed among the obsequious sentences of self-affirmation are other phrases that reveal some cracks in the armor of righteousness. "Prove me and try me. . . . do not sweep me away. . . . redeem me, and be gracious to me. . . ." In other words, "I cannot do this own my own, O God. I need you to guide and lead me. Give me some word of assurance that I am truly following your will and not my own."

The psalmist continually turns to God for affirmation and for direction. He is confident in his faith, but only to a point. Without God to validate his thoughts and actions, he is unsteady. The faith that has been unwavering up until now can easily unravel, and he knows it.

"Your steadfast love is before my eyes." This line indicates the focus of the psalmist's gaze: God. "I go around your altar," the psalm continues, as a recognition that God is at the center of the map. Like a sea captain looking to the stars for bearing, so the

^{7}singing aloud a song of thanksgiving,
   and telling all your wondrous deeds.

^{8}O LORD, I love the house in which you dwell,
   and the place where your glory abides.
^{9}Do not sweep me away with sinners,
   nor my life with the bloodthirsty,
^{10}those in whose hands are evil devices,
   and whose right hands are full of bribes.

^{11}But as for me, I walk in my integrity;
   redeem me, and be gracious to me.
^{12}My foot stands on level ground;
   in the great congregation I will bless the LORD.

Exegetical Perspective

Psalm 26 is a fairly conventional offer of the genre of lament/complaint. It consists in seven imperatives addressed to YHWH (vv. 1–2, 9, 11), two motivational clauses introduced by "for" (vv. 1, 3), and an extended statement of innocence before YHWH that likely functions as a motivational statement (vv. 4–8, 11–12). The psalm contains its peculiar surprise, but there is no surprise in the way the familiar genre is articulated.

The imperatives addressed to YHWH are framed in a judicial context. The four positive imperatives ("vindicate . . . prove . . . try . . . test") in verses 1–2 ask the judge to scrutinize carefully the evidence brought against the speaker, for the speaker knows he will be found innocent before YHWH the judge. There is a confident boldness in this appeal to the judge; the psalmist has nothing to hide before the judge "from whom no secrets are hid."[1] The fifth imperative ("do not sweep me away") acknowledges the devastating punishment of which the divine court is capable. Thus the imperative reflects a dangerous venue of judgment and punishment, but with no fear of the outcome of adjudication.

The motivational clauses in verses 1 and 3 reflect intense fidelity toward YHWH and deep

1. *Book of Common Prayer* (New York: Seabury Press, 1979), 323.

Homiletical Perspective

This psalm is striking as it paints a portrait of the one who prays it, someone startlingly self-assured. When we offer this psalm up in prayer, we find the distance between ourselves and the psalmist diminished, the gap eclipsed by a righteousness that borders on self-righteousness. When one calls upon God for judgment and vindication, an important line divides those who genuinely suffer from false testimony against their integrity from those who are deluded that they live forthrightly and steadfastly. Thus, we must engage this text as potentially dangerous, for it assumes that those who claim this psalm for themselves live a virtuous life in the context of the wider world. There is something ashamedly unabashed about declaring publicly before God one's integrity, faithfulness, and innocence, and if we preach this message, our testimony needs to take our individual and communal lot in life seriously, reflectively, and humbly.

While we should be careful in taking on this mantle of righteousness, there is something admirable about the desire to live an honorable life. However, the Jewish context in which Psalm 26 originally was penned and our present Christian context are quite different. While Jewish laws forbade certain social interactions and mandated a level of purity among observant followers, the witness and

Psalm 26

Theological Perspective

persecuted Christians. And under those persecutions some priests and bishops and lay people unfortunately succumbed, turning over precious Christian books, denying Christ, burning incense to the emperor—all things good Christians ought not do if they can help it. What do you do if your priest—the one who baptized you or married you or taught you the faith—was among the fallen? Was your baptism valid? Should it be redone? Those who argued yes came to be known (somewhat disparagingly) as Donatists, after one of their leaders. For the Donatists, baptism had to be performed by a priest in apostolic succession who never lapsed. "How can you pass on what you do not have?" Donatists asked about the apparent lack of holiness of those who apostatized. We can catch a glimpse of the agony of these fights by thinking of those Catholics affected in the clergy abuse scandal; if your priest were among the guilty, could you trust *anything* he once said or did, however good or right it seemed at the time?

Augustine had another answer: in baptism, what matters is not the holiness of the priest, but the holiness of Christ. As long as the work is performed rightly—with water in the name of the Father, Son, and Holy Spirit—baptism is valid. Those who break off from the church and claim to set up a communion of the sinless deceive themselves. The church is always full of sinners, thank you very much, and if it is not, you and I do not deserve to be part of it either. Augustine included a prediction that must haunt Protestant histories: those who break off from a supposedly apostate church will keep on breaking off into smaller and smaller bodies with more and more self-satisfied people. Ouch.

Augustine's famous *Confessions* shows why he especially would struggle with a psalm like this. The historic reason Christian apologists claimed their faith was true over against that of skeptics was to point to the holiness of Christian people. How could our faith not be true if we produce people as good as that? Augustine could say no such thing: he had fathered a child out of wedlock, he had belonged to the Manichean sect for many years. In fact, when he became bishop of Hippo, his enemies were talking. Do you really want a guy so unholy as that to be your *bishop*? Augustine's answer is his *Confessions*. He says, in effect, "You say I'm evil? Well, let me tell you just how evil I am." Christianity, for him, is not true so much because it makes the best people, but because we have the most forgiving God.

So what should we do, from an Augustinian perspective, with a psalm that calls for one's own

Pastoral Perspective

faithful keep turning to God to be sure that both our motivations and intentions are springing from a desire to please God, and God alone.

We know that putting God first is the good and right way to be, but our humanness often gets the best of us. We get caught up in trying to please everyone else: our teachers, boss, family, even people we do not know whose opinions shouldn't even matter to us, yet somehow they do. Or we go to the opposite extreme, and focus on what we want. "Look out for No. 1!" society tells us, and so we find ourselves on an ever-narrowing pursuit to place our own needs at the center of the universe. We are traipsing across an uneven landscape.

Thomas Merton (1915–68), the Trappist monk and poet, reflected on his own struggle to be faithful to God. In his book *Thoughts in Solitude*, Merton wrote: "My Lord God, I have no idea where I am going. I do not see the road ahead of me. I cannot know for certain where it will end. Nor do I really know myself, and the fact that I think that I am following your will does not mean that I am actually doing so. But I believe that the desire to please you does in fact please you."[1]

At the heart of Psalm 26, the psalmist desires to please God, and that in itself is pleasing to God. God loves an earnest believer! God is not an impossible-to-please prima donna. God seeks our affection, and delights in our devotion. It is with our seeking to please God, not being piously perfect, that God is indeed pleased. If our heart is in the right place, God knows.

It is God's steadfast love, God's loving-kindness, that "is before my eyes" (v. 3), and that entices the faithful to service. Biblical scholar Patrick Miller writes, "It is God's nature to be faithful, and it is God's nature to be merciful, to manifest a gracious love and forgiveness even against God's own inclination to reward faithlessness with justice instead of mercy."[2]

We turn to God with an expectation that God will hear our pleas and our "please." It is not an empty request on our part. God is faithful. God is the one whose intentions and motivations are pure, honorable, upright. It is God who continually, and unwaveringly, walks in integrity. To believe in, and to put our allegiance in, such a God is to place our faith and our whole being into the hands of the One who

1. Thomas Merton, *Thoughts in Solitude* (Farrar, Straus & Giroux, 1999), 79.
2. Patrick Miller, "Prayer as Persuasion: The Rhetoric and Intention of Prayer," *Word and World* 13/4 (1993): 358.

commitment to the ways of YHWH. In verse 1, it is affirmed that the speaker has lived in "integrity," that is, with a single, undivided intention; that single undivided intention is to rely upon YHWH and only upon YHWH. In verse 3, the speaker has been responsive to YHWH's covenantal loyalty (*chesed*) and has lived reliably (*'emeth*) toward YHWH. These two terms, *chesed and 'emeth,* constitute a favorite and recurring word pair in Israel's rhetoric of faith that bespeaks complete commitment to the covenantal promises and covenantal requirements of YHWH. These covenantal claims are the ground for the imperatives addressed to YHWH. The speaker will surely be judged innocent and acquitted, precisely because the speaker has gladly and fully conformed to the covenantal ways of YHWH.

Then, as though the motivations of verses 1 and 3 require further detailed substantiation, verses 4–8 characterize the life of innocent fidelity that assures an acquittal by the judge. On the one hand, verses 4–5 describe a social practice in which the psalmist has spent his time only in relation to other reliable Torah keepers and has avoided the company of the "worthless, hypocrites, evildoers, wicked." The heavy rhetoric of condemnation is conventional in the Psalter and reflects the severe "either/or" of Torah faith that is signaled already in Psalm 1 and detailed in "Psalms of Entry" such as Psalms 15 and 24. That "either/or" grows out of the "life or death" mandates of Deuteronomy (see Deut. 30:15–20). There is no compromise or middle ground. This tradition of glad covenantal innocence takes seriously "guilt by association" or, less severely, we are known by the company we keep, and eventually we become like those with whom we spend time.

On the other hand, verses 6–8 describe the speaker's active participation in the cultic life of the community. Thus to "wash hands" is, in the first instant, an act of ritual purification (see Ps. 51:7; Isa. 1:16). Activity "around your altar" consists in songs of thanksgiving that are public acknowledgments of YHWH's gifts and gestures of gratitude that eventuate in being witness in the community of the faithful concerning YHWH's wondrous, generous acts of rescue and rule. On all counts the speaker is a devoted covenant keeper!

The speaker knows that judgment is coming, because the God of the Torah will not be mocked . . . or disobeyed. The speaker, moreover, knows the sort of people who are rightly "swept away," and he is not among them. Verses 9–10 portray the rejection of covenant as a violent disruptive force within

life of Jesus overturn the priority of those obligations. In the preaching life, it is vital to remember that Jesus often subverted prevailing interpretation of Judaic laws in order to embrace those whom the laws were used to exclude. Jesus invited a tax collector to be one of his disciples, spoke publicly with a known prostitute, physically touched those ridden with disease, and otherwise acted in ways that violated certain understandings of the Jewish laws.

Given that, are we as Christians hypocrites if we preach, "I do not sit with the worthless, nor do I consort with hypocrites; I hate the company of evildoers, and will not sit with the wicked," when in fact Jesus of Nazareth did all of these things in his life? We cannot preach the goodness of nonengagement with the wicked when Jesus himself made the moral affirmation that interacting with the wicked could lead to the expansion of the kingdom of God. In the Christian faith, to name oneself innocent and all others vile is to have an acute misconception of the ordering of a world in which the last become the first, in which the dimensions of sin are not insurmountable barriers designed to hold the sinners at a distance, but portals to be opened so that the sinners might be reclaimed by God in justice and love.

Recently I heard this text preached within the complicated situation of a church working through the aftermath of a natural disaster, specifically a New Orleans church that suffered little damage when the levees broke following the onslaught of Hurricane Katrina. Without question, the members of the church had felt as though they were innocents, and literally did not want to be swept away by God. In this limited use of the text, preaching this psalm made sense, but it also raised a number of questions.

Is there an implicit assumption that the churches that were washed away were sinners, worthless, evildoers? Is this unsaid assumption made more careless when we realize that many of the churches that did not survive Katrina were populated by the less affluent, racially discriminated citizens of New Orleans, especially those in the Ninth Ward? When tragedy has demolished the houses of worship of the poor, of those already living at the margins, what right does an affluent, relatively unscathed church have to wash its hands in innocence? When do such claims of faithful innocence become the underpinnings of sinful negligence? It is a shame when we preachers believe that a biblical text is an easy one to preach, because the very nature of the Bible is that it offers messages that unsettle us, that

Psalm 26

Theological Perspective

vindication, that claims, with Augustine's enemies, to be the holiest people around? The Donatists, for example, cited verse 4 as they refused to *sit down*, literally, for a conference with the Catholics. Augustine replied that on those grounds they should not even have entered the room to "consort" with them! (How's that for literalism?)[2] There is *one* altar of the Lord around which we gather to give praise, not many—a riposte to those who shrug off care for ecumenism in any age (v. 6). And we offer praise at that altar to God, not to ourselves, as verse 7 makes clear: "telling all *your* wondrous deeds" (i.e., not our own). "To hear the sound of praise is to understand deep within yourself that whatever evil there is in you in consequence of your sins belongs to you, and whatever good there is in the setting right of those sins belongs to God."[3] The rest of the psalm must be read in this light: as praise not of our goodness, but of God's—"borrowed" or on loan from God as it were—and only so is it ours.

In this light we can see the psalm is about worship. I do not "sit with the worthless" because I sit in church, going around the altar, "singing aloud a song of thanksgiving," telling God's wonderful deeds both inside and out (v. 7). Amid our lovers' quarrels and outright fights in our denominations and congregations about what the church should or should not do, how often do we let our hair down and announce with unrestrained joy, "O Lord, I love the house in which you dwell"—that is, the church? We have no righteousness of our own to lord over those without then. All we have is a charge to tell them about the borrowed righteousness we have found, like clothes to play dress-up in, in a life of worship marked by surprising joy: "in the great congregation I will bless the LORD" (v. 12).

JASON BYASSEE

Pastoral Perspective

created us in the first place, and who seeks, always, to offer us forgiveness, hope, and new life.

Ideally, the church is the place where we come to experience that forgiveness, hope, and new life. People whose lives are broken—or even just frayed around the edges (all people, in fact)—need to know that everyone else in the congregation is not living the perfect life. Many people look as if they have it all together: the perfect marriage, family, kids, life. But most likely, these people have their hurts and heartaches and struggles too. We do not come to church to judge our thoughts and deeds against the rest of the folks gathered—nor to have them judged by others. We are all seeking God's mercy.

Within the congregation, we seek an alternative to the way society teaches us to live. Society says, "Winner take all," but the church says, "Do to others as you would have them do to you" (Matt. 7:12, NRSV). Society says, "Your worth is based on your income and status," but the church says, "Your worth comes from being loved by God." Society says, "Revenge is recommended over reconciliation," but the church says, "Strive for the greater gifts" (1 Cor. 12:31, NRSV). We hope, indeed we expect, that others in the congregation will express God's mercy and grace. As the body of Christ, we are called to put aside our prestige and our pretensions and look at one another as equals, children of God with our faults and failures, forgiven not because of our worth, but because of God's unfathomable grace.

When the *good* news of the gospel is preached, sung, prayed, heard, and lived out by the people, we leave worship feeling uplifted and blessed. "In the great congregation I will bless the LORD" (v. 12).

KATHLEEN BOSTROM

---

2. Translator Maria Boulding tells this story in *Expositions on the Psalms 1–32* (Hyde Park, NY: New City Press, 2000), 263 n. 13.
3. Ibid., 264.

Exegetical Perspective

community that cannot be tolerated. But the speaker is totally unlike those sorts of people: "But as for me!" (v. 11). In verse 11 the speaker returns to the initial claim of verse 1, again "integrity." Thus the psalm is an "envelope" of "integrity" at the beginning and end that celebrates genuine, obedient, practical faith. On that basis the psalmist finally voices two big theological imperatives: "redeem . . . be gracious" (v. 11). The speaker is in the "congregation" among those who are serious about the faith, a community of those who celebrate YHWH. The contrast is sharp and complete between "the great congregation" (v. 12) and the "congregation of evildoers" in verse 5, two statements using the same term.

This development of the familiar genre is not a surprise. But the surprise may be discerned if we focus on "integrity" in verses 1 and 11. Three lines of interpretation may be suggested:

1. This psalm, like much of the Psalter, is informed by and derivative from the tradition of Deuteronomy. In Deuteronomy 18:13, Moses commands Israel to "remain completely loyal to the LORD your God." The Hebrew term "completely loyal" is *tam*, the same term used twice in our psalm for "integrity." Thus "integrity" of the psalmist has to do with obedience to the Torah teaching of Deuteronomy.

2. The term "integrity" shows up particularly in the book of Job, concerning the man who has lived a responsible life congruent with YHWH's requirements (see 1:1, 8; 2:3, 9; 9:20–22; 27:5; and 31:6, and on the lips of his "friends" in 4:6; 8:20). These uses suggest that Psalm 26 may be understood as a presentation of the faith claims that led eventually to the poem of Job wherein a genuinely faithful person is not "vindicated" but is "swept away" along with the evildoers. This linkage to Job, moreover, is reinforced by the fact that in Psalm 25:21, just before our psalm, the word pair of Job 1:1, 8; 2:3 is exactly echoed, "integrity and righteousness." What this psalm affirms becomes for Israel, in the real world, an abiding theological crisis.

3. There is real continuity between this psalm and New Testament claims. The voice that speaks here in the Torah community of Israel is, mutatis mutandis, the same voice that speaks of the "new creation" in Christ (2 Cor. 5:17).

The psalmist is one who has found freedom and joy precisely in a life with YHWH and with YHWH's people made concrete and visible in the community of Torah practice.

WALTER BRUEGGEMANN

Homiletical Perspective

shake us out of our doldrums and reawaken us to the obligations that come with being beloved children of God living in community with other beloved children of God.

Given these concerns, how then does one preach this passage faithfully? I would encourage the preacher to take account of the situation in which both the preacher and the church membership live and serve. Is the church integrated within the concerns and pressures of its neighboring communities, and if it is not, why not? This passage can be used as a means of reminding the community that the clarion call of the Christian faith is one of engagement with the poor, the wretched, the meek, and that it is our obligation to sit with the worthless, to consort with the hypocrites, to make company with the evildoers. We have no capacity to wash our hands in innocence if all around us lies a landscape of broken relationships and societal decay. The ending of the psalm, its final two verses, is one that can be employed by the preacher through a purposeful altering of the text to encourage a communal sense of renewal, achieved by converting the singular first person into the plural first person: "But as for *us*, *we* walk in *our* integrity; redeem *us*, and be gracious to *us*. *Our feet* stand on level ground; in the great congregation *we* will bless the LORD."

This intentional call for engagement challenges our churches to step outside of the comfort zone provided by nonengagement, by stained-glass windows that obscure the needs of society outside of the church, the beautiful organ whose wafting notes drown out the cries of those in need. The church must not be a fortress within which people prop themselves up, but a shelter in which all are welcome, a harbinger of the assistance God provides to all people.

STEPHEN BUTLER MURRAY

Hebrews 1:1-4; 2:5-12

^{1:1}Long ago God spoke to our ancestors in many and various ways by the prophets, ²but in these last days he has spoken to us by a Son, whom he appointed heir of all things, through whom he also created the worlds. ³He is the reflection of God's glory and the exact imprint of God's very being, and he sustains all things by his powerful word. When he had made purification for sins, he sat down at the right hand of the Majesty on high, ⁴having become as much superior to angels as the name he has inherited is more excellent than theirs. . . .

^{2:5}Now God did not subject the coming world, about which we are speaking, to angels. ⁶But someone has testified somewhere,

"What are human beings that you are mindful of them,
    or mortals, that you care for them?
⁷You have made them for a little while lower than the angels;
    you have crowned them with glory and honor,
⁸   subjecting all things under their feet."

Theological Perspective

The quest for the historical Jesus has dominated New Testament studies for more than a hundred years. Biblical scholars continue to try to determine what the earthly Jesus actually did and said, in distinction from what his followers later attributed to him. This scholarship has deeply shaped contemporary Christologies, as is evident when contemporary statements of faith are contrasted with the church's earliest creeds. Whereas the Apostles' Creed (like the Nicene) moves directly from the incarnation to the passion ("born of the Virgin Mary, suffered under Pontius Pilate, was crucified, dead, and buried"), the 1991 Brief Statement of Faith of the Presbyterian Church (U.S.A.) devotes half of its lines about Jesus to his earthly ministry, his proclamation of a new social order (the kingdom of God), and the resistance that he encountered from religious and political authorities.

The Christology of Hebrews is better captured by the early creeds than these contemporary confessions. In Hebrews, we read nothing of Christ's miraculous healings, his compassion for the poor and marginalized, or his dramatic confrontations with the Pharisees or Roman rulers. The author of Hebrews is not trying to reconstruct the movements of the historical Jesus, or to account for why the authorities resisted his ethic of radical love. The

Pastoral Perspective

For most of my preaching life, I have avoided the book of Hebrews—somehow taking offense at what I perceived to be its exclusive and bloody interpretation of atonement theology. But now, in midlife, I am meeting Jesus again in some healing ways in these texts. As the "exact imprint of God's very being" (1:3), the Jesus in the book of Hebrews shows me the path toward polishing and reflecting the image of God in my own soul.

Educator Rodger Nishioka has helped the contemporary church understand what our dropout young adults are yearning and searching for. A palpable, passionate Jesus is at the heart of their hunger. Hebrews unveils this passionate Jesus—one who is made perfect through the excruciating sufferings of our human experience. And so Jesus embodies a paradox—the authenticity of human life and the authenticity of divine love wrapped up in incarnational reality. Jesus is the real thing—the authentic pioneer of God-drenched living, reflecting the glory of God in the flesh-and-blood experiences of earthly life.

To the Jews, "Christ crucified" was a scandal, because for them, the mysterious God, who has no name, could never be visible to human eyes. And to the Greeks, "Christ crucified" was foolishness, because for them, a God who feels, suffers, weeps,

Now in subjecting all things to them, God left nothing outside their control. As it is, we do not yet see everything in subjection to them, [9]but we do see Jesus, who for a little while was made lower than the angels, now crowned with glory and honor because of the suffering of death, so that by the grace of God he might taste death for everyone.

[10]It was fitting that God, for whom and through whom all things exist, in bringing many children to glory, should make the pioneer of their salvation perfect through sufferings. [11]For the one who sanctifies and those who are sanctified all have one Father. For this reason Jesus is not ashamed to call them brothers and sisters, [12]saying,

"I will proclaim your name to my brothers and sisters,
in the midst of the congregation I will praise you."

Exegetical Perspective

A rousing exordium: the first four verses of the epistle to the Hebrews constitute a compact synopsis of the whole of this rich "word of exhortation" (13:22). Like the classical rhetoric in which the author was trained, they display elaborate verbal devices, with alliteration (several words starting with the letter *p*) and assonance (repetition of long vowels, especially *o*) echoing through the verse. The verses are arranged chiastically, framing the reference to the act of atonement that was Christ's sacrificial death. Their theology highlights the significance of the "great high priest" (4:14), the eternal Son of God whose exaltation at the right hand of God provides firm assurance for his faithful followers. The exordium also anticipates many of the homily's major themes.

The first verse highlights God's speech, a key theme of the whole discourse. At the same time, it introduces an antithesis between the "prophets" of old, through whom God spoke to the ancestors, and the Son, through whom God has spoken at the end of days. A similar antithesis governs the central section of the text, chapters 8–10, where Jeremiah's promise of a "new covenant" introduces a contrast with the old cultic order.

The reference to Christ as Son is one of the two focal points of the Christology of Hebrews. A catena of scriptural quotations that follows this exordium

Homiletical Perspective

The opening words of the letter to the Hebrews evoke the time and space of worship. Hearing these words, we experience a sermon in the context of ongoing liturgy. This sermon is *doxological* in that the preacher glorifies God for the salvation God has achieved through Jesus Christ. This sermon, in a sense, functions as a verbal Eucharist, an offering of thanksgiving and praise that draws the hearers into God's very presence.

In this sermon we are reminded of the power of the spoken word: long ago God *spoke* through prophets, so in these latter days God *has spoken* through the Son (1:1). God's "word" (*rhēma*, 1:3) is an active force. The speaking that God did in the past brought the cosmos into being (1:2). The speaking that God has done in Christ brought news of God's salvation close at hand. In the proclamation that occurs now, in the hearing and interpretation of this text, God speaks. All this speaking is done in Christ, through Christ, and with Christ. The active power in this "word" is that same power through which God has wrought the worlds and brought salvation.

Though the preacher speaks the word, the congregation is "taken up" into this act of doxology, this verbal Eucharist. In the traditions of the Eastern churches it is understood that the congregation is taken up by the Holy Spirit into the heavenly realms,

Hebrews 1:1-4; 2:5-12

Theological Perspective

picture of Christ that emerges from Hebrews is decidedly more cosmological than worldly, and is driven more by the church's confession of faith than by scholarly interests in historical evidence and accuracy.

The beginning of Hebrews nevertheless makes clear that God's work in Christ does not float above the world or disregard its pain and brokenness. On the contrary, faith in Christ drives the believer into history and the world. For Hebrews, the historical Jesus does not first come on to the scene around 4 BCE and depart in 30 CE. Rather, the history of Jesus extends from the beginning of creation to its transformation at the end of time. The problem with the quest for the historical Jesus is not that it insists on treating Jesus and the Scriptures historically, but rather that its conception of history is too narrow.

Hebrews 1:1–4; 2:5–12 sets out nothing less than a confessional summary that embraces the entirety of time and space. It offers us a picture of history as *salvation history*, a history that derives its meaning not from scholarly interpretation of earthly actors and events, but rather from God's mysterious yet gracious purposes. What holds this history together, from beginning to end, is Jesus Christ. The One whom the book of Revelation calls Alpha and Omega (Rev. 1:8) is also for Hebrews the first and the last. The whole history of God's ways with humanity finds its hermeneutical key in Christ.

In its confession of faith, Hebrews first establishes the priority of God's revelation in Christ. God has always spoken to God's people, but in the past God spoke "in many and various ways by the prophets" (1:1). Now God has spoken to us by a Son who is "the exact imprint of God's very being" (1:3).[1] Hebrews 1:5–14 (not included in the lectionary) appeals especially to the Psalms to establish Christ's unique status as God's Son. Christ becomes the key to a right interpretation of what Christians would come to call the Old Testament.

The priority of Christ as God's revelation is paralleled by his priority in salvation history. As God's very Son, Christ exceeds every angel or spiritual being (1:4). God has created all things through Christ (1:2). Christ sustains all things through his powerful word (1:3). Drawing on Psalm 102, Hebrews proclaims, "In the beginning, Lord [Christ], you founded the earth, and the heavens are the works of your hands" (1:10).

---

1. This language anticipates the Nicene Creed, which states that Christ is "God from God, Light from Light, true God from true God . . . of one Being with the Father."

Pastoral Perspective

and dies was anathema to the Hellenistic mind. But "Christ crucified" was, for the writer of Hebrews, the tough and tender grace of a God who loves us unconditionally.

It is easy to use the hyperbolic language of this text to set up a superior Christ—so far removed from our humble, human experience that we can worship him only from afar. The comparison of Jesus in the text to the more imperfect leaders of history—the prophets and the angels and the luminaries of the Hebrew Scriptures—has all too often been twisted into an exclusive and anti-Semitic interpretation of God's love. But the use in Hebrews 2 of Psalm 8— that ode to the wonder and holiness of the human creation—*connects all people* to the glory of Christ and suggests that we too can grow toward perfection if we travel the Way of Jesus, the Way of love that gives up life in order to offer life to all.

I am more and more convinced that the uniqueness of the Christian life is the radical way we are called to embrace paradox—grace and truth, life and death, darkness and light, duty and delight. Jesus is the one who shows us how. In the rich verses of Hebrews we are given a Jesus who embodies glory *and* humiliation, power *and* suffering, authority *and* servanthood, radical grace *and* radical obedience. Each side of the paradox makes the other side possible. In stunning symmetry, we find in Hebrews an utterly majestic and cosmic God coming to touch us—up close and personal.

In this Hebrews text, as in so much of the New Testament, "perfection" does not mean an excellence out of reach of ordinary human experience. Perfection, in a gospel sense, means "completeness"—fully carrying out the purpose for which we have been created—clearing out the clutter and corruption of our living so that the "imprint of God's very being," which is in each one of us, can be fully revealed.

In 2004 I had the privilege of traveling to Colombia to meet and worship with the tiny, passionate band of disciples who call themselves Presbyterians in that beautiful, broken land. The stories of suffering—the torture and death of innocent believers, the displaced poverty of four million war-ravaged refugees, the courage of those who speak for justice and are rewarded with death threats, the passion of the young, expressed through the bravery of political action and the beauty of joyful singing—all of the stories are steeped in the glory and humiliation of the Way: the Way of the cross, the Way of Jesus, the Way paved by the intense imagery of Hebrews.

will emphasize the exalted status of the Son, set higher than any angel. Chapter 2 will emphasize the solidarity of the incarnate Son with his "brothers and sisters" (NRSV, "children") of flesh and blood. The combination of heavenly status and full humanity is the way God speaks a definitive word.

The next clause uses poetic language, similar to Wisdom of Solomon 7:25–26, in order to speak about the eternal significance of the Son. The first image, "reflection [or "radiance"] of God's glory" (1:3), anticipates language used by Christian theologians to describe the ways in which Son and Father relate as a unity with two distinct identities.

The second image, "imprint of God's very being" (1:3), uses a different metaphor, but with a similar thrust. The "imprint" or "stamp" bears the exact likeness of what is imaged. The term for God's "very being" (hypostasis) will have a long and significant history in Christian theology, with a sometimes confusing range of meaning. Our author will use the term again in 3:14 and 11:1, in each case playing on its etymology. In this verse the philosophical connotations predominate. The Son is the visible impression of the very "reality" of the God. The next usage will evoke the ethical demand that one "stand fast" for one's belief. (The NRSV translation "first confidence" [3:14] misses the crucial etymological play.) The final usage (11:1) will combine the two senses, suggesting that the hope that makes the ideal real consists in our taking a stand for what we believe in.

The next clause suggests the Son's role in creation, both at the initial moment of divine creativity and in the ongoing divine sustenance of the created order. The affirmation again evokes the figure of divine Wisdom, who was present with God at the creation (Prov. 8:22–31) and who "pervades and penetrates all things" (Wis. 7:24). Similar affirmations about the cosmic role of Christ are found in other early Christian hymnic confessions (1 Cor. 8:6; John 1:1–3) influenced by the wisdom tradition.

The exordium's central affirmation focuses on distinctive themes of Hebrews. "When he had made purification for sins" hints at the interpretation of the death of Christ as a sacrificial act, the key insight developed in chapters 8–10. Here the language is general. The later chapters will suggest that Christ's sacrificial death is the reality to which the Yom Kippur ritual pointed as a shadowy sketch.

Having completed his priestly act, Christ "sat down" at the side of the "Majesty on high," a polite circumlocution for God (1:3). The reference to Christ's session evokes a key text, Psalm 110:1, that

especially in the midst of the eucharistic celebration. So too, we can see that, in the hearing of this doxological word, the congregation is taken up in the power of Christ to be united in the Father (2:10). Those who have been sanctified by Christ are all siblings of Christ. In the hearing of this hymnic sermon of praise to God's act of salvation, we know and experience the reality of God's drawing the worshiping congregation into communion. This is our Eucharist as well, our common thanksgiving, giving thanks for what God has done and entering into the perpetual praise of God that occurs in the heavenly realms.

In the Reformed tradition the word heard and proclaimed takes the central role in the service of worship. Preaching, in many ways, becomes the place of encounter with the Majesty (megalōsynē, 1:3) of God. In Calvin's understanding of the Lord's Supper, in the Great Prayer of Thanksgiving, it is at the point of the Sursum Corda, when the congregation lifts up its collective heart, that the Spirit lifts up the congregation to the place where Christ dwells in heaven. In this heavenly feast all are nourished by the life-giving and sustaining body of Christ.

In the time and space of the liturgy of the Lord's Day service, we are fed by the life-creating Word of God by whom we are encountered in the faithful attending to that Word. We hear of God's majesty, of God's sustaining power, of what God has done in Christ, how Christ is the reflection of God's glory, and of Christ's humiliation and exaltation. This is not a moralizing text. We are not told what to do to get right with God or our neighbor. We are overwhelmed in this proclaimed word by the power and presence of God. We enter into the singing of this hymn, because we are taken up by it. We hear only of God's greatness and of the sufficiency of Christ as the author speaks of what God wants for all humanity. We are nourished by God in the hearing of the sermon.

Yet, this sermonic hymn of praise does not only evoke an ecstatic praise session. Though the focus of this sermon is on who God is and what God has done, there is a tensive point . . . a crux at the heart of the matter. We are told that Christ, in his obedience to God, has made a "purification for sins" (1:3), and has "tast[ed] death for everyone" (2:9). Hearing of God's act of sanctification through Christ draws us close to the crux of the matter: the story of Christ's passion, his suffering and death on the cross. In the midst of this hymn of praise we are drawn up not only into the unending eucharistic praise that

Hebrews 1:1-4; 2:5-12

Theological Perspective

The history of salvation moves from creation and providence to sin and salvation. Only the One who has created the world can redeem it (an insight that would receive classic theological formulation by the Cappadocian fathers in the fourth century). Christ makes purification for sin (1:3). He sanctifies us and makes us his brothers and sisters (2:11). Through his sufferings, he brings God's many children to glory (2:10). By dying, he takes on death for everyone (2:9).

For Hebrews, crucifixion and atonement point us simultaneously to resurrection and ascension. Christ's humiliation on the cross has won for him glorification as the resurrected and ascended Lord (1:3). The One "who for a little while was made lower than the angels [is] now crowned with glory and honor because of the suffering of death" (2:9).

The history of salvation does not conclude with atonement and the vindication of the crucified Christ. The redemption of humanity immediately points us to the end of time and the consummation of God's purposes for all creation. Here Hebrews profoundly identifies the eschatological tension within which Christians stand. As the redeemed, we already share in the resurrected Christ's royal office. By God's wondrous grace, God has crowned us with glory and honor, and has subjected all things under our feet (2:8a, drawing from Ps. 8). But we do not yet see everything subject to us (2:8b). Tragically, the redeemed world continues to manifest sin, evil, and disorder. As Christians, we live only by radical hope. We live by Christ's claim on our lives and the confidence that Christ has been "appointed heir of all things" (1:2). We look to Jesus, the pioneer of our salvation, who will bring all things to perfection.

The opening verses of Hebrews have creedal character. Although not in a linear manner, they nevertheless guide us through doctrines of revelation, creation, providence, sin, salvation, crucifixion, resurrection, ascension, anthropology, the Christian life, and eschatology. Unlike the Nicene and Apostles' Creeds, Hebrews' confession of faith does not fall into three neat articles, each associated with a person of the Trinity. But perhaps more strongly than these early creeds, Hebrews sets forth Christ as the one thread that runs throughout salvation history. Through him alone, we see the full work of God as Father, Son, and Holy Spirit.

JOHN P. BURGESS

Pastoral Perspective

The words of Hebrews were written to second-generation Christians—believers who were removed from the intensity, the intimacy, the passion of the early years of the movement. With the seductive pressures of a materialistic and violent world bearing down on them from every side, these disciples had become burned out, discouraged, apathetic believers. Their lethargic faith resonates with the malaise we are experiencing in our own contemporary Christian world. It is as if we are afflicted by the spiritual version of chronic fatigue syndrome—out of sync with the culture around us, weary of serving, and unable to muster either the discipline or the delight that daily discipleship can offer us. The electricity of Hebrews can reignite our faith, reminding us of the amazing grace of God's very imprint in Jesus and in us, and assuring us that endurance through suffering—as well as joy—is the power of God in us for others.

Years ago I traveled to the Middle East, and spent a delightful two days on the island of Cyprus. Our small band of pilgrims ended up visiting an ancient Orthodox monastery high up in the hills, overlooking the brilliant jewel of the sea. In order to enter the cave where the ancient hermits lived, we had to get on our hands and knees and crawl over rough-hewn rock. Once inside, we could contemplate the extraordinary paintings only by lying flat on our backs. There, glowing in the flicker of candlelight was the luminous wonder of the Pantocrator—the Risen Christ drenched in both glory and humiliation. The deep passion in the pool of his eyes was the sweet bitterness of love, a rich offering of both suffering and joy. Just by drinking in that grace, I felt myself growing in "perfection"—in the radical understanding of grace made perfect through suffering—of love so amazing, so divine that it embeds "the exact imprint of God's very being" in my living.

SUSAN R. ANDREWS

recurs throughout the homily (1:13; 8:1; 10:12). Early Christians frequently used this psalm to express their belief that after his crucifixion Christ was exalted to heaven in triumphant vindication (Eph. 1:20; 1 Pet. 3:22). One of our author's most creative moves is to use another verse from that psalm (110:4), in which a royal figure is addressed as a priest "according to the order of Melchizedek." This acclamation will ground the claim that Christ is a special high priest, whose death is a special kind of sacrifice. Christ's being seated at the right hand of God in its own right plays an important role in the psalm. In that position, Christ has achieved a heavenly glory that is now to be shared with all his brothers and sisters (2:10). There too, on a throne of grace (4:16), he is in a position to intercede for the faithful.

The exordium closes with a transitional verse using an a fortiori argument, typical of Hebrews. The note that Christ has inherited a name (1:4) introduces another important theme, inheritance, woven through the homily (6:17; 11:8). The theme will culminate in the conceit that by his death, Christ has left a will/testament that provides an inheritance for his followers (9:15–17). The "name" that Christ has "inherited" is not made explicit, although the citation of Psalm 2:7 in Hebrews 1:5 suggests that it is probably "Son," the designation used for Christ from the beginning of the exordium.

The superiority of his name parallels Christ's superiority to the angels, who are but servants (1:14). The chapter continues with a series of biblical verses that explore the theme of Christ's superiority to the angels. Some readers have thought that this contrast betokens a polemic against some form of angel worship. It is more likely a device of enco-miastic rhetoric, *synkrisis*, by which an orator exalts his subject through comparison with figures of high status. The contrast with the angels is but the first of several that occur through the homily, relating Jesus to Moses (3:1–6), Joshua (4:8), earthly priests (5:1–10), and Melchizedek (7:1–19).

HAROLD W. ATTRIDGE

resounds in the eternal realms of God. We are also confronted with the very human and inhumane suffering of Christ. We cannot escape the reality that something had gone wrong in the cosmos and that God, and only God, could set things right.

In proclaiming this text today we must follow the model of the text: our preaching is to be strongly doxological, extolling the greatness of God and praising God for the sufficiency of what God has done in Christ Jesus. *And,* in the midst of our own hymns of praise, we cannot escape the story of the cross: how things had gone wrong and still go wrong today; how our lives are caught up in the seemingly unending tale of human subjection to sin; and, how the whole created order is caught in this tension. In our experience we may forget the sufficiency of God, because the planet seems to be in such turmoil. Sin seems rampant on a global scale. The tensive place in the midst of this hymn of praise draws us all into the story of God's redemption.

Yet we do not dwell long in the place of suffering. The few phrases that refer to Christ's suffering function as reminders of the greater story. God's salvation is that much more tangible, because we know suffering. Our communal act of thanksgiving has its grounding in knowing from what God has delivered us. This text ultimately speaks of God's love. Despite all that has gone wrong in the cosmos (the very cosmos that God's word has created), God's love in Christ is sufficient to draw us from our seeming plight. In the very act of voicing this hymn of praise, at the center of which is God's speaking in Christ, we are taken up and "offered up" and, in so doing, are made sisters and brothers of Christ and of one another.

MICHAEL G. HEGEMAN*

Mark 10:2-16

²Some Pharisees came, and to test him they asked, "Is it lawful for a man to divorce his wife?" ³He answered them, "What did Moses command you?" ⁴They said, "Moses allowed a man to write a certificate of dismissal and to divorce her." ⁵But Jesus said to them, "Because of your hardness of heart he wrote this commandment for you. ⁶But from the beginning of creation, 'God made them male and female.' ⁷'For this reason a man shall leave his father and mother and be joined to his wife, ⁸and the two shall become one flesh.' So they are no longer two, but one flesh. ⁹Therefore what God has joined together, let no one separate."

¹⁰Then in the house the disciples asked him again about this matter. ¹¹He said to them, "Whoever divorces his wife and marries another commits adultery against her; ¹²and if she divorces her husband and marries another, she commits adultery."

¹³People were bringing little children to him in order that he might touch them; and the disciples spoke sternly to them. ¹⁴But when Jesus saw this, he was indignant and said to them, "Let the little children come to me; do not stop them; for it is to such as these that the kingdom of God belongs. ¹⁵Truly I tell you, whoever does not receive the kingdom of God as a little child will never enter it." ¹⁶And he took them up in his arms, laid his hands on them, and blessed them.

Theological Perspective

These passages raise theological questions on at least three levels. First, they raise the question of our proper understanding and teaching about marriage, children, and divorce. Second, because this question is set in the context of the Pharisees' "test" of Jesus, it raises the further question of who or what has the proper authority to answer our questions. Should we appeal to Scripture, tradition, reason, experience, or conscience? Third, Jesus' answer raises the question of the kingdom of God and the proper attitude of those who are to receive and enter into it. These three sets of questions are interrelated. By indicating that the proper attitude of those who are to receive and enter into the kingdom is reliance on and gratitude for God's grace, Jesus escapes the Pharisees' trap and provides a positive answer to the question of marriage, children, and divorce that is both uncompromisingly rigorous and an appeal to God's mercy.

The context of the discussion is one of many in the Gospels in which various authorities try to trap Jesus by asking him a question that they know has no good answer. Often these questions reflect ongoing controversies among competing factions or schools of thought, so any answer is likely to offend someone. If a woman successively marries seven brothers, whose wife will she be in heaven? (Mark 12:23) Should we pay taxes to the emperor? (Mark

Pastoral Perspective

She did not look like a Pharisee. She appeared harmless: a flowered-print dress, short in stature, glasses too large for her rounded face. I thought she was going to welcome me to the church. It was the reception at my very first pastorate. I extended my hand as she approached, opened my mouth—but before I could say anything, she said, "Preacher, do divorced people go to hell?"

Almost dropping my fruit punch, I thought, "I just passed my ordination exam. What is this? Another test of some sort?"

I raced through my mind's data bank for something I had learned in pastoral care, or even New Testament courses, that I might offer her (and get myself off the spot).

Finally, I spoke, "Better people than me get divorced."

I think I remember her asking the question again, "Preacher, do divorced people go to hell?" I gave her basically the same answer. I remember wondering if my attempt at cleverness had been helpful to her as she turned and walked away.

During a longer conversation in her home, she told me about her son who had recently divorced. Behind her question at the reception was a deep concern for her son, who had chosen to end a troubled marriage and was about to remarry. As a

Exegetical Perspective

No area of human life, including the most intimate that a man and woman can know, goes untouched by service in the cross's shadow, now looming in Judean territory (10:1). Great crowds, which Jesus has attracted early on (2:13; 3:7–12), ask his opinion on divorce. Some of this Gospel's oldest manuscripts identify Pharisees as the questioners (in line with 2:16–3:6; 7:1–23; 8:11–13). Other manuscripts, however, are not so specific. The interpreter is wise not to emphasize this particularity. What matters is not who asks the question but who is answering it: for the reader has traveled with members of the Twelve to the mount of transfiguration, hearing with them a heavenly admonition to pay attention to God's beloved Son (9:7).

Rabbis conventionally addressed the circumstances surrounding divorce. Mark highlights this question's adversarial tenor by indicating that it is pop quiz (*peirazontes*) sprung on the teacher (10:2). Note that the question assumes marriage's dissolution, not its maintenance. Typically (Mark 3:4; 11:29; 12:15b–16), Jesus turns the question back on his interrogators, asking them how they interpret Scripture (10:3). Correctly they answer that Moses allowed a man to draw up a certificate of divorce, letting the woman go (v. 4; see Deut. 24:1–4). The law offers a loophole. What is permissible, however, is neither necessarily

Homiletical Perspective

This text is a challenging one for preachers. The juxtaposition of these two pericopes in a single lection presents difficulties; the preacher is tempted to focus on one pericope or the other—often on the more appealing story about the children, rather than on Jesus' difficult words about divorce. One challenge for the preacher, then, is to consider the relationship between the two pericopes. A second challenge is that Jesus' difficult teaching in verses 2–12 presents serious pastoral concerns related to those who are divorced and remarried, as well as to gay, lesbian, bisexual, and transgender persons in the congregation.

In dealing with the second challenge, preachers should take seriously the particular context of Jesus' teaching on divorce and focus their sermons accordingly. The Pharisees test Jesus with a specific question about the legality of divorce. In response to this specific question, Jesus offers his teaching. Consequently, this teaching should not be used to speak regarding questions to which it is not addressed—for example, questions related to gay and lesbian relationships. To take Jesus' words in this text and use them to label such relationships as sinful would be inappropriate. In response to a specific question, Jesus discusses marriage between a man and a woman. Other kinds of relationships are simply not in the horizon of this text.

Mark 10:2-16

Theological Perspective

12:14) Here, the question concerns divorce. As indicated in the Pharisees' response to Jesus, they already know the scriptural answer: Moses allowed a man to divorce his wife. The contemporary debate concerns the legitimate grounds for this divorce. Was divorce justified only in cases of sexual impurity, or could a man legitimately divorce his wife for any fault, including perhaps the "fault" of simply being less appealing than another woman?

As usual, Jesus reframes the debate. He turns the question from the grounds for divorce to the grounds for marriage. God has created man and woman for each other. They should not be set apart. In the intervening years, the church has elaborated extensively on the grounds for marriage. In the traditional English wedding ceremony, the liturgy indicates three primary ends of the marriage between a man and woman. First, it provides for companionship and covenantal union between two people, husband and wife. Second, it provides a context for procreation and the raising of children. Third, it provides a legitimate outlet for sexual desire, although the church has often been ambivalent about sex. The first and third grounds thus stand in some tension; recall Paul's adage that it is better to marry than to burn, but better still to remain celibate and focused on the kingdom of heaven (1 Cor. 7:8–9). Over time, the emphasis in many churches has shifted from procreation and channeling of passion to covenantal union.

Changing views of marriage lead to changing views of divorce. The Pharisees' question to Jesus assumes the practice of divorce. The question is whether it is legitimate, lawful, or justifiable. As we have seen, Jesus turns the question to marriage, and, as is typical for him, radicalizes it. Moses's permission of divorce is a concession to the hardness of the human heart. Ideally, for Jesus, there would be no divorce. The marriage union would be permanent. He continues and reinforces this stricture in his private teaching with the disciples. Whoever divorces and remarries commits adultery. Contrary to traditional Jewish law but in accord with Roman thought, the demand applies equally to men and women—a man can commit adultery against his wife as well as a woman against her husband. Jesus thus shifts the question from what is legally permissible (and therefore justifiable) to a radical demand for absolute purity of heart.

But here is the difficulty: Jesus' demand for radical purity of heart appears to be an impossible ideal. Recall his claim that whoever looks at a

Pastoral Perspective

serious student of the Bible, she knew Jesus' words to the Pharisees (who put him to the "test" with the question about divorce) and his words to the disciples ("Whoever divorces his wife and marries another commits adultery against her"). Although her faith would mature later, at that time my parishioner was a distressed mother who held rigid beliefs about sin and punishment. She believed that her son was endangering his very soul.

Thus we are pushed by this text in Mark 10 to ask: how does this text address my parishioner's anxiety over her son's soul? Importantly, Jesus reframes the Pharisees' question ("Is it lawful for a man to divorce his wife?") in terms of his much larger vision of the kingdom of God. "Yes," Jesus responded, "because of your hardness of heart" (v. 5). Moses did allow you "to write a certificate of dismissal and to divorce her" (v. 4). But I say to you, "From the beginning of creation 'God made them male and female'" (v. 6).

"'For this reason a man shall leave his father and mother and be joined to his wife, and the two shall become one flesh.' . . . Therefore what God has joined together, let no one separate" (vv. 7–9). In other words, divorce is something that you can do, but it is not what God intended. Jesus is less concerned about what is allowed and more concerned about what is intended in the kingdom of God. The way that Jesus reframes the question of divorce in terms of his message about the coming kingdom is the first key to answering the parishioner's question.

In Jesus' day, when a woman received a "certificate of divorce," she lost most of her rights (like the right to own property). She could easily find herself begging for food on the street or prostituting herself for income. Clearly, Jesus had a pastoral concern for women who could have their lives torn apart by a signature on a piece of paper. In the kingdom of God, there should be mutual respect and concern for each other, not a quick certificate of divorce or a call to a lawyer to "take her (or him) for everything I can."

While marriage is not the standard for all people (there is no evidence that Jesus was married), the marriage commitment is also used in Scripture (Isa. 61:10–11; Jer. 31:32; Hos. 1–3) as a metaphor for the divine-human relationship. In some Christian traditions marriage is a sacrament. In Mark 10:9 Jesus declares, "Therefore what God has joined together, let no one separate." For Jesus, the kingdom of God was unfolding ("the kingdom of God has come near," Mark 1:15), and this meant that everything was changing. So the answer to the

Exegetical Perspective

desirable nor what God intends for God's people (thus also 1 Cor. 6:12; 10:23). With boldness reminiscent of his abolition of kosher food laws (Mark 7:14–19), Jesus asserts that Deuteronomy's prescription issues from its recipients' "hardness of heart" (*sklērokardian*: literally, "cardiosclerosis," a sinful toughening of human will [10:5; see also 3:5; 6:52; 8:17]). Again interpreting Scripture by Scripture (see 2:25–26; 7:6–13), Jesus drives his questioners back to God's intent at creation: the *union* of male and female (10:6; see Gen. 1:27; 5:2). Elaborating this point is another citation of Genesis (2:24), which stresses that human beings, male and female, are built for unity, that "the two shall become one flesh" (Mark 10:7–8a). Another text-critical question arises in verse 7: whether Mark continues the quotation with the words "and cleave to his wife" (KJV; "and be joined to his wife," NRSV). That this is Jesus' intent is beyond question: "So they are no longer two, but one flesh" (v. 8b). The point is clear: while dissolution of marriage is permissible, owing to human incompetence in sustaining their vows, God's intent at creation is wholeness, including oneness of flesh. Normatively speaking, *human beings* should not rupture what *God* unites (v. 9).

As though to place an exclamation point beside this principle, Mark 10:11–12 likens remarriage after divorce to commission of adultery against the divorced partner. This is a stunning comment in several ways. First, it is unprecedented in the Old Testament. Second, it applies to *both husbands and wives*, irrespective of which partner divorces the other. (This wording may reflect Mark's awareness of Roman law, in which—unlike its ancient Jewish counterpart—women could initiate such proceedings.) Third, it respects the integrity of the one who has not applied for divorce as an injured party. This is as radical a statement of discipleship as those dire warnings against causing little ones to stumble in Mark 9:42–50a, implicitly returning the reader to that discourse's conclusion: "Be at peace with one another" (9:50b). "In the house"—where wife and husband live—the disciples, again asking Jesus to explain himself (10:10), likely received more than they bargained for in his reply.

Other New Testament witnesses testify that Jesus' teachings about marriage got their attention and were well remembered. Indeed, the early church soon recognized circumstances that could mitigate their severity. In 1 Corinthians 7:10–11 Paul cites from the Lord the charge we know from Mark; like Jesus, Paul applies the dictum evenhandedly to

Homiletical Perspective

Within this contextual framework, preachers need to probe the underlying theological affirmations of the text, rather than remaining on the surface. This text does not represent some timeless, abstract "teaching on marriage and children." Rather, Jesus speaks about the implications of the reign of God (v. 14–15) in the context of his turn to Jerusalem (9:30–32). This deeper theological understanding of Jesus' words should guide the preacher.

The great temptation of this text is to turn Jesus' teaching into a new "law" about divorce and remarriage. But Jesus' words are not meant to be a rigid, legal principle. Such a move, in fact, runs directly counter to Jesus' underlying theological emphases. Jesus actually seeks to move beyond a legalistic approach to questions of divorce (the approach of his adversaries) toward a theological affirmation about God's purposes for marriage in the context of God's inbreaking reign. In making this move, Jesus actually uses Scripture against Scripture, rejecting the legal text cited by the Pharisees (Deut. 24:1–4) in favor of the theological affirmations present in the earlier creation stories in Genesis (Gen. 1:27; 2:24). Jesus definitely speaks some strong words about remarriage following divorce. (Notice that divorce itself is *not* the issue, but rather remarriage.) But the context is Jesus' respect for the deep bond of marriage—and possibly his sensitivity to the great pain caused by divorce[1]—not his attempt to establish a new law.

At this point the relationship between the two pericopes (the first challenge mentioned above) is instructive and may be helpful to the preacher. Scripture may be set against Scripture here, just as Jesus sets scriptural texts over against each other in his response to the Pharisees. In the conclusion to Jesus' comments about the children, he affirms, "Truly I tell you, whoever does not receive the kingdom of God as a little child will never enter it" (v. 15). Jesus here reminds the disciples that one enters the kingdom only by receiving it in complete dependence on God. One does not enter the kingdom through the fulfillment of any abstract legal principles, including those related to divorce and remarriage. The affirmation in the second pericope thus forestalls any attempt to set up Jesus' earlier teaching as a timeless law, obedience to which is requisite for entering into God's reign. Consequently, the juxtaposition of these pericopes

---

1. See Ched Myers, *Binding the Strong Man: A Political Reading of Mark's Story of Jesus* (Maryknoll, NY: Orbis Books, 1988), 266.

Mark 10:2-16

Theological Perspective

woman with lust has already committed adultery with her in his heart (Matt. 5:28) and his similar injunction, just prior to our passage, that if our eye offends us, we should tear it out (Mark 9:47). As the disciples soon ask, "Who then can be saved?" (Mark 10:26). What are we to make of Jesus' claim, not only that we should not divorce and remarry, but also that we should never look at another with desire (Matt. 5:28)?

These questions lead us back to the other levels in the text. Who is the proper authority? How are we to enter the kingdom of God? As presented in Mark, the Pharisees ask Jesus about divorce, not because they truly want to know the answer, but because they want to force him to take a stand on a controversial issue, and therefore offend someone. At one level, his answer may be even more offensive than they anticipated: Jesus claims the authority to supersede even the law of Moses. His demand for purity of heart is more rigorous than Mosaic law; more rigorous, in fact, than seems humanly possible. But, as he notes in the following passage, what is humanly impossible is possible for God (Mark 10:27). How then are we to receive and enter the kingdom of God? Not as those who try to justify ourselves, but as those who accept God's grace, like children who with purity of heart accept the grace of their parents.

Divorce remains a live issue, but most Protestant churches have concluded that respect for marriage and the institution of marriage means that some particular marriages should end. Divorce is tragic, but not the worst evil. Today, however, we might imagine someone (or a group of latter-day Pharisees) asking Jesus about sexual intercourse outside of marriage, or about marriage between members of the same sex. Is it permissible? If we learn anything from this text, it is that we must be cautious about attempting to justify ourselves. Jesus claims the authority to supersede even the law of Moses, but we are not Jesus. How might he reframe the question, turn it to its roots, and demand full purity of heart? How would he tell us to respond with gratitude towards God's grace? Might he ask whether the human was created for marriage, or marriage for the human?

JAMES J. THOMPSON

Pastoral Perspective

Pharisees' question was not what was permissible under the law, but what was now possible in this unfolding kingdom of peace, love, and justice.

Jesus was declaring the beginning of a new era in which relationships could work if each party approached the other with mutual respect and concern. It was now possible to go beyond what was just permissible to what was kingdom enhanced. Unfortunately, then and now, not everyone chooses to live out the ethics of God's kingdom. Abuse and neglect are substituted for respect and concern. As Professor William B. Oglesby once said in a pastoral-care class, "They say some marriages are made in heaven, but it appears to me that some are born in hell!" In a broken world, divorce is sometimes necessary.

In the larger lectionary passage (10:2–16), the disciples just do not get it: "Then in the house the disciples asked him again about this matter" (v. 10). The tension continues between Jesus and the disciples. He teaches them about the unfolding of the kingdom, and so often they (and we) just do not get it. Maybe that is why Jesus says in verse 14: "Let the little children come to me . . . " Perhaps Jesus was saying, "In the kingdom it is not about what is permissible but what is ethical. . . . Maybe if you receive the kingdom like a child, you will get it."

So preacher, if you are fortunate enough to get it, or at least a part of it, remember the man or woman who might be in the congregation this Sunday morning with the question, "Preacher, can I save my marriage?" Or, several folks with questions that are of pastoral concern: "Preacher, this illness . . . am I being punished by God?" "Preacher, is there any hope for my wayward child?" Prepare yourself as best you can, and then trust the Spirit to give you a grace-filled, hopeful, unfolding-kingdom answer.

DAVID B. HOWELL

Exegetical Perspective

Christian wives and husbands. But what of mixed marriages, in which one spouse is a Christian believer, the other not? Here Paul extemporizes in the spirit of Christ. The believer should not terminate marriage from fear of taint by the unbelieving spouse: to the contrary, the faith of one spouse is a means for consecrating the unbeliever (1 Cor. 7:12–14, 16). Yet, if the unbelieving partner wants out, the divorce may proceed, for finally God has called us to peace (1 Cor. 7:15). Matthew's version of Jesus' teaching allows a husband's divorce on the grounds of his wife's unchastity (Matt. 5:32; 19:9). Luke compresses Jesus' teaching by emphasizing adulterous consequences if one divorces and remarries (Luke 16:18). The author of Ephesians restates the scriptural basis of Jesus' teaching in Mark (Gen. 2:24) and pleads for marital unity, while—departing from Mark 10:9–12—placing the wife in a more obviously subservient position with respect to the husband (Eph. 5:22–33). Yet the primary dictum remains true to Jesus' spirit: "*Be subject to one another* out of reverence for Christ" (Eph. 5:21).

Beyond this scriptural context, Jesus' strict teaching about marriage in Mark 10:2–12 should be located in its social background. Mark would hardly have warned his church of divorce's consequences if Christians were not already practicing it. Moreover, both Jesus and Mark addressed a culture that provided for the divorced woman no safety net: neither alimony nor any means for legal recourse.

What may sound to our ears as relentlessly harsh assumes a different tenor when we understand that Jesus' intent is the protection and honor of the spouse as a child created in God's image, not as chattel to be discarded on selfish whim. The latter would be utterly incongruent with discipleship that cares for the vulnerable (Mark 9:42–50; 10:13–16). Although he does not address the question in Mark, it is hard to imagine that Jesus would have sanctioned a social contract in which one or both members were abusive or subject to abuse, for, as Jesus frames the matter—within the goodness of God's wholesome creation—that would be no marriage at all. From this text it is equally hard to believe that Jesus would have countenanced unbridled serial monogamy, whether in his world or our own.

C. CLIFTON BLACK

Homiletical Perspective

may in fact enable the preacher to speak a pastoral word that not only recognizes the tragedy and pain of divorce, but also comforts those divorced persons who feel they are unworthy of God's love or God's reign. Indeed, those suffering the pain and brokenness of divorce may be precisely the "least of these" who can receive the kingdom in dependence on God's love.

Finally, the preacher may look beneath the surface of the text and explore the important social implications of God's inbreaking reign.[2] At the heart of this text is the disruptive work of God in Jesus Christ, which overturns patriarchal marital relationships and elevates those at the bottom of the social ladder (children) into models for entering the kingdom. Far from simply affirming and domesticating traditional notions of marriage, Jesus' words actually subvert his adversaries' patriarchal assumptions about marriage. The Pharisees question Jesus about whether it is lawful for "a man to divorce his wife," reflecting a patriarchal framework within which only the man could seek a divorce. In the course of his answer, Jesus notes that a *man* leaves his father and mother to become one flesh with his wife (vv. 7–8). And by the end he also asserts the *woman's right* to divorce her husband (v. 12). Women are given precisely the same rights and responsibilities as men. Similarly, children, who are the least valued and most vulnerable members of society, are welcomed by Jesus, blessed by him, and offered as models for receiving God's kingdom. Jesus' teachings and actions here are revolutionary, subverting both cultural and legal presuppositions about women and children.

Preaching Jesus' words as abstract legal principles that codify traditional, patriarchal forms of marital and family relationships actually negates the underlying disruptive and revolutionary social dimensions of God's inbreaking reign, which Jesus proclaims and enacts in this text. The hermeneutical trajectory of the text is toward greater equality for and radical hospitality toward those who are most oppressed. Preachers should thus take this trajectory seriously, asking what social structures and assumptions that oppress people, particularly women and children, need to be disrupted and challenged today. Such a trajectory will enable the preacher to proclaim the unsettling reign of God that animates Jesus' words and deeds.

CHARLES L. CAMPBELL

2. Ibid., 264–71.

Job 23:1-9, 16-17

¹Then Job answered:
²"Today also my complaint is bitter;
  his hand is heavy despite my groaning.
³Oh, that I knew where I might find him,
  that I might come even to his dwelling!
⁴I would lay my case before him,
  and fill my mouth with arguments.
⁵I would learn what he would answer me,
  and understand what he would say to me.
⁶Would he contend with me in the greatness of his power?
  No; but he would give heed to me.

Theological Perspective

Life is suffering. Thus teaches the first of the Four Noble Truths of Buddhism: "Birth is ill, decay is ill, sickness is ill, death is ill."[1] In Buddhist teaching, enlightenment leads to recognition of the illusion of the self and therewith the cessation of desire, which causes suffering. While those of us nurtured in the Judeo-Christian traditions also acknowledge the painful realities of life, our starting point is very different from that of the great Indian traditions. "God saw everything that he had made, and indeed, it was very good" (Gen. 1:31). The premise of biblical religion is the goodness of God, who created a good world.

We humans are made in God's image to be the responsible stewards of what God has created. Accordingly, the self is not illusory, nor is desire per se the source of suffering. While the Bible does take with utter seriousness the human propensity toward self-aggrandizement and inordinate desire (Augustine), redemption or salvation is intended to reorient the self in an unselfish (not selfless) manner. Desire for a good and authentically happy life for oneself is not sinful (Jesus said, "I came that they may have life, and have it abundantly," John 10:10).

1. *Buddhist Scriptures*, trans. Edward Conze (London and New York: Penguin, 1959), 186.

Pastoral Perspective

Job's speech puts the congregation in one fine pickle. "Where is God?" Oh sure, that will go over really big in the church.

Isn't the church's whole liturgy a declaration that "God is here" and that we know what we are doing when we invoke the Deity? Worship in many congregations begins with a big smile and howdy from the pastor, even words like, "Thank you for coming today." (Huh? The pastor should thank people for worshiping? What are we, some sort of vaudeville show?) This is followed by, "We're glad you have come, especially if you are a visitor today. We want you to know that in the worship of First Church, God is here among us and will bless you today." Et cetera, et cetera, et cetera, yada, yada, yada, followed by, "The Lord is in his holy temple"—meaning, of course, First Church—and we are off and running.

Then comes the lesson from Job. No wonder so many churches skip the lectionary. Put this passage together with a text like Psalm 88 that goes from "You have put me in the depths of the Pit" to "O LORD, why do you cast me off?" to "You have caused friend and neighbor to shun me" and ends with the cheery "My companions are in darkness" (vv. 6, 14, 18a, 18b), and nobody would ever come back to church.

Who would preach Job 23, say, on television? The big churches and freelancers who make it onto the

⁷There an upright person could reason with him,
  and I should be acquitted forever by my judge.

⁸"If I go forward, he is not there;
  or backward, I cannot perceive him;
⁹on the left he hides, and I cannot behold him;
  I turn to the right, but I cannot see him.
. . . .
¹⁶God has made my heart faint;
  the Almighty has terrified me;
¹⁷If only I could vanish in darkness,
  and thick darkness would cover my face!"

Exegetical Perspective

This Sunday's reading comes from the long central section of the book (3:1–42:6), in which Job engages first his friends (chaps. 3–31) and then God (38:1–42:6) in a lengthy series of dialogues. These dialogues, in turn, enclose the speeches of a fourth, younger friend, Elihu (chaps. 32–37). Unlike the framing material in chapters 1–2 and the remainder of chapter 42, these dialogues are written in poetry, not prose. They usually appear in the form of laments, disputations, and in Job's case . . . well, just plain rants. They display an intricate structure, especially evident in the dialogue between Job and his friends, which forms the extended context of our passage:

	A Job's opening lament, chapter 3					
	Eliphaz	Job	Bildad	Job	Zophar	Job
Cycle 1	4–5	6–7	8	9–10	11	12–14
Cycle 2	15	16–17	18	19	20	21
Cycle 3	22	23–24	25	26	??	27

(Wisdom poem, 28)
A' Job's closing lament 29–31

Job begins and ends the section with lament. The poignant introductory lament of chapter 3 finds Job cursing the day of his birth. So much for the patience of Job in the prose introduction! This wrenching reflection on his suffering is followed by three cycles of six speeches each, in which Job's

Homiletical Perspective

What is there for the church to say as the congregation stands between human suffering and the seeming silence of God? This lection from Job 23, taken from the midst of Job's dialogue with his so-called friends, bears witness to the theological anxiety that often accompanies physical and emotional strife for persons of faith.

It is difficult enough to endure the losses that Job has suffered; now added to that hardship is his growing sense that God is eluding him. We struggle along with Job as he searches in vain for the place where he can deliver his complaint, his "lawsuit" against God.

As we join in that struggle, we would also do well to learn Job's persistence, his unrelenting conviction that he will have his "day in court." Job wants his hearing because, for all of the invective he hurls into the chasm of divine silence, he cannot let go of the conviction that God is ultimately *just*, and that God ultimately will hear him.[1] Until that day, Job's questions linger. Can the preacher let difficult questions of faith linger too? Perhaps a premature move to resolution may inadvertently undermine the power of the response that does come.

1. Cf. Carol A. Newsome, "The Book of Job," in *The New Interpreter's Bible* (Nashville: Abingdon, 1996), 4:508.

Job 23:1-9, 16-17

Theological Perspective

Within the Bible, as well as the subsequent Jewish and Christian traditions, the suffering of both individuals and communities is attributed to sin. Yet this is precisely why the problem of evil is rendered more acute within the monotheistic traditions. The assumption that evil can be sufficiently explained as the just punishment of God upon the wicked is radically called into question by the experience of all the faithful persons throughout history who had every reason to think that the magnitude of the evil inflicted upon them was completely out of proportion to any calculation of sin and punishment. For that reason, Job articulates and symbolizes their legitimate protest against God and the presumption that God rules the world with justice.

Job lifts his voice in protest. He wants his day in court so as to plead his case before the judge of the universe. He has faith that an upright person can reason with God. But how can a person argue with God? R. B. Y. Scott says of Job:

> Here speaks a free religious spirit, untrammeled either by orthodox belief or by dogmatic atheism. . . . He challenges the very world order of which he is a part. . . . Is this what the Greeks called *hubris*, the intolerable insolence of a man who would make himself God's equal? Or is it the profoundest kind of religious faith . . . a sublime confidence that to ask ultimate questions of God is not to turn away from him but to draw nearer to him?[2]

Protesting the justice of God has not been a major motif in the classical Christian tradition. It is, however, more at home in the Jewish tradition. This is one reason why Christians need to read the Old Testament more seriously than we are wont to do, and to read it without the New Testament's assurance that "all things work together for good for those who love God" (Rom. 8:28). If we take Job seriously, then we have to question the comforting belief that all suffering will ultimately be redeemed. Moreover, we must not assume that such doubt is an expression of sinful pride; rather, as Job's example shows, willingness to wrestle with God is the supreme test of whether piety or faith is adequate to our lived human experience in the world. Paradoxically, even a loss of faith may reflect a more genuine engagement with God than a faith that refuses to allow itself to be so tested.

Elie Wiesel, the Jewish writer who has spent his life attempting to come to grips with the Holocaust that he experienced firsthand as a boy in the Nazi

2. R. B. Y. Scott, *The Way of Wisdom in the Old Testament* (New York: Macmillan, 1971), 141.

Pastoral Perspective

cable system love to talk about Psalm 139: "O Lord, you have searched me and known me. . . . For it was you who formed my inward parts; you knit me together in my mother's womb" (vv. 1, 13). Here is raw material for a totalistic ideology of God, who is watching you at all times to make sure you do not sin (and especially, if you are a woman, that you do not go get an abortion). For God is inescapable—"You hem me in, behind and before. . . . if I ascend to heaven, you are there; if I make my bed in Sheol, you are there" (vv. 5, 8). God is everywhere, keeping an eye on you.

But pastors who preach on Job 23 (or Psalm 88) never make it to television. What congregation wants to start the liturgy with, "Oh, that I knew where I might find God, that I might come even to God's dwelling" (Job 23:3)? God is not here, this morning or most any other morning—but we are going to worship anyway, just in case God decides to show up? Not very persuasive, at least for most North American congregations, immersed in a culture of optimism and productivity. After all, if the mission of the church is to worship and serve God, then shouldn't the church at least be able to produce the God being served?

Most congregations are absolutely convinced that their mission is effectively advancing the cause of God in the world, that if their mission is successful, they will actually bring about what God wants. "Use these gifts for the upbuilding of your kingdom," the pastor intones over the brass offering plates, referring to cash and checks that will be used, among other things, to pay the pastor's salary and keep the lights on. Go on our mission trip, we say to our youth, to help people learn about Jesus. One Protestant judicatory calls its mission program, "Revealing Christ," and another, "Bringing People to God." Who do we think we are?

Job, who appears to be pretty much in hell here, is having no luck producing God. The passage ends in the darkness of the unknown, though even the Hebrew words are so obscure that it is hard to tell if this is Job's darkness or the darkness that covers God. Both, most likely. And in the darkness Job is left alone.

There is an odd freedom in the darkness. Matters are so dark and obscure that Job is not sure God is even watching any more. Job could, well, do just about anything or become just about anybody. Who is watching? Talk about a test of character. So what really counts now? The Christian life presents no greater challenge than finding one's way forward with integrity and responsibility in the dark.

friends Eliphaz, Bildad, and Zophar each speak in turn, with Job responding (rather loquaciously, it must be said) to each of them. All three cycles explore the ramifications of the questions raised by the doctrine of retributive justice as found especially in Proverbs. As discussed in our treatment of last week's passage, this is the common assumption, prevalent even today: that God rewards righteousness with peace, prosperity, and long life, while sin is punished. A careful reading of the friends' speeches certainly gives the impression that all three friends agree with at least half of the retributive scheme, namely, that wickedness is punished. While there is some development in the speeches as the friends become increasingly impatient with Job's rants, the detailed analysis that fills the commentaries, as well as finely nuanced attempts to differentiate their various positions, tends to obscure this basic premise of traditional religion that lies at the heart of the debate.

Where the friends go wrong is in their determined insistence upon turning the doctrine of retributive justice on its head. Many biblical texts affirm the coherence of the universe, as well as the integrity of divine justice, in language derived from Wisdom's teaching that God inflicts misfortune and suffering upon the unrighteous. But the friends argue backwards from Job's suffering to his supposed unrighteousness; since Job is clearly suffering, he must have sinned in some way that has brought God's punishment upon him. His only way out is repentance.

This is clearly seen in today's lection from the third cycle of the debate: Job's response to Eliphaz's concluding speech in chapter 22. In a series of seven rhetorical questions, Eliphaz argues that mortals are of no use to God, morally, because of human wickedness (22:2–5) providing the foundation for a double indictment of Job's "innocence": his moral failure (vv. 6–11) and his theological naiveté (vv. 12–20). He then concludes with a promise of peace and restoration *provided Job repents of his sin* (vv. 21–30).

Job's response is, in his own words, bitter (23:1, better: "rebellious," NRSV margin). His defiance is fueled by frustration. Job too understands the doctrine of retribution and even affirms God's justice and mercy; but whereas the friends say, "Since you are suffering, you must have done something to deserve this," Job has championed the other side of the same coin throughout the dialogues and especially here (23:10–12, unfortunately eliminated in the lectionary reading), saying, in effect, "No! I am innocent, I do not deserve this!" In his scathing

Pursuing the Elusive God. While he awaits God's response, Job testifies to his anguish and frustration in the face of God's seeming absence: "If I go forward, he is not there; or backward, I cannot perceive him; on the left he hides, and I cannot behold him; I turn to the right, but I cannot see him" (vv. 8–9). His bleak testimony finds many echoes in human experience.

In *A Grief Observed*, C. S. Lewis is awash in a sea of grief and pain in the wake of his wife's death. He too probes deeply into dark questions of faith, asking "Meanwhile, where is God?" In previous times of happiness, Lewis claims that he found God present everywhere he turned. But in the midst of his present anguish, searching for God is like knocking on the door of a house and hearing the door being bolted in your face. What you are left with, he says, is silence, and the disturbing fear that maybe this is what God is like after all.[2]

In bitterness upon the ash heap, Job cries out, "Oh, that I knew where I might find [God]" (v. 3). A couple of contemporary sources can be used to explicate Job's bitterness. Poet Ann Weems lost her son Todd on the day of his twenty-first birthday; in her "Lament Psalm Eight," she joins Job and the host of others who struggle with faith and loss when God is nowhere to be found. That same searching, longing for God in the face of hardship, finds voice in popular music too. At the end of the CD *Pop*, the rock band U2's singer Bono pleads for God to do something in the midst of the suffering that threatens to undo faith and life, wondering if God is busy or Jesus' hands are tied. Speaking the darkness of faith is a daring, and faithful, act.

A Case against God. The character of Job's struggle goes beyond simply lamenting the injustice and loss that he and others have experienced. Hardly the "patient" Job lauded elsewhere in Scripture (see Jas. 5:11), here Job longs to argue his case with God. Contrast Job's argument and complaint with Ivan Karamazov in Dostoyevsky's *The Brothers Karamazov*, who in the face of human suffering, particularly the horrible suffering of children, is led to deny the existence of God altogether. Dostoyevsky paints Ivan's denial of God sympathetically, for he knows that such horrid suffering is a very real threat to faith. Job too is well acquainted with suffering, but his faith endures. His mouth is full of arguments, but they are arguments *with God*.

---

2. C. S. Lewis, *A Grief Observed* (New York: Bantam, 1961), 4–5.

Job 23:1-9, 16-17

Theological Perspective

concentration camps, recounts his loss of faith in God as a result of that dehumanizing experience:

> Never shall I forget that night, the first night in camp, which has turned my life into one long night, seven times cursed and seven times sealed. . . . Never shall I forget those flames which consumed my faith forever. Never shall I forget that nocturnal silence which deprived me, for all eternity, of the desire to live. Never shall I forget those moments which murdered my God and my soul and turned my dreams to dust.[3]

Wiesel reports that other Jews in the camps continued to trust in and pray to God as their ancestors had done for centuries. Other Jews have gone even further than Wiesel by questioning the very reality of God.

The radical challenges to the basic premises of monotheistic faith represented by Job, Wiesel, and others ought not to be ignored by Christians. We too must confront honestly and courageously the possibility that many of our time-honored doctrines about God might not stand up to the test of the massive suffering experienced by individuals and communities. When the powers of nature or history so conspire against persons that their legitimate desires for a reasonable measure of happiness in life are destroyed, we dare not trivialize such suffering and despair by pointing to an ultimate consummation in which all wrongs will be righted.

Life in this world is not a fairy tale that always has a happy ending! With Marx and Freud (also Jews), we must ask to what extent our religious traditions function as opiates to numb pain or are comforting illusions about the nature of reality. For, in the final analysis, what is the truth about God?

PAUL E. CAPETZ

Pastoral Perspective

In this regard, the Job of chapter 23 is no model. Like most congregations, Job is floundering around in the dark preoccupied mainly with how to justify himself before God. "I would lay my case before him, and fill my mouth with arguments" (v. 4). God's absence has given Job lots of time to think, and what he has been thinking about is all the ways he has, in fact, been a righteous man and contributed to God's kingdom.

No wonder God is hiding (v. 9). Who wants to listen to all that? Where does God find the patience to listen to the churches trying to justify their existence, ready to provide statistics on how many people they are serving, and data on all the reasons why the old programs are not working and new ones are needed, and executive summaries of their mission and vision statements together with their goals and objectives for the new year?

The churches are full of "upright" people who want to "reason with God" (v. 7). We do not trust in God's justification but want to justify ourselves. And how better to take matters into our own hands than through rational, verbal argument, like lawyers before a judge? If we have objective data, we can prove our case.

But is God a judge? Job imagines God to be a judge because he needs God to be a judge. Job wants to make his arguments. A judge would have to listen to reason. In short, if God is a judge, then Job has a chance to get control over his fate and, like a congregation, manage his mission.

Enough, already! God has taken off the robes and left the bench. God is hiding, covered in darkness, hands over ears, waiting it out. Waiting. For us. To be quiet.

THOMAS EDWARD FRANK

---

3. Elie Wiesel, *Night*, trans. Stella Rodway (New York: Bantam Books, 1982), 32.

Exegetical Perspective

response to Eliphaz, Job's problem is not with God's attributes; Job's problem is with God's absence. He laments that he is "an upright person" and that if he could only find God and gain a hearing, God would surely hear his case and acquit him according to the very principles of retributive justice the friends are preaching (vv. 3–7). But, alas, God is nowhere to be found (vv. 8–9). This painful situation pulls Job in two directions. On the one hand, he remains confident in his belief that if God would only hear his case, he would be acquitted. On the other hand, Job is terrified (v. 16) that God's absence means that God's power will be exercised autocratically; God "stands alone [Heb: v. 13; "he is as one," perhaps meaning God is sovereign or unchangeable] and who can dissuade him? What he desires, that he does" (v. 13).

The key interpretive verse (v. 17) is, unfortunately, notoriously difficult to translate. Verse 16 states clearly that "God has made [Job's] heart faint" and "terrified [him]." But how does Job react? Two major translations provide reasonable, though different interpretations. The NRSV has Job despair that since he cannot find God, he might as well give up and be absorbed into the murky realm of oblivion ("If only I could vanish in darkness, and thick darkness would cover my face!"). The NIV, however, envisions a defiant, feisty Job, more intent than ever to press his case ("Yet I am not silenced by the darkness, by the thick darkness that covers my face"). The NRSV can point to similar despairing conclusions in Job's earlier speeches. To arrive at this translation, however, the negative particle loʾ ("not") in the beginning of the verse must be read as lu ("if only"). The NIV seems to better introduce Job's challenge of God's sovereignty in the next chapter and preserves the Masoretic Text. But how does the darkness "silence" Job? The verb in the first clause can mean either "be exterminated" ("vanish"? NRSV) or "be silenced" (NIV). Bedeviling ambiguity aside, a reading similar to the NIV has the advantage of providing a return to Job's initial lament (v. 2), thus framing his conflicted struggle in the body of the speech, and offers a smoother transition to chapter 24, his scathing indictment of what God's absence means in a world where the wicked run roughshod over the weak.

MARK A. THRONTVEIT

Homiletical Perspective

Too often have folk simply given in, resigning themselves to their misfortune: "It must be the Lord's will; I guess we will just have to accept it." Or, like Ivan, they abandon faith in God altogether. Job offers a third way: he is unwilling to accept suffering passively, *but he also refuses to abandon his faith!* Perhaps his litigious stance may stir the church to a more active struggle with faith in the face of the hardship and atrocity of our time—not only in sermons and lesson plans, but in pulpit and classroom prayers, too. From time to time, it is not a bad idea for the preacher or teacher to remind the congregation that arguing with God is an act of deep faith—deeper, perhaps, than a passive acceptance of whatever happens as God's will, or a carefully articulated theological rationalization for why things are. After all, does not God in the end vindicate Job's speech, and castigate Job's friends for not speaking rightly about God (42:7)?

God's Presence in Suffering. Finally, there is a word of hope for the church, for the God whom Job sought has indeed sought us and found us, even in the midst of our suffering. Indeed, as Dietrich Bonhoeffer noted in his *Letters and Papers from Prison*, in a world of suffering "only the suffering God can help."[3] Job's cry is answered by Jesus on the cross: "My God, my God, why have you forsaken me?" (Mark 15:34). For here, in the midst of Jesus' anguished cry, we find that the depth of human suffering has been taken into God's very being. God is very much aware of the realities of suffering, for God's Son has himself suffered. The apostle Paul reminds us, in light of Christ's suffering, that the good news of the gospel is that in Jesus Christ, we know that *nothing*—not injustice, not suffering, not even an overwhelming sense of God's absence—can separate us from God's love (Rom. 8:31–39). Safe and secure in this good news, we are set free to lament and to argue our case with God.

J. S. RANDOLPH HARRIS

---

3. Dietrich Bonhoeffer, *Letters and Papers from Prison* (New York: Collier Books, 1971), 361.

Psalm 22:1-15

¹My God, my God, why have you forsaken me?
    Why are you so far from helping me, from the words of my groaning?
²O my God, I cry by day, but you do not answer;
    and by night, but find no rest.

³Yet you are holy,
    enthroned on the praises of Israel.
⁴In you our ancestors trusted;
    they trusted, and you delivered them.
⁵To you they cried, and were saved;
    in you they trusted, and were not put to shame.

⁶But I am a worm, and not human;
    scorned by others, and despised by the people.
⁷All who see me mock at me;
    they make mouths at me, they shake their heads;
⁸"Commit your cause to the Lᴏʀᴅ; let him deliver—
    let him rescue the one in whom he delights!"

⁹Yet it was you who took me from the womb;
    you kept me safe on my mother's breast.

Theological Perspective

There are admirable religious and philosophical traditions that teach that pain can be overcome through
the adjustment of attitude. Christian Scientists,
prosperity-gospel preachers, and not a few people who
have sat in my pews think that faith is about coping
with life's psychological traumas while not getting too
depressed. These are not steeped in the biblical tradition of the psalmist or the life of Jesus, with their
explicit and agonizing wails of unabashed pain.

"My God, my God, why have you forsaken me?" is
probably the most well-known psalm line after the
Twenty-third Psalm's gentle shepherd. And what a
contrast to the Twenty-third Psalm! Here in this psalm
we have a lament of one utterly abandoned by God,
surrounded by enemies (v. 12), racked with pain
(v. 14), and not far from death (v. 15). Intermittently
the psalmist remembers God's holiness and past
mercy—to Israel's ancestors (v. 4) and to himself at his
mother's breast (vv. 9–10), but these memories do not
dull the present pain. Indeed, such memories seem
only to enhance the pain. Where is the God who is
mighty to save and gentle in nursing us into a faithful
life? Where is the God of the Twenty-third Psalm now?

What would the prayers of our communities
sound like if we took this plea for help as normative?
What if we remembered God's tender mercies so as
to demand amelioration of present suffering? At the

Pastoral Perspective

Psalm 22 reads like a verbal tennis match between
the conflicting emotions of an anguished believer.
    "God, where are you?"
    "You are the best!"
    "Why don't you answer me?"
    "You've been faithful to me since the day I was
born!"
    "How could you let this happen to me?"
    "I am so grateful for your steadfast love."
    The writer's back-and-forth proclamations of
devotion and despair swing from one end of the arc
of the pendulum of faith to the other, and his agony
is visible for all the world to see. The flames of
destitution are fanned by the cruel mockery of
outsiders. "You were so certain of God's love! Where
is your God now?" The shame of being abandoned
by God in a way that everyone else can see rubs salt
into the raw and bleeding gashes of the psalmist's
wounded spirit. If this is how God treats God's
friends, then who needs enemies?

The lack of God's response to the writer's predicament is so utterly devastating that the individual feels
less than human. He is a worm, scorned and
despised, the lowest of the low. The dilemma is
compounded by the fact that the psalmist is a person
of deep faith. The writer feels a profound, personal
connection with God. In a form of address rarely

¹⁰On you I was cast from my birth,
  and since my mother bore me you have been my God.
¹¹Do not be far from me,
  for trouble is near
  and there is no one to help.

¹²Many bulls encircle me,
  strong bulls of Bashan surround me;
¹³they open wide their mouths at me,
  like a ravening and roaring lion.

¹⁴I am poured out like water,
  and all my bones are out of joint;
  my heart is like wax;
  it is melted within my breast;
¹⁵my mouth is dried up like a potsherd,
  and my tongue sticks to my jaws;
  you lay me in the dust of death.

Exegetical Perspective

Because of the citation of Psalm 22:1 in the passion narrative of Matthew 27:46 and Mark 15:34, this psalm is the best-known lament among Christians. This psalm, a classic example of a psalm of lament, is readily divided into two parts: the *complaint* of the speaker in trouble (vv. 1–21a) and *praise and thanksgiving* after the resolution of the trouble (vv. 21b–31). Our concern here is only verses 1–15, but these verses cannot be fully appreciated apart from the later resolution of the psalm.

The verses for our consideration, verses 1–15, traverse standard elements of Israel's prayer of complaint: (a) *complaint* (vv. 1–2, 6–8, 12–15), (b) *motivation* (vv. 3–5, 9–10), and (c) *petition* (v. 11). The dramatic movement of the psalm contains no surprise; but interest for us lies in the imaginative and daring rhetoric that "pushes the envelope" of the psalmist's relation to YHWH and reflects boldness before God that is without any deference. The voice of the pray-er is of someone in dire straits who has no time for the luxury of conventional piety.

The psalm begins in a statement of intimacy, "My God, my God." Such prayers of complaint and petition are not characteristically prayed by strangers, but by those with a long history of positive interaction with YHWH. Indeed, in this case that long history has likely included promises of fidelity on the part of

Homiletical Perspective

As a preacher, I try to place myself within the contextual framework of the biblical passage. To do this for Psalm 22 is heartbreaking, especially given the limitations of what the lectionary calls us to read. While Psalm 22, following verse 22, ends with a song of thanksgiving and praise, all that our lectionary asks us to offer is the rending cry of an individual or a nation mired in the depths of terrible distress. The opening lines betray the quality of despair gushing forth from the psalmist, the prayer of one who feels forsaken and lost and suffers not only because of what others have inflicted, but because of the insufferable silence of God. The guttural, visceral pain of the psalmist is plain, "the words of my groaning," and it is important for the preacher to acknowledge, honor, and make real to the congregation how broken the relationship between God and the psalmist feels in this passage.

Preachers *need* to honor the real suffering that may go on among members of the church. Perhaps an individual faces a life-threatening illness, is caught in the overwhelming pain of divorce or addiction, or has undergone a seemingly unrecoverable betrayal. The congregation may be caught in a time of strife that threatens to undo its cohesiveness, to fetter its capacities to be worshipful, and diminishes its ability to minister to others. The larger

Psalm 22:1-15

Theological Perspective

very least we can use this psalm to encourage parishioners to cry out with pain to God. There is no need for tidied-up, buttoned-down, polite teatime prayers with the God of Israel. In fact, as though to head off such fake piety, we find in Scripture itself a formula for praying with chutzpah: God, *where in the world are you?!*

It is not suprising that Jesus prayed using the words of the Twenty-second Psalm. As one whose limbs really were wrenched out of joint on an olive shaft (v. 14), where passersby mocked and enemies snorted (vv. 7, 12), he did what any faithful Jew might have done: prayed for deliverance with the words of Psalm 22. However, for many Christians Jesus' praying of this prayer has posed something of a theological problem. How can the One whom we claim is the Son of God, and so God himself, be abandoned by God?

Several great modern theologians, like Hans Urs von Balthasar and Jürgen Moltmann, have argued that Jesus was *indeed* abandoned by God—and yet, paradoxically, was never closer to God than in this absolute abandonment.[1] In a century such as the twentieth, which saw so much God-abandonment and death on such an unprecedented scale, the church is right to insist that God does not keep divine distance from us but enters deeply into our agony. "He descended into hell," the creed pronounces, in order to "harrow" it—to dig it up.

Most ancient Christians argued that Jesus was not abandoned at all. Augustine of Hippo, for one, is quite sure that Jesus cannot have been abandoned by God, since he himself *was* God. Jesus speaks about being forsaken, not to refer to any divine abandonment by God—but so as to enter into, and *transform*, the divine abandonment felt by each of us: "What other reason was this said than that we were there, for what other reason than that Christ's body is the Church? . . . Beyond doubt, he was speaking of me, of you, of him over there, of her, for he was acting as his own body, the Church."[2]

Paul's metaphor of the body of Christ is worn so thin that we hardly notice its power anymore—until we see someone like Augustine put it to use. Christ is the head of this body, the church, and we are all members. "His" mouth cries out in pain here for the sake of all "our" suffering—as when our foot is

1. Jürgen Moltmann, *The Trinity and the Kingdom* (Minneapolis: Fortress, 1993); Hans Urs von Balthasar, *Mysterium Paschale* (Grand Rapids: Eerdmans, 1990).
2. Augustine, *Expositions on the Psalms 1–32*, trans. Maria Boulding, in *The Works of Saint Augustine: A Translation for the 21st Century*, ed. John Rotelle (Hyde Park, NY: New City Press, 2000), 229.

Pastoral Perspective

found in the biblical text God is referred to as "my God." Not "O God," or even just "God," but "*My* God." The pure and abiding trust that the writer has in God conveys his despair at being abandoned by the One who elicits that faith. God, who once seemed as close and life giving as the person's own breath, is now distant and removed. The one who has felt the security of God's proximity feels even more keenly the shattering devastation of the Almighty's presumed absence.

While the psalmist's faith intensifies the despondency, it also serves to assuage what might otherwise prove to be a hopeless situation. The personal connection between the writer and God is not eradicated even by the most agonizing despair. God continues to be "*My* God." The psalmist questions the absence of God while at the same time affirming the divine presence. There is never any doubt that God exists, even when God's seeming abandonment brings desperation and ridicule. The person of faith may question and call upon God for answers, but this very questioning implies that life is still to be found in the divine-human encounter. Faith is greater than that which seeks to destroy it.

Acknowledging one's own place in the larger picture strengthens trust in the God who does not abandon the faithful. The psalmist knows that God is faithful because, as the psalmist looks back on history, the recurring, unshakable, steadfast love of God is apparent. There are times when the community of faith (Israel, to the psalmist) is persecuted, when others threaten to destroy and erase its very existence. But always, God restores God's people; God splits the sea, guides through the wilderness, and gives daily bread. When one reviews the biblical story, one can see the record of God's faithfulness in the past, which births the hope of better times yet to come. The history of God's people gives context to our anguish and affirms that our trials and tribulations are not personal attacks wrought by an abusive God. Rather, it is God who gives the strength, courage, and hope to see us through the darkest of days.

There is a great risk in personal suffering, which has the potential to cause the sufferer to withdraw into an abyss of self-pity and feelings of persecution. "Why me?" we ask. We pull away from God and from other people, tangled in a net of fear and anger at what we perceive as an unjust sentence that we do not deserve. The world becomes an evil place, and our sense of alienation hastens our personal destruction.

Exegetical Perspective

YHWH to the psalmist and his community. For that reason, the initial address of verse 1 is immediately followed in verses 1 and 2 with an accusation against YHWH, that YHWH who promised to stand in solidarity has in fact abandoned Israel. The first part of the psalm proceeds on the assumption of divine abandonment and aims to mobilize YHWH to reengage on behalf of this helpless petitioner. John Calvin, among many interpreters, has seen how this double phrase, "My God, my God . . . why hast thou forsaken me?" contains a remarkable contradiction; Calvin, however, suggests that while the psalmist comes close to *despair*, he is in the end corrected by *faith*:

> Faith, lest he should when so severely tried sink into despair, put into his mouth a correction of this language, so that he boldly called God, of whom he thought he was forsaken, his God. Yea, we see that he has given the first place to faith. Before he allows himself to utter his complaint, in order to give faith the chief place, he first declares that he still claimed God as his own God, and betook himself to him for refuge.[1]

The complaint is against the very God to whom appeal must be made, for the psalmist has no other source of help.

The complaint is extended in verses 6–8, 12–15. In verses 6–8, the speaker is shamed and humiliated in a social context that is characteristically a deep contest between honor and shame. In the complaint, the words of humiliation tumble out: "scorned," "despised," "mock." Verse 8, in a mocking tone, allegedly quotes the mockers. The point of such utterance is to indicate that as the "unsaved" psalmist is humiliated, so is the God who has not saved.

In verses 12–15, the complaint moves toward profoundly regressive language. The "enemies" of the speaker (who remain unidentified) are likened to rapacious animals that prey upon the flesh of the speaker (vv. 12–13); in verses 14–15 the imagery changes to psychosomatic symptoms of alienation and helplessness. All that is described in these verses is derived from the pivotal complaint of verse 1: "forsaken"! Because God has abandoned, it is—in the voice of the psalmist—God's fault that all of this has come upon the speaker. The implied accusation against YHWH is a function of profound faith in which everything good or bad derives from the God of blessing and curse.

1. John Calvin, *Commentary on the Book of Psalms*, Calvin Translation Society, Comm. Ps. 22:1.

Homiletical Perspective

community in which the church resides may be dealing with a cataclysmic natural disaster or the reverberating aftershocks of a social collapse. Psalm 22 promises that such a rupture in life cannot be swept underneath the rug, and that any honest attempt to endure through such difficulty requires one to be honest about the intense feeling that God, at the very least, has abandoned those who suffer and, at worst, has brought the present predicament upon those who despair.

The beginning of this psalm is hauntingly familiar to Christian ears; "My God, my God, why have you forsaken me?" echoes out of the Judaic tradition across the centuries and into our Christian ears through Jesus' cry of dereliction from the cross, as testified in Matthew 27:46 and Mark 15:34. This recollection can help one who suffers from feeling quite so alone, for even Jesus, in his despair, shouted out in horrified wonder that God should abandon and forsake him. It can be a comfort that even Jesus, so like *us* and so like *God* all at once, not only understood, but sympathized and knew both the dimensions and ramifications of such loss. Jesus asks this exacting question of God, alongside those who suffer today, and in that common lot we are never abandoned, always with Christ who in his humanity is always with us.

The form of Psalm 22 should be noted by the preacher, for the psalm becomes a dialogue between the horrors of the present and the deliverance of the past. After the accusatory tone of the first two verses, verses 3–5 recall a trust in God's protection. This trust is reinvigorated by the psalmist's recollection that he is not alone in his history of trouble, for the greater people and nation of Israel previously have trusted in their relationship with God and called out for succor in their times of despair. Furthermore, such cries have not been ignored. The psalmist affirms that God not only heard their cries but honored their trust through providing deliverance from the circumstances that had led to their woes.

Specifically, the psalmist mentions that those of Israel who had cried out before "were not put to shame," which creates an important understanding of shame as the condition of those who not only suffer, but whose cries to God for deliverance go unanswered.

This sense of "shame" informs the originating verses of this psalm, and preachers may understand quickly that the psalmist does not take lightly the dispiriting implications of shame, compounded by abandonment and despair. One's cries to God

Psalm 22:1-15

Theological Perspective

injured and our mouth shouts. Christ does not merely name or "experience" our pain then; he takes it upon himself to transform it.

Viewed in this light, the praying of this psalm is not merely an intellectual problem to be solved. If it were that, Moltmann and Balthasar are entirely right; we should insist that Jesus is abandoned by God not less (and in fact a good deal more!) than each of us. But the praying of this psalm is more than an intellectual problem for Augustine. It is the archetype of the church's prayer, made so by Jesus' praying of it on his cross.

In biblically normed, liturgically framed prayer, we enter into the very life of Christ itself. We pray his words (the Psalms), we become participants in his stories in the gospel (through preaching), we become quite physically part of his body (in the sacraments). As we do this, the words we bring to prayer from our life experience are gathered up, transformed, and given back to us in the form of new words from God through Jesus in the Spirit's church. The same pattern as in our celebration of the sacraments recurs in prayer and worship: our bread, wine, water are taken up, blessed, and given back to make us holy.

This is how it is with this God: entering into our stuff, through Mary's womb, an ordinary rabbi's life, a nasty death, to give us everything God is. We, in turn, come to God with everything we are to become what God has given us in Christ. And this exchange takes place right there, in the words of the psalm. Or so Augustine thinks.

In the end, Augustine is not so far from Balthasar or Moltmann, though philosophical differences remain. All three theologians remind us that God enters our God-forsakenness to transform it into God's blessedness. Screech away at God from your pain. God will eventually answer with abundance. Even if he has to pass through hell to do it.

JASON BYASSEE

Pastoral Perspective

Yet suffering can also have the opposite effect. Our suffering can draw us into an awareness of and connection with the suffering of others. The heart of the mother who grieves over the death of her child is bound to the hearts of all the mothers who have ever buried a daughter or a son. The victim of a violent crime reads the newspaper with a keener eye to the plight of the other innocents whose lives are changed in an instant, forever. The employee whose job is "downsized" has a new sensitivity to those who have lost their jobs through no fault of their own. Shared suffering connects us to a larger world at the very time we are most at risk to feel isolated and alone. We are able to tap into the hope for healing and resurrection that resides in the life of that community.

That hope for healing and resurrection comes from the One in whom the community of faith is born in the first place: Jesus Christ. The suffering of Jesus is the suffering of God at the brokenness of the world, and gives context to our own suffering. Yes, the world—and life—is often painful and difficult, but our suffering is neither caused nor ignored by God. It is no accident that Jesus prayed the opening words of Psalm 22 from the cross. Jesus' cry to God "is not simply a cry of dereliction; it is an affirmation of faith in a God who, as the psalmist comes to understand and articulate, shares human affliction and enables even the dead to praise God."[1]

In times of suffering, we hold fast to the affirmation that in Christ, "suffering produces endurance, and endurance produces character, and character produces hope, and hope does not disappoint us, because God's love has been poured into our hearts through the Holy Spirit that has been given to us" (Rom. 5:3b–5).

Our affirmation of faith in the midst of pain and sorrow points to the truth of a God who holds the whole world in a divine and tender grasp, the world not just of our history, but of all eternity. The psalmist's "exuberant vision is not a mistake but a challenge, a call to enter the reign of God."[2]

KATHLEEN BOSTROM

1. J. Clinton McCann, in *The New Interpreter's Bible* (Nashville: Abingdon, 1996), 4:766.
2. Ibid.

Exegetical Perspective

When the complaint is voiced to YHWH, it is as though YHWH asks in response, "Why should I care about you?" In answer to such implied divine query, the psalmist gives God *reasons* to act (motivations). These reasons characteristically transpose the speaker's need into an interest for YHWH's own status. In verses 3–5 the motivation is an appeal to YHWH's past miracles of rescue for Israel. The appeal is that YHWH should be faithful to YHWH's own past and perform, yet again, saving miracles upon which YHWH's reputation depends, the very miracles that the mockers think cannot happen.

The second motivation, in verses 9–10, begins with an abrupt summons to YHWH: "*Surely you!*" The speaker has been YHWH's charge since birth. God has old, deep commitments to the speaker and is expected to fulfill them, for the keeping of covenantal obligations exhibits YHWH's faithfulness and reliability. (See also Num. 11:12.)

Only now, in verse 11, do we come to the first *petition* of the psalm. The psalm has delayed this long in asking anything specific of YHWH. The petition is only one brief phrase, "Do not be far from me." The remainder of the verse is an additional reinforcing motivation that underscores the urgency of the request. The petition for divine nearness suggests that it is YHWH's remoteness and detachment that have permitted the trouble to occupy the void left by divine absence. From such a verdict of *absence*, clearly, it is the sought-after *nearness* of YHWH that will turn a circumstance of trouble to one of well-being.

We may be most astonished that in the midst of the many words of accusation and motivation, the single petition to YHWH is lean and terse. It is a prayer for nearness of God. The prayer echoes the exclamation of Moses: "For what other great nation has a god so near to it as the Lord our God is whenever we call to him?" (Deut 4:7). When God is near, all will be well. When God is absent, the powers of death encroach.

The wonder of this psalm, and of Israel's prayer more generally, is the defining conviction that Israel is entitled and can insist. And while YHWH acts in freedom, YHWH's fidelity binds YHWH to hear and answer. This prayer is a covenantal interaction whereby the world is made right again, a making right to which the second half of the psalm attests.

WALTER BRUEGGEMANN

Homiletical Perspective

become all the more empty and wounding when the sole answer is that of one's tormenters, not only mocking the cries for assistance, but in effect mocking the integrity and capacities of the God with whom one is in prayerful relationship. Shame emerges not only out of the dishonoring of the self, but out of the unanswered, unaccountable dishonoring of God.

The next set of verses, 9–11, provides a return to that previous reminiscing of how Israel's cries were answered and honored, but makes an important, intimate turn toward the personal history that bonds God to the one who offers this particular prayer. Rather than relying upon God's historical relationship to Israel, now we in conjunction with the psalmist rely upon a history that each person in the congregation is able to share, a pervasively human recollection of a God who kept us safe in the womb, who brought us in care to our mother's breast, and who has been our God ever since we were infants new to the world. Invoking the vulnerability and innocence of that condition, we remind God of our personal histories with God, reiterating the utter dependence we always have had on God to be the ultimate barrier between us and all who would violate our vulnerabilities. In this passage, the preacher can move the congregation out of accusation against God and instead into a strengthening, emboldening call for God to remember and honor personal, lifelong relationship. When there is no other source for assistance, God is the only refuge.

The lectionary has us close the passage with the haunting insistence that God be aware of our present circumstances: "Many bulls encircle me, strong bulls of Bashan surround me." The time of persecution and despair is far from over, and calling upon histories both ancient and personal, the preacher and psalmist alike loudly proclaim God as their God, the congregation's God, a God of honor, compassion, and care whose silence is intolerable and whose protection is necessary.

STEPHEN BUTLER MURRAY

Hebrews 4:12-16

¹²Indeed, the word of God is living and active, sharper than any two-edged sword, piercing until it divides soul from spirit, joints from marrow; it is able to judge the thoughts and intentions of the heart. ¹³And before him no creature is hidden, but all are naked and laid bare to the eyes of the one to whom we must render an account.

¹⁴Since, then, we have a great high priest who has passed through the heavens, Jesus, the Son of God, let us hold fast to our confession. ¹⁵For we do not have a high priest who is unable to sympathize with our weaknesses, but we have one who in every respect has been tested as we are, yet without sin. ¹⁶Let us therefore approach the throne of grace with boldness, so that we may receive mercy and find grace to help in time of need.

Theological Perspective

This passage lifts up two major theological themes: the power of God's word, and the boldness by which we may draw near to God. These two themes seem to go in opposite directions. Hebrews 4:12–13 describes the word of God as a two-edged sword that lays open our innermost thoughts and intentions. The word of God places us under judgment.

"It puts your soul on the operating table," as one of my friends says. The movement is from God's majesty and holiness to humanity's weakness and limitation. Hebrews 4:14–16 moves in the opposite direction: from human weakness and temptation to Christ the high priest, who enables us to approach God's throne of grace. The NRSV even introduces a section break between verses 13 and 14, as though to indicate that we have here two different pericopes and two different trains of thought.

The lectionary nevertheless places these verses together, inviting us to wrestle with the theological tension between God's word to us and our words to God, between God's judgment that lays us bare and God's grace that empowers us to ask help of God in our time of need, and between God's claim on us and our claim on God by virtue of Christ's saving work.

It is indeed Christ alone who resolves these seemingly contradictory elements. Hebrews makes

Pastoral Perspective

In these days, when the discipline of Christian practices is regaining favor in the emergent church, these verses in the fourth chapter of Hebrews underscore the power of Scripture and the passion of prayer. One can almost feel the words of Scripture slicing into our hearts—that sword of the Word— that weapon of grace that penetrates to the very marrow of our being. Which one of us, when exegeting a text during sermon preparation, has not been convicted by the very word we are studying—a word confronting us with our own weakness, our own deception, our own pride? Which one of us has not had to set aside a particular lectionary text, knowing that we cannot, with integrity, preach a text we are simply incapable of practicing?

For the writer of Hebrews, the word of God is "living and active"—probing, slicing, carving the quotidian rhythms of our lives, refining us with a spirit and a wisdom that is fresh and alive. It is as if spiritual surgery were being performed daily— reforming us and always calling us to be reformed.

The denominational seal of the Presbyterian Church (U.S.A.) is deceptively simple—with intricate symbolism folded into every spare curve. Central to its cruciform shape are the outstretched horizontal arms of an open Bible with edges porous to the mind and the imagination. Descending with

Exegetical Perspective

This passage consists of two discrete sections. The first (4:12–13) provides a festive conclusion to the scripturally based exhortation that precedes (4:1–11). The second (4:14–16) is a transitional paragraph, offering new exhortation while introducing the theme of priesthood.

The preceding homily in Hebrews was based on Psalm 95, which called on its addressees to listen "today" to the voice of God (Ps. 95:7; Heb. 3:7). The exposition of the psalm offered a pointed warning to the addressees of Hebrews not to replicate the failure of the Israelites of the desert generation, who by their faithlessness fell away from God and perished (3:12–19). It called instead for the fidelity to stay the course and finally to enter God's "rest" (4:3, 11), not the land of Canaan but that blessed state into which God himself entered after the work of creation (4:4–5). In the hands of our homilist the text of the psalm comes alive as a word of exhortation and encouragement, threatening judgment but offering at the same time a consoling hope.

The concluding flourish, like a postlude, reflects on the whole process of proclamation in which the author has just been engaged. Although some readers have taken the "word" here (v. 12) as a reference to Jesus, Hebrews does not seem to know

Homiletical Perspective

This passage is resplendent with implications for the power of the spoken word, especially as that word is spoken by God: "indeed, the word of God is living and active" (4:12). In fact the whole opening of the letter to the Hebrews recounts the power of God's voice and how human beings respond to that power: as God has *spoken* of old, so now God has *spoken* to us by a Son (1:1). We are admonished to "pay attention to what we have *heard*" so that we will not drift away from the *message* of salvation (2:1). This message was *declared* through the Lord, *attested* by those who *heard* him. God *testifies* through signs, wonders and miracles (2:3–4). Those who have heard the message Jesus *calls* sisters and brothers (2:11) and *proclaims* to them the name of God amid the worshiping congregation (2:12). Jesus is the "high priest" of our *confession* (3:1), that is, what we *profess* through faith. We are told to *exhort* one another daily (3:13), just as the Holy Spirit has exhorted us, "Today, if you *hear* his voice, do not harden your hearts" (3:7–8, 15).

No sermon truly lives on the written page. A sermon leaps from the page in sacred sound, empowered by the voice of God. The sermon is the oral event of speaking, hearing, declaring, attesting, testifying, exhorting, calling, proclaiming, confessing, and professing the Word that God has spoken.

Hebrews 4:12-16

Theological Perspective

clear (1:2) that God has spoken most fully to us in his Son. The word of God is not an extra revelation beyond what we know in Jesus; the word of God is not a mysterious, overwhelming power that operates outside of what God does in Christ. Where God speaks, Christ is present, who has entered fully into our human condition, yet without sin. The God who places us under judgment is the very God who loves us and sympathizes with us in every respect. The One from whom we cannot escape—"If I ascend to heaven, thou art there! If I make my bed in Sheol, thou art there!" (Ps. 139:8 RSV)—is the One who bears us up on eagles' wings (Isa. 40:31).

God's judgment is gracious, and God's grace is judging. No theologian of the recent past has understood and lived this principle more than Dietrich Bonhoeffer, as he issued his call to discipleship under the conditions of Nazi Germany. Bonhoeffer called on the church to avoid cheap grace. But he also rejected new legalisms that could only become instruments of sinful human self-righteousness. Grace that is truly of God changes us and calls us into a new way of life. God's judgment is a reordering and reorienting power that gives us confidence to turn to God for help in every need.

The experience of God's gracious judgment and God's judging grace has also shaped Christians' experience of the word of God that comes to us in the words of the Bible. The Christian church has consistently affirmed that the Old and New Testaments offer much more than information about God. They set forth the living Christ and invite us into relationship with God.

In this sense, the Bible is the word of God—not because it is correct in every historical or scientific detail, but rather because it witnesses to what God has done and continues to do in Christ. In John Calvin's famous analogy, the Scriptures are like spectacles for weak, failing eyes. Without Scripture, we see only a world in chaos, driven by human ambition and failure. God's plans and purposes are blurry and hardly detectable. But if we put on the Scriptures and really look through them, allowing them to refocus our vision, God's saving work in Christ becomes crystal clear. We no longer see a world abandoned to its own devices, but see, rather, God's transforming love, which brings good out of evil and hope out of despair.

The Reformers emphasized that the church stood under the word of God. Sharply rejecting the Catholic principle that only an authoritative teaching office lodged in the pope and the bishops

Pastoral Perspective

power and promise is the dove of the Holy Spirit, reminding us that an open Bible is constantly being renewed by the fresh revelation of the Spirit. If we do not keep our own Bibles open, our own hearts unlocked, our own minds ready for God's deft sword, we may miss that liberating moment when the dis-ease of our life is cut away by the healing wisdom of a living word.

Of course, such spiritual surgery can be painful. Sometimes the word leaves us wounded, raw, and vulnerable. This is why the next few verses are so healing. Quickly the author leads us to a place of passionate prayer—an invitation to fall on our knees before the one who has been where we are now living, the one who has known temptation, weakness, suffering, agony, disappointment, and wounds so raw that they have not yet healed. Because of the intimacy we share with the one who endures every agony of our human experience, we can cry out with complete honesty: cursing, weeping, begging, whining, confessing the worst—and the best—of who we are. Having been pared down to the bare bones of our brokenness and incompleteness, we are then invited to be bold in our confession and honest in our need. How refreshing this text is, in peeling away the veneer of self-absorbed living! How generous it is, in offering us the immense pool of God's grace!

In these days of theological warfare, the book of Hebrews can be used as ammunition to bolster the battle being waged over the theology of the atonement. The high Christology and blood-soaked allusions to the crucifixion in this text have been used to underscore the doctrine of substitutionary atonement—the conviction that a perfect Jesus, once and for all, took all the sin of the world upon his own soul, doing for us what we cannot do for ourselves, dying for us so that we can live forever. Certainly, the immensity of Christ's sacrifice *is* this kind of gift.

However, this particular text suggests another more nuanced interpretation of the cross: a paradoxical mystery where the sheer grandeur and humility of Jesus' death invites us to share in this mystery completely, a paradoxical blessing where Jesus suffers *with* us, and not just *for* us. In the author's heart, Jesus' perfection is not about power or purity, but about endurance. This Lord meets us in the places of temptation and weakness, experiencing all the human foibles that separate us from God. Yet Jesus is able to endure in ways we cannot—to endure to the end, to endure the darkness until it is completely transformed by light.

Exegetical Perspective

the theology of the Word found in the Gospel according to John (John 1:1).

The first characteristics of the word, "living and active," recall the description of divine Wisdom in Wisdom of Solomon 7:22, ("subtle, mobile"), a passage to which the exordium had alluded (1:3). The second characteristic, "sharper than any two-edged sword," recalls a well-known image of the tongue as a sword. Here, as at Revelation 19:15, the image is transferred from the tongue to what it produces.

The word that "penetrates" again recalls Wisdom, which pervades all things (Wis. 7:24). What is penetrated here is specifically the interior of the human self. The description of that interiority has a paradoxical quality; the points where "soul and spirit, sinews and joints" connect would be difficult for any eye to detect. The function of the penetrating word is clear; it offers judgments on human thoughts and desires (v. 12).

The notion that God sees all is traditional (Jer. 11:20; 1 Cor. 4:5). Our homilist cloaks that notion in a new metaphor, using language of the gymnasium. There all are "naked" and exposed, particularly those engaged in wrestling, who might be caught in the grip of an opponent and have their neck "bent back" (NRSV "laid bare") to everyone's eyes. The rare word used here is also appropriate to describe a sacrificial victim whose throat is about to be slit, an allusion entirely appropriate to the sense of vulnerability that the author evokes.

The passage concludes with a play on the term *logos* ("word") with which the section had begun. The God who addresses his word to us, demands a word back, an "account" of our doing (v. 13), but also a word of trust, as "we" are called upon to say in 13:6.

The transitional verses begin with a reference to what "we" have, as at a similar transition at 10:19. The claim that Christ is a "high priest" appeared previously at 2:17, although it is not yet clear what grounds the claim. That Christ has "passed through the heavens" could be inferred from the references to Psalm 110 and the session on high (1:3, 13; 2:7–9) and procession heavenward (2:10).

The presence of Christ as a heavenly intercessor grounds the author's call to "hold to confession" (v. 14), which implies that he is addressing believers. Whether the "confession" has some specific, quasi-credal form is unclear. The author may have in mind acclamations like those he has made affirming the status of Jesus as Son.

The call to hold fast finds further grounds in a reflection on the character of the heavenly high priest.

Homiletical Perspective

The sermon is an integral and crucial aspect of our common act of worship. It is our *liturgy*, the act of the gathered people, where preacher and hearers together attend to God's human speech, that is, the living and active voice of God orally communicated, interpreted for this day.

The opening of the letter to the Hebrews speaks of the creative power of God's voice: God's Word is Jesus Christ, through whom God created the universe (1:1). The opening passages of Hebrews function as a *doxological* sermon. This sermon praises God's greatness and what God has done to achieve salvation through Jesus Christ. In our current passage (4:12–16), we are immediately confronted with the devastating power of God's voice: a double-edged sword that pierces our very being, discerning our thoughts and intentions (4:12). In the presence of this voice we are naked and laid bare, and in this most vulnerable posture we are to "render an account" of who we are, what we have done, what message we have clung to, and what words of faith we have professed. Devastated by God's word, stripped of all pretence, exposed, held up to the scrutiny of God's all-seeing eyes, we are nonetheless attentive to yet another of God's verbal acts: the pronouncement of judgment and mercy.

How has this sermon moved from *doxology* to judgment? We may need to hear a few verses that have come before. God's eternal sermon brought the cosmos into being. The *telos* of that initial sermon was God's own Sabbath rest. This sermon was proclaimed to our ancestors in the faith, through the prophets, and yet some of them failed to hear, believe, and act as if that sermon had laid claim to their lives. The "preacher" of the letter of Hebrews is concerned that God's eternal sermon be heard anew. Through God's own Son, the message of deliverance from enslavement and captivity (2:14–15) was proclaimed in the event of the cross. Those who would know God's Sabbath rest must not wander away from the message declared in their hearing.

The preacher of Hebrews discerns some act of disobedience on the part of those who would turn a deaf ear to God's voice. If God's doxological sermon has not laid claim on an individual or community, they are to beware of the piercing, penetrating aspect of that same sermon. We hear of a battle fought and won. Humanity had been held captive and enslaved. God achieved deliverance through the event of the cross. The proclamation of the cross acts as a sword that rends us free, not only from that which holds all of creation captive, but from that which holds each

Hebrews 4:12-16

Theological Perspective

(the magisterium) could rightly interpret the Scriptures, they insisted that the Scriptures were self-authenticating. The church cannot on the basis of tradition or a special claim to inspiration give the right reading of the Bible; on the contrary, the church itself is nothing without God's word in Scripture that calls it into being and sustains it. Ministers for this reason are to be understood above all as servants of the Word. They are to preach in a way that allows God's living voice in the Scriptures to be heard. Only a church focused exclusively on the word of God (*sola scriptura*) can resist the idolatries of the world, whether in the guise of power or money or sensuality.

This Reformation principle was really nothing other than what the church had long practiced, regardless of its theology. Whether in lonely cloister halls or soaring city cathedrals, in Puritan meetinghouses or Pietist small-group gatherings, Christians in worship have turned again and again to the Scriptures as God's unique witness to God's judging grace and God's gracious judgment. It is principally the Scriptures that have shaped the church's prayers, hymns, sermons, and sacraments, so as to invite Christians to encounter the living Word who is Jesus Christ. The Scriptures set forth in preaching and sacrament have given Christians the confidence that God truly speaks and calls us back to who we are before and in God.

Hebrews 4:12–16 is language about worship. It reminds us that whenever we rightly hear the Scriptures read and preached, God's word will examine us and expose our failings. But our confession of sin is inseparable from our confession of faith in the Son of God (v. 14). In Christ, the word of God becomes sacramental, drawing us into God's transforming grace. This sacramental word lifts us into heaven itself: "Lift up your hearts!" God's word like the Eucharist nourishes us within the body of Christ, so that we may "approach the throne of grace with boldness" (v. 16).

JOHN P. BURGESS

Pastoral Perspective

This endurance is not just in the midst of his own pain, but also in the midst of ours. He sticks with us, enduring our pain when we simply cannot survive for one more minute. This absolute loyalty and solidarity with our suffering sets Jesus apart—and brings us back to our best selves—offering us *at-one-ment* with God. At our best, pastors are called to imitate this healing kind of solidarity with the people we serve.

I recently practiced a silent retreat in an Episcopalian Benedictine community. In the chapel there is an icon—a Theotokos—that archetypal image of Mother and Child that has stirred Christian devotion for centuries. As I meditated upon this painting, somehow the high Christology of Hebrews became one with the degradation of the Suffering Servant.

In gold and blue and crimson, the ancient painter has given us a tender, innocent child embedded in his mother's arms—but this infant has a wise old face, softened by sadness and radiant with a fierce, forever love. I could almost hear the Word piercing, slicing into my soul; "Love one another, as I have loved you—all the way to the cross." With remorse and hope, I found myself praying, begging the one who knows my weakness to set me free. This was a live experience of the power of Scripture and the passion of prayer!

I imagine this text preached in the midst of a liturgy that shapes it and incarnates it. First an opening hymn—"What a Friend We Have in Jesus"—followed by the reading of the text and a lamentation anthem after that. Then the Word proclaimed—with narrative weakness and vulnerability on the part of the preacher—followed by extensive, honest prayer, as we dare to cast our confession before the "one who in every respect has been tested as we are," approaching "the throne of grace with boldness, so that we may receive mercy and find grace to help in time of need" (4:16).

SUSAN R. ANDREWS

Exegetical Perspective

The verse resumes a meditation on Christ's humanity that had occupied 2:10–17, which focused on the solidarity between Christ and his human "brothers and sisters." He shared with them "flesh and blood"(2:14), confronted and overcame the fear of death (2:15). He was, in short, made "perfect" through suffering (2:10), thereby made fit to be a "merciful and faithful" high priest (2:17). The current passage draws the inference that he is therefore "not . . . unable" (an example of the rhetorical figure of litotes) of sympathy with our weaknesses. The fact that he was "tested" specifically resumes the previous treatment of Christ's humanity (2:18). Christ's solidarity with humankind finds dramatic confirmation in the remark that he was "in every respect" similar, with one exception. The author maintains that Christ was "without sin," an affirmation of a piece with the image of Christ as a sacrificial victim "without blemish" as well as high priest (9:14).

The final exhortation balances the static language of "holding fast" (v. 14) with the more dynamic, "let us approach" (v. 16). A similar balance will continue to mark the exhortations of Hebrews, which constantly urges firm fidelity to tradition as well as willingness to follow the example of the patriarchs (11:8) and Christ himself (13:13). Here that movement is not defined by the conditions left behind, but by its heavenly goal (2:10; 12:1–3).

The designation of the object of the movement, the "throne," recalls the theme of the heavenly session of Christ developed through the use of Psalm 110:1 (1:3, 13). The characterization of the throne as defined by "grace" results from the identification of the one who is seated there, the sympathetic priest. The purpose of the approach, to "receive mercy and grace," defines one of the overall aims of the homily as a whole, to offer "help in time of need." The reassuring tone of this verse balances the somewhat more ominous reference to judgment that marked the previous passage. Such a balance between warning and consolation also marks other hortatory passages in Hebrews (e.g., 6:4–12; 12:15–24).

HAROLD W. ATTRIDGE

Homiletical Perspective

individual enslaved to disobedience. In the presence of God's sermon we are called to make account. God's word elicits and requires a response from us: confession.

In our liturgy we enact corporate acts of confession of sin and profession of faith. We also experience this dual pattern in our current passage: the relationship between the Word of God and our communal and individual acts of confession and profession. The Word of God that has freed us from captivity now lays claim to us. We are held captive as if before a discerning judge upon a throne. This judge is *the* Word of God, God's living sermon that requires of us an accounting (*logos*, 4:13).

Our preaching in light of this text must balance doxology, critique, and hope. We first praise God for who God is and what God has done. Then, we allow the double-edged sword of God's living Word to cut through the illusions we cling to: trusting in economic and political security instead of God's abiding presence, hoarding resources as if they were not gifts of God, believing in a cultural gospel that says what we have, whom we know, and how much knowledge, power, and prestige we possess determines who we are.

At the heart of God's eternal sermon is a calling, extended in grace, that comes to us in our time of need, in our spiritual poverty, to live into a paradoxical faith. The preacher and congregants alike are called to "hold fast" to God's Christ. What may seem like foolishness, weakness, and debasement in the world's eyes is our true hope, God's wisdom, power, and mercy.

We proclaim the hope-filled good news that before God's all-perceiving eyes we are fully known, and, because our high priest, Jesus Christ, has gained access for us to God's throne room, we can approach and attend to God's eternal sermon. Hearing God's pronouncement of mercy and grace, we return to doxology, lifting our voices in communal praise of God.

MICHAEL G. HEGEMAN

Mark 10:17-31

¹⁷As he was setting out on a journey, a man ran up and knelt before him, and asked him, "Good Teacher, what must I do to inherit eternal life?" ¹⁸Jesus said to him, "Why do you call me good? No one is good but God alone. ¹⁹You know the commandments: 'You shall not murder; You shall not commit adultery; You shall not steal; You shall not bear false witness; You shall not defraud; Honor your father and mother.' " ²⁰He said to him, "Teacher, I have kept all these since my youth." ²¹Jesus, looking at him, loved him and said, "You lack one thing; go, sell what you own, and give the money to the poor, and you will have treasure in heaven; then come, follow me." ²²When he heard this, he was shocked and went away grieving, for he had many possessions.

²³Then Jesus looked around and said to his disciples, "How hard it will be for those who have wealth to enter the kingdom of God!" ²⁴And the disciples were

Theological Perspective

The story of the rich man—described as young in Matthew (Matt. 19:20) and a ruler in Luke (Luke 18:18)—is one of the most familiar passages in the Synoptic Gospels. Like the equally familiar parable of the Good Samaritan, the story begins with a question about salvation from an earnest adherent to the law. The rich man asks, "What must I do to inherit eternal life?"

As in the parable of the Good Samaritan, Jesus turns the focus away from the petitioner's concern with his own salvation toward gracious behavior to others. The Samaritan, a religious heretic, is lifted up as the exemplar of the good neighbor. Likewise, the rich man is exhorted to go, sell all that he has, and give it to the poor, and then come and follow Jesus. On the one hand, this story clearly raises questions about our attitude and approach toward wealth, if we want to follow Jesus and inherit eternal life. On the other hand, it raises questions about our attitude and approach toward salvation itself.

Jesus' answer to the rich man shocks and dismays the disciples, and it continues to perplex many readers today. In the ancient world (Greek, Roman, and Hebrew), material prosperity was widely seen as a reward or byproduct of spiritual virtue. Things go well for the good, for men and women of good character, and poorly for the bad, for those who lack

Pastoral Perspective

Taking a step into the future can be a difficult task: getting ready for the first day at school, going out on a first date, leaving the corporate job to set up a business, undergoing experimental treatment for a life-threatening illness, selling all we have (giving it to the poor) and following Jesus. That last example was the step into the future that Jesus recommended for "the man" in Mark 10:17.

In Mark, he is first called "a man." Later, in verse 22, we find out that he is a wealthy man. He is a "ruler" in Luke and "young" in Matthew. In Christian tradition, he is often the "rich, young ruler." But for Mark he is just a regular guy, although with "great possessions."

This man, perhaps thinking he has everything else (if that is what having "great possessions" means), has the ultimate question for Jesus: "Good Teacher, what must I do to inherit eternal life?" As Jesus did when the Pharisees put him to the test with the question about divorce (Mark 10: 2–16), Jesus reframes the question in terms of the kingdom of God ("come, follow me") rather than in the language of "eternal life." After the man leaves, Jesus declares to the disciples, "How hard it will be for those who have wealth to enter the kingdom of God!"

Throughout this section of Mark's Gospel, people come to Jesus with all sorts of questions: "Is it lawful

perplexed at these words. But Jesus said to them again, "Children, how hard it is to enter the kingdom of God! ²⁵It is easier for a camel to go through the eye of a needle than for someone who is rich to enter the kingdom of God." ²⁶They were greatly astounded and said to one another, "Then who can be saved?" ²⁷Jesus looked at them and said, "For mortals it is impossible, but not for God; for God all things are possible."

²⁸Peter began to say to him, "Look, we have left everything and followed you." ²⁹Jesus said, "Truly I tell you, there is no one who has left house or brothers or sisters or mother or father or children or fields, for my sake and for the sake of the good news, ³⁰who will not receive a hundredfold now in this age—houses, brothers and sisters, mothers and children, and fields, with persecutions—and in the age to come eternal life. ³¹But many who are first will be last, and the last will be first."

Exegetical Perspective

Mark 10:17 introduces us to an unidentified supplicant ("young" in Matt. 19:22; "a ruler," Luke 18:18). There is no reason to doubt the sincerity of his approach (kneeling), his address ("Good Teacher"), or his question ("What must I do to inherit eternal life?"). Though mentioned frequently in John (3:15–16, 36; 6:27–68), in Mark "eternal life" is mentioned only in 10:17 and 30, following markers laid down in Daniel (12:1–3) and some intertestamental Jewish literature (see *Jubilees* 23:23–21; *Psalms of Solomon* 3:12b; Qumran's *Hymn Scroll* 11:3–14). Because Jesus immediately associates eternal life with the kingdom of God (10:23–24, 30), Mark probably regards the terms as interchangeable.

Jesus' reply is crisp (10:18–19). Characteristically in Mark (1:14–15, 44; 5:19) Jesus diverts attention away from himself, onto God's goodness (10:18), even though other New Testament writers highlight Jesus' sinlessness (John 8:46; 2 Cor. 5:21; Heb. 7:26; 1 Pet. 2:22). Jesus' reminder (10:19) of the Decalogue's fifth, sixth, seventh, eighth, and ninth commandments (Exod. 20:12–16; Deut. 5:16–20), supplemented by a prohibition against fraud (Deut. 24:14), yokes life in God's eternal presence with communal justice in accord with the Sinaitic covenant in this life. Though Jesus radicalizes its intent (see Mark 10:2–12), his teaching does not supplant Torah.

Homiletical Perspective

This text is rich with tensions that present both challenges and possibilities for the preacher. The tensions begin with the request of the rich man. Jesus has just proclaimed that "whoever does not receive the kingdom of God as a little child will never enter it" (v. 15). Now the rich man, who obviously did not hear Jesus' teaching, kneels before Jesus and asks, "What must I *do* to inherit eternal life?" The man's mind-set, often typical of those who are privileged, is contradictory to Jesus' teaching. Rather than receiving the kingdom in complete dependence as a little child, the rich man wants to know what he can *do* to inherit eternal life. Indeed, this tension is present even in his question. One can rarely *do* anything for an *inheritance*; by definition, an inheritance is something a person can only be given.

So the tension increases. Following the man's assertion that he has indeed kept the commandments since his youth, Jesus actually gives the man something more to *do*. Loving the man, Jesus tells him to "sell what you own, and give the money to the poor, and you will have treasure in heaven; then come, follow me" (v. 21). Jesus seems to confirm the man's orientation by simply requiring an action that is more extreme than obedience to the commandments. Faced with this new demand, the man goes away shocked and grieving, unable to

Mark 10:17-31

Theological Perspective

good character and self-discipline. There are exceptions, of course, as seen in the story of Job and similar tales of good men and women who are defeated either by circumstances or by others less virtuous than they are. The question of why the good suffer and the wicked prosper is not new. But this question concerns the exceptions that prove the rule. The ideal remains the coincidence of virtue and prosperity. The hope and expectation are that virtue and vice will meet their appropriate fate, in this world or the next.

What then are the relationships between faith and reward, or virtue and wealth? Why must this man give up his riches in order to follow Jesus? What will he get in return? A standard answer is that there is nothing wrong with wealth itself. The problem is not wealth per se but our attitude toward it. As we accumulate riches, we are tempted to trust in our possessions and our powers of acquiring them, rather than in God, for our ultimate security and comfort. Even honestly acquired and generously shared wealth can thus lead to pride. This is why it is easier for a camel to go through the eye of a needle than for a rich person to enter the kingdom of God. It is hard to let go of the immediate basis of our security and comfort—and the more we have, the harder it gets.

Jesus' promise to the disciples is thus perplexing. He promises that everyone who has sacrificed for his sake will receive, now in this age, a hundred times more than he or she has given up, and will inherit eternal life, in the age to come. This promise is perplexing, first, because it seems counter to our experience of the world. The community of disciples may provide a substitute and intensified family in place of those left behind, but the reward of discipleship in this age seems to be the way of the cross, not material prosperity.

Second, if the reason for discipleship is the promise of its reward, then discipleship seems to be no more virtuous than the naked pursuit of material gain. If faith promises a hundredfold return on investment, then it is nothing more than prudence or enlightened self-interest. Even the most narrow-minded, self-interested, and calculating spirit would be a fool not to abandon everything and follow Jesus.

To take Jesus' promise literally thus seems to push the notion of the reward for faith beyond his true intent. Faith is not simply an expedient route to friends and fortune. On the contrary, the reward for faith is of a different and higher order than what we sacrifice for it. It is only in this metaphorical sense that we will receive a hundred times more than we

Pastoral Perspective

for a man to divorce his wife?" "What must I do to inherit eternal life?" In each case, Jesus recasts the question in terms of the inbreaking of the kingdom of God and the new behavior that is required. In most cases, the disciples just do not understand. Typically, Jesus has to explain or share another parable with the dense disciples to provoke understanding. Interestingly, in this instance, the disciples comprehend, at least enough to say, "Then who can be saved?" The disciples change from kingdom language to the language of being "saved," but they at least understand the difficulty of stepping into the future.

The disciples have just witnessed a painful moment for the wealthy man who leaves "sorrowful" (my trans., NRSV "grieving"). Christian tradition has assumed that he went away sorrowful because he was unwilling to sell all that he had, give it to the poor, and follow Jesus. Another possibility is that he went away sorrowful precisely because he had decided to sell all he had and follow Jesus. That bold action would have not been emotionless. That would have been a decisive step into the future, resulting in an emotional letting go of all that he had and the relationships that came with his possessions.

In any event, the disciples are privy to just how painful steps into the future can be (whether the man did or did not give away his possessions). The kingdom of God is unfolding, but joining Jesus in kingdom activity and behavior is not easy and often it is excruciatingly painful.

For our parishioners and for us, taking a first step is often very difficult and sometimes painful: attending the first AA meeting, calling the marriage counselor, talking with the son or daughter about the marijuana in the jeans pocket, coming "out of the closet," or maybe hearing a call to ministry and literally parting with most of what we have to follow Jesus.

And what about those sitting in the pews who have not parted with all (or most) of what they have? What about their possible sense of guilt as they hear this Scripture read? "You lack one thing; go, sell what you own, and give the money to the poor . . . then come, follow me" (v. 21). Most probably they already know that their fortunate position in life is largely (or maybe even completely) due to the good fortune of being born in the Western world rather than in a developing country. What does the preacher say to these materially blessed people?

The sensitive preacher might want to explain to the congregation that giving all away at once might not be good stewardship. Planned giving and

Exegetical Perspective

Likewise, in 10:20 the questioner professes himself a lifelong, observant Jew.

In 10:21 Mark deviates from Matthew and Luke by characterizing Jesus in affective terms: He looks the man in the eye (*emblepsas*) with love (*ēgapēsen*). His interlocutor has respectfully asked a serious question; Jesus honors it and the one who has asked. The one thing lacking proves decisive. Generally, he is to sell whatever he has for the needs of the poor; particularly, he is to follow Jesus himself (v. 21). Inheritance of eternal life requires relinquishing control over this life's treasure (see also Matt. 6:19–21; Luke 12:33–34) and adhering to a new master (Matt. 6:24–33; Luke 16:10–13; cf. Prov. 28:11; 1 Tim. 6:9–10). The questioner proves unable to do the one thing because—as we now learn for the first time—he had many possessions (Mark 10:22).

This is not an isolated case (10:23, 24b), Jesus remarks; his disciples are amazed to hear it (10:24a). Why the amazement? Of all people who could expect easy access to God's kingdom, should not it be those whose very riches suggest God's blessing? On the contrary, answers Jesus: Wealth is a greater obstacle into the kingdom than a camel's bulk through a needle's eye (10:25; see also 4:18–19). Various attempts to soften this saying, like noting the similarity of the Greek term for camel (*kamēlos*) with that for a ship's cable (*kamilos*), should be resisted. The comment's sheer absurdity is in alignment with Jesus' parabolic speech (Mark 3:23; 4:1–34), as suggested by the Twelve's flabbergasted query: "Then who can be saved?" (v. 26). Repeating the action directed toward his first questioner—gazing at (*emblepsas*) them—Jesus' response drives home this passage's main point: What is humanly impossible remains divinely achievable (v. 27). In fact, this way of putting things returns the reader to the form in which the man originally framed his question: "What must *I* do?" Ultimately, salvation cannot lie in mortal hands. It resides only with God, without whose support the human will cannot achieve its deepest desires.

Here it is wise to pause, recollecting instances in Mark where God makes possible the impossible. It happens when Jesus restores sick or dead children to healthy life (5:21–43; 9:14–29). It is seen when a destitute widow, down to her last mite, deposits her very life for the sake of a temple soon to tumble (12:41–44; 13:1–2). It occurs when another woman anoints a soon-to-be-crucified Messiah with priceless myrrh (14:3–10). And it happens when Jesus, deep in prayer, receives from the Father strength to give his life for the sake of others (14:32–42; cf. 9:29; 11:20–25).

Homiletical Perspective

fulfill Jesus' requirement. The question arises, How in the world is receiving the kingdom as a little child like selling all you own and giving it to the poor?

Then things get even more confusing. Addressing his disciples, Jesus teaches that it will be *impossible* for a rich person (the very person considered divinely blessed!) to enter the kingdom of God— *more* impossible than getting a camel through the eye of a needle. And when the disciples inquire in disbelief, "Then who can be saved?" Jesus replies, "For mortals it is impossible, but not for God; for God all things are possible" (v. 27).

Now the reader must acknowledge the gracious possibilities of God, not just in relation to rich people, but for all mortals. But then, almost in the same breath, Jesus promises a reward to those who *have* left everything and followed him; they will receive houses, fields, a new family (along with persecutions!), and in the age to come, eternal life. And if that is not enough, he concludes by cryptically turning everything upside down: "But many who are first will be last, and the last will be first" (v. 31).

The preacher does well not to avoid or to try to resolve these tensions. The text contains extreme demands (sell everything, give to the poor, and follow me), extreme judgment (it is impossible for a rich person to enter the kingdom of God), and extreme promises, expressed both as grace and reward (with God all things are possible; whoever leaves everything and follows me will receive great rewards). These extreme assertions are held together with no attempt to lessen the tensions.

Consequently, despite Jesus' command to the rich man and his uncompromising challenge to the wealthy, the text should not be simplistically turned into a new "law" that requires all wealthy people literally to sell everything, give to the poor, and thereby earn eternal life. That approach stands in tension with the preceding story about the children, with other aspects of this text, as well as with other parts of the New Testament.

At the same time, however, preachers cannot dismiss Jesus' radical command to the rich man or Jesus' sharp words about the impossibility of the wealthy entering the kingdom. Jesus' sharp challenge to the wealthy is critical today, particularly in privileged, Western congregations, which must be considered rich. This important word should not be dismissed by appealing simplistically to the "impossibility of God" as a form of grace that negates Jesus' commands. Nor should Jesus' uncompromising words to the rich man be dismissed as Jesus' way of forcing

Mark 10:17-31

Theological Perspective

have given up. It is not simply more of the same, a hundred fields and houses rather than one. More paradoxically, we cannot attain even this higher reward—our eternal salvation—by striving for it. If our primary concern is our own salvation, through faith or works, then we have missed the point of both faith and works.

Jesus' answer is thus doubly shocking. First, he questions not merely greed but also wealth itself and the virtues that help us to acquire it. Certainly, those who pride themselves on their possessions or expect material prosperity to provide them with ultimate security are sadly mistaken. Even honestly acquired and generously shared wealth is dangerous to our salvation, because it prompts us to rely on ourselves rather than God.

Second, and even more shocking, Jesus questions those who pride themselves on their virtue and faith. Even honestly sought virtue and faith are dangerous, because they also prompt us to rely on ourselves rather than God. We are saved only when we stop worrying about our salvation and turn our attention to God and neighbor.

What then are we to do about our money? Jesus does not leave us with any easy response. We are left at the mercy of God, but Jesus' summons requires total transformation and commitment. For the rich man, Jesus' call meant giving up all that he had for a life of discipleship. Can it mean less for us? Our response will show whether we truly believe that we will be rewarded in this life and the next.

JAMES J. THOMPSON

Pastoral Perspective

thoughtful charity can be done over time. At any rate, the preacher will need to point out that the new life in the kingdom of God does allow for new behavior, new first steps. Maybe folks should *not* give away all they have at once, but life in the kingdom is about caring and sharing. It should not be business as usual.

Life in the kingdom of God is about transformation and character change. With the demands and temptations of life bearing down upon us, we want to cry out like the disciples, "Then who can be saved?" (v. 26). Who can live a kingdom life? How can I change? How can I take the necessary first steps?

Being in the company and presence of Jesus is a good first step. Character transformation begins with identification with Jesus ("Come, follow me"). And identification with Jesus signifies that character change is not only a slow process but also a relational process. Likewise, nestled and nurtured in the company of believers, people are enabled to take first steps into new behavior.

When the disciples exclaimed, "Then who can be saved?" Jesus responded with hope: "For mortals it is impossible, but not for God; for God all things are possible" (v. 27). Those thick-skulled disciples had finally understood something: just how hard it is to change and to live out kingdom ethics.

For them and for us, Jesus holds out the hope that, with God, change and first steps are not only possible but are already happening ("Truly I tell you, there is no one who has left house or brothers or sisters or mother or father or children or fields, for my sake and for the sake of the good news, who will not receive a hundredfold now in this age . . . and in the age to come eternal life" [vv. 29–30]). So it should not be surprising that, as the result of first steps, "many who are first will be last, and the last will be first" (v. 31).

DAVID B. HOWELL

Exegetical Perspective

Not once in Mark do we see the Twelve in prayer. Doubtless that accounts for their infidelity to Jesus on the night he was betrayed (14:27–31, 50–52, 66–72). Yet, unlike the rich man, they have left everything to follow him (1:16–20; 2:13–14), which Peter asserts and Jesus does not deny (10:28–29). Their reward for such obedience is an abundant new family to replace that relinquished by acceptance of Jesus' call (10:29–30). This comports with his earlier promise that doing God's will makes one a brother or sister or mother of Jesus (3:31–35). In exchange for much that has been abandoned, much more will be received, including eternal life in the age to come (10:30). Yet the destiny of Jesus' followers assumes a very peculiar shape. For one thing, this new family lacks a human father (paterfamilias), who in antiquity was the decisive figure. The omission is arguably deliberate, since in Mark the only true Father is God (11:25; 14:36; see also Matt. 6:9; 23:9; Luke 10:21–22; John 1:14, 18). Moreover, Jesus' disciples are not promised the extravagant rewards sometimes encountered in other Jewish eschatology (e.g., 2 Esdras 7:88–99). Until the final consummation, the good they receive will still be laced "with persecutions" (Mark 10:30; see also 13:3–27). Finally, assurance dare not become cocksure, for God's inbreaking kingdom is in the process of turning this world upside down and inside out (10:31). At no time will this become clearer than when God raises from death his crucified Messiah (15:33–41; 16:1–8).

Mark 10:17–31 presents in equipoise human responsibility and God's grace. Life in God's eternal presence depends on conduct consistent with God's eternal will for justice among his creatures. Such, however, is impossible for mortals without God's gracious help. As Augustine prayed, "Give me the grace to do as you command, and command me to do what you will."[1] This is good news only for those prepared to let go of all the fraudulent and collapsible supports, epitomized by wealth, on which in this life they are constantly tempted to rely. The God to whom Jesus points, and in whom he committed his own trust, does not want some portion of Christ's disciples. God intends to claim them entirely, without remainder or reservation. That is the promise of eternal life. Never is it realized painlessly or without sacrifice for the gospel's sake (10:29), whether by this Christ or by his followers.

C. CLIFTON BLACK

Homiletical Perspective

the man to rely on "grace alone" by presenting him with an impossible demand. Jesus' command and his word of grace must be held together, as Dietrich Bonhoeffer reminds us in his emphasis on "costly grace."[1]

Within this tension, Jesus' approach to the rich man may provide a helpful guide to preachers for speaking a difficult word from this text. Jesus loves the rich man; he does not view the man as intentionally evil. Indeed, the man appears to be faithful in many ways, having kept the commandments from his youth. Rather than condemning the "sin" of the rich man, Jesus confronts the man with his *weakness*, his captivity to possessions that prevents him from living into the full life of the kingdom. Jesus here names the "power" that holds the man captive and invites the man to step into freedom.

As Jacques Ellul has noted, the only way to live free from money is to give it away:

> How overcome the spiritual "power" of money? Not by accumulating more money, not by using money for good purposes, not by being just and fair in our dealings. The *law of money* is the law of accumulation, of buying and selling. That is why the only way to overcome the spiritual "power" of money is to give our money away, thus desacralizing it and freeing ourselves from its control. . . . To give away money is to win a victory over the spiritual power that oppresses us.[2]

Such a word needs to be spoken to persons and congregations today, most of whom are not intentionally evil, but simply captive to their wealth and complicit with powers larger than themselves. Jesus speaks his sharp words to the rich man out of love, because he wants him to be free, though Jesus is clearly aware that the depth of the man's captivity makes such freedom difficult if not impossible. But even then, Jesus promises, "All things are possible with God."

CHARLES L. CAMPBELL

1. St. Augustine, *Confessions*, trans. R. S. Pine-Coffin (London: Penguin, 1961), 10:29, 233.

1. See Dietrich Bonhoeffer, *The Cost of Discipleship*, rev. ed., trans. R. H. Fuller (New York: Macmillan, 1959).
2. Jacques Ellul, *Violence: Reflections from a Christian Perspective*, trans. Cecelia Gaul Kings (New York: Seabury Press, 1969), 166.

Job 38:1-7 (34-41)

¹Then the LORD answered Job out of the whirlwind:
²"Who is this that darkens counsel by words without knowledge?
³Gird up your loins like a man,
  I will question you, and you shall declare to me.

⁴"Where were you when I laid the foundation of the earth?
  Tell me, if you have understanding.
⁵Who determined its measurements—surely you know!
  Or who stretched the line upon it?
⁶On what were its bases sunk,
  or who laid its cornerstone
⁷when the morning stars sang together
  and all the heavenly beings shouted for joy?

. . . .

³⁴"Can you lift up your voice to the clouds,
  so that a flood of waters may cover you?

Theological Perspective

In the Bible, God is depicted as a person who acts in history: God sends a flood to destroy the evildoers of Noah's generation, God converses with Abraham, God parts the waters for the escaping Hebrew slaves, God sends the Assyrians and the Babylonians to destroy the nations of Israel and Judah as punishment for their sinfulness. Moreover, God is a moral agent. Everything God does is just and righteous. In the story about Job, these assumptions about God are put to the test by the incredible suffering of the innocent in history. Job challenges the very justice of God in ruling the universe and then waits upon God to answer this challenge.

But the answer in this text that Job receives from God out of the whirlwind puts the issue on an entirely new plane. Now God is depicted as creator of the universe whose wisdom and power far exceed anything the human mind can grasp. God replies: "I will question you, and you shall declare to me. Where were you when I laid the foundation of the earth? Tell me if you have understanding" (38:3–4). In response, Job is humbled by this disclosure of God's grandeur and majesty: "I have uttered what I did not understand. . . . Therefore I despise myself, and repent in dust and ashes" (42:3, 6). But God's answer to Job is not really an answer at all, is it? It

Pastoral Perspective

What if God really did show up at the invocation in church on a Sunday morning? What if God's voice echoed across the crowd at a rally for the presidential candidate who had just announced that America is God's chosen nation? What if God finally had enough of the bombings and wall building in the lands of the Bible and arrived to set matters straight? What would God have to say?

God's appearance in Job is startling, to say the least. But our astonishment in reading the narrative is only a modicum of the shock Job must have felt. Finally, after thousands of words of chatter among Job and his friends, myriad trial theologies, and dozens of strategies for approaching God, the voice of YHWH resounds.

Who are you (v. 2)?
Where were you (v. 4)?
What do you know (v. 5)?
Can you (v. 34)?

Job does not get answers. Job gets questions. The questions thunder across the earth, intimidating, unanswerable, leaving room for nothing but abashed silence.

What pastor has not wished to respond similarly to a querulous congregation? "We like having the sermon last—why did you change our liturgy? You

³⁵Can you send forth lightnings, so that they may go
and say to you, 'Here we are'?
³⁶Who has put wisdom in the inward parts,
or given understanding to the mind?
³⁷Who has the wisdom to number the clouds?
Or who can tilt the waterskins of the heavens,
³⁸when the dust runs into a mass
and the clods cling together?

³⁹"Can you hunt the prey for the lion,
or satisfy the appetite of the young lions,
⁴⁰when they crouch in their dens,
or lie in wait in their covert?
⁴¹Who provides for the raven its prey,
when its young ones cry to God,
and wander about for lack of food?"

Exegetical Perspective

Today's lection introduces what many perceive as the climax of the book, the "divine encounter" in which God finally appears and answers Job. As always, the material is carefully structured: Both of God's speeches (38:1–40:2; 40:6–41:34) begin with the same narrative introduction, "Then the Lord answered Job out of the whirlwind" (38:1; 40:6), followed by a challenge to Job to "gird up (his) loins" and answer questions (38:3; 40:7). The speeches are replete with rhetorical questions designed to impress upon Job the utter impossibility of comprehending the Divine and thus force him to abandon his position. These divine speeches are matched by two meager responses from Job (40:3–5 and 42:1–6) that clearly indicate God has been successful.

Three factors point to the heightened significance of this passage. First, after twenty-nine chapters of literally round after round after round of debate and rants between Job and his "friends," God finally speaks. Second, this long-awaited divine appearance occurs in the midst of a whirlwind or tempest, a frequent accompaniment to divine appearances or theophanies. Last, but not least, for the first time since the prose prologue the personal name of God, YHWH, rather than El, Elohim, Shaddai, or Eloah, appears in the text.

Homiletical Perspective

Elusive no more, the Lord speaks to Job at last. Job has poured his heart out, shaking his fist toward heaven, defending his integrity, challenging the pious orthodoxy espoused by his comforters, all the while making his case for the world according to Job.

And then, the whirlwind. No one could have been prepared for what Job experiences next. The barrage of questions for which Job has no answer comes rolling down like floodwaters, quickly subsuming him in the larger order of God's creation. This "polemical doxology"[1] certainly overrides the case that Job has been making for how things ought to be. On one hand, it may appear that the Lord's words serve to overwhelm Job into a retraction of his case. On the other hand, perhaps the Lord's words will lead Job to a renewed, enlarged vision of what it means to be human. Job's reply in 42:1–6 is treated in the lection for next Sunday; for now, we have the whirlwind.

Words without Knowledge. "Where were you when I laid the foundation of the earth?" "Who determined its measurements—surely you know!" "Can you lift

1. Walter Brueggemann, Charles B. Cousar, Beverly R. Gaventa, and James D. Newsome, *Texts for Preaching: A Lectionary Commentary Based on the NRSV: Year B* (Louisville, KY: Westminster John Knox, 1993), 549.

Job 38:1-7 (34-41)

Theological Perspective

poses a new question, namely, whether human beings can even understand God and God's ways.

John Calvin, in his sermons on Job, says that God "mocks Job, inasmuch as he was rebellious, and it seemed to him that by arguments he could win his case." The problem here dramatized is that we human beings are "so presumptuous as to glorify ourselves in our own imaginations to have power and wisdom in ourselves."[1] Before God, however, we are nothing. God's discourse out of the whirlwind thus intends to show us our lack of power and wisdom. For Calvin, the pious person humbly recognizes and consents to this truth by glorifying God, instead of boasting about human greatness and presuming to measure God according to human moral standards. While never doubting God's justice, Calvin calls us to stand in awe before the great God of glory. Calvin concludes each of his sermons on Job with this refrain: "Now we shall bow in humble reference before the face of our God."

Calvin is correct to recommend a posture of humility in the face of the ultimate mystery that is God. But what of Job's question? Are we still to believe that the great God whose power is manifest in nature is really good? Or must we choose between God's goodness and God's power? Many modern theologians have thought that an either-or decision is called for here. The theodicy problem, they claim, results from attempting to affirm simultaneously attributes that are mutually incompatible.

Process theologians have argued this point with great logical rigor. They insist that the classical doctrine of God works with a faulty notion of divine power. God is not "omnipotent," they explain, if by this term is meant that God literally has *all* the power there is. God has supreme power, but cannot determine the outcome of events unilaterally. In a relational understanding of reality, to which God is no exception, the implementation of God's good will is dependent upon the free response of creatures to embrace God's purposes for them as their own.

This critique of divine omnipotence entails that God can be affirmed as unambiguously good, since God's power is limited by the power of self-determination on the part of creatures and therefore is not directly responsible for evil. For process theologians, the book of Job exemplifies this flawed

1. John Calvin, *Sermons from Job*, trans. Leroy Nixon (Grand Rapids: Baker, 1952), 293.

Pastoral Perspective

never visit anyone at home anymore. Why don't we have more kids in the youth group? How can you justify a capital funds drive to update the heating and air-conditioning system when people in our city are hungry? When are you going to speak out against same-sex marriage?"

Finally, by chapter 38 of the congregation's whining, the pastor has had enough. In a storm of exasperation, the pastor thunders some questions in reply. "Did you give seven years of your life to educating yourself in our religious tradition so you would be prepared to be a pastor? Did you take the ordination exams? Where were you when I interviewed here and explained what my priorities would be? Do you have the skills to lead strategic planning when we lay the foundations for our mission in the next five years? I work at the breakfast for the homeless every Friday morning—why don't I ever run into you there?"

How satisfying, for sure, this setting the record straight might be. But will anybody ever be able to approach the pastor again?

Because people have other questions too. Like Job, they want to know why. Why did I get sick? Why was my son the one in that teen-driver car wreck? Why did I get stuck with a job in the third company in a row that has been taken over by a big corporation? Why am I still living when all my friends and my whole generation of the family is dead?

No pastor can answer such questions, and no pastor should. The question is much more important than any answer. The question is a cry of pain, a slash of paint across a blank canvas that offers no discernable image of what is going on here.

Why do people ask why? Especially when they know good and well that there is no answer?

Job has spent much of the thirty-seven previous chapters asking why, in one form or another, and his friends have expended many words trying to say why. Now God takes an enormous risk that Job will never want anything to do with God again, by responding, not about Job's "why" but about the grandeur, beauty, and order of the creation. If asking why is some feeble human attempt to get control of life and bring it to sense and better management, God's response gives humanity even less sense of control than before. In fact, human concerns are completely peripheral in God's queries. God has a universe to run, and human beings are only one among many species to be tended.

Will it be a comfort to Job to know that his concerns are infinitesimally minor in the grand scheme

Exegetical Perspective

But God is strikingly unconcerned with the tedious discussion of retributive justice that has exercised Job and his challengers so vigorously throughout the long central section of the book. Retributive justice, it will be recalled from previous weeks, is the doctrine, found especially in Proverbs and all too often today, that God so orders the world that everyone receives reward or punishment commensurate with his or her behavior, thus maintaining a morally coherent environment that encourages ethical responsibility.

The prologue in the opening two chapters set the stage for the long debate concerning the difficulties Job's life experience of innocent suffering presented for this doctrine. Job's friends argued exhaustively, but logically backwards, that since Job was suffering he must have sinned. But when God speaks, contrary to the expectations of the friends, there is nary a word of condemnation or chastisement. Job, in contrast, passionately maintained the truth of the other side of the retributive coin, namely, that his innocence demanded a fate diametrically opposed to his present miserable existence. So Job wanted to know why. Yet, when God speaks we hear nothing of Job's claim of innocence, and even his scathing accusations and bitter complaints are ignored.

This interpretation, that God ignores Job's bitter complaints and accusations, runs counter to the traditional explanation of chapters 38 and 39, which understand God's reproachful and even sarcastic remarks (see 38:21) as directed precisely against Job's accusations. Such a reading, however, is hard pressed to explain God's declaration in the epilogue that Job, and not his friends, has "spoken of me what is right" (42:7).

Recent attempts to deal with this apparent contradiction have suggested that since there is a second, unexpected introduction of God's speech to Job in 40:1 (cf. 38:1a), the intervening material in chapters 38 and 39 may have been intended as directed against Elihu, who has just finished speaking, and thus indirectly at Eliphaz, Bildad, and Zophar, whose arguments Elihu merely recapitulates. On this reading, God's dialogue with Job would actually be limited to 40:1–42:6. Favoring this view would be the elimination of the jarring contradiction in 42:7, a logical foreshadowing of the divine rebuke of the friends in the same verse, an explanation of the seemingly superfluous second introduction to God's speech to Job in 40:1, the otherwise puzzling delay of Job's response to God's speech two verses later, and his curious lack of response to Elihu.

Homiletical Perspective

up your voice to the clouds, so that a flood of waters may cover you?" "Can you send forth lightnings, so that they may go and say to you, 'Here we are'?" (vv. 4, 5, 34, 35)

The answer to these questions reveals a great distance between God and humanity, for it is clear that God alone has the knowledge and the power with regard to all of these things. Job does not have this cosmological knowledge, nor the power to sustain or sway the world in which he lives. Job may indeed be God's special servant, as is made clear in the prologue; but that special status does not mean that the distance between Creator and creature has been overcome. God's sovereign love extends to the whole of creation. Job has made his case; but his perspective is limited, and thus he has spoken "words without knowledge."

A sermon from this perspective may proclaim the cosmic sovereignty of God, who has made a world of abundance and sustains it with good things. Humanity has a place in this world—even a special place. But humanity is still creature, along with Leviathan (41:1–11), Behemoth (40:15–24), and the rest of the world in which the sovereign God delights. While God is challenging Job's limited, finite perspective on the world, God is also taking a great deal of delight in the vast, intricate, wondrous world of creation. William Blake's "Behemoth and Leviathan," from his *Illustrations of the Book of Job* (1826), reveals God reaching down from heaven to Behemoth and Leviathan as if they are pets awaiting God's caress.

God's World, Not Ours. The voice from the whirlwind is persuasive: this is God's world, not Job's. A sermon from this portion of Job may also sound forth a note of humility on behalf of humanity. After all, our knowledge about cosmology is derived from observation and deduction, not from eyewitness account. Like Job, we were not there when earth's "bases were sunk . . . when the morning stars sang together and all the heavenly beings shouted for joy" (38:6–7). The hymn "This Is My Father's World" is, on one hand, a hymn of trust and delight in the wonder and goodness of God's creation. On the other hand, it is a firm reminder that it is *God's* world, and not ours. Sometimes we need to hear that word.

When William Sloane Coffin was an undergraduate student at Yale, three of his friends were killed in a car accident when the driver fell asleep at the wheel. At the funeral, Coffin was sickened by the piety of the priest as he spoke the words from Job: "The LORD gave, and the LORD has

Job 38:1-7 (34-41)

Theological Perspective

view of divine power from which the theodicy problem arises in the first place.[2]

In contrast, theological ethicist James Gustafson has argued for an understanding of God that qualifies God's goodness. He believes that the problem of biblical religion is that it is anthropocentric. Since the modern sciences have shown that humanity is not the center of the cosmos, theologians must rethink inherited beliefs about God's relation to humanity. God, whose power is manifest in the ordering of nature, is not unambiguously good for human beings. God is the source of the human good but not its guarantor.[3] Furthermore, Gustafson realizes that the abandonment of assumptions about the importance of humanity in the ultimate scheme of things entails the loss of traditional religious consolations in the face of human suffering. The gain, however, is the genuine theocentrism of the tradition.

The story of Job forces a choice between at least three possibilities: first, with Calvin we might affirm both God's absolute goodness and unlimited power; second, with process theologians we might affirm God's goodness but not God's unlimited power; third, with Gustafson we might qualify God's goodness with respect to human beings, while standing in awe of God's power in the ordering of nature.

PAUL E. CAPETZ

Pastoral Perspective

of things? Will Job get caught up in the wonder of creation and forget his sores? Will the querying members of the congregation see the insignificance of their questions and trust in the God of all being?

The utter indifference of nature to the concerns of human beings is the closest we come to grasping God's response here. Nature writers and poets marvel continually at the world's opacity to human passions. "Tell me about despair, yours, and I will tell you mine," writes poet Mary Oliver. "Meanwhile the world goes on . . . meanwhile the wild geese, high in the clean blue air, are heading home again."

Is there comfort in this ordered indifference? The poets think there is. "Whoever you are, no matter how lonely, the world offers itself to your imagination," Oliver continues.[1] And this, indeed, we count on.

Images of life, of rain and sun, of accumulating clouds and silent forests, can save us from our querulousness. They are images of wonder, lifting us from our accustomed ways and amazing us that there is anything here and not nothing at all. Images of creation can build solidarity among people who otherwise may differ. Aren't images of a grand and glorious but threatened earth what human societies are counting on to motivate a global response to climate change?

Images make a difference. How people picture their lives in the future can affect the decisions they make today. The outlook of a congregation—the basic image it has of itself and of its community— makes a huge difference in how it imagines what ministry and mission it can undertake. The image we have of God's intentions for a world in which all creatures are fed and life thrives in abundance can shape the choices we make about how to live (cf. Ps. 104).

Is this good pastoral care, to offer a saving image to those who ask why? It is a risk, for sure, because it replaces the sufferer's question with another. But it is the risk God takes here, and we could do a lot worse than to risk it ourselves.

THOMAS EDWARD FRANK

2. It is important to realize that process theologians are not saying that God has made a prior decision to limit the divine power in order to respect the freedom of creatures, a position called "free will theism." The process position, by contrast, is that God's power is limited by the metaphysical structure of reality itself, since God, like all other entities, is by definition relational. Omnipotence does not even make logical sense within this theological perspective. For a succinct and lucid exposition of the position, see Charles Hartshorne, *The Divine Relativity: A Social Conception of God* (New Haven and London: Yale University Press, 1948). One should also consult the works of John B. Cobb Jr. and Schubert M. Ogden for a fully developed Christian theology based on this conception of God.

3. James M. Gustafson, "A Response to the Book of Job," in *The Voice from the Whirlwind: Interpreting the Book of Job*, ed. Leo G. Perdue and W. Clark Gilpin (Nashville: Abingdon Press, 1992), 180.

1. Mary Oliver, "Wild Geese," in *New and Selected Poems* (Boston: Beacon Press, 1992), 110.

Exegetical Perspective

Obviously, such a reading precludes this speech as an answer to Job. But then on any reading, God's response is only obliquely related to Job's questions. In fact the challenge to the preacher will be deciding just what God's "answer" entails. Last week, Job demanded an audience with God (23:1–7). This week he gets that audience, but it is hardly what he expected it to be. Formally, the speeches consist of God's *questioning* of Job, as seen explicitly in 38:3, where God says, "I will question you, and you shall declare to me," and implicitly in the sixty rhetorical questions that cascade upon our protagonist, rendering him all but speechless.

Centuries of reflection on this cryptic "answer" have failed to produce a generally agreed-upon solution. Some feel that God's avoidance of Job's questions is simply God's way of saying, "That's for me to know and you to find out!" Others remark that God's response, whatever it may be, demonstrates that God is there for us, and assures us that we are not abandoned in our suffering as Job feared. Many caution against the folly of thinking we can know the inscrutable ways of God, especially in the extraordinarily complex situation of human suffering.

In a very literal sense, the book of Job raises more questions than it answers. At the very least, however, we are assured that God is God, and we are not; and that we are human beings who struggle with things we cannot understand. Nevertheless our hope is tied to the firm conviction that this same God will take care of that which we do not understand, as we see in the created world around us.

In this regard, it is a shame that the lectionary has chosen to skip verses 8–11, in which God is presented (presents herself?) as a midwife assisting the sea as it bursts "from the womb" and wrapping it in the "swaddling bands" of the clouds and the darkness. The maternal imagery continues as God sets limits and prescribes boundaries for her charges. This imagery is worlds apart from the usual depiction of the primordial origins of the sea common in the ancient Near East and occasionally found in Israel. Instead of Marduk's triumphant, blood-drenched splitting of Tiamat, or the conquering of Yam the sea god as a depiction of YHWH's defeat of an alien, hostile chaos, we receive a picture of nurture, care, and restraint in the service of protection.

MARK A. THRONTVEIT

Homiletical Perspective

taken away; blessed be the name of the Lord" (1:21). Coffin was so outraged that he even considered tripping the priest as he processed up the aisle of the church. As he was preparing to do so, a small voice asked him, "What part of the phrase, Coffin, are you objecting to?" He says that he thought it was the second part: "The Lord hath taken away."

"Then suddenly it dawned on me that I was protesting the first: 'The Lord gave.' It hit me hard that *it was not my world*; that at best we were all guests. And 'The Lord gave' was a statement against which all the spears of human pride have to be hurled and shattered."[2]

Just as I Made You. Dazzling pictures and data from the Hubble Space Telescope continue to bear witness to the unfathomable vastness of the cosmos. Multiple *galaxies* can be seen in some images, each made up of billions of stars. In light of such amazing and overwhelming realities, it is possible for us to feel very small. "Who are we?" we wonder with the psalmist, "that God would take notice of us," given the near-infinite scope of creation?

In that context, the voice of the Lord thundering from the whirlwind comes *addressed to one of us!* The Lord speaks *about* the rest of creation, but *to* Job. For all of our seeming inconsequence, we are the ones to whom God has spoken, the ones to whom God holds out the promise of conversation about the design of creation. Outside the boundary of this lection, God says to Job, "Look at Behemoth, which I made *just as I made you*" (40:15, NRSV, emphasis added). God is not dismissing Job, but is reorienting Job within a larger awareness of God's good creation. "Who is this that darkens counsel by words without knowledge?" (38:2). The answer is Job, the one with whom the living God speaks.[3]

J. S. RANDOLPH HARRIS

2. William Sloane Coffin, *Letters to a Young Doubter* (Louisville, KY: Westminster John Knox, 2005), 107–9 (emphasis added).
3. For more on this perspective, cf. J. Gerald Janzen, *Job*, Interpretation Series (Atlanta: John Knox Press, 1985), 228–30.

Psalm 104:1-9, 24, 35c

¹Bless the Lord, O my soul.
  O Lord my God, you are very great.
  You are clothed with honor and majesty,
² wrapped in light as with a garment.
  You stretch out the heavens like a tent,
³ you set the beams of your chambers on the waters,
  you make the clouds your chariot,
  you ride on the wings of the wind,
⁴you make the winds your messengers,
  fire and flame your ministers.

⁵You set the earth on its foundations,
  so that it shall never be shaken.

Theological Perspective

What does God look like?

That question has gotten us in some trouble. Due largely to genuinely great art, like Michelangelo's Sistine Chapel, Christians have often figured that God looked like a really old guy. This image of an old guy fits with notions of wisdom and perhaps of power, and with personal images of good grandfathers that we cast on God as our divine grandpa. Such an image of a wise elder is also based on biblical images such as the "ancient of days" in Daniel 7. So the image is not totally without merit. Yet all of these images—wise, powerful old guy, divine grandpa, or "ancient of days"—are tragically incomplete. If you are a feminist, the image is incomplete because it is decidedly and exclusively male. If you are a Trinitarian, the image is incomplete because it is decidedly and exclusively solitary. Where is the Son or the Spirit in this portrait of God?

Theology at its best has insisted that God is beyond anything we can ask or imagine—and so certainly beyond our anthropomorphic images. Karl Barth was once pressed on this point: Surely we are anthropomorphizing (extrapolating from our experience and casting the image skyward) when we say God has hands, aren't we? No,

Pastoral Perspective

Imagine a world where all creation lives in perfect harmony: a world of sparkling, clean water and unpolluted air; of majestic mountains whose surfaces are not scraped and scarred by bulldozers and asphalt; a world where the womb of the earth is not gutted by mines of any kind; where forests never tremble to the sounds of chain saws. Imagine a world where "litter" refers to the birthing of animals that leap, crawl, and sleep with no fear of cages and steel-toothed traps; a world where birds are not plucked for their plumage, and fishing nets are nonexistent. Imagine a world of complete compatibility, peace, and untarnished beauty.

While many psalms can be grouped into categories—praise, lament, thanksgiving—Psalm 104 is one of a kind. The various yet distinct elements of the natural world are affirmed as perfect, quite apart from any dependence upon or interaction with human beings. Other psalms sing praise to God for creation, but no other psalm quite portrays the synthesis of the natural world void of human intervention.

Surprise! Human beings are not the center of the universe, which actually functions quite nicely without us. How vain to think that we need to "teach the world to sing, in perfect harmony" when all of

6You cover it with the deep as with a garment;
  the waters stood above the mountains.
7At your rebuke they flee;
  at the sound of your thunder they take to flight.
8They rose up to the mountains, ran down to the valleys
  to the place that you appointed for them.
9You set a boundary that they may not pass,
  so that they might not again cover the earth.
. . . .
24O LORD, how manifold are your works!
  In wisdom you have made them all;
  the earth is full of your creatures.

. . . .
35cPraise the LORD!

Exegetical Perspective

Psalm 104 is a great lyrical celebration of the goodness, order, and abundance of creation that is guaranteed by YHWH, the creator God. While it is commonly thought that the psalm is appropriated by Israel from an antecedent Egyptian liturgy addressed to an Egyptian deity, the psalm has been resituated in the orbit of Israel's faith. It is YHWH who is credited with the life-giving power that infuses all of creation and who makes life in the world possible. It is sad and absurd that the lectionary has chopped the psalm into fragments, because it constitutes a lyrical whole, a dramatic doxological formulation that runs from beginning to end.

The poem begins (v. 1) and ends (v. 35) with a summons of "the self" to "the self" to embrace, affirm, and celebrate YHWH. Such a "self" in Israel is surely a part of a doxological community, but the psalm invites the very self of the speaker to come face to face with the wonder of creation and with the creator God who orders and guarantees that life-giving wonder.

The opening of the psalm does not linger over "the self," but moves in the second line to YHWH who is acknowledged as "my God," even as YHWH is seen to be the God of all creatures. The large claim of creation is brought home to "this creature," who is

Homiletical Perspective

In sharp contrast to the previous two weeks, wherein the psalmist has begged mournfully for God's justice and deliverance, Psalm 104 allows the preacher and congregation to lighten their hearts in unabashed delight, by offering a hymn of praise to God not only as a creator, but as a provider.

This is a wonderful opportunity for a preacher to change the mood of the style of preaching from previous weeks. The last two weeks may have focused on tragedies and difficulties in the church and the community. This week's lectionary emboldens us to throw off that necessary, burdensome mantle and instead introduce the levity of celebration into the atmosphere. In the life of any relationship between a preacher and a congregation, there will be times when the preacher challenges, and there will be times when the preacher relents, allowing the congregation to breathe in deeply gulps of sweet air.

After the past two weeks in the lectionary, the congregation deserves and needs a break. The preacher deserves and needs a break. In this week, celebrate with the psalmist. Let your church be awash and resplendent in gospel, in good news. Awaken a passion within yourself and the members of your church for our awesome and wonderful God,

Psalm 104:1-9, 24, 35c

Theological Perspective

Barth responded, *only* God has hands. We only have paws![1]

Psalm 104 gives us some visual imagery for God that is even more arresting than Michelangelo's and our attempts to visualize God using human characteristics and experiences. God's clothes: light, majesty, honor. God's world: stretched out as easily as we do a tent. God's transportation: chariot, with the "wings of the wind" as charioteers. God's creation: an earth that shall never be moved. The psalm's image of God is an impressive image. Not even Michelangelo took this image on in artwork, because, well, it would be impossible. How do you draw those horses that are really winds again? The psalm's image functions, counterintuitively, to divest us of images. It is as though the psalmist were saying: "Imagine something more unimaginable than you have ever imagined. You cannot? Good, you are starting to get it." As Augustine said, "If you understand it, it is not God."

But perhaps this psalm speaks a bit more positively than that. Psalm 104 does more than give us visual aid. It recounts the saving works of God in history: here in Noah's flood above all. "The waters stood above the mountains. At your rebuke they flee. . . . You set a boundary that they may not pass" (vv. 6–9). Those who paid attention in Sunday school will immediately remember: God wiped out the whole earth for its wickedness—except for Noah and his family, and two of each of the animals. There was a fresh start after that—and a promise: God would not drown us all again. Not that God would not wipe us out again exactly—but that the method would not be water: "Not by the water but the fire next time," the old spiritual sings.

What sort of image does this part of the psalm evoke? Here is a God who cares passionately about holiness, but one who might lash out vindictively—a little like your grandfather, if you had a bad one.

Of course, if you pull on the thread that has this knot of a biblical story tied in it, lots of other knots come as well. What exactly do we make of the descriptions of God's "majesty" and "honor" here? What do those *look like*? In this as in all other questions theological, Christians start with Jesus. And we start with the assumption that Jesus is, above all, beautiful: "Fairer than the children of men," the Scripture says elsewhere (Ps. 45:2 KJV). But this is a strange sort of beauty that expresses itself in such

Pastoral Perspective

nature blends in a symphony of such synchronization it makes even our greatest music sound like a discordant, off-key whistle.

Psalm 104 captures a glimmer of the pleasure God must have felt as each new piece of life was placed in the puzzle. God's immense joy is reflected in the words of the African American poet James Weldon Johnson (1871–1938) in his poem "The Creation":

> And far as the eye of God could see
> Darkness covered everything,
> Blacker than a hundred midnights
> Down in a cypress swamp.
> Then God smiled,
> and the light broke,
> And the darkness rolled up on one side,
> And the light stood shining on the other,
> And God said, "That's good!"[1]

God's laughter and joy are so tangible that life cannot help but burst into being. This world is filled with such harmony, joy, and cohesion—what more does it need?

It certainly does not seem to need people, and might be better off without humankind, which has not always been so kind to creation. God scooped up the dust and breathed us into being. God placed us tenderly in the best organic garden the world has ever seen, to love, enjoy, and respect it. Yet from the very beginning, humanity has messed with the delicate balance of nature.

The psalmist understood the "intricate interconnectedness and subtle interdependence of air, soil, water, plants, and animals, including humans."[2] Viewing the world artistically as the writer of Psalm 104 does, one cannot but want to nurture, protect, and cherish the earth. Loving the world as God did, and does, will motivate a sincere and enthusiastic environmentalism.

Stewardship of the earth may be motivated by our concern with the kind of planet that our children and grandchildren will inherit. This is a valid and worthy motivation, for people are also God's creation, and we are inextricably linked into the ecosystem. But a theologically sound ecological awareness also arises from praising God and God's creation separately from our place in the universe. Having dominion over the earth and caring for it are

---

1. I heard Professor Nicholas Lash of Cambridge University tell this story in his seminar on "Metaphor, Analogy, and the Naming of God" at Duke University, spring 1999.

1. James Weldon Johnson, *God's Trombones: Seven Negro Sermons in Verse* (New York: Penguin Books, 1981), 17.
2. J. Clinton McCann, in *The New Interpreter's Bible* (Nashville: Abingdon Press, 1996), 4:1099.

Exegetical Perspective

to render praise to YHWH. The mood and voice of this doxology unite in the unrestrained ceding of self over to the true subject of praise. All that follows about creation is as an offering back to the creator. There is no thought that creation (or "nature") is autonomous or freestanding. It is as it is because the God of all creation has commanded it to "be fruitful" (as in Gen. 1:22, 28).

The poem then offers an inventory of all creatures, moving from the largest scope to the most specific and immediate of creatures, to "wine, oil and bread" as the elemental gifts of life upon which the human community depends and for which the human community has devised its most treasured sacramental gestures (v. 15), making final mention of "wild goats" and "young lions," as representative creatures of the wild who are in conformity with the will of the creator (vv. 18, 21).

The doxology begins by tracing the outlines of that ordered world in its largest scope (vv. 1–9). The outline is what is "observed" in a "prescientific" world that is thought to be three-storied, consisting in heavens above (v. 2), waters below (v. 3), and earth safely between heavens and waters (v. 5). There is no need to trace in any great detail that three-storied imagination, because the rhetoric is not about heaven or earth or waters; it is about "You" . . . YHWH . . . the God who is the subject of all the great active verbs in the doxology.

It is "You" who "stretches, sets, makes, rides, makes, sets, covers, sets" (vv. 2–9). The several elements of creation are the outcome of YHWH's wondrous sovereign actions, for the objects of the verbs are variously heavens, beams, clouds, wind, fire and flame (lightning), foundations, the deep, waters, thunder, mountains, valleys. The psalm has no interest in "explaining" creation. The "connect" is lyrical, doxological, and imaginative. One can fill in the "connect" of creator and creatures with the several ways the Bible has of characterizing the act of creation—by word, by molding, by evaluation, by combat—but the doxology has no interest in explanation.

In verses 5–9, the psalm voices the large conviction that the earth is a safe place, protected by the creator, even though surrounded by waters that have immense force and that could, apart from divine protection, overwhelm the safe place of the earth and bring disordering chaos and death. But the waters are not free, unencumbered agents. They are, rather, YHWH's creatures, subject to the will of YHWH. Thus YHWH can rebuke the waters when they get too "uppity" in the same way that Jesus will

Homiletical Perspective

and bask in thankfulness for this God, who loves us and our world into creation and order.

The beginning of this passage, verses 1–6, portrays the visage of God majestically, and describes each of the primal elements as contributing in some way to the greatness of God's appearance. Notably, the psalmist speaks in the present tense, invoking God's activity and agency in bringing the elements to bear, taming that which otherwise might be wild and dangerous into God's employment and demeanor. The waters, skies, earth, and fire become the very implements of God's residence with us on the earth. While the previous week's passage from Psalm 22 inferred frustration over God's seeming absence, this week's passage from Psalm 104 presumes God's company and closeness.

In Psalm 104, every element of nature reminds us of God's providence and presence, becoming an assurance rather than a symbol of uncontrolled wilderness. This steadfast sense of God's control can become the backbone of a sermon focusing on the plurality and grace of God's works in the world, which are ours to enjoy as the inhabitants of this beloved creation. The pace of this psalm is wonderful to preach out loud, each new verse a reinforcement and affirmation of the previous one.

Verses 7–9 lend a touch of history to the present activity of God invoked immediately before, naming a primordial state wherein primeval waters covered the earth and were vanquished, almost militarily defeated and contained. It is a shame that the lectionary does not continue immediately past verse 9, because there follows an inspiring description of how God's control over the waters provides sustenance and refreshment for all of God's creatures. The focus of the lectionary's boundaries here seem instead to be upon God's providence and control, rather than on the specifics of God's actions as provider. That focus is one that can assist preachers, inviting us to draw our congregations from an initial sense of unrestrained glee toward the honoring of God's control over a potentially wild and hostile world.

However, we live in a world where the elements sometimes are overtly riotous and rough, battering our communities with gusting wind, washing away our homes with surging surf. In those situations, how does one follow the lectionary wherein we speak with such affirmation of a God whose providence would seem to prevent such events? In the context of preaching on providence, how do we deal with the question of whether or not God has

Psalm 104:1-9, 24, 35c

Theological Perspective

ugliness as a crucifixion. Most people with sense do not think a life spilt out in service to the poor and not in retaliation against one's enemies is at all lovely. "He had no form nor comeliness," Isaiah proclaims, in a verse Christians also ascribe to Jesus (Isa. 53:2 KJV). What sort of beauty is this?

It is one that became ugly for our sake. Reflecting on the verse from Isaiah, Augustine wrote, "Now I am going to make a bold statement: to render [the church] beautiful [God] loved her even when she was ugly . . . more daring still, since I find it in scripture: to make her beautiful he became ugly himself."[2]

There may be some traditions in which a conquering, Zeus-like portrait of God is sufficient, but for Augustine a christologically forged theology was not one of them. The first image Christians have of this God is of Jesus, taking on all of our ugliness to give us all God's beauty—not distantly, as a nice idea, but concretely, as tangibly as the person in the pew next to us. Think of holiness that radiates from a person even if he or she is not lovely by the world's standards. Surely Mother Teresa is more lovely than any fashion model, your beloved Sunday school teacher (or grandfather) than any movie star. That beauty is a gift of God, offered to you and me also.

"If the lowliness he accepted for your sake astounds you, you will be less amazed by the eminence she enjoys because of him . . . he clothed himself in the Church."[3] God is incarnate now among God's people. God's beauty is in the people God is making holy. *That* is God's garment of light.

JASON BYASSEE

Pastoral Perspective

what we are called to do. We do this for the sake not just of humankind, but of all life.

A love for God's creation is enhanced when we see the heavens and the earth through the eyes of the Creator, who took time to stop after every act of creation and recognize the goodness of it all. If we but pause to recognize this, our spirits are lifted as the psalmist's were, in wonder and awe.

Look into the night sky out in the desert, or in open country where there is no artificial light to block the view. The multitude of stars is stunning. Are all those stars there all the time? Yes—and millions more besides.

Stand next to a thousand-year-old redwood tree, and the most powerful person in the world looks puny.

Close your eyes and take a deep breath when the lilacs come into bloom. There is not a perfume in any bottle that can compare.

Listen to the ocean waves crash and recede upon the shore or to the river as it giggles and mumbles over the rocks.

Use the same words God used when looking at the world: *That is good! That is good! That is good!*

The world has come a long way since that first declaration of God. With all the pollution and destruction, however, God still sees a beautiful world, one where God's kingdom shall eventually dwell. We long for that future time when heaven and earth are one, but it is no longer enough to hope. As stewards of the earth, we must become proactive in our duty. That means each of us doing our share: living organically whenever possible, cutting back on the overuse of natural resources, preserving water and heat, cutting back on waste.

The church needs to be a voice that calls us all to action. Members can carpool to church. Along with saving gasoline, this is a good way to reach out and get to know other people. We can cut back on the use of paper and plastic products at church meals, and recycle whenever possible. We can turn off the lights after Sunday school is over.

Use Psalm 104 as a litany of stewardship and a reminder of the great gift God has given us in providing us with a beautiful place in which to live. Amazingly, God loves us despite what we have done to the world.

We do well to remember that.

KATHLEEN BOSTROM

2. Augustine, *Expositions on the Psalms 99–120*, trans. Maria Boulding (Hyde Park, NY: New City, 2003), 111.
3. Ibid., 113.

Exegetical Perspective

later "rebuke" the waters in his role as the one who orders creation (Mark 4:35–41). The good news in these verses is that YHWH has "set a boundary" to separate dry land from the waters, in order to guarantee safe life space in the world (see Jer. 5:22). Thus Israel's *doxology about order* counters *the felt threat of disorder* that is everywhere palpable in the world. In a contemporary context that feels "out of control" in chaotic disorder, this affirmation of creation offers a profound pastoral claim in a society beset by acute anxiety.

By verse 24, the lyrical inventory of creatures has been completed. The doxology in this verse moves beyond "the creatures" back to the creator with an exclamation that celebrates YHWH's wonder, power, abundance, and wisdom, all of which are evident in creation just described. Apart from the incidental mention of "the trees of YHWH" in verse 16, this is the first utterance of the divine name since the opening phrasing of verse 1. The uses of the divine name in verses 1 and 24 form an envelope whereby the wonder of the *creator* holds the many wonders of *creation*. The poem does not flinch from the awed conviction that the creation is indeed revelatory of the creator!

The poem concludes in verse 35 with a characteristic doxology that echoes verse 1. At the end, the psalm returns to "the self" initially addressed in verse 1. We may imagine, however, that "the self" has been transformed through the lyrical process of the psalm. Now "the self" is resituated in the good, safe, abundant world of YHWH's creation just mediated in the psalm. The singers of the psalm can now depart the old, hard world of violence, threat, anxiety, greed, and despair. None of that is now appropriate in the world here exhibited as YHWH's creation.

It is unfortunate that the lectionary omits the "heavy" warning of verse 35a. That warning asserts that there is no "pass" on being YHWH's creature. The *condition* of the good earth is Torah obedience. Judgment comes to those who fail that requirement. There is an obvious move to our own ecological crisis, even if the lectionary does not want to acknowledge it here.

WALTER BRUEGGEMANN

Homiletical Perspective

willed the hurricane, the wildfire, the tornado, the earthquake, the flood?

The end of the passage, verse 35, proclaims, "Let sinners be consumed from the earth, and let the wicked be no more." How do preachers confront the very real fears of our congregations that perhaps God, in all the glory that we celebrate at the beginning of Psalm 104, has targeted a stricken community to be consumed? How, in the face of natural disasters, do we assure the members of our churches that they are not the wicked? Whether theologically correct or not, it is our human instinct to demand justice in the face of seemingly unjust difficulties, especially if we feel that we are innocent and in the right.

This psalm then invites the preacher to offer careful reflections on the nature of providence, the dynamics of God's steadfast character, and the dimensions of love present in the past and current acts of God's creation. This invitation occurs within the framework of a hymn of praise, and should bear witness to the joy emanating throughout the hymn. At the same time, our devoted thankfulness should not be blind, and we should grapple with the very real problems of a world in which disasters occur that seem outside the bounds of a providential God who loves us all justly.

As preachers, may we convert the well-earned joy that we have built at the beginning of the sermon to promise that God's providence does not play out in otherworldly ways, separate from us, but that God's providential care for the world is also enacted through the everyday miracles of mission and volunteerism by those who love God. In this way, we are able to draw upon the twinned strengths of God's providence and our thanksgiving for being a church in mission, seeking to quell the sometime chaos of the world in which we live.

STEPHEN BUTLER MURRAY

Hebrews 5:1-10

¹Every high priest chosen from among mortals is put in charge of things pertaining to God on their behalf, to offer gifts and sacrifices for sins. ²He is able to deal gently with the ignorant and wayward, since he himself is subject to weakness; ³and because of this he must offer sacrifice for his own sins as well as for those of the people. ⁴And one does not presume to take this honor, but takes it only when called by God, just as Aaron was.

⁵So also Christ did not glorify himself in becoming a high priest, but was appointed by the one who said to him,

"You are my Son,
today I have begotten you";

Theological Perspective

The book of Hebrews draws imagery from the ritual life of the Jewish temple. Jesus is the high priest who offers sacrifices on behalf of his people and mediates between God and humanity. While these ideas have profoundly influenced Catholic and Orthodox theology, Protestants have more typically turned to the language of covenant: Christian worship and ministry should proclaim God's gracious promises and call forth our obedient response. Of the three offices traditionally ascribed by the church to Christ—prophet, priest, and king—it is the first that resonates most fully with us, not Hebrews' language of priestly sacrifice.

Hebrews 5:1–10 nevertheless takes us to the heart of the Christian faith. Why did Jesus die, and did his death somehow effect human salvation from sin? Of assistance to us on answering may be Gustaf Aulén's *Christus Victor*, a minor theological classic in its effort to map out three major theological options relating to the atonement: the classic, objective, and subjective views.[1] The classic view, articulated most fully by church fathers such as Irenaeus and Athanasius, focuses on the paradoxical quality of Christ's death: the immortal Son of God subjects

1. Gustaf Aulén, *Christus Victor: An Historical Study of the Three Main Types of the Idea of the Atonement*, trans. A. G. Herbert (New York: Macmillan, 1931).

Pastoral Perspective

Because we are Christ bearers, the description of Jesus in the fifth chapter of Hebrews is about us as much as it is about Jesus. As some Protestant theologians remind us, the vision of the Reformation decisively abolishes the laity—calling all of us to be "priests." Indeed, when we are baptized into the body of Christ, each one of us becomes an essential part of the priesthood of all believers. This text also reminds us that those servants who are set apart by ordination are set aside for function and not status.

In some traditions, pastors tend to make ordination days into coronations—with long, wordy services filled with pomp, power, and prestige. This is a far cry from the only ordination Jesus ever received—that muddy baptismal bath in the shallows of the River Jordan, presided over by a locust-eating hippie. Much more appropriate are the ordination services that Presbyterians celebrate for lay leaders, when a whole host of humble servants kneel—many of them wondering if they are worthy for the task—while half the congregation, previously ordained, lays hands upon them, a reminder that ministry is something we all share as the people of God.

Central to this text are three realities of the priesthood of all believers: call, humility, and obedience. Every "high priest" is "chosen from among mortals" (v. 1), "having been designated by God" (v. 10). We

⁶as he says also in another place,
  "You are a priest forever,
    according to the order of Melchizedek."

⁷In the days of his flesh, Jesus offered up prayers and supplications, with loud cries and tears, to the one who was able to save him from death, and he was heard because of his reverent submission. ⁸Although he was a Son, he learned obedience through what he suffered; ⁹and having been made perfect, he became the source of eternal salvation for all who obey him, ¹⁰having been designated by God a high priest according to the order of Melchizedek.

Exegetical Perspective

The author of Hebrews has already introduced the notion that Christ is in some sense a "high priest" (2:17) and, immediately prior to this passage, has developed that notion further as a ground for firm faith and confident hope. In doing so, the author has insisted on the solidarity between Christ and humankind that rendered him a sympathetic intercessor on his heavenly throne. The current passage further develops the theme of Christ's priesthood, first by way of contrast with ordinary high priests (vv. 1–4). Then the author begins a more systematic grounding of his claim that Christ is a merciful high priest, first by citing Scripture (vv. 5–6), then by reflecting once more on Christ's human experience (vv. 7–10).

The consideration of earthly high priests begins with a general definition delimiting their sphere of action, "things pertaining to God," and the specific purpose of their activity, "to offer gifts and sacrifices for sins" (v. 1). This definition, compatible with the general responsibilities of Aaron and his successors (Lev. 9:1–4), focuses on the action most characteristic of the high priest, his participation in the atonement rituals of Yom Kippur (Lev. 16), which will form the basis of chapters 8–10.

The next characterization of earthly high priests (v. 2) has less to do with biblical prescriptions or narratives than with the author's homiletic intent,

Homiletical Perspective

This text evokes images of the temple in Jerusalem and of the liturgical movements of high priests making sacrifices to atone for the sins of the many. Since the temple was destroyed nearly 2,000 years ago, along with its systems of sacrifice, the images this text evokes may seem distant to us. Nonetheless, even if the practices are foreign to us, the *movement* of the text should be quite familiar to us.

In preaching we often make comparisons between the things of earth and those of heaven. We have to. How else do we speak of God, unless we can relate divine matters to the mundane? Jesus himself is recorded to have made frequent use of parables to speak of the "kingdom of God": it is *like* a mustard seed, *like* a woman who rejoices over a lost coin, *like* a master who returns from a long journey to check on his property. In each of these parables the *known* functions to reveal the *unknown*, and a parable does not often readily reveal all its secrets. The staying power of Jesus' parables lies in the open-endedness of these "stories." Deeper mysteries live at the heart of any parable for the one who would dwell with it.

Scripture itself is God's divine condescension to human language and human capacity to know more of the mysteries of God. When we speak of God, our words gesture toward divine reality through the mode of metaphor, parable, and simile.

Hebrews 5:1-10

Theological Perspective

himself to mortality, yet his death defeats death and its hold on humanity. The crucifixion of Jesus is simultaneously his glorification as the resurrected Christ.

The objective view, usually associated with Anselm (eleventh century), became the dominant theory of the atonement in the Christian West. Anselm argues that in sinning, humans have offended God's honor and owe God satisfaction beyond the trust and obedience that God originally required of them. Because of their sin, however, humans can neither return to their original condition nor make this satisfaction. Only a God-human can rescue us from our predicament. The savior has to be human because only humans owe God satisfaction, and has to be God because only God can make this satisfaction.

The subjective view has been associated with Abelard, a contemporary of Anselm. A minority view for much of Christian history, versions of Abelard's position became influential in nineteenth- and twentieth-century liberal Protestantism. The principal meaning of the cross was its moral impact. Christ's sacrifice on the cross demonstrates a complete, self-giving love that inspires us to live likewise. Feminist and liberationist theologies have picked up aspects of Abelard's position by arguing that Jesus' radical ethic of inclusion called into question the oppressive social hierarchy that maintained the privileged status of the religious and political authorities of his day. The cross should move us too to resist moral oppression and injustice in all forms and to stand on the side of society's victims.

The great church councils that formulated precise language for the Trinity and the person and natures of Christ never specified one view of the atonement as doctrinally true and exclusive of others. Although the atonement is at the heart of the Christian faith, it is so deep in meaning and mystery that no one theory can exhaust it. The Scriptures offer us, instead, several images of atonement, each of which opens us more profoundly to God's gracious, transformative work on the cross. As one contemporary confession of faith states, these various images are "expressions of a truth which remains beyond the reach of all theory in the depths of God's love for [humanity]."[2]

So too, Hebrews 5:1–10 does not give us a theory. Instead, it draws us into a drama involving priests and sacrifices. This drama operates at three levels. At

2. "The Confession of 1967," in *The Book of Confessions* (Louisville, KY: The Office of the General Assembly of the Presbyterian Church (U.S.A.), 2007), 9.09.

Pastoral Perspective

do not choose to serve God—God chooses us, and will not let us go. The only appropriate response is obedience, a commitment we keep forgetting. This is why we end up with impetuous Peter, arrogant Paul, lusty David, stuttering Moses, frustrated Martha, weeping Mary, and bitter Naomi. This is why we end up with members who annoy us, leaders who forget meetings, and fellow clergy who disappoint us. Somehow God needs each one of them—each one of us—to be the priestly body of Christ in the world.

These verses echo the paradoxical tone of the previous lectionary texts from Hebrews. Jesus is the penultimate and unique high priest of God's mysteries—the one who conquers sin and saves humanity once and for all. But he is also the humble slave, who endures and experiences every weakness, every testing that human experience can offer. And he suffers *with* us, not *for* us—not rescuing us, but strengthening us for the cruciform living that rests at the heart of our own baptized "priesthood." Powerful weakness, holy humiliation, submissive authority, priestly servanthood: Jesus models for us a kind of ministry that is complete—"perfect" not in the sense of purity, but perfect in the sense of wholeness.

So much of Christian hyperbole sets up Jesus as victorious, triumphal, judgmental, puritanical—the lofty one so far removed from human brokenness and degradation that all we can do is cower in the shadow of our own sin. But in this passage from Hebrews, Jesus calls us to kneel not in humiliation, but in humility. We are, by God's grace, imperfect priests, called and chosen by God through baptism, to claim God's image in us, to become one with the "perfect" priest Jesus—the lowly one who offers loud cries and tears on our behalf, the gentle one who models reverent submission to the empowering love and grace of God. And this priesthood that Jesus models is not set on a throne or hidden away in the rarified shadows of the Holy of Holies. Instead Jesus acts out the literal meaning of the word "priest"—that "bridge" spanning the gap between God's dream and humanity's need. Yes, as priest Jesus is called to be the reconciliation of God—and so too are those of us who bear his name.

As baptized "priests" we are given all the power, vision, and grace to be who we are called to be—not because we are perfect, but because God's grace is made perfect in us. We can be "bridge people": standing in the middle of red state/blue state politics, standing in the middle of violent conflicts, standing in the middle of broken relationships, standing in the middle of theological skirmishes, standing in the

Exegetical Perspective

already clear from 4:15, to depict Christ as a sympathetic intercessor. Ordinary priests are supposed to be able to "deal gently" (literally "moderate their emotions") with ignorant sinners. The author chooses his words carefully. Ordinary high priests are not described as "sympathetic" as was Christ. The ability to "moderate emotion" was prized in philosophical circles, especially by Aristotle. There may be here a subtle critique of real high priests, whose aristocratic pretensions may have prevented them from doing what our author thought of as their central function.

The "weakness" of ordinary high priests made it incumbent on them (v. 3) to sacrifice for themselves as well as the people. Again the writer suggests an implicit contrast with Christ, the one without sin (4:15), whose self-sacrifice was totally for others.

The final characteristic of ordinary high priests is that they did not appoint themselves to the task, but received a divine call (v. 4). This claim, explicitly based on the story of Aaron's appointment (Exod. 28–29; Lev. 8), sets up the author's constructive reflection on Christ's priesthood.

Two scriptural verses ground the claim that Christ received a divine call to be a priest. The need to make this argument arises from the fact, which the author will later acknowledge (7:14), that Jesus, understood to be a descendant of David and hence from the tribe of Judah, was not eligible to be priest. The citation of the two scriptural verses also helps to tie together the overall christological argument of the text.

The initial verse, Psalm 2:7, previously cited at Hebrews 1:5, supports the notion that God addressed Christ as Son. That verse had been used in other early Christian sources (Acts 13:33) to a similar effect. The second verse, Psalm 110:4, appears here for the first time in Christian tradition, and its use is probably an innovation by our author, although Psalm 110:1 had been extensively used by early Christians (see 1:3). The verse, which originally called a Davidic king a "priest," does not obviously give the author what is required for his argument that Christ is a "high priest." The further description of this priest as "according to the order of Melchizedek" will provide the ammunition that our author needs, and chapter 7 will be devoted to exploration of that phrase.

Instead of pursuing that argument, the author returns (v. 7) to Christ and evokes his very human experience of prayer. The author may have in mind a specific experience, such as Christ's anguished prayer in Gethsemane (Matt. 26:36–46; Mark 14:32–42; Luke 22:40–46), although his reference to Christ's

Homiletical Perspective

The writer of Hebrews is not outside the task of gesturing toward God through the mode of comparison: *just as* the people had a high priest who mediated between them and God, *so too* do we have in Jesus Christ a high priest who intercedes on our behalf with God. The author of Hebrews is careful to line out in a somewhat chiastic form a comparison between the human high priest and the divine priest.

The human high priest (1) is chosen from among mortals from the priestly clan of Aaron, (2) is put in charge of things pertaining to God on behalf of human beings, (3) offers gifts and sacrifices for sins, (4) deals gently with the ignorant and wayward, (5) is himself subject to weakness, and (6) does not presume to take this honor on himself, but is called by God to serve.

The divine priest (6) does not glorify himself, but is chosen by God, (5) learned obedience through human suffering, (4) relates to the weakness of others, (3) offered up prayers of supplication, (2) became the source of eternal salvation for all who obey him, and (1) is designated a high priest by God according to the taxonomy (*taxis;* 5:10) of the great high priest Melchizedek.

Even though the author of Hebrews uses the phrase "so also" (*houtōs kai*) (5:5) as the pivot point in comparing the earthly high priest with Christ, this term does relate any sense of "equation" between what happens on earth and what pertains to God. The earthly reality pales in the light of who God is and what God does on humanity's behalf. What happens here on earth is never "just as" what happens in heaven. If we preach, "Just as the caterpillar enters the cocoon and emerges after its seeming death as a wondrous new butterfly, *so too* does Christ enter the tomb and, though he may seem to have died, rises in a wondrously new resurrected state," we too easily equate what we know with what is inexpressible: the mysterious and radical otherness of God.

In our preaching we must speak in such a way as to show that God's reality *trumps* our own. When we speak metaphorically about God, we speak only *in part.* That small portion we can say gestures toward the qualitatively bigger and different reality of God. The writer of Hebrews is careful to do this. The earthly high priest, though he had many redeeming qualities and attended to divine matters, was still fallible and mortal. The reality of who Christ was and is *trumps* the identity of the earthly high priest.

There are multiple similarities between the two "priests." Yet, whereas the earthly high priest is a human being, chosen from among the tribe of Aaron,

Hebrews 5:1-10

Theological Perspective

one level, God and humanity are the actors. Because God in Christ has become weak, he deals gently with us in our weakness. The One who is nothing less than the Son of God makes sacrifice for us, suffers for us, and becomes the source of eternal salvation for all who obey him (v. 9). In the words of the Nicene Creed, "For us and for our salvation he came down from heaven. . . . For our sake he was crucified." In this divine-human comedy, those who were alienated have now been reconciled.

At a second level, the drama of priesthood and sacrifice takes place within the very godhead. Christ the high priest has been appointed by God, is God, and has divine power and might; nevertheless, in offering up "prayers and supplications" to the God "who was able to save him from death . . . [Jesus] was heard because of his reverent submission" (v. 7). Although a Son, "he learned obedience through what he suffered" (v. 8). The great twentieth-century theologian Karl Barth dares to speak of the Son's subordination to the Father, even though and while they are simultaneously one.

At a third level is the drama within the Son himself. Hebrews refuses to give us a picture of an immutable divine nature that cannot really know human experience or emotion. On the contrary, this God-human is "subject to weakness" (v. 2), offers up "loud cries and tears" (v. 7), learns obedience (v. 8), and is "made perfect" (v. 9). It is only by entering fully into our condition that the Son calls us to a new way of life.

For Hebrews, Christ's death results not in death but in eternal salvation and victory over death. Those who were unable to approach God on their own now have a high priest who acts on their behalf. The One who struggled within his very self to give himself completely to God now moves us to intervene morally on behalf of the weak and the wayward (v. 2; also, see Heb. 13:1–3). We see here aspects of all three theories of atonement. But what is more fundamental is the mystery of the cross itself, a mystery that we can only contemplate, and that fills us with awe and gratitude.

JOHN P. BURGESS

Pastoral Perspective

middle of the enormous gaps between rich and poor, black and white, immigrant and bigot—standing in the middle, between God's vision of shalom and the disharmony of contemporary life. Yes, as "priest," each of us is called to stretch out our arms to embrace all that is dissident, becoming a dwelling place of reconciliation where all of creation finds a harmonious home in God's heart.

This text might be preached literally in the midst of the people, incarnating the priesthood of all believers. The sermon might be sealed by leading the congregation in a renewal of baptism, where the waters of grace are shared among the people—priest anointing priest with the promises of grace.

The day I was ordained—more than thirty years ago at the Church of the Covenant in Boston—I felt anxious, unprepared, and a bit like a phony. Who was I, a sinful young woman, to claim a calling from God? At that pivotal moment of the laying on of hands, the pressure was almost unbearable, and I thought I might well crumble from the weight.

Finally the ordeal was over, my family was gone, and I could go home and crawl into bed. Yet, as I left the church, I found myself looking up into a grey, weeping sky—and there I saw a perfect rainbow. I remembered then that my ordination was not—is not—about me. It is about God, a God who chose me decades ago through my baptism and has given me, again and again, the gifts to be a priest, a bridge, an ambassador of reconciliation in all the rhythms of my daily living.

What a privilege it is for all of us to claim and share Christ's call of suffering, joy, and peace!

SUSAN R. ANDREWS

Exegetical Perspective

being "heard" does not fit that account. The general description of a pious person at prayer, found, for example, in Psalms 31:22; 39:13; 116:1–8, may color the description. The major point is that the "prayers and supplications" with "loud cries and tears" indicate the reality of Christ's very human reaction to his impending death. The picture forcefully repeats the theme of Christ's solidarity with humankind.

In this account Christ was "heard," probably in the sense that the one who could deliver him from death did so, but not before he had tasted death (2:9). Hebrews constantly affirms that Christ was exalted to heaven, and thereby vindicated, and at least once refers to Christ's resurrection from the dead (13:20).

The reason (v. 7) for Christ's being heard is his "godly fear," a virtue cited by other Jewish sources[1] in describing pious prayer. Christ thereby exemplifies the kind of behavior that the author wishes to inculcate, while grounding that behavior in a vision of Christ as sympathetic heavenly intercessor.

A concise clause (v. 8), using a long established trope in Greek literature, summarizes the christological point. Christ learned (*emathen*) from what he suffered (*epathen*). His status as Son is not incompatible with such an education, a point that the author will later develop in regard to the many "sons and daughters" (12:4–11).

As a result of his suffering, Christ was "perfected" (v. 10). This category is one of Hebrews' most distinctive features and strikes modern Christians as odd, particularly in light of the claim that Christ was sinless (4:15). For Hebrews "perfection" has not so much moral as professional connotation. The claim is that Christ, through his human experience, was made fit or suitable for the role that he assumed as heavenly high priest. The remainder of the verse indicates what that role entailed. Combining human experience with proximity to God makes Christ a "cause [NRSV "source"] of eternal salvation." The exposition of the meaning of the covenant that his death established (9:15–22) will further develop this notion.

The passage ends (v. 10) by resuming the novel verse from the Psalms (110:4) and its reference to Melchizedek. The overall argument begs for clarification of how the verse demonstrates Christ's high-priestly status, but that move will be delayed by a major piece of exhortation (5:11–6:20).

HAROLD W. ATTRIDGE

Homiletical Perspective

Christ is a Son, designated high priest by God from the far more ancient order of Melchizedek. Whereas the earthly high priest makes supplication and sacrifice to God for the expiation of sins, Christ, who is the perfect sacrifice, becomes *the* source of eternal salvation. The reality of God is always so much more than our comparisons can relate. Our hope is that the metaphors we employ to speak of God are capable of bearing the weight of the mystery.

"Good" preaching recognizes its own fallibility. We speak only in part. It is God's doing to make God fully known. God leads us into this deeper knowing. The writer of Hebrews uses the word "to offer up" (*prospherō*) at three points in this passage (5:1, 3, 7) to speak of the form of communication that occurs between the human realm and God. This term has the fuller meaning of leading to one who has the power to bestow mercy and healing. The high priest takes the pleas of the people and gestures toward the divine person. The high priest, in part, leads the people to God.

Our preaching serves this function as well. Our proclamation is an "offering up," a "sacrifice of praise," and "supplication." Our speaking of God is a verbal gesturing in which preacher and congregants are together led to the threshold of God's greater reality. We employ our words, our stories, our earthly wisdom, our interpretation of the witness to God's Word, in true hope and assurance that God's gracious and merciful condescension to us is sufficient for us.

The preacher serves a priestly function. In humility, as one who is called and chosen to discern the holy mysteries of God's living Word, he or she offers up the sermon as an act of praise and confession, always gesturing beyond himself or herself to the saving act of God.

MICHAEL G. HEGEMAN

---

1. For example Philo, *Who Is the Heir of Divine Things*, ed. F. H. Colson (Cambridge, MA: Harvard University Press, 1984), 19.

Mark 10:35-45

35 James and John, the sons of Zebedee, came forward to him and said to him, "Teacher, we want you to do for us whatever we ask of you." 36And he said to them, "What is it you want me to do for you?" 37And they said to him, "Grant us to sit, one at your right hand and one at your left, in your glory." 38But Jesus said to them, "You do not know what you are asking. Are you able to drink the cup that I drink, or be baptized with the baptism that I am baptized with?" 39They replied, "We are able." Then Jesus said to them, "The cup that I drink you will drink; and with the baptism with which I am baptized, you will be baptized; 40but to sit at my right hand or at my left is not mine to grant, but it is for those for whom it has been prepared."

41When the ten heard this, they began to be angry with James and John. 42So Jesus called them and said to them, "You know that among the Gentiles those whom they recognize as their rulers lord it over them, and their great ones are tyrants over them. 43But it is not so among you; but whoever wishes to become great among you must be your servant, 44and whoever wishes to be first among you must be slave of all. 45For the Son of Man came not to be served but to serve, and to give his life a ransom for many."

Theological Perspective

John Calvin writes that this narrative contains a "bright mirror of human vanity," because "it shows that proper and holy zeal is often accompanied by ambition, or some other vice of the flesh, so that they who follow Christ have a different object in view from what they ought to have."[1] Indeed, the problems of vanity, ambition, and other vices are not limited to followers of Christ. These problems are as old as time and as current as the daily news. It is a common insight and accusation that those who would lead often seek their own benefit and glory rather than the benefit of others.

Wherever we look, whether in government, business, charity, the academy, or the church, we face the problem of how to align the interests of leaders with the interests and needs of their followers as well as with an overall mission. Our leaders and we ourselves frequently (in the words of Calvin again) "have a different object in view from what they [we] ought to have."

To ambition and vanity, Mark adds dramatic irony. Jesus has just foretold his coming condemnation, humiliation, and death (10:32–34), but James and John are still dreaming of power and

1. John Calvin, *Commentary on a Harmony of the Evangelists* (Grand Rapids: Eerdmans, 1957), 2:417.

Pastoral Perspective

Donald Meichenbaum, one of *American Psychologist*'s ten most influential psychotherapists, tells of the time that his car was struck by lightning while he was driving. Once he was safe at home, Meichenbaum began to share his ordeal with his teenage son, expecting at least some small degree of sympathy. Instead, his son interrupted, "Dad, let's go buy a lottery ticket. They say the chances of being hit by lightning are like the chances of winning the lottery."

James and John, the sons of Zebedee, are every bit as self-absorbed as Meichenbaum's typical teenage son when they come to Jesus saying, "Teacher, we want you to do for us whatever we ask of you." Jesus politely asks, "What do you want me to do for you?" They respond, "Grant us to sit, one at your right hand and one at your left, in your glory."

In Mark's Gospel, this request follows Jesus' third prediction of his passion (10:32–34). It is surprising then, that these two disciples would ask for seats beside Jesus in his coming glory. Had they not been listening? Actually, this encounter is yet another episode in Jesus' ongoing struggle to teach the disciples about the significance of the kingdom of God being near (Mark 1:15). Jesus has taught them a new understanding about marriage and divorce (10:2–12), but they do not comprehend. Then the disciples struggle with the meaning of Jesus'

Exegetical Perspective

This passage offers last segments of a thrice-articulated, three-part cycle in Mark. Three times (8:31; 9:31; 10:33–34) Jesus predicts the Son of Man's rejection and vindication. Three times (8:32–33; 9:32–34; 10:35–41) the Twelve promptly misunderstand or reject Jesus' self-understanding. Three times (8:34–9:1; 9:35–40; 10:42–45) Jesus immediately corrects these mistakes with teaching about genuine discipleship.

Obviously, Mark is concerned with the kind of Messiah that Jesus is and with discipleship appropriate to following this Christ. In the heart of his Gospel, Mark repeatedly insists (1) that Jesus is the Son of Man who must suffer humiliation and death by human hands, (2) that his adherents either would not or could not accept Jesus' divinely appointed mission or its implications for their own, and (3) that Jesus challenged his disciples' misapprehension with clear instruction, stressing self-sacrificial service in Jesus' name and for the gospel's sake. Therefore, this week's lection truly begins at 10:32–34: On Jerusalem's threshold, for a third time Jesus foretells his arrest by Israel's religious hierarchy, his capital condemnation, his handover to Gentile authorities who revile and kill him, and his resurrection after three days. Mark 10:33–34 is a précis, with Old Testament undertones

Homiletical Perspective

On one level this text seems to be yet another example of the disciples—and not just James and John—as the fumbling, bumbling Keystone Kops who simply cannot get anything right. Jesus has just predicted his passion for the *third* time. But James and John immediately request the places of honor when Jesus enters into his glory; they do not understand that the ironic place of "glory" is the cross—and that criminals will "sit" on his right and left there.

Moreover, the two disciples seem to sense that their request is misguided. Like sheepish little children asking for something they know their parents will not give them, James and John try to trick Jesus into granting their request before they even make it: "Will you do for us whatever we ask?"—a trick Jesus will have no part of. Indeed, Matthew was so embarrassed by the disciples' lack of understanding that he got them off the hook by having the mother of James and John make this request of Jesus (Matt. 20:20–22).

James and John are not alone. The other ten disciples do not fare any better. Hearing what has happened, they get angry, and one can imagine the ensuing squabble among the disciples, which Jesus must counter with his teaching about greatness and servanthood. The scene in many ways is an almost comical counterpoint to the final passion prediction.

Mark 10:35-45

Theological Perspective

position. Not anticipating that Jesus will soon be on the cross, with a criminal on either side, they ask to be seated on his right and left in his coming glory. As Jesus tells them, they literally do not know what they are asking. Nor do they catch on when Jesus asks them if they can drink from the same cup as he, and be baptized with the same baptism. They assure him that they can, and he assures them that they will. Eager to ease into positions of power and glory, the brothers do not realize that they will soon be called upon to sacrifice everything for their cause. When the other disciples hear of James and John's impudent request, they are upset—presumably because they too are dreaming of power and position and resent the brothers' bold attempt to get ahead.

Jesus presents a stark contrast to the disciples' conception of leadership, and thus to the prevailing conceptions of status and success in the ancient and modern worlds. For Jesus, the ruler must be a servant leader, not a tyrant. The goal is to serve, not to be served. Whoever would be first must be last. This vision of servant leadership is a powerful antidote to common notions that equate servant-hood with lowly status and leadership with the ability to attain markers of success such as material acquisitions, prestige, and managerial or political power over others. We often fail to keep in view the proper object of our striving. Indeed, we frequently confuse the purposes and goal of our cause with our hope for personal success. Subsequently, even our best thoughts and actions tend to be tainted with vanity and ambition.

Jesus' rebuke of the disciples is not meant, however, to be a counsel of cynicism or despair. His rebuke is a reminder to us that we should be cautious about expecting too much of mere humans. We should be careful, for example, not to pin our hopes for salvation on those who cannot bear the weight of our expectations. Any human being who is a self-appointed savior is likely to be a disappointment. But to recognize that even the best and most committed leaders among us are subject to vanity and ambition does not imply that we should become detached misanthropes, or simply surrender to the ways of the world and aim to get ahead as best we can.

Instead, the appropriate response to our incurable tendency to put ourselves first is to be cautious and self-reflective about our motives. Likewise, just as Jesus shows compassion for the disciples even in their moment of weakness, leaders must do so with their followers, helping them to examine their motives as well. We should not accept the claims of

Pastoral Perspective

encounter with the man with "great possessions," the priorities of life in the kingdom, and "who can be saved."

Regardless of Mark's intentions, when James and John approach Jesus with their request for the best seats in the kingdom, the narrative reaches comic proportions. We have heard the story so many times that we may miss the incredible insensitivity of these two, but one has to wonder about the reaction of those who heard this story for the first time. Laughter? Amazed disbelief that James and John could make such a request on the heels of Jesus' own death prediction?

Perhaps Matthew is a bit uncomfortable with the arrogance of James and John, since he has the mother of the sons of Zebedee making their request for them (Matt. 20:20). He decides to blame the "pushy" mother. Luke's Gospel glosses over the entire incident, calling it "a dispute" over which one of the disciples would be the greatest (Luke 22:24).

Whether these differences in the various Gospel accounts are actually due to discomfort with the brazen behavior of the sons of Zebedee we will never know. But if one is not overcome with laughter at their incredible request, one has to feel a sense of embarrassment for these cherished disciples. Part of our chagrin may have something to do with the fact that we are all in some ways sons of Zebedee. Certainly we know better than to make outlandish, insensitive requests, as this narcissistic duo does, but we want the best seats in the house. We may not be upfront about our self-centered yearnings, but many of us spend our lives scheming for those kinds of privileged positions. We want that large church in a growing area with the nice, comfortable salary. We want a reputation as a strong, convincing preacher. We want our children to be at the top of the class. We want a lot of things that we never admit out loud.

So are we really that different from these greedy sons of Zebedee? We might not make outlandish requests, but in our hearts we often covet the best of the lot, the top spot, the place of recognition. Indeed, this is part of the human condition. We attempt to explain our greed for the best in a number of ways. Theologically, some would say that it is as simple as Genesis 3 (the fall); others might explain it in psychological terms such as Maslow's hierarchy of needs, Erikson's stages of development, or Freud's id impulses. In any event, this is the way we are. Or, as Jana Childers has said, we have Zebedee DNA in our genes.

However, it is only in facing our own tendencies to be a son (or daughter) of Zededee that we can

Exegetical Perspective

(Ps. 22:6–7; Isa. 50:6), of the story the evangelist will narrate in 14:43–16:6.

James and John (10:35) were among the first whom Jesus called to discipleship (1:19–20). Often in the company of Simon Peter and his brother Andrew (1:16–18), they reappear throughout Mark as representatives of the Twelve (1:29; 3:17; 5:37; 9:2; 13:3; 14:33). Their approach to Jesus is striking. Obviously, they are cozying up to the teacher, lobbying for preferential treatment. Before they have disclosed their intent, Mark's reader has already heard something similar to their self-ingratiation, "We want you to do for us whatever we ask of you" (10:35).

This reminds us of King Herod's rash offer to his daughter in 6:22. Even as Peter's refusal to accept Jesus' destiny has aligned him with Satan (8:33), the Zebedee brothers unwittingly position themselves alongside the very rulers who execute righteous teachers (cf. 10:42). Their petition to sit at places of honor in his glory (10:37; see Ps. 110:1) is drenched in irony. The request is oblivious to the status reversal in God's kingdom of which Jesus has just spoken (10:31). Further, in this Gospel the Son of Man's glory is entwined with suffering (8:38–9:1; 13:24–27; 14:61–65). Finally, those in Mark situated on Jesus' right and left are mocking bandits with whom Jesus is crucified (15:27, 32b). The reader understands the truth that eludes its addressees: "You do not know what you are asking" (10:38a; see also 14:68).

The thought in verses 38b–40 is hard to follow, for the interlocutors are talking past each other in mixed metaphors. The effect emphasizes the disciples' incomprehension while exercising a vocabulary that leans lightly sacramental. In the Old Testament "the cup" is an ambiguous image, which can connote joy and salvation (Pss. 23:5; 116:13) or woe and suffering (Ps. 11:6; Isa. 51:17, 22). At his Passover with the Twelve, a cup symbolizes Jesus' "blood of the covenant, poured out for many" (14:23–24). When he asks if James and John are able to drink from his cup, the more ominous connotation is intended (see 14:36; cf. John 18:11), though they hear the sunnier.

Likewise, "baptism" is polyvalent. While baptism is connected in Mark with repentance and forgiveness of sins (1:4), John the Baptist's beheading (6:14–29) anticipates Jesus' crucifixion (15:21–37). Jesus is acknowledged as God's Son near the Gospel's beginning, with his baptism (1:9–11), and its conclusion, with his death (15:39; see also 9:7, 9–13). In 10:39b–40 Jesus links the disciples' destiny with his own, insisting that God has readied in advance

Homiletical Perspective

In this light, preachers might explore the ways in which contemporary churches often look rather silly as they desperately compete for members in order to become the "biggest" and the "best," rather than responding to Jesus' call to servanthood.

At another level, preachers may explore the motivation behind the request of James and John, which may resonate deeply with contemporary congregants. In 10:32, we read that "those who followed [Jesus] were afraid." Understood within this context, James and John become somewhat more sympathetic characters. Maybe Jesus' ominous predictions of his passion have become clear to them. Maybe they do understand what lies ahead. And being afraid, they seek the promise of a secure future. James and John may not just be power hungry; they may rather be acting quite naturally on their fears.

This connection between fear and the quest for security certainly calls for homiletical exploration in contemporary pulpits. The fear of terrorism has led to all kinds of fateful actions, including government surveillance of citizens and preemptive war—all in the name of security. Fear over the mainline church's future—even its survival—has led to all kinds of efforts to secure ourselves (not unlike James and John), rather than risking the way of the cross. Within this context, the request of James and John becomes not just comical, but tragicomic, not unlike many of our own actions. Rather than simply criticizing the disciples for their failures, preachers might ponder deeply and sympathetically the ways in which fear breeds the desire for security.

Perhaps the connection that Jesus makes between baptism, Eucharist, and the way of the cross provides needed perspective for preaching the themes just discussed. In describing his impending crucifixion, Jesus uses the metaphors of baptism and the Lord's Supper: "Are you able to drink the cup that I drink, or be baptized with the baptism that I am baptized with?" (v. 38). Being baptized involves entering into the way of the cross—taking up the cross and following Jesus (Mark 8:34). Similarly, sharing the cup at the table invites the community of faith into the way of the crucified Jesus. The central liturgical practices of the church challenge all fear-driven quests for security, and call the church into the alternative way of Jesus—the way of servanthood.

This call, as it is issued to James, John, and the church, brings with it a promise: "The cup that I drink you will drink; and with the baptism with which I am baptized, you will be baptized" (v. 39). Sometimes these words are read as a threat or

Mark 10:35-45

Theological Perspective

anyone who sets himself or herself up to be another messiah, and we should be cautious not to develop a messianic complex of our own. But the proper response to human frailty is not to give up on the notion of leadership or action; it is to set up checks and balances within a community or organization. We must keep each other honest. We must be a community of accountability.

Furthermore, we must also carefully consider the notion of self-sacrifice. In a powerful and moving act of self-sacrifice, Jesus gives his life as a ransom for many. His sacrifice on the cross becomes the ultimate paradigm of servant leadership and self-sacrificial love, and we are called to emulate this example. But self-sacrifice must not become self-denial as an end in itself. Self-sacrifice for a disciple of Jesus Christ must be in the service of something higher than the self. The promise of the gospel is that in the sacrifice of self for others, not only will a higher and better self emerge, but the reign of God will continue to unfold. Self-sacrifice thus does not mean self-mutilation or self-extinction; we are not called to disappear. Vanity and ambition are vices, but so are timidity and sloth.

Against the image of the disciples squabbling over rank, we should remember the story of Mary and Martha (Luke 10:38–42), as well as the promises for the reward of faith in the previous passages in Mark. When we keep our minds on the unfolding reign of God, we lose the self-serving self and gain another, higher, better self. This higher, better self answers the call of Jesus Christ to be a disciple by serving others in the world.

JAMES J. THOMPSON

Pastoral Perspective

come to terms with our humanity and live the new life of discipleship. Henri Nouwen wrote, "Only those who face their wounded condition can be available for healing and so enter a new way of living."[1] When we are honest with ourselves about our condition, we can begin a journey toward wholeness.

Jesus is the model of wholeness, and thus he could come "not to be served but to serve." When we have "dealt with our issues" (in psychotherapy that phrase is code for "healing" and termination) and overcome the insecurities that drive us to greed and coveting, we, like Jesus, can be in a position to serve at least some of the time and not be served all the time.

Transformation happens through servanthood. When the man with many possessions (Mark 10:17) asks about eternal life, Jesus invites him, "Follow me." Following Jesus in a life of servanthood transforms us unto eternal life. When John appeals to Jesus to stop the man from casting out demons, Jesus responds, "Do not stop him; for no one who does a deed of power in my name will be able soon afterward to speak evil of me" (Mark 9:38–39). Following Jesus, even in unorthodox ways, can lead toward wholeness. Servanthood is a means to grace.

In light of this passage the words of Francis of Assisi take on even more meaning:

O Divine Master, grant that I may not seek so much
to be consoled as to console,
to be understood as to understand,
to be loved as to love,
for it is in giving that we receive,
it is in pardoning that we are pardoned,
and it is in dying that we are born to eternal life.

DAVID B. HOWELL

---

1. Henri Nouwen, *The Living Reminder* (New York: Seabury, 1977), 21.

Exegetical Perspective

the path both he and they tread. Blended with the images of cup and baptism, this statement simultaneously looks backward and forward: both toward the way of the Lord prepared in the wilderness for Jesus (1:2–8) and toward his Last Supper, at which everything unfolds "as it is written" for the Son of Man before he enters the kingdom (14:12–25).

Here the rest of the Twelve enter the scene, demonstrating by their anger that they are just as obtuse and self-centered as Zebedee's sons (10:41; cf. 14:27–31). Their indignation triggers Jesus' final discourse on the character of authentic discipleship (10:42–44), in terms reminiscent of those in 9:33–35:

> "Whoever wants to be first must be last of all and servant of all. . . . Whoever welcomes one such child in my name welcomes me, and whoever welcomes not me but the one who sent me" (9:35, 37; cf. 10:15, 31)
> "Whoever wishes to become great among you must be your servant, and whoever wishes to be first among you must be slave of all." (10:43–44; cf. Luke 22:27; 1 Cor. 9:19; 2 Cor. 4:5; Gal. 5:13)

The principal metaphors for discipleship in Mark 10 are "servant" (*diakonos*: vv. 43, 45) and "slave" (*doulos*: v. 44). The main idea they share is "intermediate service on a superior's behalf," which in 10:42–43a is contrasted with overweening Gentile tyranny. In the Old Testament the ideal monarch is the people's servant (1 Kgs. 12:7). In Mark the clearest expression of the Son of Man's peculiar service is "to give his life as a ransom for many" (10:45; cf. the servant's portrayal in Isa. 52:13–53:12).

Originally the market compensation required for release or "redemption" of property (Exod. 21:8, 30; Lev. 25:47–52; Num. 3:45–51), "ransom" (*lytron*) emerges in the Bible as a vital religious metaphor for the reclamation of God's people (Exod. 6:6; 15:13; Isa. 43:1–7; 44:21–23), especially through Jesus Christ (Rom. 3:23–25a; 1 Tim. 2:5–6; 1 Pet. 1:18–19). Medieval elaborations of substitutionary atonement should not be read back into Mark. Jesus freely offers his own life for the release of a murderous captive (15:6–15). The depth and power of that tale is matter enough for easily befuddled disciples to ruminate.

C. CLIFTON BLACK

Homiletical Perspective

warning from Jesus: "James and John, you too will be crucified." However, in the larger context of the story, Jesus' words may also be read as an extraordinary promise: "You will not always be driven by your fears and your need for security. Rather, you will be empowered to take up your cross and follow me. You will be faithful disciples even to the end." Here is the great promise for the church. We need not always live in fear; we need not continually seek our own security. Rather, we have Jesus' promise that we can and will live as faithful disciples as we seek to follow him. It is an extraordinary promise made to such a fumbling, bumbling group of disciples—then and now!

Finally, this text suggests the shape of the church's discipleship. Jesus calls the church to embody an alternative to what Walter Wink calls the Domination System.[1] In his concluding teaching to the Twelve, Jesus calls the disciples to offer an alternative to "the Gentiles" (the nations) among whom "rulers lord it over them, and their great ones are tyrants over them" (v. 42). The way of the cross, Jesus affirms, is the way of resistance to the Domination System, which is characterized by power exercised *over* others, by control *of* others, by ranking as the primary principle of social organization, by hierarchies of dominant and subordinate, winners and losers, insiders and outsiders, honored and shamed.

In this text the cross is not primarily focused on individual forgiveness. Nor does the cross call us simply to bear the burdens of life or to practice ascetic self-denial or passively to accept violence or abuse. Rather, Jesus calls the community of faith, in its life together, to offer an alternative to the ways of the Domination System—and to bear the suffering that inevitably comes as a result. Just as Jesus resists the Domination System throughout his ministry— even unto death on a cross—so he sets us free (ransoms us, v. 45) from that system, so we might become faithful disciples and take up his way of resistance.

CHARLES L. CAMPBELL

---

1. See Walter Wink, *Engaging the Powers: Discernment and Resistance in a World of Domination* (Minneapolis: Fortress Press, 1992), 33–104.

Job 42:1-6, 10-17

¹Then Job answered the LORD:
²"I know that you can do all things,
   and that no purpose of yours can be thwarted.
³'Who is this that hides counsel without knowledge?'
   Therefore I have uttered what I did not understand,
      things too wonderful for me, which I did not know.
⁴'Hear, and I will speak;
   I will question you, and you declare to me.'
⁵I had heard of you by the hearing of the ear,
   but now my eye sees you;
⁶therefore I despise myself,
   and repent in dust and ashes."

. . . .

Theological Perspective

Today's reading from Job carries on a theological conversation within itself. On the one hand, Job breaks through to a new experience of the Divine (42:1–6); on the other, God reiterates the theology of divine retribution that the book has been disputing for forty-two chapters (42:10–17), leaving readers to ponder for themselves which is true.

From the start of the book, Job is a sinless character, "blameless and upright, one who feared God and turned away from evil" (1:1). That means that all the catastrophes that befall the innocent Job come upon him "for no reason" (2:3). His suffering contains a totality of pain and loss; he loses his property, his children, and his health. He loses the support of his friends and, above all, he loses the comfort of the theology of which he was once an avid evangelist. He had "instructed many" and "supported those who were stumbling" (4:3–4). But in the face of the collapse of his life, his dearly held theology proves vacuous. It is not true that good things always come to good people, but it is true, as Job discovers, that new experience of life requires new ways of speaking of God.

In its exaggerations, its too-muchness, Job's suffering embraces a multiplicity of human sorrows, both ordinary and massive, and his responses of despair, self-pity, and outrage capture typical human

Pastoral Perspective

Thank God for happy endings. Hats off to the editor of Job for ending his O'Neillean *Long Day's Journey into Night* with a Shakespearean *All's Well That Ends Well*. As a parish pastor, I am a huge fan of happy endings—when the suspicious mass is benign, when the disgruntled church member comes to her senses, when an unexpected check arrives at 11:00 p.m. on December 31 to turn the financial hue from red to black. Who in his or her right mind does not love a happy ending? So, thank you, editor of Job; thank you for chapter 42; thank you for such a happy ending.

Not so fast. Job may begin with a "once upon a time" tenor and close on a "happily ever after" note, but there are forty-some chapters of misery tucked in between. Chapter 42 should have stamped across it: "Danger: Playing with Pastoral Fire." As pastors visit with folks sitting on the "ash heap," it is tempting to latch onto chapter 42 as theological proof that Job's comforters got it right. In our attempt to explain or justify suffering by defending God, we can easily be dismissive of the pain of those we love, often unmerited and inexplicable pain.

Whatever chapter 42 means, if God is just and righteous, it cannot mean that the death of Job's loved ones and the depth of his physical pain are obviated by new children and new wealth. As novelist Cynthia Ozick observes about the ending of Job:

¹⁰And the Lord restored the fortunes of Job when he had prayed for his friends; and the Lord gave Job twice as much as he had before. ¹¹Then there came to him all his brothers and sisters and all who had known him before, and they ate bread with him in his house; they showed him sympathy and comforted him for all the evil that the Lord had brought upon him; and each of them gave him a piece of money and a gold ring. ¹²The Lord blessed the latter days of Job more than his beginning; and he had fourteen thousand sheep, six thousand camels, a thousand yoke of oxen, and a thousand donkeys. ¹³He also had seven sons and three daughters. ¹⁴He named the first Jemimah, the second Keziah, and the third Keren-happuch. ¹⁵In all the land there were no women so beautiful as Job's daughters; and their father gave them an inheritance along with their brothers. ¹⁶After this Job lived one hundred and forty years, and saw his children, and his children's children, four generations. ¹⁷And Job died, old and full of days.

Exegetical Perspective

Just as there is an eye at the center of a storm, today's text is the turning point in the book of Job. Here at the center are whirling cycles of poetic gyrations and profound conversations that travel back and forth between Job and his friends, Job and God. These transcendent poetic cycles are surrounded by an immanent prose prologue (1:1–2:13) and an epilogue (42:7–17) that combine both spheres. We should keep in mind that the book of Job is also canonically positioned at the center of a collection called Wisdom literature (Proverbs—Job—Ecclesiastes). It is from this faithful center that we respond to the book of Job, and from this center that we attempt to move from the enigmatic sufferings in the book to the encounter with God near the end.

When we turn to Job's dialogue with God in Job 38:1–42:6, we notice that this conversation forms the centermost circle from which all of the other conversations flow. This tête-à-tête between God and Job is surrounded by Job's conversations with his friends—Eliphaz, Bildad, and Zophar—in 3:1–31:40 and Elihu's speech (an interpolation) in 32:1–37:24. Inside this conversational center, we discover yet another micro-concentric cycle with the minutest nucleus surrounded by two powerful outer layers. Job's tiny speech in 40:3–5 forms the nucleus: "Then Job answered the Lord: 'See, I am of small account; what

Homiletical Perspective

One of the common temptations for preachers here lies with the drive to resolve our quandaries about theodicy rather neatly. Seeking resolution seems natural enough, as the story is ending. Nevertheless, the temptation is to resolve that which the text does not seek to resolve. Clearly the Job epic is dealing with the overwhelming problems of suffering along with our theological and very human struggles to be faithful. Job's restoration, however, does not provide an explanation of suffering that satisfies our outrage or frank dismay. The homiletical task will be to explore just what sense of resolution or restoration is actually proffered by the narrative.

There are at least four significant developments in these verses that raise important questions for preaching. First, how does the dialogue with YHWH change Job's situation in suffering? Notice that this question does not yet ask how the dialogue has changed Job. With verse 5 we see that Job's perspective has been altered by God's response. The suffering has not yet ceased. Job's transformation begins even before the suffering abates. It is the awareness of YHWH's presence that transforms. The story overturns some presumptive interpretations of unexplained suffering. Job stands firm against the notion of retributive judgment in his suffering. No more adequate is the sardonic suggestion that

Job 42:1-6, 10-17

Theological Perspective

experience in the midst of loss. Job's continual, confusing reiterations of his pain, his confrontations with his caring but wrongheaded friends, and his disrupted relationship with the Creator gather up the troubles and enduring fears of anyone who knows devastation. Yet across his many speeches and against the stubborn orthodoxy of his friends, Job grows in confidence and keeps insisting on the inadequacy of his friends' orthodox views. He trusts his experience and knows that he has committed no sin sufficiently heinous to evoke these terrors. In the midst of his dark night, he dares to tell the truth of his life to his Creator. By lamenting, complaining, and shouting his discontent to the God he believes to be attacking him, he keeps his relationship with God alive.

In today's reading, Job utters his final words after he has encountered God in the lyrical poetry of the storm. Some interpreters believe the God to whom Job responds in the encounter in the whirlwind is an overpowering bully. If so, the book creates a theology of aggressive divine power that coerces human submission, no matter how unwillingly.

But Job does not think so. Instead, he utters a profound statement of faith: "I had heard of you by the hearing of the ear." In the past, Job knew God from the instructions of others, from his family, from wise sages, from his faith community. "But now my eye sees you" (42:5). Now Job meets God in his own life, on his own recognizance, in the thick of the storm that is his life. Instead of being forced into submission, Job speaks of firsthand experience, a personal meeting, a kind of seeing that surpasses known speech about God. From Job's viewpoint, this encounter overwhelms and honors him and transforms his life. The encounter in the storm calls Job to a new kind of theological knowledge; it summons him beyond himself to a heightened sense of divine presence in his life and in the world.

The poetry, however, makes it difficult to know the nature of Job's transformation, since the rest of his response to God admits of multiple interpretations and theological ambiguity: "Therefore I despise myself, and repent in dust and ashes" (NRSV). This translation reinforces a theology of fire and brimstone, of human inadequacy and divine capriciousness as Job despairs and gives in. But other translations find Job repenting "of dust and ashes," suggesting that Job gets up from his ash heap of sorrow and loss to get on with his life. His deepened experience of God summons him to new perceptions, leads him outside of himself, and creates of him a new being in the midst of his community,

Pastoral Perspective

If we are to take the close of the tale as given, it is not only Job's protests that are stilled; it is also his inmost moral urge. What has become of his raging conscience? . . . Prosperity is restored . . . but where is the father's bitter grief over the loss of those earlier sons and daughters, on whose account he once indicted God. . . . Is Job's lesson from the whirlwind finally no more than the learning of indifference?[1]

Pastors playing lightly with Job and its felicitous ending can callously try to tame the rage of those who suffer senselessly. They risk dishing up theological mush to parents grieving the random death of a child in Blacksburg or Baghdad. They can cover the wails of parents of miscarried or stillborn children with the insipid theology of "Well, God had a plan for your now dead child," or worse, "Have good cheer, you can have more children in the future." I am surprised that one of Job's comforters missed that line.

Perhaps the most dangerous theological weapon potentially unleashed in 42:6 is to read this verse as a confession by Job that he was wrong to rail at God at all. What Job "learns" in God's veiled response in chapters 40 and 41 is that there is more to God and God's reign than Job has ever imagined. What God does not answer and Job does not "learn" is why Job experiences such profound suffering while God remains mute. Like Jacob at Jabbok, Job enters the theological ring with God and will not be silenced by God's silence. He calls God out of hiding in heaven to confront unjust suffering on earth.

One of the great pastoral possibilities of this text is to invite those who suffer unjustly, often inexplicably, to give voice to their rage and despair about the silence of God. Rather than rushing in with pastoral platitudes, Job invites believers to give voice to their protest against any pastor peddling a theology that suggests God employs or endorses innocent suffering. A compassionate pastoral theology does not dash to the "happy ending" of Job, but invites those who suffer to explore what they have learned of God while sitting on the "ash heap"—no matter how they got there.

The ending of Job may leave readers with a happy ending, but it does so barbed with unresolved questions. Sam Balentine writes:

> Having protested with such passion, can Job really be expected now to return to his previously undisturbed certainties as if nothing has changed? Does

1. Cynthia Ozick, *Quarrel and Quandary* (New York: Alfred A. Knopf, 2000), 72.

Exegetical Perspective

shall I answer you? I lay my hand on my mouth. I have spoken once, and I will not answer; twice, but will proceed no further.'"

This microcenter is surrounded by YHWH's powerful words in 38:1–40:2, which begin: "Then the LORD answered Job out of the whirlwind: 'Who is this that darkens counsel by words without knowledge? Gird up your loins like a man, I will question you, and you shall declare to me'" (38:1–3). The powerful outer layers of this speech are ironically structured as they conjoin Job's softly spoken words.

The structure of the epilogue in chapter 42 combines the theological frameworks of transcendence and immanence through a careful integration of poetry and prose. We further observe several redactional layers in verses 1–6, 7–9, and 10–17. Here we can even argue for three different endings to the book of Job, at verse 6, 9, or 17. Verses 1–6 probably formed the original ending, with verses 7–9 added later. Verses 10–17 were probably composed lastly to link the book of Job to the book of Psalms.

In our exegesis of 42:1–6, we continue to see the center of this text (v. 4) surrounded by concentric circles of the texts that surround it. The difficulty with verse 4 lies in identifying the speaker. Job begins his speech in verse 1, ending his first speech in verse 3b: "Therefore I have uttered what I did not understand, things too wonderful for me, which I did not know." But to have Job then say, "Hear, and I will speak; I will question you, and you declare to me" (v. 4), is extremely obtuse, because verse 5 begins Job's second speech: "I had heard of you by the hearing of the ear, but now my eye sees you; therefore I despise myself, and repent in dust and ashes."

Verses 1–3 and 5–6 indeed belong to Job. But verse 4 is the masterful voice of YHWH bridging Job's prayers in verses 1–3 and 5–6. Ending with verse 6 places the entire book in poetic symmetry.

Prologue
    Narrator (1:1–6; 2:1)
    YHWH-Satan (1:7–12; 2:2–6)
    Narrator (1:13–22; 2:7–13)
Speeches
    YHWH (38:1–40:2)
    Job (40:3–5)
    YHWH (40:6–41:34)
Epilogue
    Job (42:1–3)
    YHWH (42:4)
    Job (42:5–6)

Homiletical Perspective

suffering is intended to teach us and therefore is divinely prescribed. God's presence begins to redefine our presumptions about suffering, even while understanding remains elusive.[1] Job's repentance begins with this acknowledgment.

The next critical consideration involves this repentance. Although the language suggests self-loathing—"therefore I despise myself, and repent in dust and ashes" (v. 6)—preachers will find that the repentance here does not suggest acceptance of judgment or sin. Instead, what is it that causes Job's repentance? It is an acknowledgment of YHWH. Some scholars suggest that emphasis on the offense to God risks limiting the actual effort of the story to overcome theological judgments of retributive suffering.[2] Surely repenting implies a realization of wrongfulness. However, we will need to decipher the focal point in Job's change of heart. The change comes when Job perceives a change in his acquaintance with God and thus of the terms of his challenge to God.

Change is a vital theme throughout this pericope. A third essential development for our homiletical exploration unfolds when God finally intervenes in Job's suffering. Again the preacher must not overlook that God's activity and Job's transformation have already begun; the promise of Job surviving or overcoming his suffering is not the axis of this narrative. The context of God's intervention is the extension of community, which becomes evident in God's appeal to Job to pray for his friends. In fact, it appears that God makes communal care a proviso. The Lord sends Eliphaz, Bildad, and Zophar to Job and will accept Job's prayer for them. In turn, God intervenes in Job's torment to use the community to overcome suffering (vv. 10–11).

Why place Job in the position of praying for his misguided and rather tormenting friends? This question holds intriguing possibilities for some homiletic movement into how we are to wrestle not only with suffering, but also with the insults to injury—that is, between injudicious scoffers and the tormented. Too often our sermons echo the ill-conceived theology of retributive suffering from Eliphaz, Bildad, and Zophar. The sermon may build upon this question, if the preacher is careful to explore how we might begin to understand God's insistence that the friends seek out Job's prayer (vv. 7–9). In short, we will need to weigh "'How' does God restore Job?"

1. James C. Logan, "Homiletical Resources: Exegesis of Four Propers Following Pentecost," *Quarterly Review* 5, no. 3 (Fall 1985): 74–76.
2. John C. Shelley, "Job 42:1–6: God's Bet and Job's Repentance," *Review and Expositor* 89, no. 4 (Fall 1992): 542–44.

Job 42:1-6, 10-17

Theological Perspective

where he bestows inheritance even upon his daughters.

But lest the happy ending settle matters theologically, the epilogue (42:7–17) reaffirms the theology of divine retribution that the book has been disputing since chapter 1. Here God praises Job and validates his resistance to the rule-based theology of his friends, which reduced Job's suffering to cause-and-effect equations. Restoring Job and doubling his blessings, God not only approves of Job's theological protests but also paradoxically reenacts the theology of divine retribution. Job the good person is rewarded, just as the friends have said all along.

Job himself refuses to acquiesce to such a view. He refuses to deny his own experience of confusion, of divine absence, and of the inadequacy of this old theology. He insists, instead, on telling God and anyone else who will listen how miserable he is, how confused and abject he has become. He plunges deeply into despair of ever being seen and heard in his suffering. Yet in this long process, he realizes that God does not follow human expectations, that God is free.

Across his speeches Job insists that God does not follow any laws, but is wildly free beyond any human calculation, yet he speaks his anger and grief to God anyway. In the midst of his abyss, Job holds fast to God; he argues, yells, and acts up in courage and fidelity. Job clings to his dignity as a human, maintains his integrity, and sets it without qualification before God. And now he receives blessing upon blessing. Is this reward or grace?

When all is said and done, several theologies of suffering continue to exist side by side in this book. Readers of Job have been brought into the thick of it and are required to try to resolve the dilemma for themselves. Job's testimony stands as witness to the inadequacy of traditional theologies to encompass every human experience. Job presses believers to hold our theologies humbly and to remember that new times require renewed and reformed theological expression for a God who transcends all speech.

KATHLEEN M. O'CONNOR

Pastoral Perspective

God really expect or require Job simply to pray for others, when Job's own prayers for help have proved so utterly useless? Such questions . . . invite us to wonder not only if the *Job* who returns to prayer in the epilogue is *fully human.* They also invite us to consider if the *God* of the epilogue, to whom he is instructed to pray once more, is *fully God.*[2]

Pastoral theology often lives on the other side of the "ash heap." Suffering has happened and people are trying to reconstruct their lives and their faith. A close reading of chapter 42 will resist all pastoral urges to make suffering simple and theology a child's connect-the-dots exercise. In chapter 8, the "comforter" Bildad tells Job to confess his guilt and good things will happen. A careful reading of Chapter 42 will resist reducing the "confession" of Job and his "blessing" by God to cause and effect. Balentine suggests the conclusion is just the opposite, "The blessing God gives seems to be Job's reward for *not* conforming to his friend's theology."[3]

For pastors who stand with those far too acquainted with unwarranted grief, the promise of God's blessing in chapter 42 cannot and should not silence the questions of God that will not be easily silenced:

> Why do the innocent suffer?
> Why are "friends" oblivious to the sincere cries of those who suffer unjustly?
> Why does God allow such suffering to stand and remain silent before the pleas of the afflicted?

Christians who read Job with the cry of dereliction never far from our ears—"My God, my God, why hast Thou forsaken me?"—dare not rush to the resurrection of Jesus or focus primarily on the unmitigated happy ending of Job. People deserve more from their pastors, and like the Job we meet throughout most of the book, they should not shy from demanding it.

GARY W. CHARLES

2. Samuel E. Balentine, *Job* (Macon, GA: Smyth & Helwys, 2006), 712.
3. Ibid., 717.

Exegetical Perspective

As expected, the conversational cycle in 42:1–6 is characterized by a careful use of "I" and "you." Centered between them is the imperative "Hear" (v. 4).

Job Answers the Lord (vv. 1–3). At the center of Job's self realization is verse 3a: "Who is this, the one who continues to hide [*hiphil* participle] counsel without knowledge?" (my translation). Job imitates the Lord's speech style without coming to any real understanding. This is the starting point of hearing.

The Lord Answers Job (v. 4). The syntactical Hebrew *na*-construction in this verse parallels YHWH's words in 38:3b and 40:7b, giving the divine imperative "Hear" the literal deferential meaning of "Would you please hear." In the end, it does sound as if the Lord has heard Job and invites Job to hear the Lord.

Job Hears the Lord (vv. 5–6). Job's conclusion is wonderfully constructed in that he demonstrates his hearing and understanding of the Lord by obeying the divine imperative. "I had heard of you by the hearing of the ear, but now my eye sees you" (v. 5). This deep theological awakening leads to humility. When we hear God, we can see what has transpired.

In final verses of the book (vv. 10–17), we witness a tripartite division: verses 10–12, verses 13–15, and verses 16–17.

Job Is Blessed (vv. 10–12). The theme of being doubly blessed is injected here for the first time. Because Job faithfully endured his trial, there is a reward—to be understood in light of Wisdom literature's emphasis on socioeconomics.

Children at the Center (vv. 13–15). In Job's world, children comprised the nucleus of all blessing. Although his society was one in which boys took precedence, we have a celebration of daughters sharing the center stage. Even their names are given: Jemimah (perhaps meaning "with YHWH"), Keziah ("YHWH's fragrance"), and Keren-happuch ("horn of the antinomy or beautifier"). The daughters also share in the inheritance (cf. Num 27:1–11).

Children's Children, to the Fourth Generation (vv. 16–17). If Job's children were the center of his blessing, then he ended his life doubly blessed, for he saw his children's children down to the fourth generation.

JOHN AHN

Homiletical Perspective

To be sure, the prospect of asking the tormented to care for their tormentors, even if they are passive victims themselves in misguided theology, will be difficult. The caution here is no less critical than trying to treat the idea that God seems manipulated into a wager, which began the spiral of suffering at hand. The risk, however uncalculated, is to render a victim theologically responsible for the restoration of an abuser.

And lastly, a fourth development builds on another promise of community. With verse 15 we encounter a fascinating transformation of culture or traditions. Job ensures inheritance for his daughters along with his sons. This verse, however, is wrought with as much difficulty as it is with potential for transformation. The text does not escape the misogyny that reduces women to some physical value in a male-dominated culture. And yet in its midst, Job's transformation begets a potential revolution of restoration. Job names his daughters to an inheritance that the culture would unjustly deny them. Job's own experience of transformation and restoration appears to drive him into a radical and innovative agency for transformation of the social order.[3]

While the narrative transcends the limitations of theological justice defining suffering, the ironic turn of events results in seeking justice for the other as a way of living. The relationship of justice to suffering is not demonstrated in arguments of retribution or judgment, but rather in how even our experience of unjust suffering and restoration from beyond our own means redirects our attention. In the encounter with God, we are compelled into redirection or self-discovery and moreover driven by restoration into some agency of justice transforming suffering.

The temptation for us in preaching from this narrative is to enter some apologetic of God's sovereign right to do anything God desires. God's sovereignty may be palpably felt in the narrative, but it is certainly not the essential point. The encounter with God itself transforms us while yet in the midst of suffering. God's inbreaking empowers us to transcend suffering. God's restoration empowers us to seek a more just way of living that overcomes the injustice of suffering.

DALE P. ANDREWS

3. Tina Pippin, "Job 42:1–6, 10–17," *Interpretation* 53, no. 3 (July 1999): 301–3.

Psalm 34:1-8 (19-22)

¹I will bless the LORD at all times;
    his praise shall continually be in my mouth.
²My soul makes its boast in the LORD;
    let the humble hear and be glad.
³O magnify the LORD with me,
    and let us exalt his name together.

⁴I sought the LORD, and he answered me,
    and delivered me from all my fears.
⁵Look to him, and be radiant;
    so your faces shall never be ashamed.
⁶This poor soul cried, and was heard by the LORD,
    and was saved from every trouble.

Theological Perspective

The central invitation of the passage is to "taste and see that the LORD is good" (v. 8). Radiating from the call to enjoy God are issues of perpetual worship, God's response to suffering, and the sensory experience of God in worship.

Perpetual Worship. What would it look like to "bless the LORD at all times"? Paul also urged believers to "pray without ceasing" (1 Thess. 5:17). Assuming that God does not demand actions beyond what humans can strive, how can believers follow this path?

Christians have explored perpetual worship through lived prayer. The Divine Office follows the ancient tradition of situating work within a rhythm of prayer multiple times a day. Habits in imitation of God build a character capable of combining love of God and love of neighbor as illustrated in the icon of the Holy Trinity. Abraham and Sarah instinctively offer hospitality to three strangers only to discover they are serving the living God. The mundane tasks humans undertake to win their daily bread or serve others provide opportunities to be mindful of God.

Basil the Great (d. 379) counseled Christians to join labor and prayer through recitation of the psalms either vocally or silently: "In this way we fulfill prayer even in the midst of work, giving thanks to him who gave both strength of hand to work and

Pastoral Perspective

Geoffrey Chaucer, in his immortal literary masterpiece *The Canterbury Tales*, includes among the several pilgrims making their way to pay homage at the shrine of Thomas Becket a strange mix of nobility, commoners, and church officials. There are knights and squires, monks and friars, nuns and parsons and priests, along with millers, cooks, lawyers, merchants, physicians, and a "parish clerk"—just to name a few of his companions!

In his description of the clerk—an unordained church official who assisted in the daily operations of the parish—Chaucer says, "Gladly would he learn, and gladly teach." Such a phrase on learning and teaching could equally be applied to the composers of many of the psalms, and especially to the author of Psalm 34.

Throughout the book of Psalms, we are instructed to praise God for unsurpassable glory, to trust God for unquenchable love, and to rely on God for unfailing nurture and grace. As in so many other texts, Psalm 34 serves two functions: liturgical prayer (in the form of petition, thanksgiving, or exhortation to praise) and instruction (which enumerates for us why we should offer our prayers and praise). This latter function eventually dominates the psalm, and we are instructed by the psalmist in the contrasting phases of prayer: the cry for help in our distress, and a song of thanksgiving for the help we have received.

⁷The angel of the L ORD encamps
　　around those who fear him, and delivers them.
⁸O taste and see that the L ORD is good;
　　happy are those who take refuge in him.
. . . .
¹⁹Many are the afflictions of the righteous,
　　but the L ORD rescues them from them all.
²⁰He keeps all their bones;
　　not one of them will be broken.
²¹Evil brings death to the wicked,
　　and those who hate the righteous will be condemned.
²²The L ORD redeems the life of his servants;
　　none of those who take refuge in him will be condemned.

Exegetical Perspective

Good News for the Brokenhearted. Today's reading celebrates God's gracious acts of deliverance on behalf of those who have been battered and bruised by life. The psalm is an individual song of thanksgiving, but it should not be construed as a personal reflection ("I") apart from community ("us"). From start to finish, the testimony of the individual and the concerns of the people of God are juxtaposed, in large measure because the two can never truly be compartmentalized. In fact, this psalm is not an individual prayer per se but a buoyant utterance of hope addressed to the congregation.

Wisdom Overtures. Wisdom overtures give this particular psalm of thanksgiving its distinctive character. As is typical of the wisdom tradition, Psalm 34 is didactic: it offers instruction on coping with life and negotiating its many twists and turns. In keeping with this tradition, the poem does not trade in categorical imperatives, systems of morality, or religious dogmas, but in pragmatic lessons derived from experience.

Also noteworthy, Psalm 34 is an acrostic poem: each verse begins with a consecutive letter of the Hebrew alphabet (with a few irregularities). In this way external structure—as well as internal vision—reflects a keen sense of order. This literary and symbolic coherence, however, cannot conceal the

Homiletical Perspective

Since the psalms are not narrative in nature, it is often fruitful for the preacher to ask: What is the story "around" or "within" the text? In this psalm of gratitude and thanksgiving, the psalmist was "delivered from all his fears." What would it mean to be delivered from "all fears," the fears of hunger or poverty, physical harm or decline, ridicule, injury, or loneliness? Is this possible? There are no guarantees against finitude, decline, or death. Does fear serve any constructive purposes? Is the challenge to learn to live creatively with all our fears, so that they do not paralyze us but prompt us to be vigilant and caring for others and ourselves? When, the preacher might ask, was I delivered from my fear? When was my congregation delivered? How about my local and global community? Stories will emerge. This time-honored practice is demonstrated in the superscription given to the psalm. The psalm's expression of gratitude brought to mind an experience that David had when he was fleeing King Saul.

It is wise for the preacher to read the verses in the psalm that are omitted from the lectionary. Often these verses are difficult or perhaps even offensive. In this instance, the verses assigned for this week are verses 1–8. This omission is confusing because the first unit of the psalm includes verses 1–10, and there seems no obvious reason to omit verses 9–10, which speak of God's providence and care.

Psalm 34:1-8 (19-22)

Theological Perspective

cleverness of mind to acquire the skill and also bestowed the material with which to work."[1]

God's Response to Suffering. This psalm proclaims God's rescue (vv. 4–7, 19–22), while admitting the problem of the suffering of the righteous (v. 19). God has a reputation for listening to the cries (v. 6) voiced by the hopeless (e.g., Abel, Gen. 4:10; Ishmael, Gen. 21:17; enslaved Hebrews, Exod. 2:23–24). Throughout the Old Testament, God's identity, and that expected of the covenant people, revolves around protecting those most vulnerable in society: widows, orphans, foreigners. In this sense, true worshipers of God who commit themselves to the Lord's justice are called to function as angels (v. 7, understood as "messenger" or "emissary") to relieve and protect any "poor soul" (v. 6).

The tricky part of this beautiful picture is reconciling God's commitment to deliverance with the persistent experience of suffering. Christian hope in the fulfillment of God's kingdom in the resurrection has traditionally grounded hope for deliverance in the long term. Short-term divine deliverance is not guaranteed. God often relies upon human cooperation in establishing justice rather than being a deus ex machina. Rescue may also entail both equanimity in the midst of troubles, which arises from trust in God, and empathy for others. God does not accept current struggles as an excuse to languish in idle self-pity, but encourages suffering to become a vehicle to address the suffering of others. Gustavo Gutiérrez observed about Job that "to go out of himself and help other sufferers (without waiting until his own problems are first resolved) is to find a way to God. . . . The needs of others cannot be left in abeyance until everything has become clear [about why suffering is happening]."[2]

Christ and the Sacraments. Christians have taken the "taste and see" metaphor to foreshadow the reality enjoyed not only in the Eucharist, but within many material aspects of worship. Sharing in the Lord's body and blood offers a very physical reception of Christ. The earliest believers recalled the Lord's sacrificial death in terms of the paschal lamb whose bones were to remain intact. Jesus' unbroken bones (v. 20) added to believers' reflections on the divine vindication of Christ (John 19:33, 36). Christ most

Pastoral Perspective

The psalmist teaches us that amid the challenges over the course of our lives God will answer our prayers, dwell with us in our fear and loneliness, and give to the faithful every good thing. In one of the verses omitted by the Revised Common Lectionary, the psalmist delights to offer from his own experience, "Come, O children, listen to me; I will teach you the fear of the LORD" (v. 11a). Or, as Chaucer would put it, "Gladly would he learn, and gladly teach."

One hard lesson we learn from the psalmist comes in verse 19: "Many are the afflictions of the righteous." No matter how faithfully we strive to live by the divine imperative to do justice, love mercy, seek peace (which Micah and the psalmist teach us), there is no guarantee that we will escape affliction in this life. Why, then, should we endeavor to be the obedient children of God if we are not promised the instant gratification of a "good life," free from conflict and rich in blessing?

The psalmist teaches us of suffering and redemption. In the New Testament lessons of our faith we comprehend *two* lives—one on either side of our inevitable death. We recognize that our full redemption does not come to us on this planet, but must wait until, as Mark Twain so succinctly stated, "we meet the Author face to face."

We are taught in Psalm 34 that simply being in need does not guarantee that our prayers will be heard by God's ears and answered by God's mercy. A prayerful life must be accompanied by an ethical life. As James Mays puts it in his commentary on the Psalms, "Seeking the Lord in supplication is not to be separated from loving good, hating evil, and seeking *shalom*."[1] Jesus himself teaches us in the Gospel of Matthew (7:21): "Not everyone who says to me, 'Lord, Lord,' will enter the kingdom of heaven, but only the one who does the will of my Father in heaven."

For all of the "teaching" in this psalm, its most enduring line is that delectable invitation, "O taste and see that the LORD is good! Happy are those who take refuge in him." No doubt this exhortation is most often heard and interpreted as a welcome to the Eucharist, and to the remembrance of Christ's continuing presence among us in the gifts of bread and wine, until he comes again.

The senses of God are highlighted more in this text than in any other of the 150 chapters of the book of Psalms. In verse 15, omitted by the

---

1. Basil the Great, Longer Responses 37, *Asketikon of St. Basil the Great*, ed. and trans. Anna Silvas (New York: Oxford University Press, 2005), 243–45.
2. Gustavo Gutiérrez, *On Job: God-Talk and the Suffering of the Innocent*, trans. Matthew J. O'Connell (Maryknoll, NY: Orbis Books, 1987), 48.

1. James L. Mays, *Psalms*, Interpretation Series (Louisville, KY: John Knox Press, 1989), 151.

anxiety and trouble bubbling beneath the surface of the text. At almost every juncture, one can discern a subtext of scarcity and palpable disease. Yet despite this background the poem remains optimistic, principally due to the conviction that God is responsive to human needs. The psalmist draws this conclusion from the tangible experience of salvation. "I sought the Lord, and he answered . . . and delivered me."

Heading. Psalm 34 begins with a superscription (not included in this volume) that recalls a crisis in the life of David (1 Sam. 21:10–15). While this heading may not be helpful for reconstructing origins, it does provide an intriguing window into the ongoing interpretive process. Apparently the interpretive community pins down and particularizes the text's indeterminate voices. An anonymous poem of survival is now rooted in the concrete textual memory of David. Informed by the superscription, the psalm recounts the tale of a desperate man on the verge of death who escapes with his life.

Call to Grateful Praise (vv. 1–3). As is customary for songs of thanksgiving, Psalm 34 begins with an invitation to give thanks. Written in the first person, the poet expresses intense desire to praise God "at all times." Praise characterizes the totality of life because "outside of God, nothing is, nothing breathes, nothing moves, and nothing lives."[1] To "boast in the Lord," moreover, is to express uninhibited delight in God (see Jer. 9:24; 1 Cor. 1:31). Grateful praise, however, can hardly be self-contained, so the psalmist invites the "humble" to join the festive throng. The "humble" are those within the community who are at risk and ever aware of their own limitations (i.e., "the afflicted" as in the NIV). The circle of joy is complete only when those at the margins participate fully in the celebration of praise.

Reason for Praise/Thanks (vv. 4–8). Rather than employing lofty theological language as a basis for thanksgiving, the psalmist relates a poignant account of deliverance. This terse testimony of hope when none seemed possible is thoroughly subjective. In a time of crisis, the petitioner cried out for help and God intervened. The rescue report spurs a series of exhortations (note also the verses left out of the lectionary, vv. 9–18).

> v. 4 deliverance testimony: "I sought . . . he answered . . . and delivered"

---

1. Henri Nouwen, *Gracious! A Latin American Journal* (Maryknoll, NY: Orbis, 1993), 49.

Psalm 34 is a wisdom psalm, acrostic in form. Though not executed perfectly, each verse of the psalm begins with consecutive letters of the Hebrew alphabet. The psalm is intended to convey a "completeness" about God's care. And, just as a collection of proverbs would do, the psalm teases us with a series of provocative and intriguing sayings that invite our attention. Consider, for instance, the following:

> I sought the Lord . . . and he delivered me from all my fears (v. 4)
> O taste and see that the Lord is good (v. 8)
> Those who seek the Lord lack no good thing (v. 10)
> Depart from evil, and do good; seek peace, and pursue it (v. 14)
> The Lord is near to the brokenhearted, and saves the crushed in spirit (v. 18)
> None of those who take refuge in him will be condemned (v. 22)

This collection of verses is interesting for a variety of reasons. Some verses bring to mind our own stories that ultimately confirm the psalmist's affirmations. We know times when we have been delivered from our fears. We know the call to be peacemakers. We know how God's presence has been a comfort to those whose spirits are crushed.

Yet not all the wisdom sayings from Psalm 34 are consistent with our experience and understanding. Is it true that those who seek God lack no good thing (v. 10)? What are good things? Do we not know of those in the past who have taken refuge in God and who have known great condemnation (v. 22)? These verses can be the tensive seeds of a sermon where the preacher, and thus the community, struggles for understanding.

A careful reading of Psalm 34 uncovers a series of repeated words and phrases that are clues for the preacher about the psalm's most important themes and meanings. Notice first the number of references to the senses. Primary are the nouns and verbs that refer to speaking and listening. Emphasized is the fact that the psalmist knows a *listening* God:

> This poor soul cried out and was heard by the Lord (v. 6)
> The eyes of the Lord are on the righteous, and his ears are open to their cry (v. 15)
> When the righteous cry for help, the Lord hears and rescues them from all their troubles (v. 17)

The psalmist knows of a God who hears those who cry out. (What does it mean that it is only the

Psalm 34:1-8 (19-22)

Theological Perspective

fully experienced "the afflictions of the righteous" (v. 19) to accomplish God's comprehensive deliverance through the Son, the victim conqueror.

Early Christians linked Moses' radiance after his Sinai encounter with God (Exod. 34:29–35) to the enlightenment or illumination of the newly baptized who died and rose with Christ in baptism (Rom. 6:4). In turning to the Lord Jesus, believers are transfigured by beholding God (2 Cor. 3:15–18). Brought into a new, intimate relationship with God in Christ, the baptized who "look to [God] are radiant" (v. 5), echoing Paul's claim that Christians "are being transformed into the same image from one degree of glory to another" (2 Cor. 3:18).

Fortified by the Jewish tradition, Christians fought hard in the second and third centuries to insist upon the goodness of creation and of humans as intentionally psychosomatic beings. At stake is the sacral nature of enfleshed life: marriage and children, appreciation of food and beauty, care of bodies—one's own and those of others—and the role of bodies in a God-oriented life. Christians argued that the whole person should have access to enjoying and receiving God: for the eyes, icons and art; for the ears, chant and music; for touch, sacraments and art; for the tongue, Eucharist; for the nose, incense and holy oil. Limiting the involvement of the bodily senses risks demeaning humanity's special creation by God and the incarnation. The incarnation healed and restored honor to matter, so that it might be used for knowing God. Theodore the Studite (ca. 759–826) explained,

> So whether in an image, or in the Gospel, or in the cross, or in any other consecrated object, God is evidently worshipped "in spirit and truth," as the materials are exalted by the raising of the mind toward God. The mind does not remain with the materials, because it does not trust them. . . . Through the materials, rather, the mind ascends toward the prototypes.[3]

Truly incarnate worship demands forms that allow a variety of means to "taste and see that the LORD is good!" (v. 8).

LISA D. MAUGANS DRIVER

Pastoral Perspective

lectionary, we read of the eyes of God, which are turned toward the righteous; and the ears of God, which bend to hear their prayers. The invitation to "taste" of the Lord, however, remains in the lectionary, as though we should not need to be reminded of the more "familiar" concepts of seeing and hearing, but the more subtle and personal concept of "tasting" God deserves to be underscored.

To understand how such a verse fits into the context of the rest of the psalm, with its emphasis on teaching, we can explore a slightly different interpretation of the word "taste." Try thinking of taste, not in terms of "savoring a delicious flavor," but rather "sinking our teeth into something of substance." James Mays suggests that "taste" is used here in the sense of "finding out by experience."[2] Such an approach brings even this seemingly detached verse back into the realm of education, and the psalmist continues gladly to learn and gladly teach.

"O taste and see!" What does such an unusual and daring exhortation mean to us?

Tasting is not a passive verb, but one that requires action. To taste anything, we must first open our mouths! The ancient responsive prayer of the church actually asks God to do that for us: "O Lord, open thou our lips!" This invocation is immediately answered by the response, "And our mouths shall show forth thy praise!" (cf. Ps. 51:15). So the psalmist invites us to open ourselves to receive the goodness of the Lord—opening not only our mouths to taste, but our minds to learn and our hearts to love. It is not enough to accept that invitation for ourselves alone, but through our lives to teach others how rich and bountiful is the feast of God's blessing for all who will faithfully receive it.

MICHAEL MORGAN

---

3. Theodore the Studite, *First Refutation of the Iconoclasts* 13, in *On the Holy Icons*, trans. Catharine P. Roth (Crestwood, NY: St. Vladimir's Seminary Press, 2001), 34.

2. Ibid., 153.

Exegetical Perspective

v. 5 exhortation: "Look to him, and be radiant"
v. 6 deliverance testimony: "This poor soul cried, and was heard . . . and saved"
v. 7 reflection: "The angel of the LORD encamps . . . and delivers"
v. 8 exhortation: "O taste and see that the LORD is good; . . . happy are those who take refuge in him"

The survival story and accompanying exhortations seek to encourage those who are debilitated by fear. Together they assert that God has been faithful in the past and will continue to act in character during times of danger and disjunction. The verses culminate in the affirmation that "YHWH is good" (v. 8) —a claim that approximates the character of God and echoes a fundamental reason for praise in the Psalter as a whole.

Much of the Psalter pivots around the binary statement that God is both great and good. Psalm 34 focuses on the latter. The psalmist urges the people of God to "taste and see that YHWH is good." When they do, they will discover firsthand that God is a sure refuge in time of crisis. And survival will in turn lead to the road called gratitude.

Concluding Testimony (vv. 18–22). The psalm concludes with a series of observations about God's involvement in the world. All exude great confidence and hope. At the same time, all recognize life's deeply strained texture: God's people have their share of "troubles" and "afflictions." The righteous inhabit a ruptured world in which they must "cry for help"; and at least some are wounded beyond words, that is, "brokenhearted" and "crushed in spirit." And yet amid the wreckage of one's life, God is "near" (v. 18) and indeed "saves . . . rescues . . . keeps . . . [and] redeems." God does not ignore cries for help but delivers the righteous from trouble. "None of those who take refuge in him will be condemned" (v. 22b). In sum, Psalm 34 is a survival story, a joyous response of gratitude to unexpected deliverance from disaster.

While such affirmations resonate with many, they raise troubling questions for those who have found it otherwise. Their lingering cries—from death camps, war-torn communities, killing fields, annihilated worlds—and the cries of their children should never be silenced, not even by the testimony of the rescued (see also the book of Job). Acknowledging the precarious presence of victim and survivor and honoring their conflicting testimonies does justice not only to the psalm but to its great cloud of witnesses.

LOUIS STULMAN

Homiletical Perspective

"righteous" who are heard?) Other senses are acknowledged in the psalm as well. The psalmist urges the community to "taste and see" God. When have we tasted and seen God's presence among us?

Psalm 34 contains an emphasis on the fear of God, as is often the case in Wisdom literature. This psalm plays with the live tension between the God who delivers us from our fears (v. 4) and the fear of God (v. 11) that guides us in life-giving ways. This interesting play on "fear" is recognized and immortalized for us in the first verse of "Amazing Grace": "'Twas grace that taught my heart to fear, and grace my fears relieved."

A primary theme throughout the psalm is deliverance. Note verses 4, 6, 7, 17, 19, and 22, which refer to deliverance, rescue, salvation, and redemption. It would be good for the preacher to review the Hebrew understandings of these great words of Old Testament faith and understanding. Redemption means being drawn out from one world into another. Salvation suggests deliverance from what restricts or oppresses us.[1]

The posture of the psalmist is one of gratitude: "I will bless the LORD at all times; his praise shall continually be in my mouth." The psalmist has decided that praise of God is not dependent on what is happening in life. God is worthy of praise "at all times." With such a commitment the worshiper knows her or his place in the world amid all things. Even in the face of adversity and contradiction, the psalmist lives with a daring commitment to search for God's presence and care, even in the midst of affliction and trouble. Material things cannot elicit this response; they are powerless to deliver us from fear, shame, and trouble. Such deliverance is the work of the one who created us and names us. The psalmist names this one as Refuge, the one to whom we turn in need (vv. 8, 22).

MARY DONOVAN TURNER

---

1. See Mary Donovan Turner, *Old Testament Words: Reflections for Preachers* (St. Louis: Chalice Press, 2003), for entries on Redeemer, Salvation, Fear, and Blessing.

Hebrews 7:23-28

²³Furthermore, the former priests were many in number, because they were prevented by death from continuing in office; ²⁴but he holds his priesthood permanently, because he continues forever. ²⁵Consequently he is able for all time to save those who approach God through him, since he always lives to make intercession for them.

²⁶For it was fitting that we should have such a high priest, holy, blameless, undefiled, separated from sinners, and exalted above the heavens. ²⁷Unlike the other high priests, he has no need to offer sacrifices day after day, first for his own sins, and then for those of the people; this he did once for all when he offered himself. ²⁸For the law appoints as high priests those who are subject to weakness, but the word of the oath, which came later than the law, appoints a Son who has been made perfect forever.

Theological Perspective

My daughter is currently reading *The Federalist Papers*. These texts are difficult for the modern reader, not just because of two centuries' worth of difference in vocabulary and style, but also because they describe federalism against the background of the system of government that was in place in this country during the 1780s—not a particularly well-known slice of American history to most of us. So my daughter will ask, "Dad, what are these trade policies that Madison says are not working?" And I think: "Hmm, trade policies under the Articles of Confederation: this is a topic about which I know almost nothing at all."

A similar problem faces the contemporary reader of the letter to the Hebrews. The author is addressing the typical adherent of first-century Judaism, explaining the positive features of Christianity in ways that would make sense to such a reader. But we are not first-century Jews, and most of us know very little about the beliefs and practices with which the writer assumes the readers are well acquainted. In addition to leaving us slightly mystified, this situation can dramatically reduce our overall interest in the topic: what good is a comparison to a system of belief that we know almost nothing about? In fact, one feels considerable sympathy for those on the other side of the argument: surely neither the first-century Jews

Pastoral Perspective

There has been much talk in church circles in recent years about leadership, fueled by a resurgence of interest in what some have called total ministry, the ministry of all the baptized or, to use the more resonant phrase beloved of Luther and other Reformers, the priesthood of all believers. This reassertion of the priestly vocation of all baptized Christians comes at a time when ordained leadership in many Christian churches has come under considerable fire. Even in our most hierarchal churches, the role of the priest or presbyter as the leader of the worshiping community—a role once unquestioned by lay people and clergy alike—is subject to sometimes withering public scrutiny. This mistrust of ordained leadership is part of a deeper general mistrust of leadership in all walks of life. Leaders of organizations—whether secular or religious—often find themselves under tremendous pressures to succeed or produce. Burnout is common. And longevity in office—particularly among leaders in churches, schools, and universities—has become rare.

In our present muddle about leadership, this passage from the letter to the Hebrews speaks with unsettling clarity. For anyone called to leadership in the church, it might even offer some measure of relief. The writer's use of priestly metaphors and priestly images to describe the work of Christ in the world

Exegetical Perspective

Christ, Our Eternal, God-Appointed High Priest.
These six verses conclude the first part of the second
major section of the Epistle to the Hebrews (7:1–
10:39). It is important to grasp the whole argument of
this chapter, in order to appreciate the full message of
the final verses. In this chapter the epistle begins to
discuss the nature of the high priestly ministry of
Christ after the model of Melchizedek, continuing a
theme that the author has already pronounced "hard
to explain" (5:11). Christ's priestly ministry has been
announced previously (1:3; 2:17–18; 3:1), and related
to that of Melchizedek at 4:14–5:10 and 6:20.

Chapter 7 is a midrashic interpretation of both
priesthoods, including a quotation from Psalm 110:4
and a reference to the story of the patriarch Abraham
paying 10 percent of his booty to Melchizedek, the
king of Salem and "priest of God Most High" (Gen.
14:17–20). The figure of Melchizedek played an
important role in early Judaism, as witnessed in the
Dead Sea Scrolls (*Genesis Apocryphon* 1QapGen
22:14–17; 11QMelch), Josephus (*Ant.* 1.10.2 §180),
the Targums, and other early Jewish literature.

The Priesthood of Melchizedek. The argument of the
chapter begins by introducing the character of Melchizedek as a priest-king (vv. 1–3). In addition to
identifying Melchizedek as "priest of the Most High

Homiletical Perspective

The letter to the Hebrews poses a challenge to the
preacher, but it also offers an opportunity for
educating a congregation about the close relationship
between early Christianity and the Hebrew faith.
Today's passage is a small section of an extended
argument in which the priesthood of Christ is
contrasted to that of the Levitical priesthood. Since
this reading represents only a small part of a larger
and rather complex argument, the preacher might
usefully spend some time clarifying the terms of the
discussion, taking care to avoid an oversimplification
that exalts Christ while condemning the God of the
Old Testament. Quoting the opening lines of the
epistle can help to forestall such misunderstanding:
"Long ago God spoke to our ancestors in many and
various ways by the prophets, but in these last days he
has spoken to us by a Son." The Christian God is not
discontinuous with the God of the Old Testament;
the author tells us that the same God who spoke
through Moses and the other prophets speaks to us
now through Christ.

A further exploration might discuss how, in
today's reading and throughout the letter, the author
proceeds by comparison and contrast. In chapter 3,
for example, Jesus' faithfulness is compared to that of
Moses, an exemplar of faith. Moses is not dismissed
or denigrated in the contrast between the two figures

Hebrews 7:23-28

Theological Perspective

nor the eighteenth-century Anti-Federalists deserve for every single aspect of their beliefs to be weighed in the balance and found wanting.

But in both cases—*The Federalist Papers* and the letter to the Hebrews—the text has endured over time *not* because it criticizes an alternative approach (about which we know very little). Rather, the classic status of these documents is due to their persuasive account of a new approach that was then being promoted, that eventually took hold, and that has remained with us to this day. In the middle section of Hebrews (chaps. 5–10), the writer is emphasizing one specific feature of Christianity as noteworthy: its understanding of *sacrifice*. We therefore need to examine that very thorny concept.

Sacrifice is something of a two-edged sword. On the one hand, we praise those who are willing to defer, or perhaps to give up entirely, instant experiences of gratification for the sake of some future good; such sacrifices are considered particularly praiseworthy if they are for the sake of another. Parents forgo their own desires so that their children can prosper; workers reduce their job-related demands so that the company can stay solvent; soldiers put their lives and limbs on the line for the sake of a greater good.

On the other hand, we also recognize that the concept of sacrifice can be easily abused. Are the workers' concessions really necessary for the corporation to stay afloat, or do they just line the pockets of the well-to-do? Are the women and men of a country's armed forces sometimes merely pawns, being used to score political points? At the very least, we recognize that those who seek to persuade people that their concessions and burdens are "a worthy sacrifice" may be seeking to maximize their own interest or profit. In fact, some writers have suggested that our fascination with sacrifice is inextricably bound up with the tendency of human beings—unique among the animal species—to perpetuate violence against our own kind.[1]

The specifically *theological* concept of sacrifice has a similarly complex range of associations. Of course, Christianity has traditionally claimed that the sacrifice offered up by Jesus—suffering the abusive treatment of the religious and political structures of his day, and eventually dying on the cross—is undertaken on behalf of the whole human race, and is therefore praiseworthy and good. But some writers have also wondered whether the Christian use of the

Pastoral Perspective

paradoxically undercuts human priestly pretensions. Only later in the history of the church did Christian leaders take on the trappings of priesthood, asserting an intermediary role between God and the believer. These trappings of priesthood—whether understood in OT terms, as this writer describes them, or in terms of priestly authority experienced in our own time—are temporary, partial, "subject to weakness." In effect, the passage declares, priests and ministers come and go, but Christ holds his priesthood permanently. In the radical rethinking of priestly authority reflected in Hebrews, only Christ holds title to the word "priest." He holds the true priestly authority—an authority characterized not by power but by humility—offering a sacrifice to God on our behalf "once for all" (v. 27) when he offered himself.

The paradoxical history of the English word "priest" reveals how deeply this passage challenges our assumptions about what pastoral leadership can look like. Although it is often thought of as a translation of the Greek word for priest (*hieros*), etymologically the word "priest" is in fact a shortened form of the Greek word for elder (*presbyteros*), the word used most frequently in the NT to describe the role of leader in a congregation, a role that only gradually came to be understood in a priestly sense.[1] This distinction between priestly and presbyteral leadership as reflected in NT language has been a bone of contention in Christian churches right down to the present day, and was particularly acute during the Reformation of the Christian churches in Europe in the sixteenth and seventeenth centuries. Denouncing "the new forcers of conscience" among the Presbyterians who held power in the revolutionary Long Parliament, the poet John Milton thundered that "New Presbyter is but old Priest writ large."[2] He objected to what he saw as a heretical backsliding toward the assertion of sacerdotal power, betraying the Protestant principle of the priesthood of all believers—and the sovereignty of Christ alone as both high priest and victim—that was the driving force of the seventeenth-century religious and political struggles in England.

A gentler, more temperate voice than Milton's from the same period of Christian history provides perhaps the best entry into the pastoral implications of this crucial passage in Hebrews—and the comfort that clergy leaders might draw from it. Consider this

---

1. See, for example, René Girard, *Violence and the Sacred*, trans. Patrick Gregory (Baltimore: Johns Hopkins University Press, 1977).

1. See the useful entry in *The Oxford Dictionary of the Christian Church*, 2nd ed., ed. F. L. Cross and E. A. Livingstone (Oxford: Oxford University Press, 1983), s.v. "Priest."
2. *The Poems of John Milton*, ed. John Carey and Alastair Fowler (New York: Norton, 1972), 298.

Exegetical Perspective

God," the author also recognizes him as "king of righteousness" (the meaning of the name in Hebrew) and "king of peace" (king of Salem, v. 2). In verse 3 Melchizedek is described as "without father, without mother, without genealogy, having neither beginning of days nor end of life, but resembling the Son of God, he remains a priest forever." This point will be taken up again in verses 26–28. Melchizedek's priesthood is described as greater than the priesthood of the Levites because Abraham paid him the tithe (vv. 4–10), and greater than Abraham because he blessed the patriarch (Gen. 14:19; Heb. 7:7). For the author, these two reasons support the argument that Melchizedek was superior to the ancestor Abraham, and that his priesthood is therefore superior to the priesthood of the Levites.

Midrash of Psalm 110:4. In verses 11–19 the epistle appeals to Psalm 110:4, the only other place in the Hebrew Scriptures where the priest Melchizedek is mentioned. As in verses 1–10, these verses form another *inclusio* with the allusions to "perfection" (*teleiōsis/eteleiōsen*) in verses 11 and 19. Two important points are made. First, the priestly ministry of the Levites (and Aaron) falls short of perfection. If it were perfect, the argument goes, why was another priesthood needed according to the order of Melchizedek? (v. 11). The second point is that the new priesthood is better because it is based on its "indestructible life" ("forever" in Ps. 110:4). So the new priesthood is better than that of the Levites and of Aaron because it replaces the old and is indestructible.

Today's reading is part of the final section of chapter 7 (vv. 20–28), which forms an *inclusio* with the reference to the "oath" (*horkōmosia*) in verses 20, 21, and 28. Here the epistle offers three major arguments as to why the priesthood according to the order of Melchizedek is better than the Levitical priesthood. First, this priesthood rests not on human merits but on a divine promise of Jesus as guarantor of a better covenant (vv. 20–22). Second, Jesus' priesthood is permanent (vv. 23–25). Finally, Jesus' priesthood is better given his character (v. 26), his deed (v. 27), and his status as Son of God (v. 28).

Hebrews 7:23–28 is better understood in the context developed at the beginning of the epistle (1:1–4), which announces the superiority of Christ over all. As the chapter exemplifies, this superiority is founded on an interpretation of both Genesis 14:17–20 and Psalm 110:4. As already stated in Hebrews 1:8; 4:15–16; 5:1, 7–9, Jesus' ministry as priest includes continuous intercession for believers.

Homiletical Perspective

in the following verses, although the superiority of the salvation attained by Christ is asserted. A sermon might be developed on how deeply the Christian message is grounded in the Old Testament Scriptures and how that understanding plays out today in relations between individuals, as well as between the church and the Jewish community. One might also stress the dangers inherent in a careless reading of the biblical text; that is, the very real and disastrous outcomes of asserting that Christian witness denies the value of or replaces the witness of Judaism.

The main contrast in today's reading focuses on the efficacy of sacrifice in relation to permanence and impermanence. Christ's sacrifice for the remission of sins is "for all time," whereas the Levitical priests, who die and need to be replaced, must "offer sacrifices day after day." A sermon might be developed around this image of daily repetition. In what ways does the regular round of our daily lives dull us to the presence of the Spirit? In what ways has the practice of our faith become routine? On the other hand, in what ways is the living Christ present in our worship and practice? How is the Christ "for all time" manifest in our lives today? How can we as individuals and as a church express our awareness of Christ's living presence to those around us?

Another sermon, or series of sermons, might explore the implications of this reading in terms of our understanding of the forgiveness of trespasses as a living process. The argument in this passage can be seen to mirror, or highlight metaphorically, how forgiveness actually works. The image of the routine of daily sacrifice by ever-changing priests can be seen to reflect the unchangeable nature of trespasses; it seems as if we are trapped in sin, since the consequences of our actions never go away. It is a closed system; intercession must be made again and again, because the atonement can only be temporary. In this closed system we are bound by our past actions; there is no real possibility of transformation, and therefore there can be no permanent release.

Hannah Arendt, the great Jewish philosopher of the last century, wrote about this closed system in her 1958 book *The Human Condition.* Arendt saw that a major predicament of the human condition is that ordinary and necessary human actions inevitably lead to a chaos of unintended and irreversible consequences. It is the nature of human beings to act, and it is the nature of action to unleash the unforeseeable and the irreversible. Without the possibility of forgiveness, Arendt asserts, we would be trapped forever in the consequences of a single action. The reflexive

Hebrews 7:23-28

Theological Perspective

language of "sacrifice on behalf of another" might not underwrite certain abuses—as when some particularly difficult sacrifice is demanded of others with the implication that such denials of self will make them more "Christlike." One thinks, for example, of the invocations of Christ's sacrifice as supposed words of comfort to those who, in various periods of history, were being oppressed on the basis of their race, class, gender, or sexual orientation.

Today's passage emphasizes that Christ's sacrifice is definitive and final; as the perfect sacrifice, it puts an end to sacrifice. In theory, this account should help us to curtail the negative and abusive elements of this language; as the definitive sacrifice, Christ's work eliminates the need for others to be cajoled into offering sacrifices that are really just a form of submission to more powerful interests. While the Christian understanding of sacrifice has certainly been put to oppressive uses, the account offered in the letter to the Hebrews can help us understand it as part of the solution, rather than as part of the problem. Rightly understood, Christ's sacrifice actually has the potential to *end* the cycle of violence that various forms of sacrifice have sometimes been employed to perpetuate.[2]

Of course, this does not mean that we will not continue to make our own kinds of sacrifices from time to time, as well as having them made on our behalf. But if, as this passage suggests, Christ's sacrifice is "once for all" (v. 27) and endures "for all time" (v. 25), this new knowledge can radically reorient our lives. We can live under the assurance that the definitive sacrifice has already been accomplished, even though its detailed ramifications are yet to be fully revealed to us.[3]

DAVID S. CUNNINGHAM

Pastoral Perspective

excerpt from the poem entitled "Aaron," by Milton's older contemporary, the poet and pastor George Herbert (1593–1633). Herbert begins by drawing a stark contrast between the holiness of "true Aarons" (Aaron was the Old Testament exemplar of high priesthood) and the weakness and sinfulness of the poet-priest who is the speaker of the poem. Recalling the elaborate priestly vestments described in Exodus 28, the poet laments that what for Aaron is "Holiness on the head, / Light and perfections on the breast," are for him "Profaneness in my head, / Defects and darknesse in my breast":

> A noise of passions ringing me for dead
> Unto a place where is no rest:
> Poore priest thus am I drest.

But then, two stanzas later, the poet turns to the Christ, the true Aaron, the high priest of the letter to the Hebrews, and finds there another head, another heart and breast, "Without whom I could have no rest":

> Christ is my onely head,
> My alone onely heart and breast,
> My onely musick, striking me ev'n dead;
> That to the old man I may rest,
> And be in him new drest.
> So holy in my head,
> Perfect and light in my deare breast,
> My doctrine tun'd by Christ, (who is not dead,
> But lives in me while I do rest)
> Come people; Aaron's drest.[3]

The poem is not just about ordained priests, nor, for that matter, is this passage from Hebrews. Christ holds his priesthood permanently, the passage declares, and consequently is able for all time to save those who approach God through him, since he always lives to make intercession for them. Given the chronic mistrust of leadership felt by many churchgoers, this passage is a source of comfort. Again, priests and ministers come and go, but Christ intercedes for us now and always. Clergy often struggle to be faithful in an increasingly stressful profession. There is equal comfort here for us, even blessing. For all our training, and whatever remaining perquisites of office come our way in a world where respect is scarce, Christ remains our "onely head," our "onely music," our "onely heart and breast."

ROGER A. FERLO

2. See René Girard, Jean-Michel Oughourlian, and Guy Lefort, *Things Hidden Since the Foundation of the World*, trans. Stephen Bann and Michael Metteer (Stanford, CA: Stanford University Press, 1987).

3. See James Allison, *Raising Abel: The Recovery of the Eschatological Imagination* (New York: Crossroad, 1996).

3. *The Works of George Herbert*, ed. F. E. Hutchinson (Oxford: Clarendon Press, 1972), 174.

Exegetical Perspective

These statements serve as affirmations to a community that struggles both with its identity and its tribulations.

Verses 23–25 contrast the temporality and plurality of the older priesthood with the permanent and single character of Christ's priesthood. Most English translations miss the correlative particle relation in verses 23 and 24. The Greek *men . . . de* construction of these verses can be better understood if made explicit, as the NASB translates it: "on the one hand . . . on the other hand." While the former priests were many and died, the priesthood of Jesus is permanent or eternal. Verse 25 offers the logical consequence of the continuous priesthood of Jesus: he is always able to save those who approach God through him. The phrase *eis to panteles* can be understood in a temporal sense ("always") or a modal sense ("completely"). The two meanings need not be taken as mutually exclusive. For the community of the Hebrews, the theological affirmation of the eternal priesthood of Christ translates into a sense of security. Not only is Jesus "always" ministering as a priest; he also is "always" (*pantote*) alive to intercede for those who approach God through him.

In verses 26–28 the chapter concludes with a summary of what has been said about Christ's priestly ministry. These verses also serve as a transition to the topic of sacrifice that will be discussed later in the epistle. The three adjectives ("holy," "blameless," "undefiled") and two participial phrases ("separated from sinners," "exalted above the heavens") together describe Jesus' moral character in his priestly intercessory actions (see also Lev. 21:11–17). The style is analogous to verse 1–3, where Melchizedek is also described with a series of adjectives. In contrast to other priests, he does not need to offer repetitive sacrifices, and he does not need to offer sacrifices for his own sins. Jesus offered himself, once and forever.

The permanent and solid character of Christ's priesthood rests on God's eternal oath. This oath appoints Jesus ("a Son") "who has been made perfect forever" (v. 28). In the epistle's view, both of these characteristics—Jesus' perfection and his permanence—make his priesthood superior to that of the Levites in the old covenant, as a priest according to the order of Melchizedek. Appointed by God's oath and exalted above heavens, his priesthood is permanent; as a self-sacrifice, his priesthood is effective for everyone.

DAVID CORTÉS-FUENTES

Homiletical Perspective

human response of striking back at injury would call forth a never-ending chain reaction of retaliation. The iron rule of vengeance would dominate all human interaction.

The preacher might use this text to help a congregation develop a mature understanding of how sin can operate in our lives, going beyond popular ideas of sin being an expression of self-indulgence in bodily pleasures. Sin cripples us because it traps us in the past; never-ending resentment and guilt can shut down our natural vitality and inhibit our growth, both individually and corporately. If we understand sin in these terms, we realize that sin is very much a reality for all of us today. Examples from our daily lives abound. We see people, ourselves included, trapped in self-destructive behavior, in addictions to alcohol, drugs, food, violent behavior, sex, shopping, TV watching. We see the effects of the consequences of past actions (our own and those of other people) in dysfunctional relationships: in marriages, in families, among friends and colleagues. We also see how the consequences of past actions can trap us in our communal lives: in extreme poverty in the midst of plenty, in greed and corruption in civic government and in corporations, in street gangs, in ethnic conflicts, in tension between nations. The list is almost endless.

Forgiveness is Jesus' amazing discovery that we do not need to be bound by our past trespasses; through repentance and forgiveness we can be transformed; we can find release from past pain and learn how to forgive ourselves and others. That Jesus "always lives to make intercession for us" means that forgiveness is always present, always available to us. We can be freed from the guilt and resentment that bind us to the consequences of past actions. Indeed, our faith can make us well. Just as blind Bartimaeus in today's Gospel reading gains sight and insight, so we too are transformed by the ongoing, ever-present healing power of forgiveness.

GINGER GRAB

Mark 10:46-52

46They came to Jericho. As he and his disciples and a large crowd were leaving Jericho, Bartimaeus son of Timaeus, a blind beggar, was sitting by the roadside. 47When he heard that it was Jesus of Nazareth, he began to shout out and say, "Jesus, Son of David, have mercy on me!" 48Many sternly ordered him to be quiet, but he cried out even more loudly, "Son of David, have mercy on me!" 49Jesus stood still and said, "Call him here." And they called the blind man, saying to him, "Take heart; get up, he is calling you." 50So throwing off his cloak, he sprang up and came to Jesus. 51Then Jesus said to him, "What do you want me to do for you?" The blind man said to him, "My teacher, let me see again." 52Jesus said to him, "Go; your faith has made you well." Immediately he regained his sight and followed him on the way.

Theological Perspective

The principal christological claim of this text is clear. Jesus, coming face-to-face with the imploring cries of a blind beggar named Bartimaeus, heals him with a simple word: "Go, your faith has made you well." At its most basic level, the passage proclaims the power of Christ demonstrated in the healing of a beggar whom the crowds want to silence. This is the compassionate Christ who brings near the good news of God's victory over the physical brokenness of the world.

It would be a mistake, however, to interpret this text simply as just another healing story. The Bartimaeus story serves as the concluding bookend to a section of Mark's Gospel in which blindness serves as a unifying theme. The section begins in 8:22–26 with a story in which Jesus struggles to restore sight to a blind man at Bethsaida. In chapters 9 and 10 Jesus confronts a different kind of blindness—a spiritual blindness among his closest followers, who seem either unwilling or unable to accept the radical, subversive claims of God's inbreaking kingdom. Jesus proclaims that the Son of Man will undergo suffering, rejection, and death only to have Peter sternly rebuke him (8:31–33). Jesus announces that the Son of Man will be betrayed into human hands, leaving his disciples confused and afraid to inquire further (9:30–32).

Pastoral Perspective

James and John, apparently confident insiders, have just been asked the same question Jesus now asks of the quintessential outsider: "What do you want me to do for you?" The answer of the presumptive faithful has varied little from the beginning: "Grant us to sit, one at your right hand and one at your left, in your glory." The plea of the presumed reprobate, crying out for God's mercy, sounds a counterpetition that is, itself, a confession: "Rabbouni, let me see again" (v. 51). The one answer rests on well-established religious laurels, the other petition issues from darkness and doubt; the one request would sidestep suffering, the other is forged out of loss, exclusion, and helplessness; the one is bent on an exclusive claim to righteousness, the other is bowed down in need before the Son who alone is righteous. This story reveals something of the nature of our ministry to both insiders and outsiders.

In the first place, Jesus is surrounded by selected and self-defined insiders as he quickly passes through Jericho. He is buffered by people who want to be identified with him. Mark does not say that they are at his side in order to be healed or taught, only that they are in his company. Often unmindful of what they want Jesus to do for them, they nevertheless want to be numbered among the faithful. Once in that number, those on the "inside" curiously act, time

Exegetical Perspective

This pericope concludes the short travel narrative that bridges Jesus' passage from his Galilean ministry to his activity in Jerusalem. The preceding verses have characterized the passion as a baptism with which Jesus would be baptized (evoking the baptismal inauguration of Jesus' ministry at Mark 1:9); this pericope foreshadows Jesus' triumphal entry into Jerusalem as the Son of David. Here Jesus encounters a blind beggar named Bartimaeus and restores his sight.

This pericope narrates the last healing in Mark's Gospel (the last mighty deed, apart from cursing the fig tree); it echoes the healing of the blind man in 8:22–26, though with noteworthy differences (unlike the paired feeding miracles of 6:30–44 and 8:1–10). In the earlier healing, Jesus remedies the man's blindness by applying spittle and laying on hands in two distinct phases; in today's lesson, he heals Bartimaeus immediately, with a word. Earlier the crowds bring the blind man to Jesus, but now the crowds try to keep Bartimaeus from hailing Jesus. The efficacy of the cure in Bethsaida seems to rest with Jesus, but Jesus ascribes Bartimaeus's recovery to his own faith. Whereas Jesus sends the healed Bethsaidan home, Bartimaeus follows Jesus—uniquely so, among the people whom Jesus heals in Mark's Gospel. These healings bracket the portion of Mark that repeats and

Homiletical Perspective

This text invites the preacher and congregation to recognize and respond to the work and person of Jesus as he leads the procession, calls others to follow, heals, and grants mercy. Perhaps the invitation contains an echo of the question that Jesus posed to his disciples on the way: "Who do people say that I am?" (8:27). Jesus is not Elijah or one of the prophets; he is the Christ. His name or title must reflect his work and person. The echo of the question is heard as our attention is directed immediately to a blind beggar. That Jesus will engage a blind person is no longer surprising, because Jesus has previously healed a blind man in Bethsaida (8:22–26). However, unlike the many other people healed by Jesus, this blind man is actually recalled by his Aramaic name, Bartimaeus, which means "son of Timaeus" or "son of honor."

The names for Jesus also find expression in this passage. The blind man uses several titles: Jesus of Nazareth (cf. 1:24), Son of David, and teacher (*rabbouni*). Many people who join the procession on the way will also welcome Jesus with the words (11:10), "Blessed is the coming kingdom of our ancestor David!" They will regard Jesus with the honor attributed to the memory and legacy of the throne of David. We can picture the early church debating and proclaiming that the highest honor must be ascribed to Jesus (12:35–37). Indeed, Mark

Mark 10:46-52

Theological Perspective

Mark portrays Jesus' disciples debating about who will be the greatest (9:33–34), with James and John jockeying for position at the right and left hand of Jesus (10:35–40) while the other apostles express anger at them for their presumptiveness (10:41). The Bartimaeus episode serves as the culmination of a section of Mark's Gospel in which Jesus confronts not only the physical blindness of Bartimaeus but, more significantly, the spiritual blindness of his closest followers who have failed to fully grasp the upside-down kingdom that Christ has brought near to the world.[1]

Thus, while the healing of blind Bartimaeus is first of all about Jesus' response to Bartimaeus's need, theologically the story serves as a metonym for the work of Christ, who in his journey to Jerusalem is seeking to cure the spiritual blindness of his disciples. This interplay between the blindness of those Jesus confronts on the way to Jerusalem and the sight-giving power that Jesus enacts in word and deed heightens the christological claim at the heart of the passage: not even the blindness of his closest followers can impede the work of Christ in the world.

To expand on this christological portrait, it is worth drawing attention to two ironic twists in this passage. First, Bartimaeus proclaims Jesus to be the "Son of David" (10:47), a deviation from the more common "Son of Man" designation that functions as the primary christological title in Mark's Gospel. In proclaiming Jesus to be the Son of David, Bartimaeus is relying on a common expectation that the Messiah was to come as a new Davidic king to restore Israel to political prominence. This expectation is borne out in the following chapter of Mark's Gospel, in which Jesus enters Jerusalem to the acclamation of crowds proclaiming with his arrival the "coming kingdom of our ancestor David" (11:10). Bartimaeus, in identifying Jesus as the son of David, demonstrates that he really does see; despite his physical blindness he can see what others who meet Jesus cannot.

But at the same time, in calling Jesus the "Son of David," Bartimaeus also demonstrates that he does not see after all. The irony is that the messianic title that Bartimaeus employs is one that Jesus himself will reject in Jerusalem. In his temple sermon, Jesus explicitly questions the identification of the Messiah as the son of David (12:35). Thus, while Bartimaeus *sees* that Jesus is the Messiah, the prevailing

Pastoral Perspective

and again, to keep others on the "outside." In spite of the fact that Jesus has just finished telling the disciples how the first must become last, Mark reports no contrary voice to the *many* that sternly ordered Bartimaeus to be quiet (v. 48). Only when Jesus himself orders the crowd to "Call him here" does the crowd feign pious hospitality, saying, "Take heart; get up, he is calling you" (v. 49).

What are we to make of Jesus' response to the crowd, and so of our ministry to the many who may want to be near Jesus while keeping their distance from another in need of his healing and succor? In the first place, Jesus' inattention to the crowd is noteworthy. Other than commanding them to call the outsider to his side, he simply lets them be. He does not upbraid them for their blindness to human need, nor does he call their faithfulness into question. Rather, in his command to "Call him here" he is also commanding the gathered crowd to become the disciples they would not be without this very specific act of obedience. Given that in Jesus the blind receive their sight, the lame walk, and the lepers are cleansed, those who simply want to be near him will find themselves in the company his love commands them to keep.

The faithful find themselves in this company today, as ministers and leaders of Christ's church command the church—in Christ's name—to be the church! Following Jesus, we need not scold those who have no idea what they want Jesus to do for them, nor call their faithfulness into question. Rather, as we call the community to attend to the other's cry for mercy, whether the other is as distant as Darfur or as close as the closet, we obediently gather a crowd around what God is doing in the world "to make and keep human life human."[1] The cry of need that caused Bartimaeus to be shunned by many becomes the occasion for their glimpse of God's final intention for creation in ordinary time.

This glimpse is called a miracle. Miracles are those events that bring people from darkness into the light. Miracles turn our attention to what really matters in life and in death. Miracles claim no power, but reveal a Power who wills to be known. Miracles point beyond the one before us to the One who made us for love's sake. "Miracle, as such," wrote Rudolf Bultmann, "means the activity of God."[2]

In the second place, then, this story invites us to consider our own ministry to the outsider, the voice

---

1. While blindness is a pivotal metaphor in this text, the preacher should be sensitive to how this image is deployed and what implicit messages are offered to those who are visually impaired.

1. Paul Lehmann, *Ethics in a Christian Context* (New York: Harper & Row, 1963), 101.
2. Rudolf Bultmann, *Jesus and the Word* (New York: Charles Scribner's Sons, 1962), 177.

Exegetical Perspective

explains the passion predictions (which the disciples nonetheless misunderstand). These clues might suggest that Mark deploys these healing stories to underline the contrast between outsiders who see Jesus and insiders who remain blind to his true identity. While this probably plays some role in the way Mark shapes the narrative, the motif of blindness remains muted, and only Bartimaeus shows explicit "faith." It seems more likely, then, that the explicit emphases of this pericope matter more than the undertones of a "blind"/"seeing" contrast.

Whereas Matthew's Gospel identifies Jesus as David's son in its first verse (and frequently thereafter) and Luke in 1:27 (repeated in 1:32, 69; 2:4; and 3:31), Mark has not hitherto so much as hinted at Jesus' royal ancestry. Thus Bartimaeus introduces a new feature to the narrative, bringing Jesus' Davidic heritage to explicit focus. He thus prepares readers for the crowd's acclamation at Jesus' entry to Jerusalem. Although Matthew uses the characterization "Son of David" frequently in healing contexts (9:27; 12:23; 15:22; 20:30–31), Mark cites it only here and in the teaching against the scribes in 12:35–37. Indeed, the crowds along the way to Jerusalem do not themselves identify Jesus as the heir of David's throne, shouting instead that "Blessed is the coming kingdom of our ancestor David" (cf. Matthew's "Hosanna to the Son of David!" 21:9). The address from Bartimaeus in these verses instructs the reader of what the crowds will not explicitly say, that Jesus himself embodies the kingship they announce. Although Jesus frequently cautions interlocutors when they ascribe greatness to him, he accepts Bartimaeus's acclamation without any reservation. In isolation, this might imply that Mark understands the phrase "Son of David" simply as a figurative compliment, as though one said that a senator was born on the Fourth of July. In Mark's narrative context, however, the succeeding incidents suggest that Mark understands "Son of David" as an assertion of Jesus' royal dignity: crowds escort Jesus into the capital city of the Davidic kingdom, and Jesus himself associates the Anointed One, *ho Christos*, with Davidic sonship in 12:35–37.

Bartimaeus urges Jesus, *eleēson me*, which the major translations render with either "Have mercy on me" (NRSV, NIV, Message) or "Have pity on me" (REB, NJB, CEV). These renderings focus a typical English-speaker's attention on Jesus' attitude toward Bartimaeus. The blind man does not ask that Jesus be kindly disposed toward him, however; he requests that Jesus do something on his behalf. Lacking an obvious comparable expression in English ("mercify

Homiletical Perspective

has already informed the reader that this Gospel is about Jesus Christ, the Son of God (1:1).

The congregation might reflect on how troubling it appears that this blind man is discouraged from seeking Jesus. Those around Jesus have often made it difficult for others to get close (2:2–4); even the disciples of Jesus speak sternly (10:13), perhaps in their efforts to keep Jesus from being overwhelmed. For Bartimaeus, would the stigma of his disability or his dishonorable trade of begging provide the justification for his exclusion from the procession?

This blind man is not dissuaded by the rebukes of the insider group. He persists until his shouts are recognized. He understands that being restored to honor, productivity, and well-being will require the mercy of the one whom he reveres as the Son of David. Bartimaeus refuses to be defined by his circumstances or by the expectations of those who are able to see, who appear to be close to Jesus, and who assume the right to speak on his behalf. He ensures that his call will be heard by Jesus.

The persistence of Bartimaeus sets in motion a wave of mercy, blessing, and change. Bartimaeus calls out to Jesus for mercy. Jesus calls for him. Those around Jesus call him to Jesus. His breakthrough of mercy begins with the recognition that those who once enjoined him not to bother Jesus of Nazareth are now transformed. They are no longer speaking sternly to him. Indeed, their excitement is palpable: Take heart! Cheer up! Get up! On your feet! He is calling you! They have become witnesses to and vessels of mercy.

The blind man is portrayed as a model of Christian discipleship. He comes to Jesus and does so by casting aside his cloak. It is quite reasonable to regard his cloak as representing his most treasured possession. It has kept him warm through the cold nights. It may also hold the meager spoils of his begging. In his act of throwing off his cloak, we see the image of one who leaves his former life behind. To those who have always known honor, power, affluence, and prestige, this image reminds us of the transforming effect of the gospel to call forth a life of renunciation and dramatic change.

Further, the image challenges us to reflect on the life circumstances of the world's poor and destitute who call out continuously for mercy. Most have no security blanket, no coats to keep them warm, and no hope for a better life. What, therefore, are the words and actions of mercy to the socially and economically disadvantaged persons who live in despair in our world?

Mark 10:46–52   215

Mark 10:46-52

Theological Perspective

assumptions about the role that the Messiah was to play in the life of Israel continue to blind him to Jesus' true mission. Like the disciples, Bartimaeus sees, but only in part. It is only in Jerusalem that the true import of Jesus' messianic mission is made manifest.

The second irony is that Bartimaeus follows Jesus "on the way," a sharp departure from the normal pattern of healing stories in Mark's Gospel, which usually end with Jesus sending the healed away from him with the command to be silent (1:44; 5:19, 37, 43; 7:36; 8:26). At one level the conclusion to the Bartimaeus episode suggests something about the life-altering consequences that accompany the granting of sight. Bartimaeus will accompany Jesus on the way. Having been granted sight, Bartimaeus can do nothing but follow the Messiah who has brought the good news of God's kingdom to bear in such a tangible way.

But the irony is this: Bartimaeus is on the way *to Jerusalem*, which this Messiah, the Lord of David, has already foretold will be the site of his own suffering and rejection. Bartimaeus and the disciples will enter Jerusalem to the raucous celebration of crowds heralding the coming Messiah. Expecting a messianic revolution, in Jerusalem these same followers will see their world turned upside down. The disciples will desert Jesus, scattering like sheep with no shepherd (14:27). Jesus will die, and those who thought that they could truly see Jesus will discover in Jesus' death that they did not see after all. The disciples will return to Galilee defeated.

But not blind. Mark's Gospel concludes with a young man, dressed in a robe of white, telling a group of women that Jesus has risen. "But go, tell his disciples and Peter that he is going ahead of you to Galilee; there you will see him, just as he told you" (16:7). In his death Christ reveals the blindness of his followers. In his resurrection Jesus gives his followers eyes to see the good news of God's ongoing reign.

VICTOR MCCRACKEN

Pastoral Perspective

silenced by institutional pronouncements, the so-called reprobate whose cry stands us still in our tracks. How easy it is to let the manageable needs of a congregation buffer ministers from those who await word of God's mercy on the margins, especially at this time of the year! There are stewardship messages to deliver, programs to get up and running, buildings to keep in repair. Yet here is a man who throws off his cloak, springs up, and comes to Jesus with great expectation and a disarming clarity. "Rabbouni, let me see again," he pleads. Think of those for whom faith is matter of life and death rather than social convention. When our ministry is marked by encounters with the blind who want to see, the lame who want to walk, the leper who wants to be cleansed, we catch a glimpse of what it must be to come close to Jesus. For through them we hear the word he speaks to us anew.

"I am thinking about Jesus," writes the woman I baptized at eighty-four. She appeared one Advent, asking about the whereabouts of our advertised brunch. She never left. "If I had been in Hitler's Germany," she once said to me, "I would be a lampshade." The crowd often wishes she would be silent and leave me alone. I selfishly seek her out. The most theologically astute member of the congregation, she reads Barth, Pelikan, Reinhold Niebuhr. But more to the point, she knows just what she wants Jesus to do for her. "Often, I think about Jesus when I have a particular difficulty with people. I think of Jesus coming into the room. I do not need to explain to him. He understands. He sees an ancient person, scorned, misunderstood. I know what he would say. I have no doubt. I know that he would understand all that I cared about with such great passion, to speak the truth, to live the truth."

CYNTHIA A. JARVIS

Exegetical Perspective

me"), we may hesitantly propose that Bartimaeus shouts to Jesus, "Help me!" Whereas the other time Jesus heals a blind man, the cure requires two applications of Jesus' miraculous saliva (8:22–25), in this case the impediment to healing comes from the crowd that stifles Bartimaeus's plea. When Jesus summons the blind man, the crowd encourages him with another hard-to-capture expression, about which the translations diverge more widely: "Cheer up!" (NIV), "Don't be afraid" (CEV), "Take heart!" (NRSV, REB), "Courage" (NJB). Of these, the NJB's "Courage" best captures the ordinary sense of the word, but misses the colloquial ordinariness of the Greek.

The directness with which Jesus accepts the connection between the "Son of David" and the Anointed One should caution preachers not to construct invidious distinctions between "political" and "spiritual" messiahship; after all, the Hasmonean dynasty had fused the offices of high priest and king years ago. Thus, the Anointed One whom 12:35–37 identifies with the Son of David will have represented a liberation that was not limited by such categories. Likewise, in the final verse of the pericope, Jesus indicates that Bartimaeus's faith has "made [him] well" (NRSV), or "healed" (NIV) or "saved" (NJB) him. The Greek verb in question, *sōzō*, serves for salvation from both physical and spiritual dangers. The highly charged Christian usage of "saved," however, would not have occurred to a Markan audience; although both meanings resonate in Mark's usage, the more ordinary Greek sense ("rescue") should prevail. Jesus is not taking sides in a Reformation debate!

Instead, Mark shows us Jesus making the transition from his role as an itinerant healer to the fullness of his identity as the regal Son. The interaction between Jesus and Bartimaeus manifestly invokes both those roles, and Bartimaeus demonstrates persistent reliance specifically upon the Son of David as the one who could restore his sight. In the healing of Bartimaeus, Mark gently affirms Jesus' identity as the anointed Son, but Jesus accepts that role by helping a noisy beggar. Together, the healer and the beggar recognize in one another more than the distracting, misguided crowd (or the imperial forces, or the temple establishment) understands: that regal authority comes to divine expression in deliverance, in persistence, in fulfilling the vocation of recognizing and strengthening one another.

A. K. M. ADAM

Homiletical Perspective

The Gospel writer locates the power of this miraculous encounter in the initiative of the man named Bartimaeus. He calls out to Jesus. He comes to Jesus. He articulates his desire to receive his sight. Jesus enables this process by asking him: "What do you want me to do for you?" Jesus asks no such question when, based on the faith of some friends, he forgives and heals a paralyzed man (2:1–12); or when the man in the synagogue comes to him with a withered hand (3:1–6). But this passage brings together faith, wholeness, and discipleship.

In this conversation, Bartimaeus uses *rabbouni* as the title of honor. It may be that he has comprehended that discipleship will involve teaching, learning, understanding, seeing, and hearing. If that is the case, then Bartimaeus is an excellent candidate. His request that he should see becomes the pathway to his salvation. In other words, he is not only allowed to see physically. He is granted the mercy that allows him to see the way of salvation. His healing may also be contrasted with that of the blind man who is led out of the village, has saliva placed on his eyes, and is healed in stages as Jesus lays hands on him twice (8:22–26). Unlike this man, Bartimaeus, in familiar Markan language, is healed immediately and follows Jesus on the way.

Finally, Bartimaeus is a model of discipleship because he is a person of faith (10:52). His capacity to see and comprehend reminds us that the disciples seem not to perceive or understand, to see or to hear (8:14–21). In this passage, Jesus draws attention to the faith of Bartimaeus (cf. 2:5); and we are invited through the words of Jesus to see the relationship between faith and wholeness, faith and salvation. These elements are powerfully combined when we hear and respond to the words of mercy: Go, your faith has made you well. Go, your faith has healed you. Go, your faith has made you whole.

LINCOLN E. GALLOWAY

Wisdom of Solomon 3:1-9

¹But the souls of the righteous are in the hand of God,
  and no torment will ever touch them.
²In the eyes of the foolish they seemed to have died,
  and their departure was thought to be a disaster,
³and their going from us to be their destruction;
  but they are at peace.
⁴For though in the sight of others they were punished,
  their hope is full of immortality.
⁵Having been disciplined a little, they will receive great good,
  because God tested them and found them worthy of himself;
⁶like gold in the furnace he tried them,
  and like a sacrificial burnt offering he accepted them.
⁷In the time of their visitation they will shine forth,
  and will run like sparks through the stubble.
⁸They will govern nations and rule over peoples,
  and the Lord will reign over them forever.
⁹Those who trust in him will understand truth,
  and the faithful will abide with him in love,
  because grace and mercy are upon his holy ones,
  and he watches over his elect.

Theological Perspective

Today's reading from the Wisdom of Solomon anticipates Christian doctrines of the communion of saints, life after death, and the justice of God. The passage celebrates human connection with the deceased and insists that human perceptions regarding the dead are not as they seem. In this Greek world that splits body and soul, the writer proclaims that the souls of the righteous are in "the hand of God." People who are not wise, people who lack faith, and who accept what only their senses tell them, think death is a disaster, an experience of destruction, and a cause for despair; but the contrary is true. The righteous have triumphed in death, and rather than being in torment, they are at peace. People may think death is punishment, but the hope of the righteous is "full of immortality." For the anonymous author of the book, death is not the end; death is not a tragedy, but a change of being, an entry into full life with God.

   The suffering that preceded death, then, for this writer is only a discipline, a trial that confirms the readiness of the righteous for eternal relationship with God. They have stood among the just, and they have been tested in the fire like gold purified in the furnace. They did not fall away, but now, contrary to human expectations, their new life after death far outstrips the true pain of their sufferings. The writer

Pastoral Perspective

Standing by the apparent finality of the grave, the *Book of Common Prayer* invites the bereaved to pray:

> In the midst of life we are in death;
> of whom may we seek for succor,
> but of thee, O Lord,
> who for our sins art justly displeased?
>
> Yet, O Lord God most holy, O Lord most mighty,
> O holy and most merciful Savior,
> deliver us not into the bitter pains of eternal death.
>
> Thou knowest, Lord, the secrets of our hearts;
> shut not thy merciful ears to our prayer;
> but spare us, Lord most holy, O God most mighty,
> O holy and merciful Savior,
> thou most worthy Judge eternal.
> Suffer us not, at our last hour,
> through any pains of death, to fall from thee.[1]

   This committal prayer has its theological roots in the Wisdom of Solomon. Canonical for some, deuterocanonical for most Protestants, the Wisdom of Solomon is an infrequent visitor to the canon of the Revised Common Lectionary. Even so, chapter 3 has etched its way into the liturgical and pastoral life of Jews and Christians.

1. *Book of Common Prayer* (New York: Seabury Press, 1979), 484.

Exegetical Perspective

There is a Christian festival of remembering and paying homage to all the saints, martyrs, and the faithful deceased. This is All Saints, also known as All Hallows (Hallowmas). In the Roman Catholic Church, it is celebrated on November 1. In the Eastern Orthodox Church, it is celebrated on the first Sunday after Pentecost. All Saints closes off and completes Easter. In select parts of Europe (particularly Spain and Portugal), Central America, and the Philippines, family members and friends visit grave sites to pray and remember the dead while others celebrate by sharing meals and singing at those graves. Some even take flowers and candles. In the evening, all those lit candles create an illuminating display of burning light—to signify the presence of God and of each beloved soul. For those in the Reformed tradition, the festival has been preserved as a day to remember those who have passed. The text before us deals with an important question of what happens to the soul after death.

The Wisdom of Solomon is a first-century-BCE exhortatory text written in Greek by a Middle-Platonist Hellenistic Jew in Alexandria, Egypt (a contemporary of Philo of Alexandria, someone with favorable outlooks on eunuchs [3:14–15]). The book is thematically divided into three broad rubrics: (a) Wisdom and Immortality (chaps. 1–6), which

Homiletical Perspective

From the onset of chapter 3, we see that the author is responding to claims against the "righteous." Death and suffering are in question here too, as with the Ruth passage this week and last week's lectionary reading from Job. This Wisdom passage attempts to overturn the judgment of the "ungodly" from the previous chapter. In chapter 2 we discover that the ungodly rationalize that our principled efforts of righteousness are in vain. As their reasoning goes, life is determined by our immediate realities. Its purpose does not point beyond libertine values and direct pleasures. In fact, life is defined by death and any escape from suffering that we can secure.

Actually, the ungodly believe a virtuous path in life to be foolhardy. The only sensible pursuit is one's own joy in life (2:6–9). This pursuit is not based in apathy, but in enmity. It argues for the exploitation of even the frail righteous (2:10–11). The call to oppress the marginalized righteous or the proponents of social justice does not find correction in its own absurd reasoning. This antagonism appears to stem from "righteous judgment" (2:12–16).

Preachers should take care here. How we preach righteousness can actually propagate enmity. Surely some of us do resent the call to virtue and justice before God that places God or the neighbor before our own pursuit of personal fulfillment. Yet, when

Wisdom of Solomon 3:1-9

Theological Perspective

exalts in their acceptance by God and offers a poetic glimpse of the fate that awaits them, when they "will shine forth" and "run like sparks through the stubble." These dead are fragments of the light, blazing into eternity with God and joining in the governance of nations. When they guide the world from their place in the afterlife, the Lord will rule over them forever. This means the dead and the living are united with each other and with God, the true ruler of all.

This passage marks a bridge between the testaments, because it elaborates on intimations of the afterlife that Christians will later expand and develop. For those left behind, the dead are not dead. Instead, it is as if they are behind a veil, their glory and vindication seen but dimly. But with full hope and confidence the poet proclaims that the righteous are alive in God. The living and the dead are still connected and related to one another. And the living can know that the suffering of those now dead has meaning, was not for nothing, and that divine justice will finally be realized. Compared to the peace and eternal life the dead now know, their sufferings are small indeed. The amplitude of love overcomes the horrors of their pain. Instead of punishment, their deaths have given them entrance into life with the Lord, a life of love, of grace, and of mercy.

The Wisdom of Solomon does not speak of resurrection from the dead in the same ways Christians understand it, but the passage stammers in that direction, anticipates it, and makes theological space for it. Because the martyrs have died in persecution and seemingly in shame and tragedy, human reflection can perceive only the successful reign of evil and injustice. But the holy ones, the righteous ones who endured their travails, now live with God. As God's elect, their souls survive and continue to be present to God and in "communion" with the living.

God's justice is at the heart of the new revelation in this passage. In face of the death of the martyrs, it appears as if evil wins over all and as if living a righteous and faithful life is meaningless. The wicked triumph and the good suffer. This passage is a lyrical challenge to such a nihilistic view. It insists in urgent terms that the justice of God is not always visible. God's justice extends beyond human seeing into the invisible world of eternity, where the righteous receive justice at last, justice so strong and desirable that it vindicates them, gives them peace, and assures them of life with God as well as continued communion with the living.

Pastoral Perspective

By the grave of loved ones, and especially on All Saints' Day, the church listens with longing faith for the promise from the Wisdom of Solomon that "the souls of the righteous are in the hand of God." Years later, John on Patmos would borrow this inspiring image to portray the souls of the righteous seated and singing around the heavenly throne of God (Rev. 4 and 5).

This Wisdom text challenges the deceptive power of appearances. Dirt being flung into a casket-filled grave suggests that the righteous finish this life exactly as the unrighteous—tossed ignominiously into the ʾadam (dirt, earth). For all appearances, it is foolish to think otherwise. That is why the author pushes readers beyond "all appearances." Just as God invites Samuel not to be seduced by the attractive appearances of David's older brothers, but to see the heart of God's chosen servant, David, so the author here invites readers to peer behind all appearances to probe the truth and purpose of God, in life and in death.

Appearances lead believers to reach foolish conclusions. In the arena of suffering, pain, and even death, appearances can easily lead the foolish to conclude that people suffer and die as punishment from God or in evidence of the absence of God. The Wisdom author draws a different conclusion. The author suggests that pain and loss, while often devastating and hardly welcome, can become occasions for the deepening of faith and the broadening of human relationships. Pain and suffering are not whips from God or signs of God's indifference or impotence, argues the Wisdom author, but can become occasions through which believers grow in hope, "For though in the sight of others they were punished, their hope is full of immortality" (v. 4).

As Michael Kolarcik reminds believers in the midst of pain and tragedy, as well as the ones who pastor to those in such circumstances,

> The Wisdom text offers a different perspective on the reality of tragedy and limitations in human life. Tragedy, loss, and death are not the destroyers of ultimate human value. The book of Job is the great precursor to the Wisdom text for modulating the perception and interpretation of tragedy in life. The tragedy of Job's life and family was not the result of his guilt, no matter how much the tradition and the three friends tried to impose such an interpretation on his experience.[2]

---

2. Michael Kolarcik, "The Book of Wisdom," in *The New Interpreter's Bible* (Nashville: Abingdon Press, 1997), 5:471.

Exegetical Perspective

contrasts the eschatological outcome of the righteous and wicked; (b) Solomon and Mortals Should Seek Wisdom (chaps. 7–10), which describes how the righteous should seek Sophia to become more righteous; and (c) Wisdom and Israel (chaps. 11–19), which describes God's favorable dealing with Israel in contrast to God's dealing against the Egyptians (Exod. 7–14).

The Souls of the Righteous (vv. 1–3). The prelude for chapter 3, "But the souls of the righteous are in the hand of God, and no torment will ever touch them," actually begins in 2:23–24, "for God created us for incorruption, and made us in the image of his own eternity [or nature], but through the devil's envy death entered the world, and those who belong to his company experience it." The author obviously has the following texts or teachings in mind: Genesis 3, *Apocalypse of Abraham* 23, *Apocalypse of Moses* 16, and Zoroastrianism (the original world was perfect but corrupted by an evil spirit). By these precepts, 3:1 has a positive disjunctive spin that all righteous souls are in God's hand—and because the souls are in God's domain, they shall not perish but have eternal life. In Wisdom, there is a deliberate concern for the soul, since it is the essence of humanity (1:4, 11; 2:22; 3:13; 4:14; 7:27; 2 Esd. 2:45; 7:13, 96). Another distinctive group that was tremendously concerned with the soul in light of Platonic philosophy, albeit centuries later (second to the fourth century CE) were the gnostics (who produced the Gospels of Thomas, Mary, and even Judas).

A powerful competing ideology of what happens after life during the time of Wisdom of Solomon was that all souls—good or bad—went to Sheol (the place of the dead) until they were judged on the final day. As questions concerning afterlife crystallized, a more developed and complex question was whether the soul went to paradise immediately upon death or whether it first went to Sheol and then, on the final day, received judgment that allowed for its entrance into paradise. Verses 1–3 speak clearly to this debate, saying that all righteous souls will experience paradise, that is, "no torment will ever touch them" (v. 1b). Here is a definitive answer that even though there may be suffering and hardship in the present era, the souls of the righteous will bypass Sheol and immediately encounter peace (vv. 2–3) in the afterlife.

The Birth of Purgatory (vv. 4–6). For the Catholic community, here is a biblical (deuterocanonical)

Homiletical Perspective

we do preach righteousness, the tragic risk would be to characterize that resentment as proof of our divine sanction. What results is a distortion of God's faithfulness, of which the passage for today intends to assure us. We therefore mistake spiritual arrogance for faith. Preachers discover another course in this Wisdom passage, however. The message arises in overcoming the arrogance of ungodly interpretations of life.

Widsom 3:4 underscores the prevailing depiction of righteousness as futile. This verse is a fulcrum to the contrapuntal claim. The author counteracts the impact of the ungodly argument embedded in our mortality. And so chapter 3 picks up the defense of faithfulness from chapter 1. Death is not the evidence of righteous futility or divine judgment. The ungodly hold that the very prospect of death liberates humanity from the demands of any righteousness defined in moral sensibilities, social ethics, or justice.

Quite to the contrary, Wisdom holds that death becomes the occasion wherein immortality vindicates righteousness. Death itself belongs to unrighteousness. God did not create the world with humanity designated for eventual death. God created us for life eternal (1:13–15). The virtuous way of life is dramatically shown to be in line with God, but not simply in some vacuous "stamp of approval." Righteousness and just pursuits are intended in the very design of creation. God created humanity to be in righteous relationship with God and with one another. The third chapter of Wisdom argues that God fulfills God's own commitment to creation with the gift of immortality to the righteous. God's faithfulness becomes the hope and source of faithfulness for the righteous.[1]

A comparison with the lectionary readings from Job and Ruth (Propers 25 and 26) underscores a theme of justice and how we interpret the experience of suffering or death. Wisdom 3:4 contends directly with the theological worldview that suffering and death indicate divine punishment or judgment. Correlation of these lectionary passages reveals that God is working toward justice and peace for the faithful and all creation. Accordingly, verse 4 explicitly identifies major trouble then in classifying suffering and death in the guilt or charge of God's judgment.

Still, another closely related question looms large: How are we to understand the language of

1. Michael Kolarcik, SJ, "The Book of Wisdom," in *The New Interpreter's Bible* (Nashville: Abingdon Press, 1997), 5:446–47, 451.

Wisdom of Solomon 3:1-9

Theological Perspective

This breakthrough extends insights articulated in the book of Daniel (12:2) regarding the afterlife, and it continues the broadly held theological assurance of the Old Testament that God makes life out of death, that God turns the empty future into a fruitful garden, that God is the ruler of all that is. When the Wisdom of Solomon picks up these themes, it introduces new insights made possible by Greek thought where the soul is separate from the body. In this passage, the souls of the righteous do not die but live forever. For Christian doctrine, however, the afterlife is not the continuation of the immortal soul passing over into the new realm of eternity. Christian doctrine extends this belief to insist on the radical nature of the life-giving power of God to raise the dead. As God raises the dry bones of dead and destroyed Israel (Ezek. 37), so Christians believe that individuals die completely, and that God raises them to new life, body and soul. Such is our hope that God will act on our behalf as God has done already in Jesus Christ. Christian belief builds on this reading from the Wisdom of Solomon, affirming the text's fundamental revelation of God's freedom and of God's control over life and death.

The celebration of All Saints' Day in Christian churches commemorates the holy ones who have died and gone before us and now are alive in God. They are the great cloud of witnesses who call us to righteous life, who are united with us even when we cannot see them. They urge us to live within the reign of God now no matter the cost. The saints are models of holiness and righteousness. Because they have lived with God and are now in the hands of God, they show us how to live, to endure, and to hold fast through loss, sorrow, and pain, as well as through honors, joys, and triumphs. They lead us to the one true thing in life: communion with God, with one another, and with all the holy ones who have gone before us.

KATHLEEN M. O'CONNOR

Pastoral Perspective

For the Wisdom writer, appearances consistently deceive the foolish into making faulty theological assumptions.

This text speaks not just a final word of assurance about "all the saints who from their labors rest"; it also encourages wise and courageous daily living for individual believers and the community of faith, as "God watches over God's elect" (v. 9). For the people of God to know that "the faithful abide with God in love" (v. 9) is to know what Paul would later declare: nothing "will be able to separate us from the love of God" (Rom. 8:39). This is more than a comforting assurance of things eternal. This assurance is a powerful motivator for the church to "trust in God" (v. 9), to live with the courage of conviction in any setting, in any age.

This Wisdom text points believers to the real power that accrues to those who "trust in God" despite their circumstances. Those who are "wise" in this way can sing for joy by a freshly dug grave in the face of death or sing in a cell with Paul and Silas (Acts 16:25–34) in the face of imprisonment or sing of peace while guards cuff them for protesting a war while on public property.

As long as All Saints' Day is exclusively a day to think back in gratitude for the saints who have gone before us or to think to a distant eternal future with God, this Wisdom text is muted. Wise ones are indeed grateful for the "great cloud of witnesses" that surrounds them and are comforted by a lasting future with God. But they are also empowered by an uncompromising "trust in God" that prompts them not to put their ultimate trust in anyone or anything less.

What would it mean for the church to trust not in a successful stewardship campaign for its future, trust not in the most dynamic pulpiteer for its future, trust not in the most appealing contemporary music for its future, trust not even in its own spiritual piety for its future? What would it mean for the church to make this sapiential word its mission statement: "Those who trust in God will understand truth, and the faithful will abide with God in love, because grace and mercy are upon God's holy ones, and God watches over the elect" (v. 9)?

GARY W. CHARLES

Exegetical Perspective

basis for purgatory.[1] In these verses, the soul is disciplined, tested, and refined— "like a sacrificial burnt offering"—in readiness to join God. This purification takes place so that the soul will meet all of God's will. According to the author, only modest discipline is required for afterlife. One can almost hear the author speaking to those caught in the anti-Jewish uprising in Alexandria, Egypt, during the first century BCE, telling them to be strong, to cling to faith despite their persecutions, because even if they die, this may be seen as an act of God, refining the soul like gold in the furnace (vv. 5–6) so that the soul will be ready for paradise.

In Heaven (vv. 7–9). For the righteous souls then, "In the time of their visitation they will shine forth, and will run like sparks through the stubble" (v. 7). Once in heaven, "They will govern nations and rule over peoples" (v. 8). In these eschaton-laden words we hear the oppressed rising to the top to govern and to rule. But the Lord will reign and watch over all the faithful; and no torment, no war, no tribulation, or sickness, or pain, or suffering shall ever reign again. Here is a glimpse of what the afterlife looks like— "love, grace, and mercy" shall abide with truth resting upon all those who "trust in the Lord."

This text brings us back to the importance of the soul or, more broadly, to the subject of the afterlife. As much as Jesus was concerned for social justice for the poor, his mission and remembered words were also about giving everlasting life (John 3:16), about believing in order to have life in his name (John 20:31), and about the ultimate fate of the soul (Matt. 10:28; Mark 8:36, 37).

The contemporary church is so very concerned about the here and now, about the so-called ushering in of the kingdom of God (that rightfully calls for justice, peace, harmony, and love), but we sometimes fail to emphasize the mission of saving souls. On All Saints' Day, preachers have a text that rightfully calls for attention to the soul and the afterlife!

JOHN AHN

Homiletical Perspective

purification and sacrifice in this passage? We preachers run some risk of promulgating the mistaken message that God intends suffering, even when we discern how the passage overturns presuppositions of divine judgment. Verses 5–6 employ the language and images of disciplining and testing to nurture or burnish faithfulness. Such language makes preaching difficult when we attempt to overcome theological distortions of suffering. An important distinction here is that God does not instigate our suffering, even for some greater good. God desires to work with us even through suffering; this is God's providential activity, which otherwise is commonly misrepresented in our preaching as some fateful divine will of suffering. How we are to understand that God "tries" us (v. 6) will be difficult to decipher for the preaching task.

As a whole, this passage is quite useful for both pastoral and prophetic preaching. Pastoral preaching might pick up on themes of reassurance for discipleship. Clearly the thrust revolves around the brunt of death and suffering that ravages faith with despair, guilt, or hopelessness. The Wisdom literature offers one of our early pastoral appeals to God's promises of eternal life to empower faithful living in the face of tribulation.[2]

This passage also speaks prophetically in the same appeal to righteousness and God's faithfulness. Mercy and love are the gifts for living both here and beyond. Social justice is upheld as God works to fulfill God's intended future in creation. The promise in chapter 3 extends from the end of chapter 2. Herein we find that the ungodly are blind to God's own perseverance to guide creation into eternal life (2:21–24). Creation is designed for life with God. This design in humanity unfolds in justice and righteousness rooted in the love of God.

Preachers today can hear the echo of Martin Luther King Jr. in such an avowal: "The arm of the moral universe is long but it bends toward justice."[3] King found moral authority for justice in God's love and purpose for creation and in God's faithfulness to work with us. This witness is a prophetic foundation of the Wisdom passage today.

DALE P. ANDREWS

---

2. Ibid., 446.
3. Martin Luther King Jr., "Our God Is Marching On!" in *Testament of Hope*, ed. James Melvin Washington (San Francisco: Harper & Row, 1986), 230; for King's theological philosophy behind this famous quote, see "An Experiment in Love," *idem*, 16–20.

1. See Jacques Le Goff, *The Birth of Purgatory*. trans. Arthur Goldhammer (Chicago: University of Chicago Press, 1981).

Psalm 24

¹The earth is the LORD's and all that is in it,
  the world, and those who live in it;
²for he has founded it on the seas,
  and established it on the rivers.

³Who shall ascend the hill of the LORD?
  And who shall stand in his holy place?
⁴Those who have clean hands and pure hearts,
  who do not lift up their souls to what is false,
  and do not swear deceitfully.
⁵They will receive blessing from the LORD,
  and vindication from the God of their salvation.
⁶Such is the company of those who seek him,
  who seek the face of the God of Jacob. *Selah*

Theological Perspective

Christian tradition prizes this psalm as a celebratory hymn to the resurrected Christ. Yet the psalm also situates salvation within God's creative activity and offers contemplation about how saints may approach the Lord's presence.

Creation and Salvation (vv. 1–2). God the Creator promised that his people would dwell in Eden-like peace where "they will not hurt or destroy on all my holy mountain" (Isa. 11:9) once the earth recovers full knowledge of her Creator. Christ the Word of God, through whom "all things came into being" (John 1:3) "became flesh" (John 1:14) for the purpose of restoring knowledge of God, transforming all "who believed in his name" into "children of God" (John 1:12–13). When the faithful proclaim that "the earth is the LORD's," they justify their hope that God will be "the God of their salvation" (v. 5). The psalm builds to a joyful welcome for the Creator who enters as king, foreshadowing Jesus' petition: "your kingdom come" (Luke 11:2).

Theodoret of Cyrus (ca. 393–457) appreciated how God's rule derives from creative goodness and provision rather than from violent coercion. Life emerges from abundant and gracious waters (v. 2) even as Christians receive life in baptism. Alternately, Augustine of Hippo (fifth century) drew attention to

Pastoral Perspective

How appropriate that Psalm 24—subtitled by Charles Spurgeon "The Song of the Ascension"[1]—should be designated in the lectionary as the psalm for All Saints' Day!

For Christian readers, this text goes beyond a celebration of the entry of the ark of the covenant into Zion (the probable theme of the Hebrew psalmist) to give us a preview of the ascension of the risen Christ into heaven (the focus of those of us who live on this side of the cross). For Christians, the remembrance of this homecoming and the promise of our own resurrection enable us to sing this particular psalm on this memorial day with heightened appreciation and deepened adoration of the God who loves us in spite of ourselves and enfolds us in places of unparalleled glory and grace.

Psalm 24 is conveniently divided into three sections, which can be interpreted in terms of the past (vv. 1–2), the present (vv. 3–6), and the future (vv. 7–10). Similarly, the three portions may be described along the more intentional lines of celebration, instruction, and expectation.

The psalm begins with a joyful acknowledgment that "the earth and all that dwell therein"—including

1. Charles H. Spurgeon, *The Treasury of David*, vol. 1 (Grand Rapids: Zondervan, 1963), 374.

⁷Lift up your heads, O gates!
 and be lifted up, O ancient doors!
 that the King of glory may come in.
⁸Who is the King of glory?
 The Lord, strong and mighty,
 the Lord, mighty in battle.
⁹Lift up your heads, O gates!
 and be lifted up, O ancient doors!
 that the King of glory may come in.
¹⁰Who is this King of glory?
 The Lord of hosts,
 he is the King of glory. *Selah*

Exegetical Perspective

Preparations for Worship. Today's reading is a lyrical performance of God's people preparing for exquisite worship at the sanctuary. The reenactment consists of three interrelated parts: a confession of YHWH as creator and lord of all (vv. 1–2), the conditions for worship (vv. 3–6), and a celebration of YHWH's return to the temple as triumphant ruler (vv. 7–10). As such, the psalm reflects a certain liturgical logic: it opens with a buoyant affirmation of YHWH's sovereignty, an astounding reason for praise; it then moves to a series of inquiries as to what is required for temple access; and it culminates in an antiphonal greeting of the divine king who takes up residence in the temple. While the poem beckons the congregation to join the festive throng, it acknowledges that worship is not to be taken for granted or treated casually. Close proximity to the "king of glory" demands court etiquette: clean hands and pure hearts are prerequisites for holy access.

Confession of YHWH as Creator and Divine King (vv. 1–2). Psalm 24 opens with a stunning confession that the world belongs to YHWH. The prepositional construction in verse 1 ("to YHWH . . .") denotes ownership. The earth is God's handiwork; it is God's possession and rightful domain. Such an assertion has polemic undertones: if the earth belongs to

Homiletical Perspective

The military language in Psalm 24 may be offensive to some. The language grows out of Israel's remembered experiences of knowing God as the one who brings victory in times of battle. It is language that intends to paint a picture of a God who has created the world and who is powerful within it. If this is not a helpful metaphorical "playing field" for preacher and community, an important question arises: what is? What are the metaphors that speak most graphically and helpfully about God's active agency and power in the world around us? This exploration could build the foundation of a strong sermon that explores theological understandings and affirmations in a local context.

"The earth is the Lord's and all that is in it, the world, and those who live in it" (v. 1). This is a simple and yet profound affirmation that is often taught to us through music even as children: "He's got the whole world in his hands, he's got the whole wide world, in his hands." This psalm provides the preacher with an opportunity to explore this affirmation with the congregation. Does God hold the world in God's hands? What are the evidences that this is the case? There may be times when we as individuals or communities may doubt this is true. If it is, then we must struggle with our own understandings of systemic evil and sin.

Psalm 24

Theological Perspective

God's creative foundation of the church, a community of salvation stabilized above the unsteady "waters" of our desires.[1]

Entering God's Presence (vv. 3–6). Coming before the Lord is serious business. The psalmist warns against approaching God too casually. Purity assumes exclusive orientation toward God: no drifting toward false gods (v. 4). At the same time the Creator is concerned with actions arising from pure hearts. Those who would "ascend" to God must be clean of thoughts and actions that harm others.

If these are the requirements, then humanity seems doomed to separation from the "face of the God of Jacob" (v. 6). Yet even Augustine, famed for his gloomy assessment of humanity, did not exclude such a God-ward orientation. He thought believers could pursue their longing to be in God's presence through the church, which consists of believers of all nations on "earth" (v. 1). Those in the church already enjoy the benefits of God working within them. The church is a community of grace where temptations can be overcome and the faithful may be lovingly prepared for immortality. When souls look to the eternal and allow themselves to be shaped by divine stability and simplicity, actions of like kind radiate toward neighbors.

Theodoret likewise contemplated how saints-in-training (v. 4 "souls") must purge false thoughts and desires (v. 4 "what is false"), thereby rooting out the source of sinful acts. In characteristic lavishness, God responds to "the fruits of these virtuous actions" with "blessing," which is always "mercy." For "all the righteousness of human beings is not nearly sufficient for gifts bestowed by God, and certainly not for those yet to come" (v. 4).

Entry of the King of Glory (vv. 7–10). This dialogue prompts reflection on the places where Christ enters. Within early Latin and Greek translations of the Psalms, "heads" was translated "princes" or "rulers," understood to be angels, demons, or even earthly elite. In either translation, the question remains: why are the gates closed to the King of Glory?

Some surmised that the heavenly gatekeepers may have balked at receiving humanity in the risen Christ. Athanasius of Alexandria (293/296–373)

Pastoral Perspective

us and every member of the family of humanity— were created by God and belong to God. The fullness of the earth is not ours, but belongs to God. The blessings of our lives—indeed, our lives themselves—are gifts from God, given for a time, but eventually repossessed by the One who lends them to us. This is the past we all share and celebrate as the heirs and stewards of creation.

The second section of the psalm (vv. 3–6) speaks to how we live our lives in the present, and instructs us in what is necessary on our part to "ascend the hill of the LORD."

The directives outlined are few, and echo more sentiment from the Beatitudes than the Commandments—clean hands, a pure heart, a humble spirit, integrity and honesty. These are infinitely more difficult to keep than the mandates against theft and adultery and the taking of another life. They are more subtle, easier to mask and deny, and can compromise us when we don't even realize it.

The Bible tells us what is expected of us: that we do justice, love mercy, walk humbly, love God above all, and love our neighbors as ourselves. And the waters of baptism are given to wash clean the dirtiest hands.

This may sound simple to our Christian ears, but since that first day of creation, when God lifted land out of water and gave order to chaos, only one being—Christ, the Word made Flesh—fulfilled the requirements to "stand in the holy place" of God, completely and perfectly undefiled.

In the last verse of this section (v. 6) we find God's grace extended to the rest of us, the "generation of those who seek . . . the face of the God of Jacob" (RSV). Even "seeking" has a sanctifying influence. What a consecrating power lies in finding and enjoying the Lord's face and favor! God knows and understands our human weaknesses, suffers and endures with us, and longs to welcome us into the divine presence.

The closing verses of the psalm (vv. 7–10) consist of questions and answers, set in a dialogue between the seekers and the gatekeepers, and it is here that the association with All Saints' Day becomes a reality for us—where our expectations of a future lived out in the presence of God find their confirmation.

With jubilation, the cry goes out for the "gates and everlasting doors" to open up and admit the King of glory. The seekers ask, "Who is this King of glory?" and are told, "The LORD, strong and mighty, the LORD, mighty in battle!" For Christians, this Lord is Jesus Christ, who through his death and

---

1. Theodoret of Cyrus, "Commentary on Psalm 24," in *Commentary on the Psalms*, trans. Robert C. Hill, Fathers of the Church 101 (Washington, DC: Catholic University of America, 2000), 159–62. Augustine of Hippo, "Psalm xxiv," in *Expositions on the Psalms*, Nicene and Post-Nicene Father, series 1, vol. 8 (1886), 61.

Exegetical Perspective

YHWH, then it does not belong to rival powers! YHWH's sovereignty subverts every competing claim of authority, including those made by rulers, nations, military complexes, and princes and principalities. YHWH reigns over all who inhabit the planet.

For a marginalized community manhandled by the empire and its fleet of self-aggrandizing rulers, this reading of reality is clearly audacious. Dangerous historical powers and unwieldy forces of nature evoke poignant questions: Who is actually in control? Is the God of Israel impotent or indifferent? Is raw political power ultimate power? Such queries are not merely intellectual curiosities, but concrete focal concerns, concerns for meaning, survival, and hope. So the psalm's initial utterance is nothing less than a bold counterintuitive assertion that YHWH is utterly reliable.

This initial confession impinges upon the assembled in another way. It suggests from the start that Israel owes undivided allegiance to this God. Since the earth and all that is in it belong to YHWH, worship defines the community's raison d'être.

Divine sovereignty is rooted in creation. YHWH has established the earth firmly on the primal sea. In ancient Near Eastern cosmology, seas and rivers represent dangerous primeval forces of chaos—forces that jeopardize both the stability of the universe and the quality of life within community. In Genesis 1, God creates order and beauty out of the life-threatening and incoherent watery abyss. With the dawning of the new heaven and earth, the "sea"—and its deluge of destructive powers—passes away (Rev. 21:1). In Psalm 24 metaphor and mythology converge in joyous celebration of YHWH's sovereign rule on earth.

Conditions for Worship and Fellowship (vv. 3–6). Although YHWH's rule is universal, the sanctuary represents the special place of YHWH's palpable presence. Here YHWH takes up residence as divine king. Here God confers blessing and righteousness. But entrance into God's presence requires great care, as a voice in the liturgical performance testifies: "Who shall ascend the hill of the LORD . . . and stand in his holy place?" Rather than responding with a long list of legal requirements or ritual obligations, another voice answers tersely: "Clean hands and pure hearts." Those who stand in God's presence must not trade in falsehood; worshipers should neither lift up their soul to what is false nor swear deceitfully. These two conditions may appear rather arbitrary but they actually

Homiletical Perspective

The psalm also gives the preacher the opportunity to explore her or his own understanding of creation theology. What is the importance of understanding God as creator? Historically, some have thought that believing in God as creator means believing in a God who has power and authority over the world. This enormous power of God is one of the potential connections between the psalm and All Saints' Day. What does acknowledging God as creator say about God's relationship to our dying? Others think that God being the creator means God knows intimately all that has been and is created.

Psalm 24 provides one of the clearest indicators that the psalms were part of the community's cultic ritual. This psalm is a liturgical song that is sung as worshipers approach the temple. Those on their way to worship are ascending the holy hill to the temple mount, the holy place. What does God hope for in those who come seeking blessing? The psalmist lists four attributes wanted by God: "clean hands and pure hearts; [those] who do not lift up their souls to what is false, and do not swear deceitfully." For the psalmist these are the four markers of a right relationship with God. What does it mean to have clean hands and pure hearts? Do these together represent inner (heart) and outer (hands) purity? Are the four qualities listed by the psalmist the four we would choose to define righteous living? What are the preacher's markers for right relationship with God? What are the community's markers? What are the ethical qualities and attributes that are emphasized in the congregation's teaching and preaching, week in and week out?

This psalm gives the preacher an opportunity to think about these very important questions. Such reflection is important, because what are emphasized as important moral and ethical standards vary radically from one community to another. When the community remembers the "saints" of the congregation or community, what are the qualities admired most in them?

The second part of Psalm 24 is a responsive reading used during worship; it is a liturgy spoken or sung upon entering the sanctuary and may have been used in association with the procession of the ark. Note the repetition of the word "glory" (vv. 7, 8, 9, 10). The preacher would do well to linger here a while. The word "glory" does not enjoy common usage in most of our contexts. What does it mean?

The Hebrew word *kabod* often translated "glory" is also translated "honor." It is used heavily in the Psalms and by the prophet Isaiah (First, Second, and

Psalm 24

Theological Perspective

observed that surely the gates were not closed to their Creator; instead Christ carried humanity on a new "path to heaven": his body. The heavenly host questions why human nature is seeking entry, for until restored in Christ, it has not approached. Looking for the King, Theodoret mused, the angels saw only Christ's human nature and battle scars, "and [did] not perceive the divinity concealed within." Western Christians often linked this dialogue with Christ's descent to hell. The fifth-century *Gospel of Nicodemus* depicts Hades behind closed gates, asking, "Who is this King of glory?" Christ, "the LORD, mighty in battle" on the cross, subsequently breaks the gates of hell, defeats death in his own realm, binds Satan, and rescues the saints.[2]

Finally, why do humans fail to welcome Christ? Augustine challenged local leaders ("rulers") to remove ("lift up") the "desires and fears" that block Jesus' entry within them. Sinners avoid inviting a God for whom suffering and humility are saving tools. Humanity fears separation from comfortable sinfulness. With the eyes of faith, believers should not be deterred by the apparent weakness which the King of glory exhibits in the bloody battlefield of his body where death was defeated.

Martin Luther berated Christians for scorning God's everyday miracles in everything from agricultural production to family life to Christ crucified. "But we are deaf, blind, and stupid; nor do we marvel at anything except at those things that appear to be extraordinary." Christ's story is too familiar to attract attention. Humanity loathes the Suffering Servant and the "inconveniences" of ordinary life. "Yet He is the Son of God, the King of glory, and the salvation of all men." Humanity deceived by worldly eyes sees only the marks of sin on otherwise good things. To see and welcome the King of glory, his ordinary miracles that sustain life, and even his humble presence in plain wine and bread, requires viewing the world through the Word which is both Scripture and Christ.[3]

LISA D. MAUGANS DRIVER

Pastoral Perspective

resurrection has won the battle with death, and of whom there could be no doubt about his authority to enter into the presence of God. Of all who ever lived, this "spotless Lamb" alone was justified.

Again the cry arises, "Lift up your heads, O gates! and be lifted up, O ancient doors!"

Hebrew poetry often uses repetition for emphasis to underscore urgency or jubilation, and here the insistence mounts beyond a request to raise the gate just high enough, or the doors just wide enough, for the King of glory to enter and then to be slammed shut in the face of the seekers. Rather, the intent is for the gates to be raised so high above the walls that they will never be shut again, and for the doors to be flung off their hinges, in order that the seekers and followers of the Lamb may follow him, redeemed and welcomed, into the courts of God.

The barriers to paradise, like the stone rolled away from the empty tomb in the garden, have been pushed aside to give us unfettered access to behold the smiling face of a gracious and accepting God, whose mercy, rather than our own merits, enables us to pass through the open door.

All Saints' Day, once an often-overlooked festival day in the church calendar, is becoming more and more a part of the life of many congregations.

In our Easter celebrations, we rejoice in the resurrection of Jesus Christ and acknowledge with thanksgiving and praise that death has been defeated. We sing "Jesus Christ Is Risen Today" with confidence that this article of our Apostles' Creed has been achieved.

But on All Saints' Day, we sing "For All the Saints Who from Their Labors Rest" and celebrate the fulfillment of the closing tenets of the creed by confessing our belief in the resurrection of the body and the life everlasting. We see the open gates and everlasting doors in front of us, through which faithful seekers in every generation have passed, and through which we too, by God's grace, will one day follow in Christ's footsteps and join the hosts gathered around the throne of God.

MICHAEL MORGAN

---

2. *On the Incarnation*, chap. 25, Nicene and Post-Nicene Fathers, series 2, vol. 4 (1892), 50. *Gospel of Nicodemus*, II. 5(21)–8(24), Ante-Nicene Fathers, vol. 8 (1871): 436–37.

3. Gen. 21:1–3, in *Lectures on Genesis*, trans. George V. Schick, in *Luther's Works*, ed. Jaroslav Pelikan and Walter A. Hansen (St. Louis: Concordia Publishing House, 1964), 4:4–8. See also *The Sacrament of the Body and Blood of Christ: Against the Fanatics*, in *Luther's Works*, 36:338.

express the core values of the Bible: love for God and neighbor.

When people "lift up their souls" to that which is false, they break the first commandment—to have "no other gods before me"—and so disfigure the face/character of God. When people "swear deceitfully" or commit perjury, they disfigure the face/character of women and men created in the image of God. Both threaten the fabric of faithful living. Both endanger the integrity of community life. And both do violence to the sanctuary. Put positively, as in the poem, those who practice covenant loyalty—to God and neighbor—enjoy access to the holy place *and* receive blessing from God. "Such is the company of those who seek . . . the face of the God of Jacob" (v. 6).

Celebrating God's Arrival (vv. 7–10). When preparations are in place, the celebration begins! The chorus of voices, perhaps the divine assembly itself, ushers in the arrival of YHWH as glorious king. Accompanied by an entourage that includes faithful Israel (vv. 3–6), YHWH is escorted to the throne. The temple gates rise in honor; indeed all welcome this valiant God with cheers of acclamation. The language is exuberant; antiphonal call and response heightens expectation. The cadence of invocation—repeated invocation—awakens the senses to another world order: the kingdom of God.

The entrance liturgy celebrates the return of One who is triumphant over world-destroying nations and chaotic forces of nature. Not unlike the song of Moses that celebrates YHWH's victory over Pharaoh's "horse and rider" (Exod. 15:1–18), the last four verses of Psalm 24 reenact YHWH's glorious kingship and unrivaled power.

Such alternative speech turns ordinary social convention on its head. Now poetry displaces raw power, and worship subverts warfare. This liturgical performance of God's reign on earth mocks pretentious world powers that claim to have the last word. It revels in the enormous power of theater. And in this theater of worship, YHWH, the "King of glory . . . YHWH, mighty in battle" eclipses every arrogant ruler and nation. What is more, the divine warrior returns to the holy place to reside with God's people. YHWH's jubilant processional empowers the wounded and vulnerable to defy despair and embrace a counter–world order. To be sure, this astonishing parade is a celebration of audacious hope. "Who is the King of glory? The LORD of hosts, he is the King of glory" (v. 10).

LOUIS STULMAN

Third) and Ezekiel. It is a poetic word that connotes something important about the nature and essence of the God we worship *and* about how we are to respond to that God.

The word translated "glory" can mean "heavy" or "weighty." It can mean the majesty or honor that is accorded to another human being. Lastly, it can refer to God's majesty. All of these meanings are interrelated and are rooted in the idea of weightiness/abundance/greatness/ importance. Thus, to honor God or to give God glory is "to make God weighty," or to give God the weight that is due.[1] We honor God's honor; we give glory to the glory of God. That the Hebrew word *kabod* holds both these meanings is demonstrated in the following two psalms:

Psalm 19 begins, "The heavens are telling the glory of God." Glory here has something to do with the enormousness (greatness/abundance) and beauty of God who created the world and all that is in it. Glory speaks a word about richness, treasure, brilliance, and the goodness of God.

Psalm 29 begins, "Ascribe [or give] to the LORD glory and strength. Ascribe to the LORD the glory of his name; worship the LORD in holy splendor." In our worship we are to acknowledge the glorious qualities of the God we serve. We give glory.

The question for the preacher, then, is how does the listening community honor the greatness of the God they worship and serve? In what ways is the glory of God that fills the earth up to the heavens acknowledged in prayer and song and word?

MARY DONOVAN TURNER

---

1. "To Be Heavy," in *Theological Lexicon of the Old Testament*, ed. Ernst Jenni and Claus Westermann, ET (Peabody, MA: Hendrickson, 1997), 2:590.

Revelation 21:1-6a

¹Then I saw a new heaven and a new earth; for the first heaven and the first earth had passed away, and the sea was no more. ²And I saw the holy city, the new Jerusalem, coming down out of heaven from God, prepared as a bride adorned for her husband. ³And I heard a loud voice from the throne saying,

"See, the home of God is among mortals.
He will dwell with them;
  they will be his peoples,
  and God himself will be with them;
⁴he will wipe every tear from their eyes.
  Death will be no more;
  mourning and crying and pain will be no more,
  for the first things have passed away."

⁵And the one who was seated on the throne said, "See, I am making all things new." Also he said, "Write this, for these words are trustworthy and true." ⁶ᵃThen he said to me, "It is done! I am the Alpha and the Omega, the beginning and the end."

Theological Perspective

We are all familiar with "stories of origin"—narratives that describe the circumstances from whence we come. We have family stories that chart the journeys of our ancestors, whether long ago or relatively recently, to the places that we have learned to call home. From childhood, we listened to fanciful tales of the origin of things, like Rudyard Kipling's *Just So Stories* ("How the Leopard Got Its Spots," among others). And of course, Christianity and Judaism point to the book of Genesis as something like the *ultimate* story of origin: how the world, and everything that dwells therein, came to be created by God.

Of course, limitless ink has been spilt over the question whether such stories ought to be regarded as literal descriptions of empirical reality, or interpreted as figurative accounts expressing a moral purpose, or even (as in the case of Kipling's tales) chalked up to the overactive literary imagination. Regardless of how such questions are resolved, however, these stories tell us something about *ourselves*; they focus our attention on our roots, the ultimate *sources* of our lives. Such stories are known, collectively, as etiologies, accounts of the origins of something (from the Greek word for "cause"). Etiologies have tremendous explanatory power in helping us understand where we came from and why we are here.

Pastoral Perspective

The book of Revelation can make parishioners nervous. One never knows what craziness someone may find in it. From the start, the official compilers of Scripture did not know what to do with Revelation. When the New Testament was put into its final form toward the end of the second century, the revelations ascribed to John the Divine barely made it into the canon.

Divine revelation, in whatever form it takes, and whatever the source, can be dangerous stuff—the stuff of ideology and violence. The images and obsessions of the book of Revelation have perhaps wreaked more havoc in people's lives—created more strife, fomented more demonic fantasies, misled more people—than any other book in the Bible. To a hostile reader (and in the history of this book there have been many such readers) the book is absolute craziness—disjointed, inconsistent, violent, madly repetitive. But even its severest critics recognize the power of its cadences, the seductiveness of its symbols, the mad glories of its theophanies, the elemental resonance of its presiding myths. The dragon with the seven heads, the women clothed with the sun, the Lamb upon his throne, what the Dante scholar Peter Hawkins has called "the cubed jewel box" of the heavenly city[1]—these are symbols

1. Peter Hawkins, "Famous Last Words," in *Heaven*, ed. Roger Ferlo (New York: Seabury, 2007), 32.

All Saints

Exegetical Perspective

The book of Revelation concludes with a word of hope and the promise of new beginnings. The beginning of the twenty-first chapter contains a double vision of a new earth and a new heaven out of which the holy city (the new Jerusalem) comes down from God (vv. 1–2). This is followed by a reference to two messages, the first from the celestial throne (vv. 3–4) and the second from the one seated upon the throne (vv. 5–8). This brief scene sets the stage for the remainder of the book with its description of the holy city (21:9–22:6) and its reaffirmation of the final coming of Jesus (22:6–21). The apocalyptic language and the images in this portion of the chapter echo the hopes of the Old Testament prophets and other early Jewish apocalypses. The message affirms God's final triumph and the outcome of the struggle of the faithful. But in this affirmation there is a significant protest against the difficulties, tribulations, and persecutions of which many Christians were victims at the end of the first century of the Common Era.

The first vision is of a new heaven and a new earth. The language echoes the message of Isaiah 65:17 ("For I am about to create new heavens and a new earth; the former things shall not be remembered or come to mind") and 66:22 ("For as the new heavens and the new earth, which I will make, shall remain before me, says the LORD; so shall

Homiletical Perspective

While presenting some difficulties of interpretation to the preacher today, the book of Revelation also offers evocative, moving images of comfort and hope to those who live in troubled times. The preacher might help the congregation appreciate the richness and beauty of some of these images by locating the book in its historical context. John of Patmos, exiled during a time of severe persecution, writes a letter of comfort to seven churches undergoing persecution, urging their members to remain steadfast and assuring them that despite all appearance to the contrary, the Roman Empire's power is not absolute; it is God who reigns supreme.

The preacher might also help the congregation understand the apocalyptic genre of writing, to which the book of Revelation belongs. A sermon might begin by describing some of the features of this recognized literary genre, symbolic language being one noticeable example, extravagant and sometimes frightening imagery another.

A prominent feature of apocalyptic writing that figures strongly in today's reading is the use of visions. John's visions lift him out of everyday life to a heavenly realm where he can view earthly existence from God's perspective. We who read John's visions can likewise be transported. We can be put in the position of suddenly seeing our own day-to-day lives

Revelation 21:1-6a

Theological Perspective

These "stories of origin" have a logical counterpart: "stories of destination," which tell us where we're going. These are not nearly as prevalent in our culture; typically, we find it easier to look into the past than to look into the future. Of course, we have access to various technologies that keep the past relatively "present" to us in ways that would have been incomprehensible to people in the ancient world. For them, the past was not that much more transparent than was the future; in both cases, *stories* were what one had to rely on in order to understand anything outside of the present—whether past or future.

In fact, it is even a bit misleading to think of "where we are going" only in terms of the future, because a *destination* is not limited to temporal sequence. To speak of "where we are headed" in a larger, broader sense is to inquire into our ultimate destiny. So, just as a story of origin offers us more than just a descriptive play-by-play account of events that led up to our present moment, so do "stories of destination" provide more than a sequence of future events. Rather, they answer the question "Where are you going?" in a much broader sense: Where are you headed? In what direction is your life taking you? What is your true destination? Such stories are the converse and counterpart of etiologies. They are eschatologies: accounts of the end (and not just in the sense of temporal finality, but also in the sense of purpose or goal).

The book of Revelation is an eschatology in this larger sense, though it is often read only as predicting a temporal sequence of events (and thus much misunderstood). Just as the book of Genesis is meant to help us understand our origins in the broadest terms, so the book of Revelation is intended to help us understand our ultimate destination. The answer to both questions—where we are from and where we are headed—is the same: God. Our ultimate origins are in God, and our ultimate end is in God as well. As T. S. Eliot wrote, "In my end is my beginning":[1] our final destination is the same as where we started. Some ancient Christian thinkers identified this pattern with the Latin words *exitus* and *reditus*: all things come forth from God, and all things ultimately return to God.[2]

As noted above, our culture is much less effective at developing persuasive eschatologies than it is at developing etiologies. We tend to operate with a

---

1. T. S. Eliot, "East Coker," in *Four Quartets* (New York: Harcourt, Brace & World, 1943), 32.
2. On this matter, as in so many others, Augustine's *Confessions* is a remarkably profound resource.

Pastoral Perspective

that have shaped the religious imagination of the West for two thousand years.

But pastorally, we know that to the credulous insider, these are no mere symbols. This book is a map of the future. It is propaganda for the elect. No detail is too trivial, no symbol too opaque for the believer who is determined to read his or her own agenda into this compendium of apocalyptic fantasies from an age long past. The book of Revelation has been used to justify all manner of things: revolution and counterrevolution, anti-Catholic polemic, Christian Zionism, pietistic quietism, sectarian violence. The book can be a happy hunting ground for bigots and fanatics, and the distortions of its purpose and its meaning are as rampant today as they were two millennia ago. One need only look at the marketing figures for the *Left Behind* series to be convinced of this book's enduring and questionable power.

So why invoke Revelation on a feast day like All Saints? In many Christian denominations, All Saints is a great feast of the church *as* church. It is a day that many liturgically minded traditions set aside for public baptisms, where the candidates are said to be newly numbered in the company of the saints, adopted children of God destined to become citizens of a heavenly city, the new Jerusalem. Further, it is no accident that this reading from Revelation, celebrating the holy city where "death will be no more," has been associated since ancient times with rites of Christian burial.

These associations are not accidental or forced. Passages like this from Revelation are neither the mad fantasy of an obsessive paranoiac nor a divinely dictated plan for the future. Revelation is at its heart a book of consolation, a vision of comfort for a people persecuted and in distress. It is often hard for Western Christians to imagine what persecution might be like—a life lived in fear and trembling, always on the run, always faithful, never sure. It is the kind of life that the emperor Diocletian inflicted on the early Christians who wrote and preserved this book. They were the first saints of the church, brothers and sisters in the faith, risking all that they had for the sake of a name—the name of Christ, which they knew was above all other names, including the name of the emperor himself. For Diocletian, what was at stake was a matter of state control, including control of the religious imagination. For Christians, what was at stake was control of their inmost identity. In putting on Christ in baptism, they had been made citizens of a heavenly city, a city not made by human hands, and

All Saints

your descendants and your name remain"). Both verses announce hope and a new future to the Israelites in exile. This new heaven and earth replace the old creation that has already fled from the presence of the white throne (20:11, "Then I saw a great white throne and the one who sat on it; the earth and the heaven fled from his presence, and no place was found for them").

A particular characteristic of this new creation is that the "sea was no more" (21:1). The book of Revelation's view of the sea is generally negative. In the Jewish apocalyptic literature, the sea is a representation of the chaos, the evil power of the underworld (*1 En.* 60:7–25; *2 Esd.* 6:49–54). For instance, out of the sea comes the ten-horned beast (Rev. 13:1–10). The great whore sits on "many waters" (17:1–2). In the new creation, there is no space for such chaos and death.

The second vision of the chapter describes the holy city, "the new Jerusalem," coming down from God (21:2; see also 3:12). As in the new creation of heaven and earth, the prophetic hope included an expectation of a restored city (Isa. 52:1; 54:11–17; Ezek. 40–48; Pss. 46; 48). Early Jewish apocalyptic literature also imagined that Jerusalem was preexistent in heaven, from whence it will come at the end of time (*4 Ezra* 7:26; 8:52; *2 Apoc. Bar.* 4:2–6). The new Jerusalem "comes down out of heaven from God." The image is not simply a description of place, but of transcendence. The new heavenly Jerusalem contrasts with the "great city" Babylon, which has fallen (18:1–24). While Babylon was a curse for humanity, the new Jerusalem is a blessing (21:3–4).

The new Jerusalem is described as "prepared as a bride adorned for her husband." Revelation has previous allusions to a marriage of the Lamb and the bride (19:6–9, see also 22:17). It seems that Revelation merges the two images of the new heavenly Jerusalem and the bride of the Lamb. We can find precedence in the Old Testament, where Jerusalem was portrayed as a woman (Isa. 1:8; 49:14–23; Jer. 4:31). In contrast to the image of Jerusalem as a bride, the city of Babylon is called a great whore (17:1–6). The new Jerusalem is the realization of the ideal community. The language echoes the propaganda language of the cities of Rome and Babylon, which promoted themselves as the ideal cities. While these cities promoted injustice, exploitation, and idolatry, the new Jerusalem promotes the continuous presence of God among God's people (21:3–4).

Verses 3–4 report a message from a loud voice (see 11:12; 12:10) "from the throne" (see also 16:7;

from God's point of view. A sermon might explore how this enlargement of vision could transform our understanding of our own reality. How, for example, might struggles and conflicts within the church look from this perspective? How might the difficulties of family life be transformed? What effect could this enlarged perspective have on our behavior as a nation? How, for example, would we respond to the fact that in the United States we incarcerate more people (mostly young men of color) than any other nation on earth, past or present? How might our imaginations, inspired by John's cosmic vision, be activated to help us respond to the impending catastrophes caused by global warming? What actions might we take?

In today's reading, the vision of the new Jerusalem is resplendent with imagery of renewal, beauty, and comfort in times of suffering and grief. The "holy city" comes "down out of heaven from God." It is a vision of the church at the end of time, and, because it partakes of the eternal, it is present and available to us now. Jesus' teaching in the Gospels that the kingdom of God is with us now finds an echo in this passage. "See, the home of God is among mortals"; community is where God dwells with God's people. A sermon might discuss this image of the new Jerusalem in terms of our church lives today. How does the understanding that God is with us now in community express itself in our worship? In what ways does our church community fall short of the understanding that God is present with us and among us now? Can our worship life be renewed by an incorporation of John of Patmos's transcendent vision? What holds us back from incorporating such a vision?

A sermon could also explore this image of the holy city in terms of our life in community in general. On the one hand, community itself can be seen as a gift from God. The human ability to work with others is a part of creation, our capacity to cooperate enabling us to achieve that which would be impossible to the lone individual. Our creativity, which expresses itself in and through community and which is not possible without community, both comes from God and is an expression of God's presence. That being said, one needs only to look around to see the fallen nature of earthly communities. Our schools, our churches, our local governments, our businesses, our police forces, our national governments—all institutions fall short of the divine purpose for which they were created. New Testament scholar Walter Wink in his 1992 book *Engaging the*

Revelation 21:1-6a

Theological Perspective

concept of time that is largely linear and points indefinitely into the future. We have some idea of where we came from, but we are less specific about where we are going. Think of the time lines that are depicted along the bottom edge of the pages in a history book: they mark certain years as important, but they have no definitive end. They just point vaguely into the future, suggesting that "time marches on" and that everything will continue to grow and develop (presumably in a beneficial, or at least a relatively benign, form). But where, exactly, are we headed? The dominant story of our culture seems to be that we are headed "everywhere at once"—which means, of course, that we are headed nowhere in particular.

One of the most significant features of the Christian narrative is its clear conception of eschatology. Of course, if that eschatology is merely a prediction of a sequence of temporal events, such as one might expect from soothsayer or a psychic, then it will have little persuasive power. But as a story of our true destination, it can provide real healing—particularly when contrasted with indistinct arrows pointed vaguely toward an indeterminate future. Christians believe that we are headed *somewhere in particular:* we are headed back to God. This is true not just for individuals but in a larger, collective, sense: eternal communion with God is the proper destiny of the church, the nations, and the entire created order.

This is the upshot of the vision of the heavenly Jerusalem in Revelation 21. God and human beings dwell together, just as they did at the beginning, before the fall—for God is the beginning and the end. No surprise, then, that the description of that new city (which continues into the next chapter) includes a garden with the tree of life, endlessly fruitful, with leaves that heal the nations (Rev. 22:2).[3]

DAVID S. CUNNINGHAM

Pastoral Perspective

could do no other than act in the name of the Christ for whom they themselves were named, the Alpha and the Omega, the beginning and the end.

How these people suffered, how they recanted, how they died, how they escaped such persecution—of these matters very little is known to us. But in passages like this, we do know how they imagined their freedom, should it ever come. And even after two millennia, in this startling vision of God's triumph, contemporary Christians can catch a glimpse of their own fears and their own hopes. What these people saw was extraordinary. They were Jews become Christians in a Roman world, members of a heretical wing of a minority faith barely tolerated by a brutal empire. Yet what they saw and preached was a vision of universal humanity, a new heaven and a new earth, a holy city coming down from heaven, prepared (in that powerful apocalyptic marrying of things heavenly and earthly) as a bride adorned for her husband. "And the one who was seated on the throne said, "See, I am making all things new." No wonder they wrote all these things down, for in a world of shifting values and imperial terror, they knew that these words of consolation and promise were "trustworthy and true."

Once you have heard them in the revival tents pitched on Wednesday nights in the impoverished neighborhoods of a Northern city, in sermons that echo the ancient cry of the persecuted and the dispossessed, it is hard to get these cadences out of your mind. To hear this reading on All Saints' Day is to hear a summons to solidarity with all those who have suffered in their witness to Christ—whether in the farthest reaches of the first-century Roman Empire or in the drug-ridden streets of an American slum; whether on an abandoned road in Central America or in the faceless precincts of a Burmese prison. When a part of the body suffers, all suffer—their tribulation is ours, and so is their hope.

"Write this, for these words are trustworthy and true."

ROGER A. FERLO

---

3. See the thoughtful commentary on this symmetry in Steven Bouma-Prediger, *For the Beauty of the Earth* (Grand Rapids: Baker Academic, 2001).

Exegetical Perspective

19:5) announcing the quality of life in the new Jerusalem. The loud voice announces that God's tabernacle (*skēnē*) is among the people, that God will dwell (*skēnōsei*) with humans (21:3). Earlier the tabernacle was the object of blasphemy by the beast (13:5–6), and it was found in heaven (15:5). That God establishes a tabernacle (dwelling place) among humans is another way of expressing God's continuous presence with the people. Community and communion unite God and the inhabitants of the new Jerusalem, which include people from "every tribe and language and people and nation" (5:9), people "from every nation, from all tribes and peoples and languages" (7:9). There is no racial, language, or ethnic discrimination in the new Jerusalem.

As announced in 7:17b ("God will wipe away every tear from their eyes"), God's presence with God's people brings welfare to all. Here the writer of Revelation echoes the prophetic hope (Isa. 25:6–8; 35:10; 65:17–25) that God "will swallow up death forever. Then the Lord God will wipe away the tears from all faces, and the disgrace of his people he will take away from all the earth, for the Lord has spoken" (Isa. 25:8). The last clause of verse 21:4 closes as an *inclusio* of 21:1 with the phrase "first . . . passed away."

Verses 5–6a report a message directly from God ("one who was seated on the throne"). It first reaffirms the statement of verse 1 ("I am making all things new") and then instructs John to write the words because they are trustworthy (see also 19:9; 22:6). The content of the writing includes both that God is making everything new and that God will dwell with the people. God's direct statement interprets the visions and the messages of the loud voice as God's action. The creation of a new community in communion with God is not the result of history but the purpose of history.

The selection ends with God's self-acclamation as the eternal God. This God, Lord of creation and community, finishes and completes the work ("It is done!"). As in 1:8, the statement "I am the Alpha and the Omega" describes God's creative power (see Isa. 48:12–13) and sovereignty.

DAVID CORTÉS-FUENTES

Homiletical Perspective

Powers says of human institutions that they are simultaneously created, fallen, and redeemed (that is, they at times may fulfill the purpose for which they were created). We become able to see this about our communities when we can enlarge our perception to include the cosmic dimension. How can John of Patmos's image of the holy city inspire us to open our eyes and our imaginations to incorporate such a transcendent understanding of our institutions? How might such an understanding affect our behavior in our various communities? What might we as individuals and as a church do to help those around us understand and appreciate the nature of our institutions, in order to work toward transforming them, toward helping them to serve their original purpose in creation?

John of Patmos's transcendent vision of the holy city is also a very appropriate reading for today, All Saints' Day. Today we view existence from the perspective of eternity. We honor the saints who have come before us, whose examples we wish to follow, and also the saints who are alive today, and the saints who will come after us. We understand also that by virtue of our baptism we are saints as well. We belong to the communion of saints—past, present, and future. In this holy community we partake of the divine.

A sermon might make this clear to the congregation by describing the lives and teachings of particular saints. The description might include people who have lived recently or who are alive today whose lives have been exemplary. A sermon could also focus on an exemplary act of an ordinary person who is not understood to be a saint in the conventional sense. Such a sermon might help us to understand how we too are saints, how in our everyday lives we too can be examples of God's love and compassion for others to follow.

GINGER GRAB

John 11:32-44

32When Mary came where Jesus was and saw him, she knelt at his feet and said to him, "Lord, if you had been here, my brother would not have died." 33When Jesus saw her weeping, and the Jews who came with her also weeping, he was greatly disturbed in spirit and deeply moved. 34He said, "Where have you laid him?" They said to him, "Lord, come and see." 35Jesus began to weep. 36So the Jews said, "See how he loved him!" 37But some of them said, "Could not he who opened the eyes of the blind man have kept this man from dying?"

38Then Jesus, again greatly disturbed, came to the tomb. It was a cave, and a stone was lying against it. 39Jesus said, "Take away the stone." Martha, the sister of the dead man, said to him, "Lord, already there is a stench because he has been dead four days." 40Jesus said to her, "Did I not tell you that if you believed, you would see the glory of God?" 41So they took away the stone. And Jesus looked upward and said, "Father, I thank you for having heard me. 42I knew that you always hear me, but I have said this for the sake of the crowd standing here, so that they may believe that you sent me." 43When he had said this, he cried with a loud voice, "Lazarus, come out!" 44The dead man came out, his hands and feet bound with strips of cloth, and his face wrapped in a cloth. Jesus said to them, "Unbind him, and let him go."

Theological Perspective

On All Saints' Day the church turns its attention to the deceased saints of her past, men and women whose lives bear witness to a hope rooted in the gospel that proclaims God's victory over death. John 11:32–44 is brimming with good news appropriate for this day. In an age of war, famine, epidemics, and genocide, the church offers its persistent countertestimony to the voices of nihilism and woe. In the raising of Lazarus, God steadfastly refuses to allow death the final word. Christ, who declares himself to be "the resurrection and the life" (v. 25) freely enters into the suffering of the world that God loves.

Theologically, this passage dances around an important issue that has plagued ancient and contemporary accounts of God's nature. Traditional Christian theology has been substantially influenced by the Greek philosophical concept of *apatheia*, an attribute that defines God as one whose perfection leaves God unaffected by the contingencies and circumstances of the created order. Calvin, for example, argues that biblical references to divine emotion need to be interpreted as anthropomorphisms intended to convey what is ultimately incomprehensible.[1] God is the

1. See, for example, Calvin's *Commentary on Isaiah* lxiii, 9: "The Prophet testifies that God, in order to alleviate the distresses and afflictions of His people, Himself bore their burdens; not that He can in any way endure anguish, but by a very customary figure of speech, He assumes and applies to Himself human passions."

Pastoral Perspective

The disciples thought Lazarus was asleep and would wake. Martha and Mary knew their brother would not have died had Jesus been present. Some opined with hostility that if a blind man could be healed by God's Word, a mortal could be kept from death. All three responses are known to those of us privileged to represent the faith in the valley of the shadow. The widower's glib denial of grief ("What is everybody so sad about?"), the pathos of a parent leaving the NICU ("Why were these prayers for my child not answered?"), the hostility of a family before an open grave ("What sort of God would allow this to happen to such a good person?") bring to mind the words of the chorus in W. H. Auden's *For the Time Being*: "We who must die demand a miracle." Or if not a miracle, we demand a reason. From the perspective of our denial, our pathos, and our hostility, we think the reason is beyond our ken and the miracle has been delayed.

This was certainly the case for Martha and Mary and their friends who had gathered to weep with them. Though in this particular case, the latecomers to the scene *had* been given a reason for the delay. Lazarus is dead, said Jesus bluntly to the disciples. He is dead so that you may believe. But believe what exactly? On a Sunday when the witness of those who have died in faith is remembered, the substance

Exegetical Perspective

The Gospel reading for All Saints' Day tells the familiar story of the raising of Lazarus. Cut off from preceding incidents, though, the pericope intensifies the uncanny atmosphere of the actions and feelings that John reports. Why is Jesus angry (*embrimaomai*, vv. 33 and 38)? Why does he cry (since he apparently knows that there will be no stench, because his Father always hears him)? What are we to make of Jesus' loud prayer "for the sake of the crowd"? The interpreter may need to expound a particular element of the passage, in the context of the day's liturgy, and not try to resolve every puzzle that the reading stirs up.

The verses of this lesson derive their intelligibility from the more extensive Bethany narrative that comprises 11:1–53. The larger story provides contextual information that helps resolve this passage's puzzles (though it provokes others). The chapter as a whole depicts Jesus as God's agent in bringing the dead to life; thus Jesus betrays no concern for Lazarus when others fear for his life (even though some scholars identify Lazarus with the Johannine "beloved disciple" on the basis of such repeated affirmations of Jesus' love for him as appear in these verses, and of the rumor reported in chapter 21 that the beloved disciple might not die). Instead, Jesus explains that "[this illness] is for God's glory, so

Homiletical Perspective

The intriguing drama of the raising of Lazarus unfolds with several important episodes preceding the scene in which the dead man comes forth from his tomb with his face, hands, and feet wrapped in cloth. He carries the stench and the look of death, and yet this final picture is worth a thousand words conveying hope, promise, and fulfillment. This moment reminds the faithful of what Jesus said earlier in John's Gospel: "Very truly, I tell you, the hour is coming, and is now here, when the dead will hear the voice of the Son of God, and those who hear will live" (5:25).

The congregation will celebrate All Saints' Day cognizant that it is surrounded by many witnesses, some of whom are wrapped in funeral clothing, standing where faith intersects with both the words and the gift of life. First come the words of life, because woven throughout the Gospel of John is the message that anyone who hears the words of Jesus and believes in the one who sent him has eternal life (5:24). Second comes the gift of life, because the figure that stands in the tomb is an affirmation of life, of eternal life, of the words of Jesus, and of the one who sent him.

The congregation may be reminded that the story begins with assurances and remembrances of love. Martha, Mary, and Lazarus are members of a family

John 11:32-44

Theological Perspective

"unmoved mover" whose perfection precludes God from experiencing real suffering and loss. For God truly to experience suffering is to render God's sovereignty over creation somehow suspect.

This text in John's Gospel, however, raises an important question about the traditional notion of divine impassibility. If Christ is, as John says, the Word made flesh (1:14), then what does this out-pouring of emotion at Lazarus's death convey about the nature of the triune God? Christian interpreters have posed numerous answers to the question. Some interpreters have adopted a dualistic understanding of Jesus' person that sharply distinguishes Jesus' divine and human natures. From this perspective, Jesus' weeping in this text is an outgrowth of his humanity, in no way related to his unique status as Son of God. Others suggest that Jesus is troubled in spirit (v. 33) because of the failure of the crowd to understand the nature of death and his own identity as God's Son.[2] John Chrysostom offers another possibility, claiming that Jesus' weeping was a rhetorical ploy, a way to arouse sympathy within the crowd by condescending to their weakness.[3]

What is common to each of these interpretations is their reticence to admit the possibility that Christ's experience of suffering bears directly on how one understands God's own relationship to suffering. If one can set aside for a moment the desire to reconcile this episode with traditional theological concerns, this text offers another possibility. The God of the church, embodied in the triune relationship of Father, Son, and Spirit, is not unaffected by the suffering and loss of the world. Jesus looks upon the grieving of Mary, Martha, and the Jews with compassion and empathy. In his weeping, Christ is not bowing to human nature, nor is he pained by the failure of the mourners to understand the nature of death. Jesus weeps for the death of Lazarus and for the pain of those who loved him. The good news of this text is that in Christ God freely enters into this suffering.

But this is not the end of the good news. The scene that John paints juxtaposes words and images that accent the finality of death—"If you had been here, my brother would not have died," "Lord, already there is a stench because he has been dead four days"—with a concluding imperative declaration that heralds a stunning new possibility:

2. See Leon Morris, *The Gospel according to John,* New International Commentary on the New Testament (Grand Rapids: Eerdmans, 1971), 557–58.
3. John Chrysostom, "Homily 63," in *Saint John Chrysostom, Commentary on Saint John the Apostle and Evangelist: Homilies 48–88,* trans. Sister Thomas Aquinas Goggin, SCH (New York: Fathers of the Church, 1960), 181.

Pastoral Perspective

of our own faith in the face of death is literally on the table.

For the most part, if people in the pews believe at all, they believe as Martha believed, in the resurrection on the last day. So they endure the death, the mourning, the crying, the pain. They grieve, yet grieve not as those who have no hope concerning those who have "fallen asleep" (1 Cor. 15:6, 18). They may even anticipate "a feast of rich food, a feast of well-aged wine" on that day when we will dine together again with Christ in the kingdom. In the meantime, the time of accident and disease, of slow dying and sudden endings, the operative eschatology is future tense, and the reigning ethic is private morality. The miracle awaits its time. Until then, we tell ourselves that we will know (the monstrous reason) by and by.

But Jesus counters Martha's future tense with his presence, speaking the words we repeat each time the great congregation gathers to weep in common: "I am the resurrection and the life. She who believes in me," Jesus must have said to Martha, "though she were dead, yet shall she live. And whosoever lives and believes in me shall never die. Do *you* (singular) believe this?" Shifting her syntax ever so slightly, Martha confesses her faith in Jesus as the Messiah, the Son of God, the one who *is to come* into the world. In most congregations, we speak of the Parousia in this way: Messiah is the One who is to come when the sun gives out or we do the planet in. It is a secular apocalyptic fit into the religious imagination. Therefore, in the interim we soldier on, doing our part to hold back the inevitable decay of our body and the demise of the earth as our home. By our ethical action in the world, we mean to deny death its victory until Jesus returns.

Finally we read that Mary comes to where Jesus was (even though the lectionary would have us begin where we can only arrive). Though she repeats, word for word, the speech of her sister, it is Mary's grief that renders God's Word silent. Jesus weeps, his tears constituting the only conscionable theological response we often can make when called to the side of the grieving. To another's lament and longing for a reason from on high, we speak of the God who weeps with us. We know this, we say, because in his weeping—over Jerusalem, at Lazarus's tomb, and in the Garden of Gethsemane—Jesus reveals the pathos of a powerless almighty God. This is not a future promise but a present reality, we confess, though our confession often stops short of the next scene.

"Take away the stone," Jesus commands. Like Martha, the realist, we balk at this dress rehearsal for

All Saints

Exegetical Perspective

that the Son of God may be glorified through it" (v. 4). Thus John presents the whole sequence as an elaborate object lesson of God's life-giving power, operative in Jesus. When Jesus says that Lazarus's sickness is not fatal, indeed that he is *glad* that he was not there to heal Lazarus (v. 15), he presumably already envisions his friend's resurrection; the appearance of callousness on Jesus' part presumably indicates that John had different features of the story in view. This sort of clue suggests that the whole Bethany narrative aims less toward unfolding the texture of Jesus' relationships with Lazarus, Mary, and Martha, and more toward illustrating Jesus' glorious power over death.

If John tells this story mainly to show Jesus' authority over death, his treatment of feelings should be read as commentary on that main purpose. This point clarifies the difficulties surrounding *embrimaomai*, which contemporary translations represent as an indication of general emotional turbulence, with glosses such as "greatly disturbed," "greatly moved," and so on. These obscure the element of anger that characterizes *embrimaomai* in conventional Greek usage in favor of depicting a Jesus who is more acceptably "distressed" at his beloved friend's death; but this gentler sense of the word seems to be attested only in conjunction with Jesus, which suggests that interpreters have sought to tone down Jesus' wrath.

Among readers who acknowledge the note of anger in *embrimaomai*, most have proposed that Jesus is angry at people's lack of faith. Others have proposed that Jesus is angry at the Jews, who weep in verse 33, but who would betray him later on ("some of them went to the Pharisees and told them what he had done," v. 46). The case for lack of faith points to the group of the Jews who responded to Jesus' tears by wondering why so powerful a healer did not protect Lazarus from dying in the first place. They phrase their question so as to indicate that they expect the answer, "Yes, one would think he could have," an attitude that indicates a guardedly positive degree of faith in Jesus.

Since John ordinarily shows no hesitancy about identifying lack of faith in his characters, the fact that he gives no such indication here undermines the claim that unbelief irritates Jesus in these verses. The charge of hypocrisy against the Jews of verse 33 likewise falters for lack of evidence. In verse 45, John notes that "many of the Jews therefore, who had come with Mary and had seen what Jesus did, believed in him." Surely these were not guilty of

Homiletical Perspective

whom Jesus loves (v. 5). Lazarus is described as the one whom Jesus loves (v. 3); and Mary is recalled as the one who anointed Jesus with perfume and wiped his feet with her hair (v. 2). Toward the end of the story, love is publicly displayed as Mary kneels at the feet of Jesus and weeps. The Jews who have come from Jerusalem to console the family are weeping with Mary. Jesus joins in the weeping, so that the observing Jews remark on his love: "See how he loved him!" (v. 36).

However, the love of Jesus for this family is superseded by his work of making God known. This revelatory work is presented in the discourse in terms of daylight and night, sleeping and waking, life and death. The work of Jesus belongs to the daylight and stands on the side of life. The figure in the shadow of the cave is called forth into light and life.

The revelatory work of Jesus has its own time and purpose. Jesus chooses his own time, and so he stays two more days in the place where he was (v. 6). Jesus chooses to return to the region of Judea where some have recently picked up stones to stone him (10:31). The disciples begin to understand Jesus' actions in terms of certain death. The disciple Thomas says to the others, "Let us also go, that we may die with him" (11:16). This setting has the signs and the aura of death: mourners, weeping, a tomb in a cave with a stone laid across the entrance, and grave cloths. In the midst of it, Jesus is visibly shaken (vv. 33–35, 38). Yet his words are about life, and his actions convey life. Jesus speaks of himself as the resurrection and the life (v. 25). He gives instructions to take the stone away. He calls with a loud voice for Lazarus to come out from the tomb. He instructs those standing around to unravel the grave cloths and set Lazarus free.

As the miracle of life unfolds, the glory of God is revealed for those who desire to see. What is revealed here is the life-giving activity of God in the person of Jesus. The followers of Jesus are invited to see the new life that Jesus represents. The story of Lazarus is now no longer about sickness or death, but about resurrection and life and the glory of God. In the same way, the disciples are invited to recognize that when they follow Jesus they are being invited into life.

The congregation will recognize that the Gospel presents Jesus as deeply moved and troubled as he is surrounded by genuine human sorrow and pain. Jesus does not stand outside of the moment as an observer. He participates in the moment and takes within himself the experience of loss that shapes and clothes that moment. In taking upon himself the sorrow and pain of those whom he loves, Jesus

John 11:32-44

Theological Perspective

"Lazarus, come out!" Lazarus, a "dead man" (v. 44) bound from head to foot in burial wrappings, emerges from his tomb. Jesus commands that the burial wrappings, the last vestiges of death, be removed. Through Christ, God, not death, has the final word: "Unbind him, and let him go" (v. 44).

In John's Gospel the resurrection of Lazarus vividly embodies God's ultimate victory over the specter of death. Jesus, who proclaims himself to be "the resurrection and the life" (v. 25), testifies to this truth by raising Lazarus from the grave. The eternal life that Christ makes available is not reserved for some eschatological future but is made available in the eschatological present that Christ inaugurates.

A final word needs to be said about the theological function of the raising of Lazarus. The revelation of the "glory of God" frames the entire episode. Jesus tells Mary and Martha that Lazarus's illness is for "God's glory, so that the Son of God may be glorified through it" (v. 4). Just prior to the raising of Lazarus, Jesus reminds Martha of his words, "Did I not tell you that if you believed, you would see the glory of God?" (v. 40). In raising Lazarus, Jesus reveals the glory of God and in so doing reveals that he is truly sent by God: "I have said this for the sake of the crowd standing here, so that they may believe that you sent me" (v. 42). Thus the raising of Lazarus validates Jesus' own identity as the Word made flesh (John 1:14).

The theological function of Lazarus's raising parallels the function of other signs and wonders in John's Gospel: "These are written so that you may come to believe that Jesus is the Messiah, the Son of God, and that through believing you may have life in his name" (20:31). Those who read John's Gospel, no less than those who witnessed Lazarus's raising, are faced with the choice whether to accept Jesus' messianic claims and to enjoy the eternal life that Christ makes available.

VICTOR MCCRACKEN

Pastoral Perspective

Easter morning. Hence Jesus must exegete the substance of what we are about to see in order that we may believe. See the glory of God, he says. See in death defeated eternal life (another word, says Robert Jenson, for God). See—here, now, *before* you lie to die—the resurrection and the life in him. See in him the God who is (present tense) victor over death. Then live as though the Eternal were now because God is. Live as though death has no power over your days. Live as though you belong, in life and death, to God. This is your only comfort, we try to say to the reasonable crowd that has assembled to pay their final respects.

Realized eschatology is what we learned to call this in seminary, but in the midst of sorrow and grief, real people who live in the face of death before the God who raised Jesus from the dead are simply called saints. They are those who realize before they die that neither death nor life, things present nor things to come, can separate them from the love of God in Christ Jesus. They are those who, therefore, may dare everything for the sake of this one true thing.

Though at the end of the day, we reason, if the story of a man being raised from the dead does not convince them, perhaps an invitation to the table will. Thomas said it well, not knowing what he was saying: "Let us also go, that we may die with him" (John 11:16). "Come unto him, all ye," we begin from behind the banquet prepared for us here and now. Take. Eat. Drink. The miracle is just this: that united in his death by his grace, you may wake from the death that is life without him and live unbound, now and eternally, to God's glory.

CYNTHIA A. JARVIS

Exegetical Perspective

hypocrisy, and this portion of the narrative does not distinguish the delegation who would later report Jesus to the Pharisees from their colleagues. A more plausible reading construes Jesus' anger in the face of death as an appropriate response of one adversary to another. Taking Jesus' anger as hostility to death itself fits the Greek usage, fits John's cosmology, and makes sense of the narrative.

The flow of John 11 begins with the challenging situation: Lazarus is suffering from a fatal affliction, so what will Jesus do about it? Jesus responds by deliberately delaying his visit for several days "so that the Son of God may be glorified." When he arrives too late to prevent Lazarus's death, Jesus assures Martha that he *personifies* resurrection and life.

At this point, the pericope for this morning picks up. Jesus sees Mary and the Jews who accompany her weeping. Confronted with death's effects, Jesus manifests his anger and grief, but even more his powerful authority as the Son. When Jesus commands that Lazarus come out of the tomb, no impediment stymies him. John cites a succession of possible obstacles: death's power as possibly greater than Jesus' (v. 37), the stone in front of the tomb, the stench of decomposition (as a sign that Jesus had already been outdone), the linen that still binds Lazarus. None of these avail against Jesus' command, "Lazarus, come out!"

This pericope, then, poses the cardinal question of 11:1–53 ("Could not he who opened the eyes of the blind man have kept this man from dying?" v. 37) and answers it not with an empty boast, but with the effectual demonstration that Jesus can indeed give life to the dead. When Jesus calls Lazarus out of the tomb, he authenticates his claim to divine Sonship, his claim to embody life itself, and his superiority to the forces of decay and death. Death still affects those who turn to Jesus in faith, as it affected Lazarus and Jesus himself; but John deploys this story to show that even though disciples may still die, death does not *end*, but *interrupts* their life. The glory of God, epitomized for John in the cross and resurrection of Jesus, also breaks forth in the resurrection of those for whom Jesus prays to his Father.

A. K. M. ADAM

Homiletical Perspective

reveals the promise available to all (3:16). In the death of Lazarus, the one whom Jesus loved, we see a precursor to Jesus' own death for those whom he loves (10:17–18). "No one has greater love than this, to lay down one's life for one's friends" (15:13). Ultimately, his act of love will reveal the glory of the one who sent him.

Jesus invites those around him to recognize that divine love and life are revealed in his words and actions. In conversation with his disciples at the beginning of the story, Jesus points to the glory of God as the primary outcome of Lazarus's condition (v. 4). At the end of the story, in his conversation with Martha, the sister of the dead man, Jesus makes the glory of God the promised response to her faith (v. 40). Then Jesus publicly lifts his head in a prayer that intimates his desire to lead the crowd standing there before the tomb in the ultimate doxology.

The final act, in which the dead man responds to the words of Jesus, reflects a very significant moment of revelation of the glory of God. However, as the glory of God is revealed, the invitation to believe that God is working in and through Jesus is presented to all. The words of Jesus to Martha ("Did I not tell you that if you believed . . . ?" v. 40) echo through the centuries to remind us of the faith of Martha and Mary who experience firsthand the glory of God. Today, those words also invite us to believe and to become witnesses to God's glory.

LINCOLN E. GALLOWAY

Ruth 1:1-18

¹In the days when the judges ruled, there was a famine in the land, and a certain man of Bethlehem in Judah went to live in the country of Moab, he and his wife and two sons. ²The name of the man was Elimelech and the name of his wife Naomi, and the names of his two sons were Mahlon and Chilion; they were Ephrathites from Bethlehem in Judah. They went into the country of Moab and remained there. ³But Elimelech, the husband of Naomi, died, and she was left with her two sons. ⁴These took Moabite wives; the name of the one was Orpah and the name of the other Ruth. When they had lived there about ten years, ⁵both Mahlon and Chilion also died, so that the woman was left without her two sons and her husband.

⁶Then she started to return with her daughters-in-law from the country of Moab, for she had heard in the country of Moab that the Lord had considered his people and given them food. ⁷So she set out from the place where she had been living, she and her two daughters-in-law, and they went on their way to go back to the land of Judah. ⁸But Naomi said to her two daughters-in-law, "Go back each of you to your mother's house. May the Lord deal kindly with you, as you have dealt with the dead and with me. ⁹The Lord grant that you may find security, each of you in the house of your husband." Then she kissed them, and they wept aloud. ¹⁰They said to her, "No, we will return with you to your people." ¹¹But Naomi said, "Turn back, my daughters, why will you go with me?

Theological Perspective

The theological ground of today's reading from Ruth is a God of fierce inclusivity, even though God remains largely in the background. The book of Ruth probably arose as a potent critique of the reforms of Ezra and Nehemiah in the period of the restoration of Jerusalem. These two leaders tried to purify Israel and cement its ethnic identity by casting out foreign wives and their children from the land. Ruth is a foreign woman and wife who does not diffuse Israel's essence by being who she is but instead, in a marvelous reversal of expectation, acts as a savior of the nation.

The story begins in dislocation and death. To escape famine in Bethlehem, Elimelech, his wife Naomi, and their two sons flee to Moab, the land of Israel's bitter enemies (vv. 1–5). Death pursues them. Elimelech and the two sons die, leaving three widows. Widows face peril, for without husband or sons they are without support. Naomi's name means "pleasant" in Hebrew, but her bitter life belies all pleasantness and she blames her fate on God. She will later say to her friends, "Call me Mara, for the Almighty has dealt bitterly with me" (vv. 20–21). She perceives herself to be utterly alone and without a future, and so gathers up the human experience of despair. Even as she blames God for her empty life, the name of her daughter-law Ruth foreshadows a reversal of fate, for Ruth means "friend."

Pastoral Perspective

This text from Ruth is a wedding favorite. The irony is that our text is set years after a mixed marriage and immediately after the death of a Hebrew husband. In the first chapter of Ruth, there is not a hint of hope for a wedding for Naomi, who is heading home, or for the alien Ruth, who chooses to follow her. A careful reading of this text would suggest that this is not a "wedding chapter" but sets in motion a "bulldozer book." Set in a situation of grief and barrenness, this chapter introduces us to two women through whom God will tear down some long-admired and carefully crafted walls.

The fact that this book holds canonical status at all is itself scandalous. The heroine in this story is not a Hebrew, but a Moabite widow who was once married to a Hebrew. In a polarized world and in a polarized church, Ruth speaks to us of possibilities, great possibilities that can emerge when we live beyond the walls that would define us and confine us. There is a lively debate about when Ruth was written. However that question is resolved, one can hear the postexilic voices of Ezra and Nehemiah calling for an expulsion of "foreign" wives, along with the strong implication that their society was being polluted by these unwelcome aliens. It is a testimony to those who carved out the canon that Ruth stands alongside these voices for "purification,"

Do I still have sons in my womb that they may become your husbands? ¹²Turn back, my daughters, go your way, for I am too old to have a husband. Even if I thought there was hope for me, even if I should have a husband tonight and bear sons, ¹³would you then wait until they were grown? Would you then refrain from marrying? No, my daughters, it has been far more bitter for me than for you, because the hand of the Lord has turned against me." ¹⁴Then they wept aloud again. Orpah kissed her mother-in-law, but Ruth clung to her.

¹⁵So she said, "See, your sister-in-law has gone back to her people and to her gods; return after your sister-in-law." ¹⁶But Ruth said,

> "Do not press me to leave you
> or to turn back from following you!
> Where you go, I will go;
> where you lodge, I will lodge;
> your people shall be my people,
> and your God my God.
> ¹⁷Where you die, I will die—
> there will I be buried.
> May the Lord do thus and so to me,
> and more as well,
> if even death parts me from you!"

¹⁸When Naomi saw that she was determined to go with her, she said no more to her.

Exegetical Perspective

Ruth is the beloved great-grandmother of King David. But Ruth is a foreigner. She crosses over the border from Moab to become one with the house of Boaz and Israel. In the prehistory of her story, Elimelech, Naomi, and their two sons had also crossed their border to live as resident aliens in Moab, a country with a negative history of religious sexual apostasy (Num. 25:1–2).

The Family Emigration to Moab (vv. 1–5). The narrator briefly relays the situation: "In the days when the judges ruled, there was a famine in the land, and a certain man of Bethlehem in Judah went to live in the country of Moab" (v. 1). This was not a good time to live, for "all the people did what was right in their own eyes" (Judg. 21:25). Without a king or a centralized government, Israel was troubled. But the more pressing problem was famine. Ironically, Bethlehem literally means the "house of food." When Elimelech and Naomi cannot find means to support their family, they seek better opportunities elsewhere. So they take their sons Mahlon and Chilion and immigrate to a new border country called Moab. But immediately, in verse 3, we learn that Naomi has become a widow. Elimelech, whose name means "My God is king," dies. Mahlon and Chilion, who are married to Ruth and Orpah, also die. At the end of

Homiletical Perspective

The transitions generated by the cycles of life present many challenges for congregational preaching. Families go through tremendous tumult with the cycles of death between generations. And the tragic disruptions of death and suffering caused by not-so-natural events make preaching precarious. Chapter 1 of Ruth begins with tragedy and suffering. Famine drives a family from home, and the horrors of three deaths leave any preaching with more problems than revelation. This opening passage is tightly woven. Even in the small details such as the names of the deceased the narrative intends to set up the crisis facing Naomi, Ruth, and Orpah. Exegetes explaining their husbands' names point to some irony or to each one's dreadful fate. Preachers need only to understand the intention to draw out the tragic theological interpretations that the main characters themselves, Naomi in particular, give to their embittered realities.

In fact, Naomi's theological worldview is most evident in the verses immediately following our text this week. Here she renames herself a bitter person (v. 20). The name echoes her claims from verse 13 when Naomi declares that God has moved against her. Naomi writhes under the theological affliction. Actually, in verse 13 and again in verses 20–21, we see that Naomi is overwhelmed by the same theological

Ruth 1:1-18

Theological Perspective

Ruth makes an improbable companion to Naomi and an unlikely character to have a biblical book named after her. She is a foreigner, a woman, a widow, and, perhaps of most importance, she is an enemy of Israel. The book repeatedly reminds readers of Ruth's enemy status by referring to her as "Ruth the Moabite" (v. 22). When Naomi learns that God has given food to the people of Judah, she begins her journey back home to Bethlehem, urging her daughters-in-law to return to their families where the Lord may provide them with new husbands and their own futures. Ruth alone refuses, but Naomi herself remains lost in the bleakness of her situation. She projects that grim world onto the future, but "Ruth clung to her" (v. 14).

Ruth's fidelity receives ample poetic expression in her famous pledge of loyalty, where God appears for the first time in the book. Ruth the Moabite leaves her own people for the sake of her mother-in-law. She will go with, lodge with, and be buried with Naomi. She will die in the same place and will take Naomi's people and Naomi's God to be her people and her God. This vow she seals with a formal oath, calling upon God to punish her and more, "if even death parts me from you" (v. 17). In the ancient world, tribal and family origins firmly fixed one's identity and one's gods, and people did not voluntarily abdicate either. Yet Ruth abandons people and gods to vow undying love for her mother-in-law and for the God of Judah. The outsider is the faithful one, the one who expresses and lives her commitment to God and God's people.

In this reading, theology is hidden and subtle. God does not break into the world in miracles that overturn nature or bring dead loved ones back to life. Instead, God acts through Ruth and her unquestioning fidelity to Naomi. This means that the stranger, widow, and enemy woman becomes the unexpected model of loyalty and devotion. In this story, the loyalty and devotion of the stranger, Ruth the Moabite, will save the line of David. The outsider keeps the nation from extinction; she saves the people, ends barrenness, and gives life to a dying seed. In view of the plans of Ezra and Nehemiah, who were trying to preserve the future by purging foreign influences, the seemingly simple story of Ruth becomes an acerbic political counterclaim and an implicit theological affirmation of God as the God of all people. The God for whom Ruth abandons everything is the God of the lowly, the widow, the stranger, and the enemy. Ethnic purity is not what God demands or desires despite the dominant efforts

Pastoral Perspective

suggesting that a Moabite widow could be an agent of God's radical possibility. Amid the rhetoric of exclusion, the story of Ruth asks us to consider what can happen when "walled worlds" collapse.

In a world suspicious of immigrants, legal or otherwise, this is a story about forced migration. Naomi and Elimelech do not cross into Gentile country because they are religious radicals. They head to Moab because there is no bread in the "house of bread"—Bethlehem. Throughout Hebrew Scripture there is a strong bias against anything good coming out of Moab. It was a place for the people of God to avoid. Moabites were a category of people to avoid. And yet, chapter 1 of Ruth begins in Moab, where not only has a Hebrew family found bread, but their sons have also found wives and a home. As the chapter closes, Ruth will intentionally leave her native land and people to accompany Naomi back to her home. Ruth will leave Moab to confront all the prejudice that such an action will entail.

Scholars debate why Naomi tells her daughters-in-law of ten years to "go back." Is Naomi glad to have this excuse to be rid of these foreign daughters-in-law? Did Naomi fear what people would say when she came home with alien relatives in tow? The fact that Ruth decides to stay with Naomi would suggest otherwise. It may suggest that Naomi knew that not only could she provide no more sons for marriage, but she could not provide enough food for her daughters-in-law to eat. Why come with her, asks Naomi, because clearly the hand of God has been raised against her? The book begins, then, with every good reason for the two Moabite widows to stay in Moab, which Orpah chooses to do, following Naomi's instructions. And yet this is the story of someone whose *hesed* (steadfast love) will not be restricted by ethnic or religious boundaries.

Ruth "clings" to her mother-in-law, ignoring Naomi's instructions and recalling for readers Genesis 2:24 ("Therefore a man leaves his father and his mother and clings to his wife, and they become one flesh"). Thus family bonds are broken and a new family is born. In Ruth, we learn that an alien woman is a distant ancestor of Jesus and a forerunner of what Jesus will ask his Hebrew disciples to do: to "cling" to him by letting go of all that "clings" to them, including their ethnic-religious presuppositions. Katharine Sackenfeld notes, "Even if her prospects in Moab were not good in her own thinking, commitment to stick with an older woman whose reception at home is uncertain is still a striking decision. . . . Whatever Ruth's motives, she was presumably wise enough to

Proper 26 (Sunday between October 30 and November 5 inclusive)

the introduction, after a period of ten years, we are left with a completely devastated family. This immigrant family has just experienced what most first-generation forced migrants encounter in times of plight and flight—suffering, loss, hardship, and pain in a new context—when they made their difficult journey to escape just such hardship.

Naomi's First Speech (vv. 6–10). Naomi hears from the fields of Moab that the Lord has visited those in Judah and given them food. As she starts the journey back, her two daughters-in-law accompany her. Naomi commands them to go back, interestingly, to "your mother's house." The Greek and Syriac manuscripts have changed the lexeme to "father" in place of "mother." Obviously, the tradents had a problem with this phrase and its implications. However, in the context of our narrative, it dramatically heightens the narrative if both Orpah and Ruth are also fatherless. "Your mother's house" literally speaks to the absence of fathers. This might explain why Ruth and Orpah, Moabites, leave their own ethnic community to marry outsiders.

Verse 8 has another important term, *hesed*, meaning loving-kindness, faithfulness, or loyalty. Just as the daughters-in-law show *hesed* to the dead, Naomi also seeks *hesed* for her daughters-in-law. Her ultimate wish for them is to "find security . . . in the house of your husband" (v. 9b). After Naomi kisses Orpah and Ruth, the women all lift their voices and weep. There is some debate about whether it is only Orpah and Ruth who cry or all three. The climax of the section seems more powerful with the bonding moment (v. 9) in which those who have lost their husbands cry out loud. Verse 10 is short, yet poignantly relays that the daughters-in-law will return with Naomi to her people.

Naomi's Second Speech (vv. 11–14). Naomi vehemently rejects this proposal. Notwithstanding the levirate tradition or even other means of producing a son, Naomi calls her life bitter; she declares that the hand of the Lord is against her. The second speech also closes with weeping aloud, but this time Orpah kisses her mother-in-law, a symbolic sign of going back. Ruth does not kiss Naomi to bring about closure or even to signal betrayal, but emotionally and ever so powerfully clings to her.

Naomi's Third Speech and Ruth's First (vv. 15–18). Naomi tells Ruth to go back, like her sister-in-law Orpah, to her people and gods (v. 15). But Ruth says,

judgment that Job rails against in last week's lectionary readings. Again it is the struggle to determine the meaning of evil and human suffering. Naomi and the friends of Job respond to tragedy in believing that God invokes suffering to punish us for some offense in sin. One name used for God, *Shaddai* (v. 20), associates the character of God with the act of judgment or punishment, and potentially of curse. As commonly used in the patriarchal period, this name appears in Job prominently. The meaning evolves around the theological worldview or judged language of guilt.[1]

Our concern with preaching from lectionary texts contending with tragedy bears similar risks to preaching in the midst of tragedy itself. Typically, someone in our congregations will be wrestling with tragedy or suffering and therefore often asks "Why?" Even more difficult ambiguities arise with some biblical narratives like Ruth. Questions of divine will or even predeterminism abound. Sometimes careless language in preaching can participate in destructive theological worldviews: "Everything happens for a reason"; "God meant to teach us something." With the terrorism of 9/11 or with Hurricane Katrina, we have heard sermons claim that God was sitting in judgment of America's misguided power and immoral privilege. Biblical traditions underscore God's efforts to speak and act against both active and passive oppression. The homiletical miscue, however, comes in charging that the experience of evil or tragedy is wrought by God, despite the harsh reality that in tragedies such as 9/11 and Hurricane Katrina many innocent lives bear the so-called judgment. Naomi seems to hold this theological worldview so strongly that she has not been able to resist even her own convictions of guilt. The book of Ruth works hard to overcome this worldview and its spurious understanding of God. Preaching from this chapter in Ruth challenges us to discern "How is God present?" or "How is God acting here?"

Naomi's resignation to embittered guilt is first disrupted by her daughters-in-law, Orpah and Ruth. Notice that the sisters-in-law are not pitted against one another. One does not represent evil and the other good. This narrative cannot be reduced to a dualistic sermon. The relationships and exchanges among the three women are critical to the narrative. Here, preachers need to consider in what manner or capacity they hope the sermon will function among their hearers. Is the goal to elicit a conversion

1. Edward F. Campbell Jr., *Ruth*, Anchor Bible 7 (Garden City, NY: Doubleday & Co., 1975), 76–77, 83.

Ruth 1:1-18

Theological Perspective

of the ruling parties. This God does not belong to one people alone but gathers peoples into this wide family.

In the book of Ruth, God is not a main character. The action takes place among humans in everyday life, but God's role is implicit in the interactions and plot reversals of the story. Ruth reverses the trajectory of Naomi's life from despair and death to fertility and hope. What starts in barrenness and negation ends with fruitfulness and new birth, not only of a baby but of a family and of the whole people of Israel. Naomi holds a grandchild in her lap, knowing that her husband's name will live in memory in the future. "Blessed be the LORD, who has not left you this day without next-of-kin" (4:14), say the women at the birth of Obed, Naomi's grandson.

Ruth, by contrast to the altered Naomi, remains a consistent figure, faithful and stalwart. She takes initiative by going out to work in the fields and steadily moves from event to event that culminates in her marriage to Boaz and the birth of her son Obed. Ruth the Moabite becomes the ancestress of King David; the king descends from an enemy widow woman who comes to be friend to another widow. Her story tells of ordinary and harsh human life in which the providence of God is manifest.

Today's reading tells the story of God, hidden yet active in human life, who brings about reversals, who turns barrenness to fertility and death to rebirth. This providential, inclusive God acts through the enemy, through the one least likely to matter in the community. Matthew's Gospel includes Ruth as a foremother of Jesus in the family tree (Matt. 1:5) making Jesus the offspring of mixed race and ancestry of dubious reputation. Jesus' own genealogy is a theological statement that includes the nations, the enemies of Israel, the excluded ones.

KATHLEEN M. O'CONNOR

Pastoral Perspective

know of potential difficulties in the path she was setting for herself."[1]

One can get a visceral sense of the decision of Ruth by tapping into sentiment toward those of Middle Eastern descent after 9/11. These "aliens" (even native-born citizens) were searched more vigorously in airport security lines, had their civil rights violated in the interest of "national security," were looked at with suspicion and contempt by even the most "enlightened" citizens. For a Moabite—and one who had been a part of a mixed marriage with a Hebrew man—to set foot in Bethlehem would have been to set off all the cultural, social, and religious detectors of the time. Leaving Moab, Ruth would face not only a language barrier, a food barrier, a social etiquette barrier, and a religious practice barrier; she would also face the constant subtle and not-so-subtle reminders that she was "not one of us." Early on in Jesus' ministry, Mark tells the story of the disciples shutting down the ministry of an adherent of Jesus because he was "not one of us" (9:38 NIV). Ruth 1 begins the story of a foreign woman who refuses to allow external boundaries to prevent her from maintaining her *hesed* for her Hebrew mother-in-law.

Lest pastors be tempted to romanticize this story, Katharine Sakenfeld offers a sobering reminder of the consequences of Ruth's decision for Naomi, "For Naomi, Ruth's presence is as much a reminder of tragedy as it is a potential comfort. Naomi has no idea how she herself will be received upon returning to Bethlehem, and now she has also a foreign companion to be explained."[2] Chapter 1 of Ruth speaks with narrative power to people often constricted by some sort of social, ethnic, racial, or religious boundary. It begins a story of how God can work across and despite the most entrenched positions and established boundaries to bring new life and new hope.

GARY W. CHARLES

---

1. Katharine Sakenfeld, in *The New Interpreter's Bible* (Nashville: Abingdon Press, 1988), 2:31.
2. Ibid., 35.

Exegetical Perspective

"Do not press me to leave you or turn back from following you!" The remaining words of the text are among the most treasured and profound testimonies of faith.

There are four components in Ruth's speech. First, Ruth is determined to be with Naomi. Even if Ruth is not sanguinely related to her mother-in-law, she will not be separated from her even by death. Instead, death has brought about a bonding more powerful than life. Second, wherever Naomi goes and wherever she decides to lodge, Ruth will do likewise. There is a unique attribute about the Hebrew lexeme *l'n*, "to lodge" (Qal), because in the Niphal, it means to "murmur or complain." This technical term is seen throughout the wilderness murmuring-complaining narratives of the Israelites living in the wilderness (Exod. 15:22ff.). Thus we understand the lodging here to be a place of discomfort, laden with complaints or bitterness. Third, Naomi's people and God will be Ruth's people and God. This is a reality of the future Ruth anticipates. Even if she is rejected in Judah as a Moabite, so that the people there murmur and complain about her, Ruth will nevertheless remain in solidarity with Naomi's people and her God. And lastly, where Naomi dies, Ruth will be buried next to her.

Just as the story began with Elimelech immigrating with his family to escape famine in order to live, we see a similar new beginning for Naomi and Ruth. The journey to Judah will be a journey back for Naomi, but a first move for Ruth. Knowing something of the marginalization, bitterness, rumors, judgments, and murmurs that may await them, the two widows migrate to Judah. In essence, Ruth is willing to die to her past so that her mother-in-law and she may live anew. In doing so, she finds God's people and God. Without her willingness to move, she would not have found God or Boaz, her kinsman redeemer.

Reading this story typologically, Ruth's story is intricately laden with christological implications. I wish to inject a new reading: it is not Boaz who redeems, but Ruth, an outsider, who moves to give life through her willingness to die.

JOHN AHN

Homiletical Perspective

moment, or perhaps to gain entry into how people may experience God's inbreaking?

The relationships in our passage function in several capacities. Most of us are immediately drawn to the climax of the chapter when Ruth confesses her loyalty to Naomi and declares her oath before God (vv. 16–17). Yet through their relationships the women already begin to break the bondage of tragedy. The various struggles in these relationships focus on how the women will be with one another. They struggle to give to each other, to act in each other's best interest. God does not appear dramatically or directly in the narrative, leaving us to say how we believe God actually does appear.

Verses 8–18 depict the women's efforts to discern how to care for each other. Orpah does attempt to stay with Naomi, but in the end follows Naomi's renewed appeals. Orpah is not unethical or unfaithful. Still, Ruth does demonstrate the extra measure. Her faithfulness and her care do not simply lead to a deeper relationship with Naomi and her own new relationship with YHWH, but also evidence how God works with us through relationships. Both Naomi and Ruth experience the inbreaking of God through their faithful relationship. An important theme to the whole narrative of Ruth is underscored in the way faithful human relationships reflect divine care and therefore the covenantal care of community.[2]

Through the care we extend to and receive from one another we encounter the gifts of God. We encounter the grace of God. God's activity has already begun in our relationships. Last week with Job and his friends, we discovered God directing relationships in restoring our own well-being. With Ruth and Naomi, we discover that God is so intimately involved in our relationships that it is hard to reduce God's presence to a linear equation of cause and effect. God is in the extra measure of relatedness we seek. God's power and character in the midst of human suffering are experienced in that extra measure. The homiletic move demonstrates how God nurtures relationships and what God does exponentially with the extra measure.

DALE P. ANDREWS

2. Katharine Doob Sakenfeld, *Ruth*, Interpretation Series (Louisville, KY: John Knox Press, 1999), 14–16, 26–35. See also James C. Howell, "Ruth 1:1–18," *Interpretation* 51, no. 3 (July 1997): 282–83; and Campbell, 80–81.

Psalm 146

¹Praise the LORD!
  Praise the LORD, O my soul!
²I will praise the LORD as long as I live;
  I will sing praises to my God all my life long.

³Do not put your trust in princes,
  in mortals, in whom there is no help.
⁴When their breath departs, they return to the earth;
  on that very day their plans perish.

⁵Happy are those whose help is the God of Jacob,
  whose hope is in the LORD their God,
⁶who made heaven and earth,
  the sea, and all that is in them;
  who keeps faith forever;

Theological Perspective

Q: What is a life committed to praising God?
A: A life consumed with allowing God to rule "for all generations" (v. 10).
Q: Who is this God?
A: The One who specifically covenanted with Jacob (v. 5), known for providing what the needy lack (vv. 7–9). Psalm 146 invites the pray-er (vv. 1–2) and community (v. 10) into a lifelong celebration and imitation of God (vv. 4–9).

Eternal Praises (vv. 1–2, 10). Life is for praising the Lord; life arises from praising God. Love of God flows through love of neighbor to such an extent that Jerome (d. 419/420) claimed, "When we perform deeds of justice we are alive; when we sin we cease to be."[1] Imitating divine justice and love shapes believers through encountering God in others. Likewise, worship ensures that they remain bound to God, who is especially present to transform the faithful. When humans turn from God in sin or in apathy, their self-chosen distance weakens access to the source of life and uproots their attempts at justice.

The great spiritual adviser Ps.-Macarius (late fourth century, Syria) asked, "For how can the one who does not seek to love God with all his soul and all his heart

---

1. Jerome, "Homily 55 on Psalm 145(146)," in *The Homilies of Saint Jerome,* vol. 1, Fathers of the Church 48 (Washington, DC: Catholic University of America Press, 1964), 393.

Pastoral Perspective

The Bible is full of surprises! Some may be gentle; others may be jarring. Some may make us smile in amusement; others may wrinkle our brows with amazement. What are we, who are so conditioned by our reason and logic, to make of such turns and contradictions as these:

- "Love your enemies" (Matt. 5:44)
- "The last will be first" (Mark 10:31)
- "Happy are those who mourn" (Matt. 5:4 TEV)
- "Go, sell what you own, and give the money to the poor" (Mark 10:21)
- "Take up (your) cross and follow me" (Mark 8:34 RSV)
- "Blessed are you poor" (Luke 6:20 RSV)
- "Behold, a virgin shall conceive . . ." (Matt 1:23 RSV)

Even those two "eternal truths" we have been taught to acknowledge—death and taxes—are covered:

- "I shall not die, but I shall live" (Ps. 118:17)
- "Render to Caesar what is Caesar's . . ." (Luke 20:25 RSV)

It should, then, come as no surprise to us that the Psalter ends rather than begins with an energetic series of "calls to worship." So much for the structure of most of our worship services today!

This inverted order is turned right side up if we think of the Psalter as a kind of citation or

⁷who executes justice for the oppressed;
   who gives food to the hungry.

The LORD sets the prisoners free;
⁸   the LORD opens the eyes of the blind.
The LORD lifts up those who are bowed down;
   the LORD loves the righteous.
⁹The LORD watches over the strangers;
   he upholds the orphan and the widow,
   but the way of the wicked he brings to ruin.

¹⁰The LORD will reign forever,
   your God, O Zion, for all generations.
   Praise the LORD!

Exegetical Perspective

Surrounded by Praise. Today's reading is enveloped in praise. It opens with a liturgical cry, "Alleluia" (v. 1), and concludes with the same primal shout (v. 10). Together the "alleluias" create doxological bookends that are both joyous exclamations and urgent invitations to praise God. Every intermediate reflection is refracted through the lens of praise.

Alleluia! As is customary of hymnic material, Psalm 146 opens with a call to worship, which in this case takes the form of a self-invocation: the summons to praise is directed to the psalmist's own self. Following this exhortation, the psalmist promises to worship God throughout life (v. 2). Accordingly, praise is more than an isolated act that takes place quickly and over a very short time. It is durative and continuous, and envelops the continuum of life. To be sure, praise of God is a fundamental commitment of life, no less essential to the faithful than oxygen is to the lungs. This initial utterance, although formulaic, is a statement of resolve, intentionality, and vocation.

What Does Praise Involve? At first the body of the psalm (vv. 3–9) appears to wander from its liturgical borders (vv. 1–2, 10). It looks as if the psalmist abandons the role of priest for that of sage. But this is not necessarily the case. At its core the psalm is a

Homiletical Perspective

Today's reading contains the Psalter's final exclamation mark: "Praise the LORD!" Beginning with Psalm 146, the last five psalms (Pss. 146–50) call us to doxology by repeating this call to praise. The psalmist praises God with the whole self (the soul). The "soul" is the integrator of all our experiences, whether positive, negative, or ambiguous. It is the seat of understanding. The psalmist commits the whole self to praising God, no matter what. This is a radical commitment to live in gratitude to God. By so doing, the psalmist chooses to live a disciplined life in which one's personal disposition, moral outlook, and worldview become sources of hope and resources for the community. "Praise the LORD, O my soul" is an alternative way of being present to and living in a world where one is vulnerable to unwanted loss, unforeseen tragedy, and grief. The psalmist warns that when we place ultimate faith or trust in material things or mere mortals, ultimately we will be disappointed. God, the creator and ever creating Lord, is alone worthy of our soul's trust and gratitude. This God, in whom we live, move, and have our being, is the source of our life and deepest sense of joy.

In Psalm 146, the psalmist is urging the community to praise God, but *not* for the ways God was made manifest in the lives of the ancestors. The psalmist, for instance, does not recount the great

Psalm 146

Theological Perspective

bestow a concern of love upon the brethren in a wholesome and sincere manner?" Prayer opens believers to God's formative grace, which in turn produces "fruits" of social virtues for nourishing both the prayers and all whom they meet. Praise transpires in opening the self contemplatively to God and actively to others through lives that redound to his glory.[2] However, worship, spiritual disciplines, and even prayer itself collapse into Sisyphean labors that accomplish nothing if they are not accompanied by spiritual growth poured out in acts of love toward others.

The Object of Trust (vv. 3–4). In offering a life of praise, how do believers' lives reflect the one they trust? Do they dutifully attend church on Sunday, yet "trust in princes" the other six days? Christians struggle with consistency in belief and action. Often the struggle spins around the fallen desire to be in control, even if it is intellectually obvious that such a desire is impossible. Yet humans continue to be crushed and resentful when their plans are thwarted, when those on whom they depended fail, and especially when death yanks down the polite curtain of denial with which they try to hide it. Augustine, prior to his commitment to God, reflected on the power of death and grief apart from God: "I had poured out my soul on to the sand by loving a person sure to die as if he would never die."[3] Every time humans put their ultimate trust in a job, a friend, an employer, or their own cunning plans, they risk grief and confusion, for none of these objects is destined to be eternal or stable. Indeed they "return to the earth" and "their plans perish" (v. 4).

God the Creator and Deliverer (vv. 5–9). The psalmist redirects attention to the particular God of Jacob. Praise and trust must be directed toward the God of justice and mercy revealed to Jacob. This unique God causes dependents to be "blessed" rather than frustrated and without help. The God of Jacob is not just any God, a nameless, impersonal force underlying all names given to the Divine. This Creator and Deliverer has a history that discloses unique divine power and reveals the relationships that are favored or opposed.

Creation displayed God's regard for interdependence: communion of God and humanity, of

Pastoral Perspective

declaration of honor, much like those we present on special occasions to special people. Such declarations begin with a lot of *whereas*es and then end with a *therefore* statement—in this case, five chapters of doxological *therefore*s.

Psalm 146 is one of the Alleluia Psalms, exhorting us to praise God—a common thread throughout the book. But here the psalmist not only gives the imperative to the listeners, "Praise the LORD!" but echoes the words internally, "Praise the LORD, O *my* soul!" How can we command others to do what we ourselves are not willing to do?

The psalmist then continues to tell us not only whom we should praise, but when, where, how, and why as well.

Whom should we praise? The answer is clear: the Lord, the God of Jacob—different names, but one living God—who is above all we can imagine, surpassing the false gods, empty idols, and earthly rulers who, regardless of their perceived power, eventually fade away. God as our Creator has a vested interest in us, with the depth of love a parent holds for a child. We honor our parents; we praise our God.

When should we offer our praise to God? Again the psalmist leaves us no room for error: as long as we have our being, from our first breath throughout future generations.

Where should we praise? With a little twist of interpretation and imagination, we can say with the psalmist, "*wherever* we have our being." No matter where we find ourselves, physically or spiritually, in the delights and challenges of life, we are instructed to praise God without ceasing.

How should we offer our praise? By singing to God, lifting our hearts and voices in psalms, hymns, and spiritual songs. We are called to praise God through music, that sublime language of sound and texture and pitch and rhythm that can lift us boldly to mountaintops with its majesty, hold us sympathetically in its warmth, and bring us to tears through its passion.

The question "*Why* should we praise God?" can be answered with one simple word: "Because!" But the psalmist is not nearly so abrupt in giving us an answer.

According to Walter Brueggemann, this psalm outlines our reasons for worship in two contrasting categories of blessing, which he defines as *cosmic* and *liberating*.[1]

---

2. Ps.-Macarius, *The Great Letter*, in *Pseudo-Macarius: The Fifty Homilies and the Great Letter*, trans. George A. Maloney (New York: Paulist Press, 1992), 263–268.

3. Augustine, *Confessions* IV.viii (13), trans. Henry Chadwick, Oxford World's Classics (New York: Oxford University Press, 1991), 60.

1. Walter Brueggemann, *The Message of the Psalms: A Theological Commentary* (Minneapolis: Augsburg, 1984).

meditation on what it means to praise God through-out life. It addresses sustaining life commitments that shape attitude, behavior, worldview, and char-acter; in other words, it attends to the building blocks of spirituality.

Two All-Embracing Approaches to Life. The poem identifies two contrasting readings of reality: one ends in failure and disappointment (vv. 3–4); the other leads to blessing and life (vv. 5–9). Both assume that the congregation is susceptible to a range of predica-ments and disjunctions. And both offer prospects for security and protection. The community can take refuge "in princes, in mortals" or look to "the God of Jacob" for help.

Trusting in Princes. The psalmist warns that the former is deeply problematic. The listening community should not trust or put its confidence in "princes," that is, those who are well positioned in the social hierarchy and enjoy a good measure of success, prestige, and power. Regardless of their celebrity and influence, kings, nobles, court officials, and other governing elite, whether foreign or indigenous, cannot provide sanctuary from life's extremities. They may *appear* to wield such power, and they may even enjoy an aura of invincibility, but "the rich and famous," like all other humans, are mortal: their lives are frail and fleeting, and their plans and prestige die with them (vv. 3–4). No matter how impressive, they are still merely children of Adam, creatures of earth who return to the place whence they came (ʾ*adamah*). To trust in human power structures, to rely on human props—whether political, military, or economic—is futile and fraught with danger. Such confidence is not only doomed to failure, but it compromises authentic faith. There is no salvation in mortals.

Trusting in the God of Jacob. The inadequacy of human categories serves as a foil for God's power to save. So the psalmist congratulates those who dare to align themselves with the "God of Jacob . . . YHWH their God." They are fortunate or happy because their hope is well founded: in contrast to conventional modes of power, YHWH makes a difference to those besieged by life (v. 5). And if that assertion by itself is not enough, the psalmist tenders a compelling list of divine acts. Like other hymns, the inventory demon-strates God's might and mercy, greatness and goodness, transcendence and involvement. Here a string of participial phrases—translated first as

stories of deliverance. There is no mention of the Israelites being led out of their Egyptian bondage and through the sea to the land of promise. The psalmist urges the community to give praise to God because of what God is *now* doing in their midst. "What, in the world, is God doing?" That is the question the psalmist answers. The psalmist teaches those who are gathered about God. In like manner, it is part of the preacher's task to instruct the community so they may become aware of their theological assumptions and affirmations. These, in ways we do not always understand, inform our living.

Contrast enriches sermons, and the psalmist uses contrast to convince the community that God is faithful and trustworthy. Some are tempted to put their trust in rulers, those who are powerful, hoping that in them they may find deliverance and help. But these, the psalmist tells us, can offer little sustained support. They are, after all, mortal. They will die. They will return to the earth. Their promises and plans will perish. This is in contrast to the God who deserves our praises. This is the God of ancestors, and this is God the creator (vv. 5–6).

This reminder of the absolute faithfulness of God is followed by a list of the things that God is doing in the world. The series of verbs used by the psalmist points overwhelmingly to the liberating work of the one who created the world and everything in it. According to the psalmist, God:

> *keeps faith* forever;
> *executes justice* for the oppressed;
> *gives food* to the hungry;
> *sets* the prisoners *free*;
> *opens the eyes* of the blind;
> *lifts up* those who are bowed down;
> *loves* the righteous;
> *watches over* the strangers;
> *upholds* the orphan and the widow;
> *brings* the wicked *to ruin*.

There is an interesting contrast set up in this list of ten active verbs attributed to YHWH. God loves the righteous but brings ruin to the wicked. The contrast is not unexpected; it is common in Wisdom literature. God loves the righteous, those in right relationship with God *and* neighbor. The righteous one, then, is one who joins God in the other liberative activities the psalmist has listed for us. The righteous one works tirelessly for justice, giving food to those who are hungry, setting free those who are bound, healing the blind, watching over strangers, and upholding those who are most vulnerable in the

Psalm 146

Theological Perspective

humanity with itself, and of humanity and the rest of creation (Gen. 1–2). In contrast, the fall manifested brokenness in all three relations (Gen. 3). The rest of Torah proceeds to outline how God initiated the Abrahamic covenant and Mosaic law to restore and protect human relationships with God, creation, and each other. Verses 6b–9 lists a classical depiction of God's justice, meant to remind worshipers that suffering is both a sign of covenant brokenness and the locus for restoring faithfulness and community. The God who reaches out to the most vulnerable in society (oppressed, hungry, prisoners, blind, bowed down, strangers, widows, and orphans) insists that people follow this example. Jesus assured doubters of his divine mandate by appealing to these very signs within his ministry (e.g., Matt. 11:2–6). In the parable of the Sheep and the Goats, Jesus made acts of love determinative for entering the kingdom: "Just as you did it to one of the least of these who are members of my family, you did it to me" (Matt. 25:40). The believer comes full circle to lifelong praise (vv. 1–2) manifested in love of God expressed through love of neighbor.

Apparent stability does not in itself inoculate anyone against suffering the oppression, hunger, captivity, blindness, alienation, and loneliness of sin. It is that vulnerability that drives humans to "trust in princes" or adopt unjust relationships to preserve themselves regardless of their economic or physical situation. The prophet Amos warned that because the people ignored the vulnerable in their midst, they will suffer a "famine . . . of hearing the words of the LORD" (Amos 8:11). Recognizing our neediness makes commitment to justice a communal expression of need not merely for God, but for each other. Involvement in God's justice through Christ, which is in reality mercy and grace, brings spiritual freedom, nourishment, vision, and community. Until the resurrection, this is how God works with and through people so that "the way of the wicked [is brought] to ruin" (v. 9b). Then "the LORD will reign forever" (v. 10).

LISA D. MAUGANS DRIVER

Pastoral Perspective

The cosmic basis for worship is found in the fifth verse, which declares that God "made heaven and earth, the seas, and all that is in them" and that God "keeps faith forever." What more reason do we need to warrant our praise than this?

But the psalmist continues with a longer list of liberating blessings that touch us more personally and immediately than the formation of the universe, when barren planets swirled in darkness awaiting the hand of God to bring order to chaos. These blessings are the covenant the faithful can claim.

We can live in the faith that God ensures justice for the oppressed—something that earthly rulers have never been able to accomplish.

We are promised that God will give food to the hungry—not simply manna for rumbling stomachs, but the nourishment for our souls and spirits that we need to live out our God-given lives as a benevolent Creator intended.

We can prosper in the hope that God will set us free from all that would bind and consume us.

We are confident that God will heal us in body, mind, and spirit.

We are assured that God will be there to lift us up when we fall, steady us when we stumble, and care for those among us who cannot care for themselves (the stranger, the orphan, and the lonely).

We are not told specifically how God will meet these needs for us, and there is no guarantee that the answers to our prayers will be what we expect—another of the "surprises" of divine providence. God does not hesitate to use us ourselves to answer our own prayers, for not all the wonders of God will "break in blessing on [our] head" (from the hymn by William Cowper, "God Moves in a Mysterious Way"). God does not promise in every instance to change *things* for *us;* sometimes *we* are changed for *things.* And a large part of our faithfulness is the wisdom to perceive the difference!

All of this is promised to those who faithfully trust in God. In a single phrase, a contrasting promise is made to the wicked: they will be frustrated and defeated.

The psalm prayer from the *Book of Common Worship* entreats the Lord: "Guard us from giving to any other the allegiance which belongs only to you."

May our faith be as strong and enduring as the Love that surprises us.

MICHAEL MORGAN

Exegetical Perspective

relative clauses and then with YHWH as subject—displays God's power and resolve to act on behalf of survivors of enormous hardship. That is to say, the recital of divine deeds accentuates God's compassion for the weak and vulnerable. The "God of Jacob . . . the LORD their God," the *maker* of heaven and earth and *promise keeper* is One who

> *executes justice* for the oppressed,
> *gives food* to the hungry,
> *sets free* the prisoners,
> *opens* the eyes of the blind,
> *lifts up* those who are bowed down,
> *watches over* the strangers,
> *upholds* the orphan and the widow,
> *brings to ruin* the wicked.

Such acts further highlight the distinction between human leaders and YHWH. Whereas "princes" are unreliable, YHWH keeps faith forever. Whereas human power brokers are inept, YHWH is adept at creating newness when none seems possible. Whereas human leaders and institutions disappoint, those who rely on YHWH are happy or blessed. YHWH's acts of kindness elicit both praise and trust (cf. Ps. 118:9). Certainly human leaders are called to act on behalf of those who find themselves on the margins, but their track record is miserable (e.g., Ezek. 34). YHWH, in contrast, uses power and privilege not to exploit but to uplift. All the more reason to congratulate the people who opt for an alternative to the conventional power structures!

YHWH reigns forever. The recital of God's decisive deeds concludes with the claim that God, "your God," "will reign forever . . . for all generations" (v. 10). This stunning affirmation—in conjunction with the commentary on anemic princes and the inventory of divine deeds—drives home with poetic force that YHWH is the true king (e.g., Pss. 93, 97, 99). And God's reign is not only just and compassionate, sovereign and gracious; it also lasts "forever . . . for all generations" (in contrast to that of "princes," who inevitably perish). All told, Psalm 146 provides a liturgical lens through which the congregation can reimagine the world and reframe conventional modes of power. Such a bold act of defiance sees through pretentious human leaders while discerning the true scope of God's power and concern for suffering people. No wonder Psalm 146 concludes with praise: "Alleluia!"

LOUIS STULMAN

Homiletical Perspective

world—the orphan and the widow. The wicked are those who do not cooperate in "mending the world." They always prioritize their own self-interest. The psalmist asserts that God brings ruin to these. The reader of the Old Testament often turns to the books of the prophets to find compelling words calling communities to justice and righteousness. An unrecognized but consistent strain in the Psalms, however, is this same insistence and call to be a justice-seeking people.

There are many sermon possibilities inherent in Psalm 146. A "praise sermon" that recounts short vignettes illustrating each of the verbs listed above is one possibility. Or preachers could focus on one of these verbs and explore the ways God has been at work in their communities—or the ways that their communities do this work for and with God.

The psalm ends again with a call to praise for all that God is doing in the world around us. To praise the kind of God who works for justice and who liberates is to live with a compassionate, yet daring and defiant, spirit. It is to turn one's own self toward those who are oppressed and hungry; who live in physical, spiritual, and mental prisons. It is to enable people to see and perceive further than they might otherwise do, to lift the heads of those who have been shamed and humiliated, to seek and bring protection to those who are most vulnerable among us. Daring acts of compassion come from a power that transcends us, yet operates through us. For the God at work in the world empowering us to live as we should, the psalmist gives praise.

The psalmist says that this is the song he will sing all his life long (v. 2). He will sing a song about the creator God who is trustworthy. This is the God who is our helper and the source of all hope. This is the compassionate and caring God who longs for justice and liberation for all those whom God has created. This is the psalmist's song. What is the preacher's song? What does the preacher know about God? What is the song of the community? How does the community understand God's activity and agency in our world?

MARY DONOVAN TURNER

Psalm 146

Hebrews 9:11-14

¹¹But when Christ came as a high priest of the good things that have come, then through the greater and perfect tent (not made with hands, that is, not of this creation), ¹²he entered once for all into the Holy Place, not with the blood of goats and calves, but with his own blood, thus obtaining eternal redemption. ¹³For if the blood of goats and bulls, with the sprinkling of the ashes of a heifer, sanctifies those who have been defiled so that their flesh is purified, ¹⁴how much more will the blood of Christ, who through the eternal Spirit offered himself without blemish to God, purify our conscience from dead works to worship the living God!

Theological Perspective

Among the many controversies that swirled around Mel Gibson's film *The Passion of the Christ* was an argument over the appropriateness (and the effect on the audience) of the film's depiction of violence. Some considered it abhorrent and tasteless; I particularly remember the hand-drawn illustration that accompanied the *New Yorker*'s review of the film, depicting the movie set with the actors covered in red stains and the director yelling out, "More blood! More blood!"[1] Other observers, even if they found flaws in the film (and most agreed that there were many), defended the graphic depictions of violence as realistic and appropriate, given what we know about crucifixion—the cruel and not-so-unusual punishment of choice during the Roman occupation of Palestine.

A similar argument might well arise over this week's reading from the letter to the Hebrews, in which there are as many instances of the word "blood" as there are verses in the passage. While the purpose of the letter (as of the movie, perhaps) was to offer a strongly positive account of Christ's sacrifice, one might well wonder whether that goal is best served by calls for "more blood." On the other hand, we may get a better grasp on this passage (and

1. David Denby, "Nailed," *New Yorker*, March 1, 2004.

Pastoral Perspective

What is a holy place? Answers to this question are often as much cultural as religious. What is holy—set apart—for one group of people may seem completely ordinary to another. Holy places usually have a history. Some have been thought of as the navel of the earth (in Greek, the ancient *omphaloi*), the thin place where things human and things divine coincide and intersect. One thinks of the Vatican hill, where the apostle Peter was said to have been martyred and buried, or the ruins at Delphi northwest of Athens, where the visitor to this day is greeted by a sign in several languages welcoming her to "the navel of the world."

And yet, as often as Christians revere and flock to their own holy places, there is embedded deep in their religious consciousness the conviction that place does not matter, that God is omnipresent, and that the holiest place—the place where God dwells—is wherever God's people gather. One can sense this tension throughout Scripture—not only in the many prophetic denunciations of worship in the "high places," but also in the prophets' ambivalence toward King David's desire to build a permanent temple on Mount Zion to replace the all-too-portable ark of the covenant. When Jesus declares that the veil of the temple will be torn from top to bottom, or that in the end time not one stone will be left on stone, he

Exegetical Perspective

Christ's Effective New Sacrifice. This chapter of the Epistle to the Hebrews describes the priestly ministry of Christ by contrasting two fundamental covenantal traditions. First, there is a contrast between Christ's ministry and the "regulations for worship" of the first covenant. Second, there is a contrast between the "earthly sanctuary" or "first tent" (or tabernacle) and a "greater and perfect tent." The first part of the chapter (vv. 1–10) describes the early tabernacle, its divisions and furniture, along with a brief account of priestly rituals and sacrifices. The author emphasizes the high priest's sacrifice on the Day of Atonement (vv. 6–8, see Lev. 16:1–19). This is interpreted as a symbol (*parabolē*), ineffective to "perfect the conscience of the worshiper" (9:9) until the time (*kairos*) when things are to be set right (9:10).

It may be helpful to offer a brief comment on the hermeneutical strategy that Hebrews employs in this passage. Although the epistle contrasts Christ's work with the first tabernacle and the rituals of the first covenant, its interpretation of the Hebrew Scriptures (and the meaning of Christ's sacrifice) is done within the framework of the Jewish faith, not in opposition to it. The epistle assumes that the reader is familiar with the faith of Israel, the Scriptures, and the sacrificial and liturgical traditions. It is within these frameworks that the death of Christ is

Homiletical Perspective

Today's reading from the letter to the Hebrews continues the discussion of the finality of the salvation offered by Christ. The passage is part of an extended contrast between the sacrificial practices of the Levitical high priest and those of Christ, and by extension between the old covenant and the new.

The metaphor of covenant appears frequently in both testaments of the Bible and lends itself to a number of themes that have meaning for us today. A possible sermon might center on how our covenant with God is also a covenant with one another, reflecting a theme pertinent to all the readings today. For the commandment to love our neighbors as we love ourselves to be more than a cliché with no impact on our lives, we need to cast a very critical eye on a prevailing myth in our culture. This is the myth of the independent individual. Here a preacher could concentrate on helping the congregation understand how much our culturally induced self-understanding in fact relies on a fiction. There is no such thing as a completely independent individual. The ideal is a heroic fantasy based on the denial of our vulnerability. Each of us exists because of other people; we would not have survived infancy and early childhood without the care of others. It may be obvious, but we are who we are, physically, psychologically, and spiritually, in relation to other people.

Hebrews 9:11-14

Theological Perspective

on Hebrews as a whole) if we are able to move beyond the graphic illustrations and into a broader understanding of the theological significance of sacrifice.

Throughout the ancient world, both in Judaism and in many forms of Greco-Roman religious life, sacrifice played an important role within various ritual structures. This activity was more sophisticated than we sometimes imagine it to be; these were not simply superstitious people imagining that their anthropomorphic gods would not be placated until the correct smells wafted up from the altars. Rather, the ritual of sacrifice was a means of enshrining, within a highly structured practice, a broader theological concept with which we are all familiar: the idea that everything ultimately belongs to God. When we return to God some small portion of what we have (whether it be grain or animals or time or money), we are underscoring our belief that what we have is not actually *ours*. It already belongs to God, and we return a portion of it to God as a sign and reminder of that reality.

Of course, as with all ritual structures, frequently repeated gestures can begin to lose their meaning and significance; we simply "go through the motions," having forgotten what we were originally intending to signify by our various acts of sacrifice. Whether (and to what degree) this was true in the ancient world is the subject of much scholarly discussion; but that it regularly happens to *us* is largely beyond dispute. Even if our practices of worship, fellowship, and congregational life are not particularly "ritualized," we are always in danger of "just going through the motions."

But this may not *necessarily* be a bad thing. The French philosopher and theologian Blaise Pascal had some interesting insights on this matter that might be particularly helpful if we're feeling a little suspicious of the ritualized use of certain gestures, bodily postures, and repeated words (particularly in worship). Pascal observed that such actions, often done without thinking, may sometimes feel "empty" to us; nevertheless, it can be worthwhile to develop them as habits, since they may eventually lead to deeper faith.[2] After all, we ask our children to develop habits long before they understand the detailed reasoning behind our expectations. We do not explain the economic details of energy supply and demand and the environmental impact of global warming to our children before

2. Blaise Pascal, *Pensées*, trans. A. J. Krailsheimer (New York: Penguin Books, 1966), no. 418, p. 152.

Pastoral Perspective

participates in this ancient prophetic mistrust of holy houses built on high places.

So too the writer of the letter to the Hebrews, who imagines Jesus as the great high priest entering the Holy of Holies. Every year on Yom Kippur, the Day of Atonement, the high priest in Jerusalem would take the blood of the animal sacrificed in the temple courtyard and sprinkle it in the temple's inner sanctum as a sign of the people's atonement and sanctification—of a reconnection with the Holy One. But now, describing the crucified and risen Lord as both priest and victim entering the Holy Place once and—literally—for all, the radical implication is that there is no longer a need for a holy space, for a space set apart from human affairs. In Christ the human and the divine coincide and intersect. God in Christ can now be worshiped anywhere and anytime— whenever Christians gather at table, break bread, pour wine, all in remembrance of him.

A mark of Christian life is this ongoing creative tension between love of holy places and the conviction that, in the end, place doesn't matter. Imagine this familiar scenario. A large, flourishing city congregation worships week in and week out in a beautiful old building that has been hallowed by use over many generations. But demographics have shifted, and people see a need to plant a new church several miles away in order to serve a growing suburban population. With the blessing of this continuing congregation, a small group of hardy souls now gathers on Sunday morning in a school cafeteria, setting out chairs and Bibles and hymnals and perhaps a portable Communion table as people gather, and breaking everything down and storing things away as soon as the service is over. As the weeks go on, this little group grows. People are attracted to the deep sense of common purpose that animates this small, hardscrabble congregation—a sense that the Spirit is present wherever they gather. A few years pass. A sizable group begins to suggest that the time has come to build a more permanent place to worship. There is considerable opposition. The congregation finds itself thrust into a crisis of identity, torn between their sense of the Spirit working in them wherever they gather, and their desire to give that Spirit a more durable home.

Now focus on that portable Communion table. What happens when it becomes permanent? Does a table then become an altar? And if we call it an altar, do we imply that what happens in this now-sacred space is a weekly repetition of the temple sacrifice? Doesn't this contradict the spirit of Hebrews, where

Exegetical Perspective

interpreted—as a better atonement sacrifice, through which the community lives and breathes. Understanding the value and practice of the sacrificial system of Mosaic tradition is necessary for a more fruitful interpretation of the Scriptures as well as the meaning of the life, death, and resurrection of Christ.

Today's reading describes the coming and death of Christ, who "with his own blood" obtained eternal redemption (vv. 11–12). This blood "purifies our conscience" and allows believers to "worship the living God" (v. 14). This central section of the chapter is followed by a discussion of how the blood of Christ becomes the "new covenant" with its effect of forgiveness of sins (vv. 15–22). The final section of the chapter affirms that in his sacrifice Christ entered "heaven itself." The implication is that this sacrifice is done once for all, to remove sins (vv. 23–28).

As the previous section described the limitations of the first covenant, its tabernacle and its rituals, Hebrews 9:11–14 describes the efficiency of Christ's sacrifice. The fundamental image becomes that of the sacrifice offered by the high priest on the Day of Atonement. But the contrast is not limited to temporal images of the first covenant versus the new covenant; it is also spatial and ontological. The contrast is also between the "Holy Place" of the perfect tent, the one "not made with hands" (v. 11) and the "earthly sanctuary" (v. 1). In the next section of chapter 9 the epistle interprets the true sanctuary as "heaven itself" (v. 24).

The section begins with an allusion to Christ as "a high priest of the good things that have come" (v. 11). As the first tabernacle and its worship were a "mere copy" of the true sanctuary (v. 24), Christ came as a high priest and entered into the Holy Place through the greater and perfect tent. In contrast to the ancient tabernacle, which was handmade, the new tabernacle is "not of this creation" (v. 11). The contrast uses the image of locality: the Holy Place of the tabernacle versus heaven itself (see 4:14; 8:1–2; 9:24).

Jesus' entrance into the Holy Place is described in terms of contrasting the blood of goats and calves with "his own blood" (v. 12). The blood of goats and calves is a reference to the blood of the sacrifices made on the Day of Atonement (9:13, 19; Lev. 16:6, 11, 15). In contrast, Christ entered the Holy Place once for all with "his own blood." As a result, he obtained an "eternal redemption" that is permanent and complete. Although "redemption" (*lutrōsis*) occurs only here in Hebrews, the concept is used in other NT places (Luke 2:38; 24:21, see also

Homiletical Perspective

Not only who we are, but also everything we have and use is based on the work of other human beings. This theme might be developed by challenging common beliefs about wealth. Those of us who resist the necessity of paying taxes, for example, could be encouraged to look at our underlying assumptions about making money. Many of us claim we are entitled to keep all of our money, believing we made it by our own hard work alone. We are, of course, mistaken. It is an impossibility to create wealth alone. Wealth is an outcome of a myriad of social interactions. Even money itself is a social construct based on trust in others. The ancient Greeks recognized this sacred aspect of money and built their mints in their temples. The myth of the heroic individual, creating economic success by his or her own efforts alone, denies the fact of our interdependence. All the cultural myths that blind us to the reality of our dependence on other human beings also blind us to the most important reality of all: our dependence on God.

Another sermon might explore other uses in the Bible of the covenant metaphor. For example, one could focus on the covenant with Noah, the widespread myth of the flood in ancient times having startling and crucial relevance for our lives now. What parallels can be drawn between human behavior and environmental destruction in the story of Noah and our story today? What can we do as individuals, as a church, and as a nation in the face of the impending catastrophe caused by global warming? Are we separate from and above the natural world, or are we too a part of nature? What does our covenant with God require of us in relation to the natural world, we who believe in the goodness of creation and in the incarnation? Does nature exist only for our use? What would wise stewardship of nature look like?

Another image that occurs in today's reading is that of sacrifice. A sermon could begin by pointing out the metaphorical use of the word in our sacramental life, moving beyond a literal interpretation. What do we mean when we say we offer a sacrifice of praise and thanksgiving to God? What self-understandings, what habits, what attitudes, do we surrender when we offer ourselves as a holy and living sacrifice to God? Is our sacrifice, in fact, a celebration? In a society that more and more focuses on personal happiness defined by external criteria— wealth, possessions, status, power—how do we understand ourselves as Christians? What is required of us as members of the Christian community? What do we gain by being part of such a community?

Theological Perspective

making them turn out the lights when they leave a room. Of course, adult believers are not children; but the ways of God are sufficiently beyond our immediate comprehension that we needn't feel compelled to give a specific detailed reason for every word, gesture, or posture we assume while in church.

I mention these details because the letter to the Hebrews is too often read as critique of Judaism and of its sacrificial rituals—or even as a critique of all ritual practice. But in fact, much of the text not only avoids offering any direct critique of those practices; it actually *depends upon* the reader's positive appreciation of those practices in order for its argument to succeed. Today we are so far distanced from the Jewish ritual practices described here that it is difficult to understand the significance of Christ's sacrifice as a kind of "perfection" of these practices.

So perhaps we can take two important lessons from this text. The first is that, as a repeated and habitual action on the part of worshipers, sacrifice is not necessarily a bad thing. Our sacrifices today do not make use of the blood of goats and the ashes of a heifer; but just as those were valuable assets in an agricultural economy, so do we do something similar when we sacrifice time, money, and energy in order to reach out to those in need—or when we offer up our "sacrifice of thanksgiving and praise" in worship.

Yet on the other hand—and this is the second lesson—we ought not to let our own sacrifices loom too large in our imagination, as if the salvation of the world depended on *us*. Only the sacrificial work of Christ is definitive, "obtaining eternal redemption" (9:12). Compared even to the most laudable sacrifices that we can imagine, Christ's sacrifice is ever greater. It is a sacrifice on behalf of all people and for all time; and thus, it is not limited to one small corner of the created world, but has cosmic significance.[3]

DAVID S. CUNNINGHAM

Pastoral Perspective

Christ entered once for all into the Holy Place, not with the blood of goats and calves, but with his own blood, obtaining eternal redemption? These are hard questions, which in many ways point to the fissures in Christian self-understanding that have separated our churches since at least the days of Reformation and Counter-Reformation. Perhaps the best pastoral response to such questions is not an either/or but a both/and—it is both altar and table around which we gather. The table at which bread is broken and wine is poured is no ordinary table; the altar at which we remember Christ's death and proclaim Christ's resurrection no longer demands the sprinkling of sacrificial blood.

If our holy places become centers of pilgrimage, it is not because they are intrinsically holy. These places are holy—whether a grand basilica in Rome or a storefront church in Poughkeepsie—because of what happened in them and what continues to happen in them. In the cathedral of San Salvador, there is a memorial to Archbishop Romero, slain by assassins as he presided at mass at the altar. For many Christians, that ramshackle cathedral in El Salvador has become a martyr's shrine, another *omphalos*—a place where matters divine coincided and intersected with matters all too human. It is hard to think about that blood shed on the altar without thinking about this passage from Hebrews. Romero was a priest and a prophet—but he was above all a pastor. His life and death were formed in Christ's own image, as both priest and victim. That altar is no ordinary table; that table no ordinary altar. To say that a martyr's blood was sprinkled there is to say that Christ's blood has sanctified us all, and that Romero's blood—like the blood of every victim of violence and terror—is a witness to the power of Christ's one and perfect sacrifice. No wonder we call these places holy.

ROGER A. FERLO

---

3. Frances Young's small book *Can These Dry Bones Live?* (New York: Pilgrim Press, 1993) provides a succinct account of various understandings of the redemptive significance of the work of Christ.

Exegetical Perspective

apolutrōsis in Heb. 9:15; 11:35; Rom. 3:24), and its Hebrew equivalent in other Jewish sources such as the Targums and the Dead Sea Scrolls (1QM 1:12; 15:1; 18:11) to express the payment for freedom. It is used in Hebrews as a metaphor for salvation.

Verse 9:13 is an argument from a lesser to a greater (a fortiori). That is: if *a* is good, *b* is even better. This first part begins with the "for if . . ." section of the statement. The second part of the comparison will come in verse 14 with the "how much more . . ." part of the rhetorical device. The references to the blood of goats and bulls, and the sprinkling of ashes of a heifer, combines traditions of the Day of Atonement and the rites of the red heifer mentioned in Numbers 19:1–22. Both the Day of Atonement and the ritual of the red heifer are called sin offerings (Num. 19:9, 17). These rituals have the effect of "sanctifying those who have been defiled." They allow such persons to engage the worshiping community and to participate in the sacrificial system. But their cleansing is external ("their flesh"). Only the sacrifice of Christ will offer the internal purification of the conscience (v. 14).

With verse 14 we arrive at the second section of the argument, the "even better" or "how much more" of the benefits of Christ's sacrifice, which are greater than the benefits of the tabernacle's sacrifice. The sacrifice by which Christ offered himself was "through the eternal Spirit." Christ's sacrifice was "without blemish," as the animals to be sacrificed in the first covenant had to be without blemish (Exod. 29:1; Lev. 1:3, 10; Num. 6:14).

The result of Christ's sacrifice is the purification of the conscience "from dead works" to "worship the living God." The inner effect in the conscience can be seen as a result of the forgiveness of sins. The purification of the conscience opens the door to free and authentic worship of the living God. Christians do not worship in order to have freedom or to clean their consciences. They worship because these gifts have already been granted them by God's grace in Christ's giving of himself.

DAVID CORTÉS-FUENTES

Homiletical Perspective

What do we lose? The discussion could also focus on the demands made by family life, again asking what we surrender and what we gain when we become parents.

The image of sacrifice might also be explored in terms of our corporate life. How are we challenged to respond to the pressing needs of the world around us? As a church and as a nation, what are our responsibilities to the rest of the world? Are we as Christians required, for example, to make sacrifices to alleviate the injustice caused by massive extreme poverty? If so, what would such sacrifices look like, and how might we make them? Surely, if the predicted catastrophes caused by global warming are to be averted, those of us in the developed world will have to make sacrifices. What can we do as individuals and as a church to help the people in our communities and in the nation at large understand the imperative to make these sacrifices? What actions should we support and which can we initiate?

A unifying image in our reading today and throughout the letter to the Hebrews is that of the living God. Through the "eternal spirit" Christ offered himself to "purify our conscience from dead works to worship the living God." This powerful metaphor offers an understanding of how to respond to the challenges facing us today. Our secular society surrounds us and tempts us with a myriad of dead works. As preachers we are called to expose the true nature of these dead gods and to proclaim the good news that our God is a living God. Unlike the dead gods whose worship leads ultimately to disappointment and despair, our God is alive and present to us every single moment, offering us forgiveness and enduring salvation.

GINGER GRAB

Mark 12:28-34

28One of the scribes came near and heard them disputing with one another, and seeing that he answered them well, he asked him, "Which commandment is the first of all?" 29Jesus answered, "The first is, 'Hear, O Israel: the Lord our God, the Lord is one; 30you shall love the Lord your God with all your heart, and with all your soul, and with all your mind, and with all your strength.' 31The second is this, 'You shall love your neighbor as yourself.' There is no other commandment greater than these." 32Then the scribe said to him, "You are right, Teacher; you have truly said that 'he is one, and besides him there is no other'; 33and 'to love him with all the heart, and with all the understanding, and with all the strength,' and 'to love one's neighbor as oneself,'—this is much more important than all whole burnt offerings and sacrifices." 34When Jesus saw that he answered wisely, he said to him, "You are not far from the kingdom of God." After that no one dared to ask him any question.

Theological Perspective

In the twentieth century a large body of theological literature has emerged that focuses on the role of *agapē* as a Christian virtue. This should come as little surprise. The apostle Paul describes *agapē* as one of the fruits of the Spirit (Gal. 5:22) and the greatest of the three theological virtues—faith, hope, and love (1 Cor. 13:13). "Whoever does not love does not know God, for God is love," declares the author of 1 John (1 John 4:8). In Mark 12:28–34 Jesus himself pronounces love of God and neighbor to be the two greatest commands of Torah. While it is relatively uncontroversial to ascribe importance to *agapē* as a quintessential feature of the Christian moral life, the import of this claim is not immediately apparent. What does *agapē* entail for how humankind relates to God? What does it mean to love one's neighbor agapically? What role does self-love play in Christian ethics, and how does *agapē* relate to other moral values like justice?

To love God is the greatest command, says Jesus, but it is important to remember that in the Christian tradition divine love precedes *agapē*. To love God agapically is wholly responsive, utterly dependent upon the love that God has made manifest first through God's covenant with Israel and then through the incarnation of Christ. As Jesus proclaims in this text, love of God entails a complete giving over of oneself to God—"you shall love the Lord your God,"

Pastoral Perspective

Civil conversation across theological divides has not been the lot of Christians in recent memory. We, rather, have grown accustomed to heated exchanges on the floor of denominational assemblies wherein one side means to expose the apostasy of the other. In most cases, the proper interpretation of Scripture underlies the import of any given dispute. The charged exchanges that precede our text in Mark's Gospel are no different. First, the chief priests, the scribes, and the elders question Jesus' authority (11:27–33). In response, Jesus speaks in parables (12:1–12). Next the Pharisees and some Herodians try to trap Jesus with a question concerning human allegiance (12:13–15a). Jesus counters with a question and a command (12:15b–17). Finally some Sadducees, whose hermeneutical bias is no mystery to Mark, put forth a hypothetical situation concerning the resurrection (12:18–27). Jesus uses the flawed exegesis to expose their ignorance of the scriptures and of God's power.[1]

When Mark's context is joined with our own, the encounter between Jesus and one of the scribes is exceptional. Given that the scribe is made privy to the preceding disputes, we can only assume he was

---

1. See James Luther Mays's excellent article entitled "Is This Not Why You Are Wrong?" *Interpretation* 60, no. 1 (Jan. 2006).

Exegetical Perspective

As the church calendar nears the end of the season after Pentecost, the lectionary (understandably) obscures the setting of this passage in the midst of Mark's account of the passion. While that decision makes sense liturgically, preachers should bear in mind that the narrative setting for the pericope bears a large part of its expressive force; this anecdote about the greatest commandment exemplifies this principle. Important as are the details of the incident, the concluding phrase depends on readers' awareness of the context for its full impact.

Mark brings Jesus to Jerusalem at the crest of a surge of popularity. The crowds associate his arrival with the advent of David's kingdom; according to 11:18, "the whole crowd was spellbound by his teaching"; his followers engender fear among his opponents (11:18, 32; 12:12); and most important, he demonstrates with his wit and miraculous power that he can accomplish anything. Mark has narrated these incidents in Jerusalem as the culmination of the feats and conflicts Jesus has been negotiating all through the Gospel; here in Jerusalem, in a sort of spirituality slam, Jesus outdoes every constituency of interlocutor. Even the inconveniently out-of-season fig tree withers at his word. When Mark concludes this pericope by observing that "after that, no one dared to ask him any question," he depicts Jesus as

Homiletical Perspective

This passage with its teaching about love of God and neighbor is one of the foundational texts that express simply and yet comprehensively the heart, spirit, and soul of Christianity. In our diverse faith communities, this text provides the framework for ethical thinking and conduct, theological reflection, and biblical hermeneutics. For example, we might ask if our words or actions reflect and embody love of God and neighbor. Similarly, as we interpret Scripture, we might ask whether the text inspires us to love God and neighbor. Saint Augustine wrote, "Whoever, therefore, thinks that he [or she] understands the divine Scriptures or any part of them so that it does not build the double love of God and of our neighbor does not understand it at all."[1]

This teaching about love of God and neighbor has a powerful and rich universal appeal that transcends the literary and cultural contexts of the biblical passage. Indeed, in Luke's Gospel, the literary context is changed, and this teaching serves as a prelude to the parable of the Good Samaritan (Luke 10:25–28). However, our engagement with this Markan text is deepened when we appreciate the literary and cultural dimensions of it. In his conversation with the

---

1. Augustine, *On Christian Doctrine*, trans. D. W. Robertson Jr. (New York: Macmillan, 1958), 30.

Mark 12:28-34

Theological Perspective

he says, with all your heart, soul, mind, and strength (Mark 12:30). The heart of Torah observance and the essence of life in God's kingdom is a stance before God characterized by this acceptance of God's beneficence.

While *agapē* toward God is wholly responsive, *agapē* toward the neighbor is of a decidedly different quality. To love the neighbor cannot mean that one gives all of oneself to the neighbor; to do so would be an act of idolatry. The priority of the first command places appropriate limits on what neighbor love can require of us. Moreover, neighbor love is fundamentally disinterested and, unlike erotic love and friendship, does not depend on the admirable traits of or my personal relationship with my neighbor. We love God because God first loved us; *agapē* toward the neighbor, in contrast, enjoins that we love our neighbor even when our neighbor refuses to reciprocate. Indeed, in God's kingdom *agapē* is a love that is due even one's enemy (Matt. 5:43–48). To love my neighbor agapically requires that I recognize my neighbor as one who is irreducibly valued. In this sense God's own love for humankind is a fitting parallel to the kind of love implied in the second greatest command.

But this text raises another possibility. Could *self-love* be analogous to the love that is due our neighbor? Jesus quotes Leviticus 19:18, "You shall love your neighbor as you love yourself." A prominent stream of the Christian theological tradition treats self-love as the opposite of *agapē*, often associating self-love with human pride and self-seeking. From this perspective "to love one's neighbor as oneself" implies that neighbor love annihilates self-love in Christian life. In God's kingdom, *agapē* displaces self-love as the foundation for human relations. In seeking after my neighbor's well-being, I also refuse to seek after what is my own.

Not all theologians treat self-love as an opposing force to *agapē*, and the reasonable sense of Mark 12:31 suggests that self-love is both natural and justifiable within certain limits. For Aquinas it is not self-love per se that is the root of human sin but rather *inordinate* love of self that turns what is natural—the love that is naturally due oneself—into an acquisitive form of idolatry. To love one's neighbor as oneself suggests that there are continuities between natural self-love and *agapē*. It is by knowing how to love oneself that one learns how to properly love the neighbor.[1]

1. See Timothy Jackson, *The Priority of Love* (Princeton: Princeton University Press, 2003), 56.

Pastoral Perspective

impressed with Jesus' interpretation of texts, even though Jesus' interpretation may have differed from his own. Jesus' understanding of Scripture drew the scribe into conversation. Whether we find ourselves on the floor of a synod assembly, in the sanctuary moderating a meeting of the congregation, or in the living room of a severe critic on the church's board, a substantive exchange rides on our theologically serious engagement with Scripture. If we mean to re-present Christ in our ministry, that ministry must be one of disciplined study and learned engagement with Scripture that leads to a theologically informed wrestling with the world in which we live. Because the scribe and Jesus were worthy theological opponents and clearly had regard for one another, they found themselves talking above the ideological divides and engaged in a kind of communication that had a redemptive ring about it.

Moreover, given his favorable overhearing of Jesus in the previous disputes, the question the scribe poses to Jesus is palpably disarming. This is not a test but an invitation to the table of theological discourse. Likewise, Jesus' response is unguarded and direct. He cites the text that interprets every text in Scripture, as well as every other revelatory claim. Jesus' response has created a space down the ages for honest conversation not only across Christian divides, but also among Jew and Christian and Muslim. That the One we confess to be the Son of God confesses the oneness of God must cause careful interfaith listeners to draw near and reconsider the suspect monotheism of Christianity. That the One who has come to fulfill the law and the prophets not only voices this command but incarnates in heart and soul, in mind and strength, such undivided love must judge our every inclination to division in his name.

The addition Jesus makes to the text from Deuteronomy is also worthy of note. Whereas Moses commands the people of Israel to love God with heart and soul and might, Jesus adds that we also are to love God with our minds. The scribe concurs. For the most part, the church does not. The life of the mind today is often the object of disdain within the congregation and among clergy, even as the growing divide between the church and the academy suggests that the disdain cuts both ways. The result is more heat than light when Christians contend with one another. Surely for this reason Karl Barth had in view the life of the mind as the service of God when he wrote, "We can even dare to say that every Christian—in however primitive and rudimentary a

Exegetical Perspective

the (publicly) undisputed champion of Jerusalem. Jesus' preeminence vests with unquestionable authority his subsequent teachings on Messiah, on the temple, and on the Day of the Lord.

Since Mark's narrative implicitly crowns Jesus with Davidic authority, and endorses his teaching as literally unquestionable, we read his response to the scribe's question carefully. First, although Mark presents Jesus as upholding the fundamental importance of loving God and neighbor, Jesus does not diminish the significance of other commandments. Jesus affirms that the love commandments are preeminently great— but does not suggest that they annul the necessity of observing other commandments. Even the scribe's embellished ratification of Jesus' answer does not imply that one who loves God and neighbor may dispense with burnt offerings and sacrifices. Jesus answers on squarely Judaic premises, just as he answered the rich man's question about eternal life in 10:17–21. The scribe recognizes the judiciousness of such an answer. Mark reports this incident not in order to introduce an unprecedented development; other contemporary Jews did not regard loving God as a matter of insignificance, and several teachers offered comparable perspectives on the greatest commandment. The story demonstrates Jesus' paradigmatic correctness, even on the terms of those who would conspire against him. At the end of this pericope, Jesus' adversaries have no legitimate ground on which to accuse him; Mark presents him as having debated them and won, on their home turf in Jerusalem, on the Torah, the topic of their acknowledged expertise.

The scene begins with a plausible query, from a character whom Mark depicts without suggesting a trace of insincerity. Which commandment matters most of all ("first," NRSV, KJV, and NJB; "most important," NIV, ESV; "foremost," NASB)? Jesus responds that the commandments to love God comprehensively, and to love one's neighbor no less than oneself, together surpass all others. The first half of the response makes the point that if one does not love God, one has no overriding reason for following the law. Mark identifies the same three faculties ("heart," "soul," and "might") as his source, while adding a term that points to intellectual deliberation; Mark quotes the LXX imprecisely (he substitutes *ischuos*, "strength," for the LXX's synonymous *dynameōs*, "power"), though in this context the addition probably reflects Jesus' outthinking all his interlocutors. Love of God motivates God's people to devote their sentiments, their piety, their thoughts, and their energies to the ways of life that God has instructed.

Homiletical Perspective

scribe, Jesus finds common ground by affirming the rich heritage that has provided the foundation for his own teaching and ministry. In other words, what has a ring of universality is actually grounded in Jewish particularity. When the scribe asks Jesus to describe the most important commandment, Jesus speaks the words of a passage known in Judaism by its first word: Hear (*Shema* in Hebrew). The Shema (Deut. 6:4–9) calls Israel's attention to the allegiance and complete commitment that is due to God alone.

How does a text grounded in such cultural particularity speak so powerfully to peoples of diverse traditions and faiths? Matthew and Luke focus directly on the command to love God and neighbor. Mark, however, includes the opening words: "Hear, O Israel: the Lord our God, the Lord is one" (12:29). Mark proceeds with the understanding that this creed calls forth absolute devotion, obedience, and commitment from the heart, soul, mind, and strength. As we deal with dialogue across diverse religious traditions and perspectives, or even within our own faith communities, this text reminds us that the impetus for radical new direction is rooted in the foundational tenets of our faith traditions.

The congregation will also observe that unlike the Gospel of John and the Johannine epistles, the theme of love does not flow through or define the Gospel of Mark. In Mark, the focus on love comes at a very critical moment in the life and ministry of Jesus. His ministry is now centered in Jerusalem, and he has set himself against the temple cult. He has overturned tables and driven people out of the temple (11:15–18); the religious leaders have engaged him in debate (11:27–33; 12:13–17, 18–27); they are angered by his teaching, and want to arrest him (12:1–12; 11:18); his death at their hands is imminent (8:31; 9:30–31; 10:32–34). In this context, Jesus speaks words whose very particular demands are foundational to the faith.

Yet these same words heard in their particularity offer a sharp critique of the teachings of the scribes, who have been guardians of the religious establishment. At every turn the scribes have opposed Jesus with questions about his authority and the source of his power (2:6, 16; 3:22; 7:1, 5). Repeatedly, Jesus has demonstrated that the scribes are on the wrong side of the work of God. In this context, however, a scribe stands in solidarity with Jesus and commends him for his insight (12:28), as well as for the soundness and truthfulness of his teaching (v. 32). He stands in solidarity with Jesus, who has just recently placed the spotlight on certain

Mark 12:28-34

Theological Perspective

A final theological note concerns the relationship between *agapē* and other values critical to God's reign, such as justice. The Christian realism that has dominated twentieth-century Protestant liberalism treated *agapē* as an ethical ideal, but one that was not achievable in history. Reinhold Niebuhr, for example, claimed that the disinterestedness implied in Jesus' vision of *agapē* was an "impossible possibility," an ideal against which human failure was to be measured.[2] For Niebuhr, justice is an approximation of love, and the best we can hope for as a regulative principle for moral life. Thus, when Jesus asserts the priority of neighbor love as the second greatest command, he is offering a vision that is not ultimately achievable. When Jesus teaches his disciples to love their neighbors as themselves, he is alluding to the intrinsic equality among humans that is basic to any conception of justice. Niebuhr fears that Christian attempts to assert the possibility of *agapē* devolve into a utopian idealism that neglects the inevitable conflict of interests that is a mark of human finitude. Humankind discovers its need for God precisely in the space between the idealistic vision of disinterested love of neighbor and the inevitable clash of human wills that characterizes historical existence.

Alternatively, some Christian ethicists disagree with this Christian realist assessment of the impossibility of *agapē* and the relationship between *agapē* and justice in Christian moral life. Paul Ramsey argues that Christ came precisely to embody *agapē* for the world and to teach his disciples both the possibility and the priority of such love. For Ramsey, the two greatest commands reveal a divine ideal that is a mark of Christian discipleship. Contrary to Niebuhr, Ramsey argues that justice is not merely an imperfect approximation of love but is simply what Christian love requires when one is confronted by the demands of two or more neighbors.[3] Christ commands his disciples to love their neighbors and in so doing enjoins upon them a way of life wholly determined by an unwavering commitment to the well-being of others. As such, *agapē* remains open to the possibility of self-sacrifice for the sake of the neighbor.

VICTOR MCCRACKEN

Pastoral Perspective

way—can and must be a theologian, and that no matter how primitive and rudimentary he can and must be a good theologian, having a true vision of the one in whom he believes, having true thoughts concerning Him and finding the right words to express these thoughts."[2]

Without hesitation the scribe, a theologian, declares Jesus to be right in his restatement of the law, repeating what he has heard (in good therapeutic fashion) to ascertain that he has also heard Jesus truly. But the scribe says more. He goes on to critique his own corner of the religious world by way of this common text. Therefore the scribe, in attempting to love God with heart and soul, with mind and strength, loves religion less. For the moment and in Jesus' presence, he has put his whole trust in the unity of the God revealed in Scripture's greatest commandment, rather than in the religious practices and pronouncements prescribed by human authorities that divide.

We would do well to attempt the same. Christian ethicist Paul Lehmann speaks of the community of faith as a diverse community called out by God's command. We are given our *human* being in the diversity of the community, he says, and yet he acknowledges that the diversities in this fellowship "cannot be preferentially used to disrupt and destroy the fellowship. They are diversities designed to express the reality and maturity of the fellowship."[3] In light of the reality and maturity of the fellowship expressed in the diversity at hand, Jesus could say of the scribe, who has neither turned from Israel nor pledged to follow Jesus, "You are not far from the kingdom of God."

Jesus' critics were silenced and the effect was momentarily deafening. Soon the same characters would conspire to arrest him by stealth and kill him. Still it is the case that we who are practitioners of religion would sooner kill his body by our divisions than obey his command to love one another. No doubt the scribe coming near and hearing the members of Christ's church disputing with one another today would be able to draw only one conclusion: we are far, very far from the kingdom.

CYNTHIA A. JARVIS

2. See Reinhold Niebuhr, *An Interpretation of Christian Ethics* (San Francisco: Harper & Row, 1963), 72.
3. Paul Ramsey, *Basic Christian Ethics*, Library of Theological Ethics (Louisville, KY: Westminster John Knox Press, 1993), 347.

2. Karl Barth, *Church Dogmatics*, IV/1 (Edinburgh: T. & T. Clark, 1936–62), 765.
3. Paul Lehmann, *Ethics in a Christian Context* (New York: Harper & Row, 1963), 66–67.

Exegetical Perspective

The second half of Jesus' answer invokes the mutuality that undergirds and strengthens obedience; disciples who do not give themselves priority over others demonstrate the kind of unstinting equity that holds community together. Conflicts arise from neighbors putting their own prerogatives ahead of another's well-being. Neighbors who love another unreservedly follow the law because the law articulates the appropriate relation of one to another. Mark (and Leviticus) does not put special emphasis on "loving oneself" in a therapeutic sense. He expects, in a common-sense way, that everyone begins with loving himself or herself. While he would frown on self-loathing, he here accentuates the love *of neighbor*, introducing "oneself" as a comparative measure for "how much one should love one's neighbor." Those who love God with every aspect of their being, and who love their neighbors as much as they love themselves, will not neglect the Torah with regard to *either* God *or* humanity.

When Jesus observes that the scribe approves of his answer, he gives the elliptical negative blessing that the scribe is "not far from the kingdom of God." The saying exemplifies Mark's habit of treating the kingdom as an enigmatic object of hope and expectation; The not-far scribe may fall into the same rough category as disciples who have been given the mystery of the kingdom, or the bystanders who will not taste death before they see the kingdom in power, or Joseph of Arimathea, who "was also himself waiting expectantly for the kingdom." Whatever the exact sense of the phrase, Jesus does not explicitly *exclude* the scribe from participation in the kingdom; if the scribe's precise status remains to be revealed, he stands in as ambiguous a relation to the awaited kingdom as do all the other characters in the Gospel (except Jesus).

Mark uses this narrative to consolidate Jesus' standing as the soundest, most insightful expositor of Scripture in the temple precincts. Jesus demonstrates his authority by identifying the priority of loving God and neighbors as the basis for all right doctrine and action. The scribe's knowledge brings him near to the kingdom of God, but Jesus has shown in other passages that participating in God's reign will entail more than knowing correct answers. In just a few short verses, Jesus will have been dragged from this pericope's pinnacle of unassailable authority to the cross of degrading death—showing the scribe and all of us the cost of fully loving God and our neighbors.

A. K. M. ADAM

Homiletical Perspective

corrupt and disconcerting practices within the temple. The scribe shares Jesus' anguish over a temple cult that has lost its soul and purpose, its moral authority, its heart for renewal, and can no longer hear, discern, or be responsive to the divine voice. The scribe proffers his strong conviction that a life marked by love of God and love of neighbor is more important than all burnt offerings and sacrifices (v. 33).

The congregation will recognize that Mark presents no treatise on love, and unlike Luke, he does not pose the question, "And who is my neighbor?" Yet our attentiveness to our cultural context reveals that the words that in ancient Israel called forth love and compassion for the widow, orphan, foreigner, poor, or slave are the words of the Gospel, proclaimed today to call forth love for migrants, poor and homeless people, the victims of ecological and economic injustice, and those ravaged by disease, war, and violence. This scribe hears Jesus say to him: "You are not far from the kingdom of God" (v. 34). He understands that love of neighbor must be combined with true worship of God.

The congregation will celebrate the kingdom of God as the proclamation of the good news of God (1:14). In the ministry of Jesus, this proclamation is accompanied by the casting out of demons (1:39) and the healing of many who are sick (1:40–42; 5:12–13). It is the good news of God that does not command, coerce, or mandate love, but rather evokes worship, love, and obedience. Love is contextualized and embodied in true worship, teaching, faith, and practice among God's people.

Perhaps Mark wants us to see the scribe as epitomizing a limited grasp of love and therefore of discipleship. For the scribe and all the characters in Mark's Gospel, including the disciples, the story of love is not complete until they see the cross of Jesus and the power of God. The Gospel presents us with love, worship, and discipleship and invites us to anticipate that the scribe will experience the full life of love of God and neighbor when love embraces him. Then he in joyful obedience will take up his cross and follow where only love can lead.

LINCOLN E. GALLOWAY

Ruth 3:1-5; 4:13-17

³:¹Naomi her mother-in-law said to her, "My daughter, I need to seek some security for you, so that it may be well with you. ²Now here is our kinsman Boaz, with whose young women you have been working. See, he is winnowing barley tonight at the threshing floor. ³Now wash and anoint yourself, and put on your best clothes and go down to the threshing floor; but do not make yourself known to the man until he has finished eating and drinking. ⁴When he lies down, observe the place where he lies; then, go and uncover his feet and lie down; and he will tell you what to do." ⁵She said to her, "All that you tell me I will do." . . .

⁴:¹³So Boaz took Ruth and she became his wife. When they came together, the LORD made her conceive, and she bore a son. ¹⁴Then the women said to Naomi, "Blessed be the LORD, who has not left you this day without next-of-kin; and may his name be renowned in Israel! ¹⁵He shall be to you a restorer of life and a nourisher of your old age; for your daughter-in-law who loves you, who is more to you than seven sons, has borne him." ¹⁶Then Naomi took the child and laid him in her bosom, and became his nurse. ¹⁷The women of the neighborhood gave him a name, saying, "A son has been born to Naomi." They named him Obed; he became the father of Jesse, the father of David.

Theological Perspective

"The Women of the Bible" can become caricatures of womanly piety as they are held to embody the essential lessons and models of femininity. Ruth stands among the ranks of these women challenging us to disturb any kind of seamless lineage of "Women of the Bible" by taking up a more ambiguous space in the canon. Ruth is substantial, she is complicated, and she seeks out meaning in her life with a kind of quiet resolve. In this way, she is a theologian's dream for the way she occupies the biblical witness—disrupting and constructing, embodying and voicing, symbolizing and acting. Her agency holds in its balance the centrality of women in the salvation narrative. Her embodied presence in the unfolding of the story is not without complexity. After all, there is more than passing suggestion that she uses her body, her sexuality, to solve the problem that she and Naomi face. Perhaps most importantly, though, she reflects the larger question of how YHWH functions and participates in Israel's mundane relationships and mores. YHWH's disposition toward social mores comes into focus here as creatively and purposefully entangled. Whether one understands this text as history, folktale, propaganda, or morality lesson, it is full of theological suggestion as to the nature and sources of redemption, as well as the character and availability of God's active participation in human life.

Pastoral Perspective

This lection, which includes the concluding verses of Ruth, recapitulates two themes that are central to the book. Then, just before the story is drawn to a close, a new theme is introduced that gives the story something of a surprise ending. All three themes have implications for congregational life.

The first theme is *hospitality*. The fate of the main characters in this story, from first to last, is dependent on the kindness of strangers. In the early verses of the book Elimelech, Naomi, and their two sons are desperate because there is a famine in Judah. Ironically, they leave a place called Bethlehem (literally, "house of bread") because there is no bread. They seek refuge in Moab, which in itself is remarkable, because there was great enmity between Judeans and Moabites. In other words, they were seeking refuge in what would be thought of as enemy territory.

Eventually the two sons marry Moabite women, and the family is able to live peaceably in this foreign land for ten years. Then, when all three men in the family die, Naomi heads back to Judah and her two daughters-in-law begin to accompany her. Naomi entreats them to seek shelter among their own kin in Moab. Although Orpah initially refuses to leave Naomi, she eventually relents and returns to Moab. Ruth, on the other hand, is insistent: "Do not press

Exegetical Perspective

Redemption in a Broken World. The most powerful instances of redemption often happen in situations of suffering or dislocation. The story of Naomi and Ruth is set within at least two contexts of marginalization. First, at the beginning of the story, Naomi is left economically desolate after her husband and two sons die (1:3–5). She is a widow who now has little or no means of financial support. The second context is the patriarchal culture that is assumed within the biblical world. Thus, this story focuses on the survival strategies of two women who must make a way out of no way in a male-dominated society. The book of Ruth's last two chapters address how Naomi and Ruth navigate these two settings of dislocation faithfully as they seek to lay hold of redemption in an imperfect world.

The selections from chapters 3–4 emphasize two events: (1) Naomi's plan for securing a future for Ruth (3:1–5); and (2) Boaz taking Ruth as his wife and providing for Naomi a next of kin (4:13–17). The two passages frame important events that help to bring this tale of redemption to a conclusion. However, much of the drama within the story is left out, requiring the preacher or teacher of these lessons to supply the missing details.

Securing a Future (3:1–5). Faithfulness and devotion can take many forms. In the book of Ruth, this

Homiletical Perspective

The book of Ruth could also have been called "The Making of a Servant of God." Obed, the "Child of Destiny" born at the end of this story, bears the name "Servant of God."

Ruth presents a recipe of ingredients by which the Holy One continues a faithful presence. It comes as a story and the telling of it offers much more animation and delight than does the academic analysis of it. It is not a holy book in which ecclesiastical structures and systems abound. God, mentioned only in passing, is assumed to be the glue in life rather than some extraneous royal being before whom all ordinary conversation stops.

The ingredients take us into all the corners of living. There is no place God's work is not in process. There are no circumstances through which God's grace cannot appear. First come the loss of livelihood and the transient life of migrants. High hopes fill the sails. Big dreams pave the way. A family settles, passes through strangeness, and begins to make its way. The young children grow up and marry their local sweethearts.

Then tragedy strikes and death claims the men of the family, young and old. Great and caring thought lies behind that even voice which then releases the two young widows to find strength in their own native culture. Deep loyalty appears, and the bond of

Ruth 3:1-5; 4:13-17

Theological Perspective

The canonical conversation is enriched profoundly by the existence of Ruth's story. She inserts into the conversation a counterpoint to the Priestly codes concerning not mixing with the unlike[1] and the vehement opposition to intermarriage clearly voiced in Ezra and Nehemiah.[2] Her ethnic identity as a Moabite holds in it echoes of Deuteronomy 23:3, "No Ammonite or Moabite shall be admitted to the assembly of the LORD." Ruth enlarges the conversation to include more expansive possibilities for those included in and identified as the "people of God."

There is an assumption of plentitude in this story, even in the midst of the social codes that Ruth must navigate. The system is complicated, but not closed in this story. Ruth is able to find inclusion. She is able to be seen, embraced, and provided for in a system that she approached as an outsider. The canon's own mixture of scarcity models of God's grace, along with arguments for the plentitude of God's grace, informs the core of the theological meaning of this text.[3] Ruth's inclusion in the community of God's people and its system of care takes its place among the other codes of conduct that guide behavior for the covenant community. Ruth embodies the ideals of a culture into which she was not born. She is a pivotal symbol of accessibility.

Ruth is also a model of a way of life, which is what allows her a way in and a way toward acceptance in the covenant community. This way of life is reflected in its ideal as one of loyalty and trust, connection, and interdependence. Ruth was already a promise maker and a promise keeper, even before she came to Judah with Naomi. Ruth is faithful in her loyalty to Naomi, and she seeks to protect her even while both women are wise to culture and convention. They know there is a system that protects those who are faithful to the rules of the game. They know there are mechanisms for generosity and for propriety. In this framework of communal life, Ruth approaches these mechanisms actively, receptively, and courageously.

These particular verses signal two moments of transformation: when Ruth is given instructions by

1. Norman Gottwald, *The Hebrew Bible: A Socio-Literary Introduction* (Philadelphia: Fortress Press, 1985, 1987), discusses the Priestly tradition and the "mixing with those who are unlike" and its effect on other prohibitions of intermarriage.
2. See Ezra 9 and Nehemiah 13:23ff. for the rejection of marriage across ethnic lines. These texts are clearly placed in the context of postexile. Ruth's context and dating is less clear. Whether preexilic or postexilic, however, Ruth disturbs the hard-line practices of a closed marital system.
3. For a helpful treatment of scarcity models in the Hebrew Scriptures, see Rita Schwartz's *The Curse of Cain: The Violent Legacy of Monotheism* (Chicago: University of Chicago Press, 1997).

Pastoral Perspective

me to leave you or to turn back from following you! Where you go, I will go; where you lodge, I will lodge; your people shall be my people, and your God my God. Where you die, I will die—there will I be buried. May the LORD do thus and so to me, and more as well, if even death parts me from you!" (1:16–17). It is an extraordinary instance of hospitality.

Normally, we associate hospitality with being able to offer something tangible, like food or shelter. But Ruth is destitute. She has no food or shelter to offer. So she offers the only thing she has left—her own continued presence. After all, these two women, made extraordinarily vulnerable by the loss of their husbands, have lived in the shelter of one another. In the midst of their grief and their need, these two women have become for one another a kind of safe harbor. In Greek, the word *xenos* can mean three things: stranger, guest, and host. These two women started out as strangers from two different cultures. But over time, in the shelter of each other, each has assumed the roles of guest and host.

This theme of hospitality, so prominent at the opening of the book, is recapitulated at the conclusion in Naomi's concern for Ruth, which leads to her instructions on how to approach Boaz ("My daughter, I need to seek some security for you, so that it may be well with you" 3:1b). Then, in turn, Boaz responds to Ruth with a kind of hospitality of his own by assuming the role of next of kin and by marrying Ruth. By the time the story reaches its conclusion, it is clear that God's story only advances through such expressions of hospitality.

Fidelity is a second theme of the book that is recapitulated in these final verses. Ruth's declaration that she will accompany Naomi to Judah is so firm and matter-of-fact that we can begin to recognize that she does not see it as a choice. It is just what one does. To be sure, Ruth is free to leave, as Orpah did. There would be no shame in that. The author of this book does not condemn Orpah, and neither should we. Besides, in following Naomi, Ruth is not making a heroic choice as much as she is simply living out her fidelity to the one who has been given to her. Naomi keeps trying to reason with Ruth. But for Ruth there is nothing to talk about, because she does not approach this as a decision. This theme returns again in the concluding verses as Naomi and Ruth—who are, after all, unrelated—care for one another with the fidelity usually reserved for family.

The family and the church are both places where we have opportunity to learn to live with people we

Exegetical Perspective

young Moabite woman left her homeland to follow Naomi after the death of their husbands. She aligned her fate to this destitute widow rather than seeking her own welfare. Similarly, Naomi begged her daughters-in-law, Ruth and Orpah, to return to their families so that the Lord might grant them security (1:8–9). In Hebrew, the word that describes such faithful actions is *hesed* ("kindness" or "loyalty"). The word appears only three times in the book of Ruth (1:8, 2:20, and 3:10). However, the characters' actions and will toward each other is best summed up in this word. *Hesed* connotes the idea of caring for another who is in need within the context of certain relationships, including covenantal partners.[1] Naomi's concern in chapter 1 was for her daughters-in-law's welfare. In 3:1–5, she continues to show *hesed* to Ruth by formulating a plan to secure a future for her through Boaz, a near kinsman.

In verse 3, Naomi tells Ruth to meet Boaz. She instructs her daughter-in-law to "wash and anoint" herself and to dress in fine clothes. These directions might signify an end to Ruth's mourning period (cf. 2 Sam. 12:20) or bridal preparation (cf. Ezek. 16:8–9). In either case, Naomi's plan is to make Ruth attractive to Boaz. She directs Ruth to wait until Boaz has retired for the evening. She is to go to the place where he is sleeping and "uncover his feet and lie down" (v. 4). The instructions, while not explicitly sexual in nature, are suggestive. The word for "lie down" in Hebrew often implies sexual intercourse. Moreover, feet are used as a euphemism for genitalia in the Bible. Though the word translated as "feet" in this passage is not the usual term, Naomi's instruction to "uncover" the lower extremities of Boaz is provocative. That this encounter happens at night makes the meeting even more suggestive.

In 3:6–15, Ruth carries out Naomi's plan. She goes to the threshing floor and waits until Boaz has fallen asleep. She quietly approaches him, uncovers his feet, and lies down. When Boaz awakes, he is startled to find this young woman at his feet. Ruth takes the initiative by asking Boaz to spread his cloak over her, an act that signifies a proposal for marriage. She adds that Boaz has the right to do this as a kinsman redeemer (*go'el*). In this tradition, a near relative fulfills obligations to a deceased kinsman. This can involve both the purchase of the deceased relative's land, in order to keep the property in the clan, and the producing of an heir for the widow

---

1. Katharine Doob Sakenfeld, *Ruth*, Interpretation Series (Louisville: John Knox, 1999), 11–12.

Homiletical Perspective

love, which holds across all differences, shines through.

The young widow and the old return to their starting place, where, of course, all has changed. Again it is countless adjustments for them. But the wily wisdom of the old woman and the courage of the young combine with the generous heart of an older man, and, through risk in the fields and self-interest in the courts, a new and thrilling love appears. An old and broken heart is healed. Tenacious faith in God proves trustworthy. The "Child of Destiny," Obed, is born. He is the father of the faithful conduit, Jesse, and Jesse of David, the very model of covenantal kingship, the seed of Messiah, the one closest to God's heart.

The date for the book of Ruth is hard to pin down. It could be from anytime between the early monarchy and the third century BCE. The theme is earthy, familiar, accessible, and real. Part of the community's strength is its realization that the Holy One is at work in the simplest, the earthiest, and the most authentic human experiences. Indeed, that is where all truths and stories of truth begin.

The editors' placement of the book of Ruth is worth noting. It is sandwiched in between the end of the wanderings and the entry into the promised land, and the beginnings of kingship and empire. In the first, leadership has arisen from among the people as they go, and the daily journey provided grist for life and faith. In the second, it is more and more a case of rule imposed from above, the thickening of tradition, the abuses of power and privilege, and the silencing of all but official voices.

The Ruth story is a firebreak between the lush, green aspirations of the whole tribe and the consuming flames of the powerful few. It calls for us to remember that God works every day. God labors on the ground, in the heart, among the folk, and through life circumstances. God weaves simple gestures, feelings, decisions, and actions in ways that bring good things. All this arises despite loss and trouble, opposition and tyranny, displacement and pain. That is huge. It shakes the powerful. It undermines the chain of command. It short-circuits the big plans of the few. It elevates the tender and dirt-real lives of the many.

The preaching possibilities here are rich. Where is God in times of upheaval? What is sacred in tragedy and reversal of fortune? How does the Deity speak through unshakable loyalties, gut feelings, and canny decisions? How does the Mighty One stand in the streets or in the courts to press for what is right?

Ruth 3:1-5; 4:13-17

Theological Perspective

Naomi about how to negotiate the customs of propriety and coupling, and when Boaz and Ruth are officially married. These are moments full of cultural content, and they are intensely embodied. The language of custom and inclusion, of safety and provision, is written on Ruth's body in the way she must "communicate" with Boaz and in the blessed result. Their communication is made acceptable, even worthy of celebration and delight, when they are married and the lineage and inheritance are secure. Risk taking and safety are enfleshed in the way Ruth encounters Boaz and, in turn, in the way he responds.

Interdependence and trust are explicitly present in this story. These are issues humanity has always struggled to live into with integrity. The covenant people of YHWH are invited into a way of life that embraces these human needs with the grace of divine guidance about what it means to make and keep promises, what it means to be loyal, and what it means to pay attention to relationship. The beauty of this grace in Ruth's story is that the artfulness of covenant law is just flexible enough to welcome and provide for her. She is welcomed and provided for as a woman who was trying to live into this kind of covenant loyalty, even before she was a part of this community.

The nature of God's covenant relationship with the people of Israel expands into a universal paradigm when it is revealed for its promise to connect and to welcome. God's interest and involvement with humanity is to be courageously and faithfully relational and to be such with loving-kindness (*hesed*). This text shines a light on the nature of God's relational grace in its generous capacity to expand into new situations and problems. Ruth also helps us to tune into the rhythm of the canon's conversation with itself. Her story enlarges and deepens the story of God's habit of welcoming the stranger and of setting the bar high for the way humanity encounters the other.

MARCIA MOUNT SHOOP

Pastoral Perspective

did not choose. Our fidelity to those we are stuck with can be a reflection of the fidelity of a God who is stuck with us all. Surely that reminder is one reason why the story of Ruth became part of the Hebrew Scriptures. Even though Ruth is a Gentile, her story reminded Jews of something important about their God. God does not abandon God's people when the going gets tough, even when they are as destitute as an ancient Near Eastern widow. God's fidelity is beyond a choice. Such fidelity simply is an expression of who God is. When we are faithful to the ones we are stuck with—as Naomi and Ruth were faithful to one another, as members of the church are called to be, as well—it serves as a reminder of the faithfulness of the God who is stuck with us all.

These themes of hospitality and fidelity can be traced through the book of Ruth. But then, in the final few verses, we learn that the child born to Ruth and Boaz is none other than Obed, the grandfather of the great King David. Through Ruth, a poor and childless foreigner, *God is at work* in surprising and unexpected ways. But it is probably a mistake to call this a surprise ending, because it picks up a theme that can be traced throughout Scripture: God often works through the most unlikely people—outsiders, strangers, and the outcast. Once again, God has been able to work in surprising ways through human hospitality. The book's concluding verses might be summarized with a variation on the admonition in Hebrews (13:2): Do not neglect to show hospitality to strangers, for thereby some have entertained the great-grandmother of a king.

MARTIN B. COPENHAVER

Exegetical Perspective

(see 4:3–5). Boaz agrees to fulfill this duty, but informs Ruth that there is another kinsman who is line before him. After receiving grain, Ruth returns to Naomi with a report of the evening's events.

Redemption through a Child (4:13–17). In the next scene, Boaz goes to the city gate, the place where justice is administered. The nearest kinsman to Naomi's husband is interested in purchasing the property but does not want to produce an heir for her. Therefore, Boaz assumes the role of kinsman redeemer by acquiring the land and by marrying Ruth. Verses 13–17 bring this act of redemption to completion when Ruth gives birth to a child. In verse 16, the plot comes full circle when Naomi nurses the baby, symbolizing the movement in the story from death to life. The child, whose name is Obed, becomes the grandfather of David. The implied message of the closing genealogy is profound. The greatest king in Israelite history can trace his beginnings to the faithful actions of his Moabite great-grandmother, Ruth.

The story of Ruth and Naomi depicts a world of struggle. Their faithful actions toward each other lead to their eventual deliverance. Though enmeshed within the problematic male-centered world of ancient Israel, these women lay hold of their salvation. They survive in the face of death and eventually secure their own redemption. God never intervenes directly in the book of Ruth. Though God's hand is behind the plot, the narrator chooses to tell this story through the faithful actions of the story's characters. The world of patriarchy does not disappear. In the end, only Boaz is mentioned in the genealogy, and the women's survival is ultimately dependent on their relationships to men. Nevertheless, this imperfect redemption points to the subtle God who works behind the scenes in order to bless the lives of these two women who embody *hesed* in their words and deeds.

FRANK M. YAMADA

Homiletical Perspective

Where is the Holy in happy endings or in the rich human tapestry that displays our best visions? How is God unseen but never absent? In what ways is God full of surprises down the road, the keeper of ultimate promises?

The style for preaching from this story seems to be story itself. Tell about the ups and down of human lives. Name the surprises. Feel the pain and joy. Lift up the importance of our human nature and sensibilities. Remind people how glad you are that our own people are so gifted and inventive and tenacious in the face of life's waves. Consider how revelation comes to you and yours. Recall the messianic personalities, the "children of destiny," who have been born into your world through a sea of trouble.

Before all doctrine, theology, and liturgical tradition, there were simply people finding profound richness in the most ordinary and unlikely places.

This story is fertilizer especially formulated to encourage weeds. The earthy, visceral range of experiences and feelings takes us outside the traditional Sunday garden with the clean smiling faces, and sets us where we and others really live, grow, languish, and die.

It is paint stripper, dissolving layers of privilege, power, and presumption, and getting us back to the natural grain of human lives in a mixed and mundane world.

This old tale is cleansing cream, rubbed in after a long, grimy day at the wars. It goes deep, loosens stubborn grit, and works as we pause, disarm, and rest.

Israel in its long life of faith has known every aspect of Ruth's journey. A thousand willing people could step forward to play any of the parts in the cast. How imaginative to tell of all the pain and glory in such a simple and approachable way. There is homiletical brilliance here. To read this story and become lost in its charm empowers that sense that each of us, no matter where we are in our ordinary living, is playing a part in the coming of the "child of destiny." The servant of God is born when we exercise our best human words and wiles across the crowded ways of life.

G. MALCOLM SINCLAIR

Psalm 127

¹Unless the LORD builds the house,
  those who build it labor in vain.
Unless the LORD guards the city,
  the guard keeps watch in vain.
²It is in vain that you rise up early
  and go late to rest,
eating the bread of anxious toil;
  for he gives sleep to his beloved.

³Sons are indeed a heritage from the LORD,
  the fruit of the womb a reward.
⁴Like arrows in the hand of a warrior
  are the sons of one's youth.
⁵Happy is the man who has
  his quiver full of them.
He shall not be put to shame
  when he speaks with his enemies in the gate.

Theological Perspective

Psalm 127 is part of the collection of Songs of Ascent, sung by pilgrims on their ascent to Mount Zion. After the wars of conquest have taken their toll, the pilgrims are less triumphal than hopeful. The fragility of their great works has become plain.

The first verse of the psalm is familiar to us through rituals of dedication. We are reminded that God the Creator is the source of all that is, including ourselves, our energies, skills, hopes, and dreams. What we make is part of God's creative work in our midst. God's people are to recognize in gratitude all the divine gifts by which they live and act. As Calvin and others have noted, this is not to diminish human labor. Rather, human labor is ennobled through participating in God's providence for all things.

The last verse of the psalm speaks of enemies at the gate. Those who sang it as they approached Zion after the destruction of Jerusalem knew that events could overturn the best protections they could erect to secure their best efforts. Yet the story goes on as long as the people survive. The true welfare of the city finally depends on God's creative action in the formation of families and the birth of children who will flourish to populate the city. God creates through human procreation as well as through human labor.

Pastoral Perspective

At first glance, Psalm 127 is a familiar tribute to God's sovereignty, a reminder of our humanity and the futility of relying on ourselves rather than on God—an important reminder of key theological understandings about who God is and what it means to be human.

But the familiarity and brevity of this psalm can belie its depth, and closer examination of this brief writing reveals a distinctly prophetic word for North American Christians. We live in a culture that values achievement, hard work, and success; where a person's value is judged by his or her commitment to the process and production of work.

God's word has something different to say about what it means to be human. Psalm 127 has another perspective, one that rings with a prophetic edge in our culture of achievement and self-reliance. In its scant five verses, Psalm 127 proclaims that our work is God's work: "Unless the LORD builds the house, those who build it labor in vain" (v. 1). It doesn't make a difference if we find a way to squeeze more time out of our day by staying up later to get work done, or rising early in the morning to start the day before the sun is up. Of course, the way we conduct ourselves in our work is important. But the prophetic word comes in the reminder that our work is

Exegetical Perspective

At first blush Psalm 127 may seem a bit schizophrenic. The first part (vv. 1–2) focuses on the building of a house, while the second part (vv. 3–5) concerns itself with the blessings of family. The key to understanding the psalm's essential unity is in the use of the word "house." House is often used as a metaphor for family, and the Old Testament authors are almost playful in their use of it. This can be seen most clearly in 2 Samuel 7:1–2, where David proposes to build God a house. God counters with a promise to build *David* a house, that is, a line of descendants through which David's throne would be established forever (vv. 11b–16).

Psalm 127 may actually be a kind of poetic meditation on the 2 Samuel 7 passage. One can imagine people appreciating God's wordplay in different ways throughout the history of the psalm's composition and use. If, as the psalm's title (not included above) suggests, it was a psalm written by Solomon (or as medieval rabbis suggested, a psalm written by David *about* Solomon), then the psalm celebrates both the tangible temple and the perpetuation of the Davidic line. The title also identifies Psalm 127 as one of the fifteen Songs of Ascents (Pss. 120–34) that were sung and prayed by pilgrims on their way to worship in Jerusalem. In

Homiletical Perspective

Psalm 127 is situated within a collection of psalms (120–34) that all bear the heading "A Song of Ascents." This particular song provides the preacher with a splendid opportunity to reflect on the long-term movement of God's people across time and to proclaim a message of God's faithful provision. The psalm is sung by people who are on the way toward giving thanks to God. As many eucharistic liturgies proclaim, "It is always right and good to give thanks and praise to God."

A sermon engendered by this particular psalm would do well to challenge a widely held view that Christian preaching, as well as Christian living, is essentially problem-centered rather than praise-centered. David Ford and Daniel Hardy address this theological and practical matter in a particularly insightful way.

> It is of the greatest importance to the whole of Christian communication that it be praise-centered. This is in contrast with the problem-centered approach that has often been dominant. . . . The essence of mission and evangelism is in the intrinsic worth, beauty, and love of God, and the joy of knowing and trusting him. . . . Problem-solving lacks the logic of overflow, and easily lets the problem be the center of attention,

Psalm 127

Theological Perspective

Human history offers no encouragement to those who assume the world they have built is under their control. The subtitle of the psalm (not printed above) reaches back to the wisdom of Solomon to recall both the beauty and the fragility of city, temple, land, and people. There is a faint echo of Solomon's declaration and prayer at the dedication of the temple in Jerusalem (1 Kgs. 8:27–30). The security of the "house" is the divine presence that meets human beings who approach the Lord with humility and gratitude, not the strength of its walls, the beauty of its design, or the magic of its liturgy. The blessing of the Lord is always grace upon grace.

When Christians and Jews speak of God's care of and blessing on the created world, human beings within it, and the people of God among them, their speech does not flow from lives always happy and blessed. The prudential and nature Psalms (e.g., Pss. 37 and 104), much of Proverbs, and the language of the Torah remind us that God's blessing accompanies trust and commitment to the will of God. Those are happy who walk in the way and are satisfied with longevity, prosperity, and a good name. By contrast, sinners who do not walk in the way do not receive such blessings. Yet it is never simple. All too often, those who do not walk in the way prosper, while those who do suffer (e.g. Pss. 73 and 89, and, famously, the case of Job).

The idea of God's providential care of all the creatures and all their actions is born in struggle. No one questions God's governing care when things go well: we are blessed because we are virtuous, lucky, or clever! The question of God's providence is raised when things do *not* go well. The link between our actions and what happens no longer makes sense, *it is vain* (v. 2 NIV). What is the point of faithful labor? When the world seems unfair, the question of God's providence is unavoidable. By contrast, those who trust the Lord know it does not all depend on them. They can commit their way unto the Lord confident that their labor is not empty (Ps. 37).

The idea of divine providence nourishes a healthy sense of security in insecure times. It does not explain evil in the world or explain it away. In a fragile world with intractable problems and things beyond our control, there is always more going on than we know. In the face of destructiveness, God continues to create the conditions for life in general and human life in particular.

Theologians often speak of providence as God's directing creativity continuing God's original creative activity through time. It is more than a

Pastoral Perspective

first God's work. We are merely instruments of God's work, which started long before we were born, and which will continue long after we are gone.

The psalmist's choice of words is significant. It is not elite work that is held up as an example of God's work. The psalmist cites common, everyday work as being God's work: building houses and guarding the city gate. God is at work in our workplaces, in our houses, in our communities, even before we arrive. That is good news! Our work does not depend solely on us. Our decision to work hard can be a grateful response to the One who called us to that work in the first place.

The second section of this psalm, verses 3–5, might present difficulties as it is used in the parish. The psalmist writes, "Sons are indeed a heritage from the Lord, the fruit of the womb a reward" (v. 3). The psalmist's priority is for sons: sons are lauded, daughters are left out. Sons provided the assurance of a line of inheritance for the family. Sons could protect their parents, so that the father "shall not be put to shame when he speaks with his enemies in the gate" (v. 5). The social and historical particularities that lead the psalmist to prioritize sons (not daughters) could make this second part of Psalm 127 complicated to proclaim liturgically in the contemporary context.

Furthermore, for men and women who have chosen not to have children, the idea that children are a reward from God may raise questions about who is eligible for God's blessing and who is not. If children are a reward from God, does a woman or man who chooses not to have children opt out of God's reward? For women and men who cannot have children, the notion that children are a gift from God, or even a reward, may stir up feelings of loss or grief and raise significant questions about God's goodness. If children are a gift from God, what does that mean for those who do not or cannot have children? Does God hold them in lower esteem than those who do have children?

There is ample support in the biblical narrative for the understanding that children are a blessing from God, and that not being able to conceive is due to God withholding children. Sarah, Rachel, and Hannah all thought that they were unable to have children, and all attributed their infertility to God's withholding (Gen. 16:1–2, Gen. 30:1–2, 1 Sam. 1:6). When each woman did become pregnant, it was understood to be the result of God's blessing (Gen. 21:1–2, Gen. 30:22, 1 Sam. 1:19b–20).

Historically in Israel, children were vital to a family. Not only did they provide able bodies to do

Exegetical Perspective

this liturgical context, the anticipation of worship in the temple and the pilgrim's arrival in the "city of David" would have enriched appreciation of the psalm. After the destruction of Solomon's temple, the psalm must have taken on a terrible poignancy for the exiles. Yet the promise of the Davidic line would have tilted their expectations toward the future and offered a spark of hope in the midst of despair. As Christians, we read the psalm through the eyes of those who recognize the surprising ways that God has fulfilled the promise through Jesus Christ, who entered the heavenly temple to sacrifice himself "once for all" and will "appear a second time, not to deal with sin, but to save those who are eagerly waiting for him" (Heb. 9:24–28).

At another level, however, Psalm 127 "works" at an almost existential level, quite apart from the themes of the Davidic covenant. It is usually identified as a wisdom psalm—an association that aligns it with books such as Job, Ecclesiastes, and Proverbs. Like those books, this psalm reflects on how to live life faithfully and well. The first two verses are a sobering reminder that human efforts are futile without God's blessing (cf. Prov. 21:30; also Pss. 124 and 115:1). The images of building a house and guarding a city are offered as examples of this reality. If we cannot relate to those, then perhaps verse 2's portrait of a workaholic will reach across the millennia to make the point. The text of the last phrase in verse 2 is somewhat garbled, but one can make sense of it in one of two ways—both of which are helpful. The NRSV renders it as a promise: "for he gives sleep to his beloved." The Jewish Publication Society's translation is somewhat more in sync with the rest of the psalm: "He provides as much for His loved ones while they sleep."

The last part of the psalm (vv. 3–5) offers another example of a situation in which human efforts are futile without God's cooperation. Seeing this image of the happy man with a "quiver" full of sons as such an illustration is the first step through these verses' pastoral minefield. Granted, human participation is required, but as the Bible often reminds us, only the Lord grants conception (Gen. 21:1; 30:22; Ruth 4:13).

Just when we think we have sidestepped the difficult issue of taking credit for the sons in our quiver, however, the second half of the poetic parallel seems to make the difficulty mandatory by identifying the "fruit of the womb" as a "reward." Again, it helps to see this psalm as part of the larger wisdom tradition. Though many wisdom passages do emphasize blessing as a reward for obedience

Homiletical Perspective

whereas praise puts what is wrong in a wider perspective from the start.[1]

Moreover, to read this psalm at the end of the Christian year, with an eye toward the final destiny of God's people, provides additional incentive for proclamation that affirms the primacy of the love of God for the world. Such God-centered proclamation, which in itself is an act of praise, will be articulated with a confidence made possible by the psalmist's confession.

First, God builds the house. Second, God watches over the city. Third, God provides while God's people sleep. The psalm effects what it claims by situating its singers in ordinary life, recalling the goodness of God's providential activity while acknowledging the primary place of God's working. It is God who ultimately builds, protects, and provides in, beneath, and through all human work and effort.

Such robust proclamation will be good news to congregations whose life is gripped by anxiety and fear; who are convinced that their existence and future are ultimately in their own hands; who feel their work is all up to them; and who believe that God has abandoned them to their own devices. No matter what the particular task or problem may be— evangelism, ministering to the poor, rendering faithful witness in the neighborhood, or challenging the assumptions of culture or the claims of the nation-state—such despair fuels the conviction that we have been left on our own and that strength from God will be given only at the end of the journey— that is, if we endure.

At this point praise-centered proclamation can announce news that is good, a gospel for weary people whose existence is not without uncertainty, whose identity is not without question, and whose resources are not without limit. While we may grant that God has had the primary role in creating the world, it seems more difficult to grant God similar primacy for the completion of creation. And while the pilgrimage to which Israel and the church have been called aims toward ever increasing praise of God, such doxological existence is often challenged by the ordinary realities of life.

The sermon could call the church to entrust itself and its future anew to the One who creates, preserves, and provides. In keeping with this theme,

---

1. David F. Ford and Daniel W. Hardy, *Living in Praise: Worshipping and Knowing God,* rev. ed.(Grand Rapids: Baker Academic, 2005), 188–89.

Psalm 127

Theological Perspective

holding operation. Although everything positive or negative has a time and a season, God has made everything "beautiful" in its time and gathers what has been scattered (Eccl. 3:11, 15 RSV). In the language of Paul, God is at work for good in everything (Rom. 8:28) even though not everything that happens is good. And that is enough to encourage builders, sentinels, and parents of children that their lives are not a fool's hope.

In this way, God's providence establishes human meaning and freedom by upholding a natural and moral order within which they can exist. The older theologians spoke of providence as divine governing or ruling, rather than as a cause with effects. Human and divine freedom are not in conflict. The Lord may build the house in the deepest sense, but it is the builders who actually design and erect it. Their activity takes place within the overall divine activity, or, conversely, God is at work through their activity.

Those who sang this and other psalms reflected the conflicts of Zion as well as their confidence in the Lord who would secure final victory. The experience of defeat is never far away. This realism has made the Psalms widely used in synagogue and church. It applies to persons and communities faced with opposition and adversaries too great to control. God is greater than whatever threatens me/us in particular situations. There will be resources and challenges we do not now see: trust God. There will be purposes served we can know only looking back: be open to learn.

This faith is a courageous hope that does not have all the answers. They must learn as they walk into the unknown future. Divine providence is not magic; it does not rescue us *from* trouble without following the way of God *through* it. Faith becomes courage to endure what we must without losing heart, and thereby losing our souls. The point was never just a building or a throne or happy family circumstances. It was always about access to God and faithfulness to the way of God in the world.

THOMAS D. PARKER

Pastoral Perspective

work, but they ensured a line of inheritance for the family. More broadly, bearing children ensured the survival of the community. "A woman's prestige was based at least partly on her demonstrated ability to produce offspring."[1] Within this historical context, it is no wonder that children were understood to be a reward, or blessing, from God.

However, we should not dismiss the notion of children as a reward from God as the culturally irrelevant product of a specific historical biblical context. Many who become pregnant after years of trying still experience the arrival of their child as a blessing from God. Many who try, unsuccessfully, to become pregnant still experience their inability to conceive as the lack of God's blessing. Even so, when dealing with the complexities of this aspect of the text, pastors will want to remember the complex tensions that exist within the OT canon: tensions between bad news understood as divine punishment, bad news understood as the product of injustice, or bad news that has no final explanation. These tensions are operative in and through our lives today. The pastor's role is to help sort out which biblical testimony best speaks to pastoral concerns in a particular congregation.

Just as the psalmist makes it clear that our work is, in actuality, not our work at all, but God's work, the psalmist also seems to be trying to underscore that God is sovereign even in matters as seemingly personal as childbearing. The parts of our lives that are the most ordinary, and the parts of our lives that are the most extraordinary, are indeed a matter of God's concern.

KATE FOSTER CONNORS

1. Jo Ann Hackett, "1 and 2 Samuel," in *Women's Bible Commentary*, ed. Carol A. Newsom and Sharon H. Ringe (Louisville, KY: Westminster John Knox Press, 1992), 95.

Exegetical Perspective

(and suffering as a punishment for sin), other parts of the wisdom corpus urge caution in this area. The book of Job, for instance, is an extended cautionary tale devoted to the dangers of reading such an equation backwards. It is one thing, after all, to remind people that obedience yields blessing and disobedience yields suffering. It is quite another to claim that those who suffer—in this case, those who are childless—are being punished for some specific sin. This larger wisdom tradition should make us appropriately nervous about assuming that those with children are being rewarded.

The last pastoral "mine" in these verses' field is their overpowering use of masculine and military imagery. Readers would do well to remember that the language here is true to its time. In order to "translate" it most truly into our own, we must remember that it is descriptive and not necessarily prescriptive. The mother—or father—who is surrounded by loyal daughters is also a formidable presence against threat.

Just as our appreciation of Psalm 127 is enriched by the "contexts" of 2 Samuel 7 and the larger corpus of the Wisdom literature, so too it is augmented when seen in the circle of the other lectionary readings. The reading from Ruth 3–4 is particularly rich with resonances. The story of Ruth, Boaz, and Naomi reads like the narrative version of Psalm 127, and could voice the prayer of one or more of the characters in that story. If one reads the whole of Ruth 3 and 4, one realizes that these characters make a full and faithful effort that is finally crowned with God's saving cooperation. As we read the genealogy in Ruth 4:17, we realize that God is using these two poor widows (cf. Mark 12:38–44) and a farmer to build up the "house and family of David" (Luke 2:4).

CAROL M. BECHTEL

Homiletical Perspective

the sermon could also provide opportunities for encouraging discouraged disciples, as well as for depicting those qualities of spiritual maturity that characterize living faith that discerns God's ordinary and often seemingly unspectacular provision. As the church nears the end of the Christian year, it continues to need fresh reminders of the God who is the source and end of its life.

Another fruitful approach for preaching might be to emphasize that a God-given heritage is the fruit of divine providence. The second half of the psalm affirms this truth: it is God who gives offspring, engendering new life that makes a family strong and secure. A people whose faith is capable of generating new life will remain confident in times of trouble. As is the case in the first half of the psalm, where God's blessings include a place for dwelling in God's presence, safety from enemies, and provision even during times of rest, so too is a way of life that bears much fruit a blessing and sign of God's providential care.

Here the preacher has a wonderful opportunity for gospel proclamation, for affirming that the life and legacy of God's people is primarily the fruit of divine activity. All our worship, work, and witness, all our service, ministry, and mission efforts are in vain unless God is always and already at work. The great surprise of this psalm, for congregations that are flourishing or fading, is its attentiveness in praising God, in remembering God's goodness, in acknowledging God's faithful activity. Some may hear this as a word of judgment; others may hear a word of mercy. Both are necessary if the church is to remain true to the way that leads to its final destiny with God.

For Israel, it was God who built the temple, God who established the city of Jerusalem, and God who blessed the lineage of David. While considerable human work was required for all of this, Israel was always dependent on God's prior working. So we too might say, "Unless the Lord builds the church, they labor in vain who build it." Such gospel proclamation directs attention to God, not as a way of escaping the problems and challenges of being God's people in the world, but in order to establish the praise of God as the beginning and end of who we are and what we are to do.

MICHAEL PASQUARELLO III

Hebrews 9:24-28

^{24}For Christ did not enter a sanctuary made by human hands, a mere copy of the true one, but he entered into heaven itself, now to appear in the presence of God on our behalf. ^{25}Nor was it to offer himself again and again, as the high priest enters the Holy Place year after year with blood that is not his own; ^{26}for then he would have had to suffer again and again since the foundation of the world. But as it is, he has appeared once for all at the end of the age to remove sin by the sacrifice of himself. ^{27}And just as it is appointed for mortals to die once, and after that the judgment, ^{28}so Christ, having been offered once to bear the sins of many, will appear a second time, not to deal with sin, but to save those who are eagerly waiting for him.

Theological Perspective

The writer of Hebrews prescribes a robust Christology as the antidote to the spiritual fatigue of a community in danger of drifting away from the gospel (2:1). In chapter 9 we are in the midst of a sermon on Jesus' priestly ministry. The metaphor of Jesus as the great high priest was introduced earlier (2:17; 4:14–5:10). Verses 24–28 advance a comparison, begun in chapter 7 and continuing through chapter 10, that demonstrates the superiority of Jesus' ministry to the old Levitical priesthood and its sacrificial system.

The author highlights four points of superiority. First, unlike the Levitical priest's entry into a desert tabernacle made by humans, the exalted Jesus has entered God's presence, providing believers with access to the living God. Second, while the Levitical priest entered the Holy of Holies to offer atonement for both his own and the people's sins (5:3; 7:27), Jesus the sinless one has done this solely "on our behalf" (9:24). Third, unlike the annual need for atonement in the Levitical order, Jesus' sacrifice has permanent efficacy, accomplishing "once for all" the forgiveness of sins (9:26). Finally, Jesus not only offers the sacrifice, but *is* himself the sacrifice (9:26).

These verses undergird John Calvin's inclusion of the priestly role in the threefold office (*munus triplex*) of prophet, priest, and king through which

Pastoral Perspective

The doors to heaven and earth get flung open in this passage. Repeated emphasis is placed on both the permanence and authenticity of Christ's living sacrifice. It is as though the author wants to shout, "Everything that we knew before was only a template, a mock-up, of the new reality made possible in Christ."

The writer begins by asserting that Jesus' power is not limited to the earthly realm where we create sanctuaries and only speak of heaven. Rather Christ has blazed a path for those who would follow him into the very presence of God. Not only that, but Christ enters into that holy space to intercede for us. We now have a champion in heaven, someone to advocate for us in the highest court.

This hopeful shift in divine/human reality brings to mind a story told by David Willis-Watkins of Princeton Seminary. He tells of his time as a parish pastor when one of his elders got a call in the night from the police station. It seems that a number of the young men of the town had gotten a bit rowdy and ended up in jail. One of them used his one call to ask the elder to come get him out. When the elder arrived at the jail, he took a look at the group of boys and asked, "How many of you are baptized?" Every boy in the cell raised his hand. The elder told the officer, "I'll take them all," and he did.

Exegetical Perspective

This passage describes the crucifixion of Jesus. But here we do not get a historical report; there is no trial before Pilate, no description of the nails in the hands and feet, no account of the cries from the cross. Instead, the author of Hebrews looks at the crucifixion from a theological perspective, telling the reader not what happened, but what it means for the world and to the human heart that Jesus died. Every observer in Jerusalem that day could have described what could be seen by the eye, but the author of Hebrews insists that the truth of the cross is hidden deeper, accessible only to the eye of faith.

In order to understand this passage, we must enter into the realm of Neoplatonic thought, which was the prevailing worldview of the Hellenistic culture out of which Hebrews comes. The writer of Hebrews is by no means a thoroughgoing Platonist, but he employs Neoplatonic words and concepts in much the same way that people today use terms like "ego," "id," and "Freudian slip," without necessarily being Freudians. Neoplatonism was the philosophical well from which the whole culture drank.

The key idea to keep in mind for this text is the Platonic distinction between the heavenly and the earthly. For Platonists, pure and perfect reality is not available in this world but exists only in heaven. Earthly, material existence is but a shadow of the

Homiletical Perspective

Preaching from Hebrews can be a challenging endeavor, first, because of the complexity of the writer's arguments for the superiority of Jesus over the established Jewish protocols for access to the Divine and, second, because of the modern Christian listener's typical unfamiliarity with those protocols. In no way are these factors diminished in this passage, which compares the tabernacle or temple with the heavenly venue where Christ made possible the eternal, unlimited access of humans to God through his exemplary work on our behalf.

The preacher may consider going into detail to explain the writer's argument here, and the preacher's listeners may even find that detail interesting. But take care not to let your homiletical ball get lost in the complex and unfamiliar weeds. Better to focus on the overarching point of the arguments in Hebrews 9:24–28, which is clear and compelling and has powerful ramifications in the lives of those who hear it well expressed.

It would be helpful to set the context of the arguments in this passage by reviewing the opening verses of Hebrews, which establish the validity of the prophets and the ways and means of holy access that God made available. The first four verses also beautifully describe the identity, the work, and the place of Jesus. He is (regarding his identity) "heir of

Hebrews 9:24-28

Theological Perspective

Jesus accomplishes his saving work.[1] As priest Jesus sacrifices himself to blot out our sin and reconcile humanity to God, and as priest Jesus intercedes on our behalf before God.

"Sacrifice" as a metaphor for the meaning of Jesus' death has disturbed some feminist and other theologians because of its potential misuse to glorify suffering and to portray God as vengeful. This focus on sacrifice and an earlier reference to purification through blood (9:22) have supported a satisfaction theory of atonement.[2] Under this theory, the sin of humanity is an offense against God that requires satisfaction before humanity can be reconciled to God; Jesus' death provides that satisfaction. But at least two dangers lie in pressing the author's theology too neatly into a classic satisfaction theory.

First, this reading ignores other language in Hebrews. Earlier Jesus' death is described in terms more consistent with a Christ-the-victor understanding. His death destroys "the one who has the power of death" and frees those "held in slavery by the fear of death" (2:14–15). We also find resonances with the moral influence theory in the depiction of Jesus' sacrifice as one of obedience and faithfulness in the face of suffering (5:8) and the call for believers to respond by bearing the abuse he endured (12:3–4; 13:13). In short, Jesus' life and ministry, no less than his death, are critical parts of his atoning work.

Second, no single interpretive model can plumb the depths of God's reconciling act in Christ. Therefore the sacrificial imagery should be held in tension with the rich variety of other biblical metaphors that partially illumine this mystery. Calvin's focus on Christ's *three* offices moves toward a more inclusive atonement theory.

This passage also introduces an eschatological theme. With its reference to "the end of the age" (9:26) and its assurance that "Christ . . . will appear a second time" (9:28), the text points forward from Jesus' saving act to the new age Jesus has inaugurated. The second coming is not a day of judgment to be feared, but a day of salvation, again because of the "once for all" nature of Jesus' reconciling work.

The entire passage trumpets liberation to all bound by the burden of guilt arising from our

1. John Calvin, *The Institutes of the Christian Religion*, ed. John T. McNeill (Philadelphia: Westminster Press, 1960), 2.15.
2. Anselm's classic articulation appears in *Cur Deus Homo?* Other theories of the atonement include Christ as victor over the powers of sin and death and the moral influence theory, under which the depth of Christ's love compels a response of gratitude.

Pastoral Perspective

By virtue of Christ's sacrifice signified in their baptism, the boys enjoyed a new reality. They found an advocate—someone willing to intercede on their behalf. So it is with our life in Christ.

This passage also offers clarity about another of the essential aspects of Jesus' ministry, linking it to the traditional Jewish doctrine of sacrifice and atonement. The writer offers a contrast of what used to be—repeated annual sacrifices by the priest—to what is now available through Jesus, the "once and for all" sacrifice of Christ.

To understand the importance of this concept of sacrifice, one has to be familiar with the Jewish understanding of sin, guilt, and the covenantal offerings that were a central part of the religious life of the early Jews. Within this context, sacrifice becomes a means of relationship between God and God's people. It has the dynamic of call-and-response as God reaches out and the people respond. According to Bernhard Anderson, "It was believed that God himself, in a sovereign act of mercy, graciously approached his people, providing the means for overcoming guilt and maintaining the holiness of the community."[1]

In this passage from Hebrews we hear a transition from a repeated ritual reenactment of God claiming the people of Israel to a once and for all claiming through Christ. The self-sacrifice of Christ is at once a declaration of the new covenant and an act of atonement and sin offering that God both provides and accepts.

In our culture we are all too familiar with paying annual fees, shelling out penalties on debts that have been defaulted, having to renew employment contracts, and enduring review processes to ensure that we will have our work contracts renewed. In a bitterly ironic and exploitative reality, there are companies today that still sell funeral insurance. Taking advantage of the fear of some people that they might die and not have the resources to be properly outfitted for the afterlife, some companies charge monthly premiums to the poorest of people with the promise that they will be taken care of and well laid out in the event of death. Failure to keep up payments results in forfeiture of their policies, and the debt can even be passed on to their families. Families are required to pay exorbitant prices to keep their contracts current.

1. Bernhard Anderson, *Understanding the Old Testament*, 3rd ed. (Englewood Cliffs, NJ: Prentice-Hall, 1975), 467.

heavenly forms and truths, something like a blurred photocopy of the original. Since human beings are confined, bodily and temporally, to this world, they are trapped in this shadow reality and cannot fully participate in the spiritual truths. Human beings yearn to be a part of the spiritual realm, but they can do so only by imitation, by vague, partial, and imperfect mimicry of the full and perfect heavenly ideas.

The author of Hebrews uses this heavenly-earthly distinction to talk about Christian worship, contrasting the priestly system of sacrificial worship (and by implication, let the preacher note, much humanly conceived worship) with the sacrifice of Christ on the cross and, finally, with the worship that Christ makes possible for humanity. In the background here is the description of the liturgy of the Day of Atonement (see Lev. 16) in which the high priest dons the holy vestments, makes a sacrifice for his own sins, enters into the Holy of Holies and, as an act of atonement for the sins of the people, slaughters a goat. Placing this old sacrificial system alongside the cross, the writer makes three main distinctions:

1. Reality vs. Simulation (v. 24). Church buildings are attempts to express holiness in wood and stone. Whether they are cathedrals with vaulted ceilings and lavish art or plain sanctuaries with simple lines and clear glass windows, churches embody human ideas about what a meeting place with God looks like. But how real are these human conceptions of holy places? On the Day of Atonement, the priest went into the holy tabernacle but, as the author of Hebrews observes, it was a sanctuary made by "human hands," a "mere copy" of the true, heavenly sanctuary. By contrast, when Jesus died, his body was not only on a cross in Jerusalem, it was in the sanctuary of "heaven itself," and he was appearing in the very "presence of God on our behalf."

At the visitors' center of the Kennedy Space Center in Florida is a massive Space Shuttle Ride on which people can have something of the thrill of an astronaut being blasted into space. Simulating a launch, this ride shakes like the shuttle and makes noise like the shuttle, but, of course, it is not the shuttle. It is a "mere copy," and the people on board are only tourists, not real astronauts. What about Christian worship? It shakes like the holy and makes noise like the holy, but there is always the fear that people are just "playing church." The author of Hebrews wants us to know that the event of Christ has saved us from simulated worship. Whether it

all things," creator of worlds, the "reflection of God's glory and the exact imprint of God's very being," the sustainer of all things, who (regarding his work) "had made purification for sins" and who (regarding his place) sits in honored authority at God's right hand (Heb. 1:2, 3). This, the writer reveals, is the Jesus whose work in heaven fully and brilliantly fulfills the work of the priests of Israel in the Holy Place of the earthly temple. Focus on Jesus, and help the congregation grasp the grace and freedom of the new way Jesus has provided.

The writer of Hebrews sets forth several arguments in this passage to develop his theme of Christ's superiority. First, he compares the earthly, human-made things—the temple, the altar, all the sacred furnishings made to precise detail for the high priest's use—with the spiritual realities of heaven into which Christ has entered, taking us with him and through him into the very presence of God. The Levitical practices the Israelites followed were mere copies or plans for the heavenly reality, and so were something like an architect's quick sketches, an artist's doodles, or a writer's outline, providing only the barest hint of what the final reality may turn out to be in all dimensions. They are, as the writer notes earlier, a "sketch and shadow of the heavenly one" (8:5). As complex, rich, and fascinating as those precise practices and intricate instruments were, the writer suggests, they offer only the vaguest foreshadowing of the work of Christ in the true heavenly place on our behalf. Why grasp onto these when the real thing is readily available?

Second, the writer compares the year after year nature of the Levitical sacrifice—made with blood that was not the priest's own—with the "once for all" nature of Christ's sacrifice, which is superior because it is eternally effective. Thanks to Jesus, salvation no longer requires an annual renewal sticker.

Third, the writer explains that when Christ returns he will not need to deal with sin in judgment, as that has all been covered already in his first incarnation. Instead, he will come to those who have already been redeemed through him and who therefore "are eagerly waiting for him," yearning to experience fully the clean and clear reality of eternal existence in God's presence—a promised reality made possible only by the infinitely superior work of Christ.

Since the writer's intended audience consisted of "the Hebrews," or Israelites of a time after Christ's first incarnation much earlier than ours, his arguments would have been quite profoundly powerful, because his listeners were well versed in

Hebrews 9:24-28

Theological Perspective

failures to "measure up" to God's desires or even our own best intentions. Forgiveness is an accomplished reality we can live into with confidence in the mercy of the God who comes to meet us in Christ. It announces good news for all who fear death and the prospect of standing before the God who indeed judges all: the Judge is none other than our Savior.

As part of a larger comparative argument for the superiority of the new covenant in Christ, this passage raises a troubling question for readers in a religiously plural society. Is its message anti-Judaic?

Biblical scholars can be found on both sides of this question.[3] Scholars are uncertain whether Hebrews was written after Christianity emerged as a sect distinct from Judaism. It contains no explicit references to "Jews" and "Gentiles," and casts no aspersions on Jews as a group. Instead, the text offers evidence of both continuity and discontinuity between the old and new covenants.

The letter begins by affirming that Jesus cannot be understood apart from God's prior revelation and promises to the people of Israel. Jesus is the Son of God, by whom God has spoken in these last days just as God "spoke to our ancestors in many and various ways by the prophets" (1:1). Moses is to be honored (3:5), and the heroes of faith in chapter 11 are all Israelites. Yet Jesus has inaugurated a new age and fulfills the old covenant with his "better hope" (7:19), "better promises" (8:6), and "better covenant" (7:22, 8:6). The author even calls the old covenant "obsolete" (8:13).

A careful look at the comparisons reveals not a wholesale rejection of Torah study and observance, but a more narrow rejection of the Levitical cultic practice of sacrifice. Whatever one's conclusion about the more faithful reading, the text's christological focus cannot responsibly become the basis for a contemporary anti-Judaism. The faithful preacher must reckon not only with the historical context that gave rise to any negative portrayals of Judaism, but also with the multivocal witness of Scripture (as in Rom. 9–11) to the one God who is faithful to God's promises to the people of Israel.

JANE E. FAHEY

Pastoral Perspective

Our contract with God is paid in full through Christ. In Jesus the relationship between humanity and God is permanent and enduring. We do not need to fear defaulting on our insurance for divine forgiveness. Our sin is removed in the sacrifice of Christ. Our fear of being rejected or coming up short is done away with in the saving death of Jesus.

This changes everything. No longer does the community need to keep track of offenses against neighbor and God, nor report to the local priest for intercession or atonement. Instead, Christ becomes both the mediating presence and sacrifice. Sin is still a reality, but so now is forgiveness. We no longer belong to a fear-based community. Instead, we find that confession becomes a regular part of our life together, because revenge and punishment need no longer be feared. Just as the child who is certain of a parent's love will come forward in trust and security rather than hide in shame, so we move toward one another and God. Forgiveness engenders intimacy between both God and neighbor.

The community that is created out of this good news is one in which all are included and all wait eagerly for Christ to return, a community that looks both forward and backward. The people of God look forward to the day when Christ returns, and they hold in their heart the memory of the saving death of Christ. This is a community whose energy can be poured into exploring, living out, and sharing the grace that is shown to all in Christ.

A liturgy that fully honors this text will highlight the confession sequence and make particular note of the link between confession and baptism. A celebration of the Lord's Supper would be ideal, since this text truly is central to that sacrament. In it, we hear the essence of the new covenant, its link with the blood of Christ, and the hope in which we wait until he returns again in glory.

ELIZABETH B. FORNEY

---

3. See Clark M. Williamson, "Anti-Judaism in Hebrews?" *Interpretation* 57, no. 3 (July 2003); 266.

takes place in a brush arbor or in St. Peter's basilica, Christian worship means being taken by Christ into the true and heavenly sanctuary and into the very presence of God.

2. Once vs. Endless Repetition (vv. 25–26). The purpose of the old priestly sacrifices was purification of the people, to get rid of human sins. According to the author of Hebrews, this kind of worship was like whitewashing a barn; it had to be done over and over again. The priest entered "the Holy Place year after year," and since he was himself a sinner, he took to the altar "blood that is not his own." The next year there would have been more transgressions and thus a need for more blood, a never-ending cycle for purging away the latest round of sins. Viewed this way, worship becomes the fearful act of guilty people, constantly on trial, week after week plea-bargaining with God. But Christ entered the true sanctuary and on behalf of all humanity offered himself, a human without sin, and achieved forgiveness once and for all. In Christ, all trials are now over.

3. Salvation vs. Judgment (vv. 27–28). Looming over much religion is the idea of judgment, that people must ultimately stand before God and account for themselves. A great deal of religious energy, therefore, is spent figuring out how to make ourselves acceptable to God in the coming judgment. In this part of the passage, the writer of Hebrews indicates that the offering of Christ makes this obsession with judgment moot. In Christ, sin has already been extinguished, and lasting forgiveness has been granted. So Christians do not have to dread the future, watching fearfully for God the judge. God's future is one of salvation and redemption. Christ is "coming again," not with a sword of judgment, but "to save those who are eagerly waiting for him." We can take down the road signs that read, "Get Right with God!" Because of Christ, we have already been made right with God. We can now put up the signs that read, "Work confidently for justice and peace. God in Christ is coming to renew all things!"

THOMAS G. LONG

the old ways that the writer compares unfavorably with Christ's way. Clearly the impact of these arguments will not be as strong on today's listeners, whose knowledge and understanding of those old ways are no doubt thin at best. In addition, focusing on the "old ways" may have dangerous anti-Semitic implications, even if the preacher does not intend them. Today's listeners may be interested in a general introduction to those ways to clarify the point of the text, but the preacher would probably use his or her time more effectively in communicating the consequences of each of these arguments, which revolve around the following affirmations that can be developed and illustrated:

First, being part of the redeemed body of Christ today means we can experience eternal reality in its fullest, richest, clearest, most profound way. Life outside of a relationship with the living Christ is two-dimensional, sketchy, a mere wisp. Life in relationship with Christ is multidimensional, offering a deep spiritual vitality that can be expressed through meaningful prayer and meditation, as well as by energetically serving others from the core of one's being in association with other believers, working together to meet real-world needs and welcome others into the mutual presence.

Second, because Christ's sacrifice was eternally effectual, we can be set free from any angst regarding the impossibility of our relating to God—not measuring up, not being acceptable, not being good enough—because our salvation has been accomplished for all time. We are set free spiritually and emotionally to live in Christ's presence and power now, always now. Our relationship with God is no longer an issue with God; it's an eternal reality—so why should it be an issue with us?

Third, because Christ will come again, we can imagine and live out of the possibilities of this deep assurance in the life of the church, whose members wait eagerly for Christ to return to live among them. Rather than lapsing into a self-satisfied, comfortable laziness at that prospect, a church engaged in expectant waiting will be throbbing with Christlike service.

This rich reality, this freedom and assurance, this abiding sense of expectation can generate a profound and effective spiritual reality within individual lives and entire congregations.

PETER M. WALLACE

Mark 12:38-44

³⁸As he taught, he said, "Beware of the scribes, who like to walk around in long robes, and to be greeted with respect in the marketplaces, ³⁹and to have the best seats in the synagogues and places of honor at banquets! ⁴⁰They devour widows' houses and for the sake of appearance say long prayers. They will receive the greater condemnation."

⁴¹He sat down opposite the treasury, and watched the crowd putting money into the treasury. Many rich people put in large sums. ⁴²A poor widow came and put in two small copper coins, which are worth a penny. ⁴³Then he called his disciples and said to them, "Truly I tell you, this poor widow has put in more than all those who are contributing to the treasury. ⁴⁴For all of them have contributed out of their abundance; but she out of her poverty has put in everything she had, all she had to live on."

Theological Perspective

The focus of the Gospel of Mark is not biographical or historical. Rather, Mark seeks to provide a theological record of Jesus as the Christ who is the mighty worker of miracles rather than the great teacher. The twelfth chapter of Mark begins with Jesus' temple teaching on the parable of the Vineyard and then moves to paying taxes to Caesar, the resurrection, the great commandment, and the question about David's son. Atypically for Mark, this chapter offers challenge and opportunity as we meet Jesus the teacher, discovering once again the power of his teachings for our lives.

Usually, we see this passage moving from a critique of ostentatious religious practices to a display of faithful sacrifice. We must be careful in making such a move, which condemns too quickly and valorizes without full understanding. Yes, Jesus does offer a strong warning against hypocrisy and overly pious behavior. The temptation is to make those who demonstrate such behaviors the poster children for sin, using them to avoid examining the ways in which we practice our own versions of liturgical overkill and encourage behavior that is really self-abnegation rather than pious sacrifice. Indeed, sacrifice is a dangerous notion. It is dangerous because we often ask those who are the most vulnerable to give the most. A quick reading of this passage encourages our doing so once again.

Pastoral Perspective

In her book *Amazing Grace* author Kathleen Norris writes about her struggle with the word "righteous."

> The word "righteous" used to grate on my ear; for years I was able to hear it only in its negative mode, as self-righteous, as judgmental. Gradually, as I became more acquainted with the word in its biblical context, I found that it does not mean self-righteous at all, but righteous in the sight of God. And this righteousness is consistently defined by the prophets, and in the psalms and gospels, as a willingness to care for the most vulnerable people in the culture, characterized in ancient Israel as orphans, widows, resident aliens, and the poor.[1]

Norris goes on to remind her readers that much of the fabled wrath of God in the Bible is directed against those who preserve their own wealth and power at the expense of the orphan, the widow, the resident alien, and the poor.

As one reads this biblical passage, Norris's thoughtful words ring true. In the first section, Jesus warns that the scribes who walk around in long robes being greeted with respect and sitting in places of honor will face the consequences of devouring

1. Kathleen Norris, *Amazing Grace: A Vocabulary of Faith* (New York: Riverhead Books, 1998), 96.

Exegetical Perspective

Religious office is not a safeguard against hypocrisy and greed. Indeed this passage, like many others, shows that unfaithfulness can masquerade as faithfulness, and pretense can parade as piety, even at the highest levels in the household of faith. Conversely, some of the greatest acts of faith occur simply, selflessly, and unobtrusively. Jesus helps his followers distinguish the reality of faithfulness from all counterfeits.

This passage concludes Mark's selected accounts (see v. 38a) of Jesus' actions in the temple and various reactions to him (11:27–12:44). After this passage, Mark presents the Olivet discourse in which Jesus warns of events before the end (13:1–37). In today's Gospel reading (Mark 12:38–44), Jesus gives a stern warning against religious hypocrisy (vv. 38–40) and offers encouragement to exercise radical trust in God (vv. 41–44).

Warning against Religious Hypocrisy (vv. 38–40). In the first portion of this passage and its parallels (Matt. 23:1–12; Luke 20:45–47), Jesus warns against succumbing to the temptations of prestige, power, and materialism. This warning is not against all scribes, for not all Jewish religious authorities had distanced themselves from God and God's kingdom, and Jesus' relations with scribes were not always

Homiletical Perspective

As the preacher comes to this text, it may be stewardship season in the congregation, the time to invite members to make pledges to the church for the coming year. The preacher knows the institutional life of the church depends upon those pledges. And so at first glance, to the delight of the preacher, the lectionary offers up this text that appears perfect for a sermon on giving.

Indeed the whole fall stewardship program that many congregations conduct is not unlike the role of the treasury of the temple in Jerusalem. That treasury was there to underwrite the religious apparatus of that day, just as most stewardship programs are designed to do in our day. And as is true in our churches today, there in Jerusalem at the temple it was the rich donors who were crucial. So in trying to use this text to invite listeners to give to the church, the preacher faces the challenge of how to do that, especially when the text does not lift up for praise those who give "out of their abundance."

But there is a deeper problem in the text that the preacher must face. Does Jesus point to the poor widow who gives her last two coins to the temple as a model for giving? Or does Jesus point to her because she is a tragic example of how religious institutions suck the life out of people?

Mark 12:38-44

Theological Perspective

Let us pause before we put the poor widow on a suspect pedestal and ask: Why do we valorize sacrifice? This valorization is more than a slow mulling over its Latin roots, which combine "sacred" and "to make" so that sacrifice is something of value offered as an act of devotion or worship to God. In today's world, sacrifice often means something very different from an act of devotion or worship. It often means giving up more than we should and less than we can. In the United States, we ask those in the working class and those who are poor to bear the weight of tax cuts that benefit those who are wealthier. Often, those who earn less pay a higher percentage of their income in taxes than those who are wealthier. This kind of sacrifice echoes Jesus' warning in the passage for us to beware.

At times, it seems that sacrifice is best when someone else is doing it. We marvel at such figures as Mother Teresa, the families of slain or injured soldiers, and teachers in tough inner-city schools. We lift them high on the pedestal with the poor widow, keeping them distinct and distant from our daily lives. The focus is on *their* giving and the inadequacy of *ours*—but nothing changes. This is one of the problems of things we put on pedestals. We do not imagine ourselves alongside them because what they represent for us is often more than we can give or more than we can imagine we are capable of giving.

Perhaps one way to break the often-fruitless common route we take with sacrifice in this passage is to explore the meaning of offering. This delicate and significant word shift may give us just the small change in perspective we need to mine this passage in new ways. It may help us both critique and embrace genuine sacrifice as we imagine ourselves in the story, not as those observing the poor widow, but as the two small copper coins.

Those coins represent more than money. They represent faith and belief and how these must be lived out in our lives in concrete acts and not solely by rituals that no longer hold religious power. Powerless rituals do not call forth deep acts of faith from us through our witness in the world. Instead, these heartless rituals have become pro forma ceremonies marking questionable status and fallow craven piety. The coins represent faith-filled offering found in presenting all of who we are and all we hope to become to God for service to the world. Indeed, offering in this sense is something other than prayer, tithes, Eucharist, or Communion. It is not so much the act of giving or receiving, as it is the act of being.

Pastoral Perspective

widows' houses while they say long prayers to keep up their righteous appearances. Few readers will have any problem with this. We have little use for hypocrites—persons who are pretentious and show off their status only to draw more attention to themselves at the expense of the less fortunate. This kind of display differs from the self-righteousness that Norris describes. Less judgmental and more officious, it still disgusts us.

In the second section, Jesus comments on a widow giving two small coins to the temple treasury. Some may read this passage as Jesus commending the widow for her sacrifice, but those who read the text carefully realize that Jesus does not do this. Rather, he simply tells his disciples that the two small coins she gave are worth more than the gifts of the rich persons who gave much more money but sacrificed very little.

Together, these two sections read as a lament for and an indictment upon any religious system that results in a poor widow giving all she has so that the system's leaders may continue to live lives of wealth and comfort. The attack is not on Jewish religious practice. The attack is on any religious practice that masks egotism and greed. The scribes are like leeches on the faithful, benefiting from a religious system that allows poor widows to sacrifice what little they have. We should be outraged by any system that appropriates the property of the poor and the near-destitute in order to perpetuate wealth for the elite. If we are brutally honest with ourselves, this is a particular dilemma for many congregations today.

Charles L. Campbell writes in *The Word before the Powers* about the challenge for the church, particularly the predominantly white, wealthy, mainline church, to recognize how it enjoys enormous privilege and status. In his call for an ethic of nonviolent resistance in preaching, he reminds us that human beings tend to preserve the systems from which we benefit:

> The reality is this: while an ethic of nonviolent resistance is inherent in the practice of preaching, the church's preaching often does not fully live up to that ethic. Even while resisting direct, interpersonal, physical violence, preaching often participates in acts and systems of domination that involve harmful forms of psychological, spiritual, and even physical coercion that must be considered violent.

Christian preachers have, after all, used the pulpit to send believers off to the Crusades and to support wars of all kinds. Christian preaching has also supported slavery, racism, and the oppression

Exegetical Perspective

conflicted (Mark 12:28–34). Rather, Jesus' warning is directed against anyone who professes to be faithful but possesses an elitist attitude and implements its tangible, unfortunate manifestations.

Initially, scribes in Israel were secular officials who could "cipher" and had charge of legal documents, especially in financial (Jer. 32:12–15; 2 Kgs. 22:3f.) and political matters (Isa. 22:15; 36:3). Scribes were also skilled in the craft of writing and were often celebrated for righteousness and wisdom (Dan. 11:32–35; 12:3; Ezra 7:6–10). Their financial acumen and literary prowess distinguished them as a class and made their associations with money, power, religion, and politics inevitable. After the exile and the Law's firm establishment at the core of Israel's life, scribes gained further prominence as interpreters and teachers of God's Law. Unfortunately, not all scribes exercised their office faithfully.

Jesus' warning against wayward scribal behavior highlights several aspects of the hypocrisy that he perceives among those who should know and do better. The first dimension of their errant attitude and action is evident in their craving for prestige (v. 38). They "desire" and enjoy being the center of attention. They long for the limelight and clothe themselves in long robes in order to signal their importance and draw the attention of others (Luke 15:22; cf. Mark 16:5). They want to be recognized and hailed in public, particularly in the professional arena, which Jesus identifies as the secular marketplace (*agora*) rather than the holy temple.

The second aspect of their departure from God's way is their desire and competition for power in the religious arena (v. 39). They crave the "best seats" (literally "first couch") in the synagogue, which for a "doctor of the Law" is akin to the "seat of Moses" (Matt. 23:2), the point from which authoritative interpretations of the law are rendered. Similar seats were offered to famous people, especially scholars, and teaching was often given from these chairs in each synagogue. Those who occupied such seats, then, wielded considerable influence and power in their communities to establish policies and execute them. Similarly, the "places of honor at feasts" were positions of status and power. Not only are Judaism's great religious feasts in sight here, but other festal religious occasions are included too. Along with status and prestige, the scribes crave control and power to promote themselves and their own agendas.

The third characteristic that Jesus opposes is merciless materialism. Here, Jesus points to an example that was not unknown in Israel (e.g., Job 22:9; 24:3,

Homiletical Perspective

This widow gives all she has to an institution that is going to be utterly destroyed. In the very next passage Jesus declares of the temple, "Not one stone will be left here upon another; all will be thrown down" (Mark 13:2). From the warning Jesus gives about the scribes, who are in part responsible for the operation of the Jerusalem temple, it is clear that he condemns them for devouring widows' houses. This whole religious apparatus has become perverted. Its operators lead privileged lives. It no longer protects widows, the poor, the vulnerable of the earth. It lives off them instead.

If the preacher decides that Jesus points to this poor widow because she is a tragic figure who has been duped by the religious apparatus, then the preacher will likely not preach a sermon that pleases the stewardship committee! But the sermon could point to the coming promise that the days are numbered for religious regimes that exist for their own well-being. On that day when the Son of Man comes, these religious regimes, like the temple in Jerusalem, will be utterly destroyed (Mark 13). The promise of Jesus is that on that day vulnerable persons will be delivered from the oppression of religion.

But if the preacher decides that Jesus points out this widow because she is a model for giving, how then might the sermon turn? Likely such a sermon would still not please a stewardship committee. For the object of the giving—the temple, in this widow's case—remains condemned. It is unworthy of the gift. Because it has not been a house of prayer for all people but has become a den of robbers (Mark 11:17), it is worthy of destruction. So from this text it would be hard for the preacher to build a case that the religious institution of the church is worthy of the gifts of the givers, particularly the gifts of the poor and vulnerable who often give to it so faithfully.

If the preacher decides that Jesus is in fact holding this widow up as a model for giving, then a key detail must be noted: Jesus calls his disciples to notice that this widow gives all that she has— literally, "the whole of her life" (Mark 12:44). She gives her whole life to something that is corrupt and condemned.

Moreover, this is the last scene in Jesus' public ministry. From here all that remains in Mark's telling is the temple discourse and the passion narrative.[1] So this widow offers a glimpse into what Jesus is about. He is on the way to giving "the whole of his life" for

---

1. Lamar Williamson Jr., *Mark*, Interpretation Series (Atlanta: John Knox Press, 1983), 234.

Mark 12:38-44

Theological Perspective

As you think through this passage, what ideas, images, stories, concepts come to mind when you think of offering as being personal? One place to begin is Christ. For Augustine, our duty is to present ourselves—all of who we are—to God in the Communion meal. However, rather than confine Augustine's compelling charge to Communion, how can we take the grace and hope we find in the wine and bread and make it live in our lives in ways that not only sustain us, but model for others the enormous power of offering all of who we are to the rest of creation? This is not something that we can do at arm's length. If we become those two small copper coins, we must *live* our lives in such a way that our offering is truly shared with others.

In this instance, value is more than being able to put monetary value on our actions or our offerings in church. This passage gives us the opportunity to explore what it means to put in everything we have, all that we have to live on as people of faith. Consider the variety of occupations or commitments of people you are in ministry with. What carefully drawn examples can you adapt to explore this authentic kind of offering? Draw widely for these examples as you take seriously the lives of the young and the old. Rather than set up a comparison and contrast between the widow and contemporary folks, focus on how the people before you represent the coins. This helps draw on the possibilities for our lives, rather than focusing, as we often do in this passage, on our shortcomings and inadequacies. In doing so, people of faith take the opportunity to explore the passage as an invitation to deep and abiding Christian witness as we live into the promise of creation.

EMILIE M. TOWNES

Pastoral Perspective

of women, gays, and lesbians. And far from resisting the economic violence that comes with capitalism, Christian preaching has been a frequent supporter of the economic status quo.[2]

Campbell pointedly reminds us that the church has all too often participated in systems of oppression and violence—psychological, spiritual, economic, and even physical—all in the name of Jesus Christ. This is a great challenge to churches whose members sit on corporate boards and vote in legislative bodies. Ironically, many of our congregational leaders and members feel as if they have little power, but this is the heart of the great illusion. Many of the scribes whom Jesus condemned also thought they were doing what was honorable, right, and good. Perhaps they too were caught up in a system over which they felt they had little control. But Jesus does not condemn only those who are aware of how they benefit from systems of violence and oppression. Jesus condemns any who benefit from such systems, whether they are aware or not. Ignorance is no excuse here.

Readers of this text must reflect seriously upon their own complicity in current systems of violence and oppression. But reflection alone is not enough. Reflection must lead to specific and sustained action by engaging spiritual practices that challenge political and economic systems in the church, the nation, and the world. Feeding the hungry and providing clothing are important spiritual practices, but the church must come to view these practices as more than programs. The church must come to understand these practices as the very life flowing out of its worship. Further, the church must call all of society to care for the orphan, the widow, the resident alien, and the poor as its primary purpose, with all other governing and political functions as secondary. In this way, the church not only exhibits God's righteousness but shapes a politic that is in itself righteous.

RODGER Y. NISHIOKA

2. Charles L. Campbell, *The Word before the Powers: An Ethic of Preaching* (Louisville, KY: Westminster John Knox Press, 2002), 83.

Exegetical Perspective

21; Ps. 94:6; Isa. 9:17; Jer. 7:6; Zech. 7:10). The law everywhere treats widows sympathetically (e.g., Deut. 10:14–19; 14:29; Ps. 146:9; Jer. 49:11) and consistently expresses God's displeasure with those who neglect or oppress them (e.g., Job 22:9–11, 29–30; Ps. 94:1–7; Isa. 1:16–17, 21–25). Thus anyone who *knows* the will of God expressed in the Law shares God's deep concern for the plight of widows and all those in need (e.g., Deut. 14:29). Here, however, Jesus asserts that the very people who should know the Law best "devour widows' houses" (v. 40). How they did this is not entirely clear, but scribes may have been exploiting widows through transactions involving their houses, personal property, and land (see Lev. 27:14–21; Num. 35:1–3; Ezra 10:8). What is clear is that scribes were preying greedily upon others for personal gain even as they were praying ostentatiously before others to "prove" their righteousness before God—as though words speak louder than actions. But faith in God always expresses itself as faithfulness; thus Jesus condemns such deliberate disregard for God, God's Law, and God's people (Mark 7:18–23; 9:42; cf. Isa. 29:13–21).

Example of Exemplary Trust (vv. 41–44). Over against demonstrations of unsympathetic religious elitism stand simple acts of genuine trust in God. In this story Jesus is sitting across from the treasury (cf. John 8:20), watching as people offer their gifts (v. 41). It is unclear whether Mark means the temple treasury itself, where a priest would announce the gift and the purpose for which it was given, or any one of the thirteen trumpet-shaped receptacles against the wall of the Court of Women on the temple mound. What is clear is that Jesus is struck by the startling contrast between the many wealthy people who bring much, giving out of their abundance, and a poor widow who offers two of the least valuable coins in Palestine. That she is both a widow and poor compounds her low social position. She represents the opposite end of the spectrum from those who have the "best seats in the synagogues and places of honor at banquets."

Many onlookers disregard her offering, but Jesus notices and calls his disciples to him. He wants them to see the true faith behind their offerings: the widow's offering demonstrates her total trust in God—"she out of her poverty has put in everything she had" (v. 44). Hers is a costly discipleship, and Jesus praises her for exemplary faith, a faith that surpasses that of many religious leaders whose faith is a sham. Her trust in God is aligned with Jesus' trust.

ROBERT A. BRYANT

Homiletical Perspective

something that is corrupt and condemned: all of humanity, the whole world.

Jesus calls the disciples, the church, to himself and points out this poor widow and her manner of giving. Watching her will not lead to unvarnished support for religious institutions. But could it reinforce the call of Christ to the church to give the whole of its life for the sake of those who do not deserve such a gift?

One governing document from a mainline church in this country declares, "The Church is called to be a sign in and for the world of the new reality which God has made available to people in Jesus Christ." How will it be such a sign? By

> healing and reconciling and binding up wounds, . . . ministering to the needs of the poor, the sick, the lonely, and the powerless, . . . engaging in the struggle to free people from sin, fear, oppression, hunger, and injustice, . . . giving itself and its substance to the service of those who suffer, . . . sharing with Christ in the establishing of his just, peaceable, and loving rule in the world. The Church is called to undertake this mission *even at the risk of losing its life.*[2]

The poor widow gives her whole life for that which is worthy only to be condemned. Is this the calling Jesus lifts up for the entire church?

PETE PEERY

2. *The Constitution of the Presbyterian Church (U.S.A.),* Part II, *Book of Order, 2005–2007* (Louisville, KY: The Office of the General Assembly, Presbyterian Church (U.S.A.), 2005), G-3.0200–3.0400 (italics added).

1 Samuel 1:4-20

⁴On the day when Elkanah sacrificed, he would give portions to his wife Peninnah and to all her sons and daughters; ⁵but to Hannah he gave a double portion, because he loved her, though the Lord had closed her womb. ⁶Her rival used to provoke her severely, to irritate her, because the Lord had closed her womb. ⁷So it went on year by year; as often as she went up to the house of the Lord, she used to provoke her. Therefore Hannah wept and would not eat. ⁸Her husband Elkanah said to her, "Hannah, why do you weep? Why do you not eat? Why is your heart sad? Am I not more to you than ten sons?"

⁹After they had eaten and drunk at Shiloh, Hannah rose and presented herself before the Lord. Now Eli the priest was sitting on the seat beside the doorpost of the temple of the Lord. ¹⁰She was deeply distressed and prayed to the Lord, and wept bitterly. ¹¹She made this vow: "O Lord of hosts, if only you will look on the misery of your servant, and remember me, and not forget your servant, but will give to your servant a male child, then I will set him before you as a nazirite until the day of his death. He shall drink neither wine nor intoxicants, and no razor shall touch his head."

Theological Perspective

Hannah occupies a space not unlike other women in Scripture who are raised out of the crowd for naming and narrative. She gestates and births a prophetic leader, and so attention is paid to her. Her story is groundwork for the construction of identity for Israel's monarchy. It is a monarchy that finds its roots in despair, in barrenness, and in humble prayer. Because this story is of great importance for the character of Israel's identity, readers could occupy themselves quite constructively by making metaphorical connections between Hannah's barrenness and despair and the emotions of a nation that was looking for a leader, for a way to feel secure and hopeful in turbulent times.

But the story of Hannah provides us with more than metaphor. She provides a kind of iconography that goes deeper. She is a meaning maker, not simply in what she points to, but in her own image, her own personage. She holds and reflects the pride and identity of a patriarchal society in how her story is told. Even so she reveals an iconic spiritual sensitivity to the ways that God is involved in and concerned about her life. She is a woman who wants a male child. She knows the import of such a gift. She lives with the humiliation of her husband's other wife's fertility and the provisions that are made because Peninnah was prolific. During her family's yearly pilgrimage to Shiloh, Hannah especially feels

Pastoral Perspective

Here, as elsewhere in the Bible, a story on an epic scale begins with a small domestic scene. Like the events surrounding the birth of Isaac and those leading up to the birth of Jesus, the birth of Samuel combines both the divine and miraculous with the human and commonplace. Although the characters are introduced briefly and sketched broadly, a pastor can recognize them in their limitations and frailties. It is not hard to imagine them as members of one's congregation, the sort of parishioners who would need a lot of pastoral care.

First, there is the tangle of relationships. Elkanah has two wives (okay, this may be one aspect of this story that is not reflected in our congregations). There is Peninnah, who has borne him numerous children, and Hannah, who has been unable to conceive because "the Lord had closed her womb" (v. 6b). In such a patriarchal culture, childbearing was a woman's only unique ability. To be unable to conceive was cause for great shame. To make matters worse, Peninnah uses Hannah's unfortunate circumstance as occasion to taunt her rival, increasing her distress.

Elkanah tries to comfort Hannah in her grief by saying, "Hannah, why do you weep? Why do you not eat? Why is your heart sad? Am I not more to you than ten sons?" (v. 8). It is not entirely clear how we

¹²As she continued praying before the Lord, Eli observed her mouth. ¹³Hannah was praying silently; only her lips moved, but her voice was not heard; therefore Eli thought she was drunk. ¹⁴So Eli said to her, "How long will you make a drunken spectacle of yourself? Put away your wine." ¹⁵But Hannah answered, "No, my lord, I am a woman deeply troubled; I have drunk neither wine nor strong drink, but I have been pouring out my soul before the Lord. ¹⁶Do not regard your servant as a worthless woman, for I have been speaking out of my great anxiety and vexation all this time." ¹⁷Then Eli answered, "Go in peace; the God of Israel grant the petition you have made to him." ¹⁸And she said, "Let your servant find favor in your sight." Then the woman went to her quarters, ate and drank with her husband, and her countenance was sad no longer.

¹⁹They rose early in the morning and worshiped before the Lord; then they went back to their house at Ramah. Elkanah knew his wife Hannah, and the Lord remembered her. ²⁰In due time Hannah conceived and bore a son. She named him Samuel, for she said, "I have asked him of the Lord."

Exegetical Perspective

The Birth of Hope. The birth of human life often serves as a symbol of hope. When a promised child is born in desperate times, the pregnancy itself becomes a site of expectation. The beginning of the book of 1 Samuel is set in such a time. The concluding period of the judges was marked by moral, religious, and social chaos. It is described as a time when "there was no king in Israel; all the people did what was right in their own eyes" (Judg. 21:25). Within this difficult situation, the character of Samuel represents a hopeful transition. He is the last of the judges, and in his role as prophet he anoints the first kings of Israel.

The opening chapter of 1 Samuel, however, does not focus on the birth of Samuel himself. Rather, it tells the moving story of his mother, Hannah. The reader learns early that Hannah is barren (v. 2 and vv. 5–6). In the Old Testament, barrenness is a common theme. Many of the mothers within Israelite tradition were confronted with this difficult condition. In the ancient world, being barren was often viewed as a sign of divine punishment. Moreover, in a patriarchal culture, where female identity was tied to childbearing, the stigma was great for women who could not conceive. In the biblical tradition, barrenness is also a site where the Lord visits the marginalized. Thus the opening of a womb becomes symbolic of God's

Homiletical Perspective

This story is a treasure. It is part of the underplanking that defines society, culture, and community. At the heart of all strife there is news of a meeting place and the promise of help on the way.

Themes we live out every day make their appearance here: broken dreams, harsh treatment by those close to us, compassion even in seemingly hopeless circumstances, the avenue of grace found in a frail place of rigid traditions, and leaders with myopic vision, clay feet, and last-minute flashes of brilliance.

This story weaves beautifully into our own situation. It is a Shiloh story, thought to come from that ancient place of meeting and worship that is no more. Many of us on the modern scene are concerned that our communities of faith shall be no more, and that all our history and achievements will tumble down with the wrecking ball. People disappear. Eras slip away unremembered. Present cultural themes and preoccupations sideline our voices and dreams.

One might begin a sermon from the vantage point of a church in decline. A site once valued goes neglected. Its opinions once sought are passed over. Leaders and traditions once in the forefront are looked on as historical oddities. The surrounding culture is after our property, our visibility, and our

1 Samuel 1:4-20

Theological Perspective

the sting of her barrenness. She leaves the banquet of her household and goes to the temple to be in God's presence. She asks God to remember her, and she makes a promise actively to acknowledge that this child is from God by dedicating him to God's service. God grants her the child, and Hannah keeps her promise.

Hannah at once embodies both the patriarchal constructions of her worth and a deep assumption that God is concerned about her. She "pours out her soul" to God from an interior awareness of her connection to God's concern—she has a God-consciousness all her own, effected but not totalized by her cultural identity.[1] Hannah's prayers are sincere expressions of her anguish and her dependence on God. Hannah's anguish is real, whether it comes from her yearning for a child or from the uselessness that she feels in a culture that puts great worth on a woman's fertility. Hers is a "prayer of groaning" that comes from a place of utter vulnerability.[2] When Hannah seeks out God's presence in this state of anguish, her prayer signals that she is aware of a divine concern for those who are of questionable cultural worth. She does not just come to God with formal petition. She does not come with traditional sacrifice. She comes in loneliness, isolation, and despair. She lays bare all the emotion and all the pain. Her disposition of prayer is a remarkable image of piety. Her "prayer of groaning" makes her an icon not simply of the mother of a son who is prophetic and powerful, but of a human being who knows herself to be known and loved by God.

It is significant that the monarchy is born in such emotion and in such surrender to God. With Hannah's mode of encounter the monarchy springs from a place of trust, a place of humility, even a place of mystical union. God is very present to her; God is responsive and close by. The monarchy is born out of barrenness, anguish, and uninhibited entanglement with God's faithfulness. God's character is full of grace, full of compassion, and audacious enough to make fertile what is barren and make abundant what is scarce. This story is a story about political power coming into its own on some level, but it is more a story about being spiritually

---

1. God consciousness (*Gefühl*) is the feeling of absolute dependence on God described by Friedrich Schleiermacher in *The Christian Faith* (New York: Harper & Row, 1963). Hannah realized her dependence; she embodied it. For Schleiermacher this signals a redemptive spiritual evolution.
2. This "groaning of prayer" embraces the immediacy of divine presence and releases spiritual experience from pure intellect in Bonaventure's *The Soul's Journey unto God* (Mahwah, NJ: Paulist Press, 1978). Hannah's mode of prayer can be interpreted as mystical experience.

Pastoral Perspective

are to interpret his response. Is Elkanah sincerely sympathetic and trying to comfort his wife by offering genuine support? Or is he dismissive of her in her loss, essentially telling her to be satisfied with her lot (along the lines of telling someone who is in grief that she should count her blessings, rather than focus on her loss)? However we interpret his words, it is a clumsy response at best. For years I convened a grief support group for those who had suffered a loss through death. At least once a year we would devote a session to reflecting on comments made by friends or family members that may have been well-meaning, but which were singularly unhelpful and perhaps even irritating in the extreme. The recurring theme of those sessions was, "God deliver me from well-meaning friends." If Hannah had been in such a group, she might well have quoted Elkanah's attempt to console her.

Indeed, in Hannah we recognize a number of common expressions of grief. There is the acute pain, which can become the consuming focus of a grieving person's life. Then there is anger, which Hannah directs most clearly toward Peninnah, but which is also evident in her response to Eli, when he accuses her of being drunk in the temple. Although both Peninnah and Eli have done something to stir the ire of Hannah, it is also clear that they are more the objects than the source of her anger, which springs more from her unfortunate fate. Bargaining is another common expression of grief reflected in this story: "[Hannah] made this vow: 'O LORD of hosts, if only you will look on the misery of your servant, and remember me, and not forget your servant, but will give to your servant a male child, then I will set him before you as a nazirite until the day of his death. He shall drink neither wine nor intoxicants, and no razor shall touch his head'" (v. 11). Every pastor has observed how deep grief can lead to desperate bargaining.

When Hannah gets to the temple to make her pleas, she ignores Eli, who is seated at the entrance, and strides right past him to make her appeal directly to the Lord. When Eli does encounter her, he misreads her spectacularly, mistaking her mumbled prayers for drunkenness. When Hannah explains herself to Eli with the ferocity of someone with nothing left to lose, Eli does offer her a blessing, but it is a perfunctory one: "Go in peace; the God of Israel grant the petition you have made to him" (v. 17–18). Indeed, two verses later we learn that the God of Israel has indeed granted her petition, and she bears a child, but this was not through Eli's blessing. Rather, it was because

Exegetical Perspective

miraculous intervention. When a formerly barren woman gives birth, the child is destined to be an important figure in history.[1]

After brief character introductions (vv. 1–2), 1 Samuel 1 divides into four parts. In the first (vv. 3–8), the narrator focuses on three characters: Hannah; Elkanah, her husband; and Peninnah, Elkanah's other wife and Hannah's rival. In the second section (vv. 9–18), Hannah makes a plea to the Lord at Shiloh, vowing to dedicate her future child to God's service. While there, she encounters Eli, the inept priest. In the third scene (vv. 19–20), after receiving a blessing, Hannah returns home with Elkanah. Shortly after, she conceives and bears a son. The final scene (vv. 21–28), which is not part of today's lesson, describes the fulfillment of Hannah's vow at Shiloh. The progression in Hannah's story resembles a familiar movement in ancient Israelite worship. Her initial suffering leads her to pray and make vows to the Lord. After words of assurance, the Lord remembers her (v. 19) and delivers her from distress through the birth of a child.

Hannah in Distress (vv. 3–8). In verse 2, the narrator contrasts the situation of Elkanah's two wives: "Peninnah had children, but Hannah had no children." Peninnah taunts Hannah, because "the LORD had closed her womb" (v. 6). This last phrase occurs here and in the preceding verse in order to emphasize the fact that Hannah is barren, and her barrenness is the subject of her rival's ridicule. Thus the two women's contrasting situations is the primary point of contention between them. Hannah's situation evokes a different response from Elkanah, who continues to love his wife in her barren state (v. 5). Annual pilgrimages to Shiloh become the occasion on which the friction between Peninnah and Hannah intensifies. In spite of Elkanah's support, Hannah is inconsolable. She refuses her portion of the sacrifice and weeps as Elkanah offers her words of consolation (vv. 7–8). In the end, her husband's love does not remove Hannah's humiliation or change her barren state.

From Distress to Prayer (vv. 9–18). In the second scene, Hannah enters the temple at Shiloh and begins to pray and weep bitterly. She asks the Lord to remember her in her distress by providing a male child. Hannah vows to offer this child to the Lord as a nazirite "until the day of his death" (v. 11). A nazirite

1. See the birth stories involving Sarah (Gen. 18:9–15; 21:1–7), Rebekah (Gen. 25:19–25), Rachel (Gen. 30:1–8, 22–24), and Samson's mother (Judg. 13:9–25).

Homiletical Perspective

place. So the body of the sermon might feature a delegation going before city council to argue for the saving and revitalization of their "Shiloh," the local faith community.

They might begin by acknowledging that they are not perfect. Sometimes the leaders get it wrong. Sometimes the response needed is not offered. Sometimes we miss the chance to serve. Eli's erroneous presumptions may well come from his exhausting treadmill of pastoral work.

The spokesperson then lays out what is lost if the sanctuary should fail. Women and men with festering and unfulfilled dreams are stuck within the range of their small circle. Where else can you go? Who else can you tell? People in families are left to be picked on and belittled with no outside help. There is no safe place to be open and heard. Lovers and dreamers have only each other to console, with no broad gallery in which to experience the life-giving visions of others and the ages.

Without the sanctuary, there is no place to slip away, to sit before the majesty, to face the gap of mystery that stretches between our little lives and the great seas of life around us.

The speaker then illustrates with one true story of a woman driven to her wit's end. She comes into the old church. She hardly knows where to begin. Agitated and seemingly inappropriate in her behavior, she attracts the attention of the old priest on guard. After a faltering start in which prejudices on both sides are challenged, the curtain of stress falls away and a real conversation ensues. The woman reunites with her husband, bringing a new outlook. They return home together in strength.

The old church is the only place left in the culture where someone actually prays for your life. It is the one place where life is lived beyond immediate gain and the satisfying of whims and wants. Strange and needful themes ring in its arches: tales of rescue by unseen hands, gifts and graces from providence, news of heroes in their real life stories and in the patina the community has laid over them by singing their praises.

At church, strange seeds are planted in the soul. As they germinate, their hosts begin to look forward, beyond one life span, beyond one set of preoccupations, beyond one political agenda, beyond personal laundry lists of hopes and fears. Promised children wait in the wings of tomorrow. They are pressing to be born. They will need witnesses, nurses, and midwives. They will require protectors, singers of songs, keepers of their story, advocates to

1 Samuel 1:4-20

Theological Perspective

awake. Strength and influence spring from this intense awareness of God's unique power and sovereignty. It is Hannah's humility and honesty that seem to get her somewhere, not her station in life. Hannah's hope that she not be regarded as "worthless" (v. 16) comes from a place of anxiety and lack of power. In order to exert power, she draws only on her relationship with God. This relationship allows her to unburden herself from her "anxiety and vexation" (v. 16). And she is "sad no longer" (v. 18). Her connection to God transforms her even before she conceives. She is empowered, not by might or by political influence, but by her intimate connection to God.

Hannah reflects all the complexity of life lived in relationship to this deity who knows and loves humanity with such proximity. Her faithfulness is embodied in how she is drawn to God in her brokenness. Here the God who is involved in the dynasty that 1 and 2 Samuel will track is the God who hears and holds people like Hannah. That Hannah is inscribed with God's grace and love is embedded in the fact that she does not just ask and promise in her prayer; she also grieves, meditates, murmurs, and stands silent. She is there as her whole self—cultural baggage, broken dreams, audacious hope, and all. This person is the person YHWH remembers in the formation of leadership for the people God loves.

The iconography of Hannah holds within it deep symbols of great import to the salvation history of the Hebrew people. Barrenness, fertility, closed and opened wombs, ecstatic prayer, intense grief, social convention, cultural limitations, and so much more create the layers of existence that form this nation of God's people. They are layers of graced existence, of miracles and surprise, of pain and promise—all of these things are written into the embodied history of who we are called to be.

MARCIA MOUNT SHOOP

Pastoral Perspective

"the LORD remembered her" (v. 19b). Eli is little more than an onlooker in this drama, and a clumsy one at that. What happens in the holy precincts does not happen through him and may happen in spite of him. That is a needed reminder to clergy and others who hang out in holy places: little, if anything, of what happens here is because of you, and some of it is in spite of you.

In reading this story a pastor might also be led to confess that Hannah, as she is depicted in this story, might be just the sort of person who would have the ability to drive a pastor a bit crazy. To be sure, it is easy to be sympathetic to her plight, but it might not be so easy to be around her. She is needy, dramatic, challenging, and insistent. She might remind us of the importunate widow of Jesus' parable (Luke 18:1–8), who wears out the judge with her continual pleas. The implication of both Hannah's story and Jesus' parable is that those who are continually persistent may wear us out, but that should come as no surprise, because God can be worn out by such persistence as well. When we are reminded that God grants the pleas of the importunate, then enduring persistence begins to look something like a spiritual discipline.

In reading this story so close to the beginning of Advent, we are pointed to another surprising birth, whose story will be recounted soon. Both Hannah and Mary are unlikely mothers to give birth to great men, one who will anoint kings and one who will be the King of Kings. And yet both births are made possible only through the extraordinary faith of the mothers.

MARTIN B. COPENHAVER

(in Hebrew, *nazir*, meaning "consecrated one") was a person who was "set apart" for the service of the Lord. The vow included: (1) abstinence from alcohol; (2) no cutting of the hair; and (3) no defilement through the touching of a corpse (Num. 6:1–21). Usually the person taking such a vow did so for a limited amount of time. Thus Hannah's promise is extraordinary in that she offers her child as a nazirite "until the day of his death" (cf. Judg. 13:7).

In verses 12–18, Hannah encounters Eli, the priest at Shiloh. As she petitions the Lord, Eli approaches her. The priest misreads her situation, assuming that she is drunk because her lips are moving without audible speech. Irony abounds in this scene. The narrator has built empathy for Hannah through a detailed description of her misery. The reader also knows that Hannah is weeping and praying before the Lord. Hence Eli's thoughtless reprimand in verse 14 deepens the incongruity between Hannah's desperation and the priest's lack of understanding. In verses 15–17, Hannah defends herself. Rather than drinking wine, she has been "pouring out" her soul before the Lord. Eli eventually blesses Hannah, assuring her of God's intention to hear her prayer. Throughout this scene, Hannah's faithfulness stands in stark contrast to Eli's lack of discernment or compassion.

The Lord Responds to Hannah. The answer to Hannah's prayer comes when the Lord remembers her (v. 19). She conceives and bears a son, whom she names Samuel. The chapter ends with Hannah dedicating her child as a nazirite just as she had promised (vv. 21–28). The divine response to Hannah's distress points to God's compassion for those who suffer unjustly at the hands of others. In the end, Hannah is vindicated from Peninnah's taunts and Eli's insensitivity. Moreover, Hannah proves to be a model of faithfulness. In the midst of her misery, she cries out to the Lord, vowing to offer her son to God's service. She defends her character when it is attacked; and, when her prayers are answered, she fulfills her vows to the Lord.

FRANK M. YAMADA

the broader community, and companions for the hills and valleys that are sure to come.

The ending of the sermon may be left open-ended, just as the old tale itself is open-ended. We do not know if councils will be convinced, or have the courage to keep the faith. We do not even know if they should. A decision either way opens one door and blocks another. We do not know the names or work of promised children already born among us. There is no guarantee that they will serve our visions. They may well end on our list of suspects and intruders.

All churches fall down. All eras end. The power of faith has always been found in the gifts of a living God, scattered among us on the move. We cannot hoard them, own them, or keep them, but only be open to their power. That is not easy, and we know it.

This Shiloh story of the birth of Samuel gives the preacher the chance to lay his or her own community alongside that of the Shiloh congregation. The church people will recognize countless moments of their own that mirror those of Samuel's mother, father, and family. It also gives the preacher the opportunity to lay out his or her church's case for its life, its mission, its history and values, and to tell its treasured stories that have given it eternal hope.

Hannah names her son Samuel, from a root word "to ask," as if he were an answer to her prayers. Linguists feel that the root of Samuel rather means "Name of God." This child, come among us through human will and the miracle of life transformation, is not ours for our ends, but belongs to and carries the name of God. It is so of each life, whether bullied in families, alone amid tormented thoughts, awkward in the community of faith, or waiting in the wings for life to begin. Such deep names are not ours to control or own. They each carry the purpose and nature of God. Each one we meet may well be that mystical, hopeful, riveting and terrifying catalyst that fuels the ongoing story of God.

G. MALCOLM SINCLAIR

1 Samuel 2:1-10 (The Song of Hannah)

[1]Hannah prayed and said,
  "My heart exults in the LORD;
  my strength is exalted in my God.
  My mouth derides my enemies,
    because I rejoice in my victory.

[2]"There is no Holy One like the LORD,
    no one besides you;
    there is no Rock like our God.
[3]Talk no more so very proudly,
    let not arrogance come from your mouth;
  for the LORD is a God of knowledge,
    and by him actions are weighed.
[4]The bows of the mighty are broken,
    but the feeble gird on strength.
[5]Those who were full have hired themselves out for bread,
    but those who were hungry are fat with spoil.
  The barren has borne seven,
    but she who has many children is forlorn.

Theological Perspective

The figure of Samuel is one of the most significant figures in the entire history of the people of Israel. He was a pivotal religious, moral, and political leader when a loose confederation of tribes and tribal leaders, beset by powerful neighbors, became a nation with an organized state and capital city (Jerusalem), a kingship (David), and, in time, the temple, the earthly abode of God. The world changed, and with it the way the people of Israel understood their relation to God, the land, and one another.

When Hannah brings her son to the priest at Shiloh to be raised as a nazirite, she does not speak of the enormous changes that will come. She sings of God the Lord, who turns wrong things right side up, who judges justly, who delivers the needy and puts down the oppressor, who upholds the world, who brings death and makes alive, and who blesses the barren with the full number of children. Her voice joins that of the prophet Miriam and Mary of Nazareth in praise of God who works deliverance through extraordinary circumstances. "Not by might does one prevail," Hannah sings, for she has personal knowledge of the divine power to work beyond the reach of ordinary human expectations. God has exalted her power to prevail even though she was barren.

Pastoral Perspective

Any person who has experienced pregnancy and then has given birth to a healthy baby, or has adopted a child and come to love that child as her own, knows that the whole process is a miracle. Likewise, watching children get older and grow into themselves is miraculous. Indeed, bringing and nurturing new life into the world has everything to do with God's holy work. Those feelings of awe must have been magnified exponentially for Hannah, for she had long ago accepted that she would never have children. In her mind, Hannah was destined for a childless life, which meant that in the eyes of the community she was considered less than whole. So when Hannah became pregnant and gave birth to Samuel, it was truly miraculous. The woman who had been labeled "barren" now had a son.

Her first response was to praise God. For Hannah, God must be the source of something so nearly impossible. God must be the source of something so unexpected, something that defies explanation. What else was there to do but sing? Hannah began her song with her own celebration: "My heart exults"; "my strength is exalted"; "my mouth derides my enemies"; "I rejoice in my victory" (v. 1). Following this first exultation, she moved quickly from expressing her own joy to

⁶The LORD kills and brings to life;
   he brings down to Sheol and raises up.
⁷The LORD makes poor and makes rich;
   he brings low, he also exalts.
⁸He raises up the poor from the dust;
   he lifts the needy from the ash heap,
   to make them sit with princes
   and inherit a seat of honor.
   For the pillars of the earth are the LORD's,
   and on them he has set the world.

⁹"He will guard the feet of his faithful ones,
   but the wicked shall be cut off in darkness;
   for not by might does one prevail.
¹⁰The LORD! His adversaries shall be shattered;
   the Most High will thunder in heaven.
   The LORD will judge the ends of the earth;
   he will give strength to his king,
   and exalt the power of his anointed."

Exegetical Perspective

Hannah's song of celebration in 1 Samuel 2:1–10 gives voice to the praise and surprise any of us might feel after a dramatic reversal of fortune. It is situated in both Scripture and the lectionary after the story of Hannah's victory over her rival, Peninnah (1 Sam. 1:4–20). After years of barrenness, bitterness, and prayer, Hannah finally gives birth to her son, Samuel. True to her word (1 Sam. 1:11), she then brings the young Samuel to the temple and "loans" him to the Lord. That she delays this parting until after the child is weaned (1 Sam. 1:21–28) testifies to the fact that this must have been an excruciating promise to keep. This context sets the tone for her song in 2:1–10 as one of poignant but powerful praise.

The very power of that praise may be confusing to modern readers/hearers, however. If we read Hannah's song solely at the level of the individual, the extravagance of her prayer may strike us as "over the top" at best and arrogant at worst. "Talk no more so very proudly" (v. 3) has a caustic quality to it that is reminiscent of the playground taunt, "Na-na-na-na-na-na." While we may be able to affirm God "guard[ing] the feet of his faithful ones," we may find ourselves faltering at that affirmation's corollary, namely that "the wicked shall be cut off in darkness" (v. 9). After all, it is one thing for Hannah to

Homiletical Perspective

On the next to last Sunday of the Christian year, we are invited to see our life as God's people in light of 1 Samuel 2, the Song of Hannah. She was a woman without children who cried inconsolably to God, pouring out her heart and vowing that if God were to grant her request to give her a son, she would set the child apart for a life of holy discipline. When Hannah and Elkanah, her husband, were finally blessed with their first child, a son named Samuel, she took the baby to the temple, where she offered him to God and dedicated him for life.

Preaching from this particular text at this time of the Christian year can be most fruitful, but there are challenges that need to be considered. For example, it will be important for the preacher to provide a clear and concise understanding of Hannah's circumstances. For example, Hannah's change from sadness to joy, following the turn of events leading from barrenness to childbirth, situates her move from prayer to praise within a larger story of God's faithfulness to Israel for the sake of the world. In addition, the diversity of views represented within a congregation related to issues surrounding children, marriage, and family may be seen in light of this larger providential story of a promise-making, promise-keeping God intent on engendering a

1 Samuel 2:1-10

Theological Perspective

In the Bible and in Christian teaching the word "God" is a power word. From the earliest stories of the ancestors to the latest visions of John in Revelation, God is actively present and powerful in the world. The Christian confessions speak of God as *the Almighty, Maker of heaven and earth*, the source and renewer of everything that exists. They speak of God as almighty ruler of the universe and of human history within it, whose glory fills the whole earth, and whose saving purposes shall ultimately triumph in a divine consummation of all things. In any imaginable situation, God's power is the transcending power by which the course of history is decided: "I work and who can hinder it?" (Isa. 43:13). Those conscious of the limits of their own power take comfort in the thought that they are not finally subject to the whims or follies of predators or oppressors. They are created and renewed by God the Lord, who redeems them in the midst of life's traumas and blessings.

God's power is never arbitrary. Creatures are empowered to be and do what they are in relation to God and one another. But God's power is finally decisive. This is the root meaning of the term "omnipotent," commonly defined as "having unlimited power." It would be a mistake to take divine omnipotence in an abstract way, as if God could, would, or should do anything without regard to creatures and their actions. A thoughtful reading of Hannah's prayer declaring God's power to redeem human life gives no support to speculations about unlimited power, about absolute goodness, or undefined evil. She sees God's power in everything that happens: in death and birth, in the grave and in triumph over it (v. 6), in poverty and wealth (v. 7), and in dishonor and honor (v. 8). Deeds have consequences, for the judge of the earth seeks equity. Those who resist shall not succeed (v. 10). It is not that God can do anything, but that God works powerfully and successfully for justice in human life.

The Christian theological understanding of God's power is born within the struggles of history through which we live and act. God's creative action is always appropriate to the environment in which God acts, a world of creaturely causes and consequences. In this sense, God's power has always been understood to be "limited," taking account of each particular context. By creating this world and not another, by creating things interconnected with one another with purposes that often conflict, and by creating moral persons whose intentions and actions express their own choices, God is self-determined to

Pastoral Perspective

affirming God's greatness. Hannah's song is indeed a song of praise for a God who works miracles.

The language of Hannah's song sounds strangely like a song celebrating victory after battle: "My mouth derides my enemies, because I rejoice in my victory" (v. 1); "The LORD! His adversaries shall be shattered; the Most High will thunder in heaven" (v. 10). Scholars agree that this language of battle made its way into Hannah's song because the song "is likely to have been taken from Israel's repertoire of public hymns."[1] Even knowing its origins, though, the language of battle seems misplaced in a song celebrating the miraculous birth of a son. But this is no ordinary birth, and perhaps the language of victory is intended to magnify its importance. It is not just a birth that Hannah celebrates in her song; it is a birth that has happened against all odds, a birth that turned social customs on their head, a birth that brought Hannah back into full relationship with her husband and her family. That, in itself, is worth singing about.

But the language of victory may also serve a larger purpose. It may celebrate and magnify what this birth means for the whole community: God stands for those who are excluded and oppressed. The victory, in Hannah's song, does not go to the one with the most military might. The victory goes to God, who stands with and lifts up the people who are most marginal and left out of society. God's gift of a son for Hannah is not only a cause for Hannah's personal celebration. Samuel's birth has become a cause for all of Israel to celebrate, because, as Old Testament scholar Walter Brueggemann writes, "The birth is not a private wonder but a gift of possibility for all of Israel."[2] The God who can bring a child to a woman who has been unable to conceive also "raises up the poor from the dust; he lifts the needy from the ash heap, to make them sit with princes and inherit a seat of honor" (v. 8). Indeed, Samuel will go on to appoint Israel's first king, Saul. Israel will become great, and their great king, David, will rise from a lowly shepherd boy to become their leader. By using battle language, the writer of this song appropriates familiar language typically reserved for military conquest and uses it to celebrate a God who breaks through hierarchies of wealth, military might, and social power.

Depending on the context of a particular congregation, God's stand for those who are

---

1. Walter Brueggemann, *First and Second Samuel*, Interpretation Series (Louisville, KY: John Knox Press, 1990), 16.
2. Ibid.

celebrate the gift of a child, but should she actively wish Peninnah ill? Then we reach the song's dramatic conclusion in verse 10:

> The LORD! His adversaries shall be shattered;
>   the Most High will thunder in heaven.
> The LORD will judge the ends of the earth;
>   he will give strength to his king,
>   and exalt the power of his anointed.

By this time—*if* we are thinking at the individual level—drama seems to have turned to melodrama, and we may well wonder if Hannah suffers from delusions of grandeur.

Our discomfort serves as a clue that Hannah's song is about far more than one woman's victory over her rival. Indeed, while it works at that level to some degree, it is better and more fully understood as a song scored for a myriad of voices. Here are some of the reasons why.

Scholars have long noted similarities between Hannah's song and Psalm 113, which also celebrates the ways God "raises the poor from the dust" (Ps. 113:7) and "gives the barren woman a home, making her the joyous mother of children" (Ps. 113:9). Such similarities (cf. Ps. 112) fuel speculation that what we know as Hannah's song/prayer may have been a psalm with history independent of the story in 1 Samuel. Its themes of victory and vindication for the oppressed, as well as its specific reference to the barren woman bearing children (1 Sam. 2:5), make it a good "fit" in this narrative context. Thus, the theory is that Hannah's song is "secondary," that is, added later by biblical editors who sought to enrich the story of Samuel's birth with this beautiful and appropriate poem (see also Judg. 4–5, as well as Mary's song in the narrative context of Luke 1).

To say that a passage is "secondary" in no way suggests that it is of any less importance, however. Quite the contrary, it simply invites us to explore the significance of the canonical shape.

If we do this with Hannah's song, we quickly realize that Hannah is not singing/praying just for herself in this passage. Actually, our first clue in that regard is that the story of the prophet Samuel's birth is one of those "near miss" stories that is so often told of a significant leader. The story of Moses in Exodus 1–2 is probably the most well-known of these. As we read about how close the covenant people came to not having a Moses—or in this case, a Samuel—it heightens our sense of awe and thanksgiving at the gift of that person's presence and leadership.

people, beloved children whose existence and way of life proclaims God's praise in and to the world.

As we approach the end or goal of the Christian year, it may be that both preacher and people are able to identify with Hannah more than they realize. Many will certainly hear in this story a strong word of hope and encouragement. For a pilgrim people, which is an apt description of both Israel and church, there will always be need for endurance, perseverance, patience, and hope. God's people live out of the past and into the future, a future that has been promised but is yet to be fully realized. We always need to offer thanks and praise to God, to acknowledge gifts graciously given, and to hope in God's continuing and surprising provision for the future.

On the other hand, the Song of Hannah may sound uninteresting or even irrelevant to a people whose pilgrimage has stalled short of its final destination and been emptied of its hope. An established, successful congregation may have difficulty sharing Hannah's longing for new life, or identifying with her exuberant praise for God's surprising gift of life stirring in her once-barren womb.

For these reasons, the preacher will need to give careful attention to the movement of Hannah's song. A great reversal, brought about by God, is being given voice in song; it is becoming reality in the life of Hannah and all who are able to join her song of praise to God. It is perhaps at this point that we find what may be the most problematic aspect of this text for many preachers and listeners. There is much about our lives as individuals, congregations, and as members of particular cultures and nations that is characterized by pride, abundance, power, and honor. Many of us may know only from a distance the lives of the poor, beaten down, weak, and lowly. Yet the vision of reality sung by Hannah invites us to see the world as God intends, to behold what God is bringing about. It is a vision that may sound surprising to some and may even be threatening for others!

As we near the end of the Christian year, God's people are given a fresh vision of the new world that is on its way, a world that is not dependent upon human efforts, plans, or strategies, but a world that is God's gift. Moreover, it will be helpful to note that Hannah's song of joy evokes fresh remembrance of Mary's song of praise in Luke 1, an outpouring of joy that marks the season of Advent and the nativity of Christ. Because the reality of the birth of God's Son to a young Jewish woman may have already faded into the distant past, it will be important to make this connection, assuring listeners that God

1 Samuel 2:1-10

Theological Perspective

be God in relation to creatures, not God in the abstract. We are not puppets to be manipulated, but responsive persons to be addressed.

In every situation God's power is specifically guided by God's gracious wisdom and God's creative purposes. God acts powerfully in relation to every creature according to its nature and circumstances. With respect to the struggles of history, this means God acts in power to establish human freedom and nourish moral responsibility, as well as to maintain accountability for our use of power.

God's power is not brute force, nor is it laissez-faire. Process theologians remind us that God's powerful activity is generative and attractive, calling forth a complex world and luring it to its best destiny. The older theologians spoke of continuous creation or of the accompanying action of God in history. Even in the dramatic moments of Israel's story such as the exodus from Egypt, God's power was hidden within the events, their leaders' actions, and the people who risked everything. It was God's liberating action, even though God's "footprints were unseen" (Ps. 77:19).

It is easier to trust in God's power to create and renew, to judge and to bless, after an unexpected rescue or recovery from threatened loss or destruction. It is more difficult to discern God's power at work in events that mask or mock the very idea of God's transcending power for good in all things. Followers of Christ embrace this paradox at its most intense when they embrace his life and bloody death as God's powerful justice and love turning the world that crucified him right side up. Even though they do not see the final realization of their hopes, they see Jesus alive and well in the world on the way to that consummation (Heb. 2:8–9, 18).

God's creating and redeeming power is at work in, with, and under the circumstances, decisions, actions, and outcomes of all the events of our lives whatsoever. Hannah speaks for persons of faith in the synagogue and in the church when she recognizes this and celebrates it and looks forward to a future in which God will complete the establishment of the rule of justice to the ends of the earth.

THOMAS D. PARKER

Pastoral Perspective

oppressed and marginalized could be either good news or threatening news. In a nation where military might, wealth, and social status prevail, Hannah's song proclaiming victory for the poor and hungry certainly rings prophetic. It also raises important questions: What does God's stand for the oppressed mean for those of us in a nation perceived by many other nations as the oppressor? What does God's stand for the poor mean for congregations in marginalized communities? What does it mean for wealthy congregations?

In this text, the very personal story of a previously childless woman bearing a child becomes a symbol of hope for the entire community. In congregations too, the personal routinely becomes a matter of public concern. Grief following the death of a child or the unexpected death of an adult can develop into a call to the congregation to take action in the community (fighting cancer, eradicating gang violence, supporting and treating substance abusers, etc.). Births are routinely celebrated in congregations and can become symbols of new life for the entire community. The challenge—and the opportunity—for churches is to find ways in the liturgical life of the congregation to honor the personal and name the ways personal experiences of those in the congregation become symbolic for the entire community.

As she breaks forth in song, Hannah connects the personal miracle of bearing a child against all odds to God's promise for the whole community. Hannah proclaims the inclusive reign of God, the coming king, and a reordering of the social hierarchy. Rarely in the worship life of a congregation is a biblical woman given such a place of importance. Hannah's song, echoed by Mary in her Magnificat celebrating the coming birth of Jesus (Luke 1:46–56), gives the planners of worship an opportunity to lift up and celebrate the power of a woman's words to form a compelling vision of hope for the community.

KATE FOSTER CONNORS

Exegetical Perspective

As Hannah's prayer grows ever more exuberant, we sense that she is celebrating a deliverance that encompasses the whole of the covenant people. In the context of the narrative they are a people who sorely need the leadership of a divinely appointed king. Thus her words anticipate the king that Samuel would someday anoint, namely, David.

The values articulated in this corporate song are extremely instructive. First of all, they give credit where credit is due. Hannah attributes her victory not to her own might, but to God's. (This is even more obvious if one follows the Hebrew at the end of v. 1 and translates "your victory" rather than "my victory.") This God who exalts the lowly and saves the feeble is the same God who creates (v. 8)—an affirmation that echoes the verse so often used at the beginning of worship services: "Our help is in the name of the LORD, who made heaven and earth" (Ps. 124:8; cf. Ps. 121:1–2). Finally, the values to which this song gives voice urge us to worship the God who is both powerful and compassionate—and they call us to look for human leaders with the same qualities.

Unfortunately, human leaders have trouble living up to such extravagant job descriptions. This must have been obvious to the biblical authors who scrupulously recorded the sins of even Israel's most beloved king, David (see 2 Sam. 11–1 Kgs. 2). And it is painfully obvious to anyone who on election day prays Psalm 72 (another biblical prayer that celebrates leaders who judge with justice and have compassion on the poor). Yet it is our very sense of frustration and failure that increases our longing for the "King of Kings," whose coming is celebrated in words quite similar to Hannah's. The difference is that in Mary's Magnificat (Luke 1:46–55), one has the sense that someone is about to be born who can actually live up to the job description. And that *is* something to sing about.

CAROL M. BECHTEL

Homiletical Perspective

has remained true to the Word spoken in Jesus. The church's identity and mission, as a sign of God's kingdom, is not in vain.

It is at this point that gospel proclamation might take shape. Hannah sings in poetic speech, her words participating in and expressive of divinely given excess and abundance. We too preach within the realm of grace, prompted by God's surprising, self-giving, extravagant love in Christ. Yet if the church is to continue on this eschatological journey, it will need more than motivational talk, moralistic scolding, and therapeutic advice.

Hannah's significance for gospel proclamation is her unabashed dependence and bold trust in God, her glad receptivity and eager responsiveness to God, her ecstatic and eccentric praise for the goodness of God. While many listeners will find it easy to affirm that we are saved by a gracious God—"Amazing grace, how sweet the sound"—they may find it more difficult to confess that we are even now being saved and are yet to be completely saved by a gracious God whose self-giving constitutes our life. Yet if our destiny is to be holy as God is holy—a people set apart to praise God for the sake of the world—then our life as church is of God, of God's grace, of God's self-sharing. As we remember the future on this Lord's Day, Hannah summons us to offer all we are and have as a holy and living sacrifice to the One who alone is worthy of such praise.

MICHAEL PASQUARELLO III

Hebrews 10:11-14 (15-18), 19-25

¹¹And every priest stands day after day at his service, offering again and again the same sacrifices that can never take away sins. ¹²But when Christ had offered for all time a single sacrifice for sins, "he sat down at the right hand of God," ¹³ and since then has been waiting "until his enemies would be made a footstool for his feet." ¹⁴For by a single offering he has perfected for all time those who are sanctified. ¹⁵And the Holy Spirit also testifies to us, for after saying,

¹⁶"This is the covenant that I will make with them
    after those days, says the Lord:
I will put my laws in their hearts,
    and I will write them on their minds,"

Theological Perspective

Having assured us for more than three chapters that Jesus the great high priest has accomplished a permanent pardon for sin, the writer now answers the question, "How shall we then live?" A description of the sanctified life forms the climax of this lection (vv. 19–25). As part of this exhortation to holy living, the writer outlines the nature of Christian hope, paints a provocative portrait of the function of the church, and ends on a note of eschatological urgency.

The entire letter to the Hebrews is a teaching sermon preached to a community deemed in need of hearing "again the basic elements of the oracles of God" (5:12). Today's opening verses therefore reprise the core message that Jesus "offered for all time a single sacrifice for sins" (v. 12). The author also reminds believers that we live in that liminal time between Christ's provisional victory over the powers of sin and death and the final victory when "his enemies would be made a footstool for his feet" (v. 13, quoting Ps. 110:1).

In the middle section (vv. 15–18), we learn that Jesus' saving work is the fulfillment of Jeremiah's prophecy of a "new covenant" in which the law is written on the hearts and minds of believers (Jer. 31:33–34). In other words, Jesus' single sacrifice has transformed ("sanctified" in v. 14) believers into people who are able to do God's will as reflected in

Pastoral Perspective

The writer of Hebrews wants his readers to know for certain that what Christ has done in his death on the cross is a "once and for all" sacrifice that frees people, not only from their debts of sin, but also from the ritual sacrifices that once surrounded them (v. 12). What is offered in this text is an invitation for a community to be organized in a "new and living way" (v. 20), not mired in the rehearsal of an "evil conscience" (v. 22).

Christ's sacrifice creates a void and a shift in the identity of the people. If they are no longer occupied with ordering their lives around sacrifices and offerings, what shall they do? How shall they live in light of this new reality? To gain a sense of the impact of this new reality, imagine the humble farmer prior to the advent of electricity or the steam engine. Time and energy that used to be spent behind the plow working by hand and lamplight is freed up, thanks to new sources of power. Far larger fields can be developed, as the day offers more possibilities than ever before. The same is true with the inbreaking of Christ into human history. Old patterns of living are broken, and fresh possibilities to heed the invitation of the living God summon the faithful to an altered identity in use of the present moment.

The author of Hebrews makes a suggestion at the close of this pericope about what that new identity

¹⁷he also adds,
   "I will remember their sins and their lawless deeds no more."
¹⁸Where there is forgiveness of these, there is no longer any offering for sin.

¹⁹Therefore, my friends, since we have confidence to enter the sanctuary by the blood of Jesus, ²⁰by the new and living way that he opened for us through the curtain (that is, through his flesh), ²¹and since we have a great priest over the house of God, ²²let us approach with a true heart in full assurance of faith, with our hearts sprinkled clean from an evil conscience and our bodies washed with pure water. ²³Let us hold fast to the confession of our hope without wavering, for he who has promised is faithful. ²⁴And let us consider how to provoke one another to love and good deeds, ²⁵not neglecting to meet together, as is the habit of some, but encouraging one another, and all the more as you see the Day approaching.

Exegetical Perspective

In this seemingly complex passage, the preacher of the sermon we call Hebrews is actually addressing a very common and familiar pastoral problem: congregational decline. His congregation is basically tired and discouraged—tired of trying to live the Christian life in a culture that offers no support for it and discouraged about the way evil still seems to persist in the world. As a result, the congregation has begun to question the value of being followers of Christ. Attendance at worship has begun to falter (10:25), zeal for mission has waned, and the kind of congregational life that is rich with love and compassion has begun to dissipate (10:24).

The preacher, who hopes to revive his congregation's spirits, does not think they need a flashy leadership gimmick or razzle-dazzle in worship. Astonishingly, what they need, he believes, is clearer Christology. The only way to overcome their despair, the preacher of Hebrews is persuaded, is to know more firmly and to believe more deeply the work and meaning of Jesus Christ. Accordingly, this passage is the climax of a long and dramatic section of Hebrews (which begins at the end of chapter 6) in which Jesus is presented theologically as the great high priest. This is not, however, abstract doctrine. Every piece of the argument is in specific response to the preacher's pastoral concern for his discouraged congregation.

Homiletical Perspective

Some preachers will have a fundamental problem with the approach the writer of Hebrews seems to take regarding Christ's work throughout this book—or at least with the approach many theologians have assumed is presented. Many believe that the blood sacrifice of Christ is the means of mollifying a God whose righteous anger at humanity's sin requires it, thereby allowing us into God's presence eternally; for them this passage (and Hebrews' entire argument) clearly bolsters their view. However, those who have difficulty with the concept of a God who must pretend that Jesus is evil in order to pretend that we are good can nevertheless find some wonderfully preachable ideas. And while the writer of Hebrews makes many careful points regarding the superiority of Christ's sacrifice to the ways of the Levitical priests, that does not mean other views of Christ's work on earth cannot also be viable.

Regardless of which atonement camp a preacher belongs to, this passage offers intriguing insights into the work of Christ. Again, as throughout Hebrews, the writer argues the superiority of Christ's once for all work over the repetitive work of the Levitical priests. This letter's original audience fully understood the priestly protocol, so that whereas the priests offered sacrifices for sin "day after day . . . again and again" with no ultimate effect regarding

Hebrews 10:11-14 (15-18), 19-25

Theological Perspective

the law. Holiness is not a matter of living under external compulsion, of compliance with the outside commands of the law. It is, rather, a Spirit-given ability (v. 15) to live as people of the new covenant.

What does this sanctified life look like? Verses 19–25 suggest five characteristics of holy living.

First, it is a life lived in a posture of *confidence* before God. Jesus' offering of himself ("through his flesh") has cleansed believers "from an evil conscience" (v. 22). With allusions to baptism and to Jesus as the one who renews Israel (Ezek. 36:25), the writer asserts that Jesus has "washed [their bodies] with pure water" (v. 22). In short, as baptized and forgiven people, believers need not be crippled by guilt or fear, but can live before God with confidence.

Second, the sanctified life is one lived in *hope*. Verse 23 urges believers to "hold fast to the confession of our hope without wavering." But this is no cockeyed optimism. Although Christ has inaugurated a new age, the world is still "waiting" for the final defeat of all God's enemies (v. 13). All believers, then and now, face the challenge of living faithfully during this "in between" time, perhaps even in the midst of "abuse and persecution" (v. 33). Christian hope is practiced *against* our outward circumstances. It is rooted not in human effort, but solely in the faithfulness of God. We are able to "hold fast" because the one "who has promised is faithful" (v. 23).

Third, the sanctified life is lived in *community*. This is a word that modern readers in a context of North American individualism might need to hear afresh. The entire community, addressed in verse 19 with the plural *adelphoi* ("friends" in NRSV), is the target of the exhortation to persevere. In fact, the writer chides them for neglecting to meet together regularly for worship and fellowship (v. 25).

In urging believers to gather, the writer names the literally "provocative" function of the church. The community gathers, in part, "for the purpose of incitement" (*eis paroxysmon*, translated in the NRSV as "to provoke one another"). The Greek can have the negative connotation of irritation, sharp disagreement, or incitement, as well as the positive meaning of encouragement or stimulation. For this author, agitation is not simply a tool of community or union organizers, but one of the functions of members of Christ's body. We are to stir up—if necessary, irritate—each other into fulfilling our baptism.

The author thus presents an ecclesiology in which the agitators are not "outsiders" but "insiders." The church is not a place where everyone "plays nice and gets along," but a place where our duties to each

Pastoral Perspective

and purpose might be. "Let us consider how to provoke one another to love and good deeds, not neglecting to meet together . . . but encouraging one another" (vv. 24–25). If there is no need for temple sacrifice, the people may have thought there was no need for community, but the writer of this text says that this is not so. The people must gather for mutual encouragement and support. The gift of Christ is not one that we receive and keep to ourselves. It is meant for the building of the whole body.

The parallels to modern life are striking. What Christian does not have a friend whom they have invited to church, only to be told that the person does not need a community of worship? They are content with solitude and personal devotion. If Christ has already died for their sins, then what reason do they have for going to church? Paul might respond that the community has need of them—for offering encouragement and for bringing fresh ideas for collaboration in the kingdom of God. As far back as Ecclesiastes 4:9 we hear that "two are better than one," for strength, healing, and support. We also read in Acts 2:44 how the early Christian community not only survived but grew strong by holding all things in common and meeting regularly for fellowship, encouragement, prayer, and study.

In many ways we have become a culture of personal piety, with little or no communal accountability for our Christian walk. The word "provoke" has an edge of intrusion in it. If we are to provoke one another to good deeds, then we will certainly have to be involved deeply in one another's lives. But here again, we face the tension between "keeping score" with ritual activities, and celebrating our freedom in Christ. Works righteousness is not the antidote to cheap grace.

Perhaps the best example I know of someone who embodies the essence of this text is an older friend of mine named Aneho. Aneho is both a Cherokee elder and a pastor. She is filled with the gracious, generous love of God and deep respect for the sacrifice of Christ. She lives by herself but welcomes all who come seeking her counsel. She calls a spade a spade. She is a truth teller, but in a way that engenders acceptance and affection. She is perhaps the most provocative encourager I know. When praying with her or sitting for counsel, a visitor will often hear her begin a challenging statement with the words, "I offer for your consideration . . . " The listener knows that what follows will be provocative for the good of the individual and the community. In the South there is a saying when a sermon hits home with

Exegetical Perspective

The main problem for the congregation is that the world of sin and evil seems to rock on unchanged, despite the resurrection of Christ. How can this be so? Does Easter make no real difference? The author of Hebrews is eager to show that the redemptive action of God addresses the world's real brokenness. God did not look down from a distant heaven and say, "There, there, it's all right," but, in Jesus, God entered into the full range of human suffering and tragedy. Therefore, as the preacher has already claimed, "We do not have a high priest who is unable to sympathize with our weaknesses" (4:15), and Jesus "learned obedience through what he suffered" (5:8). Jesus walked right into the fire of human pain, and while ordinary human beings allow the trouble of life to twist and distort them—into victims, oppressors, or a combination of the two—Jesus' suffering shaped him into a perfect offering.

Now in our text, the preacher says that Jesus, as the great high priest, placed his perfect life on the altar of heaven, offering "for all time a single sacrifice for sins" (10:12), thereby breaking the back of evil, sin, and suffering. For the author of Hebrews, the purpose of sacrificial offerings is not to meet God's needs, but to meet the human need to have a clean conscience. The goal of blood offerings is not somehow to satisfy a bloodthirsty God, but through costly yielding to bring human life to a state of perfect purity. But the sacrificial system is a never-ending cycle. Ordinary priests, because they are themselves sinners and part of the problem, are compelled to offer endless sacrifices, and these offerings can "never take away sins" in a lasting way (v. 11). But Jesus was no ordinary priest. On behalf of those who belong to him, Jesus gave the one, perfect offering of his own sinless life. Therefore, Jesus is the end of all blood sacrifice in both senses of the word "end." The perfection of humanity, embodied in Jesus, is the end, or goal, of those sacrifices, and his act on behalf of all humanity has ended the need for them. There is now forgiveness and "no longer any offering for sin" (v. 18).

But if in the cross of Christ the problem of sin has been abolished, and Easter is the validation of this claim, then why do we still see and feel so much sin and suffering all around us? To address this question, the preacher appeals to Psalm 110:1, a favorite of early Christian preachers (appearing several times in Hebrews). The psalm pictures God saying to "my lord" (originally the earthly king), "Sit at my right hand until I make your enemies your footstool." Early Christian preachers interpreted this christologically. Jesus has finished his work. He has

Homiletical Perspective

sin, Christ made a single, perfect, eternally effective offering. The blood sacrifice of Christ works, the writer argues, and it does so for everyone, for all time, wholly and completely—there's no more need for any other offering. It is a done deal.

The writer shows how completely Christ accomplished eternal atonement "by a single sacrifice for sins" by picturing Christ as sitting down and waiting. One can almost see the Lord dusting his hands with an attitude of "mission accomplished" (in this case rightly so) and slumping into an easy chair with a satisfied sigh. The writer alludes to Hebrew Scripture (Ps. 110:1), emphasizing Christ's authority to do what he has in fact done. The right hand of the sovereign is the place of ultimate authority. So when one is allowed by the supreme ruler to sit in that place, there is no doubt as to right or power. Jesus has finished and now waits for the time of the end, when his enemies will be utterly subservient and thoroughly defeated, crouching under his feet.

The parenthetical section of this reading (vv. 15–18) introduces another train of thought that, while fitting with the argument, seems a bit forced. We see the third member of the Trinity assuring believers of the covenant between God and God's people, with the explanation that as a result of Christ's work we will naturally be obedient because the Spirit will write God's laws on our hearts. There will be no need to learn them; they will be part of our spiritual DNA and thus natural behaviors. God's forgiveness of our sin is total and irrevocable, because the omniscient God has completely forgotten all the sins we have committed.

One very powerful aspect of this passage worth emphasizing is that many of us struggle under the weighty pain of regret and guilt regarding our past behaviors, especially when those behaviors have caused harm to others. It is important that we take responsibility for any and all consequences of our sinful actions in a mature and Christlike way. But it is also transparently important, and modeled here by God indeed, to forgive ourselves as God has forgiven us. This is a message congregation members need to hear: how to balance freedom from the guilt of sin with responsibility to others who have suffered in the wake of our wrongdoings. If a preacher can unfold and illustrate how that works, he or she has done some important work.

Regardless of one's views on atonement, the juice of this passage is in the final section (vv. 19–25), which lifts us out of the debate and into the real grit of living out our faith in light of the work of Christ. The writer issues a three-part resolution that flows

Hebrews 10:11-14 (15-18), 19-25

Theological Perspective

other include difficult, perhaps contentious wrestling (but always a wrestling *together*), with what "love and good deeds" (v. 24) will look like in our contexts. This ecclesiology is the vision to which Martin Luther King Jr. called the clergy of Birmingham in his famous "Letter from Birmingham City Jail." For King, the "love and good deeds" to which Christians must provoke each other include agitation against an unjust status quo.[1]

The fourth mark of the sanctified life is related to the third: Christians are called to live in *solidarity* with others. Holy living involves maturing in acts of love and Christlike service to all people. The writer is clearly concerned that the recipients of this letter are still "infant(s)" in the faith (5:12–14) and now warns against complacency, against allowing the gospel of reconciliation to become a matter of cheap grace. Sanctification is a calling as well as a gift. Believers should respond to God's gift by engaging in practices that form them into "mature" disciples ready for "solid food" (5:14). As if peering centuries ahead into America's culture of individualism, the writer emphasizes that these practices are best cultivated within the life of the believing community as it comes together to worship, enjoy fellowship, and provoke one another to acts of Christlike service.

Finally, the sanctified life is lived with a sense of *urgency* because "the Day [is] approaching" (v. 25). Invoking scriptural images of the coming Day of the Lord as one of both judgment and redemption, the writer offers both warning and encouragement. Apostasy brings judgment even upon God's people (vv. 29–30), but perseverance "great reward" (v. 35). Therefore, believers should support each other in "love and good deeds."

JANE E. FAHEY

Pastoral Perspective

particular power. "You've gone from preaching to meddling," people say in response. The writer of Hebrews invites us, as Aneho shows us, how to enter the territory of Christian meddling.

Life in Christian community also summons us to acknowledge the unfinished nature of what God has set into motion. Our transformation personally and communally is not yet complete. Yes, Christ's sacrifice has opened the gates of heaven for all to enter, but the fullness of the kingdom of God has not yet been revealed. We are a people who live in the dance of the already-but-not-yet, and to dwell in that place requires much encouragement. It is terribly easy to lose hope and focus in the face of a reality that seems to suggest that not much is different, despite Christ's having walked among us. This is yet another reason for us to gather and to testify to one another what we have seen and heard of God. It is also a reason for the Christian community to live out even more passionately the grace we have been shown in Christ.

This text is unusually well suited to a liturgy that includes a baptism or renewal of baptism. Focus on the once and for all sacrifice of Christ as well as the communal nature of the covenant would be appropriate. A litany of commitment in which the community of faith ponders new ways to encourage one another and receives permission to "provoke" one another to good deeds might also lend strength to the service in which this text is preached.

ELIZABETH B. FORNEY

---

1. See Martin Luther King Jr., "Letter from Birmingham City Jail," in *A Testament of Hope: The Essential Writings of Martin Luther King., Jr.*, ed. James Melvin Washington (San Francisco: Harper & Row, 1986), 300.

Exegetical Perspective

destroyed sin and death, and now, as Lord, he is seated in authority at the right hand of God. But the full effect of Christ's work has not yet been accomplished. God is now at work in the world subduing the "enemies" of Christ, and Christ is watching and waiting for this process to be completed (v. 13). In other words, the world today is something like Europe after the D-day invasion. The victory is sure, but there are still battles to be fought. Christ has already defeated evil, but only at the end of time (called "the Day" by the preacher, v. 25) will this triumph be clear and complete.

Now how does this christological claim build up the congregation's desire for worship? First, it underscores the urgency and importance of preaching. We cannot see the victory of Christ with the naked eye, but we can hear it with the naked ear. So the preacher of Hebrews proclaims this gospel with power and urges his hearers to "hold fast to the confession of our hope without wavering" (v. 23). In other words, if you want to know the truth, pay more attention to the gospel you hear than to the obsolete evil you see, thrashing in its death throes in the world.

Second, it takes both the dread and the toil out of worship. Instead of being burdensome or meaningless, worship becomes a zone of liberation. Worshipers do not need to slink into the sanctuary as guilty and unworthy sinners. In baptism, their bodies were washed clean and their hearts were made new (v. 22), and by the sacrifice of Christ they have become blood brothers and sisters of Jesus. They can therefore walk into church confidently, knowing that to the eye of God they appear as pure and sinless as the Christ who claims them as his own (vv. 19–22). Finally, they can live as people who know that the victory has already been won, "provok[ing] one another to love and good deeds" (v. 24).

THOMAS G. LONG

Homiletical Perspective

from a double "since": *Since* we are now able to enter God's presence confidently (v. 19), and *since* we belong to Jesus Christ under whose proven authority we live (v. 21), this is how we should live.

First, let us enter into and experience God's presence fully, honestly, authentically—knowing we are wholly clean and pure and accepted and even desired (v. 22). Let us luxuriate in God's loving, accepting presence, soaking it up. But let us not get stuck there. For many, this will involve a major step toward self-acceptance; they have been told by influential people throughout their lives that they are unlovable and unworthy and even unwanted. Stressing this point can revolutionize some people's lives. But the writer does not stop here, and neither should we. The freedom of knowing that God loves and accepts us should translate into selfless service, as unfolded in the next two points.

Second, let us believe and exercise our faith boldly, following the example of Christ, who will be faithful to his promises (v. 23). At our baptism we (or those responsible for us) made a confession of faith, and the writer encourages us to hold on to that. That confession should always be our life target. We may not always hit it—doubts and circumstances may hinder us at times—but keeping it in our sights gives us hope and purpose, and energizes our ongoing search for authentic faith.

Third, let us be creative in provoking and encouraging and pushing and pulling all those in our family of faith to "love and good deeds" (v. 24). This is all about participating in the body of Christ, working with and for and through others in the family of faith. This point speaks more directly to the gospel of Christ as our model and mentor. We are not mere spectators of God's work or simple recipients of God's grace: we are active participants in the saving work of God in the world, as we follow Christ's ultimate example of sacrificial giving, serving, and loving until the very end.

PETER M. WALLACE

Mark 13:1-8

[1]As he came out of the temple, one of his disciples said to him, "Look, Teacher, what large stones and what large buildings!" [2]Then Jesus asked him, "Do you see these great buildings? Not one stone will be left here upon another; all will be thrown down."

[3]When he was sitting on the Mount of Olives opposite the temple, Peter, James, John, and Andrew asked him privately, [4]"Tell us, when will this be, and what will be the sign that all these things are about to be accomplished?" [5]Then Jesus began to say to them, "Beware that no one leads you astray. [6]Many will come in my name and say, 'I am he!' and they will lead many astray. [7]When you hear of wars and rumors of wars, do not be alarmed; this must take place, but the end is still to come. [8]For nation will rise against nation, and kingdom against kingdom; there will be earthquakes in various places; there will be famines. This is but the beginning of the birth pangs."

Theological Perspective

Whether on a large scale or small one, apocalyptic writings are arresting. Their predictions of false messiahs, wars, earthquakes, and famines model rabbinic expressions for the kind of national calamities that usher in the advent of the Messiah. Today's passage is no exception, as Jesus foretells the destruction of the temple. Like similar passages in Matthew and Luke, these Markan verses contain predictions of political unrest, natural disasters, and the persecution of the community of believers. These three Gospels culminate in describing the cosmic upheavals that usher in the kingdom/realm of God.[1]

As we move through the New Testament, nearly one-third of the references to salvation are linked to deliverance from specific ills such as captivity, diseases, demon possession, eschatological terrors, and physical death. In the short eight verses for today's reading, Jesus begins to detail the horror of an apocalypse. The ebb and flow of creation as we know it, the relationships we have established, the cultural markers that help define us—these and more are now obliterated. This is total destruction at its sharpest. It

1. Another promising avenue to explore is the fact that Mark 13—like Luke 21, Matthew 24–25, and John 13–17—is a private address of Jesus to his disciples. Although this fact is not explored in further detail in this essay, one could develop the theme of election, in that only a select few were chosen to hear these words from Jesus.

Pastoral Perspective

Towering buildings are not supposed to crumble to the ground. Oceans are not supposed to leap out of their seabeds and flood miles inland. The ground is not supposed to shake and undulate. The sky is not supposed to form a funnel cloud and destroy a town. Yet all who have watched the World Trade Towers collapse, seen a tsunami flood a nation, experienced an earthquake, or suffered through the power of a tornado know that such events happen. Those who provide care for the victims report that all express a profound sense of loss. Not only have they lost loved ones and property, but in a deep and abiding sense they have lost their innocence. They now know that something they once believed to be sure—that a towering structure would stand forever, for instance, or that the ocean would stay securely in its seabed—is no longer trustworthy. They have lost a foundational belief upon which they once built their lives. No longer will they be able to step on the ground without wondering, if only for a moment, whether the ground is going to remain stable. No longer will they be able to look up into a darkening sky without wondering if a destructive storm is on its way.

Poet William Butler Yeats captured this sense of innocence lost in his description of the end times in the opening lines of his poem "The Second Coming":

Exegetical Perspective

Perceiving the truth can be difficult, and discerning the significance of a moment is seldom easy. Even Jesus' closest followers found this to be true (see Mark 8:32–33; 9:5–6). So, throughout the Gospels, Jesus helps his followers have "eyes to see" and "ears to hear" what is true and according to God's will (4:9, 23; 8:17–18). Here in Jerusalem, in the week of his passion and nearing the cross, Jesus continues to help his disciples look beyond appearances and trust God.

Beyond Appearances (vv. 1–2). Contrary to some interpreters, this pericope is not just a bridge between Jesus' last visit to the temple and his Olivet discourse, which in Mark is commonly called the "little apocalypse" (Mark 13; Matt. 24; Luke 21). Rather, it is a fitting introduction to the apocalyptic narrative that follows, which is Jesus' longest address in Mark. All of chapter 13 is rooted in Jewish apocalyptic thought, and central to such thinking is the belief that God controls history, that the world has become so evil that only God can save it, and that God will rescue the world from evil at the time of God's own choosing, establishing a new creation in which righteousness characterizes everyone in it. Such thinking was popular among first-century-CE Jews, but many were likely offended by Jesus' prediction of the temple's destruction.

Homiletical Perspective

In a speech delivered at the Brandenburg Gate right beside the Berlin wall on June 12, 1987, President Ronald Reagan issued a challenge: "Mr. Gorbachev, tear down this wall." That was the goal for a generation of people. Since the end of the Second World War, people in the Western world had been recruited into a massive campaign to defeat communism. We had been told it was our calling to stand up to the communists and to free the people under their oppressive grip. If this could be achieved, we were told, then a whole new world of peace and freedom would break forth. On that June day Mr. Reagan was fervently recruiting us for this cause.

Recruiters like President Reagan are clearly in the background of today's text. The text was first heard in the Jewish-Roman War of 66–70 CE.[1] This insurrection, which started in Jerusalem, was aimed at restoring the Davidic kingdom. It promised to recover the purity and independence of the Jerusalem temple and the nation of Israel. When Mark wrote this text, the temple may already have been destroyed, or its destruction may still have loomed in the future (ultimately, the temple was demolished in this war, never to be rebuilt).

---

1. Ched Myers, *Binding the Strong Man: A Political Reading of Mark's Story of Jesus* (Maryknoll, NY: Orbis Books, 1988), xxviii.

Mark 13:1-8

Theological Perspective

is unrelenting and unforgiving, and no one—not even the faithful—can escape its devastating blows as the old age is swept away for the new one.

In what is called the "little apocalypse" in Mark (because its form and content resembles Daniel 7–12 and Revelation), we find the longest speech of Jesus in this Gospel, as today's passage extends to verse 37 at the end of the chapter. Mark associates the destruction of the temple with the end of the current age and the coming kingdom of God. Today's passage is an apt one for exploring the theological meaning of salvation in the context of an apocalypse. This compelling interplay offers the preacher a rich field of possibilities to open up anew the depths of how salvation enters our lives to offer both hope and challenge. A key challenge will be to help the hearers of the word understand that salvation is a *process* of repentance, forgiveness, and new birth, and not a static event in our lives.

In two quick scene changes, Jesus moves from the grandeur of the temple to the Mount of Olives directly across from it to proclaim impending destruction. In keeping with other apocalyptic literature, Jesus uses signs and events of the day to signal the coming of the end of the current age. Yet with this end is the birth of the new age. Remarkably, in the midst of the predictions of destruction, if not annihilation, lie the seeds of salvation. It is rough sledding to help hearers of the Word continue in the midst of apocalyptic warnings once one knows that simplistic proclamations of humanity's wickedness or craven faithfulness will simply not do. The theological heft of salvation loses its power with such appeals. Rather, we should explore how we move from darkness to light, from alienation to divine community, from guilt to pardon, from slavery to freedom, from the fear of hostile powers to liberty and assurance. In short, what it means is that through abiding faith, we receive salvation through God's grace.

Theologian James H. Cone notes how the process of salvation is dominant in the black religious tradition from his Wesleyan perspective. For Cone, black worship is "the actualization of the story of salvation as experienced in the lives of oppressed black people."[2] In the context of enslavement and dehumanization, the contradiction with salvation was stark. The daily wrestling with the lived apocalypse of slavery made it difficult for enslaved

2. James H. Cone, "Sanctification and Liberation in the Black Religious Tradition, with Special Reference to Black Worship," in *Speaking the Truth: Ecumenism, Liberation, and Black Theology* (Grand Rapids: Eerdmans, 1986), 29–30.

Pastoral Perspective

Turning and turning in the widening gyre
The falcon cannot hear the falconer;
Things fall apart; the center cannot hold;
Mere anarchy is loosed upon the world,
The blood-dimmed tide is loosed, and everywhere
The ceremony of innocence is drowned.[1]

As Jesus and his disciples are leaving the temple, the disciples remark about the large stones and the buildings that appear immovable. Jesus startles them with his prediction that even the great stones that form the temple will one day be thrown down. As they sit together on the Mount of Olives gazing at the magnificent temple, the disciples must have found Jesus' words troubling, if even a little hard to imagine. Peter, James, John, and Andrew ask Jesus privately when his prediction will come to pass. In his cryptic style, Jesus warns them not to be led astray by others who will come after him, including some who will claim to speak with Jesus' own authority. Jesus tells the disciples not to be worried by wars, rumors of wars, earthquakes, or famine, as these are signs of the beginning of the end. Jesus does not answer the disciples' question directly. Instead, he sets out for them a way to live that does not focus all of their attention on the destruction of the temple or the second coming.

This is the problem with those who, invoking Jesus' name, want to draw all our attention to and focus all our energy on the end of the age. Numerous publications and Internet sites offer formulas for interpreting every tragic event, every hurricane, every war, every famine, every tornado, and every earthquake as part of God's plan for the second coming of Jesus Christ. Various groups have created their own versions of an end-time clock to tell us how close we are to Christ's return. Some provide a "rapture index," claiming that Christ's return is imminent. Others interpret each day's events in light of this text, claiming some secret revelation about God's plan for the last days.

Jesus' warning is more potent than ever. Certainly every generation has heard the voices of those who boldly claim that they are privy to insider knowledge about when Christ is returning. That is what makes the subject of the end times so attractive and so treacherous. We, like the disciples, can become so focused on discerning the signs of the times that we neglect our more important mission to witness to the gospel today.

1. William Butler Yeats, "The Second Coming," in *Michael Robartes and the Dancer* (Churchtown, Dundrum, Ireland: Chuala Press, 1920).

Exegetical Perspective

As Jesus and his disciples leave the temple for the last time (13:1; cf. 11:11, 15), an unnamed disciple comments on the splendor of the temple complex. He seems unaware of Jesus' teaching moments earlier that appearance and reality are not always the same (12:38–44). He is aware, however, that he is in the midst of a great architectural achievement. The temple in Jerusalem with its surrounding structures was magnificent by all accounts (see Josephus, *Antiquities* 15:380–425; 20:220–21; *War* 5:184–247). The Roman historian Tacitus described the temple complex as a mountain of white marble adorned with gold, a "temple of immense wealth" (*History* V. 8). Its enormous stones mystified many, and the surrounding complex included sprawling courtyards, colonnaded courts, grand porches and balconies, covered walkways, and monumental stairs. Herod the great builder built it to impress the wealthiest and most powerful rulers of the day, and he succeeded.

Jesus' response to his disciple is shocking (v. 2). It is surprising on one level because Herod's temple was so much more massive than the earlier temples of Solomon and Zerubbabel. It is surprising on another level because it is God's temple, the place many Jews believed to be the closest point of contact between God and God's people. Would God allow such a thing to happen to this magnificent temple?

A review of Mark's preceding context is instructive. When Jesus enters Jerusalem, he goes directly to the temple (11:11). He then departs to Bethany (literally "house of the poor") and the next day returns to Jerusalem, cursing a leafy but barren fig tree along the way, which subsequently withers and dies (11:12–14). Jesus then enters the temple and cleanses it, igniting the fury of the religious leaders (11:17–18). Now here, while leaving the temple, a disciple comments on the temple complex's "leafy" appearance ("Look, Teacher, what large stones and what large buildings!" 13:1), but Jesus announces its inevitable destruction. Symbolically, then, the temple continues to be barren of true worship—like the religious leaders who serve in it (see 11:15–19; 12:12, 38–40)—and it will be destroyed like the fig tree. Jesus' declaration, then, is no small reminder to his followers to look beyond appearances. True worship of God has a different center and expresses itself in different ways.

Discerning the Truth (vv. 3–8). Jesus and his disciples leave Jerusalem and ascend the Mount of Olives. For Mark, mountaintops always connote nearness to God. On a mountain, Jesus appoints the Twelve

Homiletical Perspective

Regardless of which was the case, when Mark wrote this passage, pressure was being placed on the Markan community to join the battle. Resistance fighters were going through the Palestinian countryside calling on all Jews to join this final battle, this war that would bring the end, the *telos,* the goal of the age, namely, the salvation and restoration of God's people. And the Markan community, embodied by the disciples, was clearly susceptible to joining the cause. How enamored they are by the temple, as with Jesus they leave it for the last time!

"Look, Teacher, what large (*or wonderful*) stones and what large (*or wonderful*) buildings!" The restoration of the temple's glory and the triumphal restoration of the Davidic kingdom beckoned to them as the goal of their lives. Not only was this goal alluring, but failure to join its pursuit would leave this community open to persecution at the hands of the resistance forces. They would be considered traitors to their own people.

The recruiters were out in force. They are still out in force. The goals they urge the church to pursue remain enticing. Those goals are portrayed as the destination of history. And they may be worthy goals. But are they the *telos,* God's goal for the life of this world?

The Berlin wall did come down a little over two years after President Reagan made that speech. Yet is the new world order that has emerged in the post–cold war era God's goal for humankind? Or consider the recruiting cry that rose up in the aftermath of the horrid attacks of 9/11, the cry that continues to resound, calling us to rid the world of terrorists regardless of the costs. This war against terror is held up as the way to save civilization. Yet even if the world could be freed from terrorists, would the world that remained—structured with gaping chasms between rich and poor—be God's goal for creation?

To draw closer to the place where most of the listeners to this text abide on Sunday mornings, think about churches struggling over the place of gay, lesbian, bisexual, and transgender persons in their midst. Affinity groups recruit. They proclaim their agenda is the way toward the goal of peace, unity, and purity for the church. Yet if the agenda of any of these groups is achieved, will God's goal for the body of Christ have been met?

In this final address to his disciples, Jesus tells them that many will come promising to be *messianic,* ones bringing the saving end, or goal, of

Mark 13:1-8

Theological Perspective

Africans to separate the yearning for salvation from the vision for a new humanity where people were defined by the freedom found in God's grace, rather than the enslavement meted out by human cruelty and greed. This led slaves to sing:

Oh, freedom, Oh, freedom,
oh, freedom over me.
And before I'd be a slave
I'll be buried in my grave,
and go home to my Lord and be free.[3]

Today we hear this cry for the beginning of the birth pangs as we listen to those who have been the victims of disasters such as the breaking of the levees after Hurricane Katrina in August of 2005. Those who are the survivors and victims of mental, physical, or sexual abuse are among those who may need to hear or sing this cry. Think through the many ways those who will hear this passage experience the need, the yearning, for God's grace through salvation as they face incredible—and what can often feel like (and may actually be) insurmountable—obstacles that seem to make the freedom of salvation a utopian pipe dream, rather than an act of radical witness and faithfulness.

Yes, we will be touched by the awful destruction of the apocalypse, as none escape its ravages, but for those who live with a faith that seeks a deep relationship with God—one that does not rely on trite formulas or poorly developed doctrines—we find, in and through God's grace, the pathway through devastation and suffering: salvation. For the time of destruction, which is an ending, is also a beginning for people of deep faith. The new life found in salvation helps to remind us that to have new life, all things must grow and change. It is crucial to remind the hearers of the Word that the final words of today's passage are: "This is but the *beginning* of the birth pangs."

EMILIE M. TOWNES

Pastoral Perspective

Kathleen Norris writes about how the word "eschatology" confounded her for a time, leading her to focus far too intently on the events of the day as she tried to discern the formula. Eventually she found her way through her fear of the end times, coming to regard Christ's return as life affirming in ways more subtle than any dictionary definition could convey. She writes:

What I mean is this: an acquaintance of mine, a brilliant young scholar, was stricken with cancer, and over the course of several years came close to dying three times. But after extensive treatment, both radiation and chemotherapy, came a welcome remission. Her prognosis was uncertain at best, but she was again able to teach, and to write. "I'd never want to go back," she told her department head, an older woman, "because now I know what each morning means, and I am so grateful just to be alive." When the other woman said to her, "We've been through so much together in the last few years," the younger woman nodded, and smiled. "Yes," she said, emphatically. "Yes! And hasn't it been a blessing!"[2]

So how does one survive the devastation of an aggressive cancer diagnosis or other illness, the crashing down of a building, or the aftermath of a natural disaster? How does one survive the loss of innocence? How does one live in the midst of competing voices, all full of passionate intensity, claiming that these are signs of the end of the age? Our focus must not be on the signs themselves, but rather on the one who is to come—the one who enables us to look up after such devastation and claim the certainty of blessing. Things may seem to have fallen apart. It may appear that anarchy has been loosed on the world. Nevertheless, the center will hold and—much to our amazement—we will discover that we have much faithful work to do.

RODGER Y. NISHIOKA

---

2. Kathleen Norris, *Amazing Grace: A Vocabulary of Faith* (New York: Riverhead Books, 1998), 12–13.

3. *African American Heritage Hymnal* (Chicago: GIA Publications, 2001), #545.

Exegetical Perspective

(3:13–19), prays (6:46), is transfigured by God (9:2–8), and now foretells the future (13:3–5). Here on the Mount of Olives, Jesus sits, in the manner of a teacher, "opposite the temple," and some of his closest associates—named hierarchically (cf. 1:16–20; Matt. 10:2; Luke 6:14)—begin asking about the coming destruction of the temple. There is precedent for such musings. Ezekiel foresaw the departure of God's glory from the temple to the Mount of Olives (Ezek. 9:3; 10:18–19; 11:23), and Zechariah named the Mount of Olives as the locus of redemption in the last days (Zech. 14). Moreover, the disciples' question resembles a statement of the divine messenger in Daniel 12:7, suggesting they understand Jesus' temple prophecy in eschatological terms. The prophesied destruction of the sanctuary, then, is but one aspect of "all these things" (vv. 4, 23, 29, 30), and the disciples are seeking Jesus' guidance to prepare for the arrival of God's kingdom.

Jesus responds with two commands and accompanying clarifications. First, Jesus admonishes them to screen their future leaders carefully (v. 5b). Israel has a long history of trusting false prophets and following unfaithful leaders (e.g., Deut. 13:1–5; 1 Kgs. 13:33–34; Isa. 30:9–11; Jer. 23:13, 32; 29:8–9; Mic. 3:5). Jesus warns of coming deceivers who will claim for themselves Jesus' identity and power. Consequently, Jesus' call to vigilance ("Beware") is also an implicit command to keep following Jesus' word and example (1:17–18; 2:14–15; 3:7; 5:24; 6:1; 8:34; 10:21, 28, 52; 14:54; 15:41).

Second, Jesus commands his disciples to remain calm in the unsettling events to come (v. 7a), for the approaching natural disasters and human-created catastrophes are necessary (vv. 7b–8). That is, evil is rampant in the world, it affects the earth itself, and it produces its own terror. But God's judgment and rescue are sure. The proliferation of false prophets, wars, earthquakes, and famine are but "birth pangs" (cf. Gen. 3:14–19; Isa. 13:8; 26:17; Jer. 4:31; Hos. 13:9–13; Rev. 6; etc.) of God's final judgment and the full establishment of the messianic age of God's rule. Jesus' followers may trust that God is in control.

ROBERT A. BRYANT

Homiletical Perspective

history. Urging a final battle to restore the Davidic kingdom and the temple is exactly what those Zealots were doing. But Jesus makes it evident that the temple will be no more. Its restoration and with it the restoration of Davidic glory is not the end, the *telos,* God's goal for the world. That goal is now wrapped up in the coming of the Son of Man in glory (Mark 13:26–27).

"Beware!" Jesus says. Resist the recruiters. Do not sell out and stake your life on their agenda. Their enticing promises are not the goal. Therefore do not make them the goal of your living. Instead endure, hold out for God's goal, the goal that will be accomplished only in the coming of the Son of Man.

Holding out will not be easy, for the pressure of the recruiters is intense. That is why Mark shares this discourse. That is why it is crucial for the church to hear it in this present age. The pressure on the followers of Jesus to be co-opted as champions for campaigns that promise salvation and glory is excruciating. Failure to join these campaigns, to raise even the slightest question about them, often leads to ostracism or worse. But enduring that pressure is only a birth pang. It is only a wrenching—but promising—experience that is to be endured in order to welcome the *telos,* God's goal and intention for the world that the Son of Man can and will bring.

The Markan scholar Lamar Williamson reminds us that every Gospel writer leaves the church with a challenge. John calls the church to love one another. Matthew and Luke call the church to engage in mission to the Gentiles, to those who are "other." These are daunting challenges. But perhaps the most daunting challenge for Christians in the North American context, so set on instant gratification, is this one left for us by Mark: "Beware, . . . keep awake," watch, resist, hold out for the coming of Son of Man.[2]

PETE PEERY

---

2. Lamar Williamson Jr., *Mark,* Interpretation Series (Atlanta: John Knox Press, 1983), 238.

2 Samuel 23:1-7

¹Now these are the last words of David:
  The oracle of David, son of Jesse,
    the oracle of the man whom God exalted,
  the anointed of the God of Jacob,
    the favorite of the Strong One of Israel:

²The spirit of the LORD speaks through me,
  his word is upon my tongue.
³The God of Israel has spoken,
  the Rock of Israel has said to me:
One who rules over people justly,
  ruling in the fear of God,

Theological Perspective

First Samuel begins with Hannah's poignant prayer, and Second Samuel comes toward its close with David's prayerful reflection on his reign. All the narrative material in between these prayerful bookends does not compose an easy story of the movement toward the monarchical heights of David's reign. The tendency of human beings to use and abuse power is clearly a theme that is carried through to David's "last words." As one reads this poetic song of praise, the complexity of this monarchy echoes in the background. There is much at stake, and there has been much at stake in how power has become concentrated in particular human beings for the nation of Israel. The disharmony of this monarchy has been acute at times, and what lies ahead for Solomon after David has a painful and tragic edge to it. There is a tone of wisdom that has formed in David as he has weathered his reign. Just as Hannah embodies a strong consciousness of her dependence on God in the first verses of this narrative, so now David's song points to the foundational importance of knowing the source of one's strength and worth as this chapter of Israel's monarchical success begins to close. Kingship is a gift from God. It is not something to be held with a clenched fist, but something to be held gently.

Pastoral Perspective

Last words have a special weight that other words do not. Last words are given particular significance simply because they are last words. Think of the last words that are spoken at the graveside, or the last words that are said to a child when dropping her off at college, or the last words of the final sermon before the beloved pastor retires. People attend to last words.

The Bible is full of partings, and parting words are given a prominent place in the biblical narrative.

For instance, when Moses, after leading his people out of exile and wandering with them in the wilderness for forty years, reached the verge of the promised land, he gathered the people of Israel to say good-bye to them (Deut. 32–33). He attended carefully to the moment, addressing the whole assembly at length and then speaking a particular word to the head of each tribe. Moses talked directly about his leaving, without a hint of avoidance, without false promises, because he said that the most unavoidable reality of all—the reality of God—would go with them and the promises he related were the changeless promises of God. The journey for Moses and his people was not complete. He told them that they did not yet have a homeland, and yet the eternal God was their dwelling place. For Moses,

⁴is like the light of morning,
  like the sun rising on a cloudless morning,
  gleaming from the rain on the grassy land.

⁵Is not my house like this with God?
  For he has made with me an everlasting covenant,
  ordered in all things and secure.
 Will he not cause to prosper
 all my help and my desire?
⁶But the godless are all like thorns that are thrown away;
  for they cannot be picked up with the hand;
⁷to touch them one uses an iron bar
  or the shaft of a spear.
  And they are entirely consumed in fire on the spot.

Exegetical Perspective

Tensions in Kingship. In Samuel through Kings, a conflicted picture of kingship emerges. On the one hand, the Lord makes a covenant with David, promising him an everlasting throne (2 Sam. 7). On the other, a human king is considered to be an undesirable compromise between the Lord and a faithless people (1 Sam. 8). Moreover, though a strong ideal of kingship persists throughout the history of the monarchy, the majority of the rulers from Israel and Judah fail to live up to this model. Thus both idealism and realism inform ancient Israel's royal theology. In the lesson from 2 Samuel 23 there is a tension between the ideal of the Lord's everlasting covenant with the house of David and the reality of what has transpired in this celebrated king's reign.

Second Samuel 23:1–7 is a poem that functions as David's final speech. Hannah's song (1 Sam. 2:1–10) and David's two concluding poems (2 Sam. 22:2–23:7) serve as a poetic framework for this early period of the monarchy. The motifs of justice and just rule permeate both the first and last poems. Thus David's rise and reign are interpreted within these themes. Second Samuel 23 divides into three sections. An introduction in the form of a prophetic oracle (vv. 1–3a) is followed by a description of the just ruler and his divinely appointed dynasty (vv.

Homiletical Perspective

This Sunday marks the occasion of the last words we speak before the new church year is upon us. Last words close the book on what was, and brace the community as it launches toward its future. Casting our minds across the library of the Bible, we recall how authors employed the literary vehicle of quoting the "last words" of many tribal saints and leaders. Linking these personae to their legacies made this a powerful teaching tool. As with our own advertising campaigns, if a star endorses the product, then it must be good.

Moses is given a script of last words to speak, as are Elijah (2 Kgs. 2), Jesus, Stephen (Acts 7:54–60), and in legend, Peter, Andrew, and others. It is interesting to consider the last words of each and to extrapolate from them what might be going on in the community at the time.

Moses's last words (Deut. 33) take the form of a patriarchal blessing to each of the "children," the twelve tribes. He names each one and indicates by his wish for them that he is aware of their strengths and weaknesses. He tenderly prays for each and hopes that their way ahead will be healthy, strong, faithful, and blessed. These are good last words, flexible and reusable. It is always good to let people know that the prayer that began their community life was one of love, good wishes, and blessing.

2 Samuel 23:1-7

Theological Perspective

David does not depart the scene until two chapters into First Kings, so his "last words" occupy a space not of closure but of theological reminder. God's faithfulness, God's effectiveness, and God's character are held up here as the cornerstones of the just use of power. The kingship that was David's is not to be scrutinized in terms of raw power; its worth and legitimacy rest in justice and the fear of God. Even with the shortcomings of David's rule, even with his missteps, bad decisions, and indiscretions, he remains in covenant with God. This song indicates David has, in the midst of all these lapses, kept his eye on the ball, so to speak. He has come to the end of his rule remembering that when his kingship has been at its best, it has been because he has remembered he is with God.

"Is not my house like this with God?" (v. 5) This sustained recognition of God's role in his life and in his power is what makes David a favored one of God. Within this awareness rests the vision of a good king. For Christians this vision of a good king is one of the threads that makes its way into christological understandings of kingship. How Jesus Christ filled the role of king and how he disrupted the presumptions of power grows out of this history of chosen leadership. One of the most important threads is simply that David maintained his capacity to point beyond himself to the source of his power.

There is more in this vision to check abuse of power than simply awareness of God as sovereign and as power source, however. Surely history has a long lineup of those with power who pointed beyond themselves and still abused their power with dehumanizing and destructive ways of governing. This song indicates the character of God-conscious rule when it is true to its proper or created nature—and its proper nature is characterized by the kind of justice and mercy that God so freely pours out on God's people.

Might does not make right in God's kingdom, but justice and mercy and love abound. A good king is a just king. The tragic subtext of this song is how hard it has always been for humanity to handle this sacred responsibility. The hopeful tone of this song is that there is a source of justice and love that allows those in power to scrutinize their uses and abuses of power and do better. It may sound trite, but this critical edge is what saves us from ourselves. Were it not for a vision of God's justice and mercy, the corrupting capacity of power would have its way with even more devastation than it has had throughout human history. The sound of any voice that can name injustice is a testament to the faithfulness of God's presence in the world.

Pastoral Perspective

parting was an occasion to remind the people of the eternal presence and promises of God.

We might also think of the special significance accorded Jesus' last words. Nearly the final quarter of John's Gospel consists of Jesus' parting words to his disciples. He was preparing them, at length, for his death and for their lives without him. Clearly the disciples were anxious, not wanting him to leave. They did not want to hear all that he had to say about his parting, but Jesus explained, "I have said these things to you while I am still with you. But the Advocate, the Holy Spirit, whom the Father will send in my name, will teach you everything, and remind you of all that I have said to you. Peace I leave with you; my peace I give to you. I do not give to you as the world gives. Do not let your hearts be troubled, and do not let them be afraid" (John 14:25–27). Jesus knew what the disciples would soon learn: parting is not the time for easy reassurances and false promises. Rather, it is the time to turn again to the assurance of God's continued presence and the promise that even in parting we are gathered up together into the peace of God.

It is interesting to note, as well, the way Paul concludes his letters. He knows that the way he travels is treacherous and much about his life is uncertain, so his final words are expansive, but they also are infused with a sense of urgency. The last words of his letters typically are filled with final instructions—things he has probably said before, but which need to be said again, like the final instructions you might repeat to a child who is being dropped off at camp for the summer—but then he concludes each of his letters with a kind of benediction. The last words of his second letter to the Corinthians are typical: "The grace of the Lord Jesus Christ, the love of God, and the communion of the Holy Spirit be with all of you" (2 Cor. 13:13). Paul can bring himself to say good-bye to this recalcitrant church he has loved into being only by recognizing that he is not leaving them alone, but leaving them in the grace, love, and fellowship of God.

Throughout the biblical narrative we read of leaders who in parting remind their followers of the promises of God. This lection, which consists of David's last words (appropriately enough, in the form of a psalm), is in this tradition. At first reading it might seem as if these are words of self-praise, extolling the great king's virtues: "The spirit of the LORD speaks through me, his word is upon my tongue. . . . One who rules over people justly, ruling in the fear of God, is like the light of morning, like

Exegetical Perspective

3b–5). The poem concludes with a statement about the fate of the godless (vv. 6–7). The comparison within the last two sections is reminiscent of the contrasting states of the righteous and the wicked found within Wisdom literature.

The Oracle of David (vv. 1–3a). After a brief statement, which identifies these sayings as "the last words of David" (v. 1), the poem is introduced as an "oracle" (*ne'um* in Hebrew) of the king. Usually this term is reserved for prophetic speech. Though verse 2 is likely a later insertion, the phrase "the spirit of the LORD" is consistent with the theme of prophecy established in the first line. Thus David is portrayed in this passage as a prophetic figure. His last words are to be interpreted not only as the words of an aged king, but indeed as the very words of God. This feature of the poem suggests that David's final utterance goes beyond a mere self-evaluation of his reign. The oracle serves as a prophetic evaluation of his tenure, while simultaneously reaffirming the Lord's ideals for kingship. Thus, David's reign is interpreted in light of God's standards for justice.

The Just Rule and the Everlasting Kingship (vv. 3b–5). At the heart of the poem is a comparison between the just rule of the king and the benefits of the sun. A wise leader will govern "in the fear of God" (v. 3b), and his reign will be like the light of dawn rising on a clear day (v. 4). The justice that the king establishes is compared with the nourishing effects of sunlight. Both sustain life and cause the created order to flourish. Sun imagery was often used in the ancient world, especially in Egypt, to describe the benefits of a good king's rule. Within such a setting, the king's subjects thrive and grow in a land filled with the benefits of divine and royal favor.

Verse 5 interrupts the contrast between the just rule of the king in verses 3b–4 and the fate of the godless in verses 6–7. In this interlude, David reflects upon God's everlasting covenant with his house. The syntax of the passage is ambiguous. In the NRSV, the first and last sentences in verse 5 are translated as questions; however, they can just as easily be emphatic assertions in the Hebrew ("Surely my house is like this with God"). Is David affirming with certainty that his house reflects the divine favor described in the preceding verses, or is he introducing doubt in the form of questions? The troubled conclusion to David's reign would suggest that his house was not a model of peaceful order. Adultery, murder, and a divided house characterized the end of David's life.

Homiletical Perspective

Elijah's last words encourage his young protégé. The old man is near the hour of his translation to richer things, and the young intern is hanging on to him for dear life. The old man asks what the young one most wants. It is a double portion of the old man's spirit. The youth is told, cryptically, that if he allows himself to wade into the deeps of translation into God, even though this is way beyond his depth, he may then be well on the road to spiritual power. These too are good last words. They indicate something of the glowing flame at the heart of every saint. There is that in them that cannot be controlled or fully understood, but only risked and carried on tenterhooks.

Stephen's last words form a prayer for forgiving grace. At the moment of his death Stephen asks God to forgive the blind rage of his murderers. These last words shine with great courage. Many a martyr, in Luke's time and beyond, has prayed them, and in so doing has humbled critics to think again. Indeed, Luke throws in this prayer so offhandedly that it would seem to be the daily experience of the church in his time.

Gospel writers offer us a variety of last sayings for Jesus to underpin their theological understandings of him. In so doing, they offer us the sparkling facets of a great diamond. To one dying with him he offers paradise today. Here is the gift of a companioning grace that walks with us beyond fear. To the mixed crowd before him he cries, "It is finished," and so heartens all who follow him in the church with the news that the thing is complete and that we work in that assurance.

He commends his spirit into the hands of God. Bruises and blessings, achievements and failures, his whole ministry and life, together or unraveling, are offered back to the one who called him. As we look in and listen, we sense the safety of a place for us too to go. And later, among the faithful, Jesus says that they will see him and know his companionship through thick and thin to the close of the age. You cannot find a deeper sense of security than that while working hard.

In all these instances, writers and editors are taking the broad, high road. Though we cannot see God clearly or know God's will and ways with certainty, and though it is tempting to gather what we have gleaned and to guard our treasures in the vaults of our institutional strength, these fashioners of last words press us to keep moving, to travel lightly, and to trust the one who is out there opening a way in the woods.

2 Samuel 23:1-7

Theological Perspective

This passage encapsulates the nature of divine power in the way David meditates on his life. God has not determined everything that has happened in his life, but has urged David in the best possible direction. When human intention and action can cooperate with that goad toward divine justice and love, then God's Spirit shines more clearly, with the beautiful gleam "from the rain on the grassy land" (v. 4). God promised to work with David, to stay close to him as he made his way in the world. In that proximity of relationship is the potential for all of humanity to be sanctified in its purpose and best potential. David's walk through life is full of flaws, but God's promise is everlasting. God's faithful stewarding of David expands this man's landscape of possibility and his perception, even in the midst of his flaws. The legitimacy of God's presence could well be called into question if David's flaws were regarded as somehow making null and void God's influence in his life. The nature of covenant is at stake here, and it is the nature of covenant that carries the tune of this song. David has been formed by and has lived out of the truth of God's faithfulness.

The wisdom of David in the twilight of his rule is that he knows the source of his power and he knows the character of God's justice. The vision of a just ruler is one that outlasts David's failures. There is hope for this delicate task of human beings possessing political power, because God is faithful still. In a world where abuses of power, violence, and war so often go to the drumbeat of religious overtones and undertones, David's song invites us to find our way out of violence and injustice with a song we should know by heart.

MARCIA MOUNT SHOOP

Pastoral Perspective

the sun rising on a cloudless morning, gleaming from the rain on the grassy land" (2 Sam. 23:2, 3b–4). This is not mere boastfulness, however. When one sees one's gifts as issuing from God, as David clearly does, then celebrating them is not an act of pride as much as it is an expression of gratitude and praise. David gives resounding affirmation to the promise that the God who has so blessed him, will also bless his people: "Is not my house like this with God? For he has made with me an everlasting covenant, ordered in all things and secure. Will he not cause to prosper all my help and my desire?" (2 Sam. 23:5). In parting, David reminds his people one more time of the promises of God.

And in what other way are we to part, in what other way *can* we? How else can we leave those we care about, unless we entrust them to the care of God? That is, after all, what the word "good-bye" means—"God be with you." What else can be said in parting that does not simply wither and fall at our feet as soon as it is said?

One of the roles of the pastor is to be the one who leads the congregation in saying good-bye. Whether it is offering a benediction at the close of worship, or sending off a group of young people on a service project, or offering words at a memorial service, most often it falls to the pastor to lead the community in saying good-bye. The pastor would do well to attend carefully to those last words and always to use them as an opportunity to remind the community—and the pastor himself or herself, as well—of the enduring promises of God.

MARTIN B. COPENHAVER

Exegetical Perspective

Thus the questions in verse 5 may cause the audience of the poem to reflect critically on the reign of this chosen and yet troubled leader. However, standing in tension with David's narrated past is the certainty of the Lord's divine promise, "for he has made with me an everlasting covenant" (v. 5b). Ultimately, it is not human achievement that defines God's election. The Lord alone will guarantee the prosperity of David's dynasty. God's promise transforms David's questions into affirmations.

The Fate of the Godless (vv. 6–7). The previous imagery of a just ruler is reversed in verses 6–7. In the earlier section, the king's reign is like the sun that causes the land to flourish. The godless, however, are like "thorns" (v. 6) that are eventually "consumed in fire" (v. 7). The same sun that causes the grass to grow will destroy the weeds. This second analogy has two implications. Within the context of this royal poem, the godless are equated with those who are not loyal to God's appointed servant. They will experience the negative effects of the king's reign. They do not flourish but perish in the presence of God's anointed (cf. Ps. 2:10–11). The preceding narrative context, however, provides another meaning to this curse formula. David's reign within the book of 2 Samuel was hardly a model of just and righteous rule. His house suffered from the consequences of his impropriety. In the end, God maintains the covenant, promising David an eternal throne. However, the king's responsibility to maintain justice is still taken with holy seriousness. Royal favor is like divine favor. Those who stand in the Sovereign's good graces will flourish, but those who do not fear the Lord will bear the consequences. Thus, the last two verses of the poem sound a solemn warning to all the future kings of Israel and Judah.

FRANK M. YAMADA

Homiletical Perspective

Only one such editor seems out of step. It is the one who composed David's last words. He must have heard the wolf at the door, or feared restlessness among the natives. Perhaps the administration in his day was losing its luster. Perhaps some great empire was singing its siren song. As it is, he ends up writing a harsh exit speech affirming a "teacher's pet" blessing upon David and his dynasty. All good things flow from the throne on down. That is the way it was intended from all eternity, and shall ever be. Anyone who thinks or acts differently is just a prickly pain in the royal regime and deserves to be roughly uprooted and incinerated as garbage.

These last words allow little leeway for the next generation of blessings. Only a royal monarch with all the trappings and power flowing from the top can honor this pattern. There is no place here for a manger child, a Nazareth nobody, a washer of feet, or a flesh-and-blood life susceptible to lashes, thorns, and nails. Yet that is the one who appears among us when the church year begins next Sunday.

What are we to do? Structurally we have long been tempted by that royal model with its crown and scepter. It fits better into our world of power mongers and high achiever. Yet the gracious last words of the other heroes take us into a strange world that is vulnerable and out of step with our times and neighbors. It is helpful to realize that last words are never what they appear, but are in turn taken by those who follow to be used as protagonists, antagonists, subjects, objects, verbs, curses, or love letters.

On the cusp of a new church year it seems fitting to utter the best words we can, those truest, noblest, cleanest, and closest to the heart. Such words are wide and hold open the door to the wideness of the mystery being born. Such words give broad syntax and good grammar to all those conversationalists who shall stand where we stand today.

G. MALCOLM SINCLAIR

Psalm 132:1-12 (13-18)

¹O Lᴏʀᴅ, remember in David's favor
  all the hardships he endured;
²how he swore to the Lᴏʀᴅ
  and vowed to the Mighty One of Jacob,
³"I will not enter my house
  or get into my bed;
⁴I will not give sleep to my eyes
  or slumber to my eyelids,
⁵until I find a place for the Lᴏʀᴅ,
  a dwelling place for the Mighty One of Jacob."

⁶We heard of it in Ephrathah;
  we found it in the fields of Jaar.
⁷"Let us go to his dwelling place;
  let us worship at his footstool."

⁸Rise up, O Lᴏʀᴅ, and go to your resting place,
  you and the ark of your might.
⁹Let your priests be clothed with righteousness,
  and let your faithful shout for joy.

Theological Perspective

As the pilgrims ascend Mount Zion from the scattered places they now live, their praise anticipates their arrival at the dwelling place of God on earth (v. 14). The glory of God now rests in a permanent place: the temple in Jerusalem. Those who have sacrificed to make the journey will stand in the very spot the Creator of heaven and earth has chosen to be the place where his glory is accessible and his worship pure (v. 16). Their psalm links the ideal kingdom of God with the city of Jerusalem (Zion), the temple, and the portable ark of the covenant. God's priests will be clothed with righteousness and salvation (vv. 9 and 16), while the enemies of God will be clothed with shame (v. 18 NIV; "disgrace" NRSV), so great (will be) the glory of Zion.

Where on earth does God dwell? The psalm identifies the dwelling place of God in the city of Jerusalem, perched on the lip of western Asia. It is a sacred place, a place people have found access to unsurpassable spiritual power and meaning. Are these places closer to God than others, or is it that in these places some have felt themselves touched by a divine power and love beyond the ordinary? Jacob their forefather called the place of his dream Beth-el, the house of God (Gen. 28:18–19). Yet he also wrestled with God at Peniel (Gen. 32:30) and saw the

Pastoral Perspective

Covenant is central to the identity of the people of Israel, and this psalm conveys with deep faith the significance for Israel of this mutual relationship between God and God's people. Psalm 132 turns on the psalmist's petition to God to remember. "O Lᴏʀᴅ, remember in David's favor all the hardships he endured" (v. 1). Remember, God, all the ways David sacrificed himself for your sake. Remember, O God, all the ways your faithful people have given their lives for you. "O Lᴏʀᴅ, remember . . . " (v. 1). In this psalm, formed as a prayer, the writer petitions God for the simple acknowledgment of a faithful life.

The psalmist writes from the context of the covenant between God and David, a covenant in which David promises to be faithful to God, and God promises, for the first time,[1] God's unconditional love to Israel (2 Sam. 7). Included in God's promise is the pledge to crown one of David's sons king. This unconditional love, however, does not relieve Israel of covenantal obligations. In Psalm 132, the psalmist expresses that the covenant is one of mutual expectation. God expects the people to be faithful in their obedience: "If your sons keep my

1. Walter Brueggemann, *First and Second Samuel*, Interpretation Series (Louisville, KY: John Knox Press, 1990), 257–59.

¹⁰For your servant David's sake
   do not turn away the face of your anointed one.

¹¹The Lord swore to David a sure oath
   from which he will not turn back:
   "One of the sons of your body
   I will set on your throne.
¹²If your sons keep my covenant
   and my decrees that I shall teach them,
   their sons also, forevermore,
   shall sit on your throne."

¹³For the Lord has chosen Zion;
   he has desired it for his habitation:
¹⁴"This is my resting place forever;
   here I will reside, for I have desired it.
¹⁵I will abundantly bless its provisions;
   I will satisfy its poor with bread.
¹⁶Its priests I will clothe with salvation,
   and its faithful will shout for joy.
¹⁷There I will cause a horn to sprout up for David;
   I have prepared a lamp for my anointed one.
¹⁸His enemies I will clothe with disgrace,
   but on him, his crown will gleam."

Exegetical Perspective

Most psalms are difficult to associate with specific events in the history of Israel. Psalm 132 is exceptional in that regard. James L. Mays describes it as "a liturgical version of the narrative of David's movement of the ark of the Lord from Kiriath-jearim to Jerusalem."[1] The narrative background may be found in 2 Samuel 6 and 7. This background explains some of the psalm's otherwise obscure references. For example, the place names "Ephrathah" and "Jaar" in verse 6 make sense when we remember that David is from Bethlehem (another name for Ephrathah; cf. Ruth 1:2) and goes to Kiriath-jearim (also called Jaar) to retrieve the ark of the covenant (see 1 Sam. 7:1; also 1 Chr. 13:5 and 2 Chr. 1:4). David's vow not to sleep until he finds "a place for the Lord, a dwelling place for the Mighty One of Jacob" (vv. 2–5) is a poetic version of David's words to Nathan in 2 Samuel 7:2. God's vow to build David a "house" (that is, a dynasty) is found in 2 Samuel 7:4–16.

Since this psalm is being used as one of the lections for Christ the King Sunday, only the verses that focus on David as divinely anointed king are

1. James L. Mays, *Psalms*, Interpretation Series (Louisville, KY: John Knox Press, 1994), 411.

Homiletical Perspective

On the final Sunday of the Christian year, two prominent themes that encompass the entire sweep of salvation history come to the fore. First, God is creating a holy people. Second, this people will be a dwelling place for God's reign and presence on earth. This is a lengthy psalm that voices prayer to God and affirms God's promises. This movement of prayer to praise will make for rich gospel proclamation on the day that honors Christ the King, the One who fulfills God's promise to David that a member of David's household will rule in Zion, as a place of rest for God and as the final destination of God's people.

The psalm calls upon God to remember the many struggles endured by David in his seeking to find a dwelling place for God. This significant matter is articulated at the beginning of the psalm: God desires a place to dwell, and a particular people—a holy people—will be a fitting dwelling place for God's presence and God's reign. God's reign, moreover, will be characterized by plenitude, abundance, blessing, justice, gladness, and joy; it will be the work of a promise-making God that is a gift to a promise-keeping king. Moreover, this exchange of divine initiative and human response is grounded in and expressive of the covenant, which provides a larger

Psalm 132:1-12 (13-18)

Theological Perspective

face of God in his meeting with Esau (Gen. 33:10). The "house of God" was a location, not a limitation.

It is important for Christians to grasp the power of this image of the temple and the city in the imagination of Israel. The Psalms and prophets overflow with it, and the New Testament images of the city, kingdom, and temple draw their strength from it. It was more than Paul's training that continually drew him to Jerusalem, to the temple, to the writings, and to those like James who spoke for this power center. Paul, the Christian Pharisee, longed for the purification of the central expressions of God's divine rule in the world, which Messiah Jesus would bring about. His mission to non-Jews was to open to them the privileged access to God attested in the temple and kingdom, through a direct connection to Messiah Jesus.[1] In his vision of Jews and non-Jews together, the temple on Mount Zion is the house of prayer for all humanity, the hill town Jerusalem becomes the city of God, and David's little kingdom becomes the kingdom of God. The independent histories of the synagogue and church arise from the conflicts generated by this claim.

Where in the world is God? Both the synagogue and the church answer, everywhere! This is the first thing. God is *omnipresent*. The power and wisdom of God are active in everything that is, bringing it to being and sustaining it during its time, upholding the unfolding universe, lending it beauty and meaning. "*The whole earth is full of his glory*" (Isa. 6:3). Everything speaks in voices without words. As Solomon prayed dedicating the first temple, it is not that God lives in the temple, but that God will meet the faithful there (1 Kgs. 8:27, 30). Heaven is no nearer one part of earth than another. Locality is never an issue for God.

The temple is a place of access to God, not a limit on God. If God were not actively present everywhere, God could not be present and active anywhere. God would be in heaven as in a prison, transcending creaturely reality but external to it. Jesus had it right: even the tiniest thing is clothed with the glory of God, and so human beings are cared for as well. Theologians who speak of God as the ultimate "Source" of interdependent things (Schleiermacher) or the powerful "Word" that calls everything into being (Barth) speak of the unimaginable mystery of God the Creator everywhere present and active in everything.

Yet places and times matter in the biblical story. This is the second thing. Both the synagogue and the

1. Bruce Chilton, *Rabbi Paul* (New York: Doubleday Image Books, 2004).

Pastoral Perspective

covenant and my decrees that I shall teach them, their sons also, forevermore, shall sit on your throne" (v. 12). The psalmist expects God to be faithful in God's pledge to remember: "O LORD, remember . . . " (v. 1).

Within this language of promise, the writer of Psalm 132 expresses deep desire for enduring relationship with God, a relationship that can be sustained only by God's covenant with God's people. The covenant both allows and expresses a relationship of mutual commitment, a relationship in which both God and God's people are able to expect devotion, attention, and care from the other.

In the North American church, this expression of covenant, of mutual commitment between God and God's people, could be difficult for churchgoers to relate to. Pastors cannot assume (particularly on behalf of younger generations) that the idea of commitment is highly valued. In their lifetimes, young people in North America have witnessed broken promise after broken promise. They have seen the covenant of marriage dissolve as their parents or friends divorce. They have seen the pledge of elected leaders to serve the common good dissolve as political leaders make promises and then get caught lying. Civic engagement is waning, marriage rates are declining, and people change jobs or are transferred every few years. In the daily lives of many North Americans, commitment (to the community, to family, to a particular workplace) does not hold a place of central importance. Within this context, a liturgical focus on the mutual commitment expected in God's covenant with God's people could be perceived as irrelevant or too demanding.

Yet, while those who are considered part of Generation X (born between 1963 and 1978) and Generation Y (born between 1979 and 1994) may not value commitment, they do want to find meaningful connection and relationship. In this psalm, the writer demonstrates beautifully the inseparability of God's covenant and our relationship with God. For a people wary of commitment, the psalmist's attention to such interdependence could provide an important word about the deepening of relationship with God that can happen within mutual commitment.

Ironically, however, the words themselves (even words about deepening relationship) are unlikely to convince a generation of people accustomed to broken promises and empty words that the commitment required within covenant is important. But a congregation can, in its practice of life together, communicate the gift of covenant. A young adult

Exegetical Perspective

assigned (vv. 1–12). The remainder of the psalm (vv. 13–18), optional in the lectionary, directs our attention to the flip side of this psalm, namely, God's choice of Jerusalem, the city of David, as a perpetual residence. For ancient pilgrims using this psalm as a Song of Ascents on their way to celebrate one of the religious festivals in the Jerusalem temple, both themes would have been important.

Ironically, the very themes that would have made this psalm meaningful to ancient worshipers may in fact make appreciation more difficult for modern worshipers. It is difficult to know in what sense God's choice to reside in Jerusalem is still true. Similarly, God's promises to keep a Davidic king on Israel's throne may actually distract us into the realm of modern politics in a way that is not theologically productive. Since the focus of verses 1–12 is on the latter, most of our attention will be focused there. But this much at least must be said about the interpretive hurdle of God's choice of Zion. It is important to remember the lesson that Israel itself learned during the exile. One of the primary prophets of the exile, Ezekiel, saw visions of God's throne/chariot (i.e., the ark of the covenant) moving out of the temple and east toward the exiles in Babylon. The point for both the exiles and for us is that God cannot be confined to one exclusive location, but insists on being "God with us" in whatever exile we find ourselves in. As for the other interpretive hurdle, God's promise to the house of David, perhaps the reflections that follow will help us find a place to begin.

The prayer with which this psalm begins is especially instructive for the way we read the rest. "O LORD," the psalmist says in verse 1, "remember in David's favor all the hardships he endured." The Jewish Publication Society's translation of the word rendered here as "hardships" is "extreme self-denial." Those of us who remember some of the more sordid episodes of David's story may well find ourselves completing that thought with, "and *do not* remember all the times his self-denial was anything but extreme!" But this psalm accentuates the positive, so references to those episodes remain tactfully unspoken. And the emphasis on David's self-denial is appropriate, since it highlights something that God obviously affirms in a king.

That quality of self-denial forms the psalm's most natural segue to the other Scripture passages assigned for Christ the King Sunday. Once again, Mays sees straight to the heart of the matter when he observes:

Homiletical Perspective

theological framework for understanding what Israel hopes for in light of God's desire and delight.

A sermon from this psalm might take the form of a narrative that gathers up God's past, present, and future dealings with Israel, as seen through the particular angle of David and Zion—the person of the king and the place of God's dwelling. As part of this narration, it will be important to establish the significance of what is proclaimed regarding the reign of God, the anointing of David, and the establishment of Zion as a permanent dwelling place for God in the midst of a people: God rules, God's rule is mediated by God's anointed king, and God's people are on pilgrimage to a holy city where the blessings of God's rule are generously bestowed and shared by all.

Moreover, an important aspect of this narrative will be recalling times during the course of David's life when he was required to endure hardships, and was even humbled and afflicted at the hands of his enemies, willingly subordinating his desire to the Lord's desire to establish a resting place in Zion to be the home of a holy people. It will also be important to remember how David, God's anointed ruler, exercised kingly authority in a priestly manner, becoming a humble servant in seeking a home for God. Of course, this narrative is significant for proclaiming the gospel of Christ the King, the crucified and risen One who is the fulfillment of God's promises to David's household for the sake of the whole creation.

It is therefore important to remember that the Lord made an oath to maintain David's throne, just as David swore an oath to carry out the Lord's desire. It is also significant that David, as king of Israel, ruled by serving the One who rules over all the kings of the earth, a "reverse reign" that makes visible God's presence, fully revealed in the humble obedience of Jesus. Also of importance for preaching this psalm will be holding together divine initiative and human response. On the one hand, it is possible to "spiritualize" the role of God, so that God's reign is either relegated to the past, postponed to the future, or internalized in the "hearts" of believers. On the other hand, the role of David and the action of God's people should not be allowed to obscure the providential activity of a God whose reign and presence cannot be separated from creation and its completion.

Since memory enkindles hope, the most fruitful source for preaching on this Sunday may be the movement of divine initiative and human response that has been proclaimed throughout the Christian

Psalm 132:1–12 (13–18)   323

Psalm 132:1-12 (13-18)

Theological Perspective

church remember times and places when the wisdom and power of God stood forth in compelling ways, inviting trust and obedience in definite circumstances. From the calling of Abraham and Sarah through Moses and the prophets, the kings and loss of the kingdom, and the coming of Jesus in the power of the Spirit, God's active presence is more than a universal law or influence ("the force," natural law). In these times and places, the activity of God is received as an act of grace calling forth a response of grateful faith.

Two observations bring us back to the situation within which the Songs of Ascents (Pss. 120–34) were sung. First, the vision does not die, even when the place is lost. It is transformed by a renewed hope for a better temple, a better city, land, and people, and a better son of David to sit on the throne. Second, the ongoing activity of God in the world, ever life-giving, ever challenging, ever leading to a future of hope and promise, does not cease. The faithful trust that God is still there for them. The prophets see the true temple of the Lord in the personal life of the people (Jer. 7). Neither Mount Gerizim (Samaria) nor Mount Zion is an essential place when the truly sacred place is the human heart that seeks God *in spirit and in truth* (John 4:23). The true kingdom of God is the transformation of human life by the grace and power of God.

Where then is God? In everything that exists: in the sacred places that mark remembered experiences of the nearness and greatness of God, in the ordinary places where life goes on, and in the depths of the human heart, where the decisions of life are made for good or ill. Those who celebrate the festival of Christ the King at the close of the Christian year, celebrate the real presence of Christ by the power of the Spirit wherever women and men trust him and obey his gospel by serving God's kingdom now.

THOMAS D. PARKER

Pastoral Perspective

could be invited to join a small group that requires a commitment of time, but that offers the promise of close relationships. As part of the confirmation process, mentors could pledge to take their role seriously enough that their confirmands experience God's enduring promise through a close relationship with an interested adult.

Psalm 132 reminds us that covenant is essential for faith to grow and be sustained. We expect God to listen, remember, and respond to God's people. God expects us to be obedient, and therefore faithful, to the God of Israel.

The good news for a congregation weary of broken promises is that God's promise is a different kind of promise: it is a promise that is kept. Christians claim that the purest manifestation of God's promise is, of course, the life and ministry of Jesus Christ, who came and walked among God's children to show us the abundant, inclusive, and enduring love of God. If the planners of worship can convey—in the liturgy, in the sermon, *and* in the communal life of the congregation—the good news of trust and relatedness that can grow out of covenant with God, then this psalm could provide fertile ground for a deepening of faith.

This text appears in the lectionary on Christ the King Sunday, which marks the end of the church year. Advent will begin the following week, and the church will soon begin to anticipate the coming reign of Christ. As the church year comes to a close, as congregations sing "Lift High the Cross" and "A Mighty Fortress Is Our God," this psalm might serve a central part of the liturgy by proclaiming God's promise and God's expectation. God's people were faithful, and, in turn, God was faithful: God brought forth David, and then Solomon, to lead God's people. And God indeed caused "a horn to sprout up" and "prepared a lamp for [God's] anointed one" (v. 17).

On Christ the King Sunday, the church can celebrate the reign of Jesus, the horn of David, the anointed one sent by God to walk with God's people. In Jesus, God's covenant is affirmed and made concrete.

KATE FOSTER CONNORS

Exegetical Perspective

A resonance sets in with another poem that speaks of one who took the form of a servant, and, being found in human form, humbled himself, and in his obedience unto death (Phil. 2:6–8) has become God with us and God for us, the presence and the power of the kingdom of God.[2]

When Christians read Psalm 132 in the context of the canon it is clear that Jesus Christ, "the ruler of the kings of the earth" (Rev. 1:5), is the final and best fulfillment of God's promises to and through David. If Pilate could not recognize this (John 18:33–37), it was because he was not expecting a king whose signature characteristic was self-denial. In Pilate's world—and in ours—rulers are rarely if ever defined by that quality. No wonder Jesus had to remind Pilate, "My kingdom is not from this world" (John 18:36).

The self-denial dimension of Psalm 132 also echoes the last words of David in 2 Samuel 23:1–7. In this passage, David quotes God as saying,

> One who rules over people justly,
>   ruling in the fear of God,
> is like the light of morning,
>   like the sun rising on a cloudless morning,
>   gleaming from the rain on the grassy land.
> (vv. 3b–4)

It is a rare king who can even come close to such an epitaph. Yet one gets the sense that this is the very King that even David was longing for. And this is the very King we long for still, straining our eyes toward the eastern sky with the author of Revelation, until we too can exclaim, "Look! He is coming with the clouds" (Rev. 1:7).

There is a sense in which Psalm 132 sets us up for living in a state of expectation. As Mays again points out, the psalm "gives the clear impression that it belongs to a time when there was no successor to David on the throne of Judah."[3] Those of us who live in the "already but not yet" can take a page from Psalm 132's book on the importance of keeping the memory of God's promises alive as we wait. Keeping the vision of Christ the King before us can shape the present, as well as give us hope for the future.

CAROL M. BECHTEL

Homiletical Perspective

year. James Luther Mays suggests that a canonical reading of Psalm 132 can be seen to reach its fullness in the following Pauline hymn, which sings of God with us and God for us, the presence and power of God's kingdom:

> Your attitude should be the same as Christ Jesus; Who, being in very nature God, did not consider equality with God something to be grasped, but made himself nothing, taking the very nature of a servant, being made in human likeness.
>   And being found in appearance as a man, he humbled himself and became obedient to death—even death on a cross!
>   Therefore God exalted him to the highest place and gave him the name that is above every name, that at the name of Jesus every knee should bow, in heaven and on earth and under the earth, and every tongue confess that Jesus Christ is Lord to the glory of God the Father. (Phil. 2:6–11)[1]

On the final day of the Christian year, we are encouraged by Scripture to remember the presence of God's future in the full story of Jesus Christ, a story that cannot be grasped apart from God's promises to Israel, David, and Zion. On this day of Christ the King, the One whose glory illumines all our days, the church is prompted to praise God for God's great faithfulness, to claim God's promises, and to proclaim the blessings of God's rule for the whole creation. This is a day for rejoicing and feasting, for tasting and delighting in God's presence, for being nourished by Word and Sacrament. This day is a foretaste of what is yet to come: creation's final destination and "homecoming." God has been true to the greater David, Jesus Christ, the Alpha and Omega, the One who was, and is, and is to come (Rev. 1:8).

MICHAEL PASQUARELLO III

2. Ibid., 412.
3. Ibid., 411.

1. James L. Mays, *Psalms*, Interpretation Series (Louisville, KY: John Knox Press, 1994), 412.

Revelation 1:4b–8

4bGrace to you and peace from him who is and who was and who is to come, and from the seven spirits who are before his throne, 5and from Jesus Christ, the faithful witness, the firstborn of the dead, and the ruler of the kings of the earth.

To him who loves us and freed us from our sins by his blood, 6and made us to be a kingdom, priests serving his God and Father, to him be glory and dominion forever and ever. Amen.

7Look! He is coming with the clouds;
  every eye will see him,
even those who pierced him;
  and on his account all the tribes of the earth will wail.
So it is to be. Amen.

8"I am the Alpha and the Omega," says the Lord God, who is and who was and who is to come, the Almighty.

Theological Perspective

On this Christ the King Sunday, the text from Revelation puts the lordship of God and Christ front and center. Its rich, hope-filled message addresses three themes: the power of the "Almighty" God who stands at the beginning and end of history ("the Alpha and the Omega" in v. 8), the significance of the Christ event for the church (Christology and ecclesiology), and the consummation of God's purposes for creation (eschatology). These theological themes are interwoven; in fact, theologically they cannot be separated.

Taken as a whole, this opening salutation from the seer of Patmos subversively declares to a Christian community under imperial threat that *with the Lord God*, there is always *more*: more transformation to come than the earth has yet seen, more power and authority than that claimed by earthly rulers, more dignity for God's people than earthly rulers recognize. The mode of John's theology of "more" is also subversive; its liturgy of praise to the Lord God is, at the same time, a withholding of praise from lesser lords.[1] Thus the very means by which John conveys his message communicates a theological point: the worship life of the Christian community becomes part of the work through which God is continuing to

1. The doxology in 1:5b–7 is one of several in Revelation, and a liturgical tone is present throughout the letter, especially in chapters 4, 5, and 19.

Pastoral Perspective

The Christian community is reminded both of the origin of its identity and its ultimate hope for the future in this passage. The cadence of beginnings and endings resounds over and over again in this text. The Christian community is saluted with transcendent strains of the eternal while facing a present reality that is all too immanent and deadly. During the period of history in which this text was written, the Roman Empire had made being Christian painful and dangerous. The temptation to fall away from the faith was palpable. Writing from exile himself, John summons up the titles, the images, and the eschatological promises of Christ, creating a poetic piece of inspiration and praise. Such a song of confidence and faith is as relevant to Christian life today as it was in John's time.

Despite the fact that in the United States people do not get exiled because of their faith, there are some who feel ostracized by both culture and community because of their dedication to Christ and his message of salvation. Our enlightened and scientific age leaves little room for belief in one "who is and who was and who is to come." The empire that threatens the heart of Christianity today with commercialism, self-indulgence, and increasing isolation is as deadly as the Roman Empire was when John was writing. Many are literally dying of

Exegetical Perspective

Revelation is a literary hybrid, and we can see its blended character at work in today's text. On the one hand, Revelation is an *apocalypse*, a literary form in which the author speaks in visionary fashion, giving revelations about the future (or heavenly) realm, which is depicted in sharp contrast to the present corrupt age. On the other hand, Revelation also presents itself as a more gentle literary type, an *epistle* addressed to seven Asian Christian congregations in prominent towns near Ephesus. Paul's letters had established the epistolary form as the primary means of communication in the early church, and this precedent probably influenced the author of Revelation to employ this genre.

At first glance, the letter form is the most apparent in this text. Just as letters today employ certain formulas, such as opening "Dear Sam" and signing off "Sincerely yours," ancient Hellenistic letters also contained characteristic marks. The first is naming the writer of the letter, in this case "John" (1:4a). Normally, this would be followed by a descriptor (e.g., "John, a servant of Christ Jesus"), but in the communities to which this passage is addressed, John needs no introduction. While Revelation almost surely was not written by John the disciple, it was addressed to the communities that identified with this apostle. To begin the letter by

Homiletical Perspective

Not unlike a "dramedy" television show or a "cowboys-and-aliens" movie, the book of Revelation is a double-genre piece of writing. As its title proclaims, its content is a "revelation," a message "from God's mouth to your ear." But in structure it is also a letter from John to the seven churches of Asia (v. 4a). Because this is clearly a letter from a friend and mentor, its epistolary structure helps in some small ways to make the apocalyptic visions it reveals a little less overwhelming.

According to a review in the *New Yorker*, the authors of *Send: The Essential Guide to Email for Office and Home* wrote the book to overcome the "ill-considered e-mails they had recently received, and even sent. Before long, they found themselves cobbling together a system of proper usage and protocol." Somewhat surprisingly, particularly for business e-mail correspondence, their protocol allows for multiple exclamation points!!! and abbreviations such as "LOL" (Laugh Out Loud), and encourages closings such as "All best!" and "Cheers!"[1] Such advice only highlights how mundane and vapid the vast majority of the pieces of communication we receive daily is.

1. Nick Paumgarten, "Out Box: Elements of E-Style," *New Yorker* 83, no. 8 (April 16, 2007): 48.

Revelation 1:4b–8

Theological Perspective

transform the world. Message and medium merge. John's political manifesto forces us to ask whether message and medium merge in our own lives: what do our patterns of behavior suggest about what/whom we worship as lord?

Both the Pauline-like greeting of "grace . . . and peace" in verse 4 and the closing verse of the lection (v. 8) identify God as the one "who is and who was and who is to come." By beginning with "who *is*," this departure from the linear order of past, present, and future emphasizes that God reigns *now*, even though the world's circumstances may suggest otherwise. God's rule is made visible on earth now through those who hear and obey (v. 3); Jesus Christ, "the ruler of the kings of the earth" (v. 5a), has "made" them "a kingdom" (v. 6).

The shift in verses 4 and 8 from a verb of being to a verb of action ("who *is to come*") also signals that the God who was at work to transform the world through the Christ event will accomplish yet more transformation. The God of the exodus[2] and of Jesus remains active in history. Indeed, the hearers are summoned in verse 7 to "look"—to discern the presence of the One who "is coming." The return of Christ "is to be" (v. 7); the story of God's renewal of the cosmos is not yet over.

In short, in the text's description of God, as well as in the titles and work ascribed to Jesus in verses 5 and 6, we see both the realized eschatology and the eschatological reservation of Revelation. God's rule over the powers of sin and death in the world is an "already" through the Christ event. By his death Jesus has liberated believers from sin (v. 5b). The community experiences the risen Christ's love in the present ("loves us" in v. 5b). And as the "firstborn of the dead" (v. 5a), Jesus has inaugurated a new creation. The "new earth" (21:1) is already on the way.

But God's rule is also a "not yet." There is more to come from this "coming God"[3] whose redemptive activity has the transformation of the whole cosmos in view.

What difference does the present and coming reign of God/Christ make for a Christian community under threat? Things are not what they seem. Like John's hearers, some believers today may experience oppression under state authority or other earthly powers. But the reality is that, through Jesus Christ, believers have been made a "kingdom" and "priests" (v. 6). These titles of both royal and sacral

2. Verses 4 and 8 echo God's self-identification in Exodus 3:14.
3. Jürgen Moltmann, *The Coming of God: Christian Eschatology*, trans. Margaret Kohl (Minneapolis: Fortress Press, 1996).

Pastoral Perspective

thirst for words of "grace and peace" from the eternal One, like those with which John opens his letter. In the opening lines of the letter we hear with unusual clarity both the good news of resurrection —that Christ is "the firstborn of the dead"—and a strong affirmation of the stunning sovereignty of Christ—that he is "the ruler of the kings of the earth." Such greetings serve as smelling salts, awakening the spirits of any who have lost consciousness under the domination of the empire.

To make sure we are really awake for this proclamation, John uses a dynamic trinity of verbs to tell us the salvation story. He asserts that Christ "loves us and freed us from our sins by his blood, and made us to be a kingdom" (v. 5b–6a). All of this gracious action on Christ's behalf is done in order that we might serve God. John offers these words not so much as news to anyone. Rather, he reminds us of what we already know but often forget in the trials of living in the world—or what we have allowed to be drowned out by the empire that keeps trying to give us different purpose and focus. John concludes his passionate opening salutation with praises to God and yet another assertion of God's sovereign power.

This reminding and naming language has real currency in certain circles in our world. It is often used in praise services as an introduction into intercessory prayer. Declarative language can also serve as a way to invite the congregation to focus on God and to stir up their memories about the nature and grandeur of God. Use of this type of recitation of the mighty acts of God shifts the focus of those gathered from present reality to eternal reality. It can also provide a way for the leader to direct people's attention beyond the one speaking (and beyond themselves) to the One who is worthy and able to respond to their prayers.

There is a luminous character in Atlanta named Brother Blane. His use of this type of declarative language about God never fails to lift the spirit of those who hear him. Rather than greet passersby with, "Hello, how are you," he declares, "God is worthy and God is able. Let your prayers lift you higher to the throne of glory." Somehow his warm and gracious affect conveys his conviction in the power of what he is saying. While at times it seems like crazy talk, there is also the unmistakable ring of truth about his proclamation. As one encounters Brother Blane, one realizes that he speaks not for himself, but on behalf of the God whom he loves and in whom lies his greatest hope.

claiming the name "John" invests the letter with the apostle's memory, presence, and authority.

The next mark of a letter is the naming of the recipients, in this case "to the seven churches that are in Asia." These churches are named in Revelation 1:11, and they are addressed one by one in Revelation 2–3. The number seven (used more than fifty times in Revelation) is not accidental, but instead represents divine wholeness.

The third characteristic feature of a letter is the greeting. In typical Greek letters, this would consist of the single word "greetings," and in Jewish letters, the word *shalom* (peace). Since the word "greetings" is quite similar to the Greek word for "grace," early Christian letters, including this one, often replaced the term "greetings" with "grace" and then added the Jewish *shalom*; thus, "Grace to you and peace" (1:4b).

The fourth feature of an ancient letter is the thanksgiving section, usually a brief section in which the writer would reconnect with the recipient by expressing warm and affectionate thoughts. Christian epistles at this point frequently bring God directly into the equation, replacing the horizontal sender-to-recipient expression with a prayer of thanksgiving or, as in this passage, a doxology: "To [Christ] who loves us and freed us . . . be glory and dominion forever and ever" (1:5–6).

So we have here the typical features of an ancient letter, but this text is doing much more than simply filling in the blanks in the typical epistle structure. The apocalyptic themes that will dominate the rest of the book are already at play. The text first invites the reader to look up. "John," as will soon be made clear (1:9–20), has taken a visionary journey up into the heavenly realms, and he reports on "all that he saw" (1:2). The idea is that heaven is an unseen reality above the earth, with events taking place simultaneously with earthly history. On the earthly plain, John's community is troubled, experiencing faith-quenching distress of some kind, including violence and persecution (see, e.g., 11:7–10 and 20:4). The exact source of the persecution is unknown, but it is most likely a local conflict rather than a more generalized and widespread Roman campaign.

In response to this crisis, John, "in the spirit on the Lord's day" (1:10), has traveled up to this heavenly realm, and now returns with a report on what he witnessed. What he sees is good news for the community below. Down below, their robes are drenched in the blood of violence, but in heaven the saints are gathered in praise around the throne of God, their robes washed "white in the blood of the

Unlike contemporary e-mails, however, John's letter from the outset comes across as weighty, vital, and serious, commensurate with his subject: the risen Christ, the one who reigns. John has some difficult and intense but ultimately healing and hopeful words for these churches, some of which labored under constant Roman persecution.

First, as part of his letter protocol he greets his readers, extending "grace to you and peace"— commodities of great value at the time and today— in the name of the one who authorized and, through visions, provided the content John shares. This one is described in Trinitarian language: the timeless and eternal one "who is and who was and who is to come"; the sevenfold Spirit or perfect presence; and Jesus Christ, who is further described in three parts as faithful witness, firstborn of the dead, and ruler of earth's kings.

On this Sunday celebrating the Reign of Christ, this passage provides fascinating insights into his person and work, as well as into our response to his reign. Understanding the flow of this passage can be helpful in the preparation of the sermon: First, John describes who Jesus is; second, he explains what he has done for us; and third, he reveals what our response should be to all that.

First, *who is this Jesus* who is coming? John provides a three-part portrait in verse 5a. (1) As "faithful witness" Jesus lived and moved authentically among us as a mentoring teacher, a model of sacrificial service. The word "witness" is also used to mean "martyr," which speaks of his death. He would not yield to the opposition but continued to overturn both money-changing tables and spirit-strangling religious assumptions—to the death. (2) As "the firstborn of the dead" he overcame that death and assumed his rightful place in heaven. (3) As "the ruler of the kings of the earth" he possesses ultimate authority over all creation—and even over human-made political divisions.

Second, the description of *what Jesus has done for us* continues in verse 5b as part of an expression of praise (whereby John continues to follow epistolary etiquette): he "loves us and freed us from our sins by his blood." Notice the tenses: Christ's love for us is always present, but his work on our behalf is in the past, though its effects continue perpetually.

The next phrase, "and made us to be," moves us transitionally from the descriptions of Christ and his work to the description of *our work under his reign*: We are to live both as members of "a kingdom,"

Revelation 1:4b–8

Theological Perspective

authority suggest that believers already possess a power and dignity that the state may refuse to recognize. Because Christ is "ruler of the kings of the earth," all other lords who claim dominion are mere pretenders. Like Jesus Christ, who is the "faithful witness" (v. 5a), the church is called to witness to the lordship of God by its opposition to all earthly powers that seek to usurp the place of God. This "witness" (in Greek, *martys*) may extend to giving one's life, as was true of Jesus, of Antipas in 2:13, of the two witnesses in chapter 11, and of those on whose blood Rome is drunk in 17:6. But the ultimate vindication of Christ's lordship is coming, when "all the tribes of the earth" (v. 7) will see the God who reigns.

For twenty-first-century North American Christians, Revelation presents an urgent challenge. What does it mean to be a "faithful witness" to Christ's lordship in a time that some social critics have labeled a time of American imperialism? The Christian stance vis-à-vis the state may require fresh confessions of the lordship of Christ, as in the Theological Declaration of Barmen, the response of some German Christians to Nazism in 1934. But competing claims for loyalty do not come only from the state. What does it mean to be a "faithful witness" in a time of alarming evidence of the destructive impact of human behavior on God's creation? What does it mean to be a "faithful witness" in a time of growing disparities of wealth and income?

When the curtain is drawn back and the powers of this world are shown to be pretenders—when the Lord of history, the slaughtered Lamb (5:6), is revealed for *all* to see—will we be among the "faithful witnesses" who, by our worship of the Lamb and resistance to pretenders, have been making this reality visible and hastening the arrival of the "new Jerusalem" (21:2)?

JANE E. FAHEY

Pastoral Perspective

After John's greeting in today's text, he tells his readers that he too writes and speaks on behalf of God. Entering into a word of prophecy, John paints a picture of a victorious, cloud-riding Messiah. John clearly expects the return of Christ to be one of judgment and power. Christ will be revealed to everyone: "every eye will see him, even those who pierced him." John does not predict this as a happy occasion, but rather tells us that "all the tribes of the earth will wail" (v. 7).

This declaration of Christ's return is woven into the heart of the communion liturgy. Those who share the elements hear the announcement that "as often as you eat this bread and drink the cup, you proclaim the Lord's death until he comes" (1 Cor. 11:26).

Today's passage from Revelation invites us to reflect more deeply on just what we expect of Christ's return. Often we hear it spoken of in great anticipation. In the final page of this book John himself prays, "Come, Lord Jesus" (Rev. 22:20). John gives voice to a longing to be in the real presence of Christ, having no longer to survive on faith alone—even if that presence is one that causes us to wail as we are transformed into the likeness of Christ.

Echoing God's first appearance to Moses, John uses "I am" language to conclude this passage: "I am the Alpha and the Omega." Indeed, God is our beginning and our ending. In the words of the Presbyterian Brief Statement of Faith, we take great comfort in knowing that "in life and in death we belong to God."[1]

ELIZABETH B. FORNEY

---

1. "A Brief Statement of Faith," in *The Book of Confessions* (Louisville, KY: Office of the General Assembly, 1999), 269.

Exegetical Perspective

Lamb" (7:14). While things look bleak on the earthly plain, the glimpse of the heavenly realm reveals a different truth. Even as the suffering goes on, the victory of the saints is already accomplished in the heavenly realm.

Our passage provides a first taste of this triumph when it greets the community from the God "who is and who was and who is to come" (1:4; see also Exod. 3:14). This is a God who is served by a complete ensemble of spirits (again the number seven; see also 4:5 and 5:6) and who holds all time—past, present, and future—in the divine hand. To know that this God rules eternally provides reassurance and confidence for those who have fallen under the wheel of a seemingly indifferent history.

John also sees and brings greetings from Jesus Christ, who is "the firstborn of the dead, and the ruler of the kings of the earth" (1:5), signaling that Jesus' resurrection is the first act in the creation of a holy people whom death cannot destroy (see also Rom. 8:29 and Col. 1:18). Naming Christ as "the ruler of the kings" also assures the reader that no earthly power, regardless of how toxic, can ultimately loosen the grasp of Christ upon his followers.

But if heaven and earth remain forever on parallel tracks, this text would be cold comfort. "All hell is breaking loose on earth, but don't fret," it would coo. "Things are just fine in heaven." But in John's apocalyptic vision, parallel lines eventually meet, and the triumph of heaven becomes an earthly victory. Therefore, after asking readers to look up into the heavenly realm, John next asks them to look forward into the future: "Look! He is coming with the clouds; every eye will see him" (1:7–8). What is now visible only to the eyes of faith—that Christ is the Alpha and Omega of human history and the Lord of all—will one day be known by the whole cosmos, saint and foe alike. It is this proclamation of Jesus Christ as the Lord of all time and space that firmly connects this passage to Christ the King Sunday.

THOMAS G. LONG

Homiletical Perspective

under his authority, and as "priests serving his God and Father" (v. 6).

It would be helpful, especially in cultures where a monarchy is not established, to explain how a ruler's subjects live, work, and serve. In America, the only insights most people get come from tabloid and TV reports of the shenanigans of Britain's royal family—certainly a skewed, sensationalized, and one-dimensional view. Those in Canada, Great Britain, and other European nations may possess deeper insights, yet the image of rulers today is far from what John's readers would have known or understood. In modern Thailand, by huge majorities the Thai people adore their king, Bhumibol Adulyadej, who has ruled the southeast Asian nation for more than sixty years along with a generally democratic parliament. When a European living in Thailand was caught drunkenly defacing a poster honoring the king, he received a "mere" ten-year prison sentence. But true to his benevolent nature, the king pardoned him and he was deported.[2] Though there are plenty of detractors for any human monarch of any place or time, this example may provide a hint of the sort of servant leader John speaks of, though Christ's reign as a slaughtered lamb raised is infinitely more radical. Once again, Revelation uses the culture's imagery while undermining it.

So, how do we live under the reign of Christ the King? How do we operate as priests who serve God? Consider this: We reflect within our everyday spheres John's threefold description of Christ: (1) we follow Christ's example as a faithful witness; (2) we seek ardently to understand his will for us, to deny ourselves, and take up our crosses and serve others sacrificially; and (3) we make it our life's goal to bring others into his reign of love and praise, which will last forever.

Christ is not a tyrant; he is a lover. He is not a power-mad despot we are forced to serve or else; he is a servant witness. And he calls us to be the same sort of loving and serving witnesses to others. When we grasp that calling, our lives become sources and avenues of praise for "the Alpha and the Omega . . . who is and who was and who is to come, the Almighty." Amen!

PETER M. WALLACE

2. "Thailand: Man Who Insulted King Pardoned," *New York Times*, April 13, 2007, http://www.nytimes.com/2007/04/13/world/asia/13briefs-king.html.

John 18:33-37

³³Then Pilate entered the headquarters again, summoned Jesus, and asked him, "Are you the King of the Jews?" ³⁴Jesus answered, "Do you ask this on your own, or did others tell you about me?" ³⁵Pilate replied, "I am not a Jew, am I? Your own nation and the chief priests have handed you over to me. What have you done?" ³⁶Jesus answered, "My kingdom is not from this world. If my kingdom were from this world, my followers would be fighting to keep me from being handed over to the Jews. But as it is, my kingdom is not from here." ³⁷Pilate asked him, "So you are a king?" Jesus answered, "You say that I am a king. For this I was born, and for this I came into the world, to testify to the truth. Everyone who belongs to the truth listens to my voice."

Theological Perspective

Arraignments involve the formal reading of a criminal complaint that spells out the basic facts and legal reasons that those filing the charges believe are sufficient to support a claim against another person or entity. This is done in the presence of defendants to inform them of the charges against them. The accused are expected to enter a plea that answers the charges being made against them. The normal plea is either "Guilty" or "Not guilty." Today's passage does not follow the norm, helping us rethink the important difference between trying to access the facts and trying to seek the truth.

As is the case in the three other Gospels, Pilate reenters the praetorium to question Jesus and asks him the famous question, "Are you the King of the Jews?" Jesus' reply is also well known, "Do you ask this on your own, or did others tell you about me?" From this initial question and counterquestion, the passage moves to Pilate's rejoinder—making this dialogue unique to the Gospel of John. As this arraignment continues, John records another statement by Jesus, unique to this Gospel, regarding the origin of his kingdom and the clearly drawn distinction between that kingdom and the world.

Jesus expands on his messianic mission as the witness to the truth in wording that is distinctly Johannine. In intellectual terms, we tend to think of

Pastoral Perspective

Most children at some time in their childhoods get frustrated enough at their families that they decide to run away. This decision often happens in some dramatic fashion. Pronouncements are made. Important items are packed, and some food is gathered for what will no doubt be a long and arduous journey. For many years, the prevailing wisdom offered by specialists recommended that parents and caregivers engage in conversation with the children, acknowledging their frustration and then discussing with them logically where they would go and how they would live, eventually dissuading the children from running away. This advice, while certainly reasonable, has given way lately to an alternative response. Now it is recommended that parents and caregivers simply tell children, "No," explaining that they may not run away because "we belong to one another" and that when persons belong to one another, even when they are frustrated and upset, they stay with one another.

The question of belonging is at the heart of this conversation between Jesus and Pilate. Pilate is trying to determine if Jesus claims to be the king of the Jewish nation. Jesus responds by asking questions of Pilate and then explaining that the nation, the kingdom to which Jesus belongs, is not a political reality but a theological one. Ultimately, Jesus and

Exegetical Perspective

The church proclaims that Jesus is king and his kingdom is coming. The truth of this testimony, however, is not self-evident; thus many still ask, "Who is Jesus?" and "Where is his kingdom?" In the Gospel lesson, Pilate questions Jesus, face to face, and Jesus makes an astonishing statement about his kingship and realm.

The context of this passage is crucial. It belongs to the larger unit of 18:28–19:16a, Jesus' trial before Pilate. Pilate moves between "the Jews" and Jesus in seven scenes that occur inside or outside the praetorium (18:29–32, 33–38a, 38b–40; 19:1–3, 4–7, 8–11, 12–15). In context, it becomes evident that at least two trials are underway: one between Pilate and "the Jews" (18:29–32, 38b-40; 19:4–7, 12–15)—who in John are most often Jesus' opponents and must not be interpreted anti-Semitically—and the other between Pilate and Jesus (18:33–38a; 19:8–11). The centerpiece of this unit is the ironic mock coronation of Jesus as king (19:1–3), which is described also in both Matthew (27:29) and Mark (15:18). In John, however, the soldiers use the definite article and hail Jesus as *the* King of the Jews (19:3). At issue in both trials are Jesus' royal identity and the responses of others to Jesus. Indeed, Jesus' identity as king dominates John's narrative from here through Jesus' crucifixion (cf. 19:19–22).

Homiletical Perspective

What is Pilate's goal in this trial? And what does Jesus, the one supposedly on trial, offer Pilate? Perhaps a sermon lies between these two questions.

This text is called "the trial before Pilate." It might better be called "Pilate on trial," for Pilate knows that Jesus should not be on trial (see 18:28–19:16). "What accusation do you bring against this man?" Pilate asks the Jewish leaders. "Take him yourselves and judge him according to your law" (18:29, 31). Obviously Pilate—who is charged with maintaining Roman rule in Judea—does not consider Jesus a threat to that rule. So why does he try Jesus, find "no case against him" (18:38), but then have him flogged (19:1) and hand "him over to them to be crucified" (19:16)?

Something seems strange here. What is Pilate's goal in this trial? Pilate likely considers himself the most powerful, most in-control person in Jerusalem. He is "the local representative of the greatest world power of that time."[1] In his encounter with Jesus he brags about the position and the power he possesses, saying, "Do you not know that I have power to release you, and power to crucify you?" (19:10). But Pilate, though supposedly in control, is absolutely trapped in fear. The Jewish leaders want Jesus

1. Lamar Williamson Jr., *Preaching the Gospel of John* (Louisville, KY: Westminster John Knox Press, 2004), 254.

John 18:33-37

Theological Perspective

truth in terms of reliability and dependableness. In religious terms, it expands beyond this to an unwavering conformity with God's will so that we think in terms of reality and understanding. In the New Testament, it is possible to speak of truth as something that is done rather than something that is simply believed or thought of. Indeed, it is possible to set truth in contrast to unrighteousness. For contemporary Christians, the truth as revealed in Jesus Christ takes precedence over all other human understandings of truth. All of these dynamics are at play in this passage from John.

The interplay between the more intellectual understanding of truth (which Pilate represents in this passage) and truth as revelation (which we find in Jesus Christ) is an important one to explore for contemporary hearers of the Word. Though important in helping establish and maintain many social norms, intellectual truth does not fill all of our needs. We are compelled to go beyond merely understanding and making sense and order in our world. We must seek to know God and live as active witnesses on this journey into God. Jesus' life and mission is a model of this for us. In Jesus, we learn that truth is a stimulant for faithful living and witness, rather than only a matter for contemplation. It is something we do.

Theologian Dorothee Soelle offers one model for how we might accomplish this. In her classic book *Beyond Mere Obedience*, Soelle counsels against a form of truth-seeking that emanates from an authoritarian model of obedience.[1] This kind of obedience becomes blind to the world and ultimately to God. Rather, Soelle urges us to practice discerning obedience, which is in response to the proclamation of Jesus. Discerning obedience is "an obedience which has its eyes wide open, which first discovers God's will in the situation."[2] For Soelle, this means that freedom, change, and spontaneity coalesce so that we not only accept responsibility for the world around us but seek to be a part of God's transformation of the world. Freedom, restored through the liberatory power of Jesus, begins this process for Soelle. The power we need to change things is found in spontaneity that then inspires new freedom. In discerning obedience, we practice freedom daily through seeking to understand and live anew the truth found in Christ, which sets us free to discover God's will in a future that is open to possibilities.

---

1. Dorothee Soelle, *Beyond Mere Obedience*, trans. Lawrence W. Denef (New York: Pilgrim Press, 1982), 3–17.
2. Ibid., 25.

Pastoral Perspective

his followers belong to a kingdom that is not earthly bound. Ultimately, Jesus and his followers belong to the truth. Gerard S. Sloyan writes that the words "king" and "kingship" touch on a different sphere from that of this world. Jesus gives the words new meanings. Pilate understands "king" and "kingship" in earthly terms. Jesus redefines "king" and "kingship" to belong to what Sloyan refers to as the "sphere of belief in him who came in to the world to testify to the truth."[1] This sphere of belief occurs among all those who both hear and heed Jesus' voice. Proclaiming the truth, being the truth, and even belonging to the truth are what make Jesus a king. His kingdom—his nation—is not defined by earthly terms, but neither is it some ethereal, imaginary concept. Jesus comes from and belongs to God's kingdom.

The question of belonging continues to be a crucial if troubling one. Just as children test the resilience of their belonging to their families in times of frustration and disagreement, so too do adults. We test our belonging to our families. We test our belonging to our communities of faith. We test our belonging to our nation. These tests appear in a variety of ways. Unlike children, many adults have the ability to leave relationships, and some do—for a few hours to calm nerves, for a few days to ponder the durability of the relationships. Some eventually leave permanently. Communities of faith are no different. Some persons test their belonging by delivering ultimatums. Some persons test their belonging by simply drifting away quietly, wondering if anyone will notice. Others take time to engage in thoughtful conversation with the community's leadership and then, through measured prayer and discernment, decide whether to stay or to leave.

Even our citizenship is tested. For some communities of faith, the placement of the national flag in the place of worship is a deeply contentious issue. Some see the presence of the flag in the sanctuary as a symbol of idolatry. Others see the symbol of the flag as an obligation, signifying our gratitude to God for the freedom of the expression of religion framed in this country's founding texts.

The underlying assumption in all of these situations is the profound emphasis in American culture on the individual. All of these tests of belonging are focused on the individual's own decision making. But is this what Jesus meant when

---

1. Gerard S. Sloyan, *The Gospel of John*, Interpretation Series (Louisville, KY: John Knox Press, 1988), 206.

Exegetical Perspective

A comparison of this text with its Synoptic parallels (Matt. 27:11–14; Mark 15:2–5; Luke 23:2–5) is also instructive. In the Synoptics, Pilate asks Jesus only if he is the king of the Jews, and Jesus answers cryptically, "You say so." In John, Jesus and Pilate have an extended discourse that amplifies key Johannine themes.

Who Is on Trial? Jesus' opponents bring him from the house of Caiaphas to the Roman praetorium, called the Antonia fortress, built along the northern wall of the temple complex. They want Pilate to condemn Jesus. Pilate senses their lack of clarity regarding their charge against Jesus (v. 30), and he attempts to persuade "the Jews" to issue their own judgment, but they refuse (v. 31–32). Pilate then enters the praetorium, "calls" Jesus to him, and questions him there (v. 33).

Pilate's first question addresses Jesus' identity as king of the Jews. The title of "king" is loaded with political—insurrectional—meaning for the Romans, who have little tolerance for any king but Caesar. As Rome's chief authority in Palestine, then, Pilate is pressing Rome's full authority against Jesus when he asks the question. Boldly, Jesus withstands the pressure and does not answer the question. Rather, he challenges Pilate with a question of his own. Taking control of the conversation, he wants to know the source and motivation of Pilate's inquiry (v. 34). Pilate's response is telling (v. 35).

First, Pilate asserts his Gentile status and reveals no personal interest in Jesus' status among the Jews. He cares nothing for Jewish kings and messiahs. Second, Pilate's response suggests that Jesus' suspicion of a conspiracy against him is well-founded: the people and their chief priests handed Jesus over to him (see 1:11; 11:47–53). Modern readers would do well to keep in mind the larger context of John's Gospel—which does not everywhere disapprove of Jews or affirm Gentiles—and so not overstate John's case against "the Jews" here.

The King and His Kingdom. Pilate then asks Jesus: "What have you done?" Those outside the "court-room" know. Jesus' opponents, witnesses to Jesus' ministry, and the recipients of John's Gospel—then and now—are all aware of Jesus' activity. Pilate, however, does not know. Once again, Jesus evades Pilate's question and asserts his royal identity. He begins speaking about his kingship and kingdom (cf. 3:3–5).

Jesus claims twice that his kingdom is not of this world, and the proof he offers is that his followers

Homiletical Perspective

crucified. If Pilate does not give them what they want, can he stay in control? Does he have enough troops to quell the trouble those leaders might stir up? How will it play back in Rome if on his watch he is not able to handle matters in Jerusalem?

So when Pilate summons Jesus and asks him, "Are you the King of the Jews?" is that really his question? Does he truly believe Jesus is an insurrectionist? Or is he trying to find a technicality on which to condemn Jesus in order to placate the leaders? Is he free or bound in his effort to stay in control? Is that Pilate's real goal, regardless of the cost—to stay in control? Trapped, Pilate has to hide his true convictions, his honest questions, and his haunting fears.

The preacher might speak to the reality of how fearful, and thus how trapped, are we who hear this text in this day. Evidence of that captivity may be clearly seen in some of our politicians. For instance, there is the account of one U.S. senator who wanted to declare that his vote to authorize the war in Iraq was wrong. But in three drafts of an op-ed piece he wrote to make that confession, his aides deleted the confession or tempered it to say only that he had been misled.[2] Those political aides were sure that being honest could not be the goal of the senator. Rather, staying in power had to be his goal. Authenticity would have to be jettisoned. The senator was trapped.

But evidence of this captivity is present in the pews of many congregations. In mainline churches, most members have every creature comfort imaginable, including houses, cars, and freedom to travel on expensive vacations. Yet dare these members be real at work or in public life? Dare they reveal who they are, what they truly believe, how they actually perceive things? Or are they trapped by their fear of losing their position and with it the continuing path of upward mobility on which they bank to pay the mortgage, the car payments, and the credit card debt? Must they hide themselves, doing and saying things they do not want to do or say in order to "stay in control"?

On this Sunday, the church proclaims Christ the King. The church announces that it bows only to Jesus the Christ. The church declares that it does not give allegiance to any other person, principality, or power claiming to be sovereign. Yet will the church live out its profession? Forever fearful in this increasingly post-Christian era of losing members and thus losing influence in the community, does the

2. Jonathan Darman, "I'm Real. Really," *Newsweek*, February 19, 2007, 36–38.

John 18:33-37

Theological Perspective

We are aided in accepting the challenges of discerning obedience by remembering that the truth Jesus calls us to, in this passage and others, originates in God and not in humanity. This truth is neither relative nor provisional. It is eternal and an intricate part of God's ongoing revelation in our lives and in creation. God truly is a God of love and grace, who wills the blessings of creation in our lives. This can be brought out with compelling effect by exploring Jesus' words, "Everyone who belongs to the truth listens to my voice" (v. 37), and then following this with Pilate's question, which Jesus does not answer: "What is truth?" (v. 38).

This important two-step in John's dialogue between Jesus and Pilate brings the journey of discovery about truth into bold relief. Truth can be transforming if we seek it through discerning obedience that asks us to look deeply into who we are and what we have become, to try to live into what we can and should be. By looking deeply, we must look at what is right and wrong in our actions and attitudes toward others and within ourselves. This means that we challenge ourselves to look beyond what *we* think to the truth found in God as represented by Jesus. The truth that Jesus represents is found in God, who is love and grace. This means we carry on an intense individual and communal dialogue to help ground ourselves. We do so in private and communal prayer, worship, religious education, meetings, and all the other ways we gather as people of faith as active witnesses in the world.

Ultimately, truth is an essential element in helping us sort through the miasma of life. We must be alert, open, and willing to walk into this truth through a discerning obedience that listens wisely, and then encounter truth as the challenge and gift God gives to us through infinite love and grace.

EMILIE M. TOWNES

Pastoral Perspective

he said that those who belong to the truth listen to his voice? Is it really up to the individual to decide?

Bruce J. Malina writes that one of the greatest challenges for Americans in reading the Bible is to understand the difference between the U.S. emphasis on the individual and the Mediterranean emphasis on the community. Malina explains that in the world of the New Testament, a person did not think of himself or herself as an individual who acts alone, regardless of what others think and say. Rather, the person is "ever aware of the expectations of others, especially significant others, and strives to match those expectations. This is the group-embedded, group-oriented, collectivistic personality, one who needs another simply to know who he or she is."[2]

In the example of children who are testing their belonging to the family, the best response is to remind them of their place and participation in the family. When Jesus tells Pilate that all who listen to Jesus' voice belong to the truth and are part of his kingdom, he is saying, in Mediterranean fashion, that belonging is less about individual decisions and more about collective participation in a community that transcends the self. He even hints at this for himself when he speaks of being born and coming into the world to testify to the truth. The reign of God is larger than any individual, even Jesus himself.

Surely the kingdom is present wherever Jesus is present. It is present wherever we experience the reign of God through God's invitation, healing, and restoration—but our belonging is not up to each one of us alone. Our belonging is up to God. That is the new reality that Jesus proclaims. That is the new truth to which all of us—the community of those invited, healed, and restored—belong.

RODGER Y. NISHIOKA

---

2. Bruce J. Malina, *The New Testament World* (Louisville, KY: Westminster John Knox Press, 2001), 74.

Exegetical Perspective

are not fighting for his release (v. 36). On the surface, Jesus asserts that his kingdom presents no threat to Roman rule and power. As the previous context of John and the other Gospels reveal, however, Jesus' rule and kingdom are profoundly subversive to any worldly authority that demands allegiance over loyalty to God. The religious leaders have come to recognize this; Pilate does not yet see it.

Jesus' insistence upon his kingdom's otherworldly nature also makes its association with the kingdom of God inescapable. It is the kingdom of God that Jesus has been proclaiming and revealing (1:9–13, 49–51; 3:1–21; 6:1–14, 29–40; etc.); Jesus now claims to rule it. Pilate understands Jesus' comment in this way, but he sees here no threat to Roman authority and is willing to accept Jesus' claim to such a kingship (v. 37a). Jesus accepts his assessment (v. 37b). At this point, Jesus makes a startling assertion. Not only does he relate his kingship and the kingdom to the purpose of his birth (cf. 1:1–5, 9–14), but he claims that his kingdom is also present—in part—upon the earth. The reign and rule of Jesus are present wherever anyone accepts the truth of his identity and witness.

The Johannine theme of truth is central to this text. Indeed, the final references to truth in John occur here. John began his Gospel by identifying Jesus with God's truth (1:1–5, 9–14, 32–34; etc.), demonstrated the truthfulness of Jesus' perceptions (1:47; 2:25; etc.), and proved that Jesus' teaching bears witness to the truth (4:23–26; 5:33; 8:32, 40, 45, 46). Jesus also imparted truth to his disciples (14:6; 15–17, 25–26; 15:26; 16:7, 13–15; 17:17, 19). The opponents of Jesus, however, have rejected the "truth" (8:44) and sided with the "world" (11:47–53). In this last reference to truth, Jesus declares that his kingdom is present in everyone who hears and accepts his testimony.

But what has Jesus done? In John's Gospel, he has enabled people to face the truth about themselves, their relationships, their faith, and the world in which they live. Now Pilate has the possibility of recognizing the truth, and he is looking Truth in the face (14:6). But Pilate, like many others, is not interested in the truth and asks contemptuously, "What is truth?" (v. 38a).

In truth, Jesus is the judge and king.

ROBERT A. BRYANT

Homiletical Perspective

church temper its message and its mission in a desperate effort to maintain position?

Yet notice Jesus. As Pilate asks that question designed to catch Jesus in a capital offense, "Are you the King of the Jews?" Jesus says to him, "Do you ask this on your own, or did others tell you about me?" (v. 34). There, before Pilate, Jesus seeks to encounter the real Pilate, the one who in truth is utterly trapped in his desperate effort to stay in control. There Jesus gives himself to be with the true person who is Pilate. There Jesus invites Pilate to be transparent, to share how it is with him, to utter the truth of his own life.

It is exactly what Jesus does at the beginning of his ministry with the Samaritan woman at the well.[3] And here in the very last encounter Jesus has with a human being before his death, an encounter that leads to his death, he makes an offer to Pilate. "Everyone who belongs to truth listens to my voice," says Jesus to Pilate. Even to Pilate Jesus offers to be the good shepherd, the good shepherding king, who, when his sheep listen to his voice, are led into abundant life (John 10).

This is always Jesus' offer. But to receive it means facing the truth about our lives, the truth Jesus holds up before us. Pilate refuses to face that truth. "What is truth?" he declares dismissively.

What about those confronted by Jesus as this text is heard today? Jesus still offers the invitation to be authentic about how it is with us, and being authentic, to be led by the shepherding king into abundant life.

PETE PEERY

---

3. Williamson, 252.

John 18:33–37   **337**

Contributors

A. K. M. Adam, Professor of New Testament, Seabury-Western Theological Seminary, Evanston, Illinois

Harry B. Adams, Professor Emeritus, Yale Divinity School, New Haven, Connecticut

Patricia D. Ahearne-Kroll, Assistant Professor of Religion, Ohio Wesleyan University, Delaware, Ohio

John Ahn, Assistant Professor of Old Testament, Austin Presbyterian Theological Seminary, Austin, Texas

Dale P. Andrews, Martin Luther King Jr. Professor of Homiletics and Pastoral Theology, Boston University School of Theology, Boston, Massachusetts

Susan R. Andrews, Executive Presbyter, Hudson River Presbytery, Scarborough, New York

Loye Bradley Ashton, Assistant Professor of Religious Studies, Tougaloo College, Tougaloo, Mississippi

Harold W. Attridge, Dean and Lillian Claus Professor of New Testament, Yale Divinity School, New Haven, Connecticut

Carol M. Bechtel, Professor of Old Testament, Western Theological Seminary, Holland, Michigan

C. Clifton Black, Otto A. Piper Professor of Biblical Theology, Princeton Theological Seminary, Princeton, New Jersey

Ruth L. Boling, Minister of Word and Sacrament, Presbyterian Church (U.S.A.), Forest Hills, New York

Kathleen Bostrom, Copastor, Wildwood Presbyterian Church, Grayslake, Illinois

Walter Brueggemann, Professor Emeritus of Old Testament, Columbia Theological Seminary, Decatur, Georgia

Robert A. Bryant, Associate Professor of Religion, Presbyterian College, Clinton, South Carolina

John P. Burgess, James Henry Snowden Professor of Systematic Theology, Pittsburgh Theological Seminary, Pittsburgh, Pennsylvania

Jason Byassee, Director of the Center for Theology, Writing and Media, Duke Divinity School, Durham, North Carolina

Charles L. Campbell, Professor of Homiletics, Duke Divinity School, Durham, North Carolina

Paul E. Capetz, Associate Professor of Historical Theology, United Theological Seminary of the Twin Cities, New Brighton, Minnesota

Kenneth H. Carter Jr., Pastor, Providence United Methodist Church, Charlotte, North Carolina

Gary W. Charles, Pastor, Central Presbyterian Church, Atlanta, Georgia

Kate Foster Connors, Parish Associate, Brown Memorial Park Avenue Presbyterian Church, Baltimore, Maryland

Martin B. Copenhaver, Senior Pastor, Wellesley Congregational Church, Wellesley, Massachusetts

David Cortés-Fuentes, Associate Professor of New Testament, San Francisco Theological Seminary, Pasadena, California

David S. Cunningham, Professor of Religion, Hope College, Holland, Michigan

Kathy L. Dawson, Associate Professor of Christian Education, Columbia Theological Seminary, Decatur, Georgia

Carol J. Dempsey, OP, Associate Professor, Department of Theology, University of Portland, Portland, Oregon

Mark Douglas, Associate Professor of Christian Ethics, Columbia Theological Seminary, Decatur, Georgia

Lisa D. Maugans Driver, Assistant Professor of Theology, Valparaiso University, Valparaiso, Indiana

Jane E. Fahey, Pastor, Druid Hills Presbyterian Church, Atlanta, Georgia

Roger A. Ferlo, Associate Dean and Director for the Institute for Christian Formation and Leadership, Virginia Theological Seminary, Alexandria, Virginia

Elizabeth B. Forney, Minister of Word and Sacrament, Presbyterian Church (U.S.A.), Clarksville, Tennessee

Thomas Edward Frank, Professor of Religious Leadership and Administration and Director of Methodist Studies, Candler School of Theology, Emory University, Atlanta, Georgia

Lincoln E. Galloway, Associate Professor of Homiletics, Claremont School of Theology, Claremont, California

Ginger Grab, Chaplain, Bard College, Tivoli, New York

Douglas R. A. Hare, William F. Orr Professor of New Testament Emeritus, Pittsburgh Theological Seminary, Pittsburgh, Pennsylvania

J. S. Randolph Harris, Pastor, Highland Presbyterian Church, Winston-Salem, North Carolina

Michael G. Hegeman, Coordinator of the Engle Institute of Preaching, Princeton Theological Seminary, Princeton, New Jersey

Susan T. Henry-Crowe, Dean of Cannon Chapel and Religious Life, Emory University, Atlanta, Georgia

H. James Hopkins, Pastor, Lakeshore Avenue Baptist Church, Oakland, California

Amy C. Howe, Parish Associate, Evergreen Presbyterian Church, Memphis, Tennessee

David B. Howell, Editor of *Lectionary Homiletics*, Midlothian, Virginia

Cynthia A. Jarvis, Minister, The Presbyterian Church of Chestnut Hill, Philadelphia, Pennsylvania

Nathan G. Jennings, Assistant Professor of Liturgics and Anglican Studies, Episcopal Theological Seminary of the Southwest, Austin, Texas

E. Elizabeth Johnson, J. Davison Philips Professor of New Testament, Columbia Theological Seminary, Decatur, Georgia

Stephen C. Johnson, Assistant Professor of Preaching, Abilene Christian University, Abilene, Texas

Susan B. W. Johnson, Senior Minister, Hyde Park Union Church, Chicago, Illinois

Peter Rhea Jones, Professor of Preaching and New Testament, Mercer University, Atlanta, Georgia

Thomas G. Long, Bandy Professor of Preaching, Candler School of Theology, Emory University, Atlanta, Georgia

Jennifer L. Lord, Associate Professor of Homiletics, Austin Presbyterian Theological Seminary, Austin, Texas

Victor McCracken, Ph.D. Candidate, Emory University, Atlanta, Georgia

Martha L. Moore-Keish, Assistant Professor of Theology, Columbia Theological Seminary, Decatur, Georgia

Michael Morgan, Seminary Musician, Columbia Theological Seminary, Decatur, Georgia, and Organist, Central Presbyterian Church, Atlanta, Georgia

Stephen Butler Murray, Chaplain, Skidmore College, Saratoga Springs, New York

Rodger Y. Nishioka, Benton Family Associate Professor of Christian Education, Columbia Theological Seminary, Decatur, Georgia

Julia M. O'Brien, Professor of Old Testament, Lancaster Theological Seminary, Lancaster, Pennsylvania

Kathleen M. O'Connor, William Marcellus McPheeters Professor of Old Testament, Columbia Theological Seminary, Decatur, Georgia

Thomas D. Parker, Emeritus Professor of Systematic Christian Theology, McCormick Theological Seminary, Chicago, Illinois

Michael Pasquarello III, Granger E. and Anna A. Fisher Professor of Preaching, Asbury Theological Seminary, Wilmore, Kentucky

Pete Peery, Pastor, First Presbyterian Church, Asheville, North Carolina

Charles E. Raynal, Director of Advanced Studies and Associate Professor of Theology, Columbia Theological Seminary, Decatur, Georgia

Allison Read, Assistant Rector, Christ Church in Short Hills, Short Hills, New Jersey

Sharon H. Ringe, Professor of New Testament, Wesley Theological Seminary, Washington, D.C.

Marcia Mount Shoop, Minister of Word and Sacrament, Presbyterian Church (U.S.A.), Chapel Hill, North Carolina

Richard M. Simpson, Rector, St. Francis Episcopal Church, Holden, Massachusetts

G. Malcolm Sinclair, Preaching Minister, Metropolitan United Church, Toronto, Ontario, Canada

Archie Smith Jr., James and Clarice Foster Professor of Pastoral Psychology and Counseling, Pacific School of Religion, Berkeley, California

Louis Stulman, Professor of Religious Studies, University of Findlay, Findlay, Ohio

Barbara Brown Taylor, Butman Professor of Religion, Piedmont College, Demorest, Georgia, and Adjunct Professor of Christian Spirituality, Columbia Theological Seminary, Decatur, Georgia

James J. Thompson, Assistant Professor of Philosophy, Presbyterian College, Clinton, South Carolina

Mark A. Throntveit, Professor of Old Testament, Luther Seminary, St. Paul, Minnesota

Emilie M. Townes, Associate Dean and Andrew W. Mellon Professor of African American Religion and Theology, Yale Divinity School, New Haven, Connecticut

Mary Donovan Turner, Vice President and Dean, Pacific School of Religion, Berkeley, California

Aaron L. Uitti, Rector, Episcopal Church of Saints Peter and Paul, Marietta, Georgia

Leanne Van Dyk, Dean and Vice President of Academic Affairs, Western Theological Seminary, Holland, Michigan

Peter M. Wallace, Vice President and Dean, Alliance for Christian Media, Atlanta, Georgia, and Producer and Host, "Day 1" Radio Program

Haruko Nawata Ward, Associate Professor of Church History, Columbia Theological Seminary, Decatur, Georgia

Dawn Ottoni Wilhelm, Associate Professor of Preaching and Worship, Bethany Theological Seminary, Richmond, Indiana

Telford Work, Associate Professor of Theology, Westmont College, Santa Barbara, California

Frank M. Yamada, Director of the Center for Asian American Ministries and Associate Professor of Hebrew Bible, McCormick Theological Seminary, Chicago, Illinois

Scripture Index

Author Index

Martin B. Copenhaver	Proper 27 OT PP, Proper 28 OT PP, Proper 29 OT PP	Michael G. Hegeman	Proper 22 E HP, Proper 23 E HP, Proper 24 E HP
David Cortés-Fuentes	Proper 25 E EP, All Saints NT EP, Proper 26 E EP	Susan T. Henry-Crowe	Proper 17 OT PP, Proper 18 OT PP
David S. Cunningham	Proper 25 E TP, All Saints NT TP, Proper 26 E TP	H. James Hopkins	Proper 19 OT HP, Proper 20 OT HP, Proper 21 OT HP
Kathy L. Dawson	Proper 19 E PP, Proper 20 E PP, Proper 21 E PP	Amy C. Howe	Proper 17 G PP, Proper 18 G PP
Carol J. Dempsey, OP	Proper 19 PS EP, Proper 20 PS EP, Proper 21 PS EP	David B. Howell	Proper 22 G PP, Proper 23 G PP, Proper 24 G PP
Mark Douglas	Proper 19 E TP, Proper 20 E TP, Proper 21 E TP	Cynthia A. Jarvis	Proper 25 G PP, All Saints G PP, Proper 26 G PP
Lisa D. Maugans Driver	Proper 25 PS TP, All Saints PS TP, Proper 26 PS TP	Nathan G. Jennings	Proper 19 G HP, Proper 20 G HP, Proper 21 G HP
Jane E. Fahey	Proper 27 E TP, Proper 28 E TP, Proper 29 NT TP	E. Elizabeth Johnson	Proper 19 E EP, Proper 20 E EP, Proper 21 E EP
Roger A. Ferlo	Proper 25 E PP, All Saints NT PP, Proper 26 E PP	Stephen C. Johnson	Proper 17 OT HP, Proper 18 OT HP
Elizabeth B. Forney	Proper 27 E PP, Proper 28 E PP, Proper 29 NT PP	Susan B. W. Johnson	Proper 19 PS TP, Proper 20 PS TP, Proper 21 PS TP
Thomas Edward Frank	Proper 22 OT PP, Proper 23 OT PP, Proper 24 OT PP	Peter Rhea Jones	Proper 17 E HP, Proper 18 E HP
Lincoln E. Galloway	Proper 25 G HP, All Saints G HP, Proper 26 G HP	Thomas G. Long	Proper 27 E EP, Proper 28 E EP, Proper 29 NT EP
Ginger Grab	Proper 25 E HP, All Saints NT HP, Proper 26 E HP	Jennifer L. Lord	Proper 17 PS HP, Proper 18 PS HP
Douglas R. A. Hare	Proper 17 G EP, Proper 18 G EP	Victor McCracken	Proper 25 G TP, All Saints G TP, Proper 26 G TP
J. S. Randolph Harris	Proper 22 OT HP, Proper 23 OT HP, Proper 24 OT HP	Martha L. Moore-Keish	Proper 19 G TP, Proper 20 G TP, Proper 21 G TP
		Michael Morgan	Proper 25 PS PP, All Saints PS PP, Proper 26 PS PP